EPISTEMOLOGY AND COGNITION

EPISTEMOLOGY
and
COGNITION

Alvin I. Goldman

HARVARD UNIVERSITY PRESS
Cambridge, Massachusetts, and London, England   1986

Publication of this book has been aided by a
grant from the Andrew W. Mellon Foundation.

This book is printed on acid-free paper, and its
binding materials have been chosen for strength
and durability.

Library of Congress Cataloging in Publication Data

Goldman, Alvin I., 1938–
    Epistemology and cognition.

    Bibliography: p.
    Includes indexes.
    1. Cognition.   2.   Knowledge, Theory of.
I.   Title.
(DNLM: 1.   Cognition.   2.   Philosophy.
BF   311   G619e
BF311.G582   1986   153.4   85-21906
ISBN 0-674-25895-9 (alk. paper)

In memory of Frances and Nathan Goldman

Preface

THE IDEA of this book germinated while I was a fellow at the Center for Advanced Study in the Behavioral Sciences during 1975–76, with support from the Guggenheim Foundation. Conceived there was the idea of *epistemics:* an enterprise linking traditional epistemology, first, with cognitive science and, second, with social scientific and humanistic disciplines that explore the interpersonal and cultural processes impinging on knowledge and belief. The intention was to enrich epistemology while preserving its own identity. This book articulates the first part of epistemics: the relation between epistemology and cognitive science. A sequel is planned to delineate the second part: social epistemics.

In trying to lay a satisfactory conceptual foundation for epistemics, I was aided at the Behavioral Science Center by discussions with John Perry, Keith Donnellan, Michael Bratman, and Holly Smith, and by later debates with Richard Nisbett during a seminar we taught jointly. Initial programmatic statements appeared in "Epistemics: The Regulative Theory of Cognition," *The Journal of Philosophy,* 75 (1978):509–523, and "Varieties of Cognitive Appraisal," *Nous,* 13 (1979):23–38. Other precursors of material in this book include "What Is Justified Belief?" in G. Pappas, ed., *Justification and Knowledge* (Dordrecht: D. Reidel, 1979), and "The Internalist Conception of Justification," in P. French, T. Uehling, Jr., and H. Wettstein, eds., *Midwest Studies in Philosophy,* vol. 5, *Studies in Epistemology* (Minneapolis: University of Minnesota Press, 1980). Themes from "The Relation between Epistemology and Psychology," *Synthese,* 64 (1985):29–68 (written in 1981), form the basis for parts of Chapters 4 and 5. "Epistemology and the Theory of Problem Solving," *Synthese,* 55 (1983):21–48, is the basis for much of Chapter 6. A version of Chapter 11, "Constraints on Representation," appears in Myles Brand and Robert Harnish, eds., *The Representation of Knowledge and Belief* (Tucson: University of Arizona Press, 1986).

Writing of the book began in earnest in 1981–82, when I was a fellow of the National Humanities Center. (I feel fortunate to have enjoyed the marvelous research opportunities of two fine centers.) Work continued in 1983 under a grant from the National Science Foundation (SES-8204737).

I owe deep thanks to many colleagues and friends for valuable comments on portions of the manuscript at different stages of its evolution. First and foremost, I am indebted to Holly Smith, who read virtually every version of every chapter. Her probing criticisms and generous advice have significantly improved the book. Other reviewers of hefty chunks of the manuscript were Charles Chastain, Robert Cummins, Robert M. Harnish, John Pollock, Lance Rips, and Stephen Schiffer. Kent Bach, Fred Dretske, Keith Lehrer, and Carl Posey commented on some selected chapters. In all cases chapters emerged somewhat scathed, but (I hope) improved. I have also benefited from the helpful comments of many students in graduate seminars, both at the University of Illinois at Chicago and at the University of Arizona.

Contents

Introduction

I.1. *Epistemology as a Multidisciplinary Affair*

The aim of this book is to redirect and restructure the field of epistemology. One central theme is that epistemology should be a multidisciplinary affair, not the province of pure, *a priori* philosophy. Though philosophy is the chief conductor or orchestrator of epistemology, many other disciplines—including empirical disciplines—are important parts of the ensemble. This book is the first part of a larger project, and the full conception of epistemology I envisage will only emerge from the whole work. In this introduction I sketch the larger conception, although much of it outstrips what is actually developed in this volume.

Epistemology, as I conceive it, divides into two parts: individual epistemology and social epistemology. Individual epistemology—at least *primary* individual epistemology—needs help from the cognitive sciences. Cognitive science tries to delineate the architecture of the human mind-brain, and an understanding of this architecture is essential for primary epistemology. Social epistemology needs help from various of the social sciences and humanities, which jointly provide models, facts, and insights into social systems of science, learning, and culture. The connection between primary epistemology and the sciences of cognition is treated in this book. The nature and structure of social epistemology will be examined in a future study.

To some readers the interdisciplinary theme may sound banal. Epistemology deals with knowledge, which is the property of individual minds. So *of course* epistemology must be interested in the knowing mind. Similarly, most knowledge is a cultural product, channeled through language and social communication. So how could epistemology *fail* to be intertwined with studies of culture and social systems?

Despite these truisms, strong countercurrents in the history of epistemology run against the interdisciplinary theme. Here is a sampling of such countercurrents (not all mutually compatible, being drawn from different traditions).

(1) As the study of method, epistemology should be autonomous. It should

be prior to the sciences; so it must not seek help from them. (2) Epistemology should only be concerned with the analysis of concepts, specifically epistemic concepts such as 'knowledge', 'warrant', 'rationality', and the like. But conceptual or linguistic analysis is the province of philosophy; so epistemology needs no help from behavioral or social sciences. (3) The true aim of philosophy is to "show the fly the way out of the fly-bottle,"[1] that is, to dissolve puzzles and paradoxes that lead to skepticism. Such dissolution requires only linguistic analysis, not a model of the mind-brain or empirical models of intellectual influence. (4) Epistemology is the study of methodology, and proper methodology is the province of deductive logic, inductive logic, probability theory, and statistics. Epistemology reduces to these subjects, all of which are *formal* disciplines. *Empirical* sciences are not needed. (5) Epistemology is normative, evaluative, or critical, not descriptive. So empirical sciences, which are purely descriptive, cannot help epistemology. The psychology of reasoning, for example, cannot shed light on proper reasoning, on logically or scientifically sound reasoning. In view of these metaepistemological currents, the proposed interdisciplinary theme is controversial, not trivial. It needs sustained clarification and defense.

Furthermore, the interdisciplinary theme is only one of my themes. Of equal or greater importance is the specific epistemological framework to be proposed, which specifies the particular ways in which disciplinary collaboration should proceed. This framework contrasts with other systems of epistemology that would equally favor an interdisciplinary orientation. Let me briefly mention a few components of this framework.

One crucial component is the evaluative mission of epistemology. Along with the dominant tradition, I regard epistemology as an evaluative, or normative, field, not a purely descriptive one. This makes it far from obvious how *positive* science can have inputs to epistemology. How, exactly, do *facts* of cognition or social intercourse bear on epistemic evaluations or norms?

A few other recent characterizations of epistemology also link it with psychology. But these characterizations depict the field as a descriptive one. On a purely descriptive conception it is not surprising that epistemology should be indebted to psychology—should even reduce to it. Thus, on W. V. Quine's naturalistic conception, the epistemologist would study how the human subject responds to certain input; how, in response to various stimulus patterns, the subject delivers a description of the external world and its history. In studying the relation between this "meager input" and "torrential output," epistemology "simply falls into place as a chapter of psychology and hence of natural science."[2] Similarly, Donald Campbell advances a conception of the field which he calls "evolutionary epistemology." On this conception epistemology takes cognizance of "man's status as a product of biological and social evolution."[3] Campbell explicitly characterizes his conception as descriptive: descriptive of man as knower.[4]

If epistemology is a branch of psychology, or evolutionary theory, the field's empirical status needs no clarification. But this approach, though perfectly tenable, neglects the evaluative strain pervading most of historical epistemology.[5] Epistemologists have traditionally been interested in whether beliefs about the world are justified or warranted; whether we are rationally entitled to these beliefs. Epistemologists seek to discover or invent proper methods of inquiry and investigation, often dismissing established procedures as irrational. Clearly, 'justified', 'warranted', and 'rational' are evaluative terms; and the advocacy of particular methods is a normative activity. So traditional epistemology has a strong evaluative-normative strain. I aim to preserve that strain.

The emphasis on evaluation invites parallels with moral philosophy and normative social theory, and these will be important elements in my discussion. In studying various epistemic terms of appraisal, I will inquire into their basis: Is it objective or subjective? Is it deontological or consequentialist? Should epistemic norms be absolutist or pluralist?

My epistemological framework prominently features an objectivist standard or set of standards. The central epistemological concepts of appraisal, I argue, invoke *true belief* as their ultimate aim. So the evaluation of epistemic procedures, methods, processes, or arrangements must appeal to truth-conduciveness, an objective standard of assessment. While this emphasis on truth is hardly startling, the framework contrasts with many studies of science and opinion that explore properties of social systems and institutions. Specifically, studies in the history and sociology of science characteristically shy away from considerations of truth.

Truth-linked standards may seem useless, because of circularity or vacuousness. To decide whether such a standard is satisfied, we have to employ our present beliefs about the truth. Isn't this circular? Or doesn't it imply automatic endorsement of current procedures, by which our present beliefs have been formed? Wouldn't it preclude criticism and revision, to which normative epistemology ought to be committed?

None of these objections is warranted. To be sure, application of a standard requires recourse to present beliefs. In Otto Neurath's metaphor we can only rebuild our intellectual ship while floating upon it at sea.[6] But the same point holds for any standard, truth-linked or not. So there is no objectionable circularity here. Second, criticism and revision are not precluded. We can criticize (at least some of) our belief-forming processes even with beliefs created by those very processes. I will treat all these points more fully in due course.

I.2. Objects of Evaluation

Granted that epistemology is an evaluative enterprise, its scope and direction depend heavily on its *objects* of evaluation. *Which* things are to be evaluated? Epistemologists have often held that the prime objects of evaluation are arguments, or forms of inference. Now one thing meant by 'inference', or 'argument', is a set of sentences or propositions. If inferences in this sense are the objects of epistemic evaluation, epistemology need only enlist the aid of deductive and inductive logic. On this approach epistemology need not evaluate psychological processes. Nor are social institutions, or properties of intellectual communities, proper objects of evaluation.

Against this choice of evaluative objects, a number of points must be made. First, although epistemology is interested in inference, it is not (primarily) interested in inferences construed as argument forms. Rather, it is interested in inferences as processes of belief formation or belief revision, as sequences of psychological states. So psychological processes are certainly a point of concern, even in the matter of inference. Furthermore, additional psychological processes are of equal epistemic significance: processes of perception, memory, problem solving, and the like.

Why is epistemology interested in these processes? One reason is its interest in epistemic justification. The notion of justification is directed, principally, at beliefs. But evaluations of beliefs, I contend, derive from evaluations of belief-forming processes. Which processes are suitable cannot be certified by logic alone. Ultimately, justificational status depends (at least in part) on properties of our basic cognitive equipment. Hence, epistemology needs to examine this equipment, to see whether it satisfies standards of justifiedness.

The architecture of cognition does not constitute the focus of all epistemology, not even all *individual* epistemology. But it does constitute the focus of what I call *primary* (individual) epistemology. The notion of primary epistemology may be introduced by consideration of a passage from Francis Bacon. In his *Novum Organum*, Bacon wrote:

> Neither the naked hand nor the understanding left to itself can effect much. It is by instruments and helps that the work is done, which are as much wanted for the understanding as for the hand. And as the instruments of the hand either give motion or guide it, so the instruments of the mind supply either suggestions for the understanding or cautions.[7]

Bacon's point should be granted. Just as man's technological achievements have not been executed by the naked hand, most advances by the human intellect have not been achieved by the understanding *left to itself.* In both cases instruments, tools, or "helps" have been essential. In the intellectual domain such tools include systems of language and notation, proof techniques in mathematics, methodologies of empirical science, and all the other symbolic structures and heuristics by which science and scholarship have been guided. With this granted, it might seem as if the job of normative epistemology is to appraise *instruments* proffered to the mind, and to devise new instruments. On this conception logic, probability theory, and statistics fall within normative epistemology, since they offer important scientific and intellectual tools. But studying the understanding considered by itself—the fundamental architecture of human cognition—should be of no significance to epistemology.

This conclusion, however, goes awry. While few intellectual feats are achieved without any "helps" for the mind, the intrinsic properties of the mind still hold significance for epistemology. First, unless the mind has a suitable structure, it cannot *use* tools properly or successfully. Second, the invention, acquisition, and selective retention of intellectual tools must ultimately rest with native cognitive mechanisms, with the understanding "considered by itself." It is fully appropriate, then, for epistemology to inquire into cognitive architecture, to assess its strengths and weaknesses. At a minimum, this is a job for primary epistemology.

Within primary epistemology, then, the objects of epistemic evaluation are cognitive processes, structures, and mechanisms. But this only touches individual epistemology. What are the objects of evaluation in social epistemology?

Social epistemology is concerned with the truth-getting impact of different patterns and arrangements of social intercourse. For example, there are different possible forms, or styles, of interpersonal argument, debate, or controversy. How would these affect the resultant beliefs of the participants? More generally, social intercourse involves a variety of communications structures and channels. Informal channels, involving face-to-face conversations, are one end of a continuum. Other channels, such as classrooms, courtrooms, and assemblies, are also face-to-face, but more formal. Finally, there are non-face-to-face channels involving the public media. Given the informational or misinformational impact of communication channels, the motivations and resources of people involved in channel transactions are critical. What variables affect which messages a potential communicator would like to transmit? What variables affect the decisions of channel controllers—such as editors, media owners, or boards of education—in their selection of candidate messages? What variables affect the activities of potential message receivers in their search for messages of interest and in their response to messages they receive?

Interwoven in such structures and acts of communication, various positions and patterns are found. There are positions of power and authority, and patterns of cooperation and conflict. The task of social epistemology, as I conceive it, is to evaluate the truth-conducive or truth-inhibiting properties of such relationships, patterns, and structures. What kinds of channels, and controls over channels, comprise the best means to 'verific' ends? To what degree should control be consensual, and to what degree a function of (ascribed) expertise, or 'authority'? To what extent should diversity of messages be cultivated? Which principles of selectivity are suitable for different sorts of channels? What distinguishes the canons of science from other systems of investigation and communication? These questions are the domain of social epistemology.

I.3. *Continuities and Discontinuities with Historical Epistemology*

How my conception of epistemology converges with, or diverges from, the subject's history merits discussion. First, does the psychological orientation mesh with epistemology's history? If we consider its full history, the psychological orientation fits well. The historical literature is replete with descriptions and classifications of mental faculties and endowments, processes and contents, acts and operations. Psychological theories that occupied historical epistemologists also had a motivation similar to mine: to assess the mind's powers and limits in its quest for knowledge. Many writers emphasized the limits of knowledge, urging us to 'rein in' reason's excessive pretensions. Kant is famous for this thesis, but the idea was expressed earlier by Locke: "If by this inquiry into the nature of the understanding, I can discover the powers thereof; how far they reach; to what things they are in any degree proportionate; and where they fail us, I suppose it may be of use to prevail with the busy mind of man to be more cautious in meddling with things exceeding its comprehension".[8] Other writers were more optimistic, even Hume in certain moods: "'Tis impossible to tell what changes and improvements we might make in [the] sciences were we thoroughly acquainted with the extent and force of human understanding."[9]

Psychologistic epistemology, then, is in the mainstream of historical epistemology. My proposal differs in rejecting introspectionism in favor of experimental psychology. But the relation envisaged between normative epistemology and mental science closely parallels the classical tradition.

As is well known, however, epistemology of the twentieth century took an antipsychologistic turn. Influenced by Gottlob Frege, positivism, and ordinary-language philosophy, 'psychologism' became suspect in all branches of philosophy. Frege opposed psychologism in logic and the philosophy of mathematics. Positivism viewed all legitimate philosophy as the 'logic' of the sciences. Ordinary-language philosophy stressed the study of natural language, and often (like positivism) favored a behaviorism that denied the relevance (or existence!) of interior mental operations. Through much of this period it was viewed as a confusion to introduce psychology into epistemology. Rudolf Carnap separated these sharply, as did Hans Reichenbach with his distinction between justification and discovery.[10] Discovery was relegated to psychology, while epistemology was supposed to address questions of validity, an issue of logic rather than psychology. Epistemology was to elucidate the logic of science, or analyze key epistemic concepts. The paradigms of epistemology became the logic of confirmation, the analysis of 'S knows that p', and the theory of justification or warrant. None of these tasks, it was felt, called for collaboration with empirical investigators.

I do not reject these inquiries. I shall myself sketch an analysis of knowing (Chapter 3), and present a theory of justification (Chapters 4 and 5). What I do reject is a radical bifurcation of epistemology and psychology. When correct accounts are given of knowledge, justification, and other pertinent epistemic concepts, it emerges that the empirical study of belief genesis becomes most relevent to epistemology. So, at least, I shall argue. While I endorse (a form of) psychologism in epistemology, I do not endorse it in logic. Validity or invalidity of arguments, as far as I can see, is not a matter of psychology. Truths of model theory, proof theory, and recursive function theory—the main branches of logic—do not depend on psychological truths. I am open to persuasion that psychology undergirds logic. But I am not inclined toward this view, and nothing said here depends on it.

In linking epistemology with cognitive science, I use the term 'cognitive science' (or 'cognitive psychology') neutrally. Some use the phrase in an 'ideological' way, to advocate a particular brand or style of theorizing. For example, it may designate a computational approach, or an approach that focuses on a certain level of abstraction, say, functional as opposed to neural. In this usage cognitive science contrasts with neural and biological approaches to cognition. But my usage is not ideological in any of these ways. It includes any scientific approach to cognition.

Though my general outlook is catholic in principle, I in fact draw mostly on cognitive psychology in the narrow use of the term. Rather little is said about neuropsychology. Although I pay attention to neurally inspired models in Chapter 15, the present state of neural modeling does not permit very much in the way of epistemological applications.

Little is said in this book about the tenability of this or that theoretical approach in psychology or cognitive science generally, though the examples I use doubtless betray my preferences (in this epistemological context). A detailed treatment of theoretical stances belongs to the philosophy of psychology, which I do not pursue here. To be sure, the philosophy (methodology) of psychology is part of the philosophy of science, which is in turn part of epistemology. But the focus of this book is primary epistemology, which does not address the special problems of particular sciences. (That would be treated under *secondary* epistemology.) Since the choice of psychological method depends on epistemology, and epistemology depends on psychology, there is (in Quine's phrase) "reciprocal containment" between the disciplines.[11] But nothing is objectionable in this relationship.

Let me turn now to continuities and discontinuities in my approach to social epistemology. Although modern epistemology—from Descartes to Kant—was preoccupied with the individual knower, there has been plenty of interest in its social dimensions. This interest goes back at least to Plato and the Socratic elenchus. Probably influenced by the sophists of his day, Plato treated inquiry as an interpersonal, dialectical process, in which two inquirers try to sustain their opinions against the disputations of their opponent. This dialectic was regarded by Plato as an essential epistemic device.

In more recent times the epistemology of science has often emphasized social elements. Pragmatists like C. S. Peirce and John Dewey stressed the corporate aspect of scientific inquiry, and positivists also stressed the intersubjectivity, or publicity, of scientific knowledge. Thomas Kuhn is identified with a different social perspective on science, with his emphasis on the paradigms that scientific communities share and transmit.[12] Historians and sociologists of science are generally concerned with the communities, or schools, that have marked scientific controversies.

A different social slant to epistemology was introduced by Wittgenstein, who viewed epistemological criteria as portions of language games, understood as species of social practices.[13] This Wittgensteinian slant underlies Richard Rorty's recent formulation of a social conception of epistemology. For Rorty, knowledge is "the social justification of belief," and rationality and epistemic authority are supposed to be explained by reference to "what society lets us say."[14]

Precedents for social epistemology are plainly legion, but most of the current approaches strike me as unsatisfactory in various ways. Historians and sociologists of science typically devote their energy to descriptions of scientific practice and development. Little attention is given to the evaluative issues that are characteristic of epistemology. When evaluative questions are broached, they are seldom tackled with a firm theoretical foundation. I shall try to remedy some of these deficiencies in my subsequent work on social epistemology.

The territorial instinct may incline some philosophers to view the proposed interdisciplinary conception of epistemology as a regrettable surrender of philosophical autonomy. But *epistemology's* lack of autonomy would only parallel that of other branches of philosophy. Neither moral nor social-political philosophy can proceed without recourse to other disciplines. How can moral philosophy abstract from contingent facts of the human psyche: the sources of aggression and sympathy, the sense of fairness and reciprocity? How can it abstract from our feelings about ourselves, our offspring, and infrahuman creatures? How can social philosophy neglect the feasibilities and infeasibilities imposed by economic, historical, and political contingencies? Admittedly, *foundational* questions of ethical and social theory may be addressable without appeal to particular social facts. But *substantive* conclusions of social theory must rest in part on human nature and economic and political feasibilities. Therefore, substantive ethics and social theory must be multidisciplinary affairs.

The same holds for epistemology. Although foundational questions may be autonomous, substantive individual and social epistemology need help from other disciplines. The present book develops this theme for individual epistemology. Part I addresses foundational issues and is squarely within philosophy by anyone's conception. But a major conclusion of Part I is that substantive evaluations of (primary) individual epistemology require inputs from the psychology of cognition. I present illustrations of this idea in Part II, but I must stress that these are only illustrations. I do not purport to present a finished primary epistemology. My intention is to delineate the general contours of primary epistemology, as I envisage it. With continued growth in the sciences of cognition, we will be able to do the job better and better. I am merely trying to illustrate the *modus operandi.*

The multidisciplinary conception of epistemology I like to call *epistemics,* to distinguish it from other, more autonomous, conceptions of the field. It is not the only possible conception of the subject, but it is potentially the most fertile. There are current interests and developments in the study of knowledge processes and knowledge systems (using 'knowledge' loosely) in many disciplines. Epistemics is a suitable way of integrating those widely shared interests.

part I

THEORETICAL FOUNDATIONS

chapter 1

The Elements of Epistemology

1.1. Beliefs, Assertions, and Propositions

Epistemology deals with affairs of the intellect. In common parlance 'intellect' often refers to the remote reaches of the mind. This is not what I mean. I mean the whole range of efforts to know and understand the world, including the unrefined, workaday practices of the layman as well as the refined, specialized methods of the scientist or scholar. It includes the entire canvas of topics the mind can address: the nature of the cosmos, the mathematics of set theory or tensors, the fabric of man-made symbols and culture, and even the simple layout of objects in the immediate environment. The ways that minds do or should deal with these topics, individually or in concert, comprise the province of epistemology.

It is controversial whether different topics call for fundamentally different intellectual approaches or processes. But certain elements are common to virtually all efforts of the intellect; and these form the basic building blocks of epistemology. Deployment of the intellect involves either *mental* acts or states, or *public* utterances, frequently both. Among the mental states, *beliefs* are usually singled out by epistemologists. Among linguistic acts, the ones of central concern are *assertions.* Most intellectual endeavors try to arrive at some belief on a designated topic, or to formulate a statement on the problem at hand. Accordingly, the 'product' of the scientist or scholar is typically a body of assertions—presumably accompanied by a body of beliefs. So epistemology naturally focuses on either beliefs or assertive claims. In this book I will largely abstract from natural language and public speech acts, since there will be enough complexities on our hands without the complexities these topics introduce. I will concentrate on the mental side of epistemology, without implying that this is its only side.

Belief is not the mentalistic concept of choice for all epistemologists. Belief is normally a categorical, or binary, concept, an all-or-nothing affair. You either believe something or you don't. But epistemologists commonly point out that there are degrees of conviction or confidence in a statement.

They urge us to do epistemology in terms of degrees of belief, or perhaps subjective probabilities. In describing someone's view of tomorrow's weather, you needn't confine yourself to saying 'He believes it will rain', 'He believes it won't rain', or 'He's undecided'. You can describe him as 'believing-to-degree-.78' that it will rain, or something of this sort.

Whatever the exact concept we select—a categorical or graded notion of belief—some sort of belief-notion seems critical for mentalistic epistemology. Let us now place belief states within a larger map of the mental terrain. This map is implicit in what philosophers call 'folk psychology', that is, a network of assumptions and views about the mind that is expressed in everyday language. Whether these folk psychological concepts succeed in picking out real mental entities is a controversial question, to which I will return shortly and in subsequent chapters (especially Chapter 8). But first let us see where folk psychology, as presented by philosophers, places the concept of belief.

Philosophers commonly divide mental states into two sorts: those that have and those that lack propositional content. The former are *propositional attitudes*, and the latter *sensations, qualia*, or the like. Propositional attitudes are recognized by the sentences used to ascribe them, the telltale sign being an embedded 'that'-clause. Typical examples of such sentences are: 'He wishes that the siren would stop', 'She doubts that it will snow this weekend', and 'He fears that war will never end'. Embedded that-clauses apparently pick out contents of the indicated attitudes, contents commonly referred to as 'propositions'. Hence the term 'propositional attitudes'. Propositional attitude types include wanting, hoping, wishing, fearing, doubting, suspecting, and believing. A particular mental state of this type consists in a person having a specific attitude type directed at a specific proposition. In addition to propositional attitudes, the class of mental states includes sensations like pains, itchy feelings, and perceptual experiences, all of which are said to have qualitative character. However, some theorists hold that even these mental states have propositional content; and a few theorists try to explain away qualitative character in terms of propositional content.

Among propositional attitudes, we distinguish those with a conative or optative attitude toward a proposition—favoring or opposing the proposition's realization—and those with a purely intellectual assessment. The latter involve a stance on the question of whether the proposition is true, quite apart from whether it would be nice if it were true. Such intellectual attitudes include believing, being certain, thinking it likely, doubting, and suspending judgment. These sorts of states are called *doxastic attitudes*, or sometimes *credal attitudes*. They are central to epistemology.

In calling beliefs or other doxastic attitudes *mental* states, philosophers do not imply that they are phenomenological states. Beliefs do not have to occur in consciousness to count as mental. The belief that you reside at 3748 Hillview Road may be held for many years, though you only 'think about' your address intermittently during this period.

Many issues about beliefs and belief ascriptions are controversial. Most of the controversy concerns belief contents. Does a mental state really have a determinate content? If so, what is the source of this content? Is content determined exclusively by what's 'in the head', or by external factors as well? If external factors are relevant, can we really say that belief states (including their contents) are purely mental, that is, inner states of the individual considered in abstraction from his or her environment or causal ancestry?

Another problem concerns the objects (or relata) of beliefs. The term 'propositional attitude' naturally suggests that the objects in question are propositions. And this is a common way of talking, both among philosophers and psychologists. But propositions are problematic entities. As classically interpreted, they are logical or abstract entities, somewhat akin to Platonic forms. Philosophers widely regard this sort of ontological status with suspicion. There are other theories of propositions, but none is free from criticism. In place of propositions some philosophers posit sentences of an inner language, a *lingua mentis,* as the relata of beliefs. But this sort of posit is also controversial.

These sticky issues about beliefs are relevant to my enterprise. They are relevant, first, because it is hard to do any mentalistic epistemology without using something like the belief construct. Second, they are relevant because of the intended bearing of psychology on mentalistic epistemology. Beliefs may not be a kind of entity with which psychology is capable of dealing. Or, being a construct of folk psychology, scientific psychology may choose to replace the belief construct entirely and work with different theoretical resources.

While all these issues are relevant to my undertaking, they cannot be fully resolved here. That would require a full-scale treatment of difficult topics in the philosophy of mind and the philosophy of language, which go beyond the scope of this book. Several of these issues will be addressed squarely in Chapter 8, but even there they will not receive a full-dress discussion. Nonetheless, some remarks are also advisable at this juncture, to indicate roughly where I stand on these issues.

For convenience, I will proceed on the assumption that the objects, or relata, of beliefs are propositions. The utility of proposition-talk is that it nicely unifies the treatment of mental attitudes, overt speech, and truth-value ascriptions. Suppose Alex says 'The moon is round', and Kurt says 'Der Mond is rund'. It is natural to say not merely that both asserted a truth, but that they asserted the *same* truth, namely, that the moon is round. But this single truth cannot be their two sentences, since these were different.

The suggestion is that the two sentences expressed one proposition, which is the truth in question. Suppose further that Oscar utters no such sentence, but has a belief he could express as 'The moon is round'. Then it is tempting to say that he *believes* the *same truth* that Alex and Kurt *assert.* How can this be explained? Again, proposition-talk can do the job. If Oscar's belief content is a proposition—the same one expressed by Alex's and Kurt's sentences—then it is easy to identify the single truth with this very proposition. Thus, by letting propositions be (1) the contents of verbal assertions, (2) the contents of beliefs, and (3) the bearers of truth, we nicely unify a whole range of discourse.

Given the utility of proposition-talk, I shall avail myself of this talk, but only as a *façon de parler.* I regard propositions as a temporary theoretical posit from which we should ultimately ascend to a better theory. Since such a theory may be quite complex, and its details probably would not seriously affect my project, it is an issue to which I will devote little attention.

The bearing of psychology on the belief construct, however, is more central to my concerns. So let me briefly anticipate a fuller discussion of this matter in later chapters. What stance should cognitive science adopt toward beliefs? At least four approaches are possible: reduction, replacement, neutrality, and refinement.

A reductionist says that beliefs are perfectly fine entities for a serious cognitive science, only they need to be reduced to, or explained in terms of, scientifically respectable elements. Since propositions, for example, are dubiously respectable, beliefs need to be understood as relations to syntactic entities, such as sentences in a language of thought.

An advocate of replacement holds that beliefs are not scientifically tenable posits. As part of a radically false theory, a degenerating research program, they will ultimately be discredited and abandoned like phlogiston.

An advocate of neutrality holds that cognitive science can remain neutral about beliefs. It can proceed perfectly well without them, but this does not imply their overthrow or illegitimacy. Cognitive science may not be in a position to ascribe (propositional) content, or to say how such content should be ascribed. But it may allow that a suitable theory of interpretation—a good 'psychosemantics'—*can* ascribe content, or show how content is standardly ascribed.

The refinement position I have in mind is not an *alternative* to the preceding approaches, mainly because it does not address the problem of content. Content is not the only dimension of interest in the belief construct. Psychology should also be interested in the range of contentful states. Cognitive science could endorse the notion of content but stress the need for acknowledging a richer array of distinct content-bearing states. Many different states, it may hold, are all lumped under the folk-psychological label of 'belief', and these need to be sorted out for the purposes of an adequate science of the mind.

I favor a combination of the neutrality and refinement approaches. I do not expect cognitive science to force the total abandonment of content states. But I do expect it to foster a more fine-grained set of descriptive resources. This richer set of resources should help epistemology; not by making it easier, but by making it (psychologically) more realistic.

1.2. Truth-Values and Knowledge

Beliefs are commonly said to be true or false, and so are assertions. But, strictly, it is not *acts* of assertion, or *states* of belief, that are true or false. It is the *contents* of these acts or states. Since we are taking propositions to be the contents of beliefs and assertions, they have the role of bearers of truth or falsity. What is primarily true or false is a proposition. A belief qualifies as true only derivatively: when its content is a true proposition.

Ignoring assertions, then, there are three basic categories that need to be distinguished. First, there are psychological, or mental, states. Second, there are propositions, which are the contents of (certain of) these states. Third, there are truth-values, such as true, false, and perhaps indeterminate. (The possible need for a third truth-value arises because some propositions may be neither true nor false, for example, propositions with vacuous referring terms, like the one expressed by 'The present king of France is bald'.)

It is essential to distinguish carefully between these categories. In general, the mere fact that someone believes a proposition does not make it true, or false. The proposition's truth-value is not determined by its being the content of some belief state. (Of course, there are exceptions. If the proposition is 'There are beliefs', then the mere fact that someone believes it guarantees its truth.) Moreover, there are true propositions that nobody believes. Presumably there is a true proposition saying precisely how many people will have a toothache in 1993. But nobody believes that proposition now, and probably nobody will ever believe it.

What makes a proposition have the truth-value it has? The natural answer is: the way the world is. I believe this natural answer is right, and philosophically defensible. Philosophers of this persuasion are often called realists, so I am a realist (of sorts).

Although a full discussion of truth and realism is deferred until Chapter 7, some preliminary clarificatory remarks must be entered here. In discussing truth one must distinguish firmly between the question of what *makes* a proposition have a certain truth-value and the question of how people can *determine* its truth-value. The former question concerns the nature of truth. The latter concerns the *evidence* for a proposition's truth-value, or the methodology of trying to figure out a proposition's truth-value. This distinction is elementary, but it still needs emphasis. Some philosophers hold, to be sure, that a proposition's meaning (or truth-conditions) is a function of the evidence that would count for or against it. Still, at a minimum, one must distinguish between a proposition's *being true* and people *having evidence* in its favor. Surely there are plenty of cases of true propositions for which nobody now (or perhaps ever) has good evidence. The example of the 1993 toothache sufferers is a case in point.

Since many people, including philosophers, insist on conflating truth with other notions—mostly related to evidence, justification, or the like—it is worth dilating on this point at this early juncture. To take a recent example, consider Richard Rorty's claim that there is a sense of 'true' in which it means (roughly) "what you can defend against all comers."[1] The idea of "what can be defended against all comers" is some sort of social justification notion. According to Rorty, there is a sense of 'true' in which it is necessary and sufficient for a proposition's truth that somebody can defend it, presumably successfully, against all who argue against it.

There is no such sense of 'true'. To appreciate what's wrong with this definition, suppose you are an unfortunate victim of circumstance and misidentification. A horrible crime has been committed of which you stand accused. You are totally innocent—such is the truth. But you are a lookalike of the dastardly criminal, and numerous witnesses come forward to identify you as the doer of the deed. Sadly, you have no alibis. You were out for a walk at the time of the act, and nobody can vouch for your whereabouts. Meanwhile, the real criminal has died in an accident. Given these facts, the real truth cannot be successfully defended against all comers. You cannot defend it successfully, for there are too many eyewitnesses to make your case believable. (Furthermore, we may suppose, you actually did have a motive for the act, though it did not motivate you enough to do it.) Nor is there anyone else who could successfully defend your innocence against all comers. Nonetheless, the truth is: you are innocent. The only correct sense of 'true' makes truth independent of how well it can be defended. Its defensibility is a separate matter, which may depend on a variety of extraneous circumstances. Any innocent person accused of a crime surely wants the *real* truth to emerge; and the real truth is all that is normally meant by 'true'.

The innocent defendant case shows that "what can be defended against all comers" is not a necessary condition of truth. But neither is it sufficient. A totalitarian regime may arrange a successful defense of certain false propositions against all comers (at least all comers in that society); but this cannot make the false true.

I will examine more sophisticated attempts to explain truth in terms of evidential, or justificatory, notions in Chapter 7. At this point it is important to distinguish truth and justification, whether social justification or intrapersonal justification.

It is equally imperative to distinguish truth from knowledge. A proposition may be true without being known, just as it may be true without being believed. Let me pause here to make a few remarks about the concept of knowledge. There is a loose and a strict sense of 'knowledge'. In a loose sense a person knows something (a proposition) if he believes it and it is true. If he believes the truth, he is not ignorant of it. He is cognizant of the fact, and so, in a loose sense, knows it. Many writers, especially in the behavioral and social sciences, use 'knowledge' in an ultra-loose sense, to mean simply belief, or representation of the world. This is probably a misuse, though one so common that perhaps it has achieved legitimacy. In more proper usage, to which I shall cleave, no proposition can be known unless it is true.

To repeat: in the loose sense of 'know' someone knows proposition p if and only if he believes p, and p is true. This suffices to show that knowledge is not equivalent to truth: truth does not require belief, but knowledge does. There is also, however, a strict sense of 'know', which has much occupied epistemologists. In this strict sense knowledge requires more than belief and truth. It requires satisfaction of some third, and perhaps fourth, condition beyond belief and truth. Since epistemology has often been regarded as 'the theory of knowledge', many epistemologists have devoted great energy to analyzing this strict sense of 'know'. I too shall pay it a fair bit of attention, especially in Chapter 3. But the analysis of knowledge will not be one of my sustained points of preoccupation. I will use it partly as a jumping-off point for an examination of the notion of justification, which will be one central focus of my discussion. For the present, it suffices to note the complexity of knowledge and to distinguish it from truth.

A principal reason for resisting a realist construal of truth is an alleged threat to knowledge. Many philosophers fear that if truth is definitionally prized off from evidence, or justification, it will be impossible for anyone to know the truth. Truth(s) will be epistemically inaccessible, or unknowable. But this dire consequence is not at all indicated, at least not without lengthy argumentation. The mere fact that extramental reality is what makes a proposition true (or false), as realists maintain, does not imply that no truths can be known. The mere fact that truth does not (definitionally) require knowledge, or justification, does not mean that it *precludes* knowledge, or justification. (These comments do not convey the most serious historical or contemporary arguments against realism. I mention them only in an introductory fashion, to forestall very simple confusions that may befall those unfamiliar with epistemology.)

I have already had occasion to introduce a central epistemic concept, the concept of justification. This has been a doubly important term in the field. First, it is important in its own right, as a term of epistemic evaluation, or appraisal, which is widely applied. Second, it is often linked to knowledge, which, as I have noted, is traditionally central to epistemology. Its connection to knowledge will be discussed later on, in Chapter 3. But I want to turn now to justification in its own right; more precisely, to the larger family of terms of epistemic evaluation of which 'justification' is one member.

1.3. Epistemic Evaluation

The Introduction stressed the fact that epistemology is an evaluative, normative, or critical discipline. Let me now address the possible scope and nature of such evaluation. First, what do we mean by 'evaluation', or 'norm'? We mean a judgment that pronounces something to be good or bad, right or wrong, proper or improper, and the like. Since we are concerned exclusively with epistemological evaluation, we do not mean to raise questions of moral, aesthetic, or legal goodness or badness, rightness or wrongness. We mean to ask about specifically intellectual virtues or vices, proprieties or improprieties.

Notice that the term 'value' is not always tied to the above sense of evaluation. When the mathematician or logician speaks of the values of a variable, he is not talking about a variable's good or bad aspects. He merely refers to the object or class of objects over which the variable ranges. Similarly, when a mathematician evaluates a function, he does not judge it to be good or bad; he merely calculates the output of the function for a specified input. The term 'truth-value', I believe, also uses 'value' in a nonevaluative sense. To assign a proposition a truth-value does not, as I understand it, involve any evaluative judgment. It does not say that the proposition is good or bad, intellectually proper or improper, or anything of the sort. It just says (roughly) that the world is the way the proposition says it is.

But there are many terms and phrases that do register epistemic evaluations. Some of these were mentioned in the Introduction and in the preceding section. But let me discuss these more thoroughly.

On a traffic citation form in Cook County, Illinois, the following clause appears: 'This complainant ... states that he has just and reasonable grounds to believe and does believe that such defendant committed the above offense'. The phrase 'just and reasonable grounds' is an example of an epistemic evaluation. An officer issuing such a citation affirms not only that he believes that the defendant committed a specified offense, but that this belief is justly and reasonably grounded, and in this sense, is epistemically proper or in order. More generally, terms like 'justified' and 'unjustified', 'warranted' and 'unwarranted', 'well-grounded' and 'ill-grounded', 'reasonable' and 'unreasonable', 'rational' and 'irrational', when applied to beliefs or other doxastic attitudes, typically express epistemic evaluations. They are used to grade a belief along some evaluative epistemic dimension.

In studying epistemic evaluation, a number of separate categories should be addressed. Four categories may be usefully distinguished: (1) the domain of evaluation, (2) terms or dimensions of evaluation, (3) standards of evaluation, and (4) styles of evaluation.

(1) Domain of evaluation. Which 'things' are evaluated in epistemic evaluations? Prime examples, we have seen, are beliefs and other doxastic attitudes. But these are not the only objects of evaluation. Methods are also objects of epistemic evaluation. Philosophers of science often debate whether certain inductive methods are scientifically proper or improper. The term 'methods', however, is ambiguous. It can refer to purely abstract, 'logical' objects like argument forms (such as modus ponens and universal instantiation) and principles of confirmation (such as the special-consequence condition and the converse-consequence condition). But it might equally refer to psychological processes, especially belief-causing, or belief-generating, processes. Important differences in epistemological directions might flow from different conceptions of methods. It is important to settle, therefore, which of these conceptions is most central for this or that epistemological purpose. I will turn to this issue in later chapters.

Even among psychological processes, doxastic attitude-forming processes are not the only candidates for objects of evaluation. Other candidates include hypothesis-forming processes, concept-forming processes, search processes, and even second-order processes, for example, processes for forming new belief-forming processes.

In addition to mental states, processes, and methods, there are other types of candidates for epistemic appraisal. Certainly speech acts, both oral and written, should not be exempt. Nor should it be assumed that a verbal claim, or assertion, must be evaluated on the same basis as a belief. Evidential standards for a public claim may differ from those for a private belief. Similarly, constraints on public argumentation may differ from constraints on intramental inference. Furthermore, single assertions or arguments are not the only plausible verbal units deserving evaluation. Larger discourses like speeches, articles, and books are also natural units; in fact, they are more prevalent units of intellectual evaluation than single assertions or arguments.

Finally, a variety of institutional arrangements with intellectual import, and many social structures and processes, may be objects of evaluation. Whether these are objects of epistemic evaluation will depend on one's conception of epistemology. But given my conception of social epistemology, as sketched in the Introduction, it should be clear that I regard these as potentially suitable topics of epistemic evaluation. Most issues in this area, though, are postponed to a future work.

(2) Dimensions of evaluation. Most evaluations treated in academic epistemology have been in the category of evidential evaluations (loosely speaking). I have in mind such evaluations of beliefs as justified, warranted, well-grounded, reasonable, rational, and the like. It should not be supposed that these are all equivalent; in fact, I doubt their equivalence. One point of this section is to highlight the variety of terms of epistemic appraisal, to prepare for needed distinctions.

Many terms of widespread intellectual evaluation have not figured prominently in analytic epistemology, although there is no good reason why they should not. Consider the term 'intelligent'. In most walks of life, as well as in educational and psychological settings, this is the most common term of intellectual appraisal (a term fraught with difficulties and controversies, to be sure). There is no reason why this should not figure prominently in the mission of epistemic evaluation. Admittedly, precise and culturally acceptable standards for intelligence are needed to make the term useful, but that does not affect the present point. 'Intelligent' is especially worth mentioning here because it does not fall (wholly) in the evidential category. Intelligence does not seem to be just a matter of restricting one's beliefs (or subjective probabilities) to the evidentially warranted, as I will discuss in later chapters.

That intellectual evaluations are not exhausted by evidential ones should be clear from various strands in the philosophy of science, and from social practices of reward and approbation. Many philosophers of science, Karl Popper most consistently,[2] have stressed the value of strong, or bold, theories. A theory that explains more is more desirable than a weaker theory. A scientist who invents and substantiates a more powerful theory receives more approbation than one who invents, and provides equal substantiation to, a weaker theory. In science, and in all avenues of the intellect, importance or significance counts for a lot. Nobel prizes are not awarded simply on the degree of evidence a scientist marshals for his claims. The importance or significance of these results is a critical component. So epistemology should not confine itself to treatment of evidential dimensions of appraisal.

Still other dimensions of appraisal that figure prominently in intellectual life are generally neglected in twentieth-century epistemology. For example, discourses (and other cultural contributions) are regularly appraised on the dimension of originality. Originality is not just a matter of evidential appropriateness, argumentative soundness, or even importance or significance. Rather, it is a matter (roughly) of how difficult it must have been to make the contribution against the historical and cultural background of the contributor, given the intellectual context that existed at the time. I will explore the possible basis for such evaluations in Chapter 11.

(3) Standards of evaluation. In making an evaluation, a speaker assumes some factual basis, or grounds, for the evaluation. In judging an athlete to be outstanding, for example, a speaker presumably relies on some set of actual feats that the athlete has performed. In appraising a student as superior, a speaker bases the judgment on some set of achievements, such as percentage of correct answers to questions or problems. In general, evaluative status does not enter the world autonomously. It always 'supervenes', as philosophers sometimes put it, on purely factual states of affairs. It is often

controversial just which factual states are, or should be, linked with specific evaluations. This is notoriously problematic in the ethical domain. But few writers, except perhaps emotivists, doubt that some factual basis (whether objective or subjective) underlies evaluative judgments, or should underlie them. A central problem for epistemology, equally, is the factual basis on which epistemic evaluations are made. Since there are numerous different terms of epistemic evaluation, it must be expected that different bases will be paired with different terms. Some terms may be vague, or ambiguous, in which case a family of different factual bases may be associated with a single term.

An illustration from ethical theory should help concretize the idea of factual grounding for evaluative judgments. 'Right' is a core term of moral appraisal. But what factual circumstances make an action right? A sample answer is provided by Act Utilitarianism. This theory counts an action A right if and only if A causes, or would cause, as much net happiness as any alternative action open to the agent. The rightness of an action is determined, on this theory, by the relative amounts of happiness that actions in the agent's alternative set would produce. This is a purely factual matter (using 'factual' in a broad sense, to include counterfactual states of affairs). There is a fact of the matter as to what quantities of happiness and unhappiness would result from sundry actions. So there is a fact of the matter—however hard it may be to *know* this fact—as to whether action A would produce as much net happiness as other actions in the alternative set. Thus, Act Utilitarianism provides a factual basis on which rightness (allegedly) supervenes. It is doubtful, of course, that this theory is correct. But it provides a clear *example* of a factual basis.

In the case of epistemic status, we also want to know the factual, or substantive, conditions on which it supervenes. Consider justifiedness. What has to be true of a belief for it to qualify as justified? What factual standard determines justifiedness?

What kinds of answers to this question are legitimate? It is not admissible to answer by using other terms of epistemic appraisal, such as 'rational', 'well-grounded', or the like. We need nonevaluative terms or conditions. Some principal categories of 'facts', or substantive conditions, are the following: *(a)* logical conditions, *(b)* probabilistic conditions, *(c)* psychological conditions, *(d)* 'social' conditions, and *(e)* metaphysical conditions.

Let me briefly illustrate these categories. A theory might say that a person's belief in proposition p is justified if and only if p is logically implied by other propositions the person believes. Such a theory only invokes notions in categories *(a)* and *(c)*: logical relationships and psychological states. Notice that this theory makes justifiedness arise from logical implications among propositions actually believed, not justifiably believed. A theory that invoked justifiable belief would be inadmissible, for it would employ a term of epistemic evaluation where substantive conditions are sought. (This problem could be averted with a recursive, or inductive, specification of justifiedness. But then at least the base clause or clauses of the specification would have to omit terms of epistemic evaluation.)[3]

Another admissible theory would let justifiedness arise from the corpus of a cognizer's beliefs plus probabilistic relationships between the target belief and the beliefs in this corpus (or rather, the propositional contents of these beliefs). But here a theorist must tread carefully. The term 'probability' is notoriously ambiguous, and some of its proposed explications implicitly render it a term of epistemic evaluation (tied to what an epistemically rational person would do). For present purposes, 'probability' would have to be restricted to some other meaning, for example, a frequency, or propensity sense.

Most theories of justifiedness appeal heavily to psychological conditions, especially the antecedent beliefs of the cognizer. A different sort of theory would appeal to *other* people's beliefs, or perhaps their overt statements. This would fall into category *(c)*: social conditions. The inclusion of socially accepted practices, or 'language games', would also fall into category *(c)*. These are admissible as long as it is merely the existence, or acceptance, of the practices that are invoked.

Under category *(e)* I include a number of sorts of factual conditions: for example, conditions invoking the truth or falsity of certain propositions, conditions invoking the notion of cause, and conditions invoking nomological necessity or any other modal notions.

Theories that invoke solely psychological conditions of the cognizer are naturally called 'subjective', or 'internalist', theories. Theories that invoke such matters as the actual truth or falsity of relevant propositions are naturally called 'externalist' theories (assuming, at any rate, some realist approach to truth). The invocation of logical or probabilistic relations may be harder to classify. These are not purely subjective, internal states of affairs, but they have often appeared in theories that would normally be classified as internalist rather than externalist. I shall explore these points later, especially in Chapters 4 and 5. This is only a preliminary introduction, to prepare the reader for some of the directions the inquiry will take.

My interest in factual standards of epistemic terms sounds similar to an interest in 'criteria of application', or 'indices' or 'measures' associated with predicates (as these notions are used, for example, in the behavioral sciences). But all of these terms have a verificationist connotation. They all seek observational standards, which could directly be used to *determine* whether the evaluative term in question applies in specific cases. By contrast, when I speak of factual standards, I do not restrict such standards to observable, or verifiable, standards. I want standards that specify, in general, when an evaluative epistemic term *does* apply, whether or not it provides a way of *telling* that it applies.

This contrast can be illustrated with the Act Utilitarian theory of moral rightness. Such a theory provides substantive conditions of rightness, but not a verification procedure for determining rightness. For example, the theory invokes the notion of happiness without offering any observational reduction of happiness. It presupposes truth-values for various counterfactual statements, without specifying verification procedures for such counterfactuals. These omissions are not objectionable for the purposes in question. No such verificational, or observational, reductions are being sought. Similarly, in offering factual standards for epistemic terms, it is admissible to include truth-linked standards, despite the fact that 'true' is not an observational, or directly verifiable, term. I stress this point because my own approach will feature truth-linked standards prominently. So it needs emphasis at the outset that this is quite unobjectionable, given the goals in question.

(4) Styles of evaluation. Evaluative, or normative, discourse appears in different styles. Some specimens of such discourse include deontic terms, like 'obligatory', 'permitted', and 'forbidden', or more familiarly, 'right' and 'wrong'. Often such terms have systems of rules associated with them. Let us call this kind of normative discourse *deontic.* There are other forms of evaluative discourse, however. Some evaluative terms merely appraise certain qualities as good-making or bad-making features, relative to some suitable dimensions. In other words, they pick out certain traits as virtues or vices. This contrast is found among terms of epistemic appraisal. Epistemologists often try to identify rules of rationality, and they sometimes talk about what is rationally required. This is deontic language in the epistemic domain. By contrast, terms like 'careful' and 'original' might be used to evaluate intellectual performances or traits, but such terms apply no deontic category. They merely identify certain good-making characteristics.

Let me mark the foregoing contrast by saying that evaluative terms can register either deontic classifications, on the one hand, or virtues and vices, on the other. Both styles of evaluation will be employed in this book. I will treat justifiedness (Chapters 4 and 5) as a deontic notion and examine it in a framework of rules. But other evaluations to be studied will be in the virtue-vice style.

A different division of styles distinguishes *regulative* and *nonregulative* normative schemes. A regulative system of norms formulates rules to be consciously adopted and followed, for example, precepts or recipes by which an agent should guide his conduct. A nonregulative system of evaluation, by contrast, formulates principles for appraising a performance or trait, or assigning a normative status, but without providing instructions for the *agent* to follow, or apply. They are only principles for an *appraiser* to utilize in judging.[4] Many epistemologists have sought regulative precepts: principles to guide a cognizer's reasoning processes.[5] But it is also possible to do epistemic evaluation—even in a *rule*-based framework—without seeking action-*guiding* principles. Indeed, when it comes to fixed or automatic psychological processes, it is pointless to offer principles of guidance. Nonetheless, such processes can be the subject of epistemic appraisal.[6]

For the most part, my evaluative approach will be of the nonregulative variety. This will be true especially when the issue revolves around basic psychological processes, as it will in the heart of the book. This nonregulative style will be adopted even in talking of justificational rules. However, a regulative perspective is not entirely excluded, in *some* contexts of my discussion.

1.4. Reliability, Power, and Speed

By way of preview, let me introduce three standards of evaluation—all truth-linked standards. Each can be applied to a variety of objects in the intellectual domain, including both psychological processes and social forms and institutions.

The first standard is *reliability*. An object (a process, method, system, or what have you) is reliable if and only if (1) it is a sort of thing that tends to produce beliefs, and (2) the proportion of true beliefs among the beliefs it produces meets some threshold, or criterion, value. Reliability, then, consists in a tendency to produce a high truth ratio of beliefs. This, of course, is a categorical notion of reliability. But a corresponding quantitative notion of reliability is easily introduced, proportional to the true-belief ratio. (Notice that 'reliability', as used here and in other epistemology literature, corresponds to the behavioral scientists' term 'validity'.)

The reliability standard will be invoked in connection with the evaluative notion of justifiedness. More precisely, reliability is one component in a complex standard appropriate to justification. But reliability is of interest independently of epistemic justification. It is of interest in the epistemic evaluation of social arrangements that produce beliefs, even if these arrangements are not judged on the dimension of justifiedness.

To be clear about reliability, it helps to distinguish two different intellectual misadventures: error and ignorance. Error is false belief; ignorance is the absence of true belief. A reliable process, method, or procedure is an antidote to error. The greater the reliability of one's methods, the smaller one's proportion of errors. But reliability is no antidote to ignorance. Complete reliability can be achieved by extreme caution, or conservatism: producing beliefs only in the 'safest' circumstances, where it is virtually impossible to go wrong. But such radical caution would probably be purchased at the price of (extensive) ignorance. If hardly any beliefs are produced, hardly any true beliefs are produced. This spells (extensive) ignorance.

If the antidote to error is reliability, the antidote to ignorance is (intellectual) *power.* Power is the capacity of a process, method, system, or what have you to produce a large number of true beliefs; or, slightly differently, the capacity to produce true beliefs in answer to a high ratio of questions one wants to answer or problems one wants to solve. As these alternative formulations suggest, there are several variants on the notion of intellectual power. I will focus primarily on the second of these variants, the problem-solving, or question-answering, conception of intellectual power (see Chapter 6). Although power, like reliability, incorporates the ingredient of true belief, it is clearly a distinct standard. A method or system can be very reliable without being very powerful; and a method or system can be pretty powerful but not terribly reliable.

I believe that the power standard, especially the problem-solving variant, is associated with the evaluational term 'intelligent'. One mark of intelligence is a relatively high problem-solving capacity. As indicated earlier, 'intelligence' is an evaluative term that could be central to epistemology. So it is appropriate to explore the substantive standards linked to it, such as problem-solving power. However, I will not attempt a detailed elucidation of intelligence. That term has too long and controversial a history, and may be too vague to make analysis profitable.

A third standard I will explore is *speed,* that is, speed in getting true beliefs. In many intellectual tasks, getting a true answer sooner rather than later is a desideratum. Often there is a specified deadline, after which information loses value. So problem-solving speed is a virtue of a cognitive system. It is also linked to intelligence. In evaluating the strengths and weaknesses of the human cognitive system—a task that will occupy me in Part II—speed is a standard to be considered.

In addition to *first-order* reliability, power, and speed, I will have occasion to consider *second-order* reliability, power, and speed. First-order reliability is a property of belief-forming processes (methods, systems, or what have you). But there are also second-order processes, processes that produce or modify belief-forming processes or methods. A second-order process may be called second-order reliable if the processes it tends to produce are reliable, or, alternatively, if the modifications it introduces tend to increase reliability. Analogous notions of second-order power and second-order speed are readily introduced.

I will not attempt to analyze, or specify standards for, all terms of epistemic evaluation. The salient omission here is rationality, which has figured prominently in epistemology. This notion is so vague in ordinary usage, and so disparately employed by different philosphers and social scientists, that it has limited usefulness. In portions of the book (especially Chapter 14) I will address and criticize other people's discussions of rationality, but I will not try to provide a positive account of my own.

chapter 2

Skepticism

2.1. Varieties and Grounds of Skepticism

I have claimed continuity between my project and historical epistemology, but some readers may wonder. A chief preoccupation of traditional episte-mology is the problem of skepticism. Does my conception of the field—epistemics—come to grips with skepticism? Can psychological investiga-tions of cognitive processes bear on skeptical puzzles? And what about the traditional interpenetration of epistemology, metaphysics, and the philoso-phy of language? The outlines of my conception seem to place little weight on these connections. Doesn't that belie my claim of continuity? This chap-ter is devoted to this constellation of issues.

Let me begin with an overview of skepticism, not a historical overview, but a systematic classification of *types* of skepticism, *grounds* for skepticism, and possible *responses* to skepticism. This overview will help locate my po-sition vis-à-vis epistemology's concern with skepticism and some of its other traditional affiliations.

Skepticism comes in many shapes and colors.[1] These varieties can be ca-tegorized by focusing on three dimensions: *(a) theme, (b) scope,* and *(c) strength.* Let us look first at alternative skeptical themes.

Skepticism goes back, of course, to the ancient period. The two most im-portant ancient schools were the Academics and the Pyrrhonians. The Aca-demics, such as Arcesilaus and Carneades, maintained that no assertions about what is going on beyond our immediate experience are certain. The Pyrrhonians did not endorse the negative dogmatic conclusions of the Aca-demics, in that they did not *deny* that knowledge of the nonevident was possible. Instead, they suspended judgment on the question. The Pyrrhon-ians attributed the origins of their views to Pyrrho of Elis, who was re-garded as a model of the skeptical way of life. He tried to avoid committing himself to doctrines about the nature of reality, while living according to appearances and attempting to attain peace of mind. The fullest presenta-tion of Pyrrhonism was given by Sextus Empiricus.[2] In response to opponents who portrayed the attitude of skeptics as a definite view, Sextus said that it was like a purge that eliminates everything, including itself.

Pyrrhonian skepticism, then, might be characterized as the *cultivation of suspension of judgment,* or doubt. This kind of skeptical theme does not make pronouncements on the possibility of knowledge, certainty, or justification. It only urges suspension of belief—though it is accompanied by arguments to support this attitude. This form of skepticism contrasts with other forms, which are constituted by *theses* about knowledge, certainty, or other epistemic attainments. (In other historical periods, the term 'skeptic' was often applied to anyone who rejected, or failed to endorse, widely accepted views.)

In contemporary epistemology, as well as in much of its history, skepticism is primarily some sort of negative thesis about epistemic attainments. I will focus on two of these attainments: *knowledge* and *justification* (or warrant). Skepticism has often been directed against certainty, but we can interpret this formulation as a special case of either skepticism about knowledge or skepticism about justification. Certainty can be viewed as either the highest grade of knowledge or the highest grade of justification. So skepticism directed against certainty falls either within the knowledge theme or the justification theme.

Skepticisms differ not only in theme, but in scope. Some skepticisms are universal, denying all knowledge or justification. This extreme sort of skepticism is rather rare. Even the ancient skeptics tended to exempt propositions about appearances from the scope of their doubts. Most skepticisms, then, are somewhat less comprehensive, restricting themselves to selected domains such as ethics, mathematics, other minds, the past, the future, the unobserved, and the external world. More global skepticisms tend to focus on a selected theme, such as knowledge or justification, and try to show what makes it impossible, or difficult, to achieve in any domain. More local skepticisms tend to focus on the peculiarity of the selected subject matter—for example, the external world, or the future—and try to show what makes it inaccessible to knowledge or justified belief.

Skepticisms vary not only in theme and scope, but in strength. Roughly, a skepticism's strength is inversely related to the strength of the epistemic achievement that it disputes. A common form of skepticism, we have seen, is the denial of certainty. Certainty can be thought of as either the highest grade of knowledge or the highest grade of justifiedness. Certainty-denying skepticism disputes the existence of such high-grade epistemic attainments. But this is a relatively weak sort of skepticism. Significant forms of knowledge or justification may be weaker than certainty. We might be moderately justified in believing something even if not completely justified. Such lower grades of epistemic accomplishment are not disputed by this kind of skepticism. A stronger form of skepticism, however, would deny even lower grades of knowledge or justification. It might hold that we are not the *slightest* bit justified in believing propositions in the selected domain(s).

A subtopic under strength is modality. Skepticism might be formulated as a doctrine denying the *actual* existence of knowledge, or justified belief. More commonly, however, skeptics dispute the *possibility* of the selected epistemic attainment. What is sometimes left unclarified, though, is the nature of this possibility. Is the skeptic denying the 'logical' possibility of knowledge or justified belief? Is he saying that *no being* could have such knowledge or warranted belief? Or is he just saying that it is humanly impossible to attain such knowledge or justification?

Some of the most common brands of skepticism address what is attainable by *humans*. Many of these skepticisms are explicitly founded on alleged shortcomings of human faculties. Here we can immediately discern how the psychology of human cognition might be relevant to skepticism. Where skepticism is predicated on the frailties or inadequacies of human cognitive powers, the psychology of cognition may address this claim. Of course, the psychology of cognition might be the foundation for new brands of skepticism, by unearthing previously undetected human frailties. But whether it ultimately promotes or impedes the cause of skepticism, psychology can certainly be *relevant*. This point will be explored further below.

Another subtopic under strength emerges when one distinguishes *direct* and *iterative* skepticism.[3] A sample of direct skepticism is the thesis that we cannot know anything. A sample of iterative skepticism is the thesis that we cannot *know that we know*. Although iterative skepticism is an interestingly weaker variant of skepticism, I will focus my attention on direct brands of skepticism.

Given this classification scheme for varieties of skepticism, I can now proceed to survey different kinds of *arguments*, or *grounds*, for skepticism. The single most pervasive ground for skepticism, especially when directed at the knowledge theme, is the *possibility of error*. Many famous skepticisms arise from this source. We can motivate this skeptical strategy by noting that a person does not know a proposition, in any strict sense, if for some suitable sense of 'could', he or she could be mistaken. Even if the target proposition is in fact true, a person's belief in the proposition is not knowledge if it could have been wrong. Suppose the belief was arrived at unsystematically, by a wild guess or by wishful thinking. Then it is just accidental, just lucky, that the belief is true, and it is not something really known (in any strict sense of 'know'). Saying that it is just accidental that the belief is true means that it could easily have been false, and this error possibility excludes possession of knowledge. Knowledge requires more than true belief obtained by lucky guess. Exactly which error possibilities must be foreclosed is controversial. But in some sense, knowing must rule out the threat of error. So the skeptic's denial of knowledge often takes the form of insisting that the threat of error is serious.

Three kinds of error possibility are prominent in the skeptical literature: (1) the fallibility of our cognitive faculties, (2) the relation between the mind and the objects of cognition, and (3) the logical relation between hypothesis and evidence.

Fallibility of the faculties is the earliest and perhaps most common ground for skepticism. Foremost is the fallibility of the *senses*, but the fallibility of *reason* runs a close second. Deception by the senses was intensively discussed by Sextus Empiricus, and most later skeptics including Descartes employed similar ideas. The deceptiveness of reason was commonly demonstrated by showing how it yields incompatible conclusions. In the seventeenth century Pierre Bayle argued that most theories are "big with contradiction and absurdity," that man's efforts to comprehend the world rationally always end in perplexities and insoluble difficulties.[4] Similarly, Kant undermined the pretensions of Reason with his antinomies, a classical skeptical device intended to show the equal strength of contrary lines of reasoning.[5]

Problems about the relation between mind and cognized objects also cut across many periods and topics. Some of these dwell on the character of the objects in question, and some on the nature of the relation. In the former category there is the problem of mutability or change. Plato, following Heraclitus, held that physical objects are constantly in flux, and felt that such flux precludes knowledge. Only unchangeable, immutable objects such as mathematical entities and Forms can be known. In more recent philosophy just the opposite conclusion has been drawn: only physical objects, not abstract entities, can be brought within our ken. In both cases, however, the trouble arises from the possibility of error. Change is a problem because the real properties of a changing object are difficult to detect.[6] Abstractness is a problem because it is hard to see how the mind can get reliable information about an abstract entity, which inhabits a nonspatiotemporal realm.

The difficulty of knowing about an abstract entity may be assigned to the mind-object *relation*, rather than to the composition of the object itself. The problem is: how can the mind get access to an abstract entity? How can it reliably form opinions about the entity's properties? A similar worry underlies skepticism about the external world, skepticism about other minds, and other famous skepticisms. If the mind has direct acquaintance only with its own contents, how can beliefs be reliably formed about physical objects? If mental phenomena are intrinsically private, how can you form reliable beliefs about another person's mind? Whatever external behavior the person displays, there is always the possibility of erroneous diagnosis of the underlying mental causes. Indeed, the assumption of any mental life at all may be erroneous. The 'person' may be just an elaborately programmed robot. How can mere behavioral access to a humanoid creature preclude this possibility of error?

The third source of error possibilities is evidential gaps. If evidence fails to entail a conclusion, alternative hypotheses are compatible with the evidence. So anyone drawing the specified conclusion *might* be wrong. No evidence available to us, Hume indicated, guarantees that the sun will rise tomorrow, or that bread will continue to nourish.[7] None of our evidence, Bertrand Russell pointed out, rules out the possibility that the world came into existence just five minutes ago, complete with ostensible memories and records of a wholly unreal past.[8] These evidential relationships can generate, respectively, skepticism about the future and skepticism about the past.

It would be a mistake to try to squeeze all arguments for skepticism into the error possibility category. At least two other arguments may deserve different treatment. One such argument is that any attempt to achieve justification incurs the dilemma of either circularity or infinite regress. One variant of this argument is of ancient vintage, involving an attempt to find a 'criterion' of justification. A belief is justified, we may say, only if it is approved by a suitable criterion. But how is such a criterion to be chosen? The Pyrrhonian skeptic claimed that any attempt to identify a criterion involves either circularity or infinite regress. This dilemma was posed by Sextus Empiricus:

> In order to decide the dispute which has arisen about the criterion, we must possess an accepted criterion by which we shall be able to judge the dispute; and in order to possess an accepted criterion, the dispute about the criterion must first be decided. And when the argument thus reduces itself to a form of circular reasoning *(diallelus)*, the discovery of the criterion becomes impracticable, since we do not allow them to adopt a criterion by assumption, while if they offer to judge the criterion by a criterion we force them to a regress *ad infinitum.* And furthermore, since demonstration requires a demonstrated criterion, while the criterion requires an approved demonstration, they are forced into circular reasoning.[9]

The circularity argument appears in a number of epistemological contexts; the problem of induction is perhaps the most famous. Is the inductive method (assuming there is a unique such method) legitimate? Attempts to validate induction all too readily appeal to induction itself. Yet this, the skeptic objects, is circular. The proper conclusion, he says, is that induction is illegitimate. Since there is no other method by which beliefs about the future (or the unobserved) can justifiably be formed, the circularity problem appears to doom the possibility of justified beliefs in this domain.

Another skeptical argument that might not go in the error possibility file is the 'rival hypothesis' argument. Some of the most famous skeptical arguments introduce hypotheses intended to rival ordinary, external world beliefs. These rivals include Descartes's dreaming and evil genius hypotheses as well as their modern, brain-in-a-vat counterpart. These rival hypotheses are all intended to raise doubts about our warrant in believing standard, external world propositions. These ploys *might* be construed as demonstrating the possibility of error. But, alternatively, another style of argumentation can be attributed to this sort of skeptic.

The skeptic might be arguing that a person is justified in believing p only if there is no other hypothesis q which explains the phenomena as well as p. The evil genius and brain-in-a-vat hypotheses might be adduced to show that for any selected external world proposition p, a rival hypothesis can always be constructed that is equally explanatory. This kind of strategy is often used in the philosophy of science. If, for any scientific theory T, a nonequivalent but equally explanatory theory can be constructed, perhaps we are never justified in believing any scientific theory.[10]

I suspect that the rival hypothesis stratagem is more commonly motivated, at least in historical writings, by the possibility-of-error worry. Certainly Descartes, in the first *Meditation*, seems to have been thinking along these lines. The other construal of the rival hypothesis stratagem is mentioned for the sake of completeness. As the discussion proceeds, however, I shall pay much greater attention to the error possibility category.

2.2. *Responses to Skepticism: Metaphysics, Analysis, and Psychology*

There are five kinds of epistemological response to skepticism that are noteworthy: (1) *concession,* either total or partial; (2) *metaphysical reconstruction;* (3) *conceptual analysis;* (4) *defense of cognitive powers;* and (5) *construction of a theory of evidence.*

The first category of response is to concede all or part of the skeptic's claims. At one extreme is concession to global skepticism, even strong global skepticism, which claims that we know little or nothing, or that we have not the slightest justification for believing anything. Toward the same end of the continuum is concession to certain important local skepticisms, such as skepticism about the external world. To concede any of *these* forms of skepticism, I think, is to *become* a skeptic.

We have seen, though, that there are weak forms of skepticism. Indeed, in some of these cases, it is debatable whether the view merits the label at all. Suppose you admit that people are never *completely* justified in believing any empirical proposition. Or that people are never justified in believing any scientific theory with certainty. Does this make you a skeptic? Not in current philosophical parlance. Lots of current philosophers hold these views but do not style themselves skeptics. So agreement with very *mild* versions of skepticism does not constitute capitulation to skepticism as it is usually understood.

The remaining categories of response to skepticism are all one or another form of rebuttal. Their suitability, of course, depends on which argument the skeptic marshals. Where the skeptic attacks the cognitive faculties, the opponent can defend these faculties; either the very faculties attacked, or different ones instead. (For example, if the skeptic says that knowledge is unattainable through the senses, it may be countered that knowledge *is* attainable through reason or innate faculties.) Where the skeptic claims that objects of certain kinds are unknowable, the opponent can retort that the objects do not have the uncognizable properties the skeptic alleges. Where the skeptic claims that a rival hypothesis precludes justification, the opponent can construct a theory of explanation to show that the rival is not as explanatory as the target hypothesis. And so on. Let us now examine these responses in greater detail, to see exactly where they lead. Which strategies of response the epistemologist selects will heavily influence the direction of his epistemology.

We proceed to the second category of response on our list: metaphysical reconstruction. Metaphysical theorizing has often been a parry to the thrust of skepticism. When certain domains seemed epistemically inaccessible, philosophers have sought to avert epistemic catastrophe by inventing metaphysical theories to reconstitute the target domain, thereby making it more accessible to the inquiring mind. When it appeared that the physical world could not be 'reached' by the mind, Berkeley introduced idealism to avert disaster,[11] and Mill introduced phenomenalism.[12] By constituting trees and tables out of 'ideas', or 'permanent possibilities of sensation', Berkeley and Mill intended to save the knowability of these objects.

Similar stratagems have been employed in mathematics. Kant felt that mathematics is knowable *a priori* and with certainty. But if the external world is what makes mathematics true, this kind of knowledge seemed unattainable. Kant's solution was a metaphysical theory that interiorized mathematical facts. Mathematical truths were said to be a function of the mind's own structure, which imposes determinate forms on all experience. This mental structure is knowable by transcendental means, and hence is knowable *a priori* and with certainty.

Even in this century philosophers of mathematics have advanced ontologies designed to cope with skepticism. Mathematical platonism breeds the puzzle of how the mind can know about abstract, nonspatiotemporal objects. Formalism, logicism, and constructivism are all (construable as) responses to this worry. If, as formalism claims, mathematical truths are reducible to truths about marks, or inscriptions, they should be more readily knowable, since marks are perceivable (or introspectible) entities. If, as logicism claims, mathematical truths are reducible to truths of logic, they are more readily knowable, since logic (it was assumed) does not have so problematic an epistemic status. If, as constructivism claims, mathematical truths are a matter of proofs that have been or can be constructed, then these truths should be within human ken.

The general pattern here is plain. Metaphysical reductionism is attractive because the reducing entities are thought to be more epistemically accessible than the sorts of entities being reduced or eliminated. The reduction is intended to avoid the skeptical conclusion that we cannot have knowledge of the specified domain. The epistemic theme, however, is not always knowledge or justification. It might feature other epistemic notions, even a quasi-epistemic notion like reference. Hilary Putnam advocates a metaphysical view he calls "internal realism," which seems principally designed to avoid a skeptical threat of no determinate reference relation.[13]

The attractiveness of the metaphysical reductionist strategy depends on two things: first, how plausible the advocated reduction is; and second, whether the advocated reduction really facilitates knowledge of the target domain. Most historical reductionisms have foundered on the first point. The reduction of physical objects to ideas, or sense data, has not fared well; nor did Kant's efforts to interiorize the domain of mathematics. In general, reductive metaphysics has usually proved more costly in overall philosophical perplexity than the epistemological benefits it promised. So cost-benefit analysis has turned the tide of philosophical opinion against it. Frequently, moreover, the epistemological fruits have not proved as sweet as billed. None of the twentieth-century movements in the philosophy of mathematics, for example, has been the epistemological panacea its proponents proclaimed.

I would not make the sweeping claim that all metaphysical reductionism is doomed to failure, that it is never advisable to use such a strategy to cope with skepticism. But the track record of these strategies is not good, and my own inclination is to steer in other directions. This is one reason why my epistemological program does not venture deeply into metaphysics.

Let us turn next to the third category of response: conceptual (or linguistic) analysis. Two different strains of this response must be distinguished: *(a)* analysis of the sentences (or statements) in various special domains, and *(b)* analysis of key epistemic terms, such as 'knowledge' and 'warrant'.

The first kind of conceptual analysis breeds many of the same kinds of theory as metaphysical reductionism, only the theories assume a linguistic form. Thus, linguistic phenomenalism of the twentieth century sought the same style of refuge from skepticism about the external world as Berkeleyan idealism and Millian phenomenalism. Similarly, logical behaviorism was a linguistic reductionism, which (among other things) aimed to salvage the knowledge of other minds. Another kind of conceptual reduction was Hume's treatment of cause and effect. By tracing the idea of causation to constant conjunction, Hume may have hoped to preserve the possibility of knowledge of causation (though this interpretation does not sit well with

Hume's skeptical tendencies). At any rate, twentieth-century Humeans who offer regularity analyses of causation do so partly because they hope to vindicate the prospects for knowledge of causation.

My doubts about this use of conceptual analysis parallel my misgivings about metaphysical reductionism. Most linguistic reductionisms of this sort have been abortive. Linguistic phenomenalism proved no more successful than its metaphysical forebears. And logical behaviorism was a similar flop. Again, I do not oppose *all* uses of conceptual analysis of strain *(a)*. Clearly we *do* need analysis of causal statements, for example, before claims to knowledge of causation can be made good. But I will not pursue ventures of this sort in detail.

My feeling about the second kind of conceptual analysis is quite different. Here I feel no reservations. Any adequate response to skepticism must involve, or presuppose, analyses (or 'accounts') of key epistemic terms like 'knowledge' and 'justification'. Such analyses will be important parts of my undertaking. Only the specific accounts offered of such epistemic terms will rationalize the relevance of psychology to epistemology. (Actually, *certain* details of my accounts are not crucial to the relevance of psychology. But if correct accounts of these notions run along *very* different lines, psychology is much less relevant, or entirely irrelevant.)

To illustrate the pertinence of analysis to the resolution of skepticism, consider the mind's access to various classes of objects. The fear that physical objects may be inaccessible to the mind presupposes some sort of account of access. I will not try to say what accounts of access (explicit or implicit) have led to skeptical worries. One way to allay these fears, though, is to give an adequate account of access, which shows how the mind does, or can, have access to the external world. *Causal* theories of knowledge try to do just this. They suggest that a causal, or causal-subjunctive, relationship between external objects and the mind, mediated by the perceptual systems, can be a sufficient condition for acquisition of knowledge about those objects. Whereas the access metaphor conveys the impression that the mind must somehow make its way 'to' the external world, the spirit of the causal theory is that it suffices for the objects to 'transmit information' to the mind, via energy propagation, sensory transduction, and the like. In short, the direction of epistemic access is not from the mind to the object, but from the object to the mind. If this is roughly right, there is no need to reconstruct objects out of materials that are 'closer' to the mind, namely, the mind's own contents. Knowledge is possible as long as it is possible for objects and minds to stand in the right sort of causal relationship.

Of course, there are problems of detail with a purely causal theory of knowledge.[14] Nonetheless, the causal approach clearly illustrates how an analysis of knowledge can, in principle, resolve skeptical worries without a revisionary metaphysics.

Let me further illustrate how conceptual analysis can help answer skepticism, and how different proposed answers guide epistemology down alternative paths of inquiry. One approach to justification says (roughly) that a belief is justified if the believed proposition better explains what it purports to explain than any rival proposition.[15] Furthermore, this 'best-explanation' approach may be presented as a theory of *evidence.* That is, it may claim that evidential support for a proposition is to be understood in terms of the position of that proposition in an explanatory network. Two comments are in order about this argument. First, if the account is right, it stands a good chance of resolving certain skeptical challenges, specifically, those that arise from rival skeptical hypotheses. To make this response stick, though, the epistemologist must show that ordinary physical object beliefs *are* better explanations of the phenomena than, say, the Cartesian demon hypothesis or the brain-in-a-vat hypothesis. This will necessitate a satisfactory theory of explanatoriness. (How does simplicity, for example, affect degree of explanatoriness? How is simplicity measured? And so on.) In addition, the epistemologist will be called upon to defend the view that a best-explanation account of evidence is the right sort of theory of evidence. My second comment, then, is that this sort of theory of justification not only bears on skepticism but also bears on the direction of one's epistemological inquiries. Obviously, this approach to justification points more in the direction of the theory of evidence (the fifth response listed above) than in the direction of psychological scrutiny of cognitive mechanisms.

By contrast, suppose an account of justification asserts that a belief is justified if it results from reliable cognitive processes. Such an account is relevant to various forms of skepticism, specifically those forms of skepticism that impugn our cognitive faculties. If this account of justification is correct, then the skeptic may be right in insisting that our beliefs are justified only if our cognitive faculties are not excessively error-prone. A full account of justification would shed light on what is excessive or tolerable in the way of fallibility. (Total infallibility is presumably a misplaced demand.) Finally, there would be the question of whether human cognitive processes *are* sufficiently reliable. This question, in turn, breaks into two components: *(a)* What cognitive processes do human beings in fact have? and *(b)* What is the reliability of these processes? At least question *(a)* falls in the province of psychology. Hence this account of justification would lead epistemology down a path that fosters collaboration with cognitive psychology. And it leads to a version of the fourth response to skepticism (the defense of cognitive powers).

Conceptual analysis is sometimes deployed against skepticism in a much more direct fashion. Some philosophers try to show that skepticism can be defused by purely conceptual dissection of the skeptical position. I have in mind here so-called transcendental arguments, at least semantic versions thereof. Recent transcendental arguments have tried to show the absurd or paradoxical nature of skeptical questions. They try to show that if the skeptic's claim makes sense at all, it must be false.

For example, Sydney Shoemaker has argued against the other-minds skeptic as follows.[16] To assert, as the skeptic does, that it is logically impossible for one person to know of another that he's in pain is to imply that the word 'pain' has no established meaning. But if the word 'pain' has no established meaning, then the putative statement that it is logically impossible for one person to know of another that he's in pain has no established meaning either. Therefore, either what the skeptic says has no established meaning, or it is false.

Barry Stroud has critically examined transcendental arguments of this sort and shown that they depend on a very dubious semantic principle, which he calls "the verification principle."[17] I am inclined to agree with this diagnosis. Attempts to rebut skeptical challenges by such *a priori* means rest on questionable semantic assumptions. So I do not see conceptual analysis as undermining skepticism quite so easily. Still, it is relevant to the possible defeat of skepticism in ways I have sketched above.

Since I have stressed the role of analysis in response to skepticism, let me digress a bit to comment on conceptual analysis. Most philosophers these days are cautious of this enterprise, principally in view of Quine's attacks on analyticity and general problems about the notion of meaning.[18]

Three comments on this issue are in order. First, while there are doubtless severe theoretical problems concerning the notions of meaning and synonymy, there must be *some* substance to the commonsense notions suggested by these terms. Certainly we can distinguish better and worse definitions of a given word, whether dictionary definitions or definitions offered by casual speakers. Moreover, it is clear that the speech of a child or a foreigner can often profit from a reasonable definition, and the better the definition, the better the learner's resulting usage. So there must be *some* phenomenon of meaning that remains to be clearly elucidated.

Second, although many philosophers preach the abandonment of analyticity, their practice sometimes belies their preaching. People do things very much *like* conceptual analysis even if they officially reject it. It is hard to do much in epistemology (or other branches of philosophy) without feeling constrained to do something like conceptual analysis.

Third, people often mean by 'conceptual analysis' the presentation of strictly necessary and sufficient conditions for a term. But given the longstanding failure of philosophers (or lexicographers) to devise accurate definitions of this kind for very many (if any) words, it is doubtful whether such analyses are indeed possible. I share theorists' doubts about this form of definition.[19] In the meantime, however, I will follow the working practice of trying to give necessary and sufficient conditions for important epistemological terms. This can be regarded as a first approximation to a better way of treating meaning, if such a better way can be devised.

2.3. How Important Is Skepticism?

It is clear that epistemologists cannot respond satisfactorily to skepticism without accounts of key epistemic terms, especially 'knowledge' and 'justification'. This is one reason I shall devote the next three chapters to these topics. However, the nature of knowledge and the nature of justification are matters of independent interest, quite apart from the tenability of skepticism. Thus, while I remain mindful of skepticism in these discussions, it does not wholly dominate them. Skepticism is only *one* concern of epistemology; its significance should not be blown out of proportion.

To help keep my treatment of skepticism in proper perspective, let me amplify this point. The two principal questions of (global) skepticism are: is it (humanly) possible to have knowledge, and is it (humanly) possible to have justified belief? On the main accounts I shall offer of knowledge and justified belief, the attainment of both knowledge and justified belief depends critically on the use of sufficiently reliable cognitive processes. Hence, whether knowledge and justified belief are humanly possible hinges on the availability or nonavailability of sufficiently reliable processes. Suppose that this matter—the availability or nonavailability of such processes—is settled, whether in the affirmative or in the negative. Would it follow that nothing is left for epistemology to do? Certainly not.

Suppose first that the threat of skepticism were thwarted. Suppose we were guaranteed that there are sufficiently reliable processes to make knowledge and justified belief possible. Still, much work would be left. Epistemology should be concerned with not only whether there are reliable processes, or methods, but which ones these are. Epistemology should be interested in *specifying* the good procedures, not simply ensuring that there are such. To be assured that knowledge or justified belief is possible is to be assured (on this theory) that *some* satisfactory processes are available. But how many such processes are there? And which ones are they?

Notice that even in the history of epistemology, the central issues have not always been couched in terms of skepticism. Consider the rationalist-empiricist controversy, for example. This was a debate not so much over whether knowledge can be attained as over how it can be attained: by principal reliance on the senses, or by greater reliance on reason? Rationalists questioned the ability of the senses and induction to deliver the goods; they advocated the power of innate concepts and principles, intuition and demonstrative proof. Empiricists challenged the existence of innate ideas and *a priori* principles; they doubted the ability of pure ratiocination to achieve intellectual ends. This debate continues today among neorationalists and their opponents. Both parties to the dispute can cheerfully admit that knowledge is attainable (or perhaps that knowledge in a *strong* sense is not attainable). The dispute centers on the *means* by which knowledge—or true belief—is to be attained.

Now let us assume that global skepticism wins the day. Would that spell the end of epistemology? Not necessarily. Even if there are not any *sufficiently* reliable cognitive processes to qualify a person for either knowledge or justified belief, there might still be differences among processes in degrees of reliability. A worthy epistemological task is to identify the *comparatively* reliable processes, to discriminate the better from the worse. This would indicate how to maximize one's truth ratio, or maximize the probability of getting a high truth ratio. Even if epistemic honors like knowledge or justified belief are beyond our grasp, that does not mean all distinctions should be abandoned.

The next point to notice is that knowledge and justifiedness, at least on my accounts, critically invoke one particular standard of appraisal: reliability. But that is not the only standard of epistemological interest. Even if no cognitive processes are sufficiently reliable to confer knowledge or justifiedness, indeed, even if all are equally unreliable so that none stands out above its peers, distinctions could still be drawn according to other standards. I have already mentioned the standards of power and speed. Procedures might differ in the range of questions to which they can deliver correct answers and in the speed of getting these answers. Such differences are certainly of epistemic interest, even if the reliability of all processes is too low to qualify for knowledge or justifiedness.

Another dimension of appraisal possibly orthogonal to skepticism is *rationality*. This is a widely cited epistemic desideratum, one that may be feasible for human beings even if both knowledge and justifiedness are not. It may be possible to have rational beliefs even if knowledge is unattainable. This point is often taken for granted in the dominant philosophy of science tradition, which commonly pursues questions of scientific rationality without concern for standard problems of skepticism.

It should be noted, in this connection, that the weapons in the skeptical arsenal are usually best equipped for demolishing the epistemic qualifications of full-fledged beliefs. When it is claimed that we cannot know, this is often on the grounds that we do not have a right to be sure or completely confident. It is more difficult for the skeptic to provide grounds for saying that we have no right to even *partial* beliefs, say, to subjective probabilities of .60. Theories of rationality often try to lay down conditions for rational subjective probabilities. And such conditions may be important for epistemology even if prospects for *knowledge* are foreclosed.[20] I shall not myself offer any theory of rationality. But I shall tentatively tender an account of justifiedness for partial beliefs. This would be of interest even if skepticism—at least in the knowledge theme—wins the day.

The issue of skepticism, then, is not the be-all and end-all of epistemology. A balanced epistemology should have a place for it without allowing it to overshadow other issues. This book tries to present a balanced perspective. But since one of my aims is to redress the imbalance of previous epistemologies, which have exaggerated the significance of skepticism, the space devoted to skepticism will be comparatively small.[21]

chapter 3

Knowledge

3.1. Knowledge and Causal Processes

What is knowledge? More specifically, what is propositional knowledge: what is it to know that something is the case? To know a proposition p is to know that it is true. But you cannot know that p is true unless it *is* true. So a necessary condition for knowledge is truth. Equally, you cannot know that p unless you are of the 'opinion' that p is true, unless you believe p. So belief, like truth, is necessary. But true belief is not sufficient for knowledge, at least not in the strict sense of 'know'. If it is just accidental that you are right about p, then you do not know that p, even if you are correct in believing it.

Suppose you wake up in a foul mood one morning and think to yourself, 'Today is going to be a miserable day'; and lo, a miserable day ensues. It does not follow that you *knew* in the morning that it was going to be a miserable day. It is just a fluke if such a feeling is right, and flukes are not sufficient for knowledge.

One traditional proposal for strengthening the requirements is to add a justification requirement. A true belief is not knowledge unless it is a justified belief. I do not reject this suggestion, but it is a complex matter to establish conditions for justifiedness. So let us see what can be said about conditions for knowledge without yet invoking a notion like justifiedness.

A first factor to consider about knowledge is a *causal* factor. Whether a true belief is knowledge depends on why the belief is held, on the psychological processes that cause the belief or sustain it in the mind. This is illustrated by the miserable day example. In that example the only cause of the belief is your foul mood, which produces a gloomy forecast. But this kind of cause is not adequate for knowledge. If we change the cause, the same belief could qualify as knowledge. Suppose you get a call from an officemate, who reports on excellent authority that the boss plans to fire half the staff today, yourself included. You believe as before—that it's going to be a miserable day—but now you *know* it (assuming, at any rate, that things go as reported). In this variation, the cause of your belief is suitable for knowledge.[1]

The next question to ask is: What makes a cause, or causal process, the right kind of process for producing knowledge? What distinguishes knowledge-producing causes from other causes? Why isn't a feeling, or mood, an appropriate kind of cause? The natural answer seems to be: because belief formation based on mere feelings, or moods, can easily go wrong. It would be easy to be in a bad mood in the morning although the day is not going to be miserable. So if a belief gets formed in this fashion, it has a very good chance of being false. The belief does not qualify as knowledge—even if it happens to be true—because the style of belief production is error-prone, or unreliable. If, however, the belief-producing process is reliable, that helps qualify the belief for knowledge.

We have here a sample motivation for a *reliability* approach to knowledge. Coupled with the earlier suggestion that the cause of the belief is crucial, we have a *causal reliability* approach. But causal reliabilism is not the only form of reliabilism. Let me briefly mention and discuss an alternative brand of reliabilism: the reliable-indicator approach.

D. M. Armstrong has proposed such an account of knowledge.[2] The model on which he bases this account—especially the account of *noninferential* knowledge—is the model of a reliable thermometer. In a reliable thermometer the temperature reading is a reliable indicator of the actual ambient temperature. Similarly, he proposes, a noninferential belief counts as knowledge when it is a reliable indicator of the true state of affairs. Reliable indicatorship is explicated in terms of a nomological, or lawlike, connection between the belief and the state of affairs that makes the belief true.[3] If the having of the belief is nomologically sufficient for the belief's being true, then the belief is a reliable indicator and qualifies as a piece of knowledge.

Let B stand for a particular brain state, and suppose that whenever a human being believes he is in brain state B, this nomologically implies that he *is* in brain state B. This might happen because the only way to realize belief in this proposition is to be in brain state B. It follows from the reliable-indicator account that whenever any person believes he is in brain state B, and hence the content of that belief is true, this true belief qualifies as knowledge. But this result is readily susceptible to counterexample. Suppose that what causes a given person to believe he is in brain state B is not any genuine understanding or information concerning brain states, in particular, no knowledge of the cited nomological fact. Further, suppose that he has no autocerebroscope to monitor his brain states and give readouts about them. He just has a firm hunch that he is in brain state B (it is a state he heard described in a recent lecture, but he dozed through most of that lecture and knows nothing of what was said about the state). Surely, he does not *know* he is in brain state B, although his belief to this effect is a reliable indicator of the truth.[4]

It is worth stressing that even a *stronger* variant of the reliable-indicator condition would not suffice to capture knowledge. Even if the indicator relation is strengthened from nomological to logical sufficiency, the desired result is not secured. Even if the having of a given belief 'logically' guarantees the truth of the belief, the belief may not qualify as knowledge.

Suppose young Humperdink considers a proposition having fifteen disjuncts, the eighth of which is 'I exist'. Schematically, then, the proposition is: '1 or 2 or . . . or I exist or . . . or 15'. Now Humperdink is not logically sophisticated enough to realize that this proposition is entailed by 'I exist', so he does not believe it *for this reason*. Nor does he believe it because he already knows (or believes) one of the other fourteen disjuncts to be true. He only believes it because he is inclined to believe *any* complex proposition with ten or more disjuncts. The very thought of such a complex proposition overtaxes his meager mental powers and induces belief. If these are the facts, one would hardly say that Humperdink *knows* this fifteen-disjunct proposition to be true. Nonetheless, his believing it is logically sufficient for its truth. This is because his believing it logically guarantees that he exists, which in turn logically guarantees that the disjunctive proposition is true. Thus, his belief is a logically reliable indicator of the truth. Yet this does not raise the belief to the status of knowledge.

Once again, the process that causes the belief is critical to the knowledge question. Since the causal process in Humperdink's case is just being overwhelmed by sheer complexity, and since this is an unreliable process, the resulting belief fails to qualify as knowledge. The fact that the belief happens to be a reliable indicator of the truth is irrelevant to the knowledge question.

3.2. Alternative Reliable-Process Theories

Given the attractions of causal reliabilism as an approach to knowledge, it is worth pursuing further. In particular, let us focus on the attempt to account for knowledge in terms of reliable *processes*. The reliable-process approach was first formulated, in kernel form, by Frank Ramsey.[5] There are now several variants under discussion, and we need to explore the prospects of the various alternatives.

Three pairs of options can help generate a field of alternative reliable-process theories. (To repeat, these are theories of *knowledge*. There are also reliable-process theories of *justifiedness*, to which I shall turn in Chapter 5.) First, we may distinguish a process's *global* reliability and *local* reliability.[6] (This has nothing to do with the global-local distinction for types of skepticism; that distinction does not enter here.) The difference lies in the range of uses for which the process is reliable. Global reliability is reliability for all (or many) uses of the process, not just its use in forming the belief in question. Local reliability concerns only the reliability of the process in the context of the belief under assessment. However, this might include its reliability in certain counterfactual situations centered on the target belief.

This brings us to a second distinction among reliable-process approaches: the *actual-counterfactual* distinction. Some approaches might invoke the process's reliability only in actual applications. Other approaches might invoke its reliability in counterfactual situations as well.

If counterfactual applications are allowed, a third distinction comes into play. On the one hand, the admissible counterfactual situation may be restricted to the one determined by the *pure subjunctive:* what would happen if proposition p were false? Alternatively, more counterfactual situations could be invoked, for example, all situations involving *relevant alternatives* to the truth of p.

Combinations of options chosen from this menu determine an array of reliable-process approaches. Let us see how current versions of reliabilism fit into the resulting classification. Robert Nozick's version of reliabilism—what he calls the "tracking" theory—can be seen as a choice of *local* reliability, in *counterfactual* applications, as specified by the *pure subjunctive.*[7] In first approximation his account features the following four conditions for knowledge: (1) p is true, (2) person S believes that p, (3) if p weren't true, S wouldn't believe that p, and (4) if p were true, S would believe that p. Nozick adds the proviso that beliefs in the counterfactual situation(s) must result from the same method M, used in the actual situation.

Condition (3) is obviously the critical one in this account, and introduces the local subjunctive as the linchpin of the analysis. Unfortunately, the local subjunctive is too weak. Here are a few examples to show why.

Suppose a parent takes a child's temperature and the thermometer reads 98.6 degrees, leading the parent to believe that the child's temperature is normal, which is true. Suppose also that the thermometer works properly, so that if the child's temperature were not 98.6, it would not read 98.6 and the parent would not believe that the temperature is normal. This satisfies the first three conditions of Nozick's analysis. Presumably the fourth condition is also satisfied: in (close) counterfactual situations in which the child's temperature is normal, the parent would believe that it is normal.

But now suppose there are many thermometers in the parent's medicine cabinet, and all but the one actually selected are defective. All the others would read 98.6 even if the child had a fever. Furthermore, the parent cannot tell which thermometer is which; it was just luck that a good thermometer was selected. Then we would not say that the parent *knows* that the child's temperature is normal, even though Nozick's analysis is satisfied.

Another case will solidify the point. Suppose S sees a smiling stranger on the street, and concludes that the man just won a lottery. His only basis for this belief is that the stranger is smiling. S knows nothing else about him that forms the basis for this belief. As it happens, this stranger *would not* be smiling unless he had just won a lottery; the only thing with the power to make him smile is a lottery prize. So if he had not won a lottery prize, the cognizer would not believe that he had. According to Nozick's account, S knows that this man just won a lottery. But intuitively that is not right.

Prior to Nozick, Fred Dretske offered a very similar analysis, although the formulation of his analysis is slightly more complex.[8] However, Dretske's analysis succumbs to the same sorts of counterexamples as I have just presented.[9]

Another version of reliabilism was presented in my paper "Discrimination and Perceptual Knowledge."[10] That paper also invokes counterfactual situations in accounting for knowledge attributions; but it does not employ the pure subjunctive. It says (roughly) that a true belief fails to be knowledge if there are any *relevant alternative situations* in which the proposition p would be false, but the process used would cause S to believe p anyway. If there are such relevant alternatives, then the utilized process cannot *discriminate* the truth of p from them; so S does not know.

This relevant alternatives account works better than the pure subjunctive one. The pure subjunctive account is just too permissive. Suppose Sam spots Judy across the street and correctly believes that it is Judy. If it were Judy's twin sister, Trudy, he would mistake her for Judy. Does Sam know that it is Judy? As long as there is a serious possibility that the person across the street might have been Trudy rather than Judy (even if Sam does not realize this), we would deny that Sam knows. This is handled properly by the relevant alternatives account, since the possibility of its being Trudy would presumably qualify as a relevant alternative. But the pure subjunctive account would not necessarily give the correct verdict. We may suppose that what *would* be the case if Judy weren't across the street is that *nobody* would be across the street; or we may suppose that if Judy weren't there, her colleague in the mathematics department would be there. (Say they had flipped a coin to see who would fetch lunch, and Judy lost. If the colleague had lost, *he* would be the person walking down the street.) In these counterfactual situations, Sam would not believe that Judy is across the street. So Sam's belief would survive the pure subjunctive test, and that account would incorrectly say that Sam knows.

Notice that the no-relevant-alternatives condition can handle Gettier and post-Gettier cases.[11] Consider Brian Skyrms's case in which a pyromaniac believes that the next Sure-Fire match he strikes will light.[12] It is true that it will light, but not because of the usual chemical condition of previously encountered Sure-Fire matches. This particular match is defective, but it will light because of a coincidental burst of Q-radiation. Here the pyromaniac does not know that the match will light. Why not? He does not know because there is a relevant alternative situation in which the pyromaniac's evidence is exactly the same but the match does not light, that is, a situation in which the match is defective (as in the actual situation) *but* there is no burst of Q-radiation. Other Gettier and post-Gettier cases can be handled similarly, as I will show in section 3.4.[13]

In "Discrimination and Perceptual Knowledge" I emphasized what I here call a *local* reliability requirement for knowledge. But I did not mean to endorse local reliability to the exclusion of global reliability. Indeed, in other papers I have made the global reliability requirement quite explicit.[14] Notice that local and global reliability are not mutually exclusive. A theory can require *both*, and I mean to require both in a theory of knowing. To qualify as knowledge, a true belief must result from a generally reliable process, not just one that is (counterfactually) reliable for the case in question.

Another variant of reliabilism, by contrast, selects global reliability to the exclusion of local reliability. This is Colin McGinn's recent adaptation of the discrimination approach.[15] McGinn's theory also contrasts with the two kinds of theories discussed thus far in eschewing counterfactuals. In terms of our classification, it selects global reliability; purely factual, not counterfactual, situations; and the no-relevant-alternatives option (although this third option does not invoke counterfactual alternatives).

The discrimination theme I stressed in "Discrimination and Perceptual Knowledge" calls attention to the fact that one sense of 'know' listed in the Oxford English Dictionary is "to distinguish (one thing) from (another)." Examples of such a sense are "I know a hawk from a handsaw" *(Hamlet),* "We'll teach him to know Turtles from Jayes" *(Merry Wives of Windsor),* 'I don't know him from Adam', and 'He doesn't know right from left', as well as other current sayings that readily come to mind. The conjecture is that the propositional sense of 'know' is related to this underlying meaning, in that knowing that p involves discriminating the truth of p from relevant alternatives. On my development of this theme, the alternatives are counterfactual alternatives. McGinn develops the discrimination theme slightly differently. He wants us to consider the truth-discriminating power of the belief-forming process (or 'method') within some relevant class R of propositions, where R is not restricted to proposition p and contraries of p. We are to look at the propensity of the process to form true beliefs across a range of propositions whose truth-values are taken as fixed in the actual world.[16]

One of McGinn's examples that motivates his approach, especially his eschewal of counterfactuals, is this: You visit a hitherto unexplored country in which the inhabitants have the custom of simulating being in pain. You do not know that their pain behavior is mere pretense, and so you form the belief, of each person you meet, that he or she is in pain. In this way you acquire many false beliefs. One person, however, is an exception to the cus tom of pain pretense: this hapless individual *is* in constant pain and shows it. You also believe of this person, N, that he is in pain. In this case your true belief is not, intuitively, knowledge. But the relevant counterfactual 'If N were not in pain, you would not believe that N was in pain' is *true*, since if N were not in pain, then (unlike the pretenders), he would not behave as if he was, and so you would not believe that he was. Since this counterfactual is true, it cannot accommodate the absence of knowledge in this case. So a noncounterfactual version of reliabilism, McGinn surmises, is needed to handle it.

Notice, though, that this case is only a problem for the pure subjunctive variant of the counterfactual approach. The relevant alternatives variant can handle it. A relevant alternative possibility is one in which N is not in pain but is a pain simulator, like the other people around him. In this counterfactual situation you would falsely believe that he is in pain, which is why you do not know in the actual situation.

McGinn's dismissal of counterfactual conditions is unconvincing for other reasons. First of all, he does not offer a fully formulated analysis. He does not tell us exactly what the discriminative range of the belief-forming process must be in order to be capable of knowledge production. Moreover, there seems to be a general pitfall for his strategy. A process might be *wholly* reliable in *actual* situations. This would apparently imply that every true belief it produces counts as knowledge. But that seems implausible: there might still be cases in which counterfactual possibilities defeat a knowledge ascription. My worry on this score cannot be nailed down in the absence of a fully formulated analysis from McGinn; but the outlines of his approach incur this probable difficulty.[17]

Although I differ from McGinn on the appropriateness of a counterfactual requirement, especially a local requirement, we are in agreement on the need for a *global* reliability requirement. This comes out clearly for knowledge of necessities, such as the truths of mathematics. Can such knowledge or nonknowledge be handled by invoking such counterfactuals as 'if it were not the case that $7 + 5 = 12$, S would not believe that $7 + 5 = 12$'? One problem is that we have no adequate account of counterfactuals with impossible antecedents. Another problem is that it is not clear that such a counterfactual is true in the case of someone who *does* know that $7 + 5 = 12$. So Nozick's third condition might be violated by someone who knows this proposition. (The no-relevant-alternatives approach would not be imperiled, though, because there may *be* no alternative in which $7 + 5$ does not equal 12.) Also, while Nozick says that his fourth condition is designed to handle true beliefs in necessities that do not qualify as knowledge, McGinn shows that this claim does not succeed.[18]

How *should* we handle true beliefs in necessities that do not qualify as knowledge? My suspicion is that they are mostly cases in which the belief-forming processes, or methods, are not globally, or generally, reliable. General reliability refers to the notion of reliability explained in Chapter 1, that is, a statistical or dispositional property of a belief-forming process *type*. We may take it to refer to the truth ratio of beliefs generated by the process on all actual occasions of use, and probably some possible occasions as well. So global reliability may also involve counterfactuals.

Leaving the topic of necessities, let us reflect more on general reliability. As indicated, general reliability is probably best understood as a propensity rather than a frequency. This avoids the possibility that actual uses of the process are numerically too limited or skewed to represent an intuitively appropriate ratio. If we move to the propensity idea, though, there is the problem of specifying the range of possible uses that should be countenanced. I do not know exactly how to do this, but it seems plausible to restrict possible uses to situations rather similar to those of the real world. I will return to this theme in Chapter 5.

Another problem for the global reliability approach is the 'generality problem'. The approach speaks of *the* (psychological) process that causes a belief. But commitment to a unique process is problematic. Global reliability is a ratio among instances, so, strictly speaking, it only holds of a process *type*. But whenever a given belief is produced, the process token that generates it may be described in different ways.[19] Correlated with these different descriptions are different process types, and these types may have different reliability properties. The question is: which of these many types should be used in fixing reliability? Should the relevant type be sliced broadly or narrowly? In the case of a perceptual belief-forming process, for example, should the relevant type simply be 'perceptual causation'? Or, at the other extreme, should it include detailed features of the retinal stimulation peculiar to this specific instance of belief causation?

Before addressing this problem, I must note that it is not peculiar to the reliability approach, but probably faces any *process* account of knowledge. Since some such theory, I have argued, is essential, the problem is not peculiar to reliabilism.[20]

The generality problem was identified in my earlier paper "What Is Justified Belief?" but the dilemma posed by the problem has been emphasized by others.[21] If type selection determines very broad types, there is the No Distinction problem. Every case of perceptual belief causation will be categorized the same way, including both cases where the object is far away and seen only briefly and cases where the object is close at hand, observed at leisure, and in optimal viewing conditions. This seems wrong because our temptation to credit the cognizer with 'knowledge' differs in these cases, and this ought to be traced to general reliability differences. But if type selection determines extremely narrow types, there is the Single Case problem. When the type is extremely narrow, there may be only one actual instance, namely, the instance in question. Since this instance by hypothesis yields a true belief (otherwise it would not even arise as a serious candidate for knowledge), the type will have a truth ratio of 1. Intuitively, it might not be a case of knowledge, but the reliability approach would not have the materials to imply this judgment.

Now the Single Case problem arises only if global reliability is determined exclusively by actual frequencies. As suggested above, however, a propensity approach is preferable. Since we can thereby put aside the Single Case problem, we are in a position to favor a narrow principle of type individuation. Certainly narrow types are needed to draw the desired distinctions between processes, those that intuitively do yield knowledge and those that do not.

But how is it determined, in each specific case, which process type is critical? One thing we do not want to do is invoke factors external to the cognizer's psychology. The sorts of processes we're discussing are purely internal processes. Let me advance a conjecture about the selection of process types, without full confidence. The conjecture is: the critical type is the *narrowest* type that is *causally operative* in producing the belief token in question.

To illustrate this idea, suppose (purely for illustrative purposes) that there is a template mechanism for forming perceptual beliefs. The mechanism takes feature inputs from the sensory systems and tries to match them to various templates, each template representing some category C, for example, the category of dogs, or the category of cars, or the category of chairs. Suppose the mechanism so functions that there is a value T such that if the input features match the template of category C to degree T or more, then the mechanism generates a belief that the stimulus object belongs to C. Now if the value of T is very low, then even when a stimulus is highly degraded—partly obscured, or seen under adverse lighting conditions—feature inputs resulting from the stimulus may prompt a belief that the stimulus belongs to C. Suppose such a belief on a given occasion is true. Should we call it knowledge? Doubtless we would be leery of doing so. Our reluctance can be explained by pointing to the unreliability of the mechanism. A mechanism of the sort postulated, with a *low threshold* for matching, will tend to be quite unreliable. So as long as the value of the matching threshold is included in the chosen process type, we will get the right answer on this knowledge ascription case.

But notice that the mechanism has lots of different matching properties. It has the property of producing a belief when the degree of match is T; the property of producing a belief when the degree of match is T + .1; the property of producing a belief when the degree of match is T + .2; and so on. Is the appropriate process type always one that includes the first of these properties, namely, the *minimal* degree of match sufficient for belief?

Presumably not. For consider a case in which the perceptual input is not degraded, and the actual degree of match to the template is, let's say, .99 (on a scale of 0 to 1). Then presumably we will want to say that this is adequate for knowledge (if everything else goes well). But if the selected process type still includes the *minimal* value T, the type as a whole may not have sufficient reliability.

My proposed account would handle this case by noting that the mechanism's property of having T (say, .70) as minimally sufficient is not causally operative in this case. The property of having this threshold value does not play a critical causal role in eliciting the belief. The degree of match in this case is actually .99. So the critical aspect of the mechanism's functioning that produces the belief is the propensity to produce a belief when the degree of match is .99. If *this* property, rather than the others, is included in the selected process type, an appropriate degree of reliability is chosen that meshes with our knowledge ascription intuition.

Clearly, this proposal needs to be developed and refined, but I will not try to do that here. I present it only as a promising lead toward a solution of the generality problem.

3.3. Second-Order Processes

For a belief to count as knowledge, I am arguing, it must be caused by a generally reliable process. Exactly *how* reliable I have not said. Nor do I think this can be answered with precision. The knowledge concept is vague on this dimension, and an analysis need not impose more precision than the common sense concept contains.

I want to turn now to another wrinkle in the reliable-process theory. So far, attention has been restricted to immediate causes of a belief, not remote cognitive ancestry. But the attainment of knowledge may depend on such extended ancestry.

Knowledge may depend on remote cognitive ancestry for two reasons. First, when a person believes p by inference from antecedently held beliefs, whether he knows p depends on more than the reliability of this final inference procedure. It also depends on the antecedent beliefs and how they were derived. Those beliefs must themselves be known, or at least believed justifiably, and this implies (as I shall argue in subsequent chapters) that they must have been caused by reliable processes. Since those beliefs' causal ancestry may be remote, so may be the relevant ancestry of the belief in p.

A second reason why knowledge depends on cognitive ancestry concerns second-order processes, that is, processes used in acquiring processes. To illustrate, suppose our friend Humperdink has attended a series of talks on mathematics by a certain Elmer Fraud. These talks are not under the auspices of any certified educational institution, and Humperdink has been

warned that Fraud has no credentials in mathematics. Humperdink hears
Fraud enunciate numerous principles and algorithms, almost all of them
defective. Nonetheless, being a complete novice—and a gullible one at
that—Humperdink blindly accepts and applies them all. In one case, however, Fraud happens to teach a perfectly correct algorithm. Humperdink
internalizes this one along with the others, and applies it to a relevant class
of problems. In using this algorithm to solve a problem, Humperdink gets
the answer right and forms a true belief in the answer. This belief is the result of a reliable process, namely, the algorithm. (Later I will call such algorithms *methods,* rather than *processes,* but the distinction will be waived for
now.)[22] Clearly, though, Humperdink should not be credited with knowledge. He does not know because it is quite accidental that he has hold of a
reliable algorithm. Using blind faith to acquire algorithms is notoriously
unreliable; an algorithm so acquired cannot transmit knowledge, though
the algorithm itself may be perfectly reliable.[23]

This example suggests that a further requirement for knowledge is
needed. Not only must the belief result from a reliable process, or method,
the process or method used must have been acquired (or sustained) by a
suitable second-order process.

Can this further requirement be dispensed with? Can Humperdink's failure of knowledge be explained by the fact that his belief in the answer is
based on a belief in the correctness of the algorithm, which is an *unjustified*
belief? This might work in the present example, but it will not be generally
adequate. Many of our belief-forming procedures are not believed by us to
be correct; we may not have any belief about them at all. They may be
merely automatized procedures, not objects of 'declarative' belief (in the
terminology of cognitive science.)[24] If these procedures have been unsuit-
ably acquired, however, they cannot yield knowledge, even if they are completely reliable. Suppose, then, that in addition to the principle below,

(1) S knows that p only if S's belief in p results from a reliable belief-
forming process,

we also accept the following principle:

(2) An acquired belief-forming process (or method) can generate knowledge only if it is acquired (or sustained) by an appropriate second-order
process.

The question immediately arises: What determines 'appropriateness' for
second-order processes? The reliability theme readily suggests an answer,
already mentioned in Chapter 1. The obvious proposal is that a second-
order process is appropriate just in case it is second-order reliable. But what
is second-order reliability? One answer (also mentioned in Chapter 1) is that
the ratio of reliable processes among the processes it generates must be very

high. However, this requirement might be too strong. A weaker requirement may suffice: the second-order process need only acquire processes that
are *more* reliable than previous ones used in the same contexts. Whichever
of these proposals is adopted, second-order reliability seems to be a promising kind of ingredient for the appropriateness of second-order processes.[25]

Second-order processes are of special importance to one of the book's
general themes: the link of epistemology to psychology. Many first-order
procedures used to form beliefs are not deep-seated psychological processes. They are learned algorithms or domain-specific inference precepts.
But when we ascend (descend?) to second-order processes, or perhaps even
higher-order processes, we eventually come to processes that clearly are
deep-seated psychological processes: parts of the architecture of cognition.
If, as my recent ruminations suggest, such processes are relevant to questions of knowledge, it becomes clear how portions of psychology that study
basic cognitive mechanisms are relevant to judgments of knowledge. Only if
(some of) our basic cognitive processes are either reliable or higher-order
reliable can we qualify as knowers. Therefore, whether we so qualify
hinges, in part, on facts in psychology's bailiwick.

Parenthetically, I might add that similar points hold for other themes of
epistemological interest, though not specially pertinent to knowledge
ascriptions. Take the topic of evidence-gathering strategies. These too may
be learned strategies, which are partly domain-specific. But they are doubtless learned with the help of higher-order processes, which may be wired-in
features of our cognitive architecture. Since these processes are also of
epistemological significance, we have another area in which psychology can
contribute to epistemology.

3.4. Knowledge and Justification

Still another refinement is needed to achieve a fully adequate account of
knowledge. There are cases in which beliefs are caused by globally and locally reliable processes, yet the person has reason to believe they are not
reliable. These are cases where the belief, though caused by a reliable process, is not *justified*.

Two examples should be mentioned. In the first Millicent in fact possesses
her normal visual powers, but has cogent reasons to believe these powers
are temporarily deranged. She is a subject of a neurosurgeon's experiments,
and the surgeon *falsely* tells her that current implantations are causing
malfunction in her visual cortex. She is persuaded that her present visual
appearances are no guide at all to reality. Yet despite this belief, she continues to place credence in her visual percepts. She ignores her well-justi-
fied belief in the incapacitation of her visual faculty; she persists in
believing, on the basis of visual appearances, that a chair is before her, that

the neurosurgeon is wearing a yellow smock, and so on. Now these beliefs are all, in fact, true. Moreover, they are formed by the usual, quite reliable, perceptual processes. But are they specimens of knowledge? Intuitively, no. The reason is that Millicent is not *justified* in holding these beliefs; they contravene her best evidence. It seems, then, that causation by reliable processes is not sufficient for knowing.

Another example is this: Maurice uses a reliable—but not perfectly reliable—heuristic to arrive at a certain belief p. Now the fact that the process is not perfectly reliable does not by itself preclude knowledge. I do not assume that perfect reliability is required. But there is another heuristic Maurice knows, which is more reliable than the first (though still not perfect), and Maurice believes it is more reliable. He even suspects, in this case, that the better heuristic might yield a different result, since it has differed from the first in similar cases before. But despite these beliefs, Maurice neglects the superior heuristic. Had he used it, it would indeed have led him to a different conclusion: to believe not-p rather than p. But in this particular case the first heuristic gets things right: p happens to be true. Does Maurice know p? Intuitively, no. He does not know, once again, because his belief in p is not justified. He should have consulted the superior heuristic.

If knowledge requires justifiedness, as these cases suggest, I cannot complete my account of knowledge without a theory of justifiedness. But does it follow that the reliable-process theory is on the wrong track entirely? That justifiedness is a wholly different element, quite out of spirit with the themes I have stressed until now? That of course is possible. It might be supposed that once the justificational element is introduced into knowledge, it will change our picture of knowledge dramatically. But that is not what I shall argue. On the contrary, my account of justified belief will feature some of the same ingredients discussed thus far, though couched in a different format. Further requirements will be added, however, to handle the foregoing cases (especially the Millicent case).

The reader may wonder whether my account handles the standard examples in the post-Gettier knowledge trade. What about the original cases in which the (true) belief in p is (justifiably) inferred from false premises? And what about the so-called social dimensions, where things known to other cognizers, but not to S, may keep S from knowing p? These cases can be handled, I believe, by the local reliability requirement, the no-relevant-alternatives condition.

Suppose S believes that either Jones owns a Ford or Brown is in Barcelona, and his justification consists in evidence for Jones's owning a Ford. In fact, Jones does not own a Ford, but by sheer coincidence Brown is in Barcelona. S does not know that either Jones owns a Ford or Brown is in Barcelona, although this is true.[26] Why doesn't he know? S's true belief is not knowledge because it is defeated by the following relevant alternative, which is compatible with all his evidence: Jones doesn't own a Ford and Brown isn't in Barcelona. This counterfactual situation is one that S cannot discriminate (with his evidence) from the actual state of affairs.

Similarly, consider the case in which you apparently see Tom Grabit steal a book from the library. Unbeknownst to you, Tom's mother has said that Tom is miles away while his twin brother, John, is in the library. This may be enough to defeat any claim on your part to know that *Tom* stole the book, even if it is true.[27] My explanation of this case is that you cannot discriminate this truth from *John's* stealing the book. Furthermore, the latter alternative seems to be relevant, as long as Mrs. Grabit says what she says. When it transpires, however, that there *is* no twin John—he's only a figment of Mrs. Grabit's demented imagination—this ceases to be a relevant alternative, and you can be credited with knowing. In this fashion, the no-relevant-alternatives element of my account seems able to handle Gettier and post-Gettier examples.

3.5. Knowledge and Skepticism

Where does this reliable-process approach to knowledge leave us on the issue of skepticism? Can it help meet skeptical challenges? Or does it present any new avenues to skepticism? Finally, what does it imply about the relationship between psychology and skepticism?

On the reliable-process account, of course, the critical factor in knowledge is the acquisition of true belief via processes that are both locally and globally reliable. It seems clear that it is at least logically possible to acquire true beliefs via processes that satisfy these requirements. So at least the 'logical possibility' of knowledge seems to be secured. Furthermore, this may be all that can reasonably be expected of an analysis. An analysis cannot be expected to entail that we *do* know, or that we know very much or very often. Indeed, it cannot even be expected to entail that it is *humanly possible* to know. That may depend on human powers—in this case, the possession of sufficiently reliable belief-forming processes. And the existence of such powers cannot reasonably be secured by an *analysis* of knowing per se.

However, some analyses might open the door to skepticism wider than others. For example, an analysis of knowledge that requires the exclusion of all logically possible alternatives would open the door very wide indeed. My account, however, which requires the exclusion of only 'relevant' alternatives, does not open the door quite so wide. In particular, I assume that I can know there is a computer keyboard in front of me because I do not have to discriminate that state of affairs from the possibility that I am merely a brain in a vat being artificially stimulated to make it appear as if there is a keyboard in front of me. The brain-in-a-vat alternative just is not a *relevant* alternative. (I do not, however, have a detailed theory of relevance.)

There is, however, a related argument for skepticism not handled by this reply: the problem of closure. It is an initially plausible principle that knowledge is closed under known logical implication. If I know that p and I know that p logically implies q, then I must know that q. In the present case let p be that there is a keyboard in front of me, and let q be that it's *not* the case that I am a mere brain in a vat . . . Since I know that p logically implies q, I only know p if I know q. But do I know q? Do I know that the envatment hypothesis is false? It does not seem as if I discriminate that from *its* relevant alternatives. So it seems as if I do not know q. But that seems to imply that I do not know p.

Dretske and Nozick have argued, plausibly, against the principle of closure.[28] To legitimate the rejection of closure, though, one needs an account of knowledge that sustains this rejection. But, as McGinn points out, the discrimination account does sustain nonclosure.[29] Different propositions carry with them different requirements as to the discriminative capacities necessary for knowledge of them. And knowledge of logically weaker propositions can require greater discriminative powers than knowledge of logically stronger propositions. It can be easier to know p than q although p implies q (and not vice versa) because q requires more in the way of discrimination than p. To know there is a keyboard before me I needn't discriminate this state of affairs from envatment. But to know I am not envatted, I do need to discriminate this state of affairs from envatment. So I may not know I am not envatted. Yet this possibility does not preclude my knowing there is a keyboard before me.

The kind of knowledge skepticism I have principally examined is *direct* skepticism, which claims that it is impossible to know. But there is a different sort of question, concerning *iterative* skepticism (see Chapter 2), that may perturb many people regarding the reliable-process approach. Granted that such a theory leaves open the possibility of knowledge, does it allow us to know that we know? Many discussions in epistemology go astray in failing to distinguish questions of first-order and higher-order knowledge (or justification).[30] But once the distinction is carefully made, there is no objection to raising questions and doubts about the prospects for higher-order knowledge, and the implications different theories have for such knowledge.

Is the reliable-process theory worse off than other theories vis-à-vis higher-order knowledge? No. At least it isn't worse off than a good theory ought to be. We have already seen that it makes knowledge a logical possibility. By the same token, it makes it logically possible to know that one knows. To know that we (sometimes or often) know, we would have to know that we (sometimes or often) use reliable processes of belief formation. But since the analysis makes it (logically) possible for us to know what processes we use, and makes it (logically) possible for us to know all sorts of truths about the world (which is essential for knowing the reliability of our processes), the analysis makes it possible for us to have higher-order knowledge. To be sure, the analysis does not entail the actual existence of higher-order knowledge. It does not even entail that *if* we know, then we know that we know. But no analysis of knowledge should entail this. A plausible theory ought to have the property that knowing that one knows is more difficult than simply knowing. It is a virtue of this theory that it has this property.

Granted that my analysis allows the possibility of both first-order and higher-order knowledge, what does it say, or imply, about whether we *do* in fact know (very much of the time)? As indicated earlier, the analysis per se does not speak to this question. It does imply, though, that we *do* know only if we have reliable (and higher-order reliable) cognitive processes. It follows that to find out whether we know, we need to ascertain the properties of our native cognitive processes. This is where psychology enters the picture. Psychology can (in principle) tell us about the nature of our cognitive processes. When these processes are spelled out, we can try to determine their reliability. (It is doubtful, though, that psychology alone can determine their reliability. For this we need help from a variety of intellectual fields, probably including logic and statistics.)

Notice that psychology is needed not merely to tell us whether we do know, but whether it is humanly possible to know. The reliable-process theory of knowing entails the *logical* possibility of knowledge, but it does not entail that knowledge is humanly possible. It is humanly possible only if humans have suitable cognitive equipment. And this is something of which we can best be apprised only with the help of psychology.

In saying that whether we do or can know depends on psychological facts, I partially concur with Quine when he says that "sceptical doubts are scientific doubts."[31] But my agreement is only partial. Some, but not all, skeptical doubts are scientific doubts. Some routes to skepticism arise from concern over the propriety of crediting someone with knowledge if certain logically possible alternatives cannot be excluded. The best way to counter *this* skeptical maneuver is through a satisfactory analysis of knowledge, not through psychology or other branches of science. (Of course, any piece of linguistic analysis is plausibly viewed as applied psycholinguistics, and hence as part of science. This is not what Quine had in mind, though, given his strictures about analysis and analyticity.) But this sort of maneuver, as I have discussed, can be met by the reliable-process account.

chapter 4

Justification: A Rule Framework

4.1. Justification and Rules

There are several reasons for interest in the notion of justification. First, we may have a purely intrinsic interest in the question of when people's beliefs are justified. Second, we may be concerned with skepticism, which is sometimes couched in the justification theme: Is it possible to have justified beliefs? Third, our interest in justification may derive from an interest in knowledge. Justified belief, I have shown, is necessary for knowing. So ascriptions of knowledge, and questions about the possibility of knowledge, hinge on justifiedness.

These reasons for interest in justification all arise in theoretical contexts. But judgments of justifiedness can also arise in practical contexts. Suppose I am trying to determine whether or not p is true. So far, my evidence is very scant. I now learn that Delphine believes p. How much does that help me in my determination? Not very much; it is not very decisive unless I know whether Delphine's belief is justified or unjustified. If her belief is unjustified, then her believing p is not much of a guide to the truth or falsity of p. But if her belief is justified, I have much stronger evidence for the truth of p. I have a practical reason, then, for wanting an assessment of Delphine's belief on the justifiedness dimension.[1] (Notice how this point meshes with a reliabilist theory of justifiedness. It makes sense to regard someone's justified belief in p as evidence for the *truth* of p if justified belief is belief formed by reliable processes.)

There are multiple reasons, then, for interest in the notion of justifiedness. For these reasons, and because it has played a central role in traditional epistemological theory, I shall devote two chapters to the topic. It should be acknowledged from the start that there is much vagueness in the (epistemic) use of 'justified'. No unique conception of justifiedness is embraced by everyday thought or language. This will emerge in Chapter 5, where I present several distinct accounts of justifiedness, each with some hold on intuition. However, these accounts form a close-knit family; so there seems to be a core idea of justifiedness, which my theory will seek to capture.

I approach justification in terms of a rule framework. This is warranted by purely semantic connotations. Calling a belief justified implies that it is a *proper* doxastic attitude, one to which the cognizer has an epistemic right or entitlement. These notions have a strong deontic flavor, as indicated in Chapter 1. They are naturally captured in the language of 'permission' and 'prohibition', which readily invite a rule formulation.

There are two additional reasons for the rule framework. First, it helps formulate a comprehensive classification of theories of justification. It provides a neutral structure within which competing conceptions can be articulated. Second, it lends itself to instructive parallels between epistemic evaluation and moral and social evaluation. Questions about objectivity and subjectivity, absolutism and relativism, are points of lively controversy in all of these domains. The rule framework helps formulate such questions with greater theoretical rigor than would otherwise be possible, and thereby helps us see the issues clearly.

We should be reminded, however, of the caution expressed in Chapter 1. Talk of rules naturally suggests a regulative conception of evaluation: an attempt to provide advice, decision guides, or recipes, for making doxastic choices. But the rules I shall be discussing should not be understood as rules for guiding a cognizer's intellect. A person need not even understand the rules, and if he does, he need not be able to apply them in the process of belief formation. Perhaps rules advanced by *some* theorists could serve as (first-person) decision guides; perhaps I too would endorse such rules for secondary epistemology. But the rules I envisage for primary epistemology would not have this property.

A good first pass at a rule framework for justification is presented by the following principle:

(P1)   S's believing p at time t is justified if and only if
       S's believing p at t is permitted by a right system of justificational rules (J-rules).

This principle can be generalized for all sorts of doxastic attitudes, not just beliefs. But I will not be concerned with this generalization until Section 5.7.

Principle (P1) is intended to express a semantic truth about the language of justified belief. Indeed, it is intended to be a purely formal, largely neutral, principle. Although it is not wholly uncontroversial, I would expect it to be acceptable, at least as a necessary condition, to epistemologists of very different persuasions. It is not intended to identify any particular factual standards for justified belief. To obtain a full theory of justifiedness, one must go well beyond principle (P1). Indeed, two additional levels, or stages, of theorizing are needed to get a complete account. I will return to these levels shortly.

Several other comments about (P1) are needed. First, a comment about the term 'right'. Obviously, all sorts of different justificational rules, or systems of rules, might be proposed. Many candidate rules are quite silly, and would not be endorsed by any epistemologist (for example, 'A cognizer is permitted to believe any self-contradictory proposition on Tuesdays'). I certainly do not want to say that justified belief consists in belief licensed by *any* rule, even a silly rule. The only sensible linkage is with correct, or right, rules of justification, not mere candidate rules. Nor does justifiedness necessarily consist in conformity with widely accepted rules. Widely accepted rules could be wrong, and if they are, conformity with them does not guarantee justifiedness.[2] If justifiedness is to consist in rule conformity, it must be conformity with *right* rules.

Second, why do I insert the qualifier 'justificational' before 'rules'? What is the import of this? It reminds us that there are different terms of epistemic appraisal, and a similar rule framework might be used to explicate those other terms as well. For example, we might explicate 'rational belief' as belief permitted by right rules of rationality. Since 'rational' and 'justified' are different terms of appraisal, rules of rationality (R-rules) might well be distinct from rules of justification (J-rules). Hence we need to distinguish justificational rules, or J-rules, from other possible rules.

Third, (P1) links justifiedness and conformity with systems of rules. Why systems, and not simply single rules, are involved cannot be explained now and is deferred for later treatment.

Fourth, (P1) links justifiedness with J-rule *permission,* rather than obligatoriness. Why not say that a belief is justified just in case it is *required* by a right system of J-rules? The answer is that right J-rules may be quite permissive, allowing cognizers leeway in their doxastic attitudes. For example, if a person has a certain corpus of prior beliefs, the rules might permit him to infer a further proposition that logically follows from this corpus. But the rules might not *mandate* this inference. To take another kind of example, if there are J-rules for subjective probabilities, they might permit someone in a certain cognitive state to assign to proposition q a subjective probability in the interval from .70 to .80. No determinate subjective probability is mandated; any credence in this interval is permitted. So if a cognizer in this cognitive state forms a subjective probability of .77 vis-à-vis q, this doxastic attitude is justified, even though it is merely permitted by the rules, not required.[3]

Fifth, systems of J-rules are assumed to permit or prohibit beliefs, directly or indirectly, as a function of some states, relations, or processes of the cognizer. For example, J-rules might permit a cognizer to form a given belief because of some appropriate antecedent or current state. Thus, someone being 'appeared to' in a certain way at t might be permitted to believe p at t. But someone else not in such a state would not be so permitted. Alternatively, the rules might focus on mental operations. Thus, if S's believing p at t is the result of a certain operation, or sequence of operations, then his belief is justified if the system of J-rules permits that operation, or sequence of operations. Here the belief in p would be not directly, but only indirectly, sanctioned by the rules—because it is an output of licensed operations. Principle (P1) does not try to settle just what the J-rules should be. In that respect, it is quite neutral.

In introducing (P1), I called it a good 'first pass' at a framework principle. But there is the issue of whether it is strong enough. Although it provides a necessary condition for justifiedness, whether it provides a sufficient condition is questionable.

Two possible ways of strengthening it might be proposed. First, in addition to requiring that the belief *be* permitted by right rules, it might be required that the cognizer *know* that it is permitted, or believe *justifiably* that it is permitted, or something along these lines. Of course, there is a problem of circularity if we build justifiedness, for example, into the framework principle. For we would then use the concept of justifiedness to set conditions for justifiedness. The same circularity problem arises if we require *knowledge* of the permission, for knowledge implies justifiedness. Recall (from Chapter 1) that we want a theory to give nonepistemic conditions for justifiedness.[4]

The circularity problem might be circumvented, though, by proposing a principle like the following:

(P2) S's believing p at time t is justified if and only if
    (a) S's believing p at t is permitted by some right J-rule system R, and
    (b) R permits S to believe at t that the (or a) right J-rule system permits his believing p at t.

Is (P2) a better principle than (P1)? Note first that any reason for endorsing (P2) as over against (P1) ought also to be a reason for endorsing *further* iteration of the permission requirement, with a *(c)*-clause that parallels *(b)*, a *(d)*-clause that parallels *(b)* and *(c)*, and so on. Of course, imposing such an infinite number of requirements could make it humanly impossible to have justified beliefs. This is precisely the result a skeptic would welcome, so this sort of strengthening of (P1) is likely to appeal to epistemologists with a skeptical streak.

The mere fact that such strengthening would play into the skeptic's hands should not disqualify it. Perhaps the strengthening is really required for a correct account of justifiedness. We must not assume the skeptic to be mistaken without argument, or without fair examination of the terms or notions in question.

However, it is indeed a level-confusion to replace (P1) with (P2).[5] Our analysandum is *being justified*, not justifiably believing that one is justified. So (P2) is just ill-motivated. To see this, consider young children and other philosophically unsophisticated cognizers. People in these categories—*most people*—do not even have the concept of J-rules, so they do not have beliefs, and presumably cannot be permitted to have beliefs, about whether their beliefs conform to right J-rules. But it is counterintuitive to suppose that only philosophers, or other methodological sophisticates, even have a chance at justified beliefs. To take just one example, why can't ordinary perceptual beliefs be justified without higher-order sophistication? It seems clear, then, that (P2) is an excessive strengthening of (P1).

There is a weaker form of strengthening, however, which seems quite well motivated. Suppose S's belief in p is permitted by a right J-rule system, but S believes that it is not so permitted. Alternatively, suppose S's belief in p is permitted by a right J-rule system and S is *justified* in believing that it is not so permitted (whether or not he actually believes that it is not permitted). In either case, it is counterintuitive to regard S's belief in p as justified. In these cases S's belief, or justification for believing, that the belief in p is not permitted *undermines* its permittedness. That is, although the belief *is* permitted, this does not intuitively suffice for its justifiedness. A well-motivated strengthening of (P1), then, is one that requires no undermining of a belief's permittedness.

One kind of undermining described in the previous paragraph occurs when S is justified in believing that her belief in p is not permitted by right J-rules. Since we are seeking a principle of justifiedness, however, we should not use the notion of justifiedness in explaining the notion of undermining. So let us revise the foregoing description by saying that a permission for S to believe p is undermined if S is permitted (by right J-rules) to have a belief in the denial of this (lower-level) permission.

I have mentioned two ways, then, in which a belief's permittedness might be undermined. First, the belief can be undermined by the cognizer's being permitted to believe that the belief is not permitted. Second, the belief can be undermined by the cognizer's believing that the belief is not permitted, even where the higher-order belief is not itself permitted. But additional possibilities should be entertained. The cognizer might not have the concept of belief permissibility, or even of right rules. But suppose the cognizer believes that certain conditions are not satisfied, where those conditions are *in fact* necessary for belief permissibility. This is a third way, I think, in which the belief's permittedness may be undermined. I will not try to give a full theory of undermining, but will say more about it in section 5.6 where it will play an important role. Meanwhile, I can strengthen (P1) by adding the no-undermining condition, thereby yielding the following principle:

(P3)   S's believing p at t is justified if and only if
      (*a*)   S's believing p at t is permitted by a right system of J-rules, and
      (*b*)   this permission is not undermined by S's cognitive state at t.

Although (P3) is the real framework principle I mean to endorse, in most of what follows I will be mainly interested in clause *(a)*, in other words, in principle (P1). For convenience, then, I will often refer to (P1) as the framework principle, and I will make reference to (P3) only when it is specially pertinent.

4.2. *Rightness Criteria for J-Rules*

Principles (P1) and (P3) are formal principles of justifiedness. They do not give much in the way of substantive standards on which epistemic justifiedness supervenes. But substantive standards are precisely what we want, as indicated in Chapter 1. We want to know under what conditions a belief is justified.

While principle (P1) does not answer this question, it does tell us something we need to know to answer it, namely, what system (or systems) of J-rules is right. How this right system is identified involves a *two-stage* approach. First, we need a *criterion* of rightness. Second, we need to determine which system of J-rules in fact satisfies the chosen criterion. Now if we regard (P1) as a prior stage of theorizing and add these two stages to it, the theory of justification consists of three stages or levels: (1) the level of the framework principle, (2) the level of the criterion, and (3) the level of the J-rule system. Most of my attention to justifiedness in Part I (the remainder of this chapter and Chapter 5) focuses on the second stage: the criterion of rightness. Hefty portions of Part II will be devoted to the consequences of this choice. But I shall not attempt to specify in detail any system of J-rules that satisfies the chosen criterion.

What is meant by a criterion of rightness? First of all, I mean a standard of rightness that fulfills the requirements mentioned in Chapter 1. It must specify factual, substantive conditions for rightness of J-rules. These cannot be conditions that themselves invoke, or rely upon, epistemic notions. To illustrate, consider the following putative criterion:

A system R of J-rules is right if and only if
    R is the set of rules an ideally rational inquirer would instantiate.

Such a proposal is inadmissible because it employs the term 'rational', itself an epistemic term. We want only nonepistemic notions to appear in a criterion of rightness.

Second, I do not mean by 'criterion' what many philosophers (such as Wittgenstein and Wittgensteinians) have meant, namely, a test or way of determining whether the term in question is satisfied. A criterion of rightness is simply a very general set of conditions that are necessary and sufficient for a system of J-rules to be right. Such a criterion can be correct whether or not it is easy, or even feasible, to *ascertain* what systems satisfy the criterion. There is an understandable propensity to crave a set of truth-conditions, or satisfaction-conditions, that can actually be *applied,* indeed, easily applied. Unless one can figure out what system satisfies a criterion, of what use is the criterion? How could we execute the third stage of epistemological inquiry into justification, the stage of identifying a right system of J-rules?

Despite these natural cravings, we must not confuse the question of what *makes* a system right with the question of how to *tell* if it is right. The first of these questions is fundamental. Only once we can say what makes a system right can we worry about identifying a right system. So let us understand by 'criterion' only a set of *satisfaction*-conditions for rightness, not a test of rightness, or set of *verification*-conditions for rightness.

It is time to drop this abstract mode of discourse and give some examples of possible criteria of rightness. However, before turning to the epistemological sphere, I want to give some analogous examples from other domains, where similar enterprises are undertaken.

Morality is a domain in which right rules are commonly sought, or assumed to exist. What makes a system of moral rules a right system? Many answers are possible, but let us choose one for purely illustrative value, a theological criterion of rightness:

A system R of moral rules is right if and only if
  R is a system of moral rules decreed by God.

This proposal has the virtue of simplicity. It makes it quite clear what is necessary and sufficient for a system of moral rules to be right. But it does not follow that it would be easy to determine what system is right. Assuming the correctness of this criterion, one would have to determine which system was in fact decreed by God. This might raise controversial issues as to which texts or alleged revelations are authoritative expressions of God's will; or for that matter, whether God (whose existence and uniqueness are assumed for the sake of argument) ever delivers decrees in overt verbal form, and whether such verbal formulations should be interpreted literally or otherwise.

Another example of a criterion of rightness can be taken from the theory of justice. John Rawls's theory of justice exemplifies a three-level structure very analogous to mine.[6] Here is my reconstruction. Rawls first introduces the idea that a basic social institution is *just* if and only if it conforms with correct principles of justice. This parallels principle (P1). Second, he offers a theory of what makes a justice-principle correct; that is, he offers a criterion of rightness for justice-principles. That criterion is:

A justice-principle p is right if and only if
p would be chosen by parties in the Original Position.

Third, he formulates two specific principles and argues that they satisfy this criterion, that they would be chosen in the Original Position.

In the area of the law we also find analogous examples, though in this sphere the criteria are those of a 'genuine', or 'valid', law, not necessarily a 'right' (meaning, morally right) law. Here we have such examples as that of John Austin (the nineteenth-century legal theorist):

L is a law if and only if
L is a dictate of the sovereign.[7]

There is also the criterion of so-called legal realism, that the law is what judges say (or will say) it is. There are two possible variants of this position:

L is a law if and only if
L is what the courts have said is the law,

Or

L is a law if and only if
L is what the court of highest authority will (or would) say is the law.

One of the underlying motivations of legal positivism, and of legal realism, is a conception of law that makes the law more readily knowable, which is a severe problem under the natural law conception. The foregoing criteria were intended (in part) to meet that desideratum. It is questionable, however, whether they fully succeed in this. For example, suppose the court of highest authority has not addressed the validity of a given statute, and will never address it. Then it is not readily verifiable whether the statute is a valid law.

Issues of verifiability have strongly colored much theorizing in the law. This is unfortunate from the standpoint of theoretical clarity. Thus, H. L. A. Hart introduces the notion of a "rule of recognition" in the law, which is close to what I am calling a 'criterion'.[8] Unfortunately, Hart conflates the two questions that must be distinguished: what makes something a valid law, and what the procedures are for recognizing, or verifying, that something is a valid law. Failure to separate these questions can and has led to some confusion in jurisprudential theory.[9] The same problem exists in epistemology. It is therefore imperative to understand by 'criterion' of J-rule rightness only a set of conditions that make (a system of) J-rules right, not a test, or verification procedure, for J-rule rightness.

It is time to turn to examples of criteria for rightness of J-rule systems. The examples to follow only give a flavor of the different criteria that might be advanced, including some variations on popular themes. Obviously, no attempt is made at exhaustiveness. In all cases the notion for which the criterion is offered is: 'A system R of J-rules is right'.

Possible criteria include:

(C1)   R is a system of rules derivable from logic (and probability theory).

(C1°)   R is the system of rules that would be chosen by someone who believes all truths about logic (and probability theory), but is ignorant of all contingent facts.

(C2)   R is the system of J-rules accepted by the players of one's language game (Wittgenstein).[10]

(C2°)   R is the system of J-rules accepted by members of one's disciplinary matrix (Kuhn).[11]

(C2°°) R is the system of J-rules accepted by one's peers (Rorty).[12]

(C3)   Conformity with R would guarantee a coherent set of beliefs.

(C4)   R permits doxastic attitudes proportioned to the strength of one's evidence.

(C5)   Conformity with R would maximize the total number of true beliefs a cognizer would obtain.

In trying to identify an acceptable criterion, what method should be used? The strategy I endorse is best expressed by the Goodman-Rawls conception of "considered judgments in reflective equilibrium."[13] We examine what rule systems would likely be generated by each candidate criterion. We reflect on implications of these rule systems for particular judgments of justifiedness and unjustifiedness. We then see whether these judgments accord with our pretheoretic intuitions. A criterion is supported to the extent that implied judgments accord with such intuitions, and weakened to the extent that they do not. But our initial intuitions are not final. They can be pruned and adjusted by reflection on candidate rule systems. There are other tests of a criterion's adequacy as well. Does it generate any rule systems at all? Does it generate a *complete* rule system, that is, one that would imply justifiedness or unjustifiedness for all cases of belief and all doxastic attitudes?

This procedure need not involve empirical psychology or social science. I do not claim that psychology plays a role in selecting a criterion of J-rule rightness. This is not the level at which psychology enters the epistemological enterprise. It enters the picture only if and when a criterion is selected that makes reference to cognitive processes. In other words, psychology is relevant to stage 3 of a theory of justification, which involves the choice of particular J-rule systems, not stage 2, which involves the choice of a criterion.[14]

With these general comments in mind, let us return to the list of candidate criteria and look briefly at some of their characteristics and problems. This is only a preliminary examination, to get a feel for possibilities and difficulties.

Criteria (C1) and (C1°) invoke truths of logic, or rules of logic, as the basis for a J-rule system. This reflects a widespread view that principles of logical inference provide justificational procedures. On this approach, then, proper rules of justifiedness are to be generated by truths of logic, or by someone omniscient about logical truths.

The first point to raise about such an approach concerns completeness. At most, deductive logic can generate a proper subset of desired rules of justification; not all appropriate rules can be derived from it. Where nondeductive inferences are appropriate—and such cases are certainly legion—truths of deductive logic are of little or no help. Are there truths of inductive logic to fill the breach? That is very dubious. Many epistemologists and philosophers of science now question whether there is a body of truths we can call 'inductive logic'.[15] *Perhaps* probability theory can be adduced to provide a relevant class of truths. But, again, the epistemological pertinence of probability theory is complicated and problematic.[16] Presumably, some rules of justification should pertain to perceptual beliefs, and some to beliefs involving memory. Neither truths of deductive logic nor of probability theory can generate J-rules in these domains. Hence, criteria (C1) and (C1°) are inadequate on grounds of incompleteness.

There are, moreover, further fundamental weaknesses in (C1) and (C1°). They both assume—(C1) most explicitly—that *some* J-rules can be derived from truths of logic. But that is not so, as we shall see in Chapter 5. A typical truth of deductive logic is that modus ponens is a valid argument form. But no (correct) rule of belief formation is derivable from this sort of truth. Validity of argument forms has no immediate implication for belief-forming practices.

It might seem as if belief-forming rules can be derived from logical truths. Such rules could simply permit a cognizer to believe any proposition in the corpus of logical truths. This is perhaps what (C1°) envisages: a logically omniscient cognizer formulating rules that allow people to believe, at a minimum, what the cognizer himself believes, namely, all logical truths. But this would have unacceptable implications. It would imply that whenever a person believes a truth of logic, the belief is justified. That is clearly wrong. It is possible to believe a truth of logic unjustifiably. I will elaborate on this point in Chapter 5.

Criterion (C1°) articulates a common stance in epistemology. The epistemologist is allowed to appeal to truths of logic, and perhaps probability theory, in formulating methodological rules; but appeal to contingent propositions (except perhaps first-person experiential statements) is disallowed. This idea bears some resemblance to Rawls's conception of the Original Position, the position in which hypothetical parties are to choose principles of justice. In Rawls's Original Position the parties are behind a "veil of ignorance." They do not know what their own situation in society is or will be. But they are imagined to have ideal knowledge about relevant laws, such as laws of economics and sociology. Similarly, the hypothetical agent envisaged in (C1°) is supposed to choose a system of J-rules and is endowed with a certain combination of ideal knowledge and ignorance. He knows all truths of logic and probability theory, but no contingent truths. So we might call his position an *Epistemologically* Original Position.

Why is this the right position from which to choose a system of J-rules? Is it because truths of logic and probability theory are *necessary?* Is it because they are knowable *a priori?* But why should these properties make the described position a suitable Original Position? Is it because such truths are knowable with epistemic *certainty,* whereas contingent propositions are not? This assumption is dubious. Prior to theory, many contingent propositions seem to be known with as much certainty as many truths of logic (especially higher-order logic). Finally, the whole idea of equating J-rule rightness with what would be chosen in an Epistemologically Original Position is a questionable one.[17]

Let us turn now to criteria in the (C2) family. The members of this family all share a social perspective: they make rightness a function of what is accepted by a society, or culture, presumably that of the target cognizer. On this approach a person has a justified belief only if his method of forming or defending the belief satisfies the J-rules of his community (linguistic community, disciplinary community, or what have you). Any such proposal invites an obvious objection. Why should we assume that what is accepted as justification-conferring by the members of a particular community really is justification-conferring? Can't such a community be wrong? Why should authority be lodged in a cognizer's own community? What is privileged about it? Generations of scientists and mathematicians have used methods of inquiry and proof that they regarded as sound but were later shown to be somehow unsound or defective. Why couldn't the same failing hold for any arbitrary community of inquirers?

Next let us look briefly at (C3). (C3) presents a coherence criterion of justifiedness, and this raises the old question of whether coherence (in any of its interpretations) is a strong enough requirement for justification. I shall challenge the coherence approach on precisely this point in Chapter 5. At this juncture, let me merely note that coherence may enter the picture at other levels as well. Even if coherence is not selected as the *criterion* of rightness, a right J-rule system might demand that cognizers be consistent and use their total evidential corpus. In short, traditional coherentist themes could be correct even if coherence is not the proper criterion of J-rule rightness.

Proposal (C4) is next on our list. This criterion has the virtue of being applicable to all doxastic attitudes, not just beliefs. But it appears to be formally inadmissible, since it employs the term 'evidence', an epistemic term. This point is correct, but probably remediable. (C4) would need to be revised so as to indicate, in purely factual, nonepistemic terms, what the class of evidence beliefs are. There are also other objections to be raised against (C4). I shall present these objections early in Chapter 5.

Criterion (C5) belongs to a family of possible criteria that invoke truth. It is what I call a 'truth-linked' criterion. One possible objection to (C5) is an objection against truth-linkedness in general. Is it appropriate to invoke truth in a criterion of J-rule rightness? Won't this raise a serious problem of *determining* which system(s) of J-rules satisfies the criterion? Won't it be either impossible or circular to use such a criterion? Since I shall ultimately advocate a truth-linked criterion (or family of criteria), this is an important issue. But I must defer its full treatment until the end of Chapter 5. The rationale and plausibility of a truth-linked criterion will be spelled out gradually as I proceed. It should be recalled, however, that a criterion is not intended as a test or verification procedure for J-rule rightness. So the possible difficulty of determining which J-rule system(s) satisfies a truth-linked criterion is not an insuperable objection.

Apart from truth-linkedness, (C5) is not a proposal I deem acceptable. The substance of (C5)—maximizing the number of true beliefs—just isn't the correct ingredient for justifiedness. Also, (C5) omits elements that an acceptable criterion must include. But these will not be explored until Chapter 5.

In short, I do not endorse any of the proposals in this sample list. Still, they are useful illustrations, to give a sense of the options available and the considerations that may be brought to bear in assessing candidate criteria.

4.3. *Objectivism, Relativism, and Related Issues*

Discussions of morality and moral rules often provoke the following questions. Is there a unique moral code, a system of moral rules, valid for every person and culture? Or are different moral codes valid for different persons or cultures? Are there objective standards that make a moral code valid, or is it just a matter of preference, taste, and subjective attitude? Answers to these sorts of questions give rise to theoretical oppositions. *Relativists* hold that valid codes vary from person to person, or culture to culture. *Absolutists* hold that a single code is valid for all people and cultures at all times.[18] *Subjectivists* maintain that validity, or rightness, of moral rules is just a matter of subjective opinion. *Objectivists* believe that objective facts determine the validity of a moral rule.

Similar questions arise in epistemology. They are most frequently voiced in discussions of 'rationality',[19] but have equal force for 'justification'. Is there a unique system of right J-rules that holds for all inquirers at all times? Or does the right system of J-rules vary from culture to culture, or even individual to individual? What about objectivity versus subjectivity? Are there objective facts that make one system of J-rules right and other systems wrong?

I propose, first, a change in some of this terminology, and a slight refocusing of problems. Let us first distinguish three views on whether there is a uniquely right system of J-rules. These views are: *monism, nihilism,* and *pluralism.* Monism says there is exactly one right system of J-rules. Nihilism says there is no right system of J-rules. Pluralism says there is more than one right system of J-rules.

Nihilism is a species of skepticism. If there is no right system of J-rules, no cognizer can ever have a justified belief, because principle (P1), and (P3), says that a belief is justified only if it is permitted by a right system of J-rules. If there is no right system, no such system permits any beliefs. Skepticism is normally combined with another view, that doubt or suspension of judgment *is* a justified attitude toward the target class of propositions. This view cannot be shared by nihilism. For if there is no right system of J-rules, then no right rules can permit any doxastic attitude whatever, including suspension of judgment. So nihilism is a species of skepticism, but should not be identified with all versions thereof.

Turning to pluralism, two species of pluralism may be distinguished. *Relativistic* pluralism says that one system of J-rules is right for one person or culture, while another is right for another person or culture. The cultural variant would, of course, yield epistemological cultural relativism, analogous to moral cultural relativism. But there is a second, *nonrelativistic* species of pluralism. This view holds that two or more systems of J-rules are each right for every person and culture.

To understand nonrelativistic pluralism, consider a parallel with justice. It is plausible that there is a unique criterion of justice or a set of demands that justice makes for all societies. But many alternative sets of social institutions could satisfy these demands. Thus, there is a plurality of sets of institutions each of which would be fully just. For example, justice may demand some sort of mechanism of equal opportunity, but different mechanisms might work equally well. Again, justice may demand some method of compensating victims of unjust harms, but different mechanisms might do this equally well. And perhaps any of these mechanisms would be just in *any* society. Similarly, there might be different systems of J-rules, each of which would be right, as judged by a single criterion of rightness. This would not imply relativism; for it would not suggest that rightness of J-rule systems varies from culture to culture, or individual to individual.

My position will favor nonrelativistic pluralism. But the picture will be clouded somewhat by different conceptions of justifiedness, all of which I shall regard as defensible. Under some of these conceptions relativistic pluralism will be sanctioned.

Let me turn now to objectivism and subjectivism. Objectivism (on the topic of justification) holds that the correct criterion of rightness invokes some sort of objective facts, not merely the opinions or attitudes of individuals or groups vis-à-vis competing schemes of justifiedness. By contrast, subjectivism holds that the rightness of rules is only a matter of what some individual or group thinks.

Several variants of subjectivism may be distinguished. *Individual* subjectivism says that rightness of rules depends on what some individual thinks. *Social* subjectivism says that rightness depends on what some group, or community, thinks. It is common to pair subjectivism with relativism. Thus, if an individual thinks that a system of J-rules is right, then that system is right for him—but not necessarily for others. Similarly, if a community thinks that a system of J-rules is right, then it is right for them—but not necessarily for other communities. Criteria (C2), (C2*), and (C2**) are all variants of social subjectivism. Although they are not formulated to entail relativism, this would be a natural interpretation. In other words, if a given system of J-rules is accepted by a certain linguistic community, then that system is right for that community—but perhaps not for other communities.

Another variant of subjectivism is *indexical* subjectivism. Indexical subjectivism is especially common in metaethical theory, but is readily carried over to the epistemological sphere. Individual indexical subjectivism would be the view expressible as, 'A system of J-rules is right just in case *I* think it is right'. Social indexical subjectivism would be the view expressible as, 'A system of J-rules is right just in case *we* (indexing some relevant group) think it is right'. Like other forms of subjectivism, indexical subjectivism is readily paired with relativism.

Not all versions of indexical subjectivism are first-person versions (either singular or plural). They do not all fix rightness by the opinions of the speaker, or even the speaker's own group. For example, Stephen Stich and Richard Nisbett propose the following criterion of rightness for J-rules: Rule R is right if and only if R accords with the reflective practice of the group of people I (the speaker) think appropriate.[20] This criterion uses an indexical reference to the speaker. But it does not link rightness to the speaker's own appraisal of the J-rule; rather, it is linked to the appraisal of a designated group.

Returning to the basic opposition between objectivism and subjectivism, what kinds of facts should be regarded as objective? Two prime candidates come to mind. First, the verific, or truth, properties of the procedures the rules sanction. Assuming some realist conception of truth, the issue of whether a given system of J-rules promotes truth (that is, belief in truth) is an objective matter of fact, which transcends any individual's or group's opinion about the issue. So truth-linked criteria of rightness are objective criteria. Second, logical and mathematical properties are objective. So any criterion that invokes logical properties of propositions, or probabilistic properties (at least if they are either frequencies or propensities), would count (to that extent) as objective. For example, a criterion that requires rule systems only to ensure logical consistency of a belief corpus is objective.

Although traditional epistemology has not often formulated J-rules very explicitly, it is clear that the traditional conception of such rules would have them deal almost exclusively with a person's subjective states.[21] They would permit beliefs as a function of present 'appearances', antecedent beliefs, and the like. But this does not mean that traditional epistemology is wedded to a subjectivist criterion of rightness. The *content* of right rules may be wholly subjective; but the *criterion of rightness* may be objectivist.

This point is worth elaborating in connection with coherentism. Coherentism can be formulated as a criterion of rightness, as in (C3). Suppose we interpret 'coherence' there as logical consistency (this is only one possible interpretation, of course). Then whether a system of J-rules is right, on this criterion, is an objective matter. It is an objective matter whether conformity with a given system of rules would or would not guarantee logical consistency.

One could modify (C3) to obtain a subjectivist (and relativist) coherentism. Such a criterion follows:

(C3*) System R of J-rules is right *for* cognizer S if and only if
          S *believes* that conformity with R would guarantee the logical
          consistency of a belief corpus.

It might be tempting to equate what I have been calling 'objectivism' and 'subjectivism' with what recent epistemologists have called 'externalism' and 'internalism', respectively. But this is not quite right. Most internalist epistemologies invoke logical relationships as determinants of justificational status. But logical relationships are objective matters of fact. So these internalist theories would also be (at least partly) objectivist theories. Personally, I am no longer anxious to use the terms 'externalism' and 'internalism', which readily convey misleading impressions. I find 'objectivism' and 'subjectivism' more useful (though they too can be misleading).

It should be clear that I favor an objectivist, at least a largely objectivist, criterion of rightness over a subjectivist criterion. This seems to make best sense of the strategies employed by most epistemological methodologists. When a statistician recommends a certain statistical procedure and criticizes others, he usually appeals to the relative rates of error, or probability of error, that the different methods would yield. Such benchmarks are objective benchmarks, not simply the statistician's personal opinion. When a philosopher of science criticizes rules of detachment because they lead to the lottery paradox, the criticism appeals to the prospect of inconsistency. Again, this appeals to an objective standard: genuine inconsistency, not simply what is believed by this individual or group. More generally, when methodologists have historically argued in favor of this or that piece of methodology, their arguments have never simply appealed to their own opinion. They have always rested on such factors as the comparative propensities of the competing methods to avoid error, to yield greater accuracy, or to yield greater logical and/or probabilistic consistency.[22]

Unless there is some objective criterion, it may be impossible even to make *sense* of methodological disagreement. Under relativistic subjectivism, at any rate, individuals and groups do not really disagree, since one only claims that a given rule system is right *for him* (or his group), and the other claims a different rule system right *for him* (or his group). There is no disagreement here, only the semblance thereof. This kind of point is familiar from metaethics, which has examined subjectivist and relativist doctrines in the moral domain. Many objections to these positions have been well stated in this literature, and apply *mutatis mutandis* to the epistemological domain.[23]

Despite these points, I think a case can be made for *mixed* conceptions of justifiedness, conceptions that include both objective and subjective components, especially socially subjective, or culturally subjective, components. I shall elaborate this possibility a bit in Chapter 5.

Let me turn now to a crucial distinction that will sound similar to some of the distinctions already drawn, but which is really quite different. What I have in mind does not mark properties of rightness criteria. Rather, it is a distinction between senses of 'justified'. I shall mark this distinction with the phrases 'really justified' and 'apparently justified'. The same sort of distinction is more commonly marked by the phrases 'objectively justified' and 'subjectively justified'.[24] This terminology is avoided since I am already using 'objective' and 'subjective' to mark different distinctions.

The distinction drawn here parallels one frequently drawn in moral theory, a distinction between actions that are objectively right and subjectively right. If an agent performs an action that he believes, or even justifiably believes, to be right, then it is said that the action is subjectively right. It is objectively right only if it is really right. Similar cases can arise in epistemology. Suppose that a given belief of a cognizer is not permitted by any right system of J-rules. Then according to (P3) this belief is not justified. I shall say that it is not *really* justified. But suppose the cognizer believes, even believes justifiably, that this belief is permitted by a right system of J-rules. Then I shall say that his belief is *apparently* justified.

In the moral realm it is a tricky question whether praise or blame should be allocated as a function of objective rightness or subjective rightness. A number of writers have suggested that these acts or attitudes should be predicated on subjective rightness rather than objective rightness. The matter is far from clear and raises some sticky problems.

Similar issues can arise in legal contexts. Suppose someone violates a law but justifiably believes at the time of action that it is not a violation. For example, a prior court ruling had indicated that such actions are legal, and our agent reasonably infers that this is the law. As it turns out, he is mistaken; for a higher court later overturns the earlier ruling. Is the agent culpable? Since he has violated the law, he is legally culpable. But surely his justifiable belief in the legality of his deed affects our appraisal of him (and the deed).

Now turn to similar cases in the epistemological realm. Suppose that J-rule system R is not a right rule system, but a cognizer thinks R is right, and correctly thinks his belief in p is permitted by R. (However, he does not infer p from his belief about R; he infers p from other propositions. He just concurrently thinks that this inference procedure accords with R, which it does, and that R is right, which it is not.) In fact, his believing p is not permitted by any right J-rule system. According to our framework principle, his belief in p is not really justified, but it is apparently justified. The question is: does this cognizer deserve epistemic praise or blame for this belief?[25] On the one hand, by hypothesis his belief is not (really) justified, so it looks as though he deserves epistemic blame. On the other hand, he is justified in believing that the belief is justified, so perhaps epistemic blame is ill-deserved. Indeed, perhaps he deserves epistemic credit for his intellectual conduct. I think we are pulled in both directions, and this is a proper and irresoluble tension. The only way to relieve the tension is to acknowledge the distinction I have drawn and note the category of problematic cases. Nothing about these problematic cases, I suggest, gives us reason to withdraw or revise principle (P3). But we should be prepared to understand our reaction to certain examples concerning justifiedness by calling attention to the derived sense of 'justifiedness', namely, apparent justifiedness.

4.4. J-Rules as Cognitive-State Transition Rules

The last two sections were devoted to rightness criteria for J-rules, and to some properties of such criteria. But I have said little about J-rules themselves. It is time to rectify this omission. One thing already implied about J-rules is that they permit or prohibit beliefs (and / or other doxastic attitudes), either directly or indirectly. Let us restrict our attention to permission rules. A direct form of J-rules would expressly permit certain beliefs, or would present *schemas* for belief permission. For example, a rule might permit belief in any proposition that has a certain *type* of relation to other propositions already believed. An indirect form of J-rules would license the execution of certain belief-forming processes or operations; the rules would not specify the permitted beliefs, but would indirectly sanction the belief output of these licensed processes. This is just an indication of two possible forms of J-rules. We now need to inquire more generally into the form that J-rules should take.

Two importantly different approaches to J-rules should be scouted first: *interpersonal* and *intrapersonal* approaches. An interpersonal approach says that J-rules should permit a person to believe things as a function of some relation to other persons. An intrapersonal approach says that J-rules should permit beliefs only as a function of some properties intrinsic to the cognizer himself.

A prime example of the interpersonal approach focuses on reason giving as an interpersonal activity. The idea here is that justifications are things we *give* to other people, which the latter either accept or reject. A person is justified in holding a certain belief only if he actually gives others, or could give them, acceptable reasons for the belief. This interpersonal approach is succinctly characterized by Rorty:

> Justification is not a matter of a special relation between ideas (or words) and objects, but of conversation, of social practice . . . We understand knowledge when we understand the social justification of belief.[26]

As this passage indicates, the interpersonal approach may also be called a 'social' approach to justification. But notice that I am addressing here J-rule contents, not criteria of rightness for J-rules. A social approach to rightness criteria is an entirely separate matter, which I have discussed in the previous sections.

On an intrapersonal approach, permission-conditions of J-rules would make no reference to other people. They would restrict themselves exclusively to the cognizer's own mental contents, such as prior beliefs, perceptual field, ostensible memories, cognitive operations, and the like. Most traditional epistemologies have indeed focused on such mental states; but they have not been exclusively mentalistic. They have usually included such conditions as logical relationships between prior beliefs and the target belief. Such logical relationships are not themselves mental. However, since they make no reference to other people, I shall classify approaches of this sort as intrapersonal, and I will even speak of them (loosely) as 'mentalistic' approaches.

There are a number of solid reasons for rejecting the social, or interpersonal, approach to J-rules. Before marshaling these reasons, however, let me remind the reader that I do not mean to neglect social dimensions in my overall conception of epistemology. These dimensions will be explored in a future work. But the theory of *justification*—at least the theory of *primary* justification—does not require reference to social dimensions.[27]

The first reason I prefer an intrapersonal approach to a social approach is that a theory of justification should pertain to all propositions, including propositions about the existence of other people. A conception of justification that presupposes the existence of others leaves no room for the question of their existence, which a full theory should be capable of addressing. This is one legitimate reason why the tradition has opted for an intrapersonal approach.

Second, interpersonal reason giving really depends on intrapersonal reasons. Whatever a person can legitimately *say* in defense of his or her belief must report or express mental states: his or her premise beliefs, perceptions, and the like. What justifies a person is not the *statements* that might be uttered but the mental states those statements would express (or describe). Perhaps it will be replied that the cognizer could justify a belief by appeal to the physical world, not the mental state. A justifying statement might be: 'The meter reads 9.57'. But if the cognizer is to be justified in accepting this statement, it is not enough that the meter *does* read 9.57. The meter reading must have some impact on the cognitive state. The believer's mental condition, or the mental operations he or she executes, are fundamental for justifiedness. Ability to *report* these things is, at best, only of derivative significance.

Third, a prime motivation for a theory of justifiedness is the desire to complete the theory of knowledge. As discussed in Chapter 3, justified belief is necessary for knowing. But if we are interested in the conception of justification most closely associated with knowledge, the interpersonal conception of J-rules is too stringent. One can know without being able to give a justification in the sense indicated by the interpersonal theorist. One may possess good reasons for belief without being able (fully) to state or articulate them in verbal form. Our perceptual beliefs, for example, often depend on cues of which we are not wholly conscious, or which we could not characterize in words. Many theoretical beliefs depend on a host of background assumptions that are hard, if not impossible, to bring to the surface, much less itemize exhaustively.[28]

Fourth, it begs important questions to assume that current justificational status depends on what the cognizer can say *now* in support of his or her belief. Justifiedness may involve *historical* factors—how prior beliefs originated—that the cognizer no longer recalls and hence could not deploy in argument with an interlocutor. Then, too, what people can say in a debate or defense depends partly on their psychological constitution: how adept they are at dealing with pressureful situations. Some people who have excellent reasons for their beliefs might choke or clam up. So dispositions to say things in an interpersonal situation are not the proper measure of justifiedness.

Finally, the guiding idea behind the interpersonal conception is that cognizers are justified only if they can show to others that their view is plausible. I already gave some arguments against this in Chapter 1, but there is more to say. *Which* other potential reason-receivers are relevant? What if those persons are too stupid or stubborn to follow one's arguments or abandon prior prejudices? One's inability to convince them might only reflect badly on them, not on the believer. If nobody else had been capable of understanding Einstein's theory of relativity, Einstein would not have been able to satisfy anyone with his reasons. But it would not follow that Einstein was not justified in believing his own theory (at least once appropriate observations had been made, such as those concerning the perihelion of Mercury). Collectively, these are strong reasons in favor of the intrapersonal approach, and that is what I shall mainly pursue in this book.[29]

To help develop J-rules within the intrapersonal approach, let me initially propose a format involving *cognitive state transitions.* I shall argue for a replacement of this format later on, in Chapter 5; but it will be instructive to use it as far as it seems satisfactory. Since principle (P3) links justifiedness with permission, we may focus exclusively on permission rules.

On the present proposal a J-rule permits transitions from prior cognitive states to beliefs. (The generalized version would permit transitions from prior cognitive states to *any* doxastic attitudes; but I will continue to concentrate on beliefs.) Prior cognitive states may consist of perceptual appearances, ostensible memories, doxastic attitudes, or any combination of such states. So, for example, a J-rule may say that a person is permitted to make a transition from a prior state of being appeared to in such-and-such a way to a successor state of believing that p. Or a J-rule may say that a person is permitted to go from a prior state of believing propositions q, r, and s to a successor state of believing propositions q, r, s, and p.

As indicated earlier, we may want J-rules to present *schemas* for transition permissions. For example, if what permits a transition is a certain logical or confirmational relation between antecedent beliefs and succeeding beliefs, the pertinent logical or confirmational relation may be specified in the rule's antecedent. So we may have a rule-schema: If proposition p is logically implied (or highly confirmed) by propositions q, r, and s, then a cognizer is permitted to go from a prior state of believing q, r, and s to an (immediately) succeeding state of believing p.

To facilitate the expression of such rules, let M be the permission operator, and let / represent a momentary state transition. An expression flanking / on its left will represent a prior cognitive state; an expression on its right will represent a belief—or other doxastic attitude, in the generalized version. (Of course, it need not represent the totality of permitted beliefs.) The whole expression will be enclosed in parentheses. Let B serve as the belief operator, and let p, q, and so on, be variables. We may then symbolize the foregoing rule in the following notation:

If (q & r & s) logically implies p, then M (Bq & Br & Bs / Bp).

An important constraint must be placed on conditions that appear in the antecedent: they must not include any *epistemic* terms. Remember (Chapter 1) that we are trying to provide factual, or substantive, standards for evaluative notions, in this case justifiedness. Working within a rule framework, this means that rules should invoke only factual conditions. Therefore, epistemic terms must be excluded from rule-conditions.

Some theorists may wish to say that certain beliefs are permitted automatically, no matter what the cognizer's prior state. Some epistemologists have held, for example, that a person is always justified in believing a tautology, no matter what his prior evidence or beliefs. I can express this in transition notation by letting V stand for the *universal* cognitive state: a state one is automatically in, no matter what other states one is in. Then the foregoing idea could be expressed with the following rule:

If p is a tautology (or logical truth), then M (V / Bp).

This says that a cognizer is unconditionally permitted to believe any tautology.

Theories may differ over whether they permit transitions based on partial cognitive states or based on total cognitive states only. The second kind of theory would assume that all segments of a total cognitive state are relevant to belief permission, whereas the first kind would imply that proper segments of a total cognitive state can sometimes suffice for belief permission. Coherentists would probably favor the *total* cognitive state requirement. But my notation can accommodate either approach.

We can now see more clearly the connection between justifiedness and a system of J-rules. Suppose a cognizer believes p as a result of an inference permitted by a certain J-rule. This does not guarantee that his belief in p is justified. For suppose that the prior beliefs (in, say, q, r, and s) were not justified. Then even though the most recent transition accords with a J-rule, even a correct J-rule, the belief in p is not justified. At least it is not justified in a strong sense, the sense most closely associated with knowledge. Making a permitted inference from *unjustified* premise-beliefs does not help yield a cognizer knowledge. Rather, the prior beliefs must themselves have been acquired by permitted transitions from still previous states. But these transitions (if they were permitted) may fall under different J-rules.

In this fashion the justificational status of a belief in p is, first of all, a function of the belief's cognitive *ancestry,* possibly stretching back quite far. Second, whether or not there has been a licensed, or permitted, history may well depend on a group of rules, not any single rule. This is one reason we need to consider rule systems, not just individual rules. Justifiedness depends on conformity with a right system of rules, not ordinarily on conformity with a single rule.

With a picture of J-rules now before us—at least one possible picture—

we can reflect on some traditional theories in terms of that picture. Consider the foundationalist and coherentist approaches to justification. These can now be seen as different views about the substantive contents of a right system of J-rules. Coherentism was earlier viewed as a criterion of rightness. But I think it is better viewed as a theory—or family of theories—of right J-rule contents. So too foundationalism.

The core of foundationalism is a commitment to some special class of beliefs—so-called basic beliefs—from which all justification derives.[30] This would be reflected in a J-rule system that ultimately permits all other beliefs only by their relationship to members of this special belief-class. By contrast, coherentism's rule structure would not feature such a distinctive status for any belief-class.

Many versions of foundationalism go beyond this core version. For example, some foundationalists hold that each member of the special belief-class is permitted *independently* of the cognizer's other beliefs. Roughly, their justificational status is inferentially impenetrable. A second special doctrine of some foundationalists is that all basic beliefs have the *highest* possible justificatory status. Neither of these theses, though, is essential to foundationalism.[31]

Still another inessential feature is the doctrine that justification guarantees truth. This point is worth stressing because some writers attack foundationalism by reference to this feature. In so doing, they perhaps refute a radical version of foundationalism, but not its core. Both Richard Rorty and Keith Lehrer launch this form of attack. Lehrer, for example, writes:

> The fundamental doctrine of foundation theories is that justification, whether it is the self-justification of basic beliefs, or the derivative justification of non-basic beliefs, guarantees truth.[32]

Rorty makes the same sort of assumption.[33] In fact, he goes much further. He assimilates all epistemology to foundationalism—somehow ignoring coherentism entirely—and takes himself to refute the possibility of epistemology by refuting foundationalism. Now it may well be that historical writers, such as Descartes and perhaps Spinoza, held some such view. But certainly not all recent writers have held it. Indeed, it is possible to endorse the core of foundationalism without saying anything about the relation between justifiedness and truth, much less implying that justification guarantees truth.

Turning briefly to coherentism, this doctrine might take the form of a J-rule system with a single rule:

> If p coheres better with one's total set T of beliefs than does any competitor of p, then M (T / Bp).

In spelling out this rule, one would obviously have to spell out (nonepistemically!) the meaning of 'coherence', which admits of various interpretations. (More on this in Chapters 5 and 9.) Also, there are other possible ways of formulating coherentism within a J-rule system. Without necessarily appealing to some special notion of coherence, one could still insist—in a holistic spirit—that every permitted transition depend on the total set of prior beliefs, never a mere subset of these.

If foundationalism and coherentism are just particular styles of J-rule systems, each may be compatible with a variety of different rightness criteria. Different criteria could each be satisfied by a foundationalist rule system; and different criteria could each be satisfied by a coherentist rule system. Furthermore, since a single criterion can be multiply satisfied, it is conceivable that the same criterion be satisfied by both a foundationalist rule system and a coherentist rule system.[34]

It is not a central purpose of my argument to defend either foundationalism or coherentism. I am principally interested in finding a criterion of rightness; in particular, I shall advance a *reliabilist* criterion. It will then be an open question whether J-rule systems satisfying such a criterion would be foundationalist or coherentist (or both). Which rule system(s) satisfies the criterion is an empirical question.[35] It is part of epistemology, of course, to address this question. But the prior issue concerns the selection of a criterion. That is the task to which most of Chapter 5 is devoted.

Justification and Reliability

5.1. *Logic, Psychology, and J-Rules*

In this chapter I gradually wend my way to a criterion—or family of criteria—of J-rule rightness. The strategy is to examine candidate criteria, or types of criteria, by their implications. I ask which J-rules a criterion would authorize, and which beliefs would be permitted, and hence deemed justified by those rules. If the implications of a candidate criterion conflict with intuitions, there is evidence, sometimes conclusive evidence, of its inadequacy. But I also judge criteria by general plausibility, and I am mindful of considerations of 'reflective equilibrium'.

Some of the criteria scouted in Chapter 4 appeal to truths of logic, specifically criteria (C1) and (C1*). This accords with a widespread assumption that logic provides us with proper methods. Since 'proper method' is easily construed as 'justification-conferring method', it is natural to assume that J-rules—at least those governing reasoning—can be derived from logic. This assumption is false. As I shall argue, no J-rules may be derived from logic *alone.* For this reason, no criterion like (C1) or (C1*) is satisfactory.

In Chapter 4 I indicated that a criterion like (C1) is incomplete: it cannot generate *all* needed rules. But what I'm about to point out has nothing to do with incompleteness. I deny that *any* correct J-rules can be generated by logic. First, J-rules cannot be derived from truths of logic in a strict sense of 'derive'. Second, even if J-rules are loosely derivable, the rules so derived would be wrong. So logic cannot serve as even a partial criterion of J-rule rightness.

Are J-rules derivable from logic? Let me first make it clear that by 'logic' I mean formal logic, which consists of three branches—semantics (model theory), syntax (proof theory), and recursive function theory—of which I will concentrate on the first two. Semantics primarily studies validity and implication, where the validity of a sentence consists of its being true in all models, and implication of one sentence by another consists of the first being true in all models where the second is true. Proof theory studies what sentences are provable in various axiomatic systems. An important part of logic also studies the connections between semantic and syntactic properties of formal systems.

One thing formal logic does not study, in any form, is psychological states. Logic is completely silent about states of belief, or other cognitive subject matter. Yet that is precisely the concern of J-rules, namely, transitions to states of belief (or other doxastic attitudes). There is no way, then, in which J-rules are literally *derivable* from, meaning entailed by, truths of formal logic. Admittedly, I shall shortly find reason to replace the cognitive-state transition format with a slightly different format for J-rules. But even under the new format it still will not be possible to derive J-rules from logic.

There is a further reason why J-rules cannot literally be derived from truths of logic. Truths of logic are purely descriptive, factual statements. They formulate certain facts—presumably necessary facts—concerning semantic and syntactic properties and relations. By contrast, J-rules are normative statements. They say what cognitive-state transitions are permitted. But factual propositions concerning semantic and syntactic matters cannot literally entail any permissions or entitlements, at least no permissions vis-à-vis cognitive states. Such normative conclusions just do not follow from semantic or syntactic truths.

It is widely assumed that logic deals with principles of good reasoning. Logic is often characterized as the art of reasoning. Unfortunately, such a billing is a bit of a sham. It isn't that logic courses are not useful for good reasoning, it's just that there are no well-established principles of good reasoning (good cognitive-state transitions), and no satisfactory theory of how good reasoning is related to formal logic. In short, there is not really a well-established discipline of informal logic. If there is to be such a discipline, I think it must be a branch of epistemology. But that is a subject which has yet to have its foundations firmly established (which is what I am trying to do here). The relations that would obtain between this branch of epistemology and formal logic are in need of delineation. They are not yet well understood.

The notion that logic yields norms gains credence from the fact that formal logic formulates rules of inference, which appear in both axiomatic systems and natural deduction systems. But these rules are not *belief*-formation rules. They are simply rules for writing down formulas. Furthermore, formal logic does not really endorse any inference rules it surveys. It just tells us semantic or proof-theoretic properties of such rules. This is undoubtedly *relevant* to belief-forming principles, since these properties bear on whether certain sentences are true if others are. But it does not in itself tell us whether, or how, such rules may be used in belief formation. This will become clearer below.

Granted that J-rules are not literally entailed by truths of logic, can't we construct J-rules on the basis of formal logic? If a certain argument is valid, isn't a transition from belief in the argument's premises to belief in its conclusion justificationally permissible? So aren't (right) J-rules derivable in a loose sense from facts of validity? No.

Before defending this answer, I need to expand framework principle (P1), to make it more determinate. This should be done, I believe, by reformulating it as a *historical* principle:

(P1*)   A cognizer's belief in p at time t is justified if and only if
it is the final member of a finite sequence of doxastic states of the cognizer such that some (single) right J-rule system licenses the transition of each member of the sequence from some earlier state(s).

Of course, our *real* framework principle, (P3), should also be recast in this manner, yielding (P3*). First let us distinguish two sorts of J-rules: *belief-independent* and *belief-dependent* J-rules. Belief-independent J-rules (possibly an empty class) permit beliefs to be formed independently of prior belief states (or other doxastic states). They might include perceptual J-rules that permit beliefs as a function of *sensory* cognitive states only. (However, perceptual J-rules might make provisions for prior beliefs, thereby becoming belief-dependent rules.) Belief-dependent J-rules permit beliefs as a function of prior beliefs, and perhaps other prior doxastic states as well. They would include rules that permit inferences from old beliefs to new, and rules that permit retention of old beliefs from one time period to another.[1] Now according to (P1*), the justificationally relevant history of a belief may reach back quite far. If a belief is inferred from previous beliefs, whose permissibility is in turn traceable to still earlier beliefs, and so on, the justificational history may be extensive.

Let us now return to the question of deriving J-rules from logic. Before defending my denial of such derivability (even in a loose sense of 'derive'), a technical point must be noted. Although I have introduced rightness as a predicate of J-rule *systems*, I also want to discuss, especially here, rightness of individual rules. The relationship is straightforward: an individual J-rule is right if and only if it belongs to some right J-rule system.[2]

I have two arguments against (loose) derivability. The first has been stressed by Gilbert Harman.[3] Suppose p is entailed by q, and S already believes q. Does it follow that S ought to believe p; or even that he *may* believe p? Not at all. Even if he notices that q entails p, it is not clear that an appropriate move is to add p to his belief corpus. Perhaps what he ought to do, upon noting that q entails p, is abandon his belief in q! After all, sometimes we learn things that make it advisable to abandon prior beliefs.[4] We might learn that prior beliefs have a certain untenable consequence. For example, you might discover that your prior beliefs jointly entail that you don't have a head. Instead of concluding that you don't have a head, you may be better advised to infer the falsity of some prior belief or beliefs.

We see, then, that the mere validity of an argument—for example, < q, therefore p>—does not imply that a believer in its premise or premises should become a believer in its conclusion. This should come as no surprise. An inconsistent set of premises implies every proposition. But this does not mean that someone who believes an inconsistent set of propositions should (or even may) form a belief in any random (further) proposition.[5]

This point can be explained as follows (though it need not depend on this explanation). Rules for forming beliefs should promote the formation of true beliefs. Drawing conclusions by valid inference patterns promotes this goal *if* prior beliefs are true. But prior beliefs are not always true; nor is it likely that they will always be true even if they are formed in accordance with right rules. (Even right rules are likely to allow some falsehoods to sneak in.) So it does not follow that right rules should always license the acceptance of any logical consequence of prior beliefs.

In view of this consideration, J-rules like the following are incorrect J-rules:

If <q, therefore p> is a valid argument, then M (Bq / Bp).

If *this* is the envisioned pattern by which J-rules are derivable from truths of logic (truths of validity), logic would only generate incorrect J-rules.

The second argument for the nonderivability of (right) J-rules from logic runs as follows. Again let us examine the candidate rule that permits formation of belief in any logical consequence of prior beliefs. I now raise a different kind of difficulty for the rightness of such a rule.

Suppose Claude believes proposition x, at which he arrived earlier by transitions permitted by a right J-rule system. In other words, given (P1°), Claude's belief in x is justified. Suppose further that x entails y, but this entailment is extremely complex (since, say, both x and y are very complex). Even a sophisticated logician would have a hard time determining that <x, therefore y> is a valid argument, and Claude is just a logical neophyte. Claude does not 'see' that it is valid, prove that it is valid, or learn this on anyone else's authority. Nonetheless, he proceeds to believe y. He 'makes a transition' from a state of believing x to a state of believing y (as well). Is his belief in y justified? Intuitively, no. But if the target J-rule *were* right, the belief would be justified. Claude would have arrived at his belief in y via a sequence of transitions permitted by right rules. Since the belief is not justified, the rule in question is not a right J-rule.[6]

The problem with the foregoing J-rule is that it permits any old transition that accords with valid inference patterns. In particular, it places no restrictions on *how* the transition is made. It does not require the cognizer to understand why the inference is valid, nor to see the connection between premises and conclusion. It places no constraints on the *process* for arriving at the target belief, no constraints on the specific causal path by which the belief is formed. As long as the consequent belief 'succeeds' the premise belief, it is permitted. That just seems wrong.

On reflection, the very format of state transitions is a source of the problem, since state transitions imply nothing about causal processes. To talk of state transitions is to talk simply of states arrayed in time, without addressing the processes that may be causally operative in producing this array. And this leaves a lacuna that underlies the inadequacy of the foregoing rule and other rules of its type.

Now the reader might say, OK, let's just understand by 'state transition' something a bit stronger. Let's understand that the prior state must *cause* the successor state. But this does not resolve the problem. There are many possible causal chains that could connect the two states. *Which* precise causal chain connects them is a critical determinant of justifiedness. Like knowledge, justifiedness is sensitive to specific causal generators of belief. Principles of validity, by contrast, are entirely silent on such matters. This is why logic alone cannot provide conditions of justifiedness.

One upshot of this discussion is that we must strengthen our conception of J-rules in order to arrive at a satisfactory criterion of rightness. Instead of conceiving of them as specifying mere cognitive-state transitions, we must conceive of them as specifying cognitive *processes*, where by 'process' we mean a determinate kind of causal chain.[7] This is the sort of thing that logic, by its nature, cannot provide, but precisely the sort of thing naturally sought from psychology. Notice there is nothing here that casts doubt on our framework principle (P3*). The only moral I wish to draw is the need for a constraint on an acceptable criterion of rightness: no criterion will be plausible unless the rules it authorizes are permission rules for specific (types of) cognitive *processes*.

Is this a rash conclusion? Are there other ways to handle the Claude case? Wouldn't it suffice to make a small revision in the proposed J-rule? Let us not only require that an inference <q, therefore p> be valid in fact, but that a cognizer believe in this validity. Further, let us require that the validity belief be justified. These requirements will correctly deny justifiedness to Claude's belief, since *ex hypothesi* Claude is not justified in believing that <x, therefore y> is valid. The proposed revision can be written in the following way:

If <q, therefore p> is valid, then M (Bq & B (<q, therefore p> is valid) / Bp).

It is not apparent from this formulation that the validity belief must be justified. But this requirement is an implication of (P1*). Where a belief results by inference from others, it cannot be justified unless those other beliefs are justified (that is, generated in conformity with right J-rules). So inclusion of

the validity belief in the rule means that if Claude's belief in y is to be justified, he must not only believe <x, therefore y> to be valid, but that belief
must be justified.

Does this ploy work? No, it has two problems. First, it is too strong, at
least if it is to serve as the prototype for deductive J-rules. Not all inferential
J-rules can include the provision that the cognizer believe in the inference's
validity. Children and adults untrained in formal logic presumably use inference procedures before they acquire the concept of validity. Lacking the
concept of validity, they have no *beliefs* about validity. Nonetheless, they
presumably form justified beliefs by justification-transmitting inferences.

Second, the revised rule is still too weak, for the same reasons as its predecessor. It still does not impose any requirements on the causal processes that
produce the successor belief states. In fact, it does not even require the
prior belief states to be causes of the successor state. This allows counterexamples to be readily constructed. For example, suppose a person (justifiably) believes x and (justifiably) believes that x entails y, but the latter belief
is merely stored in long-term memory and is not presently activated. Under
these circumstances, he may start to believe y on a mere hunch. His belief
may not 'connect up' with his prior beliefs in x and the validity of <x,
therefore y>. If so, his belief in y is not justified, contrary to the implication
of the currently proposed J-rule.

Would it help to amend the rule to say that prior beliefs are 'activated'?
No, this would still leave it open whether a causal connection is established
between predecessor and successor beliefs; and it would leave open the details of any such connection. By leaving these matters open, similar counterexamples as before are still constructible.

Since this kind of problem is intrinsic to the state-transition framework,
we really do need the previously proposed revision. To be right, J-rules
should not merely permit state transitions; they should permit selected
cognitive operations or processes—processes that sometimes output beliefs.
Thus, right J-rules should take the form of process permissions, which may
be represented schematically as

M (Proc 1),   or
M (Proc 1 & Proc 2 & . . . & Proc N),

where the latter represents a complex process formed from elementary
processes by serial concatenation, parallel composition, or other composi-
tional devices.

The conclusions for which I am currently arguing are bolstered by further reflection on a logic-based criterion and a state-transition rule format.
In Chapter 4 I noted the possibility of J-rules that grant unconditional belief
permissions. One such J-rule, mentioned in Chapter 4, is this:

If L is any truth of logic, then M (V / B(L)).

This sort of J-rule has been endorsed by many confirmation theorists (such as Carnap), though usually formulated in terms of 'rationality'. For example, if one assumes that it is rational to place credence in a proposition to the degree it is confirmed by one's total evidence, and assumes that a logical truth is automatically confirmed to degree 1 no matter what one's evidence, then it is always rational to place degree of credence 1 in any truth of logic. Translating this into talk of (all or none) 'belief' and 'justifiedness', we get the principle that one is always justified in believing a logical truth, no matter what one's prior state.

This J-rule runs into the same trouble as its earlier cousins. Since it places no constraints on how a belief in a logical truth is produced, it implies, together with (P1*), that such a belief is justified even if it is arrived at by sheer hunch or guesswork. No matter how complex the proposition L, no matter how naive the cognizer, no matter how weak or undeveloped his cognitive capacity to interrelate L's constituents so as to determine its logical necessity, his belief in L is justified. This is clearly unacceptable. As before, the J-rule runs into trouble because it licenses beliefs irrespective of the cognitive processes that produce them. Correct J-rules can only permit belief formation via appropriate cognitive processes; this is what the newly envisaged rule format proposes. But appropriateness cannot be specified by pure logic. Logic is silent about cognitive processes, so it cannot yield correct J-rules.

Again, it might seem as if we could improve the foregoing J-rule without reference to cognitive processes. One of the following two revisions might be proposed:

If L is any *self-evident* truth of logic, then M (V / B(L)).

Or

If L is any *obvious* truth of logic, then M (V / B(L)).

One trouble with the first proposal is that 'self-evident' may be an epistemic term, in which case it is inadmissible. If it is not epistemic, it must be covertly psychological; it must refer to what is psychologically easy, or simple, to ascertain. This is surely what 'obvious', in the next proposal, conveys. Obviousness, ease, or simplicity are not notions of formal logic. So while these principles have better prospects than their cousins, they are not derivable from logic alone.

These cases not only illustrate the impotence of pure logic in generating proper J-rules, but reinforce the relevance of psychology. To say that a logical truth is obvious is to say that there are psychologically simple processes which would disclose its truth. It follows that the proposed belief permissions depend not only on facts of logic but on facts of psychology. What is simple for one species of cognizer is not necessarily simple for others. Simplicity is relative to innate cognitive architecture, to the class of processes or operations that are available, or naturally utilized, by the system.[8] So what is obvious for human beings is not a function of logic, but of human psychological structure.

Moreover, it is not enough for a J-rule to permit beliefs as a function of obviousness or simplicity. To say that a truth is obvious is to say that it *could* be believed as the result of simple—and approved—operations. But suppose that a given cognizer believes it as a result of completely different, and unapproved, operations. Then his belief is not justified. So an acceptable J-rule would not grant belief permissions on the basis of the mere 'availability' of suitable processes, as the previously mentioned candidates would. It would only grant belief permissions on the basis of actual utilization of suitable processes. Thus, J-rules must specify which processes are permitted. This returns me to the process format for J-rules, which I earlier saw reason to endorse.

Before closing this section, let us look at a point some people raise concerning the relation between logic and J-rules. Even if logic alone cannot generate permissive J-rules, maybe it can generate prohibitive rules. Maybe it can tell us when it is *un*justifiable to believe certain propositions, even if it cannot say when it is justifiable. The following would be a possible rule:

If proposition N is logically inconsistent, then there is *no* state K such that M (K / B(N)).

This rule says that a cognizer is not permitted to believe a logical inconsistency, no matter what his prior condition. But this rule is blatantly mistaken. Suppose N is a complex inconsistency, which Stella does not recognize to be inconsistent. Moreover, Stella is advised by an expert logician, who is normally careful and honest, that N is actually a logical truth. Since Stella has good reason to believe in this logician's honesty and expertise, and since she reasons accordingly, she forms a belief in N. Such a belief is justified, contrary to the rule in question.

Perhaps it would help to weaken the proposal to the following:

For any logical contradictories, q and ~q, there is no state K such that M (K / Bq & B~q).

Even this rule may be objectionable. If a pair of contradictories are both quite complex, it may be difficult to tell that they are contradictories. If, as in the Stella case, the cognizer does not herself appreciate their actual logical relationship, but has testimonial evidence for their joint truth, she may be justified in believing them both. Of course, we could weaken the proposal still further:

For any *obvious* logical contradictories, q and ~q, there is no state K such that M (K / Bq & B~q).

Inserting the qualifier 'obvious' improves the chances of the rule being correct. But it also surrenders the hope of providing a purely logic-based rule. Again it is imperative to invoke a psychological notion, making tacit reference to human cognitive powers. This again reinforces the unavoidability of reference to cognitive factors in getting accurate rules of justifiedness or unjustifiedness.

An analogous point holds concerning possible *permissive* J-rules. Suppose we waive Harman's problem about the relation between deductive validity and right J-rules. Couldn't we then say that while arbitrary valid argument forms do not generate right J-rules, *some* valid argument forms do. In particular, doesn't modus ponens have a right J-rule associated with it? Now this might be correct. But if it is, it is only because modus ponens represents a fundamental, primitive cognitive operation. Only this *psychological* status can make modus ponens have an associated right J-rule. Once more, what makes for rightness is not just a matter of logic; it is also a matter of psychology. After all, modus ponens is no more *valid* than other valid argument forms. It is just psychologically simpler than others.[9]

5.2. Evidence Proportionalism: Confirmation Theory and Statistics

In the first section I introduced the idea that J-rules must be process rules, rules that permit selected belief-forming processes (or, more generally, doxastic attitude-forming processes). The process approach goes against a substantial tradition concerning the nature of justification (or rationality). So I want to spend more time looking at that tradition and contrasting my approach with it.

Perhaps the root idea of the tradition I am opposing can be given the label *evidence proportionalism*. It is the idea that justifiedness consists in proportioning your degree of credence in a hypothesis to the weight of your evidence. This idea appeared in Chapter 4 as criterion (C4). This criterion presupposes some way of scaling the weight of evidence, for example, on the interval from zero to unity. It then suggests that a proper J-rule is only one that permits a cognizer to fix his degree of belief as a function of evidential weight. If degrees of belief can also be scaled on the unit interval, then degree of belief should be identical to weight of evidence. It is normally assumed that weights of evidence are derivable from certain formal facts together with the cognizer's present evidential corpus. The critical formal facts are either of a semantic nature—so Carnap viewed statements of inductive probability, or confirmation theory[10]—or a mathematical nature—belonging to statistics, for example. Logical implication is a special case of such formal facts, where the premise proposition confers a confirmation of degree 1 on the conclusion.

If this approach is correct, then all talk of 'processes', especially psychological processes, seems to be irrelevant. It is therefore important to examine this approach and see where it goes wrong. Let me stress at the outset that I shall not be claiming that statistics, for example, is irrelevant to epistemic justification; on the contrary, I shall try to show where it properly enters the picture. But I shall be arguing that fields like statistics and confirmation theory cannot *by themselves* give us an adequate theory of justifiedness.

A preliminary point should be mentioned first. Evidence proportionalism normally assumes that a large range of credal intensities, or 'subjective probabilities', are available to a cognizer. This is a substantive psychological assumption that is open to question. Indeed, I shall raise doubts about it in Chapter 15. At this point, though, I will let this facet of evidence proportionalism go unchallenged. Instead, I will assume whatever repertoire of credal states the evidence proportionalist wishes to postulate, and criticize the theory on other grounds.

The main point to be made here is essentially that of the previous section. Whatever the degree of confirmation of evidence on hypothesis, whatever the degree of statistical or probabilistic support the hypothesis receives from the evidence, these relationships cannot fix the justifiedness of allotting a selected degree of credence vis-à-vis the hypothesis. The question will always arise: What understanding does the cognizer have of these relationships? If he lacks proper understanding, then he is not generally justified in assigning the indicated degree of credence. But 'understanding' can only arise from use of suitable cognitive processes. So a specification of justifiedness must make reference to such processes.

To illustrate this general theme, suppose a detective is investigating a crime, and seven suspects are under study. The detective has a large body of evidence, including material about individual suspects (their alleged whereabouts, their past relationships to the victim, and so on) and a great deal of base-rate data concerning personality types, kinds of interpersonal relationships, and incidence of criminal acts vis-à-vis partners in these relationships. Now let us suppose there is such a thing as a 'proper' statistical analysis of all this information, an analysis on which all expert statisticians would agree. (This is, of course, a fiction, given the differing views among statisticians themselves.) And suppose that ideal statistical analysis would say that the probability of suspect S_1 having committed the crime, given all of this evidence, is .85. But suppose that the detective himself is ignorant of statistical methodology, and is not even wise enough to consult a statistician. Suppose he simply eyeballs his evidence and leaps to the conclusion that the probability of the hypothesis 'S_1 did it' is .85; and thereupon forms a degree of belief of .85 in this hypothesis. Is this degree of belief (or subjective probability) justified? Clearly not. Once again, the psychological processes actually executed in forming the judgment are critical to the judgment's justifiedness. Justifiedness is not fixed by an ideal statistical, or confirmational, analysis of the evidence (even assuming there is such a thing, which is problematic).

At this point the statistical methodologist may object. All right, he may say, justifiedness is not simply a function of the end results of a statistical analysis. If the detective forms some degree of belief in S_1's culpability by sheer guesswork, and this fortuitously coincides with the assignment prescribed by the proper statistical analysis, that does not mean his degree of belief is justified. But what if the detective actually *uses* the statistical analysis? What if he applies the prescribed statistical method, that is, psychologically 'realizes' or 'instantiates' that method? Wouldn't it then follow that his resulting degree of belief is justified? That is all the statistician (or the epistemologist-cum-statistician) claims. As long as the statistical method is 'used', justifiedness is guaranteed. Admittedly, talk of 'using' the method implies agreement with the claim that psychological processes are critical for justifiedness. But this does not mean that statistical method is an irrelevant, or even secondary, issue. It just means that statistical methods must be psychologically instantiated in order to yield justifiedness.

That this argument does not succeed is in effect shown by the Humperdink-Fraud case of section 3.3. But let me elaborate the point with another example. Begin with the claim that as long as the proper statistical method is used, justifiedness is guaranteed. For simplicity, let us move from the statistical domain to another domain where suitable methods or algorithms are uncontroversial. Take the methodology of deriving square roots. Here there is a clear algorithm for getting the right answer. And it may be suggested that anyone using this algorithm will be guaranteed not only a true belief in the calculated answer, but also a justified belief. Is this so?

Suppose Gertrude's mathematical education is seriously deficient: she has never learned the square root algorithm. One day she runs across the algorithm in a pile of papers written by someone she knows to be a quirky, unreliable thinker, and no authority at all on mathematical matters. Despite this background knowledge, she leaps to the conclusion that this rule for deriving square roots (the rule is so labeled) is a sound method. She proceeds to follow, and form beliefs in accordance with, this algorithm. She forms beliefs in propositions of the form 'x is the square root of y'. Are these beliefs justified? Clearly not, for Gertrude has no adequate grounds for trusting the results of this algorithm. She herself has inadequate understanding to realize that it works correctly: nor has she checked to see that the answers are right; nor does she have good inductive grounds for supposing that a random algorithm in this room is correct. So her belief is unjustified; yet she has used a correct algorithm to arrive at her belief.

This case, like the Humperdink-Fraud case, shows that unless a method is properly acquired (or properly tested after its original acquisition), it cannot yield a justified belief. The mere fact of usage is not enough. We must now determine what kinds of acquisition processes are proper. Of course, some reference may again be made to learned algorithms or techniques suitable for appraising the soundness of other methods. But the same question will arise for them. What is their pedigree in the cognizer's mind? Were they suitably acquired? Ultimately, the question of justifiedness must rest on some unlearned processes, on some psychologically basic processes that are never themselves encoded or stored as recipes, algorithms, or heuristics. These processes are just executed, not 'applied' in the way that an algebraic or statistical technique is 'applied'.

We arrive in this fashion at the same conclusion tentatively put forward earlier. Justifiedness centrally rests on the use of suitable psychological processes; and by psychological processes I here mean basic, elementary processes, not acquired techniques that are mentally encoded and applied.[11]

Now suppose statistics indeed provides us with 'ideal' methods. (It is questionable whether statistics incorporates methods of belief formation, or credal-state formation. However, various forms of statistical inference do seem to prescribe credal-state-forming methods. So let us allow this supposition to pass.) Should we then conclude that unless our native cognitive apparatus instantiates this very set of methods, we never have justified beliefs? This demand would almost certainly lead to skepticism (in the justification theme), for it seems highly unlikely that our native cognitive architecture would realize these methods. In fact, certain psychologists have recently been engaged in arguing that native inference propensities do not match those of 'normative' statistical methodology.[12] If our native processes do not match these statistical methods, then, first of all, ordinary beliefs formed without the methods cannot be justified. But, worse yet, even beliefs based on method utilization cannot be justified. Utilization of the methods does not confer justifiedness unless the methods are acquired by justification-conferring processes. Ultimately such acquisition must utilize native processes (including second-order processes). But, *ex hypothesi*, these native processes do not include the 'ideal' statistical methods. So it will be humanly impossible to form justified beliefs.

Is the prospect of landing in the skeptical ditch enough to refute the foregoing proposal? Perhaps not. That would involve too strong an antecedent commitment to skepticism's falsity. But there are independent reasons for thinking that the requirements of a refined, or optimal, procedure should not be imposed at every level of cognition. Suppose we can imaginatively construct perceptual devices that are superior (say, in reliability) to our own. Does this mean that none of our perceptual beliefs are justified? Suppose we can devise a memory system that is better (again, say, in reliability) than ours. Does it follow that none of our memory beliefs are justified? Surely not. So why should the fact that we can design more refined *inference* procedures than our native ones show that the latter cannot yield justified beliefs? Another parallel may be instructive. Suppose that before Russell presented his paradox, all existing set theories were paradoxical. Does it follow that nobody before Russell had any justified beliefs about sets? Surely not. Just because more refined conceptions of sets were later generated is not enough to show that all earlier beliefs about sets were unjustified.

All I have been arguing here is that the norms of ideal statistical methodology need not be imposed on basic cognitive processes. But it remains to be seen just what the proper J-rules do require, and just what criterion of rightness should be chosen to fix correct J-rules. Although I have here fended off one specter of skepticism, I do not mean to preclude the possibility that skepticism might enter through another door. Once we choose a criterion of rightness, it might still turn out that no J-rule system that satisfies the criterion is humanly realizable.

One main result of this section is to emphasize the importance of the distinction between basic psychological processes, on the one hand, and various sorts of algorithms, heuristics, or learnable methodologies, on the other. Let us call the former simply *processes* and the latter *methods*. I shall now argue that a good theory of justifiedness should systematically separate these two classes. There is a family of different conceptions of justifiedness, each having some pull on intuition, which can only be dissected with the help of this separation.

5.3. *Processes, Methods, and Levels of Justifiedness*

I have just distinguished native psychological processes from acquired methods, including algorithms, heuristics, skills, and techniques of various sorts. The former mark the province of primary epistemology, while the latter mark that of secondary epistemology. I now wish to distinguish two corresponding levels of justification: *primary justifiedness* (P-justifiedness) and *secondary justifiedness* (S-justifiedness). Roughly, P-justifiedness results from the use of approved processes, and S-justifiedness results from the use of approved methods.

The natural theory of *full* justifiedness requires the use of both approved processes and approved methods (if methods are used at all). However, there are several reasons why proper use of processes is more fundamental. First, as we have seen in the previous section, use of correct methods is not sufficient for justifiedness. Methods must also be properly acquired; and this ultimately rests on the use of right processes. Second, questions of full justifiedness must not only deal with the matter of how methods are acquired when they *are* acquired, but also why they *fail* to be acquired even when they are available. If a cognizer has plenty of opportunity to acquire certain correct methods but fails to do so, his subsequent failure to use such methods may render his resultant beliefs unjustified. Here failure to use proper methods is not a flaw at the level of methods so much as a flaw at the level of processes. The processes are defective because they fail to add things to the cognitive repertoire that ought to be added.

This sort of case reminds us that within the class of processes are not only first-order processes but also second-order processes. Second-order processes were originally defined as processes that produce new processes. But with our distinction between 'processes' and 'methods', we should reinterpret second-order processes as ones that produce new methods, or are involved in method acquisition. In the previous section I indicated that a belief produced by right methods is not ipso facto justified—is not *fully* justified, as we should now say. These methods must be acquired by suitable processes. The best way to phrase this requirement is that the methods must be acquired by permitted *second-order* processes. A complete account of P-justifiedness, then, must provide not only a rightness criterion for first-order processes, but also a rightness criterion for second-order processes.

The use of proper methods not only depends on suitable processes of method acquisition, but also depends on suitable processes of method selection. In any cognitive problem-solving task, a cognizer must choose which methods to apply. A mature cognizer has an enormous number of stored methods—principles and heuristics of various sorts that he has either devised by himself or been explicitly taught by others. The task is to determine which of these methods is relevant and applicable to the problem at hand. The cognizer can misfire in this task in two ways. He may choose an *incorrect* method, or he may *fail* to choose a correct method (which he possesses). Either of these mistakes can result from poor processes of two sorts: *(a)* poor retrieval processes, or *(b)* poor reasoning processes. Poor retrieval processes might result in failure to access the best, or most relevant, methods stored in memory. Poor reasoning processes might result in a poor choice among the methods that are retrieved. So inadequacy of method may be a fault assignable to processes for either of two reasons: a flaw in method-acquiring processes or a flaw in method-selecting processes.

These points having been made, it remains true that full justifiedness depends partly on the propriety of methods—either ones actually used or ones omitted—not just on the suitability of processes. So a complete theory of justifiedness must deal with rightness for methods as well as for processes.

Later in this chapter (in section 5.5) I will present an *objective* criterion of rightness for process rules, more specifically a *reliabilist* criterion. (Actually I will present a family of three criteria, each with substantial appeal.) Still later (in section 5.7) I will sketch a similar criterion (or family of criteria) of rightness for second-order process rules. It would be reasonably expected that a parallel criterion for *methods* should be presented as well. Indeed, I have strong sympathy for an objective, reliabilist conception of rightness for methods. But some considerations favor a different conception, which I shall now note.

Consider examples from early stages of science or mathematics. Somebody invents methods that, in hindsight, are naive and unreliable. Relative to the information available at the time, though, practitioners were P-justified in believing those methods to be sound. We may well be prepared to credit those early practitioners with *fully* justified beliefs. If so, we must be employing some nonobjective conception of S-justifiedness. Specifically, we may be employing a weaker, *culturally relative*, conception of S-justifiedness.

How might we formulate a socially subjective, relativistic, criterion of rightness of the sort I have in mind? It might run as follows:

> A method M is right for culture C at time t just in case M is widely believed by members of C to be the best method (or a good method) for the class of problems at issue.

If a scientist belongs to scientific culture C, and if he uses methods widely endorsed at the time by members of C, then the beliefs formed by these methods are S-justified.

Let us assume that the rightness criterion at the primary level is some sort of objective criterion. Then the pairing of that criterion with the socially subjective rightness criterion at the secondary level yields a *mixed* criterion, partly objective and partly (socially) subjective. I noted this possibility in passing in Chapter 4. I do not mean to endorse this approach, as contrasted with a fully objective approach. I only mean to air some of the possible approaches.

Although S-justifiedness is clearly an important component of full justifiedness, the remainder of my discussion of justifiedness in this chapter is confined to P-justifiedness. Elsewhere in the book I occasionally return to questions of methods, but the bulk of my attention is devoted to processes. Methods will be addressed more fully in the future volume on social epistemology.

5.4. Consequentialism

In earlier sections I endorsed a process format for J-rules, arguing that right J-rules (at the primary level) can only permit basic cognitive processes. This is really a partial specification of a rightness criterion for J-rules. An acceptable criterion must, at a minimum, require J-rules to be process rules, not state-transition rules, for example. What further conditions should appear in an acceptable criterion remains to be seen. But let us pause and reflect on this constraint.

This constraint plays a critical role in vindicating the claim that psychology has a role to play in the theory of justifiedness. If right J-rules must specify basic psychological processes, then cognitive psychology has an important role to play in determining right J-rules. For cognitive psychology (or, more broadly, cognitive science) is the field that explores the human repertoire of basic cognitive processes. Unless and until these processes are identified, no selection can be made of the ones that should be licensed by a right rule system.

Of course, further conditions must be included in a rightness criterion. As I develop my account of an acceptable criterion, the argument may conceivably go astray at any point. But if my contention up to this point is correct—that right J-rules must be basic process rules—then I have already substantiated one central theme: the importance of psychology for individual epistemology (at least at one level). I stress this point because the rationale for investigating psychological processes in Part II does not hinge on *all* my epistemological theses of Part I. Although Part II does investigate psychological processes with an eye to the truth-linked criteria I embrace in Part I, a proper place for psychology is already established by the theses defended thus far, independent of truth-linkedness. Thus even if the rest of my account of justifiedness (and power) should fail, psychology's role is secure.

One objection needs to be considered in this connection, though. The proposed partnership with psychology in the epistemological enterprise—specifically in the theory of justifiedness—assumes that part of epistemology's task is the choice of specific J-rules. But some readers might take exception to this assumption, asking: Why shouldn't epistemology stop at the selection of a rightness *criterion?* Why should epistemology include the job of identifying the J-rules (or J-rule systems) that actually satisfy the criterion?

There are three answers here. First, epistemology has traditionally been concerned not simply with abstract criteria for good methodology or procedure, but with the endorsement of particular methods or procedures. This is especially clear in the philosophy of science wing of epistemology. Since psychological processes, I have argued, are the suitable class of 'procedures' in primary justifiedness, it is appropriate for primary epistemology to actually specify the approved processes, not simply to lay down a criterion they must meet.

Second, it is just part of a full theory of justifiedness to say *which* J-rules (or J-rule systems) are right. To stop epistemology at stage 2, the level of the criterion, is to abort it at an unnatural juncture. Admittedly, the job of articulating a detailed J-rule system goes beyond the horizon of this book; nonetheless, that job is still an epistemological one.

Third, once a criterion of rightness is chosen, it may be an open question whether any J-rules satisfy it. Perhaps no human psychological processes meet the constraints of the criterion. In that case skepticism (in the justification theme) is victorious: it is not humanly possible to have justified beliefs. But since the prospects for this sort of skepticism stand or fall with the existence of nonexistence of J-rules satisfying the criterion, examining the satisfiability of the criterion is certainly an assignment for epistemology.

With these points in mind, let us now work toward a more specific rightness criterion. The next step is to distinguish two possible approaches, familiar from ethical theory: *consequentialism* and *deontology.* Consequentialism holds that rightness is a function of consequences; in this case it would hold that rule(-system) rightness is a function of the consequences of conforming with, or realizing, the rules (or rule system). In opposition to consequentialism is deontology, which makes rightness rest either wholly or partly on nonconsequential factors. Criteria discussed earlier are examples of justificational deontology, namely, the criteria appealing to truths of logic—(C1) and (C1*)—and evidence proportionalism—(C4). Evidence proportionalism is a particularly good example. It says that justificational rightness is a matter of proportioning strength of conviction to weight of evidence, no matter what the consequences. This is analogous to the deontological theory of punishment, which says that punishment should be proportioned to the seriousness of the crime, no matter what the effects may be.

No deontological criterion examined thus far has proved satisfactory. This does not prove, of course, that none will. But I cannot construct other good prospects, so I shall look elsewhere. I suspect that some form of consequentialism is correct, and I will now explore varieties of epistemic consequentialism to find the most promising. Of course I restrict my attention to *rule* consequentialisms, for I am interested in rightness of rules (or rule systems). I ignore entirely the suggestion that the justificational status of each belief is a function of that very belief's consequences. I also assume that we are only interested in the direct consequences of rule conformity, not indirect consequences.[13]

Consequentialisms can differ along two dimensions. First, they may differ on the issue of which consequences have (positive or negative) *value.* Second, they may differ on which *measure* of valued and disvalued consequences is relevant to rightness. One familiar measure is *maximization* of net value; another possibility is some sort of *satisficing* measure. Let me begin with the question of value. It should be emphasized that I am not concerned with epistemic value in general, but only with justificationally relevant value, for I am presently interested in rightness of J-rules.

Several candidates of justificationally valuable consequences are readily suggested.

(1) *verific* consequences: believing truths, not believing falsehoods
(2) *coherence* consequences: achieving coherence in one's belief (or credal probability) corpus
(3) *explanatory* consequences: believing propositions that explain other believed propositions
(4) *pragmatic* consequences: realizing one's practical, nonintellectual goals
(5) *biological* consequences: surviving, reproducing, propagating one's genes

One feature of these candidates, which complicates the picture, is their causal interdependence. Believing truths often helps a person achieve practical goals. Realizing practical goals, such as food, shelter, and mating, typically promotes biological ends. There is also plausibility in supposing that many cognitive functions subserving the attainment of true belief, or goal realization, were selected for in evolution because of their biological consequences, that is, their contribution to genetic fitness.

Since consequentialisms often focus on 'ultimate' values, these causal interdependencies and evolutionary possibilities might incline one toward a biological theory of epistemic value. But I think this would be a mistake. For one thing, causal interdependence is not identity or equivalence. Believing truths does not always promote pragmatic or biological ends; witness the threat to our survival posed by our belief in truths of nuclear physics. Furthermore, while some cognitive processes promote happiness or goal realization by way of producing true means-ends beliefs, others promote happiness by inhibiting true belief. They may shore up the ego with false, but pragmatically convenient, self-ascriptions.

Second, even if the desire for truth acquisition is ultimately traceable to biological fitness (curiosity about one's environment can promote survival), it still appears in the organism as an 'autonomous' desire. People do not desire true belief merely as a *means* to survival, or the achievement of practical ends. Truth acquisition is often desired and enjoyed for its own sake, not for ulterior ends. It would hardly be surprising, then, that intellectual norms should incorporate true belief as an autonomous value, quite apart from its possible contribution to biological or practical ends.

These considerations, among many others, lead to the unremarkable conclusion that true belief is a prime determinant of intellectual value, and in particular, a critical value for justifiedness. At any rate, they suggest that verific consequences are a better candidate for justificational values than pragmatic or biological consequences. But what about coherence and explanatory consequences? These have figured prominently in many theories of justification and science. Why choose verific value over these forms of value in an account of justificational rightness?

Let us first examine coherence consequentialism. 'Coherence' admits of many interpretations. In a weak sense a corpus of beliefs is coherent just in case it is logically consistent. But surely this kind of coherence is not strong enough to serve as a benchmark of justificational rightness. If the promotion of logical consistency suffices for rightness, it is compatible with the promotion of completely fanciful belief corpora. Mere logical consistency can be satisfied by belief systems concocted out of thin air, fabricated by paranoia or neurotic defense mechanisms, or otherwise generated by sheer fantasy. These sets of beliefs certainly do not count, intuitively, as justified. But under a consistency criterion of rightness, such beliefs would count as justified.[14]

The notion of coherence is readily applied to systems of subjective probability. Credal, or personal, probabilities are coherent if and only if they conform to the probability calculus. If the personal probability for hypothesis H is .75, then the personal probability for not-H must be .25, and so on. Subjective Bayesianism is a theory that makes such probabilistic coherence necessary and sufficient for rationality. If it were presented as a sufficient condition of *justificational* rightness, it would be a species of justificational coherentism. (Of course, Bayesians do not normally present their theory as a form of consequentialism; but that construal, I take it, is innocuous.)

A somewhat stronger version of probabilistic coherentism is kinematic probabilistic coherentism. This requires not only that credal systems be probabilistically coherent at any given moment, but that they obey certain requirements over time: that there be certain continuities between a person's subjective probabilities at time t_1 and time t_2.[15]

Both forms of probabilistic coherentism—static and kinematic—suffer the same sorts of difficulties as logical consistency coherentism. Mere fantasizers and deluded paranoids can satisfy their requirements as long as they are excellent probabilists. Yet the subjective probabilities of wild fantasizers and deluded paranoids certainly are not justified doxastic states.

Actually, some qualifications must be added to the sketched counterexamples. We must not suppose that the cognizers in these examples are *total* fantasizers. They cannot merely fantasize about the probability calculus, if they are going to make their credal systems conform to it. Nor can they merely fantasize about their past credal systems, if their present credal systems are going to display the requisite continuities. They may need genuinely accurate memories. Apart from these requirements, though, they may fantasize as much as they wish. They need not pay attention to their perceptions, for example, but may discount them as thoroughly as they wish. Surely, such cognizers provide strong enough counterexamples to these forms of coherentism.

There are stronger senses of 'coherence', however, beyond logical consistency and conformity with the probability calculus. Some epistemologists, such as C. I. Lewis and Roderick Chisholm, formulate a conception of coherence which requires that a coherent set of propositions mutually support and confirm one another.[16] We might call the weaker forms of coherence *negative* coherence. This only requires the absence of logical or probabilistic conflict. The stronger form of coherence may be called *positive* coherence.[17] It requires positive (mutual) support.

Even positive coherence, however, may suffer from the fantasizer difficulty. For systems of belief that satisfy the mutual support requirement could be constructed through idle (though clever) fantasy. Even the positive coherence theory, then, is not strong enough. Yet in some respects it is too strong. Why should right J-rules require promotion of a belief system that is wholly mutually supportive? Couldn't there be little islands of belief unsupported by the rest of the mainland corpus? I may now be justified in believing that I have an itch in my left thigh even though this belief neither supports nor is supported by any other belief of mine. The theme of holism in the theory of justification has, to be sure, many attractions. But it should not be carried too far.

Any theory of justification that neglects coherence relations entirely is liable to be defective. But it does not follow that coherence requirements should be built into the *criterion* of rightness. My contention is that coherence is not the highest standard of justificational rightness but a derivative, subsidiary, standard. The fundamental standard concerns the formation of true belief. Coherence enters the picture only because coherence considerations are generally helpful in promoting true belief. On the assumption that prior beliefs are largely true, new prospective beliefs should be examined for consistency with prior beliefs, since a *necessary* condition of a belief's being true is consistency with all other true beliefs.

I turn next to the explanatory approach. First, I need to distinguish two senses of 'explain', a truth-implying sense and a truth-independent sense. In the former proposition q explains proposition r only if q is true; here 'explains' has a truth-condition, like 'know'. In the latter sense there is no such condition: q can explain r in the sense that it *would* be a good explanation of r *if* it were true. It has all other earmarks of explanatoriness, whatever exactly these are.

In the truth-implying sense of 'explain' the explanatory approach is not a distinct rival to the verific approach. How much the two compete depends on whether the explanatory approach holds *(a)* that *only* explanatory true beliefs are valuable, or *(b)* that explanatory true beliefs are just *more* valuable than others, though not the only valuable ones. I question the correctness, though, of either view.

First, cognitive operations can confer justifiedness because they detect truths even if the truths have no explanatory value. The truth that I now have an itch in my thigh does not explain anything else I believe; nor, perhaps, is it explained by any of my other beliefs. Still, it is justified. (On the reliabilist view that is because introspection is a reliable process.) Similarly, it is doubtful whether propositions of pure mathematics or logic explain anything; but beliefs in these propositions can still be justified.

Second, there seems to be nothing distinctively justification-conferring about the production of explanatory beliefs. Explanatory power does not seem to increase, or contribute to, justifiedness. This is compatible with the view that explanation is itself an important epistemic desideratum, certainly an important part of the aim of empirical science. It does not follow from this view that explanatoriness is critical for *justifiedness*. The most explanatory propositions, it is generally held, are highly theoretical propositions of empirical science. This would seem to imply, on the view under scrutiny, that inference processes leading to such theoretical beliefs are the best at conferring justification. But this seems quite wrong. Processes like perception or even introspection seem to be better at conferring justification, though their outputs may have much less explanatory power. Presumably, this is because they have a higher truth propensity than theoretical inference processes.

What about the truth-independent notion of explanation? Such an approach may be favored by someone who is attracted by consequentialism but who questions the suitability of verific values. This approach, however, falls prey to the fantasizer counterexamples. Clever imagination can construct elaborate potential explanations, perhaps even simple and elegant explanations, of what we antecedently believe. But if these fanciful constructions were consistently false, I would feel little inclination to say that this sort of process confers justifiedness. Certainly it would not yield the kind of justifiedness that brings us close to 'knowledge'. As in the case of coherence, it may turn out that explanatory factors have an appropriate place at the level of J-rules, should explanatory processes indeed be truth-conducive. But explanatoriness should not replace verific values at the level of the *criterion*.

Finally, I want to examine an approach that is a consequentialism of sorts, but a rather different style of consequentialism than others under discussion. The approach I have in mind is epistemic decision theory, as developed by Hempel, Hintikka and Pietarinen, Levi, Hilpinen, and Lehrer.[18]

Epistemic decision theory views belief, or 'acceptance', as an action, and lays down a principle of rational, or justified, belief that is very similar to the Bayesian principle of rational decision making. The theory assumes that the cognizer has epistemic 'utilities', specifically, the verific utilities of accepting truths and avoiding falsehoods. It also assumes that the cognizer has subjective probabilities. It proceeds to identify a rational, or justified, doxastic act as one that maximizes *expected epistemic utility*, as determined by the verific utilities and subjective probabilities.

Since epistemic decision theory makes reference to the prospective out-comes of a doxastic choice, it is ostensibly a kind of consequentialism. But it is a quite different form of consequentialism from the others I have been discussing. It makes epistemic correctness not a function of the genuine consequences of doxastic actions, but rather a function of their expected consequences. This is a very fundamental difference.

All other forms of consequentialism under discussion have been 'objec-tive' consequentialisms. They all deem a rule system to be right if confor-mity with it would *really* achieve certain values. This parallels the standard example of consequentialism in ethics, namely, utilitarianism, which makes moral rightness of actions or rules a function of the happiness and unhappi-ness that would *really* result from them (and their alternatives). By contrast, epistemic decision theory makes rightness a function of the *expected* conse-quences of a doxastic action. If this is a consequentialist view at all, it should be classed as a different variety: a 'subjective' consequentialism.

Matters are complicated somewhat, however, because epistemic decision theory offers a rule of rationality, or justifiedness, not a criterion. The other theories surveyed have all been criteria for rule rightness. This complica-tion interjects an element of incomparability among the views. I find it dif-ficult to say what sort of criterion tacitly underlies the epistemic decision theoretic rule. But I will not press this point.

I now offer some criticisms of epistemic decision theory, considered as an approach to justifiedness. The first and main criticism is that it allows beliefs to be formed on the basis of subjective probabilities without placing any constraints on how those subjective probabilities are formed. Apparently, the latter may be formed in any fashion at all, including hunch, fancy, and the like. But if a belief is based on subjective probabilities of that ilk, there are no grounds for regarding the belief as justified. It certainly is not justi-fied in any sense that links up closely with knowledge.

Of course, epistemic decision theory could be supplemented with condi-tions for the proper formation of subjective probabilities. These might re-quire attention to observed frequencies, for example. But now a *new* theory is required, which may have little or nothing in common with the initial, epistemic decision motif. One then wonders whether some entirely differ-ent criterion isn't needed—for example, an *objectively* verific criterion—to fill out the approach. At a minimum, this supplement would destroy any semblance of a *unified* approach to doxastic justifiedness.

A third critical comment pertains to an element of epistemic decision theory hitherto neglected. In characterizing epistemic 'utilities', I men-tioned only acceptance of truths and avoidance of error. There is another wrinkle in the approach, however: acceptance of 'stronger' truths—truths with greater content measures—has more utility than acceptance of 'weaker' truths.[19] Aside from the difficulties of content measurement, I do

not think this is an appropriate determinant of value for the theory of justification. It may be appropriate for other epistemic terms of appraisal, but
not for justifiedness. Consider two J-rule systems R_1 and R_2. Conformity
with R_1 would yield true beliefs with greater content than conformity with
R_2, but in other verific respects (such as truth ratio) the rule systems are
equivalent. It is unclear to me that the processes licensed by R_2 are *justificationally* inferior to the processes licensed by R_1. R_2's processes may be inferior on *other* dimensions of appraisal, but not on the dimension of
justifiedness.

Having excluded its principal competitors, I conclude that the verific approach to justificational value—in the objective consequentialist style—is
the most promising. True belief is the value that J-rules should promote—
really promote—if they are to qualify as right. But so far, this is just a theory
of *value* and a choice of objective over subjective consequentialism. We still
do not have a determinate criterion of rightness.

5.5. Reliabilism

Thus far I have narrowed the class of acceptable criteria, first to *process*
criteria, then to *consequentialist* process criteria, and finally to *verific* consequentialist process criteria. But this still does not pick out a unique criterion. The task of this section is to narrow the class of acceptable criteria still
further. I will advocate a particular criterion as best, but also acknowledge
several related criteria as legitimate conceptions of justifiedness. Thus, instead of plumping for a uniquely correct criterion, I will endorse a small
family of criteria, all in the 'truth-ratio' category.

Within the class of verific consequentialisms, there are two important
subclasses to notice: criteria invoking number of true beliefs, and criteria
invoking ratio of true beliefs. It is clear that J-rule rightness is not solely a
function of the number of truths that would be produced. The 'process' of
believing everything one can think of, including each proposition and its
negation, might produce as large a total of true beliefs as any other process.
A criterion that required (just) maximization of the *number* of true beliefs
could be satisfied by a J-rule that permits such a process. But, obviously,
beliefs so formed are not justified.

This strongly suggests that what is critical to J-rule rightness is ratio of
true beliefs, not total number. The trouble with the foregoing process (assuming it is psychologically feasible, which is doubtful) is that its ratio of
true beliefs to total beliefs would only be .50. These considerations prompt a
reliability approach to justifiedness. A justificationally permitted process must
be one that yields a high truth ratio, higher—perhaps appreciably higher
—than .50. Further support for reliabilism comes from a survey of cases.

Among the prototypical cases of justification-conferring processes are: (1)

forming beliefs by standard perceptual processes, (2) forming or retaining beliefs by memory, and (3) certain patterns of deductive and inductive reasoning. Among the prototypical cases of non-justification-conferring processes are: (1) wishful thinking, (2) sheer hunch or guesswork, and (3) failure to take account of all one's relevant evidence (or failure to take account of obviously relevant evidence). What the former processes seem to share is a reasonably high truth ratio. What the latter processes seem to share is a low(er) truth ratio.

Support for reliabilism is bolstered by reflecting on *degrees* of justifiedness. Talk of justifiedness commonly distinguishes different grades of justifiedness: 'fully' justified, 'somewhat' justified, 'slightly' justified, and the like.[20] These distinctions appear to be neatly correlated with degrees of reliability of belief-forming processes. Not all perceptual processes or memory processes, for example, confer equal grades of justification. A belief based on fleeting or careless perceptual exposure is generally less justified than a belief based on ample and attentive perceptual examination. A belief based on a hazy recollection is less justified than one involving vivid memory. These intuitions of justificational strength are traceable to truth ratio. Perceptual processes featuring more extensive, leisurely observation tend to have higher truth ratios. Vivid recollections yield a higher truth ratio than hazy ones. Thus, what seems critical is the ratio of truths produced by a process, not the total number produced.[21]

Even within the class of ratio criteria, there are choices to be made. Let us first distinguish *resource-independent* and *resource-relative* criteria. A resource-independent criterion fixes an acceptable truth ratio without regard to the resources of the (type of) cognitive system in question. A resource-relative criterion fixes an acceptable truth ratio as a function of the target cognitive system's resources, in the present case, human cognitive resources.

Resource-relative criteria are likely to be comparative. One such criterion is a *maximizing* criterion. It would say that a rule system is right if and only if the processes it permits would maximize truth ratio, that is, maximize relative to humanly available processes. This is what some writers call a criterion of "doing the best one can."[22] A different sort of resource-relative criterion is a *satisficing* criterion. For example, a criterion could say that a rule system is right just in case the processes it permits have a truth ratio of a level humans commonly attain, or that it is easy for them to attain.

A resource-independent criterion is liable to be absolute rather than comparative. It would set an absolute truth ratio that must be met, whether or not human resources are capable of meeting it. Such a criterion might say that a rule system is right only if its realization would produce a truth ratio of at least .90. Given such an absolute, resource-independent criterion, it becomes an open question whether any system of J-rules is right for human beings. Human beings might possess no set of basic cognitive processes that allow the criterion to be satisfied. Less dramatically, such a criterion might exclude belief permission rules for one class of processes, for example, inductive processes, though not exclude belief permission rules altogether. Human perceptual processes might be capable of generating beliefs with a truth ratio of .90, but perhaps no human inductive processes could generate such a high truth ratio.

Notice that a maximizing, resource-relative criterion could have implications that are either stronger or weaker than some specific resource-independent criterion. Take an (absolute) resource-independent criterion that sets the acceptable truth ratio at .80. If it turns out that human resources include processes capable of a truth ratio higher than .80, then a maximizing, resource-relative criterion would require (at least) that higher ratio. But if human resources are weaker, a maximizing resource-relative criterion might only require a truth ratio of, say, .70. In principle such a criterion might even count a rule system as right with a truth ratio *less than .50*.

Is a criterion that permits a truth ratio of less than .50 a 'reliabilist' criterion? Probably not. This means that not all the criteria that fall into the truth-ratio category qualify as reliabilist criteria. Perhaps only the absolute, resource-independent criteria should be so labeled. In that case among the family of criteria that I am prepared to count as legitimate—that is, as capturing *some* intuitively satisfying conception of justifiedness—not *all* are reliabilist criteria. They are, however, all truth-ratio criteria.

The satisficing, resource-relative approach has its attractions. In many domains we make evaluations based on what the 'common man' does, or what it is reasonable to expect people to do given their capacities. Plausibly, this is what we (sometimes) do in appraising belief formation too. We expect people to use better, more reliable, processes as long as they are relatively easy, or natural, processes. We do not expect people to use very difficult, or sophisticated, cognitive process sequences, even if these could increase the truth ratio. Omission of such processes does not preclude justified belief, on one plausible conception of justifiedness. In Part II I will have several occasions to distinguish the relative difficulty of cognitive feats and to link judgments of justifiedness to these distinctions. The satisficing, resource-relative criterion would neatly accommodate such judgments.

All three of the aforementioned approaches have their merits. In most of what follows, though, I shall opt for an absolute, resource-independent criterion of justifiedness. One virtue of this approach is that it makes the challenge of skepticism both serious and credible. If some fixed level of truth ratio is necessary for justifiedness, it is an open question whether human processes ever yield justified belief, whether they are even capable of yielding justified beliefs. By contrast, the maximizing, resource-dependent criterion guarantees that *some* human processes can yield justified beliefs. And the satisficing, resource-relative approach also makes it easy to have justified beliefs.

There is room for disagreement, of course, on the question of how seriously global skepticism should be taken. Some epistemologists might favor the resource-relative approaches precisely because they soften, or eliminate, the threat of (global) skepticism. But I am inclined to take skepticism as a serious challenge, so I would not back away from the absolute, resource-independent approach on that account. Another virtue of this approach is that it effects an intimate thematic tie between accounts given here of justification and knowledge. Recall that the global reliability requirement was central to the theory of knowing (Chapter 3). Of course, knowledge has other requirements not needed for justifiedness. Unlike a piece of knowledge, a justified belief need not be true. And the local reliability requirement for knowledge ('no relevant alternatives') is not imposed for justifiedness. But otherwise, the two concepts turn out to be very close.

Let me now formulate the absolute, resource-independent criterion of justifiedness:

(ARI)   A J-rule system R is right if and only if
         R permits certain (basic) psychological processes, and the instantiation of these processes would result in a truth ratio of beliefs that meets some specified high threshold (greater than .50).

Since (ARI) does not designate any particular threshold, it is really a criterion-*schema*. A determinate criterion would be fixed by choice of a threshold parameter. However, I am content to leave the theory with this degree of vagueness, since the ordinary concept of justifiedness is similarly vague. Before the theory could actually be applied, however, a specific threshold value would have to be chosen. One cannot decide whether a particular J-rule system is right—even if one knows its truth ratio—until a required truth ratio is selected.[23]

I will not formulate here the two resource-relative criteria, but their formulation should be fairly straightforward. Although I will have occasion to refer to them from time to time, (ARI) is the main criterion(-schema) I shall utilize, one which is obviously reliabilist in character.

At this point the following question arises: Is the rightness of a rule system determined by its truth ratio in the *actual* world, and in that world only? Or should the performance of the rule system also be judged by its performance in other possible worlds? Or is a still different performance measure appropriate? Obviously, a given rule system could perform well in one possible world—say the actual world—and poorly in another. Which possible worlds are relevant to the rightness of a rule system, and ultimately to the justifiedness of a belief formed in compliance with the system?

Before addressing this issue, we should ponder the following related question. Is a J-rule system that is right in one possible world also right in all possible worlds? In other words, is rightness a 'rigid' designator? Or can a system vary in rightness across different possible worlds? Rightness is easily relativized to a possible world by saying that, for any world W, a system is *right in* W just in case it has a sufficiently high truth ratio *in* W. A different theory would be chauvinistic toward the actual world. It might say that a rule system is right in any world W just in case it is sufficiently reliable in the *actual* world. This kind of actual-world chauvinism would of course imply that each rule system has the same rightness status in all possible worlds.

I think that neither of these answers is correct. At any rate, neither seems to capture our intuitions about justifiedness in hard cases. The answer that best accords with our intuitions—as will emerge in the next section—runs as follows. We have a large set of common beliefs about the actual world: general beliefs about the sorts of objects, events, and changes that occur in it. We have beliefs about the kinds of things that, realistically, do and can happen. Our beliefs on this score generate what I shall call the set of *normal worlds.* These are worlds consistent with our *general* beliefs about the actual world. (I emphasize 'general', since I count worlds with different particular episodes and individuals as normal.) Our concept of justification is constructed against the backdrop of such a set of normal worlds. My proposal is that, according to our ordinary conception of justifiedness, a rule system is right in any world W just in case it has a sufficiently high truth ratio *in normal worlds.*[24] Rightness is rigidified for all worlds; but it is rigidified as a function of reliability in normal worlds, not reliability in the actual world. Rightness of rules—and hence justifiedness—displays normal-world chauvinism.

Obviously, the notion of normal worlds is quite vague. But I do not find that objectionable. I think our ordinary notion of justifiedness is vague on just this point. But let me expand on the approach by putting it in a more general, nonepistemological, context.

The idea of actual-world chauvinism is related to the causal theory of names and natural kind terms proposed by Saul Kripke and Hilary Putnam.[25] On this view the reference and/or meaning of a term is derived from the actual sample of objects to which the term was applied in some original baptismal acts, or meaning-giving contexts. Words like 'gold' or 'cat', for example, acquire reference and/or meaning from the class of things to which they were originally applied. Objects sharing the same nature or essence as that sample, or class, are also gold pieces, or cats. Without reviewing the many discussions of this theory, let me turn to a problem case raised by Peter Unger, a case which also provides rationale for normal-world chauvinism.[26]

In an early paper Putnam introduced an example in which the things we have always taken to be cats have really been inanimate robots, placed on earth by Martian scientists.[27] Unger now introduces the case of feline robots in the past and feline animals in the future. Starting *now*, the Martian scientists (unbeknownst to us) replace all the feline robots with feline animals. According to the causal theory, the feline animals would not correctly be called 'cats'. The theory implies that 'cats' would refer to the nature or essence of the things originally dubbed 'cats', namely, feline robots. Since the feline animals do not share that nature or essence, they are not cats. But this is intuitively incorrect. Surely the feline animals would be cats.

Furthermore, I find it intuitively wrong to say that the feline robots are cats, even though they are what humans in the example have been calling 'cats' all along. This suggests that the reference and/or meaning of 'cats' is fixed not by the actual nature of objects so called, but by their presumed nature. What we *believe* about the things we call 'cats' determines the meaning.

Similarly, I suggest that the meaning of the term 'justified' (in its epistemic use) is fixed by certain things we *presume* about the world, whether we are right or not. Specifically, beliefs are deemed justified when (roughly) they are caused by processes that are reliable in the world as it is presumed to be. Justification-conferring processes are ones that would be reliable in worlds like the presumptively actual world, that is, in normal worlds.

Let me trace an implication of this theory. Suppose it turned out that the actual world is not as we think it is. Suppose it is a Cartesian demon-style world, in which we are radically deceived about 'external' things (though we are not deceived about the nature of our cognitive processes). This means that our cognitive processes are not reliable in the actual world. At least our perceptual processes are unreliable, and perhaps our inductive processes as well. It does not follow, on my theory, that our actual-world beliefs are *unjustified*. The cognitive processes we use may still be reliable in *normal* worlds, in worlds similar to the *presumed* actual world. This possibility follows from normal-world chauvinism vis-à-vis J-rule rightness.

I do not suppose that the fundamental world regularities that define the class of normal worlds extend to properties of our own cognitive processes. Thus, what we believe about our cognitive processes in the actual world need not hold in (all) normal worlds. For this reason, my proposal does not imply that the processes *believed* to be reliable (in the actual world) *are* reliable in normal worlds. Consequently, the processes we believe to be justification-conferring need not really *be* justification-conferring. We could be mistaken in thinking that certain cognitive processes of ours are reliable in normal worlds. For example, we may presume that our processes of estimating the chances of future events are quite accurate, but we may be quite mistaken about this. Hence, it is still a contingent and empirical question whether the processes we take to be justification-conferring really are so;

indeed, it is left open whether there are any justification-conferring processes available to humans at all. Thus, normal-world chauvinism does not beg the question of skepticism.

Does the current stratagem turn my theory of justifiedness into a subjectivist account rather than an objectivist one? I think not, for the reason just indicated. Whether a given rule system is right does not simply depend on what we believe about the world. It depends on whether the processes permitted by the specified rule system really *do* have a high enough truth ratio in normal worlds. This is something that hinges on the 'facts' about these processes, not simply on our opinions. Hence, the proposal is objectivist, not subjectivist, in contour.

One final point. My proposal to judge reliability by reference to normal worlds is made in the spirit of trying to elucidate the *ordinary* conception of justifiedness. I am prepared to be persuaded that this ordinary conception can be improved upon. I would lend a receptive ear to proposals to 'regiment' the concept of justifiedness so as to judge rightness by reliability in the *actual* world, or by reliability in the possible world of the belief in question. Either of these approaches might seem preferable from a systematic or theoretical point of view. Nonetheless, they do not seem to be what is implied by the ordinary conception as it stands; and that is all I am currently trying to capture.

5.6. Counterexamples and Replies

Previous versions of reliabilism have been the objects of a number of counterexamples and criticisms. Let us look at the most prominent of these, to see how the present version of reliabilism fares.

Reliabilism may be inadequate for either of two reasons: it may not be *sufficient* for justifiedness, or it may not be *necessary*. One charge of insufficiency comes from Putnam.[28] Suppose, Putnam says, that the Dalai Lama is in fact infallible on matters of faith and morals. Then anyone who believes in the Dalai Lama, and who invariably believes any statement the Dalai Lama makes on a matter of faith or morals, uses a method which is 100 percent reliable. Such a person's beliefs in matters of faith and morals should all be justified, according to reliabilism, even if his argument for the belief that the Dalai Lama is never wrong is simply "the Dalai Lama says so." But obviously these beliefs are not justified.

A second set of arguments for insufficiency is presented by various authors, including Laurence BonJour.[29] BonJour presents four cases, in all of which the cognizer has a completely reliable clairvoyant power. According to earlier versions of reliability theories of justifiedness, the clairvoyance-caused beliefs of these cognizers should be justified.[30] BonJour makes it plausible that his four cognizers' beliefs are not justified. In some cases the cognizer has explicit counterevidence against his or her possession of a clairvoyant power but ignores it. In another case the cognizer has no reasons to believe that he or she is clairvoyant but has counterevidence against the clairvoyance-caused belief, namely, that the President is in New York. The cognizer persists in believing that the President is in New York in the face of the counterevidence. And so on for the other cases.

A third sort of counterexample purports to show that reliability is not *necessary* for justifiedness. Consider a possible world in which a Cartesian demon systematically deceives a certain cognizer (or lots of cognizers). The cognizer employs the very same psychological processes that you or I use, but the result is a massively false set of beliefs. Since his processes are not reliable, reliabilism implies that his beliefs are not justified. But intuitively they are justified.[31]

Let us start with Putnam's counterexample. Notice, first, that the method of believing whatever the Dalai Lama says on matters of faith and morals is just that, a *method,* in the slightly technical sense I have given that term. But my theory does not say that being produced by a reliable method is sufficient for justifiedness. For one thing, I have not really offered a theory of secondary justifiedness, although I do lean in the direction of a reliability theory thereof. But let us set that issue aside. I have committed myself to the view that, however reliable or right a method may be, it does not confer justifiedness unless it is acquired by suitable processes, for example, metareliable processes (see section 5.7). Now this condition is not clearly met in Putnam's example. Putnam says that the person's only argument for the belief that the Dalai Lama is never wrong is simply "the Dalai Lama says so." But what are we to infer from that? The person's only defense of the method seems to be another application of the method. But this still leaves open the question of what *processes* have led him to acceptance of this method. Pending specification of some legitimate (metareliable) psychological process, one is left with the suspicion that no metareliable process has been used, that the believer has simply stumbled upon a method which, by chance, is infallible. In that case the belief is not justified, on my theory. If it turns out that metareliable processes were used in acquiring the method, then I think that the person is justified in believing the method to be reliable, and hence the beliefs that issue from it may be justified. (Even this result, though, will not suffice for justifiedness on my theory. The method itself must be certified as right. Under a culturally relative criterion of rightness, trusting the Dalai Lama may not be a right method, even if it is in fact infallible; for the relevant culture might not approve of such a method.)

Before turning to BonJour's examples, which are rather like the Millicent case introduced in Chapter 3, let us see how my theory handles the Millicent case. Millicent has perfectly normal and (we assume) reliable visual powers. She also has a false though justified belief that her visual powers are seriously impaired. Despite this belief, Millicent forms other beliefs that endorse the testimony of her visual appearances. Intuitively, these beliefs are not justified. But doesn't our reliability theory imply that they are justified? No. To appreciate this, we must simply recall the *nonundermining* clause of our framework principle (P3*). The nonundermining provision is violated in the Millicent case; at least that is how the provision should be understood.

Recall the initial discussion of permission undermining in section 4.1. A sufficient condition for undermining was suggested there: the cognizer believes—justifiably or not—that he or she is not permitted to hold the target belief. Now Millicent does not fulfill this condition, we may suppose. Let us say she does not possess the concept of permission by a right J-rule system, and therefore possesses no beliefs featuring this concept. What *is* true of Millicent, though, is the following. She believes that her visual powers are impaired, so that the belief-forming processes that utilize her visual powers must not be reliable. What she believes, then, is such that *if* it were true, the beliefs in question (her visually formed beliefs) *would not* be permitted by a right rule system. Satisfaction of this condition, I now propose, is sufficient to undermine permittedness. In other words, it is sufficient for undermining that a cognizer believes that certain conditions obtain which, if they did obtain, would entail that the target beliefs are not permitted by a right rule system. The cognizer need not actually have any beliefs about rule systems, rightness, or criteria of rightness.

Millicent's visually formed beliefs are permitted by a right J-rule system. But according to my framework principle, the beliefs still are not justified, since their being so permitted is undermined. This yields the result needed for handling the *knowledge* question: Millicent's visually formed beliefs are not pieces of knowledge because they are not justified. And they are not justified despite the fact that the producing processes are indeed reliable.

Let us now turn to BonJour's examples. A difference between BonJour's cases and the Millicent case is that the characters in BonJour's examples do not *believe* they *are not* using reliable processes. However, undermining should be so construed that the permittedness of their target beliefs is undermined nonetheless. For although they do not in fact believe that the target beliefs are unreliably caused, they are *justified* in so believing (in a sense to be specified below).

Let us look at these cases in detail. Maud has a completely reliable clairvoyance power, and uses it in forming a belief N that the President is in New York. Maud believes herself to have the power of clairvoyance. But Maud also has been inundated with massive quantities of apparently cogent scientific evidence that no such power is possible. Intuitively, then, Maud is justified in believing that she has no reliable clairvoyance power, although she does not believe this. And she is justified in believing that her belief in N is not reliably caused, although again she does not believe this. Since she is *justified* in believing the latter, however, that should suffice to undermine the permission of her believing N. (Use of her clairvoyant powers would be permitted by a right rule system because they are reliable.)

To make this proposed treatment stick, I need to go a bit beyond the theory of justifiedness offered thus far. The account I have offered is a theory of when an *actual* belief is justified. It is a theory of what I call (in "What Is Justified Belief?") *ex post* justifiedness. But the present undermining deals with being justified in believing a proposition one does not actually believe. The idea is that it is a proposition one would (or could) be justified in believing, given one's present cognitive state, although one does not in fact believe it. This is what I call *ex ante* justifiedness. A theory of *ex ante* justifiedness can be constructed, I think, along lines very similar to my account of *ex post* justifiedness, though I will not pursue all the details. One difference is that we may have to require right rule systems to feature obligation rules as well as permission rules. Thus, we might suppose that a right rule system would *require* Maud to utilize certain reasoning processes, processes that would lead her from the scientific evidence she possesses to belief in the proposition that she does not have any reliable clairvoyance power. And similarly, she would be required to infer that her belief in N is not caused by any reliable processes. On the proposed account she would be justified *(ex ante)* in believing that her belief in N is not reliably caused. And this suffices to undermine the permittedness of her belief in N.

BonJour's case of Casper would be handled similarly. Casper has attempted to confirm his allegedly clairvoyant beliefs on numerous occasions, but they have always turned out apparently to be false. Given this evidence, he ought to use processes that would lead him to believe (permissibly) that he lacks reliable clairvoyant processes. This undermines the actual permissibility of his belief in N.

BonJour's next case, the case of Norman, is arguably a little tougher, and indeed it is introduced to show that even a nonundermining condition still does not produce an adequate reliabilist theory. BonJour describes this case as one in which Norman possesses no evidence or reasons of any kind for or against the general possibility of clairvoyance, or for or against the thesis that he possesses it. But it is hard to envisage this description holding. Norman *ought* to reason along the following lines: 'If I had a clairvoyant power, I would surely find *some* evidence for this. I would find myself believing things in otherwise inexplicable ways, and when these things were checked by other reliable processes, they would usually check out positively. Since I lack any such signs, I apparently do not possess reliable clairvoyant processes.' Since Norman ought to reason this way, he is *ex ante* justified in believing that he does not possess reliable clairvoyant processes. This undermines his belief in N. Thus, the nonundermining clause of (P3°) handles BonJour's cases.

Let us turn now to the Cartesian demon example. This case is intended to show that reliability is not *necessary* for justifiedness. Intuitively, a cognizer being massively deceived by an evil demon is still forming justified beliefs. But in an evil demon possible world, the cognitive processes being utilized just are not reliable. So reliability is not a necessary condition for justifiedness.

The solution to this counterexample is straightforward. The counterexample rests on the assumption that the justificational status of a belief in possible world W is determined by the reliability of the belief's processes in W. But this is what I have denied (in the previous section). The justificational status of a W-world belief does not depend on the reliability of the causing processes in W. Rather, it depends on the reliability of the processes *in normal worlds*. Now an evil demon world is a paradigm case of a non-normal world. So it does not matter that the processes in question are highly unreliable in that world. It only matters whether they are reliable in normal worlds, and that is apparently the case. (At any rate, that is what our intuitive judgment of justifiedness presumes, I think.)

The same treatment of the putative counterexample applies if the counterexample is revised to make it an actual-world case. Imagine, the objection goes, that our *actual* world turns out to be an evil demon world. (Or imagine we are actually brains in a vat being deceived by scheming scientists.) Intuitively, our beliefs would still be justified; yet the belief-forming processes being deployed are not reliable. Again the case is easy to handle. Its apparent strength rests on the assumption that the justificational status of the beliefs is determined by the reliability of their causal processes *in the actual world*. But this does not accord with our theory. Reliability is measured in normal worlds; and in this case, the actual world is an abnormal world! So reliability in the actual world just does not matter.

The reader can now see how the normal-worlds account of reliability fits our intuitions very naturally in the evil demon class of cases. Indeed, reflection on these cases (partly) prompted the normal-worlds approach. Once formulated, though, it seems to work naturally for other cases as well.[32]

5.7. *Calibration and Second-Order Processes*

This section picks up several loose ends in my theory of justification. I take up, briefly, three topics. (1) I suggest a way to generalize the truth ratio approach from categorical to partial beliefs (subjective probabilities). (2) I indicate why rightness has been defined in the first instance for rule systems rather than individual rules. (3) I discuss rightness criteria for second-order processes.

First, note that the theory presented thus far addresses only the justificational status of binary belief. It is generally assumed, however, that there are degrees of belief, that people believe propositions with more or less confidence; and it is often claimed that confidence levels can be scaled on the unit interval. Many theorists therefore seek an account of epistemic norms for these different confidence degrees or subjective probabilities. Can the reliabilist framework accommodate such a refinement?

It certainly can, as I shall outline below. Before proceeding, though, let me register my reservations about the psychological reality of degrees of belief. Although there is unquestionably *some* (introspective) basis for the notion of degrees of confidence, I question whether the psychological facts warrant a systematic treatment of belief states as subjective probability states. Grounds for these doubts will be scouted in Chapter 15. Meanwhile, I will make the working assumption that the psychological issues can be resolved. I will try to show how truth ratio consequentialism is a well-equipped framework for doing the epistemology of partial beliefs. Doubts I harbor about the psychological tenability of this construct will be deferred until Chapter 15.

What I want to do, then, is generalize the truth-ratio (ARI) criterion of rightness, so that it applies to processes that generate partial beliefs. I assume that partial beliefs can take any real value in the interval from 0 to 1. Very simply, the proposal is that a J-rule system is right if and only if it is 'well calibrated'.

The notion of calibration is presented and defined by Sarah Lichtenstein, Baruch Fischhoff, and Lawrence Phillips as follows: "A judge is calibrated if, over the long run, for all propositions assigned a given probability, the proportion that is true equals the probability assigned."[33] Application of this definition to J-rule systems would run as follows. First, assume that instantiations of (that is, compliance with) a given J-rule system R would produce some partial beliefs. (I am interested in instantiations of R in normal worlds, but I will focus on the actual world as presumably one such world.) Now among the partial beliefs so produced, let those of the same degree be grouped together: all of degree .50, all of degree .70, and so on. Then a system R is well calibrated if and only if, for each degree D, the truth ratio of propositions believed to degree D is approximately D. For example, approximately half of the propositions at .50 subjective probability are true, approximately 70 percent of the propositions at .70 subjective probability are true, and so on. Finally, a J-rule system is *right* if and only if it is well calibrated.

Given this rightness criterion, the framework principle for justification, (P3°), is directly applied. A token partial belief is justified if and only if *(a)* it is the result of a sequence of (basic) processes permitted by a right rule system, and *(b)* the permittedness of this sequence is not undermined (for the cognizer in question).

Good calibration as an epistemic norm is not without its problems.[34] These would have to be resolved before the good calibration approach could be finally accepted. But I am only interested here in outlining a good-calibration approach to justification, and showing how the truth-ratio conception readily lends itself to a related treatment of justification for partial beliefs.

The second loose end I wish to pick up in this section concerns the choice of rule systems, as opposed to individual rules, as bearers of justificational rightness. The rationale for this need not occupy us at length. The point is that rules are *interdependent* with respect to their epistemically relevant properties. In particular, they are interdependent with respect to truth-ratio properties. This is especially clear for inferential rules. A rule of 'detachment', for example, might not spell trouble if complemented by certain rules, but will breed what is known as the lottery paradox if complemented by other rules. A sound inferential rule will generate additional true beliefs when applied to true input beliefs. But if other rules permit false beliefs to be formed, then even a sound inferential rule may produce innumerable errors. Truth-ratio propensities, then, only make sense as applied to rule systems, not isolated rules. A similar point holds, I suspect, for different epistemically relevant properties that other theories might advocate.

The third loose end I wish to pick up concerns second-order processes. In section 5.3 I noted that a complete theory of primary justifiedness should include a rightness criterion for second-order as well as first-order processes. It is now time to adumbrate what this criterion should be.

Given my truth-ratio approach to first-order rightness, the natural expectation is a truth-ratio approach to second-order rightness as well. This indeed strikes me as promising; but there are several permutations to consider. Two of these were suggested in section 1.4, where I first introduced the notion of second-order processes. A second-order process might be considered metareliable if, among the methods (or first-order processes) it outputs, the ratio of those that are reliable meets some specified level, presumably greater than .50. For example, suppose a threshold of .80 is set for both reliability and metareliability. Then a second-order process is metareliable if and only if at least 80 percent of the processes (or methods) it produces are at least 80 percent reliable.

A weaker conception of metareliability would merely require *increases* in reliability, not an absolute ratio of reliability. On this conception a second-order process would be metareliable if it modifies or replaces processes (or methods) so as always to increase levels of reliability. Even more weakly, a second-order process might be metareliable if the modifications or replacements it produces usually (rather than always) increase reliability.

In addition to these possibilities, there are possibilities obtainable by adapting either of the resource-relative conceptions of J-rightness introduced in section 5.5. Corresponding to the maximizing resource-relative criterion would be a criterion of second-order rightness that requires use of second-order processes with maximum metareliability (for humans). Corresponding to the satisficing resource-relative criterion would be a criterion of second-order rightness that merely requires a level of metareliability that is easily, or commonly, achieved. Each of these criteria can be combined with either of the themes examined above: *(a)* the proportion of reliable processes (or methods) that get produced, or *(b)* the tendency to increase the reliability of one's repertoire.

It is worth emphasizing that second-order processes should be judged not simply by their acquisition performance, but also by their retention performance. Even if a set of second-order processes frequently acquires poor methods, this will not be so bad if the poor methods are weeded out quickly. But if poor methods are *retained* over considerable periods of time, it is a much more serious deficiency. In assessing the quality of second-order processes, retention (and modification) characteristics should be weighed as heavily as acquisition characteristics.

I will not try to choose a unique criterion from among the candidates sketched above. I will rest content with this family of criteria (though I will return to the topic in Chapter 17, where further complications will be introduced). I suspect that our ordinary conception of justifiedness is simply quite vague about the constraints on method acquisition and retention, so no unique criterion is saliently indicated. In any case these candidate criteria all confirm the notion that truth ratios (or improvements in truth ratios) are central to second-order rightness.

This notion is further confirmed if we turn our attention from second-order processes for categorical belief-forming processes to second-order processes for partial belief-forming processes. To complement our good-calibration criterion of rightness for partial belief rules, the natural suggestion is that second-order processes are permissible if they usually produce reasonably well-calibrated processes (or methods); or at least *improve* calibration by managing, over time, to discard poorly calibrated processes.

5.8. *Truth-Linkedness*

The rightness criteria I have proposed are all verific consequentialist criteria, and these are a species of *truth-linked* criteria. Many people are suspicious of such criteria. There are charges of circularity and worries about the difficulty of *applying* a truth-linked criterion. This section is intended to answer the charges and allay the worries.

Let us begin with a charge of definitional circularity. This charge (in slightly different words) is leveled by Putnam:

> Truth, in the only sense in which we have a vital and working notion of it, is rational acceptability . . . But to substitute this characterization of truth into the formula 'reason is a capacity for discovering truths' is to see the emptiness of that formula at once: 'reason is a capacity for discovering what is . . .

rationally acceptable' is *not* the most informative statement a philosopher might utter. The . . . epistemologist must either presuppose a 'realist' . . . notion of truth or see his formula collapse into vacuity.[35]

If truth is indeed rational acceptability, Putnam is right in claiming that a reliabilist—or more generally, a truth-linked—account of justifiedness is circular (or "vacuous"). I therefore need to show that truth is not rational acceptability. In short, I need to argue for a realist theory of truth. This task will be undertaken in Chapter 7. Until then, I simply presuppose a realist understanding of truth.

A different charge of circularity is posed by Roderick Firth.

> Each of us decides at any time t whether a belief is true, in precisely the same way that we would decide at t whether we ourselves are, or would be, warranted at t in having that belief . . . If we are rational we must assume . . . a correlation between warrant-conferring rules and true beliefs . . . in order to identify true beliefs. Our reasoning is obviously circular if we then use beliefs so identified as data for inferring a correlation between warrant-conferring rules and true beliefs.[36]

The worry here (as indicated by the final sentence of the passage) seems to be directed at what we have been calling a reliabilist 'criterion' of justifiedness. Firth appears to be charging that in order to substantiate that criterion we must presuppose it. This charge rests on a misplaced assumption. It is apparently assumed that we can only substantiate the criterion by generalization from observed 'data'. We observe warranted beliefs, we observe their truth, and we infer a correlation between the two. This picture of criterion substantiation is misplaced. We do not have to observe warranted beliefs and determine their actual truth-values to decide whether the criterion is correct. As in other cases of analysis, one can proceed entirely by hypothetical cases. We can simply ask whether an *imagined* belief caused by unreliable processes would count as warranted. We use hypothetical cases to elicit our intuitions. The procedure does not require us to determine the actual truth-values of actual beliefs.

Another passage from Firth raises the specter of a different sort of circularity. He writes:

> [If by] 'warrant-conferring rules' . . . we *mean* statistically reliable rules . . . is there any way to decide rationally whether or not a particular set of rules . . . is or is not warrant-conferring? To decide this, which involves predicting the future, would require an inductive argument based on the past failure or success of those rules in generating true beliefs. But if we are rational, how can we identify true beliefs except by assuming, explicitly or implicitly, that some particular set of rules is warrant-conferring?[37]

This objection concerns not the choice of a criterion, but the determination of which rule-system (if any) *satisfies* the criterion. The objection is that in the attempt to decide which rule system satisfies the criterion, one must already assume some system as right. Some system must be presupposed in order to form beliefs at all, including beliefs about which system satisfies the criterion's requirements. This is apparently viewed as objectionable on grounds of circularity.

Does the suggestion that a rule-system must be assumed, or presupposed, mean that one must already have *beliefs* about what rule system is right? That is not so. One need only *use* cognitive processes (and perhaps methods) to decide whether a target rule system satisfies the criterion. Using cognitive processes does not in general—nor in this case—require beliefs in the epistemic properties of rule systems.

Firth is also wrong in suggesting that application of a reliabilist criterion requires *prediction of the future.* One can identify a truth propensity in normal worlds—at least an approximate truth propensity—without worrying about the exact course of events in the future segment of the actual world. Consider, for example, assessment of the truth propensity of visual mechanisms. By studying their underlying structure, one can determine that they would breed illusory impressions in a certain class of stimulus conditions. If one has a rough idea of the frequency of this class of conditions in normal situations, one can assess the degree of unreliability this property engenders. Some inductive reasoning is involved in the study of any mechanism's properties, but no prediction of individual future events is required.

The next point to notice—and emphasize—is that truth-linked criteria are no worse off than any other criteria in the matter of application. To apply *any* sort of criterion, some reasoning and other cognitive processes are required. How else could one decide whether a particular rule-system satisfies a given criterion? This fact does not reflect *adversely* on truth-linked criteria as compared with other criteria.

Perhaps the intended challenge is not whether a truth-linked criterion can be applied at all, but whether it can be applied either *(a)* correctly, or *(b)* rationally (or justifiably). Firth's formulation concerns *(b)*, but let us start with *(a)*.

First, again note that the issue does not reflect adversely on truth-linked criteria as compared with other criteria. There can always be a question of whether antecedent cognitive processes or methods will work *correctly* in trying to apply a criterion. Consider a criterion that says that a rule system is right if and only if conformity with it would maximize 'positive coherence'. An attempt to apply such a criterion would first involve an assessment of just how much coherence would be produced by each of a number of specified rule systems (given some measure of positive coherence). Next one would have to determine that all possible rule systems had been surveyed, at least all strong candidates. Clearly, all sorts of mistakes might be made in this selection process. Even much weaker criteria would feature the possibility of mistaken application. Suppose a criterion says that a rule system is right if and only if it guarantees a consistent belief corpus. Application of this criterion is also tricky. Even famous logicians have made mistakes about the consistency of certain formal systems. It is no trivial matter to determine whether any given rule system ensures consistency.

It might be argued that some criteria would be *easier* to apply correctly than truth-linked criteria. Some criteria would not require empirical investigation of psychological mechanisms, and this would alleviate some of the difficulties posed by (ARI), for example. But notice that the cited difficulty does arise not from the truth-linked feature of (ARI), but rather from its reference to basic psychological processes. That feature of a satisfactory criterion is independent of truth-linkedness. Second, notice that in a certain sense, truth assessments are involved in application of *all* criteria. For example, to decide whether a candidate system R satisfies a coherence maximization criterion one has to decide whether it is *true* that R maximizes coherence.

Third, even if it is granted that truth-linked criteria are harder to apply than others, what reason is there to suppose that relative ease of application must be a property of a *correct* criterion? No argument has been given to this effect. (This might be a plausible constraint if the criterion and rule systems were intended to be regulative, or action-guiding. But they are not so intended.)

I offer no guarantee that (ARI), or any of the other truth-ratio criteria proposed here, can be correctly applied. But as we have seen, no such guarantee can be offered for other criteria either. Still, it may be replied, can't we at least provide a guarantee that it is *possible* for truth-ratio criteria to be applied correctly? Surely such a minimal guarantee ought to be forthcoming for any adequate criterion.

At this point we need to distinguish logical possibility from factual possibility. We can certainly guarantee that it is logically possible for truth-ratio criteria to be correctly applied. It is logically possible that our native processes, together with our antecedently accepted scientific methods, should lead us to identify one or more rule systems that really do satisfy (ARI) or my other truth-ratio criteria. When it comes to factual possibility, though, the matter is open to doubt. It is conceivable that our actual cognitive resources are so poor, and our currently accepted scientific methods so weak, that they are incapable of correctly applying these criteria. I say that this is *conceivable,* but I am not inclined to think it is true. I am much more inclined to think that our native processes and our current methods offer a serious possibility of correct application, though the task would not be easy. However, since I cannot prove that our actual processes and methods are adequate to the task, I cannot offer a guarantee to this effect. Once again, though, no invidious judgment is implied vis-à-vis truth-linked criteria. If our native cognitive processes and currently accepted methods are *too* defective, they will not allow *non*-truth-linked criteria to be applied correctly either. Indeed, if our processes and accepted methods are *so* flawed, almost any worthy intellectual endeavor is doomed to failure.

Some philosophers would insist that such a dire scenario can be excluded *a priori*. Proper principles of 'interpretation', or belief ascription, they would say, guarantee that most of a person's beliefs are true. So belief-forming processes cannot be *too* defective. I can live with this suggestion, but I do not wish to insist upon it. In particular, I want to stress a strong *contingent* component in process reliability (see Chapter 8). But a modest *a priori* component could be allowed as well, if the argument for it could be made good.

Although I am leery of the thesis that our belief-forming processes could not *be* too defective, I acknowledge that nobody could *believe* that his or her own processes were defective in a wholesale way; at least nobody with a modicum of logical acuity and reflectiveness. How could anyone think that *all* his or her belief-forming processes are radically defective? A little reflection would indicate that this very belief is thereby undermined, since it too must have been formed by putatively defective processes. Still, while wholesale self-deprecation is excluded, a person can certainly believe that *some* of his or her belief-forming processes are faulty.

Let us now turn to a slightly different argument, which states that there is no point in seeking a right rule system under a reliabilist criterion, because there is no possibility of improvement. If we unfortunately start out with an unreliable set of processes, any attempt to identify proper processes and methods (right rules) will fail. So we would be stuck in an epistemic quagmire. If, however, we are fortunate to start with a reliable set of processes, any attempt to identify proper processes will be pointless, since we will already be using such processes.

It is evident, though, that this argument is a flop. First of all, even if we natively use (mostly) reliable processes, it is another matter to identify what those processes are. Second, no convincing argument has been given against the possibility of improvement, of epistemic bootstrapping. The main sort of bootstrapping scenario runs as follows. We start with a set of available processes with varying degrees of reliability. We use the more reliable processes to identify good methods. We then use the more reliable processes, together with some of the good methods, to identify the various processes and their respective degrees of reliability. The superior specimens are so identified, and their use is said to be justification-conferring. The inferior specimens are so identified, and their use is said to be non-justification-conferring. If the faulty processes are subject to direct or indirect control, we try to avoid those processes. Or we try to devise methods to minimize their impact. In this manner epistemic melioration is possible.

One must now ask whether it is possible to apply a reliabilist criterion rationally, or at least justifiably. This is (logically) possible. As long as we have some sufficiently reliable processes (which are not undermined by any of our beliefs), and they are the sorts of processes needed for the question at hand, a right rule system would permit the use of those processes. So we *could* arrive at a justified belief about which particular rule system is right. (Of course, even a justified belief could be false. So justified application of the criterion does not ensure correct application of the criterion. But we have already addressed the problem of correctness.)

My conclusion is simple. There is nothing wrong with truth-linked criteria in general, nor with a reliabilist criterion in particular. Given the strong arguments I have marshaled on behalf of such a criterion (or family of criteria), we have every reason to accept it.

chapter 6

Problem Solving, Power, and Speed

6.1. Intelligence and Goal-Directedness

In chapter 1 I called attention to a *variety* of terms of epistemic appraisal and standards attached thereto. But thus far all discussion has centered on knowledge and justification, which invoke one principal standard of epistemic evaluation: reliability. It is time to broaden our perspective, to expand the range of terms and standards within our purview. No apology is needed for the lengthy treatment of knowledge and justification. These are critical to skepticism, and skepticism is historically critical to epistemology. But skepticism, knowledge, and justification should not be the whole province of epistemology. Nor should reliability be the only pertinent standard. There are other terms, dimensions, and standards with an equal right to occupy the epistemological limelight.

For example, 'intelligence' is a more prevalent term of cognitive evaluation in extraphilosophical contexts. Though doubtless very vague, it deserves more attention in epistemology than it has hitherto received. I shall not undertake a full scale analysis of intelligence. However, I wish to explore some standards of cognitive appraisal that appear to be *among* the criteria for intelligence, and defend the importance of these criteria for epistemic purposes.

The main standards I will emphasize are power and speed. Both are distinct from reliability and comparable in importance. As noted in Chapter 1, reliable cognitive mechanisms are an antidote to error, but not necessarily an antidote to ignorance. Reliable processes guarantee a high truth ratio among the beliefs they generate. But they may generate very few beliefs indeed; they may leave the cognizer with very little information, even on the issues that interest him or her most. The antidote to ignorance is not reliability, but (intellectual) power. Powerful cognitive mechanisms are (roughly) mechanisms capable of getting a relatively large number of truths.

An intelligent cognitive system, it seems clear, is not simply a reliable system. Intelligence is at least partly a matter of power: a capacity to com-

bat and relieve ignorance, not simply error.[1] To be sure, an intelligent creature may be lazy, and may therefore remain mired in ignorance. But an intelligent creature is at least capable of relieving its ignorance.

It would be a mistake to equate intelligence with power, at least if power
is equated with number of truths that can be obtained. First, it is not entirely clear that number of truths, rather than, say, complexity, is the appropriate standard of intelligence. Suppose system A is capable of getting more
true beliefs than B, but B can solve more complex problems. B might be
credited with more intelligence. This could be accommodated by building a
complexity parameter into a measure of power. But I have no proposals for
a metric of complexity.

Second, a system may be capable of acquiring numerous truths, but
mostly incidental ones, unrelated to its needs or interests. For example, a
system may be capable of indefinitely expanding its true-belief set by adding disjuncts to truths it already believes. But a system that just cranks out
more and more disjunctive true beliefs, oblivious to other pressing questions
left unanswered, might well be considered very stupid.

The last point is really twofold. First, intelligence probably has something to do with breadth of answerable questions, not simply their number.
Second, a system oblivious to the questions it wants to answer, which
blindly computes answers to irrelevant questions, is not very intelligent. Intelligence is partly a matter of *goal-responsiveness.*

If we seek to crystallize a standard of (intellectual) power that is reasonably close to intelligence, we need to distinguish several conceptions of
power. One simply makes power a function of the number of true beliefs a
cognitive system can generate. A second makes it a function of number plus
breadth. A third makes power a function of the proportion of questions it
wants to answer that it can answer (correctly), or the proportion of problems undertaken that it can solve correctly. Only the third conception
makes power a goal-responsive notion, so it is the best conception in this
group. Notice, though, that we should restrict attention not to questions or
problems actually posed by the cognitive system, but rather to those it
could pose.

Further comments on goal-responsiveness are in order. Biological cognitive systems are typically deployed to help the organism satisfy its practical
needs or ends. This involves the choice of actions, designed to achieve specified goals. Good choices of action—ones that lead to a high level of goal
satisfaction—typically depend on good information, that is, true beliefs or
relatively high confidence in truths. Thus, cognitive mechanisms are used to
try to get true beliefs on *pretargeted* questions, questions relevant to the
practical tasks at hand. Even when no practical task is at stake, cognitive
activity involves prespecified questions. Purely intellectual questions commonly engender a host of subsidiary problems, solutions to which become

targets of inquiry. Intelligence is the ability to succeed in such inquiries, to find the answers, or solve the problems, antecedently posed. Getting true beliefs on incidental matters does not count (as much). It is like a game of billiards, where a player calls his shots, saying which ball he will get in which hole. If he sinks a different ball, or the right ball in a wrong hole, it does not count. Success in cognitive matters is also measured mainly by solving the problems one is *trying* to solve, not forming a lot of incidental true beliefs along the way. (Of course, incidental truths may be useful later, when one's goal structure alters, so incidental true beliefs are not valueless. The issue is not as sharply defined as in billiards.)

Unlike power, reliability has nothing to do with goal-responsiveness. Cognitive processes could be wonderfully reliable but wholly unresponsive to current goals. Thus, the notion of power I am placing on our agenda invokes considerations of a different order than those invoked by reliability. I suggest that intelligence involves some such goal-responsive parameter, and any total, well-balanced evaluation of a cognitive system should do so as well.

It would still be a mistake to suppose that intelligence can be equated with power. In addition to complexity, at least one other variable must be included: speed. Other things equal, a more intelligent person is one who solves problems relatively quickly. It is possible that speed can be *partly* subsumed under power. First, the faster one solves problems, the more problems one can solve in a given time period. Second, many cognitive goals, or tasks, can be conceptualized as finding an answer to a given question by a certain time. When the time limit is short, slower problem-solving processes will not satisfy the constraint, hence will not be able to execute the specified task at all. But time constraints are not always built into intellectual tasks. So it is best to retain power and speed as two distinct standards of evaluation.

The human cognitive architecture clearly has design features sensitive to power and speed. Its attentional control mechanisms respond to current goals, and its memory seems structured for retrieval of relevant information. The system also appears to have a number of devices that shortcut belief formation: heuristics that enable a belief to be formed by nonalgorithmic and nonexhaustive procedures. These are obviously conducive to speed. I shall explore a variety of such mechanisms in Part II.

It may be asked, however, whether such features of the human system are normatively acceptable. Don't they conflict, in some cases, with reliability? Clearly there are going to be trade-offs between speed and reliability, as well as trade-offs between goal-responsiveness and reliability. How does possession of the indicated mechanisms stack up against a proper balancing, or weighting, of the several standards I have introduced?

If there were an attractive way to fuse these variables into a single measure, I would cheerfully endorse it. But I know of no such formula. We must live for now with an irreducible multiplicity of standards. This may be a bit disappointing, but not surprising. Consolation may be taken from ethics and the law, where analogous complications arise. It is hard to balance the competing claims of justice and mercy, of public good and individual rights. We should not expect an easy formula for epistemic evaluation either. Distinct standards need to be treated separately. That is why I qualified all talk of rules in Chapters 4 and 5 as *justificational* rules: they were not rules for overall epistemic status. Still, all appropriate standards need to be kept in mind. Thus, my assessments of cognitive mechanisms in Part II will heed power and speed as much as reliability.

6.2. Problem Solving and Truth

Implicit in the preceding discussion is a truth-linked conception of problem solving: getting a true answer to a question. But recent epistemological discussions of problem-solving contexts have not all so interpreted 'problem solving'. Indeed, the most extended use of problem-solving terminology, namely, that of Larry Laudan in *Progress and Its Problems*, expressly divorces truth from problem solving.[2] A more precise account and defense of my truth-linked usage is therefore in order. This will also pave the way for a view of the cognitive activities involved in problem solving and unveil a fuller vision of the cognitive processes that are proper *objects* of epistemic evaluation.

The language of problem solving has cropped up intermittently in epistemology and the philosophy of science. John Dewey's theory of inquiry, for example, rested on a notion of a "problematic situation."[3] More recently, philosophers of science like Karl Popper, Thomas Kuhn, Imre Lakatos, and Laudan have all talked of problem solving, or puzzle solving, as an important facet of science.[4] Some of this usage, however, has only selected points of contact with mine. For example, Kuhn, Lakatos, and Laudan view problem solving as a property of theories, not an activity of cognizers, which is what my usage will indicate.

However, a number of recent philosophers of science have linked the language of problem solving with that of questions and question answering, as I shall do. Jaakko Hintikka, for example, proposes an 'interrogative' model of scientific inquiry.[5] And both Sylvain Bromberger and Bas van Fraassen make question answering central to their theories of scientific explanation.[6] My own approach is intended to be even more general. It is intended to subsume every sort of intellectual question: scientific or nonscientific, theoretical or nontheoretical. This is appropriate for a general epistemological framework.

Why interpret problems as questions in the first place? For the purposes of epistemology, a problem is an intellectual problem. This makes it natural to view problems as questions, to which cognizers (or groups of cognizers) either need or want answers. Doubtless there are other senses of 'problem' not covered by this approach. Emotional problems are sources of trouble, or distress, but are not (typically) questions (though they may give rise to a question: How can the person be rid of the distress?). But for epistemological purposes, identification of problems with questions should prove congenial.

To analyze problems and problem solving, let us begin with the issue of what it is to *have* a problem, in the intellectual sense that concerns us.

S has problem Q if and only if:
    (1)   Q is a question,
    (2)   S wants to have a (true) answer to Q,
    (3)   S does not believe that he has a (true) answer to Q, and
    (4)   S does not have a (true) answer to Q.

This account is somewhat stronger than it needs to be. There might be a sense of having a problem that is compatible with believing that one has an answer, contrary to (3). A cognizer could have a problem without realizing it, because he thinks he's got the answer. In this sense, though, having problems will not necessarily motivate one to try to find answers. Since I am ultimately interested in activities *directed* at finding answers, I am inclined to neglect this possible sense. Another definition weaker than the above one would delete condition (4). This would make having a problem compatible with having an answer (but not realizing that one has it). This can occur if you believe a proposition that *does* answer Q, without believing it answers Q. (Perhaps you just haven't noticed that it answers Q.) However, this sense can be neglected for simplicity. The central cases are those captured by the definition provided.

An important feature of this definition is the desire element. Clause (2) implies that S *has* Q as a problem only if S *wants* to have an answer to Q. (Compare Bromberger's notion of a "p-predicament.")[7] Thus, someone ignorant of a certain question's answer, but wholly uninterested in it, does not have that question as a problem; he does not make it one of his questions.

Notice that wanting to have an answer to Q is not the same as wanting to be told an answer to Q. In general, my discussion focuses on intrapersonal questions and answers, not interpersonal question asking and answering. A teacher, who already knows the answer to Q, may want to be told the answer by a student. But this is incidental to the having of a problem.

Another central feature of the definition is that having a problem involves wanting a *true* answer. This seems natural enough. When you ask a question, you don't just want a random candidate answer; you want the real, correct, answer. Sometimes people do want merely candidate answers.

But then their question is: What are some candidate answers to that question? and there again a correct answer is desired, namely, things that *are* candidate answers.

Given this definition of having a problem, the natural definition of a problem *solution* is:

Proposition A is a solution (answer) to problem (question) Q if and only if
(1) A is a potential answer to Q, and
(2) A is true.

Erotetic logic studies the logical relations between questions and answers. This includes the study of which propositions are potential (relevant) answers to which questions. By a potential answer, I mean roughly what Nuel Belnap and Thomas Steel call a "direct" answer: a proposition that answers the question completely, but just completely.[8] I will not survey or endorse any theories of erotetic logic. I will just presuppose our ability to recognize potential answers.[9]

Given the controversy over the truth-condition, it is worth underlining its appropriateness further. Its suitability is especially clear for the terms 'problem' and 'solution'. In common usage one does not solve a problem unless one gets a correct solution: a real solution is a correct solution. Nobody is credited with solving a mathematical problem unless he or she finds (is credited with finding) a true solution. Nobody is credited with solving a game problem or puzzle, such as Rubik's cube or cannibals-and-missionaries, without getting a correct solution. A detective does not solve a mystery without figuring out who really committed the crime. In crediting someone with a solution, we *mean* that he or she has a true solution—although we can, of course, be wrong about this.

Is a solution to a problem necessarily a proposition, as our definition implies? In the Rubik's cube puzzle, or other such puzzles, a solution might appear to be a specified *end state*, such as a configuration of the cube; and this is not a proposition. However, the propositional formulation can readily handle this and similar cases. A solution may be construed as a propositional description of an appropriate end state. Or, when the problem is to find a series of moves that will transform an initial state (such as a certain cube configuration) into a specified end state, then a solution consists in a proposition that describes a series of moves from the initial state to the end state.[10]

There are two senses in which someone may be said to *have* a *solution* to a problem, a weak and a strong sense. The weak sense is this:

S has a solution to problem Q if and only if
there is a proposition, A, such that
(1) A is a true answer to Q, and
(2) S *believes* that A is a true answer to Q.

The strong sense is this:

> S has a solution to problem Q if and only if
>   there is a proposition, A, such that
>   (1)   A is a true answer to Q, and
>   (2)   S *knows* (or believes *justifiably*) that A is a true answer to Q.

Both of these senses are legitimate. If a student gets a correct solution to a problem by mere guessing, he still has a solution, even if his belief in it is neither a justified belief nor a piece of knowledge. However, in saying that someone has, or has found, a problem solution, we often imply some sound method of belief formation, sufficient (along with the satisfaction of other conditions) for knowledge or justified belief.

This concludes my analysis of problem solving. It is extremely simple, which is a virtue, not a defect. However, there is much more to say, even in an 'analytical' vein, about problems and their solutions.

As writers on erotetic logic stress, there are many varieties of questions: *whether* questions (yes-or-no questions), *why* questions, *where* questions, *how* questions, and so on. Some examples are: Is it possible to find true happiness? Who is the mayor of Tucson? What element has atomic number 94? What is a proof of such-and-such a theorem? How can I fix this leaky faucet?

There are other ways we might categorize questions. One taxonomy might be: *(a) theoretical, (b) practical,* and *(c) productive.* Theoretical questions would include those of science, mathematics, and philosophy. Practical questions would include how-to questions like, How can I fix this faucet? and others directly linked to practical needs or desires, such as, Where can I get immediate medical attention? Notice that most practical desires or needs have associated questions, namely, What actions can I perform to satisfy this desire or need? This is the sense in which practical problems normally have associated intellectual problems. (However, *solving* a practical problem consists in *effecting* a desired result, not merely getting a true proposition that specifies a way of effecting that result. This is another reason why the intellectual conception of problem solving does not exhaust all senses of 'problem solving'.) Productive questions are really a species of practical questions. But it is worth highlighting the fact that creative, artistic, and technical activities generate problems and solution-seeking activities. A painter may ask, What pattern or color in this portion of my canvas will achieve such-and-such an aesthetic effect? and a composer might ask an analogous question while composing a quartet.

Another possible taxonomy would classify by number of correct answers. Questions can have zero, one, or many correct answers. Normally a person wants one correct answer, even if he believes there are more. It is also possible, of course, to want an answer to a question when there aren't any: one can mistakenly believe that there are. Philosophers used to study a special class of such questions, 'pseudoquestions'. Pseudoquestions were said to be meaningless, or irresoluble, philosophical questions that have a semblance of meaningfulness and answerability. This status was invested with some philosophical importance. Of course, questions can also lack true answers for philosophically uninteresting reasons. What is a proof of this formula? has no true answer if the formula is not a theorem. Where is a good restaurant in town? has no true answer if the town has no good restaurants. ('Nowhere' is not a true answer so much as a denial of the question's presupposition. Typically, questions have presuppositions, the falsity of which can imply the absence of any true answer.)[11]

Some questions delimit, either explicitly or implicitly, a fixed set of potential answers. Yes-or-no questions are a special case, where the two candidate answers are 'yes' and 'no' (or corresponding full sentences). Other questions enumerate a list of possible answers, for example, Who is the oldest: Sally, Mary, or Beverly? Many questions, however, delimit no finite or fixed set of possible answers. These include, What explains the moon illusion? and What is a cure for cancer? For epistemological purposes, this is the most interesting class. To find an answer to such questions, a cognizer must *construct* possible answers. He cannot simply assess truth-values of the specified candidates. This cognitive task is clearly more complex. Admittedly, truth-value assessment is often difficult enough, but not always. It may be easy to determine whether a proposed proof of a putative mathematical theorem really is a proof. So it is easy to answer the question, Is this putative proof a genuine proof? But constructing or inventing a genuine proof may be extremely difficult, requiring lots of creativity. So it is much harder to answer, What is a proof of this statement?

Science characteristically asks questions for which it is difficult both to devise plausible answers and to verify their truth-value. Because of verificational difficulties, there are often deep methodological disputes over principles of verification. Does this mean that truth should be dispensed with as a scientific desideratum? Surely not. Just because something is hard to get, even hard to recognize if and when you've got it, does not imply that it should not be sought. There is ample reason, moreover, for understanding scientific inquiry as a quest for truth, like other inquiries. One significant scientific activity is the devising of new kinds of equipment, technologies, and methodologies that can facilitate theory testing. The natural explanation of such activities is that better devices, better statistical methodologies, and so on, will enable researchers to identify, or get closer to, the *truths* they seek.

I will say more about truth seeking in science in Chapter 7. But let me add a few remarks here about some authors' explicit rejection of truth in the conception of scientific problem solving. Laudan, in particular, offers a conception of problem solving, applied to theories, in which a theory can solve many problems without being true. Is this usage legitimate? If so, how can it be reconciled with my truth-requiring analysis of problem solving?

The predicate 'solves a problem' sometimes *is* applied to admittedly false theories. As Laudan indicates, we can say that Ptolemy's theory of epicycles solved the problem of retrograde motions of the planets, though Ptolemy's theory was admittedly false.[12] One possible use of 'solves' is merely in the quoted sense, analogous to the occurrence of 'knew' in 'The ancients knew that the sun goes around the earth'. A speaker who utters this sentence does not really mean to assert that the ancients knew this; he would just be putting the matter as the ancients themselves would have put it (language differences aside).

To understand a different usage of 'solves', suppose we grant a non-truth-implying sense of 'problem solving', which is applicable to theories. Let it be what Laudan suggests, roughly, that a theory solves an (empirical) problem if it (together with suitable auxiliary assumptions) implies a statement describing the problematic phenomenon, while competing theories fail to imply it. The question remains: Is the scientist's main theoretical aim to find theories that solve problems in *this* sense? Or does the scientist have a deeper, truth-linked aim? I suggest there is a deeper aim. The scientist typically wants to find a true theory, wants to answer the question (solve the problem), What theory *really explains* the phenomena in the specified domain? where no theory can 'really explain' a phenomenon unless it is true. Now a theory's ability to solve problems in Laudan's sense is readily understandable on this truth-linked aim. One piece of evidence in favor of a theory's truth is that it implies actual phenomena that rival theories do not imply. Thus, I propose that scientists are interested in this *non*-truth-linked 'problem-solving' property of theories as a *means* to finding a *true* theory.

Of course, the fact that scientists often settle for mere approximations to truth must be reconciled with the claim that they are really after truth itself. This large topic cannot be fully addressed here. But the main lines of an answer, I think, have to do with the idea that in settling for approximations, scientists live with a temporary stage of what they view as a longer enterprise. Since scientific theory deals with the most complex scientific questions, they do not expect to find fully accurate theories soon, perhaps even in their lifetime. Still, progress has been made (toward the truth) if outlines, or general features, of a true theory are identified. They settle for such an outline, or model, as a momentary step toward a more distant goal. (Of course, scientists may err in thinking that what they have is even an outline, or an approximation, of a true theory. But such fallibility is granted by all. The present question is why scientists settle for a theory sketch, which is *admittedly* not correct in all details. *That* is what the 'means toward a distant end' explanation is supposed to explain.)

What I am endorsing here is 'aim realism'. This should be distinguished from other brands of scientific realism, such as so-called convergent realism, the doctrine that science has in fact been getting closer to the truth; or the doctrine that scientists try to make new theories continuous with their predecessors. More will be said about these varieties of realism in Chapter 7.

The proposed truth requirement for problem solving is precisely analogous to the truth requirement for knowledge, and equally appropriate. Some people might object that it makes problem solving harder than a weaker sense would allow. Certainly. But it does not make it *unnecessarily* harder. In its central sense, problem solving *does* require truth, just as knowledge requires truth. So our analysis does not impose anything excessive on the concept of problem solving. If it turns out to be hard to solve certain problems, so be it.

6.3. Cognitive Components of Problem Solving

Whether a cognizer actively seeks an answer to a given question depends on the relative strength of the desire for an answer, as compared with other desires. It also depends on his beliefs about the comparative ease or difficulty of (his) finding an answer. If he thinks it would be hard, and if he has better uses of his time and cognitive resources, he may skip the quest. Suppose, however, that he devotes at least some cognitive resources to the question. What specific activities, or operations, will be utilized? This raises the more general question: What are the components of problem-solving activity?

Activity aimed at problem solving frequently involves overt actions, such as opening books, asking experts, and physically intervening in the world to get relevant data and responses. But I shall focus on purely *mental* operations. This follows from my central interest (here) in primary epistemology. Furthermore, physical activities aimed at problem solving are always controlled by psychological processes. So the latter have a natural priority.

What are the cognitive components, then, of problem solving (often called 'inquiry')? The positivist tradition tended to focus on *(a) hypothesis generation, (b) test,* and *(c) doxastic decision,* where *(c)* consists in a 'decision' (though not necessarily a voluntary decision) to accept, reject, or assign some probability to a hypothesis.

This list of components is easily expanded. In addition to hypothesis generation, there is also concept formation (also discussed by the positivists). Recent philosophers of science have stressed a further component, namely, *pursuit*.[13] In trying to find an answer to a theoretical problem, one decision the scientist makes is which of various research programs to pursue, that is, which general approach to a problem is worth refining or amending, in the hopes of getting an optimal theory.[14]

Cognitive scientists interested in problem solving are normally concerned with more detailed, microcomponents of the foregoing categories. Their studies are not fundamentally at odds with those of philosophers. Sometimes, though, the categories do not correspond to one another in obvious ways. Let us look at a few aspects of problem solving, as often discussed by cognitive scientists.

One such aspect is the way a cognizer understands, formulates, or 'represents' the problem to himself—how he conceptualizes it. One conceptualization of a problem can make it hard to solve, while another makes it easy. An example from Michael Posner is the following:

> Two train stations are 50 miles apart. At 2:00 P.M. two trains start toward each other, one from each station. Just as the trains pull out of the stations, a bird springs into the air in front of the first train and flies ahead to the front of the second. When the bird reaches the second, it turns back and flies toward the first. It continues to do this until the trains meet. If both trains travel at 25 miles per hour and the bird flies at 100 miles per hour, how many miles will the bird have flown before the trains meet?[15]

If the problem is conceptualized in terms of the bird's *trajectory*, one must calculate how far the bird goes on each trip between the trains. The problem is then difficult. But if it is conceptualized in terms of flight *time*, it becomes trivial. The trains must travel one hour before meeting (50 miles at a closing speed of 50 miles per hour), and at 100 miles per hour the bird will fly 100 miles.

The importance of how a problem is 'represented', or 'framed', cannot be underestimated.[16] Researchers have therefore explored the factors that influence representation. What stimuli prompt the cognizer's representation, and how easy or hard is it to revise initial representations? Initial representations, it has been found, often tend to structure subsequent thinking, sometimes to confine thinking to rigid 'loops', in which the cognizer keeps recycling the same themes. The mathematician G. Polya, noting the threat of rigidity, advised problem solvers to avoid commitment to an initial representation.[17] Successful problem solving sometimes depends on holding hypotheses in check.

The impact of initial representations is illustrated by Posner from studies of impression formation.[18] These studies indicate that the items first encountered on a list structure one's mental organization of the list. When subjects are asked to determine which of the following four words is *inappropriate* (to the rest)—'skyscraper', 'cathedral', 'temple', and 'prayer'— they tend to respond 'prayer'. Since 'skyscraper' occurs first, the list has apparently been organized in terms of buildings, so 'prayer' is the odd entry.

When the same list is presented in a different order—'prayer', 'cathedral', 'temple', and 'skyscraper'—one tends to organize the items by the theme religion, and 'skyscraper' is the odd item.

The significance of representation is explored in other contexts too. One such area is the differences in representation between experts and novices. What enables an expert to solve problems better than a novice—solve more of them, and more quickly? Part of the answer appears to consist in how experts conceptualize the problem domain. For example, expert chess players seem to group or chunk configurations on a chessboard into larger units than do novices. They have more global, or abstract, categorizations of the problem space.[19]

The importance of *abstraction* is cited by many researchers in cognition. Walter Kintsch and T. A. van Dijk's theory of story understanding emphasizes increasingly abstract 'macrostructure' representations of a prose passage, representations that correspond to summaries of the passage at high levels of generality.[20] Such abstraction is also held to be essential in devising analogies deployed in problem solving. Breakthroughs in problem solving often occur when the problem solver discerns an analogy between the target problem and previously encountered problems, possibly from different domains. The psychologists Mary Gick and Keith Holyoak have explored the function of analogy, indicating the critical value of an appropriate *level* of abstraction before analogies in different domains can be discerned.[21]

I suggested earlier that cognitive scientists are interested in many of the same categories of inquiry as philosophers. But sometimes the cognitive science perspective can transform those categories. Consider the category of evidence gathering, for example. As usually construed by philosophers of science, gathering evidence would consist in making observations of the world. But the perspective of cognitive science suggests a further sense of 'evidence gathering'. It is normally assumed that the main work of problem solving occurs in the active portion of the mind—sometimes called 'working memory', or 'short-term memory'. But most of a cognizer's information is stored in long-term memory. Whatever has previously been learned and might be useful for the problem at hand will not be utilized unless it is *retrieved* from long-term memory (LTM). Indeed, it may often happen that relevant information—relevant 'evidence'—fails to be retrieved from LTM, and the target question goes unanswered as a result. This means that a cognizer's evidence-gathering task includes not merely making suitable observations, but also gathering (retrieving) information from LTM. Success or failure in answering a question depends on retrieval effectiveness. Hence, the problem-solving power of a cognitive system—at least any system with a dual memory structure—depends on retrieval properties of that system. This aspect of intellectual power has been largely ignored.

The importance of information retrieval should be obvious in the case of

inductive inference, where any piece of evidence might override, or undermine, other evidence. But even in deductive tasks, retrieval from LTM is
essential. Suppose that the innumerable beliefs in your memory bank include the following:

(1) Barney sent Betty a valentine.
(2) Betty loves Barney.
(3) Mary can't stand Mike.
(4) All lovers love any lover.
(5) Sally is sad.
(6) Billy is Sally's brother.
(7) Sally secretly admires Betty.
(8) Mary loves Bill.
(9) Bill didn't send Betty a valentine.

Suppose you now pose the following question to yourself: Does Mary love
Betty? Relevant to this question is whether anything you know (or believe)
entails this proposition. To determine this, you must probe your memory for
such items. Under my hypothesis, there *are* propositions you believe (stored
in LTM) which jointly entail that Mary loves Betty, namely, (2), (4), and (8).
But will a probe of LTM access these items? Will memory 'report' them to
you, that is, 'activate' these items so that you can perform deductions from
them? Whether LTM does this depends on how these items are organized in
your LTM, and how retrieval from LTM works in general. These factors are
critical in determining whether you will correctly answer the question at
hand. More generally, they are critical in determining a human cognizer's
problem-solving power (as will be discussed more intensively in section
10.3).

Now if memory retrieval is one of the determinants of problem-solving
power, and if power is one of the standards of epistemological interest, then
not all operations of epistemic interest are matters of rationality or irrationality. For memory retrieval is not naturally classed as rational or irrational.
Traditionally, epistemic evaluation has tended to confine itself to questions
of rationality, or similar questions. But under the approach advocated here,
other dimensions of epistemic evaluation are also of interest. Specifically,
the efficiency or inefficiency of various cognitive operations can be subjected to epistemic scrutiny, where by 'efficiency' I mean effectiveness in
getting problems solved.

Another critical aspect of problem-solving activities is the *sequence* of
problem-solving steps. This aspect is emphasized by studies of problem-
solving 'strategies', especially in artificial intelligence. These studies explore
various principles for searching a problem space for a solution, by successively examining various 'moves' or 'states' in the problem space. One stock
example of a search strategy is hill climbing. Assume that a cognizer can
specify a respect in which a move from one state to another brings him or
her closer to the goal state of the problem. Then the hill-climbing strategy

tells the cognizer always to seek and choose a move that goes up the present hill, brings the cognizer closer to the goal state. The notion of closeness is frequently fairly natural. In the cannibals-and-missionaries problem, for example, a move that results in two cannibals and two missionaries being on the other side of the river gets one closer to the goal than the initial state. (The initial state is no cannibals or missionaries on the other side; the goal state is all three cannibals and all three missionaries on the other side.) Hill climbing has its defects as a general strategy. For example, it can get one stuck on a local hill (a local maximum), and give no method for ultimately climbing the mountain (getting to the real goal state). But it illustrates the idea of a strategy that results in a series of search steps.[22]

A cognitive system must operate sequentially, by a series of steps. (I do not mean to exclude parallel processing.) In trying to solve a problem, it always faces the implicit question: What should be done next? Furthermore, it must perform its operations in real time, not in some idealized situation where time is suspended. Since cognitive tasks often have time constraints—especially when linked to practical exigencies—the exact temporal sequence of operations is critical. The epistemic adequacy of cognitive 'heuristics', or short cuts, must be assessed in light of these constraints.[23]

Traditional epistemology and philosophy of science have largely neglected the temporal and operational constraints on the intellect. Discussions of justification and rationality have typically proceeded in terms of logical and probabilistic relations between theory and evidence; but these sorts of relations abstract from temporal and operational considerations. The so-called historical wing of philosophy of science, to be sure, emphasizes diachronic factors. But this tradition has not attended to cognitive operations, in the sense intended here. It seems clear, though, that an adequate primary epistemology must be centrally concerned with the real-time situation of a cognitive system and the sequences of operations it executes. Cognitive science, of course, studies cognition in precisely this fashion.

The importance of sequential operations does not just result from our concern with the epistemic standard of speed. To reason effectively even without deadlines, a cognitive system must ensure that relevant premises are accessed at the time they are needed. Suppose that I periodically think of the fact that the university library opens on Sundays at noon. That will not be of much help if I neglect to access this fact on Sunday mornings, when I actually contemplate going to the library. If I fail to retrieve this fact on Sunday mornings, I may make some futile trips. Thus, the *timeliness* of mental operations is an important facet of cognitive life, which must not be neglected in a comprehensive primary epistemology. But it is readily neglected without detailed study of cognitive operations.

I have focused predominantly on stages of inquiry *prior* to the doxastic decision stage, primarily because past epistemology has riveted its attention on the latter stage. Past emphasis on the doxastic decision stage may partly be rooted in the dominant interest in justification, which seems mainly concerned with this stage. But if intelligence, or power, is of equal importance, there is no good rationale for this concentration. Arguably, a cognizer can have justified doxastic attitudes just by using suitable doxastic decision processes.[24] But one cannot solve problems effectively just by using good doxastic processes. Doxastic decision processes only serve to *select* from the available candidate solutions. At best, selection can reject false candidates and accept a true candidate if one is generated. But if no true solution is generated, even the best doxastic decision process cannot produce belief in a true solution. To be a good problem solver, then, one needs good hypothesis-constructing processes. Similar remarks apply to processes governing sequential search.

6.4. Social Problem Solving and Product Epistemology

I have concentrated on individual problem solving. But problem solving can also be a group enterprise. All sorts of groups have shared interests in finding answers to specified questions. Salient examples are scientific and scholarly groups, but there are also committees, juries, government agencies, and whole societies. So the theory of problem solving, both descriptive and normative, extends into the social arena. Problem-solving power is an appropriate standard for social epistemology. For any number of group practices and structures we may ask whether they promote or inhibit problem-solving power. Although detailed reflection on this issue will not be undertaken here, a few general comments may be made, as a preview of future research.

How might collective efforts at problem solving outstrip those of an individual? Some obvious possibilities are these: (1) People can pool their factual information, yielding more data for each individual. (2) Ideas and hypotheses can be multiplied more easily, each cognizer profiting from the larger menu of candidate solutions. (3) Critical assessment of candidate solutions can be facilitated, since an isolated cognizer is easily seduced by the allure of his own ideas, and defects are easier to detect, and weed out, in the concoctions of others. (4) Because complex solutions often need many skills to refine and test, division of labor can facilitate execution of the several tasks. (5) Incentives can be offered that make intellectual specialization possible, which may be needed for the long-term investment required for solving complex problems. (6) Sanctions can be imposed for behavior inimical to truth (lies, fabrications, and the like).

All these are commonplace reasons why scientists and scholars form professional and academic communities. There are equally commonplace features of collectivities that may work against problem solution. Social groups generate systems of status, authority, and (social) power. When those accorded a high status get things wrong, their false doctrines may gain wide currency and may be difficult to eradicate, even in the face of striking counterevidence. The influence of authority figures may congeal ideational frameworks and inhibit novelty and invention.

Setting aside these issues, which are too large for present scrutiny, notice that there are questions to be raised about what it even means for a *group* to solve a problem. Does it mean that all members of the group believe a true answer? Presumably that is much too strong. Exactly which members, then, or how many, need to believe a true answer? Once this issue is raised, it becomes obvious that a finer-grained treatment of the topic is in order. Take the case of governments. Certain experts in the State Department, or the Defense Department, may know the truth about a certain question, but cannot persuade their higher-ups of this truth. Perhaps they cannot even have timely communication with decision makers to get the truth heard. If the decision makers lack (belief in) the truth, it is arguable that the government does not have the solution, even though some of its members do.

In any case, the *distribution* of information (or belief) within an organization is certainly of paramount importance. This topic should be placed on the agenda of social epistemology. But the point is also of interest because of analogies with (primary) individual epistemology. As noted in section 6.3, the mind also has functional locations, such as working memory and long-term memory. Just as it matters to an organization where information is located within it, so it matters to the mind where information is located. If information in an organization resides only in some lower-echelon official, and never gets persuasively communicated in a timely fashion to higher officials, its value to the organization may be nil. Similarly, information only stored in LTM, and never accessed at all or in a timely fashion, has little value to a cognitive system, either for purposes of behavioral decision or further problem solving.

Evidently, a critical facet of social problem solving is the process of communication. This brings into prominence the units of communication by which individuals hope to shape the thinking of others. These units include oral discourses, books, articles, research reports, theorems (or proofs), legal opinions and briefs, and various forms of fiction. Let us call all such works intellectual *products*.

I have said that epistemology's aim is intellectual evaluation. Thus far, our attention has been engaged by the evaluation of mental events and processes, such as, beliefs and belief-forming processes. In fact, intellectual evaluation far more frequently centers on what I am calling products than on internal states and operations. In everyday intellectual and cultural commerce, it is not mental acts that comprise the chief objects of appraisal; it is discourses and published works. It would be a lean epistemology indeed that did not feature such objects in its purview. Social epistemology, at a minimum, must be concerned with these objects, since they are the life-blood of cooperative intellectual endeavor. So let us momentarily shift our focus from *belief epistemology* to *product epistemology.*

However, I doubt that product epistemology can be divorced entirely from belief. A principal aim of most intellectual products is to inform an audience, to induce beliefs in putative truths. Several dimensions of evaluation flow naturally from this aim. First, a premium is placed on products that present *new* truths, truths not already circulating in the public forum. If some true contents have previously been aired, people have had the opportunity to learn and believe those contents. So their significance is reduced. But this needs some qualification. Even if a given truth has previously been presented, a product that presents it more cogently, persuasively, or comprehensibly is still highly valued. Thus, second, the mode or manner of presentation counts substantially in a product's appraisal. Third, value is placed not simply on truth per se, but on truths that interest the audience. Where individuals or groups place high priority on answering certain questions, products that succeed in answering those questions—or are judged to answer them successfully—receive special plaudits.

Still another determinant of product evaluation may also be traced to mental factors. The grading of a product typically involves the question of originality, or creativity. By how much does this product go beyond previous work in the field? How difficult was it to produce this work, given the common knowledge and tools of the discipline? A certain mathematical lemma, for example, may never have been stated or proved before, but it might still be an obvious consequence of a well-known theorem. The magnitude of an intellectual achievement is partly a function of the difficulty of generating it. Clearly, such judgments of difficulty presuppose some metric of originality or creativity, and the question arises of the basis of such a metric. It can only be based, I believe, on some conception of normal, human cognitive capacities, a matter on which cognitive psychology may be able to shed some light. I shall return to this theme in Chapter 11. Meanwhile, I content myself with the remark that even the evaluation of products in the social arena may be illuminated by reference to human psychology.

6.5. *Multiple Values: Adjunct and Specialized*

A recurring theme of the past several chapters is the epistemological importance of true belief. My accounts of knowledge, justifiedness, and problem solving were all variations on this theme. This may convey the impression that I favor a monistic approach to intellectual value. But I wish to correct any such impression. Value monism is an inappropriate posture for a complete epistemology.

Nevertheless, I do wish to preserve the centrality of true belief in the network of intellectual values. The envisaged network is partly expressed in the following conjecture. We have various cognitive faculties and operations that seem to promote true belief (or accurate representation), and this is their principal utility. Still, we do not value these faculties and operations solely as means to true beliefs. The exemplary exercise of these cognitive faculties is a pleasure in itself. We enjoy and admire the free exercise of perceptual, calculational, imaginative, and recollective powers quite apart from our interest in the truths they reveal. Thus, although the *fundamental* value of these cognitive powers consists in their promotion of truth acquisition, they also have *adjunct* value. The cognitive activities themselves, and the external products they generate, may be cherished for their own sake. Indeed, these activities and products may often conflict with the pursuit of truth, and they may be valued in spite of this. Hence, at least from a descriptive vantage point, a theory of intellectual activity must embrace *value pluralism.*

Let me briefly illustrate and concretize this idea. A pervasive aspect of cognition is sensuous experience, that is, mental events associated with the sense modalities. By sensuous experience, I mean not only perception itself but the use of visual, auditory, and other 'codes' in imagery and imagination. The existence and nature of such processes is controversial, a matter I will explore further in Chapter 12. Meanwhile, appealing to both introspection and psychological experimentation, I will assume that modality-specific codes are a facet of our mental operation. My conjecture is that the underlying function of such equipment is to help form accurate representations or true beliefs. This is realized primarily in perception of the environment, but secondarily in imaginative construction of possible patterns and scenarios.

While the evolutionary, or adaptive, value of modality-specific codes may be linked to accurate representation of reality, we delight in our sensuous powers for their own sake. The visual and musical arts clearly draw their pleasures from the creation and apprehension of sensuous forms and patterns. Virtually every art form has a close link with modes of sensuous representation. Values embedded in these art forms arise from deep-seated features of our inner sensuous life.

A second pervasive aspect of cognition is imagination itself, by which I mean the mental construction of new patterns, combinations, sequences, structures, and so on, out of old elements or parts. The elements can be either sensuous or purely conceptual. Thus, imagination can consist of the mental construction of a visual scene or the construction of a hypothesis out of antecedently existing concepts. The child who imagines a battlefield, the composer of a sonata, and the mathematician framing a new conjecture, all construct new mental combinations out of old mental materials.

The primary use of imagination is in the formation of accurate representations about reality. To answer questions about the world, one typically has to generate candidate answers, and such generation typically involves new permutations of familiar conceptual ingredients. But while imagination is therefore critical to problem solving, or question answering, it is clear that free exercise of the imagination is a joy in itself. Children's play largely consists of fashioning combinations of actions or plots out of previously encountered materials. Such play has no intended effect on true belief; the spontaneous pleasure attached to it is manifest. (At the same time, spontaneous pleasure in multiple generation of new combinations itself promotes problem-solving ability. Perhaps the young learn faster than the old because they are quicker and more indefatigable in generating new hypotheses.)

Since virtually all cognition is laden with imaginative constructions, most of this activity is taken for granted. A baseline of such constructivity is assumed for all humans. One could not be human without generating combinations out of antecedently present elements. Furthermore, the general lines of construction may be largely species-specific. This would account for the commonality of the concepts we generate, the predicates we project, the possibilities we envisage. But certain constructed patterns we recognize as relatively unusual or exemplary. These are what we dub 'imaginative' creations. Imaginativeness is not a characteristic of *all* products of the imagination: only those surpassing the routine outputs thereof. This is the theme sketched at the end of the previous section, and one I will develop further in Chapter 11.

In addition to the adjunct values attached to our cognitive powers, the plurality of cognitive values has another source: the institutionalization of specialized branches of science, scholarship, arts, and culture. First of all, these fields often develop a specialized interest in a selected class of truths. Second, traditions of pursuing these truths may draw disproportionately on selected cognitive skills. So habits of criticism in the field may place relatively more emphasis on those sorts of skills.

Consider first scientific and scholarly fields that (pretty) clearly aim at truth. Some of these are specially interested in certain sorts of truths. The nomothetic sciences are interested in lawlike, causal, or theoretical truths. They prefer truths that are comprehensive, full of explanatory power, and simple. Historical subjects, by contrast, may not aim at lawlikeness or theoreticity. Simplicity of a historical account may be regarded as a defect. History arguably disdains the abstract in favor of richness of detail, individuality of the personages or economic circumstances of the episode in question.

In this context recall my rejection in Chapter 5 of explanatory power as a value to be linked with justification. That point can now be clarified. It is undeniable that science aims at explanation. But this is a *specialized* aim, which is not obviously present (or present to the same degree) in all cognitive undertakings.

Other specialized aims and vehicles account for specialized values attached to diverse traditions and genres. Although language and symbolism are the medium of the sciences, humanities, law, and the arts, the aims and uses of language and symbolism differ widely, and the values emphasized differ accordingly. In law and philosophy, disputation and argumentation play a central role. The skills of the debater and the controversialist are emphasized. In other fields, such as the fictive arts, different kinds of rhetorical styles are emphasized; disputation plays little role. While the lawyer, the philosopher, and the playwright may all aim at some sort of truth, the formats and techniques for expressing their respective ideas are very divergent. Similarly, canons of science and mathematics require precision and rigor, whereas the literary fields call for expressions that are evocative and rich in connotation, possibly precluding precision and rigor.

It may indeed be suggested that different disciplines and genres have fundamentally different *modes* of conveying truths. Science, scholarship, and philosophy concentrate on the assertive mode of expression, whereas literary works may try to convey truths by showing, or depicting, them. The novelist shows what it is like to be a certain kind of person, to live in a certain era or culture. This is a commonly valued way of getting understanding of human and cultural facts; important information is somehow conveyed. Epistemology must be concerned with such diverse modes of communication, and it must countenance multiple values specifically keyed to these diverse modes. Even among purely assertive communications, differences in style are crucial to the mental or doxastic upshots in an audience. Style affects perspicuity, which affects how well a message is understood, comprehended, or represented by the audience. This too is reflected in critical evaluations of intellectual products.

Epistemology has focused heavily on statemental units of communication and on propositional units of mentation. But this may be an inadequate approach if epistemology seeks to deal with *understanding* or *comprehension*. How does a cognizer comprehend a large body of data or a highly complex theory? Can such comprehension be well represented by a list of believed propositions? Does incomprehension simply consist in failure to grasp the relevant propositions (whatever 'grasping' is)? Recent work in psychology and artificial intelligence posits different sorts of mental structures—schemata, frame-systems, scripts—that encode complex informational structures. An adequate belief epistemology may want to make use of such mentalistic constructs. At the same time, a product epistemology may want to appraise, or elucidate appraisals of, discourses in terms of how well they succeed in effecting suitable sorts of mental structures. Thus, true 'belief' may be too restrictive a conception of epistemic aims, even when other adjunct and specialized values are set aside.

chapter 7

Truth and Realism

7.1. Varieties of Realism

The notion of truth is important for almost every epistemology, but it is central to my epistemology for special reasons. I have invoked truth not only, as is commonly done, as a condition for knowing, but also as a critical element in two dimensions of epistemic appraisal, namely, 'justification' and 'intelligence'. The roles to which truth is assigned in my epistemology may be a source of queasiness to some. As we saw in section 5.8, some philosophers think they discern a circularity in using 'true' in an account of the epistemic term 'justified', because the notion of truth is *itself* epistemic. Other philosophers might hold that it is misguided to assign truth or even the pursuit of truth, a central role in problem solving, because at least one central domain of problem solving—the domain of scientific theory—involves no pursuit of truth at all, but only predictive power, calculational convenience, or the like. For these and other reasons, a discussion of truth is an important item on our agenda. It must be shown that the truth concept can perform the functions to which my epistemology assigns it, and that it has the 'realistic' properties that I have attributed to it throughout.

As I have indicated, I do wish to defend some kind of realistic view of truth. But not everything called 'realism', not even every variety of realism about *truth*, is a doctrine I mean to endorse. So I need to disentangle different conceptions of realism, in order to keep our bearings.

In recent years the most influential work on truth and realism has been done by Hilary Putnam and Michael Dummett.[1] Much of my discussion will therefore relate to theses that they have advanced or explored. Dummett conceives of realism as a family of doctrines about different subject matters; you can be a realist about one subject matter and not about another. He prefers to say that realism is a view about a certain class of *statements,* for instance, physical object statements, mathematical statements, ethical statements, or statements in the future tense. Here is a recent formulation of realism he offers: "The very minimum that realism can be held to involve is that statements in the given class relate to some reality that exists independently of our knowledge of it, in such a way that that reality renders each statement in the class determinately true or false, again independently of whether we know, or are even able to discover, its truth-value."[2]

There are two components in this characterization of realism. First, there is the principle of *bivalence:* every statement in the class is determinately either true or false. Second, there is the principle of *verification-transcendent truth:* a statement is true or false independently of our knowledge, or verification, of it (or even our *ability* to verify it). The second of these theses will figure prominently in my discussion. But the first, the bivalence principle, is tangential.

It is not clear just how firm a criterion of realism bivalence should be. Dummett regards it as necessary for realism, though not sufficient.[3] But it is not even clear that it should be accepted as necessary. Why can't a philosopher be a realist about a given class even if he takes the Frege-Strawson line that a singular statement containing an empty proper name—such as, 'The present king of France is bald'—is neither true nor false? Why can't he be a realist even if he acknowledges *vague* statements within the given class, which are neither true nor false?[4]

Setting these points aside, suppose we grant Dummett the label 'antirealist' for philosophers who deny the principle of bivalence for a given class of statements. Is it important for my purposes to defend the corresponding kind of realism, as a general claim? Not at all. There is nothing in my epistemology that requires defense of the principle of bivalence for all classes of statements. I could readily admit the failure of this principle for any number of classes of statements: statements about the future, subjunctive conditional statements, even statements of mathematics. What is critical is that when any such statement *is* true (or false), what makes it true (or false) is independent of our knowledge or verification. Thus, the second of the two realist theses explained above, verification-transcendence, is critical. To put it another way, truth must not be an *epistemic* matter. But the issue of bivalence does not affect my epistemology.

Admittedly, the two theses are interconnected in some philosophies. Some denials of bivalence are consequences of a denial of verification-transcendence. The constructivist in mathematics denies verification-transcendence, saying that a mathematical statement is true only if there exists a proof of it, and is false only if there exists a proof of its negation. The denial of bivalence readily follows. However, people may also deny bivalence for other reasons. Nothing in my epistemology requires any quarrel with bivalence per se.

My concern with realism, then, is a concern with truth; with what makes a statement, or belief, true, if it is true. So I shall primarily be concerned—in much of the chapter, at any rate—with the theory of truth.

In calling my principal topic the theory of truth, two clarifications should be made. First, I am interested (roughly) in the 'meaning' of truth, not in procedures or marks for telling which propositions are true. Classical defenders of the coherence theory of truth probably failed to observe this distinction. They ran together coherence as a *test* of truth and coherence as a *definition* of truth. As a test of truth, coherence has some attractions; as a definition, it has no plausibility at all. I, of course, am only interested (here) in the definition of truth. A theory of tests for truth is better understood as a theory of justified belief.

The second clarification is that I am not concerned here with the formal theory of truth, with an account of truth that resolves the liar paradox, for example. Rather, I am only concerned with the metaphysical questions surrounding the notion of truth. There are many philosophers who doubt whether there are any interesting metaphysical questions, whether there is anything informative that can be said about these questions. They maintain that Alfred Tarski's work on the semantic conception of truth, or the idea of truth as disquotation, resolves all the legitimate questions that can be raised about truth. I believe that Putnam has given decisive arguments for rejecting this claim: the Tarskian, or disquotational, theory does not give us an adequate analysis, or understanding, of the notion of truth.[5] Substantial, classical questions remain, questions that divide realists from antirealists. These are the ones that will engage my attention.

I have isolated one central dispute about truth that I shall address: whether truth is verification-transcendent or not, whether it is a purely nonepistemic notion or in some sense epistemic. This will be the topic of the next section. But there is another important dispute about truth that standardly divides realists from antirealists; that is, whether truth consists in 'correspondence' with reality. This is another way of thinking about realism versus antirealism. Whether a realist account of truth needs to be committed to correspondence, and if so, what kind of correspondence, will have to be explored. That will be the topic of section 7.3.

7.2.   Truth as Nonepistemic

Putnam writes of two conceptions of truth: an *externalist* versus an *internalist* conception,[6] which he earlier dubbed "metaphysical realism" and "internal realism," respectively.[7] Metaphysical realism sees truth as "radically non-epistemic".[8] Internal realism, by contrast, finds an epistemic component in truth. I do not find any of Putnam's terminology optimal. In particular, his "internal realism" is best regarded as a form of antirealism. So I shall count the nonepistemic approach to truth as realism *sans phrase,* and the epistemic approach to truth will be counted as (a species of) antirealism.

How, exactly, would an epistemic account of truth go? As we will see, the proponent of an epistemic approach is caught on the horns of a dilemma. If a strong epistemic component is introduced, the resulting account is liable to be *unnecessary* for truth. If he weakens the epistemic component, the resulting conditions are liable to be *insufficient* for truth. Before considering some sample accounts, let us consider some dimensions along which epistemic theories of truth might vary.

First, there is a choice between actual verification and merely possible verification. For example, constructivism is depicted as maintaining that a mathematical statement is true only if we are (actually) in possession of a proof of it, and false only if we are (actually) in possession of a refutation.[9] This can be contrasted with a weaker possible view, namely, that a mathematical statement is true only if it is *possible* that we should possess a proof of it.

Second, there is a choice between *present* verification and verification at some time or other, for example, at some future time. C. S. Peirce defined truth as "the opinion which is fated to be ultimately agreed to by all who investigate."[10] This is clearly a weaker requirement for truth than one which requires, for p to be true, that p is agreed to *now*.

Third, there is a choice between conclusive verification and inconclusive, or prima facie, verification. A very strong requirement for the truth of p is that it be conclusively verified. A weaker requirement is that, for p to be true, it must be supported to some degree. Of course, either of these requirements can be weakened by taking the possibility option in the first choice: p is true if it is merely possible for p to be conclusively verified.

The fourth choice concerns the person or persons for whom the proposition must be verified. Dummett regularly speaks with an indefinite first-person plural: "we." In the constructivist's approach, cited above, a mathematical statement is true only if *we* possess a proof of it. But who, exactly, are "we"? *All* human beings? One or more human beings? Or should the restriction to human beings be lifted entirely?

Clearly, many permutations of the epistemic approach to truth can be generated from these options. Let's quickly look at some sample accounts and the difficulties they encounter.

(a) All of us now have conclusive evidence for p.
(b) Somebody now has conclusive evidence for p.
(c) Somebody will some day have conclusive evidence for p.
(d) Somebody now has prima facie evidence for p.
(e) Somebody will some day have prima facie evidence for p.
(f) It is possible for somebody to have prima facie evidence for p.
(g) It is possible for somebody to have conclusive evidence for p.

Considered as necessary and sufficient conditions for 'p is true', each of these suffers from palpable defects. Each is either too weak or too strong; some of them are both.

Let us examine them as conditions for the truth of ordinary physical object propositions. Clearly, *(a)* is much too strong. It could certainly be true that Julius Caesar had a mole on the nape of his neck although it is false that all of us now have conclusive evidence for this. Similarly for *(b)*: this could be true even though *nobody* now has conclusive evidence for p. Even *(c)* is still too strong. This minor historical fact about Julius Caesar may be one for which nobody will *ever* have conclusive evidence. Even *(d)* is too stringent. Perhaps nobody now has even prima facie evidence for this fact. This would not keep the proposition from being true.

Not only is *(d)* too strong, it is also too weak. Suppose some historian does have prima facie evidence for this proposition. That surely does not entail that the proposition is true. For example, suppose a Roman text of the period attributes a remark to Brutus that seems to indicate the presence of a mole on Caesar's neck. That evidence is not sufficient for the truth of the proposition. The same twin problems arise for *(e)*, for similar reasons. It is both too strong and too weak.

Turning to the 'possibility' formulations, *(f)* is too weak for the same reasons as *(d)* and *(e)*. The mere possibility of prima facie evidence for p does not guarantee p's truth. The difficulties for *(g)* are slightly harder to assess. They depend on how 'conclusive evidence' is interpreted. If it is interpreted very strictly—so that conclusive evidence *entails* truth—then it is doubtful whether it *is* possible for somebody to have conclusive evidence for any proposition, at least any physical object proposition. So *(g)* would be too strong. If 'conclusive evidence' is interpreted less strictly, so that it does not entail truth, then *(g)* is too weak.

There is another plausible objection against *(g)*, if it is interpreted strictly. On the strict interpretation we are to understand 'p is conclusively verified (for some person S)' to *entail* (by virtue of its meaning) 'p is true'. But if this is right, truth is covertly contained in the analysis of 'p is conclusively verified'. And then it would be circular to employ the latter locution in the analysis of 'p is true'!

This point is worth underlining because it should also figure in the assessment of the epistemic account of truth endorsed by Putnam. Putnam writes:

> Truth is an *idealization* of rational acceptability. We speak as if there were such things as epistemically ideal conditions, and we call a statement 'true' if it would be justified under such conditions.[11]

To clarify this proposal, let me reformulate it as follows.

(h)   If someone were in epistemically ideal conditions vis-à-vis the question of p versus not-p, then he would be justified in believing p.

The correctness of this proposal depends on how 'epistemically ideal conditions' is defined. Is there a way to define it so that the equivalence is correct? There is a definition, I think, in which the equivalence could succeed. Suppose we define 'S is in epistemically ideal conditions vis-à-vis p' as: S is so situated and so constructed that he would believe p if and only if p is true. Being in epistemically ideal conditions vis-à-vis p might consist, for example, in (1) being in a perfect position for observing p, (2) having perfect detector organs vis-à-vis states of affairs like p, and (3) having belief-forming processes perfectly coordinated with these organs' outputs. On a suitable theory of justifiedness, then, proposal *(h)* might be right.

But this stratagem obviously incurs the sort of problem we posed for *(g)* under the strict interpretation. It makes the equivalence work only by making it *circular*. The problem, of course, is that the proposed definition of 'epistemically ideal conditions' reintroduces the notion of truth!

Putnam obviously cannot use this way of defining 'epistemically ideal conditions'. He hints at this himself when he restricts 'verified' to an "operational" sense.[12] Is there an alternative way of defining 'epistemically ideal conditions' so that (1) no nonepistemic notion of truth is presupposed, and yet (2) *(h)* turns out to be equivalent to 'p is true'? That has yet to be shown. I doubt that there is any such way. In short, there is no reason to think that Putnam's epistemic equivalence can succeed unless its crucial epistemic notion is cashed out circularly, in terms of the (realist) notion of truth.

The difficulty facing Putnam's proposal is a specimen of a difficulty facing any epistemic approach to truth. How are the epistemic notions appearing in any such account themselves to be understood? How are 'justified', 'verified', 'rationally acceptable', or other such terms to be analyzed? Putnam and Dummett seem to take these terms as primitives. But I find this highly counterintuitive. Epistemic notions strike me as far more in need of explication than truth. Furthermore, given the plausibility of my sort of theory of justification—a truth-linked theory—the onus is on Putnam, Dummett, or like-minded theorists to show that these notions have non-truth-linked explications.

Let me not rest this contention on the details of my theory of justifiedness. I can argue more broadly for the necessity of having recourse to truth in explicating epistemic standards. First, as I have noted, many epistemic notions countenance degrees of strength, for example, degrees of confirmation, weight of evidence, and the like. What accounts for these degrees? What is the continuum on which these gradations occur? The only plausible answers, I think, would appeal to truth. My own theory of justifiedness appeals to true-belief-conducive psychological processes (and methods). But other theories might appeal to an evidential link between evidence and hypothesis. One has stronger evidence for p to the extent that the evidence makes p *more likely*. But 'more likely' must mean 'more likely to be *true*'. Of course, we could define a technical notion of confirmation that has no commitment to truth, where the truth of the evidential propositions has no linkage—logical, probabilistic, subjunctive, or what have you—with the truth of the hypothesis. But in that case who would suppose that this technical notion has anything to do with the intuitive notion of evidential support?

Second, take the notion of epistemic 'access' to a state of affairs, such as perceptual access or memory access. Again we have the notion of better and worse epistemic situations. And again this can only be spelled out in terms of truth. Perceptual access to a situation is better just in case it is easier, in that situation, to form *true* beliefs about the objects or events in the scene. The optimal distance and viewing conditions are those that promote the greatest chance of truth and accuracy.

Third, the history of science and philosophy is filled with controversies over methodology. Contending schools have vied over the right procedures for fixing belief. It is hard to make sense of these debates save as debates over which methodology is most conducive to *true* convictions. However difficult it may be to settle such questions, they seem to presuppose the notion of truth. So truth is conceptually prior to any operational specification of epistemic methods or standards. Antirealists, who seek to define truth in epistemic terms, are proceeding precisely backwards.

We must not ignore, however, an underlying impetus behind many moves toward an epistemic account of truth. Antirealists are doubtless worried about the epistemological consequences of a realist conception of truth. If truth is definitionally detached from evidence, either actual or possible, is there really any prospect that we can have epistemic access to the truth? Isn't there a threat of skepticism? Some antirealists might be prepared to concede that the ordinary, naive conception of truth is nonepistemic. But they may feel that *replacement* of this naive conception is required to avert epistemic catastrophe.

Given this problem, we must determine whether candidate epistemic accounts of truth really help, whether antirealist proposals really improve our epistemological opportunities. The answer is: not necessarily. Putnam's proposal, *(h)*, is a case in point. Truth is there equated with what people would be justified in believing if they were in epistemically ideal conditions. But since none of us ever *is* in epistemically ideal conditions with respect to any proposition, how are we supposed to tell—from our actual standpoint—what a person would be justified in believing in that hypothetical situation? To assess the truth of p according to this proposed equivalence, we would have to assess the truth-value of the indicated subjunctive conditional. But that is no mean task! If anything, it imposes an even nastier epistemic predicament than the one feared from realism.

The nonepistemic nature of truth is well described by Brian Loar.[13] Our ordinary (realist) conception of truth can best be understood, he says, in *modal* terms. The idea of a proposition's being true is the idea of a state of affairs such that it could happen (or could have happened) that it be true even though we are not in a position to verify it. Furthermore, he asserts, it is part of our theory of nature that this is generally so. Whether p concerns objects in the garden, in Antarctica, or in the Andromeda galaxy, p's verifiability by us depends upon various contingent circumstances not entailed by laws of nature. For us to verify such propositions, light, sound, or some such energy must reach our sense organs. But the regions of space through which such energy must travel might have (or might have had) distorting properties. There might be black holes in the relevant regions that 'soak up' the light. Also, for us to verify such propositions (indeed, *any* propositions), our brains must be constructed in certain ways. But they might not have been suitably constructed. So it might have happened that these propositions are true although we are not in a position to verify them.

As this way of explaining truth indicates, a sharp distinction must be drawn being a proposition's being true and the proposition's being verified. The latter, but not the former, involves processes by which the truth is detected or apprehended. (Here I have in mind both extracognitive processes—for example, the traveling of light from object to retina—as well as intracognitive processes.) Indeed, only such a sharp distinction—characteristic of realism—can make good sense of certain of our verifying procedures.

In seeing how realism makes sense of verification, I follow the suggestions of William Wimsatt, who in turn credits Donald Campbell and R. Levins.[14] Our conception of reality is the conception of something robust, an object or property that is invariant under multiple modes of detection. The use of multiple procedures, methods, or assumptions to get at the same putative object, trait, or regularity is commonplace in ordinary cognition and in science. Wimsatt lists many examples, including the following: *(a)* we use different perceptual modalities to observe the same object, or the same sense to observe the object from different perspectives and under different observational circumstances; *(b)* we use different experimental procedures to (try to) verify the same alleged empirical relationships, that is, alternative procedures are used to 'validate' one another; *(c)* different assumptions, models, or axiomatizations are used to derive the same result; *(d)* we use agreement of different tests, scales, or indices as a sign of validity of a trait-construct; and *(e)* we seek matches of theoretical description of a given system at different levels of organization. In short, our verification procedures, when they are careful, seek to 'triangulate' on the objects or relationships under study.

We can best make sense of a need for triangulation on the assumption that the truths, or facts, about the object or system under study are sharply distinguished from the processes of verification or detection of them. Any particular method might yield putative information partly because of its own peculiarities—its biases or distortions. This is a potential danger as long as the properties of the studied object are distinct from the process of detection. Triangulation hopes to correct for such biases on the assumption that independent methods will not have the *same* distorting characteristics (if any at all). Obviously, we cannot use no method *at all* to make observations, to 'get at' the system or relationship under investigation. So we run the risk of getting mere artifacts of a measurement or observation process, rather than the real character of the object. Using multiple methods of detection minimizes this risk. In general, we try to get away from the idiosyncracies of the verification procedure in order (better) to get at the verification-independent properties of the target object. All this makes sense on the assumption that there are truths about the object independent of this or that verification procedure.

Admittedly, this realist stance is not the only possible diagnosis of the need for triangulation. Triangulation may be viewed as a variant of coherentist methodology; and coherentism is an epistemology fully available to the antirealist. However, the antirealist must take coherentism simply as a brute fact about our epistemic procedures. He cannot offer any principled rationale for triangulation, of the sort available to the realist. The realist, by contrast, can explain the fallibility of our detection procedures, and hence the need for triangulation, in terms of the distinction between the real facts and the verification processes used to get at them.

As an aside, it is noteworthy that our perceptual systems seem 'designed' to mark properties of the distal stimulus as opposed to those of the organic process of detection. So-called object constancies are a case in point. A moving observer does not see the stationary stimulus as moving or varying in size, though such displacements do occur at the retinal level. The perceptual system suppresses these displacements, apparently on the presumption that they are observer-induced changes. What the system seeks are properties of the observation-independent object. When input is diagnosed as resulting from observer characteristics—in the present case, observer movement—it simply is not communicated to higher cognitive levels.

Readers of Dummett may feel that I have thus far neglected a principal reason for a verificationist account of truth. Dummett approaches the topic of realism and antirealism from the context of a theory of meaning or understanding. In that context the question arises whether it is possible for us to understand, or grasp, any verification-transcendent conception of truth. Do we have a capacity to understand statements whose truth transcends their verifiability? If a proper theory of understanding, or meaning, precludes such a capacity, then no sense can be made of a realist, verification-transcendent, account of truth.[15] And none of the foregoing arguments can carry any weight.

I cannot enter in any depth into the theory of meaning or understanding. That clearly exceeds the scope of this work. Nor can I comment in detail on Dummett's proposals concerning a "use" theory of meaning, and the requirement that uses must be "manifestable" in behavior. I am inclined to regard these proposals with some skepticism, but I will not venture into this tricky terrain.[16] Instead, I put forth the following argument.

The claim that we cannot mean or understand verification-transcendent statements can only refer to verification *by us*, that is, by human beings. But as I have already argued, in the case of many if not most physical object statements, their truth certainly appears to be possible independently of human verification. For example, it might be true that such-and-such happened in the Andromeda galaxy although no human beings were (or are) in a position to verify it. (To hold otherwise would involve an untenable form of epistemic *speciesism.*) Moreover, this modal fact seems far more certain than any (interesting) doctrine in the theory of meaning. So if we are confronted with a choice between this modal fact and a meaning doctrine that excludes verification-transcendent meaning, we are better advised to doubt, or reject, the meaning doctrine.

7.3. Truth and Correspondence

I have now completed the discussion of whether truth is an epistemic notion. I have defended the realist position that it is wholly *non*epistemic. In this section I turn to another facet of the debate over truth: whether truth consists in 'correspondence'. Antirealists are often anxious to pin a correspondence doctrine on their foes, because they find grave difficulties with that doctrine. But it is not clear that a realist must be committed to correspondence; that depends on what, exactly, is meant by 'correspondence'. Realism is in trouble on this score only if there is an untenable version of the correspondence doctrine to which realism must adhere.

One version of a correspondence doctrine, the Tractarian version, says that the world is a totality of *facts* and that a proposition is true just in case it corresponds with a fact.[17] A familiar objection to this is that the world does not contain factlike entities, the kinds of entities that would exactly correspond to sentences or propositions. It is implausible to suppose that there are disjunctive facts in the world, existential facts, conditional facts, universal facts, and so on. Language or thought constructs disjunctive statements, existential statements, conditional statements, and the like. But it is misguided to suppose that structures of this sort constitute the world. If the correspondence doctrine is committed to this picture, it is an untenable doctrine.

The foregoing correspondence doctrine portrays the world as being prestructured into truthlike entities. This is one thing the antirealist opposes. A closely related view, also opposed by (some) antirealists, is that the world comes prefabricated in terms of categories or kinds. This is another facet of the correspondence theory to which Putnam objects.

> For an internal realist like myself . . . 'objects' do not exist independently of conceptual schemes. *We* cut up the world into objects when we introduce one or another scheme of description . . . [For an externalist the world contains] Self-Identifying Objects, . . . the *world*, and not thinkers, sorts things into kinds.[18]

The point here is essentially a Kantian point, and one also stressed by Nelson Goodman.[19] The creation of categories, kinds, or 'versions' is an activity of the mind or of language. The world itself does not come precategorized, presorted, or presliced. Rather, it is the mind's 'noetic' activity, or the establishment of linguistic convention, that produces categories and categorial systems. When truth is portrayed as correspondence, as thought or language *mirroring* the world, it is implied that the world comes precategorized. But that, says the antirealist, is a fiction.

Let us use 'correspondence$_1$' for the constellation of views just canvassed, namely, that the world is prestructured into truthlike entities (facts), and that truth consists in language or thought mirroring a precategorized world. Although this is *one* conception of correspondence, a realist need not be wedded to it. Weaker variants of correspondence are still compatible with realism. Let me try to sketch—admittedly metaphorically—a less objectionable style of correspondence theory, to be called 'correspondence$_2$'.

The mirror metaphor is only one possible metaphor for correspondence. A different and preferable metaphor for correspondence is *fittingness:* the sense in which clothes fit a body. The chief advantage of this metaphor is its possession of an ingredient analogous to the categorizing and statement-creating activity of the cognizer-speaker. At the same time, it captures the basic realist intuition that what makes a proposition, or statement, true is the way the world is.

There are indefinitely many sorts of apparel that might be designed for the human body, just as there are indefinitely many categories, principles of classification, and propositional forms that might be used to describe the world. Although the body certainly has parts, it is not presorted into units that must each be covered by a distinct garment. It is up to human custom and sartorial inventiveness to decide not only what parts to cover, but what types of garments should cover which expanses of the body, and whether those garments should be snug or loose. For many bodily parts (or groups of contiguous parts), there is a wide assortment of garment-types used to clothe them. In outer footwear, for example, there are sandals, slippers, shoes, tennis shoes, snowshoes, fishing boots, and hiking boots. In inner footwear there are anklets, calf-length, and over the knee stockings. Among trousers there are shorts, knickers, and full-length pants. For the torso there are short-sleeve and long-sleeve shirts, jackets, vests, tunics, robes, saris, capes, and huipils.

Despite all this variety—humanly invented variety—there is still the question, for any specified type of apparel, whether a specific token of that type fits a particular customer's body. This question of fittingness is not just a question of the style of garment. It depends specifically on *that* customer's body. Similarly, although the forms of mental and linguistic representation are human products, not products of the world per se, whether any given sentence, thought sign, or proposition is true depends on something extra-human, namely, the actual world itself. This is the point on which realists properly insist.

In inventing or evolving sartorial styles, people devise standards for proper fittingness. These may vary from garment to garment and from fashion to fashion. Styles specify which portions of selected bodily parts should be covered or uncovered, and whether the clothing should hug snugly or hang loosely. This is all a matter of style, or convention, which determines the *conditions of fittingness* for a given type of garment. Once such fittingness-conditions are specified, however, there remains a question of whether a given garment token of that type satisfies these conditions with respect to a particular wearer's body. Whether it fits or not does not depend solely on the fittingness-conditions; it depends on the contours of the prospective wearer as well.

The case of truth is quite analogous. Which things a cognizer-speaker chooses to think or say about the world is not determined by the world itself. That is a matter of human noetic activity, lexical resources in the speaker's language, and the like. A sentence or thought sign, in order to have any truth-value, must have an associated set of *conditions of truth*. Exactly what determines truth-conditions for a sentence or thought sign is a complex and controversial matter. But let us assume that a given utterance or thought, supplemented perhaps with certain contextual factors, determines a set of truth-conditions. The question then arises whether these conditions are satisfied or not. The satisfaction or nonsatisfaction of these conditions depends upon the world. Truth and falsity, then, consists in the world's 'answering' or 'not answering' to whatever truth-conditions are in question. This kind of answering is what I think of as 'correspondence$_2$'. Notice that *which* truth-conditions must be satisfied is not determined by the world. Conditions of truth are laid down not by the world, but only by thinkers or speakers. This is the sense in which the world is not precategorized, and in which truth does not consist in mirroring of a precategorized world. Unlike correspondence$_1$, correspondence$_2$ is compatible with what is correct in the constructivist themes of Kant, Goodman, and Putnam.

While these philosophers are right to emphasize constructivism, they carry it too far. There is a strong suggestion in Goodman's writing that "versions" are all there is; there is no world in itself. Although Goodman speaks of truth as being a matter of "fit," it is not fitness of a version to the world, but fitness of a version to other versions.[20] This, of course, a realist cannot accept. To return to our sartorial metaphor, the realist insists on the existence of a wearer: clothes don't make the world.

A chief motivation for the Goodman-Putnam view is epistemological. One strand of their position holds that we can never compare a version with "unconceptualized reality," so as to determine whether the world answers to a thought or statement. Comparison of a theory with perceptual experience is not comparison with unconceptualized reality because perceptual experience is itself the product of a sorting, structuring, or categorizing process of the brain. So all we can ever do, cognitively, is compare versions to versions.[21]

Conceding this point, however, does not undermine realism. Since correspondence$_2$ does not embrace the mirroring idea—nor the idea that true thoughts must resemble the world—the epistemology of getting or determining the truth need not involve comparison.

Can the same problem still be posed for my theory? It may be reexpressed by saying that, on my theory, we can never grasp or encounter the world, so as to determine whether some thought or sentence of ours fits it. And if the realist's world is unconceptualized, how can it be grasped or encountered in a manner to determine fittingness?

I see no insuperable difficulty here. Perception is a causal transaction from the world to the perceiver, so perception does involve an encounter with the world (at least in nonhallucinatory cases). To be sure, the event at the terminus of the transaction does not *resemble* the event at the starting point. The terminus of perception is a perceptual representation, which involves figure-ground organization and other sorts of grouping and structuring. The initiating event does not have these properties. Still, the transaction as a whole does constitute an encounter with something unconceptualized. We are not cut off from the world as long as this sort of encounter takes place.

But is this sort of encounter sufficient for knowledge or other forms of epistemic access? As far as I can see, realism about truth does not preclude such knowledge. Suppose that the (unconceptualized) world is such that the proposition 'There is a tree before me' fits it, that is, is true. And suppose that the perceptual process is a reliable one, both locally and globally. Then, according to my account of knowledge, I may indeed *know* that there is a tree before me. The world that I learn *about* is an unconceptualized world. But *what* I learn about this world is that some conceptualization (of mine) fits it. *How* I learn this is by a process that begins with the unconceptualized world but terminates in a conceptualization.

Does this (realist) theory make the world into a noumenal object, an object that cannot be known or correctly described? Not at all. On the proposed version of realism we can know of the world that particular representations fit it. So the world is not a noumenal object.

I cannot leave Putnam's critique of realism without commenting on a central component in his antirealist argument on which I have thus far been silent. In arguing against a correspondence theory of truth, Putnam has pointed out that there are *too many* correspondences. Correspondence has traditionally been construed as a word-world relationship. Putnam contends that there are too many word-world relationships of the requisite sort. Briefly, while there may be one satisfaction relation under which a given sentence turns out true, there will also be other satisfaction relations under which it turns out not to be true. So for any word-world relation purporting to be the 'intended' truth relation, there are other, equally good candidates. Since no unique word-world relation can be identified with truth, the correspondence notion of truth is untenable.[22]

Actually, the multiplicity of relations Putnam discusses are often candidates for the reference relation rather than the truth relation. But since the principal topic of interest is truth, the significance of his attack on a determinate reference relation lies in its implications for truth. What we have, then, is an indeterminacy argument against a word-world relation of truth, which is taken by Putnam to be a general critique of ('metaphysical') realism.

I believe there are two sorts of replies to this critique. First, one can challenge the indeterminacy argument by denying that Putnam has taken all relevant parameters into account. This point has been argued persuasively by Alvin Plantinga.[23] Putnam seems to suppose that the terms of our language get their meaning or extensions, somehow, by virtue (solely) of the set theoretical models of first-order formalizations of the body of our beliefs. In other words, roughly, our terms get their meaning and extensions by virtue of a vast network of implicit definitions. But this theory is extremely dubious. There must be further constraints at work in fixing our meanings and extensions. So the multiplicity that Putnam identifies of possible assignment functions to our terms does not have the implications that he alleges.

Second, the problem posed by Putnam, if it is a serious problem, is not really a problem about truth. Rather, it is a problem about interpretation, or the establishment of truth-conditions. These must be distinguished. Questions of truth cannot arise until there is a suitable bearer of truth-value, with an established set of truth-conditions, about which it can be queried *which* truth-value it has. Sentences or thought events construed as meaningless marks or nerve impulses are not bearers of truth-values. Only when a sentence or thought event is interpreted—when it has suitable semantic properties (including reference of singular terms and sense or reference of general terms)—is it even a candidate for being true or false.

Now Putnam has worries, as do other theorists in the field, about *how*, exactly, words and thought signs get their meaning and reference. How, in other words, do they get truth-conditions attached to them? These are important issues, which I will not in any way try to resolve. But unless and until sentences and thought signs are conceded to have interpretations, or truth-conditions, the question of truth cannot even arise. However, once we concede a determinate interpretation, or set of truth-conditions, for sentences and thought signs, we have assumed that Putnam's problems can be resolved. We can then turn to the question of truth, to the possession of this or that truth-value. I see no insurmountable obstacle here to the realist theory I have sketched. *Given* truth-conditions for a sentence, or thought, what makes it true or false is surely the way the world is, or whether it fits the world.

7.4. *Scientific Realism*

The doctrine of realism discussed thus far is a doctrine about truth. It is the doctrine commonly called 'metaphysical realism'. But another epistemological issue concerning realism is that of scientific theories and theorizing. Whereas scientific theories are ostensibly designed to describe the world, frequently the unobserved 'fine structure' of the world, some philosophers of science contend that this is an improper or injudicious portrayal of scientific theories. These philosophers—variously known as instrumentalists, fictionalists, and empiricists—deny that theories purport to give literally true stories of what the world is like. Rather, they are just calculational instruments for predicting the course of experience, devices to predict (and perhaps explain) what is empirically observed. Denying the face-value meaning of theoretical statements, philosophers of this ilk try to convey the meaning of these statements in purely observational terms, or other constructions out of empirically acceptable materials. Against such reductionist maneuvers, scientific realists hold out for a literal interpretation of theoretical statements. Acceptance of such statements is seen as an ontological commitment to entities ostensibly designated by their theoretical terms. And such ontological commitment is viewed as epistemologically conscionable.

I construe scientific realism (henceforth 'SR') as having a core consisting of three interconnected theses. First, there is a *semantic* thesis: SR says that theoretical statements in science are to be interpreted literally and referentially. Their meaning should not be purged of its (ostensible) extra-empirical content. Second, there is a thesis concerning the *aim* of scientists: SR says that what theorists are (generally) trying to do is to find and believe true descriptions of the world. Third, SR advances the epistemological claim that this aim is *legitimate,* since scientists sometimes are justified in believing scientific theories so construed. Or, in a slightly weaker variant, it is a legitimate aim because it is (humanly) possible for scientists to have justified belief in scientific theories realistically construed. (I will address both variants of the third thesis, but will not always announce switches from one to the other.)[24]

Although I have supported metaphysical realism as a theory of truth, the question of SR is quite independent. One could be a realist about truth while opposing SR. One could be, say, a reductionist about theoretical statements, but go on to say that the truth of any theory, given such a reduction, still depends on how the world is, nonepistemically. For example, the theory's truth would depend on whether the world really has a propensity to obey the specified observational regularities.[25] I am inclined to be a scientific realist as well as a metaphysical realist, as intimated in Chapter 6. But these doctrines are distinct. Moreover, I am *more* committed to metaphysical realism—especially its view of the nonepistemic nature of truth. My epistemology does not hinge so much on the SR issue. But to clarify my general stance, a brief excursus into SR is appropriate.

In the writings of (early) Putnam, Richard Boyd and W. H. Newton-Smith, SR has been given a new twist, rendering it a stronger doctrine than the core view I presented above.[26] SR is depicted as holding not merely that theoretical terms purport to refer, but that they (often) succeed in referring. Not only do scientists aim to describe the world with their theories, but they succeed in doing so. Or, more cautiously, their mature theories gradually get closer to the truth. In short, SR is viewed not merely as a doctrine about scientific aims, but as one about scientific success. (By 'success' I mean not merely predictive success, but success in delineating the fine structure of the world.)

This brand of SR is sometimes called 'convergent realism', or 'historical progressivism'. What I wish to emphasize about this doctrine is that it is an *addition* to the core of SR; one can therefore embrace SR's core without embracing convergent realism. This is the posture I mean to assume. More precisely, although I feel some attraction to convergent realism, at least in a modest, scaled-down version, I recognize that the historical record, viewed from our present vantage point, is not entirely clear.[27] Moreover, the thesis of convergent realism is at a different epistemological level than the core of SR. And in the present context I want to remain neutral about that level.

Am I really entitled to accept SR's core while remaining neutral about convergent realism? As I shall indicate shortly, there is reason to hesitate on this point. To assess this matter, we need to look back at the three core theses of SR. The semantic thesis of SR certainly does not depend on historical progressivism. The meaning of theoretical sentences may exceed their empirical content *however* scientists have been faring at limning the structure of reality. The second thesis of core SR, the aim component, also does not imply convergent realism. It may be true that scientists typically *intend* their theories to get at fundamental, transobservational truths; but they may nonetheless be falling flat, or achieving only modest success, in this endeavor.

It is only when we move to the third thesis of core SR that convergent realism may be implicated. If scientific theorizing has indeed fallen flat, historically speaking, how can it be epistemically *legitimate* for scientists to aim at getting theoretical truths? How is it possible for them to be justified in believing scientific theories so construed? This seems to be a particular problem given my theory of justifiedness. After all, if beliefs are justified only when caused by reliable processes, and if scientific methodology has a poor historical track record, the processes in question must not be reliable. But then belief in scientific theories, at least construed realistically, is not and cannot be justified. So the justifiedness of accepting scientific theories appears to depend on the truth of convergent realism, or at least a good *average* record of true theoretical beliefs, even if there is no continual forward *progress.*

The problem is crystallized in what Putnam calls the "disastrous meta-induction" of scientific theorizing.[28] Suppose scientists decide that no term in the science of more than fifty years ago referred, and no theory of that vintage was true. If this keeps happening, shouldn't we be led to the meta-induction that no theoretical term now or in the future will refer, and no present or future theory will be true? From this, conjoined with my theory of justification, won't it follow that we are not, and could not be, justified in believing any theoretical statement?

No, there are several lacunae in this line of reasoning. Let us look first at the "disastrous meta-induction" itself. Upon inspection, the meta-induction is really self-undermining. We judge past theories to be false only by the lights of our present theory. If we abandon our present theory, we are no longer in a position to judge past theories false. So if we use the meta-induction to conclude that no present scientific theory is true, we thereby eliminate all grounds for believing that past theories were false. But then we are no longer entitled to believe the premises of the meta-induction.

But, it might be replied, couldn't those premises still be *true?* And if so, wouldn't this reinstate the difficulty for any prospect of justified theoretical belief? Let us see, then, whether the meta-induction might be vulnerable on other grounds. I think it is. In deciding whether we can inductively infer the falsity of present and future theory from the falsity of believed theories of the past, we have to assess the bases of those past theoretical beliefs. Scientists in previous eras may have used different—and poorer—methodologies than we now have available. After all, there have been dramatic and continued developments in statistics and other evidential procedures. Furthermore, we now have vastly more powerful instruments of discovery and detection in many domains. Perhaps these differences in instrumental and evidential tools can outweigh past failures. Thus, our present scientific situation may not be relevantly similar to past science. Suppose you are going on a long automobile trip, and on all your previous long trips you had a flat tire. Should you expect a flat on this trip too? Not necessarily. If you began all previous trips with bald tires, but this time you start with a freshly purchased set of tires, the induction would be weak. (This response may not be conclusive, but it should give us pause.)

Setting aside the force of the meta-induction, we need to look more carefully at the implications of my theory of justification for the present question.[29] There are several reasons why a poor track record of positive belief in scientific theory need not ruin scientists' chances for justified theoretical belief according to my account. By 'positive' theoretical belief let us mean a belief that a theory is true; by 'negative' theoretical belief let us mean a belief that a theory is false, that is, a belief in the denial of a theory. Since the same methods are used to arrive at negative theoretical beliefs as positive theoretical beliefs, even if scientific methodology (assuming, inaccurately, that a single methodology has continuously been in use) has consistently generated false positive theoretical beliefs, it may still have generated lots of true negative theoretical beliefs. Moreover, the latter class is probably much larger than the former. Think of all the scientific theories we now reject and of the innumerable theories that past scientists rejected. When the entire class of outputs of scientific methodology is included, both negative and positive, the overall truth ratio may be rather impressive.

The next point concerns the distinction between primary justifiedness (P-justifiedness) and secondary justifiedness (S-justifiedness). Recall that P-justifiedness turns on the truth ratio of basic psychological processes; and S-justifiedness turns on properties of methods. Now the basic psychological processes used in assessing scientific theories probably are no different from those used for many other tasks; only the methods, at most, are distinctive. So even if these processes have a poor track record in this very special domain, it does not follow that they have poor reliability *in general*.

When we turn to S-justifiedness the matter is up in the air, because I did not fully commit myself to a criterion of J-rightness at the secondary level. While I am certainly attracted to an objectivist, truth-ratio criterion here too, I feel a tug in the direction of a culturally relative criterion (see section 5.3). Perhaps a belief is S-justified if it results from methods that are approved by a relevant community, say a community of experts. This might suffice, then, to make present positive scientific beliefs S-justified as well as P-justified.

Furthermore, we should not forget the wider *family* of truth-ratio criteria presented in section 5.5. This family included not only the absolute resource-independent criterion, (ARI), but also two resource-relative criteria. There was the maximizing resource-relative criterion and the satisficing resource-relative criterion. Either of these approaches could be extended to S-justifiedness. For example, a method could be counted as right if it has the highest truth ratio among all available methods. This comparative criterion might deem some of our present scientific methods to be right even if their absolute truth ratio is not terribly high.

These points indicate that, within my *full* theory of justification, a poor track record of scientific beliefs—especially positive theoretical beliefs—need not preclude the possibility of justified belief in scientific theories. That suffices to show that *core* SR is independent of convergent realism. However, a few further comments are in order to guarantee a fair-minded assessment of just how good or bad the track record of theoretical beliefs may be.

One point is that philosophers and historians of science have a tendency to concentrate on the most encompassing theories in science, those at the highest level of generality, which also typically postulate entities or forces that are least amenable to observation. Philosophers and historians of science are preoccupied with quantum theory, or problems of evolutionary theory. They spend little time citing more prosaic theories, such as the theory that the liver's function is to detoxify the body. It may well be true that once-accepted theories at the highest level of generality are frequently found in hindsight to be mistaken. But it is unfair to restrict consideration to these kinds of theories. Lower-level theories also occupy scientists, and these typically have much greater staying power.

We should also notice that any large-scale theory normally has numerous components, and scientists who believe the whole theory also believe its several components. Even when the theory as a whole is subsequently overthrown, the several components are not necessarily all overthrown. The general theory of the electron has certainly changed over time. But the view of the electron as a basic unit of electrical charge, not resolvable into smaller units, has been retained. That component has stayed constant. If, in this fashion, we take account of beliefs in all *components* of theories, not just entire theories, the specter of a "disastrous meta-induction" is much less forbidding. It does not look, from our present vantage point, as if science has been doing so poorly at all.[30]

One final point. I have been trying to show how, given my account of justification, it could well turn out that positive belief in scientific theories is justified. But it is not critical to my epistemology that this be so. Maybe a large-scale scientific theory is such a risky intellectual commitment, and the alternative possibilities are so numerous, that scientists are not entitled to believe such theories. This admission would not lead to general skepticism, nor to any general problem for my account of justification. Even if *global* skepticism were fatal to a theory of justification (which is not obvious), it is not so objectionable for a theory to imply local skepticism, that beliefs in one special arena are unjustified. There is nothing in my account of justification, then, that forces me to endorse SR, especially its third thesis. Scientific realism plays a less essential role in my view than metaphysical realism. Still, for the reasons indicated, I am inclined to accept it, and to believe in its compatibility with other tenets of my epistemology.

I draw this discussion to a close, having shown why realism about truth is a plausible and defensible doctrine. Truth is not an epistemic notion; and in a properly softened form, even a correspondence theory of truth is tenable. We have seen how *core* scientific realism, while distinct from realism about truth, is an attractive view, and ultimately compatible with my general epistemology.

chapter 8

The Problem of Content

8.1. *Epistemology and Content*

Having defended a realist, nonepistemic conception of truth, I am almost ready to proceed to Part II, which elaborates the projected relation between primary epistemology and cognitive science. However, there is one last 'foundational' issue that needs to be broached before turning to Part II, namely, the problem of content.

My epistemology, like most others, assumes the existence of beliefs and other propositional attitudes. A propositional attitude, of course, is a mental state with (propositional) *content.* But recent literature abounds with worries and doubts about contents, especially the possession of contents by *mental* states. These worries are directly relevant to this book, partly because they challenge one of my basic presuppositions, and partly for other reasons to be explained below. Unfortunately, many of these issues lie at the heart of philosophy of mind and philosophy of language, and I can only hope to paint the landscape with very broad brushstrokes. Still, I must reconnoiter the territory to inspect the possible pitfalls. I must consider, if only broadly and provisionally, whether the alleged threats are genuine, and if so, whether and how they can be met.

To say that something has content is to say that it has semantic properties: meaning, reference or truth-conditions, for example. Given my epistemological perspective, truth-conditions are especially important. Unless mental states have truth-conditions, there can be no true or false beliefs; *a fortiori* there can be no mental processes with the epistemological properties that interest us, such as, power and reliability. My investigation of such properties of mental processes could not get started: it would be devoid of relevant subject matter.

It should be emphasized that the absence of content—specifically, truth-conditions—would be a problem for most epistemologies. Any epistemology that takes knowledge seriously must take true belief seriously. Even an epistemology that ignores knowledge and truth-values, but instead stresses interpersonal agreement and disagreement, must take semantic content seriously. For how can there be agreement or disagreement without the sharing of content?

It would be hasty to assert that every epistemology needs the notion of content, especially mentalistic content. Quine's formulation of the mission of naturalistic epistemology suggests a concern with what people say, with their concrete noises, rather than with their internal ideas and beliefs.[1] The main aim is to explain how it comes about that people say what they do, that they utter the conjectures they utter. For this purpose, there need be no contentful mental states. So the untenability of mentalistic content need not be a doomsday scenario for *all* brands of epistemology.

Setting aside utterance (or speech-act) epistemologies, however, your standard, run-of-the-mill epistemology would be in a sorry state without mentalistic contents. Certainly my epistemology invokes such contents throughout. So any challenge to such contents, or any ground for thinking that empirical psychology can have no truck with such contents, needs to be confronted.

In this chapter I shall consider three theses concerning belief content that (if true) might imperil my epistemological project. The first thesis is that there are no contentful mental states. If true, this would imperil my argument for obvious reasons. This thesis will be addressed in the next section. The second thesis concedes contentful mental states but asserts that scientific psychology has nothing to say about them. If this were true, there would seem to be no way in which epistemology could profit from scientific psychology. Hence my proposed alliance between primary epistemology and scientific psychology would crumble. This line of argument will be examined in section 8.3. The third thesis seeks to undermine the notion that the reliability or rationality of our belief-forming processes could be ascertained by *empirical* means. On the contrary, it is claimed, the very ascription of content presupposes the reliability and rationality of believers. Reliability and rationality are guaranteed *a priori*, so questions of rationality or reliability find no place on the agenda of empirical science, as my conception of epistemology proposes. This challenge will be confronted in section 8.4.

My consideration of all these challenges must be briefer than they merit. They raise fundamental questions in the philosophy of mind and language that require a full length book in themselves. I can only afford a cursory look at selected lines of argument and rebuttal. In particular, there are two large problems in the field that I shall not try to address.

First is the question of the objects of belief. Assuming that beliefs are relational, what are their relata? Are they propositions (in some guise or other)? Are they sentences of mentalese? Are they both propositions and internal sentences?[2] This admittedly significant question will receive no sustained attention here. It is true that I shall give sympathetic treatment to the notion that cognition operates with some sort of 'representations', or 'data structures' (whether or not these are viewed as sentential). But even if there is an internal code, or a multiplicity of codes, it does not follow that belief is best analyzed, or paraphrased, as a relation between a cognizer and a formula in the language of thought. Nor is it clear how (or whether) the semantic properties of belief are inherited from properties of mental sentences. As Putnam suggests, even if cognitive psychology properly seeks a functionalist account of the mind in terms of representational systems, it does not follow that such a system of representation yields the semantic contents that a theory of belief requires.[3]

This brings me to the second main problem I shall not address systematically: the topic of *interpretation*. If mental states do have contents, how do they acquire these contents? What confers semantic properties on mental states; what makes them have the truth-conditions they have? The issue of interpretation is perhaps *the* central problem in the philosophy of mind. But although I will say a few relevant things about this problem, I make no pretense of having a positive theory.

8.2.   Challenges to Content

Let me begin, then, with challenges to the very existence of mentalistic contents. The strongest statement of such a challenge has been presented by Paul Churchland.[4] He accepts the popular idea that propositional attitude notions are embedded in folk psychology, and that folk psychology is a *theory*. Taking the theory-theory seriously, Churchland insists that, like any theory, folk psychology runs the risk of being false. If it is false, he adds, its principles and ontology should be replaced. Churchland apparently holds that folk psychology probably *is* false. In Lakatos's terms it is part of a stagnant or degenerating research program.[5] While philosophers have touted the explanatory and predictive utility of folk psychology, Churchland stresses its explanatory failures. He argues that it cannot explain mental illness, creative imagination, intelligence differences between individuals, the ability to catch a fly ball, or the nature and functions of sleep. He also expresses skepticism about the "inner language" model of the mind that folk psychology embraces. Finally, he maintains that folk psychology is "irreducible" to neuroscience. In this fashion Churchland argues for the falsity of folk psychology, and for the ultimate abandonment of the propositional attitude terms it employs.

To reply to Churchland, let me start with two smaller points. First, why does the fact that folk psychology cannot explain mental illness, creative imagination, or intelligence differences support its falsity? Perhaps the theory just has a limited domain and does not purport to explain such phenomena. Narrowness of scope needn't in itself disconfirm a theory. Second, folk psychology need not be committed to mentalistic sententialism. There are possible construals of propositional attitudes that do not invoke a *lingua mentis.* So even if mental sententialism is indeed misguided, that is not grounds for the elimination of propositional attitudes.

Let us now turn to larger points that render Churchland's conclusions debatable. To begin with, is it really so clear that folk psychology is a *theory?* Philosophers have been at pains to extract a theory of mind from ordinary mentalistic discourse, but it is questionable whether these attempts have succeeded. Efforts to elaborate the functionalist program in the philosophy of mind, which sees mentalistic concepts as embedded in a theory, have run into serious problems.[6] But if propositional attitude concepts are not theoretical concepts, it is an open question whether they should be abandoned for the kinds of reasons that scientists abandon theoretical posits.

However, assuming that folk psychology *is* a theory, and that propositional attitudes are posits of that theory, the issue that then comes to the fore is: Under what circumstances should one theory in science be overthrown by another (successor) theory? And under what circumstances is it proper to abandon a theory's ontological commitments?

As already mentioned, Churchland holds that folk psychology is irreducible to neuroscience. He apparently thinks that the only alternative to reducibility is replacement. He therefore expects folk psychology ultimately to be replaced by neuroscience. But this expectation might be forestalled for one of two reasons. First, the comparative plausibility of reduction versus replacement is partly dependent on how 'reduction' is construed. Strong forms of reduction are indeed unlikely to be realized. But some weaker forms of reduction might be more tenable. Second, reduction and replacement may not be an exhaustive set of alternatives. Some third alternative might be the most reasonable.

It is indeed implausible that folk psychology should be reduced to neuroscience in the strong sense of 'reduction', formulated by Ernest Nagel.[7] This kind of reduction requires 'bridge laws' that establish a one-to-one correlation between the predicates of the reduced theory and the predicates of the reducing theory; and that is unlikely to be available. In general, it is unlikely that folk psychology is sufficiently precise for this kind of correlation.

But there are alternative conceptions of reduction in science that might be more favorable to the present case. In Kenneth Schaffner's account of reduction, three theories are distinguished: (1) the original theory, (2) the corrected version of the original theory, and (3) the reducing theory.[8] Schaffner points out that predecessor theories can seldom be derived from successor theories in their original form, but corrected versions of them may be derivable. For example, classical Mendelian genetics may not be derivable from modern molecular genetics; but it is conceivable that a corrected version of Mendelian genetics—modern transmission genetics—is derivable from modern molecular genetics.[9] Current formulations of folk psychology may not be derivable from any future neuroscientific theories, but some corrected or refined version of folk psychology may be so derivable. In this imagined version folk psychology would retain its commitment to propositional attitudes—states with contents—but might considerably refine its laws and perhaps its terminology as well.

It is doubtful, however, that even a corrected version of folk psychology would satisfy Nagel's requirements for reduction. The requirement of a one-to-one correlation between folk psychology's predicates and those of neuroscience is probably unsatisfiable. Different species of higher organisms might achieve the same psychological states and regularities by way of a wide variety of neurological means. Thus, it is unlikely there can be a *type-type* correspondence between folk psychological predicates and neurological predicates. This point is stressed by Jerry Fodor, *inter alia*, who points out that, in general, such type-type correspondences do not obtain between the "special sciences" and more basic sciences.[10]

However, the absence of such correspondences should not preclude multiple schemes of taxonomy and theory for the same type of system. Whether a biological system, an economic system, an information-processing system, or what have you, units and states can be delineated at different *levels* of analysis. Each of these levels can be scientifically respectable, even if they are not aligned by way of type-type correspondences. Furthermore, it is unclear that they must compete with one another for predictive power in order to maintain respectability. Even if a higher-level set of units is inferior in predictive potential to some new, lower-level grain of analysis, it is not obvious that the higher-level units must be abandoned. Replacement is not the only alternative to reduction.

In applying this theme to propositional attitudes, it is especially important to emphasize the distinction between a theory's laws and its ontological commitments. the laws of current folk psychology may be imprecise, and hence relatively weak for predictive purposes. But this does not show that the favored terms of folk psychology have no reference. There may indeed *be* belief states and desire states, even if our commonsense dealings with such mental states have not evolved very precise or powerful laws to describe their relationships.

This point needs elaboration. The putative linkage between a term's predictive power and its ontological respectability should not be accepted uncritically. There are many terms used in language that seem ontologically unproblematic, despite the fact that their predictive utility is comparatively weak. Consider ordinary expressions like 'tree', 'automobile', 'alive', 'wealthy', and 'holds a Ph.D.'. These terms appear in no strict laws of contemporary science. Any generalizations made with their help are very rough indeed. Nonetheless, there is little cause to deny the referential status of these predicates. There *are* trees, automobiles, living things, wealthy people, and holders of Ph.D.'s. Similarly, even if words like 'belief' and 'desire' have modest predictive utility—compared with projected predicates of a maturing cognitive science—this should not be taken to establish their referential bankruptcy. The thesis that the genuinely referring terms are only those that occur in generalizations with maximal predictive power (within a given domain) is very dubious.

Another challenge to mentalistic content is presented by Stephen Stich, who sometimes seems to make a more cautious claim, namely, that the belief construct is unsuitable *for cognitive science.* At other times, however, he seems to call the very existence of beliefs into question. Stich claims that cognitive science must pay a very heavy price if it adheres to the program of a "strong representational theory of mind (RTM)," that is, a program that couches generalizations in terms of content. Predicates of the form 'believes that p' are both vague and context sensitive. The folk language of belief characterizes a person's cognitive state by comparing it to our own. So people who differ fairly radically from us in doctrine, or ideology, will fall outside the reach of belief description altogether. But some of these subjects may have minds that work very much as ours do. Thus, Stich argues, if there are important generalizations that cover both us and such exotic folk, a cognitive science embodying strong RTM is bound to miss them.[11]

One of Stich's examples is that of aged Mrs. T, who suffers from severe memory loss. Whenever she is asked 'What happened to McKinley?' she says, 'McKinley was assassinated', but she is quite unable to say what an assassination is, or what its consequences are. It seems inappropriate, says Stich, to describe Mrs. T as believing that McKinley was assassinated. Indeed, no definite content ascription seems available to us. Thus, Mrs. T's states are beyond the reach of a cognitive theory that cleaves to descriptions in terms of content.

Is Stich's conclusion warranted? It is doubtless true that we often have inadequate resources for describing the content of a person's belief. In particular, simple sentences of English (and other natural languages) cannot be counted on to get things right. Our language marks certain distinctions but not others. This means that it is difficult to phrase a set of distinctions drawn by a given cognizer but not well marked in English. This holds, for example, of Daniel Dennett's case of a six-year-old child who says that his daddy is a doctor.[12] The child does not yet have a full understanding of 'doctor'; he may not know that this precludes being a quack or an unlicensed practitioner. So perhaps the English word 'doctor' does not *exactly* capture the content of the child's belief. Still, this should not imply that the child has no belief at all.

This point is especially clear if we individuate propositions in terms of a possible-worlds analysis, as does Robert Stalnaker.[13] The content of what the child believes can be captured in terms of the range of possibilities, or possible worlds, that the child envisages. This set of alternative possibilities will doubtless grow as the child matures, and then he will have another belief content associated with the same English sentence. This will be captured by a different demarcation in terms of possible worlds. There are difficulties with pinpointing belief content with English sentences, but this does not undermine the existence of contentful states.

As previous cases illustrate, the fact that a cognizer assents to a given sentence does not guarantee that his belief content is well captured by that sentence. This conclusion applies to other examples in the literature. One is drawn from Saul Kripke's paper "A Puzzle about Belief."[14] Kripke assumes that the language user in the following example is sincere, reflective, and not conceptually confused. Two further assumptions he takes as noncontroversial principles are: (P1) If a speaker of a language L assents to 'p', and 'p' is a sentence of L, then he believes that p; and (P2) if a sentence of one language expresses a truth in that language, then any translation of it into another language also expresses a truth in that other language. A problem case Kripke then describes is as follows. Pierre, a native, initially monolingual Frenchman, has heard or read about 'Londres' being beautiful. He has perhaps seen pictures. So he assents to the sentence 'Londres est jolie'. Later he emigrates to England and takes up residence in London. However, he does not learn that 'London' refers to the same city as the French name 'Londres', which he had learned many years ago. He learns English by exposure, and, given his observation of his surroundings, assents to 'London is not pretty'. Given that 'London' and 'Londres' have the same fixed semantic value, it follows from the disquotation principle, (P1), and the translation principle, (P2), that Pierre believes that London is pretty and he believes that London is not pretty. Yet he has not made any logical blunders.

The way to deal with this puzzle is to reject the disquotation principle. As we have seen, the relation between belief content and what a person *says* (even sincerely) is not at all simple and straightforward.[15] A person's thought content may be either richer or narrower than a given sentence he utters suggests, depending on his grasp of the words used and his background beliefs or ideology. This point also applies to some cases presented by Tyler Burge. In one of Burge's best-known examples, a man says: 'I have arthritis in the thigh'. This man is unaware that the term 'arthritis' is properly reserved for inflammation of the joints.[16] Should we say that this man believes that he has arthritis in the thigh? This may seem innocuous enough, and certainly would do for most practical purposes; but it does not capture his cognitive content in an ideal fashion.

There are additional reasons for doubting that belief content can be captured with simple sentences of a natural language, even one the believer speaks. A person's *perceptual* representation of an object should probably be included in the content of a belief concerning that object. But there may be no satisfactory way of identifying this perceptual content with any simple sentence of a natural language. Of course, since we often want to communicate about the content of perceptual beliefs, we need some vehicle of communication, especially a handy, efficient one. So we employ simple sentences of a natural language. It is a mistake to suppose, however, that such sentences can provide anything but a very rough *approximation* of belief contents. Even in expressing one's own beliefs, it is doubtful that one's utterances convey them very fully or accurately. None of this, however, constitutes negative evidence against the existence of contentful beliefs.

Let us return now to Stich. Stich's worries are not exhausted by the difficulty of pinpointing belief contents in puzzle cases. He presents two other problems for the viability of the belief construct in cognitive science. First, he claims that folk psychology's belief construct requires that beliefs be the cognitive causes of both verbal and nonverbal behavioral effects. But certain psychological experiments show that verbal and nonverbal behavior have *distinct* cognitive causes. Hence, he claims, the right thing to say is that there are no such things as beliefs.

Second, Stich contends that beliefs should be identical with "naturally isolable" parts of the cognitive system, but there are possible network models of the mind within cognitive science that would violate this isolability (or modularity) requirement.

These arguments are effectively countered by Terence Horgan and James Woodward.[17] I briefly summarize their principal responses. First, even if the dual-control thesis is partly right, it is still plausible to posit beliefs as the two sets of causes. (Notice that Stich himself concedes that there would be "belief-like" states.)[18] Second, in *many* cases people display integrated verbal and nonverbal behavior: for example, lecturing while doing a logic problem on the blackboard. Here it seems inescapable that the same states must be causing both verbal and nonverbal behavior. The control systems must not be wholly independent. So belief states causing both verbal and nonverbal behavior must be posited at least for this class of cases.

In reply to Stich's second argument, Horgan and Woodward reveal the implausibility of the natural isolability, or modularity, requirement, pointing out that it is an enormously unattractive intertheoretic compatibility requirement. There is no reason why beliefs could not be identical with highly complex, even 'gerrymandered', conglomerations of lower-level events. Such complex events could still play the causal role that folk psychology imputes to them.

I have surveyed a variety of recent arguments against the existence of beliefs and found none of them conclusive.[19] So let us proceed to the two other challenges to my epistemological undertaking.

8.3. Can Psychology Address Content?

I seek to enlist psychology's aid in determining the truth-conducive properties of mental processes. But can psychology do this? Only, it seems, if it can address cognitive states in terms of their content. But there are arguments in the literature that psychology does not, or should not, do this. While mental states may *have* content, psychology is allegedly *silent* about it. If that is right, how can psychology shed light on truth-conducive properties of mental mechanisms? Truth-conduciveness is obviously fixed by properties related to content.

Let me introduce this argument with some familiar background. According to most recent theories, the truth-conditional content of a belief is a function not just of what is in the cognizer's head, but of external things as well. This sort of point has been made most influentially by Putnam with his Twin-Earth examples.[20] But it is equally a consequence of many kinds of functionalism, which would link the identity conditions of propositional attitudes to their causal and counterfactual relations with external stimuli and bodily movements.

Now consider the additional claim that psychology deals exclusively with what's in the head. In particular, a proper cognitive science is only concerned with the 'formal', 'syntactic', or computational properties of mental processes. This thesis has been advanced in several quarters, chiefly by Jerry Fodor. Fodor calls it the "formality condition."[21] There is some question as to whether Fodor really intends the thesis in question; I will return to this in a moment. But let us examine the passages that suggest it.

Fodor distinguishes the *formal* properties of a mental representation from its *semantic* properties. "Formal operations are the ones that are specified without reference to such semantic properties of representations as, for example, truth, reference, and meaning".[22] The former are purely internal characteristics of a representation, while the latter relate the representation to the external world. Fodor goes on to assert that cognitive psychology proceeds (or should proceed) purely in terms of formal properties, that is, computationally. This apparently means that truth-conditional content is to be ignored.

> The formality condition, viewed in this context, is tantamount to a sort of methodological solipsism. If mental processes are formal, then they have access only to the formal properties of such representations of the environment as the senses provide. Hence, they have no access to the *semantic* properties

of such representations, including the property of being true, of having refer-
ents, or, indeed, the property of being representations *of the environment.*[23]

However, there are other passages in Fodor's writing that appear inconsistent with the foregoing. In another article he writes: "Propositional attitudes interact causally and do so *in virtue of* their content."[24] And in the
introduction to the volume collecting the papers from which I have quoted,
he writes: "In order to specify the generalizations that mentalistic etiologies
instantiate, we need to advert to the contents of mental states."[25] It appears
from *these* passages that psychology does need to deal with contents, a conclusion that apparently conflicts with the other cited passages. But Fodor
may here intend 'content' to refer to *narrow* content, which is not a semantic notion.[26] Since we are restricting attention to wide, *truth-conditional*
content, Fodor can indeed be interpreted as holding that cognitive psychology ignores (or should ignore) *that* kind of content (wide content). In any
case, there are other exponents of this view. Stich, for example, forthrightly
endorses the view that cognitive science should proceed purely
"syntactically."[27]

How, then, would the presently envisaged challenge to my enterprise go?
It might be formulated in the following argument:

(1)   Cognitive psychology proceeds purely syntactically, formally, or
      computationally.
(2)   Truth-conditional content is not (just) a function of syntactic processes
      or relations. It is partly a function of external objects, of mind-world
      relations.
Therefore,
(3)   Cognitive psychology does not deal with truth-conditional content.
Hence,
(4)   Cognitive psychology cannot shed any light on truth-conditional prop-
      erties of mental processes, including truth-conducive properties of be-
      lief-forming processes.

Once laid out in this fashion, though, the argument is clearly unsound. Most
importantly, (3) does not follow from (1) and (2). Any appearance of validity
trades on an ambiguity between *opaque* and *transparent* readings of 'deals
with', in (3). If psychology were confined to purely formal descriptions, it
would not deal with contentful states on an opaque reading of 'deal with'; it
would not talk about contentful states *in terms of* their content. But assuming that mental states *are* contentful, psychology would still deal with contentful states on a transparent reading. The states it addresses in contentless
terminology would in fact *be* contentful states.

So even if cognitive psychology proceeds purely nonsemantically, it can
still tell us things about beliefs and about various causal processes that generate beliefs. Even if it describes beliefs and belief-causing processes purely

formally, once the contents of these states are assigned, one would be in a position to assess the truth-conduciveness of the processes. In other words, even if cognitive psychology does not participate in the assignment of truth-conditional contents, it can still play the role in primary epistemology that I have assigned it, that of identifying—in *some* descriptive terms or other!—the various belief-forming processes available to the organism. This completely undercuts (4), which comprises the challenge to my project being considered in this section.

Although this completes my main response to this challenge, a few other comments are in order, apropos of premise (1). First, one might reject premise (1) as *descriptively* false. Many parts of psychology in fact deal with the world-mind interface. Perceptual psychologists study the relationship between physical inputs and perceptual representations, in order to determine when and why perceptual illusions occur. And even when cognitive psychologists do not study environment-organism interactions, they commonly *do* employ content descriptions to characterize internal events.[28]

But suppose (1) is construed as a *prescription*, rather than a description of current practice. Perhaps it is a prediction of psychology's practice in some ideal, future incarnation. On what would such a prescription be based? One consideration, of course, is the computational model, which has inspired many of the themes of cognitive psychology. But notice that even the computational model makes use of extrinsic descriptions. When we describe states of a computer in terms of numbers and the arithmetic function addition, we are not giving intrinsic descriptions of those states; we are interpreting the states in terms of some external, abstract objects. So the computational model itself makes use of semantic interpretation.

A second possible reason for a purely formal psychology is that the true laws of the system can be formulated only in syntactic, intrinsic terms. But is this correct? It is admittedly plausible to suppose that if there are any laws of the system statable in extrinsic terms, there must also be laws statable in intrinsic terms.[29] But this would not show that no laws are statable in extrinsic terms. Furthermore, some writers argue that one cannot state *all* laws of the system without including laws formulatable in semantic terminology.[30] Laws stated in intrinsic terminology would be different laws. So if psychology wants to include all laws of the system, it must work at the semantic level as well as the intrinsic.

A different kind of defense of psychology's use of content descriptions would reject the heavy emphasis on laws. According to a recent model of psychological explanation offered by Robert Cummins, the main style of psychological explanation is not subsumption under laws.[31] Rather, it is "functional analysis": explaining a system's possession of one property by appeal to properties of its components. If this model of psychological explanation is correct, psychology would not be forced to abandon content descriptions even if it turned out that the best (or only) *laws* of the system were statable syntactically. Psychology might still want semantic descriptions of the organism at certain levels of description, which would ultimately, of course, be explainable in terms of lower-level organization.

8.4. Content, Rationality, and Reliability

I turn now to the final challenge concerning content attribution. This challenge is based on the claim that certain questions I regard as questions for psychology are already tacitly answered by the very ascription of content. These answers are given, as it were, *a priori*, or transcendentally; they are not questions for empirical psychology. Hence, psychology need not, and cannot, play the role I ascribe to it.

This line of argument comes in two forms. First, it is claimed that the ascription of content presupposes *rationality*. We automatically attribute rationality to a being just by imputing propositional attitudes to him. But rationality involves certain kinds of inferential processes. Hence, what inferences people make is (largely) an *a priori* matter, not one to be settled by empirical psychology. Second, it is claimed that the ascription of content presupposes *reliability*. In imputing propositional attitudes, we must so interpret a creature's beliefs that most of them come out true. So questions of reliability cannot be *empirical* questions. Since we are already committed to (a large amount of) reliability by the very ascription of beliefs, the matter of reliability is (largely) settled before psychology even enters the picture. Strands of these theses have been endorsed by a number of authors. But they are emphasized most heavily by Donald Davidson; so I shall pay closest attention to his formulations.

The principal source of these themes, though, is Quine. In discussing interpretation of a speaker's utterances, Quine advocates a "charity principle": "Fair translation preserves logical laws . . . Assertions startlingly false on the face of them are likely to turn on hidden differences of language . . . One's interlocutor's silliness, beyond a certain point, is less likely than bad translation."[32]

Davidson has enunciated similar themes in several papers. Regarding rationality, he writes: "If we are intelligently to attribute attitudes and beliefs, or usefully to describe motions as behavior, then we are committed to finding, in the pattern of behavior, belief, and desire, a large degree of rationality and consistency."[33] In the same vein (but apropos of preferences rather than beliefs), he writes: "I do not think we can clearly say what should convince us that a man at a given time (without change of mind) preferred *a* to *b*, *b* to *c*, and *c* to *a*. The reason for our difficulty is that we cannot make good sense of an attribution of preference except against a background of coherent attitudes."[34]

Concerning the imputation of reliability (to use my term), Davidson writes: "Charity is forced on us;—whether we like it or not, if we want to understand others, we must count them right in most matters."[35] "Since knowledge of beliefs comes only with the ability to interpret words, the only possibility at the start is to assume general agreement on beliefs. We get a first approximation to a finished theory by assigning to sentences of a speaker conditions of truth that actually obtain (in our opinion) just when the speaker holds those sentences true."[36] "What makes interpretation possible, then, is the fact that we can dismiss *a priori* the chance of massive error. A theory of interpretation cannot be correct that makes a man assent to very many false sentences: it must generally be the case that a sentence is true when a speaker holds it to be."[37]

A similar stance on rationality is taken by Dennett. In a recent paper he says that propositional attitudes are premised on the following principles: (1) a system's beliefs are those it *ought to have*, given its perceptual capacities, its epistemic needs, and its biography; (2) a system's desires are those it *ought to have*, given its biological needs and the most practicable means of satisfying them; and (3) a system's behavior will consist of those acts that it *would be rational* for an agent with those beliefs and desires to perform.[38]

Returning to the reliability theme, several others have sketched approaches to interpretation guided by the idea that representation derives from the capacity of a system to be a reliable indicator of its context. These writers include Stephen Schiffer, Hartry Field, Brian Loar, Fred Dretske, and Jerry Fodor.[39] However, I will not undertake to detail their proposals.

To turn to critical discussion, let us look first at the thesis about rationality, restricting attention to that segment of rationality concerned with beliefs and inferences (rather than, say, preferences). So restricted, rationality is often equated with 'logicality'. An initial problem with this equation is that logic does not entail any inference principles, an observation I stressed in Chapter 5. So it just is not clear what it means for a belief system to be logical.

At least two interpretations, though, readily come to mind. First, a belief system may be regarded as logical (and therefore rational) only if it is consistent. Second, a belief system may be regarded as logical only if it is characterized by deductive closure: the agent believes all logical consequences of his beliefs. Neither of these principles is very plausible as standards for belief attribution. Deductive closure is especially unattractive. Surely no human being infers all the logical consequences of his beliefs, yet we do not hesitate to ascribe beliefs to people.

On reflection, the consistency principle is not plausible either. Acceptance of this principle would imply that nobody could possibly have an inconsistent set of beliefs, since any apparent inconsistency would disqualify the person's mental states from being *beliefs* at all. But surely we do not withhold belief ascriptions for this reason. Russell showed that the axiom of comprehension leads to inconsistency; but this does not mean that people who previously (ostensibly) accepted the axiom of comprehension did not really have any beliefs.

Of course, Davidson does not claim that believers must always be rational or consistent. He only says that propositional attitude attributions commit us to finding a "large degree" of rationality and consistency in the subjects of our attributions. But then it emerges that there is no *a priori* determination of the specific logical operations that believers must always, or even regularly, employ. So, as I wish to contend, it presumably rests with empirical science to determine just what these deductive operations are.

I may put the point this way. Since perfect logicality is not a presupposition of belief attribution, belief attribution at best presupposes minimal logicality. This point has been emphasized by Christopher Cherniak.[40] But what, exactly, does 'minimal logicality' imply? Precisely which deductive inferences must a cognizer make, as a prerequisite of having beliefs at all? I do not see how any plausible conditions can be laid down *a priori*. Formal logic catalogs all sorts of argument patterns. How should we pick from these the ones that a believer, qua believer, *must* (always?) execute. Even if we laid down a disjunction of such patterns as requisite for believing, no conclusion could be drawn about which of these disjuncts *human beings* regularly, or typically, or easily, execute. As far as human inference capacities are concerned, the matter is surely an empirical one.

The point can be brought home another way. Before teaching a course in logic, it is not obvious to the trained Ph.D. exactly which inferences freshmen will find easy or hard, natural or unnatural. This is manifestly an empirical matter, and quite appropriately studied by the psychology of reasoning. (See Chapter 13 for further discussion.)

I have failed to identify any plausible *a priori* logicality constraints, even in the domain of deductive logic. But *a priori* constraints of rationality, if there are such, should also include inductive logic. Here one hardly knows where to begin. Principles of inductive logic are very controversial, in the first place. Assuming we could settle on some such principles, are they really to be required as conditions for belief ascription? What about principles of probability and statistics? Are creatures who violate such principles necessarily devoid of propositional attitudes? That is extremely dubious.[41] Empirical studies strongly indicate that people have little native grasp of probability (as I will discuss in Chapter 14). But this hardly keeps them from qualifying as believers.

It is time to turn to the second form of the present challenge, the one concerning *reliability*. The first comment I need to make is that, contrary to what Davidson avers, our procedures of content attribution do allow the ascription of belief systems that are 'massively' false (in the ascriber's opinion). Cartesian demon scenarios are apt for illustrating this suggestion. But let me give a slightly more realistic variant of Descartes's demon.

Imagine a child who grows up normally and develops a mastery of English. Several cognitive catastrophes then befall him. He is stricken by diseases that distort his visual powers and his memory—except his memory for language. As a result, he now describes his visual environment in ways we regard as massively false. And when he recalls things from his personal past, his accounts are systematically erroneous. To ensure his health and well-being, he is placed in the hands of a guardian, who feeds and treats him well except for instruction in cognitive matters. The diabolical guardian reads him specially concocted newspapers and encyclopedias full of falsehoods. So the child gradually acquires a radically false picture of the world. The guardian even teaches him fallacious inference patterns, which take him even further from the truth. His misconceptions are expressed in avowals of belief, and since there is nothing amiss with his linguistic memory, we have every reason to interpret his utterances homophonically. We would then be strongly disposed to ascribe to him a system of belief that is massively false.[42]

Suppose, nonetheless, that we concede a kernel of truth in the notion that *some* sort of truth constraint is presupposed by the ascription of content, though of a more modest nature than those Davidson endorses. What would be the repercussions of this concession? A theory of interpretation still would not fix a belief set's reliability, so the determination of just what that global reliability is would still be an empirical matter.

Furthermore, even if Davidson were right in claiming that massive error is excluded *a priori,* this would not damage my theory. Suppose belief ascription commits us to an accuracy rate of 50 percent. The criterion of justifiedness presumably requires a higher truth ratio, say 80, 90, or 95 percent. Can people's belief-forming processes attain such higher levels? This would be an empirical question, not foreclosed by the theory of interpretation.

Notice next that even if the theory of interpretation requires a high truth ratio across the corpus taken as a whole, there might be small slums of defective belief-forming processes, perhaps infrequently employed. The task of identifying a right system of J-rules would include the identification and rejection of such defective processes. More generally, for purposes of the theory of justifiedness, it is not enough to know the global truth ratio of a cognizer's actual beliefs. One needs to know the specific cognitive processes that are employed and available for employment, since it is only such processes that a right J-rule system will specify. Identification of the available processes is an empirical task.

Finally, all of the foregoing questions concern reliability. But epistemology is also interested in *power* and *speed.* Evaluation of basic cognitive processes along these dimensions is not at all affected by the theory of interpretation. (At least, no argument has been given for any such thesis.) Thus, many questions of importance to primary epistemology would require contributions from cognitive science—even if some of Davidson's more radical suggestions were correct.

I conclude that any plausible interpretation theory is compatible with the role assigned by my framework to empirical psychology. Let us proceed, then, to concrete illustrations of the contributions that psychology might make.

part II

ASSESSING OUR COGNITIVE RESOURCES

chapter 9

Perception

9.1. *An Agenda for Primary Epistemics*

The principal way that cognitive science can contribute to epistemology, I claim, is to identify basic belief-forming, or problem-solving, processes. Once identified, these processes would be examined by primary epistemology according to the evaluative dimensions and standards adduced in Part I. How do the processes fare in terms of justification, rationality, and intelligence? How well do they stand up, as judged by the three standards of reliability, power, and speed?

My extended treatment of justification, in Chapters 4 and 5, may suggest to the reader that I regard justification as *the* central term of epistemic appraisal. Indeed, the reader may be expecting a full-scale system of J-rules, with permissions granted to a specified coterie of basic cognitive processes. Any such impression, however, needs correction.

My extended attention to justification is somewhat disproportionate to the importance I attach to it. I have devoted so much attention to it partly because of its pivotal role in traditional epistemology, and partly because I have a positive theory to advance. This does not mean that I regard evaluative terms like 'rational' and 'intelligent' as less important. I simply have no fully developed positive accounts of those notions to present. (I also find them intrinsically vaguer notions.) Nor do I mean to assign the standard of reliability a higher intellectual status than power or speed. I decline to offer any such ranking.

As far as the construction of a right J-rule system is concerned, it would be greatly premature to essay such a construction at this juncture. Cognitive science is still groping its way toward the identification of basic processes. Many different theories are afloat. This is understandable, since the mind-brain is an enormously complex system, with a wide range of subsystems, all of which are extraordinarily difficult to study experimentally. Furthermore, it is no trivial task to relate the sorts of processes tentatively delineated by cognitive science to questions on the epistemological agenda.

Even an initial survey of the field and sampling of the possibilities will occupy us at length. Finally, a truly complete set of J-rules would have to register an interplay between different components, or functions, of the mind-brain. I shall have enough on my hands in identifying relevant processes *individually,* and exploring their properties.

For all of these reasons, Part II presents only some *first steps* toward a full-fledged primary epistemics: a prolegomenon, if you will, to the subject. Clearly, a full development of primary epistemics will require continued research and collaboration by many people from several disciplines.

I have said that in this part of the book I will illustrate prospective contributions of cognitive science to epistemology. The term 'illustrate' needs emphasis. It is not crucial to my view that any particular item in Part II should prove to be correct. I am not wedded to any particular candidate as a basic cognitive process; nor do I have a significant stake in the normative assessment of any such candidate. My aim is to show what *might* be among the basic cognitive processes and what the epistemological implications of this may be. Relative to this aim, no specimen hypothesis I adduce about psychological processes is critical. The structure of the inquiry concerns me, not the correctness of specific details. However, I naturally select themes taken seriously by at least part of the cognitive science community. And I pay *some* attention to the evidence supporting various hypothesized processes, although I do not do this systematically or rigorously. Weighing evidence is the task of cognitive science itself (using currently accepted scientific methods). The strict role of primary epistemology is to borrow the results of cognitive science and assess the epistemic repercussions of these results.

While the principal contribution of cognitive science is to identify basic belief-forming processes, there is another contribution as well: *refinement* of the descriptive categories with which epistemology operates. For example, epistemology commonly deploys the category of belief. But belief is a very coarse-grained category from the standpoint of mental science. Primary epistemology needs a more subtle and flexible set of doxastic state categories. Drawing on psychological materials, I shall introduce a few such categorial refinements among doxastic states, distinguishing 'perceptual' from 'central' beliefs (this chapter), and 'activated' from 'unactivated' beliefs (Chapter 10). The whole topic of uncertainty or degrees of confidence, standardly handled with the category of subjective or 'judgmental' *probabilities,* also needs to be addressed with increased psychological sophistication. I shall draw on psychological materials to tender a new approach to acceptance and uncertainty in Chapter 15.

Of course, any complication in the array of doxastic categories threatens to complicate the picture of normative assessment. When activated and unactivated beliefs are distinguished, questions arise about the meaning of 'reliability' and 'power'. Are these to be defined in relation to activated beliefs or unactivated beliefs? Such complications cannot be avoided in a serious and realistic theory. (I shall have other reasons also, in Part II, to tinker with some of our normative standards. But no major thematic changes will be introduced.)

What are the implications of Part II for the global assessment of native cognitive processes? Within the cognitive science community, perspectives on human endowments span a wide spectrum, ranging from rosy to gloomy, from admiring to depreciating. The admirers are struck with the remarkable capacities of the system's endowments. Indeed, it is hard not to be impressed when one reflects on the ease with which the mind learns enormously complex language systems, or the mind's plasticity in problem-solving activity (neither capacity being adequately understood). Human mechanisms must be doing something—many things—right! But deprecators within the cognitive science community point an accusing finger at the 'dirty' heuristics the mind seems to employ: procedures which do not measure up to statistical or probabilistic standards that are widely accepted as normatively correct.

I shall present examples of both outlooks in this part of the book. But my own tentative assessment will be neither warmly glowing nor severely disparaging. It will be more qualified and moderate in tone. The mind uses all sorts of cognitive processes and process variants. In terms of, say, reliability, they are a mixed bag: some good, some not so good. Moreover, most of them have significant *trade-offs*. The less reliable processes are often quicker. They may be good from a pragmatic standpoint, even if they do not confer maximal power. So I shall not be arguing for any sweeping conclusions here. I adduce no reasons to think that the human mind, on the whole, is either strikingly better or strikingly worse, epistemically speaking, than others have supposed. The main conclusion, perhaps, is that it takes much careful sifting and analysis both to identify the basic processes and to weigh their strengths and weaknesses.

My discussion will sometimes suggest conclusions, however, that are at variance with doctrines many epistemologists and methodologists have held. For example, the appropriateness of a strong 'total evidence' requirement will be called into question (Chapter 10). The softening of principles for belief revision will be proposed (also Chapter 10). Greater approval will be tentatively conferred on 'imagistic' thinking (Chapter 12). 'Acceptance' of hypotheses, rather than continued uncertainty, will be viewed more favorably than many theorists would condone (Chapter 15). And processes that breed 'order effects' will be seen as nonetheless sanctionable (Chapter 16).

The importance of my analysis in Part II, however, is not the depth of *disagreement* with other epistemologists that it exemplifies. Its importance lies in the exploration of largely uncharted problems. Epistemology simply has not had the opportunity to inspect and assess fine-grained cognitive processes, because the kinds of processes at work in the mind-brain have not been dissected (in a scientifically adequate manner) until recent years. The importance of Part II, then, consists more in the formulation of new questions than in the answers I propose here.

A final comment is in order on what this part of the book *does not* seek to accomplish. I have already stressed (in Chapter 8) that this is not an essay on the philosophy of mind. Thus, I am not seeking to resolve such issues as the nature and source of semantic properties for mental states. I now wish to indicate with equal emphasis that this is not an essay on the methodology of psychology. This means two things. First, I shall not spend time defending the empirical cognitivist approach to the study of the mind, as opposed to generic rivals, such as phenomenology, introspectionism, or behaviorism. Second, I shall not discuss systematically the divergent research methodologies *within* cognitive science, nor seek to choose among them in a principled fashion. I assume that some variant or variants of cognitive science are good ways to study the mind. Working on this assumption, I draw on any materials that strike me as plausible and interesting for epistemological purposes.

It may be observed that the methodological details of the study of mind surely belong to epistemology, at least to that wing of epistemology called 'philosophy of science'. So why don't these issues fit squarely into Part II? The answer follows from my distinction between processes and methods. Insofar as epistemology deals with proper methods, especially methods of the several sciences, the methodology of psychology does belong to epistemology. But this volume deals principally with *primary* epistemology, which concerns itself with acceptable processes, not methods. That is why the methodology of psychology falls outside my purview.

9.2. *Bottom-Up and Top-Down Processing*

Perception is a central topic in both psychology and epistemology, and therefore a suitable starting point in exploring the interface between psychology and epistemology. But there is a drawback to this strategy. The psychology of perception is such a huge and complex topic that my treatment of it will, of necessity, be extremely selective and shallow. Nonetheless, since it bears on such central issues in epistemology, it cannot be neglected. I will start, then, with a brief foray into this domain.

A standard approach to perception is to view it as *pattern recognition*. People regularly recognize presentations of a certain pattern—such as the letter 'A'—as instances of that pattern. How is this recognition accomplished?

Before turning to this question, note that the language of recognition imputes a doxastic act. It views the output of perception as a *classification*, or *categorization*, of the stimulus. This suggestion is not inadvertent. Cognitive psychology studies perception as a species of information processing, where 'information' necessarily has *content*. (However, as used by psychologists, 'information' needn't be *true* content.) In view of this, I think it expresses the dominant outlook in cognitive science to describe the output of perception—the percept—as a doxastic state or event. The percept is not a mere feeling, or 'quale', but a classification of some segment of the environment. A percept is a representation of the world, not a contentless bit of phenomenology. It is congenial to this view, then, to construe a percept as a *belief*, a distinctive kind of belief, which we might call a 'perceptual belief'. Subclasses of such beliefs are visual beliefs, auditory beliefs, and so on. I will say more about this proposal a bit later.

It is a little misleading, though, to portray all perception as recognition, that is, as *re*-cognition. This terminology is appropriate for cases in which perceptual representation involves the matching of present material to previous perception or to a category drawn from memory. But it is doubtful whether all perception involves this. We frequently perceive a thoroughly novel shape, and perceive it in its full individuality. There is no question of recognition, or prior familiarity, here. This point is stressed by Irvin Rock, who in *The Logic of Perception* distinguishes different stages of perception and different perceptual outputs.[1] The first stage he calls "form perception." This can occur without recognition of the stimulus. The perceptual output of form perception characterizes the stimulus as 'round', 'elongated', or the like. Other stages involve the accessing of memories that lead to further perceptual descriptions. (For example, the stimulus is seen as a dog.) However, Rock emphasizes that both form perception and higher-order perceptual stages involve *descriptions*, though descriptions of different sorts. Even form perception is the description of an external stimulus, description of the stimulus as having a certain shape, organization, orientation, and the like.

A popular approach to perception, at least in the 1960s and 1970s, has been *feature analysis*. Although current writers question its adequacy,[2] it will be convenient to conduct my discussion in terms of this approach. According to the model, stimuli are thought of as combinations of elemental features. Features for the printed English alphabet, for example, might consist of horizontal lines, vertical lines, lines at approximately 45-degree angles, and curves. Thus, the capital letter *A* can be seen as consisting of two lines at 45-degree angles and a horizontal line. The pattern for *A* consists of these lines plus a specification of how they should be combined.

There is physiological evidence that the nervous system 'extracts' such features as horizontal lines;[3] and there is behavioral evidence for the existence of features as components in pattern recognition. For instance, where

letters have many features in common—as with *C* and *G*—evidence suggests that subjects are particularly prone to confuse them.[4] However, even
though our perceptual system may extract features, what we perceive are
patterns composed from these features. The feature-extraction and feature-
combination processes underlying pattern recognition are not available to
conscious awareness. What we are aware of are the patterns.[5]

The processing described above is referred to as *bottom-up*, because information flows from little perceptual pieces to larger units built from
them. Bottom-up processing is assumed to be operative in recognizing
words out of letters, sentences out of words, and so on. In addition to bottom-up processing, there is considerable evidence for *top-down* processing,
in which higher-level beliefs, or background beliefs, influence the interpretation of low-level perceptual units. Psychologists have particularly shown
that (knowledge of) a pattern's *context* influences how one perceives that
pattern.

Consider the example in Figure 9.1. We perceive this stimulus as *THE
CAT*, interpreting the middle letters of the words as *H* and *A* respectively.
But in fact the *H* and the *A* are identical stimuli. Presumably, these identical stimuli are interpreted differently because of our knowledge (or beliefs)
about adjacent letters, and our knowledge (or beliefs) about which letter sequences are most likely to be presented. These are pieces of 'higher-level'
knowledge.

Dramatic evidence for the role of context involves speech perception,
specifically, the *phoneme-restoration effect*. R. M. Warren had subjects listen to the sentence, *The state governors met with their respective legislatures
convening in the capital city*, with 120 milliseconds of pure tone replacing
the middle *s* in *legislatures*. Only one in twenty subjects reported hearing
the pure tone, and that subject was not able to locate it correctly.[6]

In this example context causes subjects to hear what *is not* there. But
there are plenty of cases in which context facilitates *correct* identification.
G. A. Miller and S. Isard presented sentences to subjects in noise; subjects
were to listen to the sentences and report them back.[7] Some sentences were
normal; others were semantically anomalous, though grammatical; and still
others were ungrammatical. Successful identification was clearly best for
the normal sentences, second-best for grammatical but anomalous sentences, and worst for ungrammatical sentences. Subjects obviously improved their speech perception both through the use of meaning constraints

Figure 9.1

and grammatical constraints. That is, they were able to use their background knowledge about meaning and grammar to facilitate correct identification.

Cognitive psychologists generally believe that perception uses a mixture of bottom-up and top-down processing. The occurrence of top-down processing is the basis for the widely made claim that perception is 'intelligent'. All one's knowledge about the world—or a lot of it, at any rate—can aid the construction of a percept.

One dissenting voice is that of Jerry Fodor.[8] Fodor defends the thesis that so-called input systems—including perceptual systems—are *modular*, and one significant feature of these modules is that they are "informationally encapsulated." This means that pieces of information represented elsewhere in the organism are not available for use by such systems. Obviously, the thesis of informational encapsulation conflicts with the claims of many proponents of top-down processing.

However, Fodor's statements of his position make it less radical than it initially appears, as is clear from this passage:

> The claim that input systems are informationally encapsulated is equivalent to the claim that the data that can bear on the confirmation of perceptual hypotheses includes, in the general case, *considerably less* than the organism may know. That is, the confirmation function for input systems does not have access to *all* of the information that the organism internally represents.[9]

Fodor does not deny, then, that *some* top-down processing takes place. Rather, he wishes to register three points. First, he argues that some information which the organism represents—in the 'central' systems—cannot feed back on perception. That is, this information cannot influence the construction of a percept. In a Müller-Lyer illusion, one line looks longer even when we know that the two lines are equal in length. What we know apparently does not (in Zenon Pylyshyn's terminology)[10] cognitively "penetrate" the perceptual process. Second, Fodor disputes the interpretations of some of the experiments standardly cited in support of top-down processing. There is a question, for example, of whether subjects are really reporting how things look or sound, rather than, say, guessing. Third, Fodor claims that where there is top-down information flow, it occurs within the perceptual module. The input system cannot access outside information, but it can deploy *internal* high-level information to help construct a percept.

It seems hard to deny that memory information influences perception. The most striking cases are with fragmented or incoherent figures, for example, pictures that initially appear to be an assortment of dots, globs, and unrelated lines. Once we succeed (perhaps with the help of a hint) in identifying such a figure as a particular object or group of objects, such as a dal-

matian or a rider on horseback, we have no difficulty seeing the figure in the
same way on subsequent occasions. A memory-schema obviously shapes
later perceptual acts.[11] Of course, it needn't be that *all* knowledge lodged in
memory affects perception.[12] But at least memory traces of previously *perceived* figures seem to do so.

This is not the place to try to settle this delicate issue. It suffices for my
purposes to register the widespread acceptance of at least *some* top-down
processing in perception, which even Fodor accepts. Let me now begin to
explore some possible epistemological morals of this kind of psychological
material.

9.3. Reliability, Speed, and Power in Perception

The main question I want to raise in this section is whether top-down processing heightens or lowers the reliability of perception. First, however, I
pause to consider a different question about top-down processing, which
has received lively discussion in the epistemological arena. This concerns
the possibility of 'objective', or 'neutral', theory choice in science.

Epistemologists have not been slow to draw conclusions from the apparent influence on perception of background knowledge, theories, and expectations. The most prominent and extreme example, perhaps, is Thomas
Kuhn. Appealing to Gestalt and New Look psychology, Kuhn has con-
tended that scientists with different theoretical "paradigms" *see* things differently. Hence there is no independent way to settle disputes among
holders of competing paradigms.[13]

The tenability of this significant epistemological thesis obviously hinges
on facts of perception. It is therefore important to stress that several considerations render the thesis dubious. First, as indicated in section 9.2, not *all*
theories and background beliefs are capable of shaping perception. In addition to the Müller-Lyer illusion, there is the familiar stick-in-the-water case.
Even when a person knows that a particular stick is straight, it still looks
bent when immersed in water. His background theoretical beliefs do not
penetrate his perceptual processing so as to make the stick look straight.[14]

Second, even if there is a tendency to interpret what one sees in terms of
background theories, this interpretation is arguably a *post-perceptual* phenomenon, a nonperceptual belief. If so, the percept itself may be a non-the-
ory-laden component of cognition. If that is right, there is a theory-free
element in the cognitive system to which appeal can be made in trying to
settle theoretical disputes.

Third, even if some percepts are theory-laden, it may be possible to reduce and even eliminate theory-ladenness. Many psychological experiments
involving top-down processing feature very brief exposure times, or large
quantities of 'noise'. Perhaps context and prior expectations predominate

over low-level determinants *only* when exposure times are brief, or when there is a lot of noise, so that no perceptual conclusion can be reached by bottom-up processing alone. Given more time and/or less noise, bottom-up processing may predominate. For example, when one looks leisurely and carefully at the stimulus in Figure 9.1, one sees clearly that the second letters of each word are identical.

It is possible, then, that even if theory-ladenness sometimes occurs, it can be excluded *in scientific contexts* by appropriate experimental designs. In the case of scientific observation, there is (in general) no bar to ample observation time and noise reduction. Furthermore, the context of observation can often be manipulated, so the impact of context can be minimized or eliminated.

Finally, even when a percept is affected by categories stored in memory, it is normally possible to switch back to a prerecognition stance: to see the form independently of the familiar category. For example, even if one normally sees a drawing of a cube as a cube, with appropriate perspective, it is also *possible* to see it in a prerecognition, two-dimensional mode, namely, as a square and two parallelograms joined together at their edges, as suggested in Figure 9.2. This again illustrates how perception is capable of releasing itself from the influence of theory.

I now turn to the more central issue of this section: the impact of top-down processing on the reliability of perception. Primary epistemology is concerned with this point for the following reason. Let us assume that perceptual processes can occur with variable amounts of top-down processing, ranging from none at all to substantial amounts. If there is a substantial difference in reliability among these different processes, this could well have an impact on approved systems of J-rules. Suppose, for example, that heavily top-down perceptual processes—those using large amounts of contextual information—are much less reliable than purely bottom-up processes. Then perhaps no rules permitting these top-down processes would be included in any right system of J-rules.

We have already encountered reasons for being suspicious of top-down processing. In the phoneme-restoration effect, for example, subjects hear

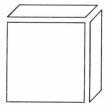

Figure 9.2

legislatures even though the sound corresponding to the first *s* has not actually occurred. Only some nonspeech sound, such as a pure tone, has occurred. Clearly, reliance on context *can* breed error. It does not follow, however, that top-down processing *generally* promotes error. On the contrary, the contexts used by speech perceivers may generally be reliable indicators of the target phonemes, and hence may generally foster reliability.

Some further experiments make this point clear. One important line of research on top-down effects comes from experiments on letter identification, especially experiments by G. Reicher[15] and D. D. Wheeler.[16] In these experiments subjects were given a very brief presentation of either a letter (such as *D*) or a word (such as *WORD*). Immediately afterward they were given a pair of alternatives and instructed to report which they had seen. If they had been shown *D*, subjects might be presented with *D* or *K* as alternatives. If they had been shown *WORD*, they might be shown *WORD* or *WORK* as alternatives. The two word choices, of course, differ only in the *D* and *K* letter. Results of the experiments showed that subjects were about 10 percent more accurate in the word condition. They more accurately discriminated between *D* and *K* in the context of a word than as letters alone, even though they had to process more letters in the word context.

Similar effects have been obtained at the multiword level. In an experiment by E. Tulving, G. Mandler, and R. Baumal, for example, subjects were given varying amounts of context before being shown a target word in a brief exposure.[17] The greater the number of context words preceding the critical word, the higher the percentage of correct identifications.

As these experiments clearly indicate, top-down processing can *increase* reliability, at least for some kinds of tasks. It is noteworthy, indeed, that the initial example of *legislatures*, in which top-down processing leads to perceptual error, was a deliberately contrived case (like all experimental cases). One might well speculate that in more ecologically natural settings, top-down processing does not often produce such errors. At present, then, we have no reason to think that top-down processing per se is a negative characteristic of perception, at least from the vantage point of reliability and justifiedness.

It is worth elaborating this point in a slightly different way. In the literature on perception it is common to distinguish *realist* and *constructivist* theories of perception. Roughly, constructivism holds that the mind adds things to the incoming stimulus in the course of producing a percept, whereas realism tends to deny such activity. For my purposes, the label 'realist theory' is likely to be misleading. So let me substitute a preferable phrase suggested by Rock: *stimulus theory*.[18] On Rock's characterization stimulus theories hold that nothing more is necessary by way of explanation of perception than the relevant stimulus. Such theories would of course allow that various processes transduce the physical stimulus, encode it neurally, and transmit it deeper into the brain. But as long as these processes are "perfectly correlated" with the sensory input, what goes on internally is a "direct function" of the incoming stimulus, and can therefore be ignored by perceptual psychology. The most promising forms of stimulus theory would stress, however, that proper identification of the effective stimulus is a subtle matter. The stimulus for perceived size need not be the size of the object's visual angle subtended at the eye: it could be the relationship (the ratio) of the visual angle of the object to that of other neighboring objects. This emphasis on higher-order features of the stimulus derives from the work of J. J. Gibson, the most prominent perceptual realist, or in my terminology, stimulus theorist.[19]

Contrasting with the stimulus theory are the various sorts of constructivist theories. As indicated, the common ground of such theories is that some internal constructive process occurs that mediates between the incoming stimulus and the percept; something gets added to the stimulus.

We might say, very roughly, that constructivist theories tend to postulate top-down processing, whereas stimulus theories postulate purely bottom-up processing. Furthermore, the contrast between constructivist and stimulus theories seems to invite conclusions about reliability. If the perceptual processes add things to the stimulus during perceptual processing, isn't this likely to *distort* the perceptual output? Won't there be a tendency for the percept to get things wrong? Conversely, if stimulus theories are correct, doesn't this bode well for the accuracy of perceptual processes? Indeed, this prospect of accuracy, or truth, is already intimated by the very term 'realist' (which is why I prefer to avoid it).

However, these conclusions are completely unwarranted. As the experiments I have cited indicate, the deployment of information obtained from sources other than the target stimulus need not be distorting. On the contrary, proper use of accurate contextual information can enhance reliability. Furthermore, real-world regularities may have been incorporated into perceptual systems in the course of evolution. So if, as constructivism often suggests, perceptual systems automatically add such information in the course of processing—or reveal innate preferences for certain kinds of answers or solutions to perceptual questions—this need not be detrimental to reliability.

Until now my discussion has been restricted to the standard of reliability. But other standards of appraisal should also be explored. Let me turn first to the standard of speed (or, rather, the combination of reliability and speed). The relevant literature is readily interpreted as demonstrating the contribution of top-down processing to increases in speed, the ability to make correct perceptual judgments in less time. In the Tulving, Mandler, and Baumal study, for example, subjects were shown a target word, such as *disorder*, for varying brief exposure times. In one condition this word was preceded by no context at all; in another it was preceded by eight words of context, for example, *The huge slum was filled with dirt and.* For an exposure time of 40 milliseconds, the percent of correct identifications with no context was about 15 percent, whereas the percent of correct identifications with the context was about 50 percent. Clearly, use of context facilitated accurate beliefs when speed was critical.[20]

This certainly seems to show that perceptual systems gain speed by using auxiliary information. But, interestingly, Fodor argues that speed is acquired by perceptual systems' being designed to ignore lots of the facts, by their informational *encapsulation*.[21] The argument runs as follows. If perceptual systems were allowed access to *all* information possessed by the organism, and they tried to search out all relevant information in long-term memory before making a perceptual 'decision', speed would be greatly reduced. So the very unavailability of auxiliary information fosters speed, according to Fodor.

Although there appears to be a conflict in these contentions, they are in fact reconcilable. Fodor is assuming that if information were available from central systems, the accessing of this information would have to be very slow. If this were right, then access to all information in central-system memory would indeed sacrifice speed. But it is not clear that accessing of information from central systems is so slow. Moreover, I have conceded (see note 20) that the information actually used in top-down processing of linguistic stimuli may not be in the central system, and hence can be very fast on anybody's view.

Since Fodor makes so much of speed as one of several defining characteristics of input systems, we should pause to question the idea that perceptual systems always work faster than central systems. Perceptual systems, like central systems, sometimes take their time in arriving at a final conclusion. Consider Rock's experimental work in which an observer is placed inside a large, opaque, rotating drum.[22] After a period, the drum appears to the observer to stop turning and he experiences *himself* as rotating instead (in the opposite direction). There is generally a transitional period in which the drum appears to be slowing down and the observer experiences himself as beginning to turn slowly. Thus, the perceptual system ultimately 'prefers' the self-motion interpretation, rather than depicting the surrounding environment as moving. But it takes the system some time to arrive at this interpretation; it does not happen virtually instantaneously.

In any case, everyone apparently agrees that perceptual systems have mechanisms that contribute to their speed. It is also widely acknowledged that speed is a sensible trade-off for (some amount of) reliability, at least for perceptual systems. First, life-threatening objects in the environment need to be identified quickly. Second, many stimuli are potential need satisfiers; they deserve at least preliminary identification. If such identifications were slow, it would take too much time to make them all. From a pragmatic vantage point, then, some accuracy is worth sacrificing for speed.

Now I have not thus far endorsed *pragmatic* values, such as need satisfaction or desire satisfaction, as species of epistemic values. But an appeal to such pragmatic factors certainly makes sense. Although I rejected this pragmatic approach to *justifiedness* (in section 5.4), this does not bar the pragmatic dimension from appearing in a more inclusive survey of epistemic values. It is worth asking, then, how well the perceptual systems perform from this pragmatic standpoint.

In particular, let us consider how perceptual pattern recognition may be influenced by affect: by strong desires and aversions, or other emotions. Suppose that pattern recognition proceeds in terms of matching sense-derived materials to a stored pattern representation. Then make three other assumptions: (1) A match can be effected even if there is only *partial* correspondence with the stored pattern. (2) Greater *activation* of a stored pattern facilitates the matching of that pattern. (3) Patterns with high *affective* value—either positive or negative—receive a higher level of activation.[23]

Given these assumptions, there will be an enhanced tendency to perceive stimuli in high-affect categories. For example, a young child who has a strong desire to see her mother will recognize lots of women in the distance as her mother. The parent in the shower, listening for its infant's cry in the next room, may hear such a cry when in fact it is only the noise of the shower. A gardener fearful of snakes will see a snake when it is really only a piece of garden hose.

These characteristics of a cognitive system probably deserve high marks from a pragmatic standpoint. Pragmatically, erring on the side of false positives is prudent. Nothing much is lost if the child mistakes another woman for her mother, if you mistake your garden hose for a snake, or shower noise for your infant's cry. It is cost-effective to accept some false positives in order to minimize errors of omission.

But processes that apply desire and aversion parameters are not conducive to reliability. Affect-caused increases of activation are not well correlated with the actual probability of a pattern's instantiation. The desirability or danger of a category is a poor indicator of whether an instance of it is actually present. So the class of perceptual identifications that result essentially from this sort of process will have a lower truth ratio than other perceptual identifications. There is reason to suspect, then, that right systems of J-rules would not permit these sorts of processes. In other words, right systems of J-rules might not license perceptual belief formation that includes affect heightening of pattern activation. When perceptual beliefs are formed *in this way*, they may not be justified.

A few words, finally, on the standard of power. The concept of power stressed in Part I, it will be recalled, is a goal-responsive sense of power:

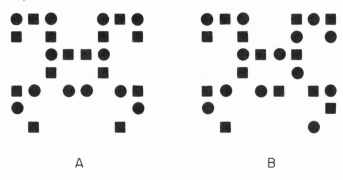

A   B

Figure 9.3

getting answers to the questions you *want* to answer. Now perception is often described as a highly automatic process, which is surely true. But goal-responsiveness is built into perceptual operations in certain ways. One kind of responsiveness to desire or aversion was just mentioned in the preceding paragraphs. But a more pervasive mode of goal-responsiveness involves *attention*. Attention allows perceptual systems to be selective about the information they gather.

Two sorts of attentional mechanisms can be distinguished. First, the organism can orient the sensory organs: it can turn the head, focus the eyes, extend its limbs for touching, and so on. Second, it has internal attentional mechanisms that allow it to filter out certain sensory input in favor of other input. The classical studies on this topic involve dichotic listening experiments, in which subjects wear a set of headphones and receive a message through each. When asked to follow one of the two messages, most subjects have little trouble. They tune out one message and attend to the other, just as a person at a cocktail party tunes out the conversation of the group he's facing and tunes in the conversation of an adjoining group.

Another example of attention, this time in the visual modality, involves the decision to focus on the global shape of a figure as opposed to specific details. Dramatic differences in a percept can result from such differences in focus. Consider Figure 9.3. If one attends only to the global characteristics of the two figures, they will appear virtually identical. But this impression quickly recedes when their parts are examined carefully. Indeed, half of the homologous parts are different. It is clear, then, that perceptual systems can be guided by goals. This speaks well of them in terms of power.

9.4. Foundationalism and Coherentism

In this section I turn to a slightly different application of perceptual psychology to epistemological concerns. A long-standing controversy in epistemology revolves around the *structure* of epistemic justification. The classical contending theories are *foundationalism* and *coherentism*. In Chapter 5 coherentism was rejected as a criterion of J-rule rightness. In so rejecting it, however, I noted its possible tenability at a different theoretical level: the level of substantive J-rule systems. The reliabilist criterion of rightness is neutral about the precise character, or content, of right J-rule systems. As far as reliabilism goes, a system—or its rules—could be either foundationalist or coherentist in character. Assuming that at least one right J-rule system is feasible for human beings, what the rules in such a system are depends on psychological facts. I want to examine this issue now in connection with perception. Perception is relevant because perceptual beliefs comprise one class of candidates for 'foundational', or 'basic', beliefs.

I am proposing that the foundationalist-coherentist controversy depends for its resolution on psychological facts, but I do not maintain that it depends on these facts exclusively. Part of the controversy hinges on one's exact conception, or definition, of these doctrines. The terms 'foundationalism' and 'coherentism' have been used for a wide variety of distinct doctrines. Greater terminological precision is therefore needed before the controversy can be resolved. Once a clear choice of terminology is made, however, psychological facts have an important bearing. Certainly this is so if perceptual beliefs are one candidate class of basic beliefs. The viability of their candidacy for justificational 'basicness' depends on the processes that generate such beliefs. This is a matter to be settled by the psychology of perception.

Let us begin with the terminology: What is meant by 'foundationalism' and 'coherentism' (henceforth 'F-ism' and 'C-ism')? These doctrines are commonly formulated as theses about the structure of reasons or evidence. For example, F-ism can be construed as the view that some justified beliefs are directly or immediately justified, that is, not justified in virtue of being supported by other beliefs. And the relation of 'support' may be taken as a relation in which one belief provides reasons or grounds for another.[24]

The reasons or evidence formulations, however, are not congenial to my theory of justifiedness. Within my approach, F-ism and C-ism are best viewed as theses about the contents of right J-rule systems. Before turning to this manner of construing the doctrines, though, let us survey more traditional formulations.

Descartes is the originator of the F-ist idea. He thought that knowledge should be placed on a firm foundation, and he sought to identify the nature of that foundation. Descartes maintained that beliefs can be epistemically firm, or secure, only if they are based on "certain" or "indubitable" foundations. This is often reexpressed as the view that foundational beliefs must be infallible or incorrigible, that is, incapable of being false. This position now has few adherents. If there is a special class of foundational beliefs—so-called basic beliefs—few theorists would hold that they must be incorrigible. The essential requirement for basicness, then, remains to be specified.

Another facet of Descartes's F-ism held that the class of foundational beliefs consists in beliefs about one's own current mental states (or one's own existence—as a purely mental entity). And this aspect of Cartesianism is also unfashionable nowadays. F-ism could allow other kinds of beliefs to be basic, for example, perceptual beliefs about physical objects or events in the environment. Current epistemologists tend to formulate F-ism as a doctrine that is neutral about the specific subject matter of the basic beliefs. I will follow this neutralist mode of formulation.

Even within this core, neutralist conception of F-ism, there are two distinct variants: *strong* F-ism and *weak* F-ism. Strong F-ism says that the justificational status of basic beliefs is wholly independent of the rest of one's doxastic corpus. Basic beliefs are justified no matter what other beliefs the cognizer currently holds. Weak F-ism says that the justificational status of basic beliefs is partly independent of the rest of one's doxastic corpus. There is some nondoxastic source of justificational status, or warrant—but perhaps some doxastic source as well. This characterization would still allow a distinction between basic and nonbasic beliefs, since nonbasic beliefs would get whatever warrant they have *entirely* from other beliefs.[25]

We come now to the formulation of C-ism. One approach to C-ism sees it as the denial of F-ism, another sees it as an autonomous doctrine. Viewed in the first way, C-ism is the doctrine that there are no basic, or foundational, beliefs. But this doctrine admits of different interpretations, given different versions of F-ism. Thus, one version of C-ism is the denial of strong F-ism, another is the denial of weak F-ism. The former doctrine would hold that no beliefs receive their justificational status wholly from nondoxastic factors. The latter would hold that no beliefs receive their justificational status even partly from nondoxastic factors: *all* justificational status derives from relations with the cognizer's other beliefs.

The second approach to C-ism, the autonomous approach, would avoid characterizing the doctrine as merely the denial of F-ism. It might give the following sort of generic formulation:

A belief is justified if and only if it belongs to a coherent system of beliefs of the cognizer.

This leaves at least two questions to be answered: *(a)* what is it for beliefs to 'cohere'? and *(b)* which system of the cognizer's beliefs must cohere in order for a member belief to be justified?

Concerning question *(a)*, answers might take a *negative* or a *positive* form.[26] A negative answer might be: beliefs cohere just in case they are not inconsistent. A positive answer might be: beliefs cohere just in case they mutually support one another.[27] Concerning *(b)*, answers might again be of two sorts: *holistic* and *nonholistic.* Holistic C-ism says that the relevant system for purposes of the coherence theory is the cognizer's *entire doxastic system.* Nonholistic C-ism would admit proper parts of an entire doxastic system.

Under the influence of Quine's holism, many current formulations of C-ism tend to be holistic. But there is a problem with this approach. Suppose that the construal of 'coherence' implies that the lack of inconsistency of the relevant corpus is a necessary, if not sufficient, condition for coherence. Then if one requires holism, coherence of the *entire* doxastic corpus, someone with an inconsistent set of beliefs cannot have *any* justified beliefs. This is strikingly counterintuitive. If some inconsistency has arisen in one corner of your doxastic corpus, it should not disqualify *all* the rest of your beliefs from being justified. So it is doubtful that an optimal formulation of C-ism is one that requires holism. Notice too that C-ism viewed as the denial of F-ism need not involve holism.[28] Clearly, not all varieties of C-ism need be holistic.

Turning now to my own theory of justifiedness, the question is, What is it for a given J-rule system to be F-ist or C-ist in character? Again, the different conceptions of F-ism and C-ism sketched above will dictate different replies. On one conception the critical question is whether any rules in the set of J-rules permit the use of belief-forming processes whose inputs are *wholly nondoxastic.* If so, this set of J-rules would instantiate strong F-ism. If not, it would instantiate C-ism viewed as the denial of strong F-ism.[29]

On an autonomous and *holistic* conception of C-ism, however, the foregoing would not be the critical question. According to holistic C-ism, a set of J-rules will be C-ist only if the rules authorize only holistic processes, processes that take as inputs *all current doxastic states.* In other words, a process must be (in Fodor's terminology) "Quinean," in the sense of being sensitive to the cognizer's entire belief system.[30]

My reliable-process criterion of rightness implies that whether a set of J-rules is right depends on two things: (1) the cognitive processes available to human beings, and (2) their reliability. Whether there are any right *F-ist* J-rule systems, or any right *C-ist* J-rule systems, also depends on these facts. Hence, whether right J-rule systems are F-ist or C-ist in character depends on psychological facts.

Let me apply these points to the area of perceptual processes. It should be recalled, in this context, that I interpret a percept as a belief, a perceptual system's judgment about environmental objects (see section 9.2). Such a belief can be rejected by the central system. This is just what occurs when vision 'says' that the stick immersed in water is bent, and the central system 'says' that it is straight. Admittedly, calling perceptual outputs 'beliefs' diverges from ordinary usage; but it is theoretically fruitful. It makes sense of the intuitively compelling feeling that the central system *disagrees* with the visual system when it judges the stick to be straight. Disagreement is best construed as conflict in belief.

Thinking of percepts as beliefs, we confront the question, Are these beliefs justificationally basic beliefs? This must be investigated by reference to perceptual processes. First, are any of these processes sufficiently reliable to be included in a right set of J-rules? If so, the second question is: What is the nature of these processes? Do they take prior doxastic states as inputs? In particular, do they take *all* prior doxastic states as inputs? Are they sensitive to the entire doxastic corpus?

If perceptual processes take *no* prior doxastic states as inputs, the resulting beliefs would qualify as basic according to both strong and weak F-ism. However, if my analysis of top-down processing is correct, it is unlikely that perceptual processes ignore other doxastic states entirely. Thus, the psychological facts are not congenial to strong F-ism, at least if the candidate class of basic beliefs are perceptual beliefs.

However, several versions of C-ism also fare poorly if such theories of perception are correct. First, *holistic* C-ism cannot be very plausible. As we have seen, it is doubtful that perceptual processes have access to the cognizer's *total* doxastic corpus: it is doubtful that they are Quinean. But if, despite this, perceptual processes are sufficiently reliable to be sanctioned by a right J-rule system, then holistic C-ism is undermined.

Another form of C-ism I defined also holds scant prospects for vindication. C-ism as the denial of weak F-ism says that there is no source of justifiedness *except* other doxastic states. Within my framework this implies that the only processes licensed by right J-rule systems would be processes that take *only doxastic states* as inputs. But surely perceptual processes take some sort of sensory events, or transducer activity, as inputs. And these sorts of inputs presumably are not doxastic. Hence, assuming that some of these perceptual processes are permitted, some licensed processes would contravene the constraints of this version of C-ism.

I need not review all the variants of F-ism and C-ism to sustain my principal conclusion. It should be amply clear how facts of perceptual processing have a direct bearing on the viability of various forms of these doctrines. Thus we see how epistemological conclusions in the area of justifiedness hinge on facts that need to be determined by cognitive science.

chapter 10

Memory

10.1. *Two Kinds of Belief*

Another central component of cognition, and a main source of belief, is memory. Admittedly, to call memory a 'source' of belief is a bit misleading, since memory, when veridical, does not originate belief. But we can think of the matter as follows. Belief is a dated affair. Though you believe a proposition now, there is no guarantee you will believe it later. That depends on memory *power*. (This sense of 'power' is slightly different from that of problem-solving power, a distinction I pursue in subsequent sections.) Similarly, though you believe a proposition now, because you seem to remember it from an earlier time, it does not follow that you did believe it earlier. That depends on the *accuracy* or *reliability* of your memory. So what you believe at any given time, whether correctly or incorrectly, often depends upon memory. Epistemology, then, is rightly concerned with properties of memory, in particular, with the power and reliability of memory. Memory is an important item for epistemology's agenda.

Before proceeding, one matter of terminology should be mentioned. The term 'remember' is often used in a *factive* sense. That is, 'S remembers that p' entails the truth of p; and 'S remembers event E' entails that E really occurred. For present purposes, though, I set aside this factive sense. When I speak of remembering a proposition or event, I do not mean to imply that the recalled proposition is true, or the recalled event actually occurred. 'Memory' will refer, roughly, to *ostensible* memory.

Questions about the power and reliability of human memory will be treated in later sections. First I wish to address another issue to which the psychology of memory is highly germane. This concerns the concept of belief.

One way psychology can impinge on primary epistemology, I have suggested, is by *refining* its descriptive resources. In this chapter I shall illustrate this point by arguing that memory research demands a revision—or enrichment—in the concept of belief. Twentieth-century epistemology has largely rested content with the conceptual tools of ordinary language, including the belief concept. But this concept is really psychologically inadequate. In the first two sections of this chapter, I will identify this inadequacy and suggest how the psychology of memory can improve the situation.

Many recent writers have worried about the *content* aspect of the belief concept, as we saw in Chapter 8. The inadequacy of the belief concept on which I focus here is quite different. There are (at least) two different *kinds* of belief, and failure to distinguish these kinds and heed this distinction systematically undermines the attempt to provide satisfactory and realistic epistemic principles.

In Chapter 9 I proposed a dichotomy between perceptual and nonperceptual beliefs. In this chapter, though, I will ignore perceptual beliefs entirely. The distinction examined here is a further distinction, wholly within the more commonly acknowledged class of beliefs, so-called central-system beliefs.

To believe a proposition at a given time, a person need not think of it, or entertain it, at that time. Five minutes ago you doubtless had a belief about where you were born, but you probably were not ruminating on your birthplace five minutes ago. Yet a person often does entertain beliefs; they occupy attention and get actively invoked in cognitive tasks. These two classes of belief are sometimes noted by philosophers of mind, who use the phrases 'dispositional belief' and 'occurrent belief' to mark the two classes.[1] But cognitive psychology would have us think of these two classes in a slightly different way.

According to the popular 'duplex' theory of memory, the mind has two memories: *long-term* and *short-term* (or *active*) memory. (A third kind of memory, sensory information storage, is ignored here.) Long-term memory (LTM) is a place where information can be stored for very long periods of time, perhaps indefinitely. Information in LTM decays very slowly. Short-term memory (STM), by contrast, has a much faster decay period. Unless refreshed, or rehearsed, information fades fairly rapidly from STM. There is also a big difference in the *amount* of information retainable in LTM as compared with STM. LTM is virtually unlimited in capacity, whereas STM has a very restricted capacity. Furthermore, whereas information lies dormant in LTM and is not capable of influencing cognitive activities, STM is a sort of 'workplace', where various operations and transformations can be performed on data, and new items can be constructed. In order to utilize material stored in LTM, that material must be retrieved and copied into STM. That's what it is to 'think of' something one has previously known or believed.

Although this duplex portrait of memory has been popular for about a decade and a half, experiments during the 1970s have posed difficulties for it, particularly for the notion of STM as a single entity. The properties used to define STM have been split apart, so it is no longer clear which of them (if any) should be taken as constitutive of a short-term store.[2] However, I shall stick with the older model in my arguments. If anything, the new research suggests that belief-state phenomena are even *more* complicated than the older model suggests, an idea that would strengthen my case for making distinctions. For expository purposes, it will be convenient to rest content with the older model. It should be recalled, throughout, that my discussion is only *illustrative* of the potential impact of psychological research. Not all details of contemporary findings need detain us.

John Anderson's recent treatment of memory in *The Architecture of Cognition* departs slightly from the duplex theory.[3] Anderson views active memories not as events occupying a special location, but as activated states of LTM. Activation is something like a light bulb lighting up. Indeed, on Anderson's theory, it is like a light bulb governed by a dimmer switch: activation can take on a continuous range of levels, not just on and off. For present purposes, though, I will confine my attention to on and off states: 'activated' and 'unactivated' states. These can be identified with the two sorts of belief states I spoke of earlier, which I will call activated beliefs—A-beliefs—and unactivated beliefs—U-beliefs.[4]

Two objections might be lodged against the attempt to identify so-called dispositional beliefs with states of LTM. First, it may be claimed, not all states of LTM are belief states. Second, not all dispositional beliefs are states of LTM.

The first objection has three elements. (1) Not all LTM states are belief states because some LTM states are *goal* states. Our long-range goals, or intentions, are stored in LTM; but these are not belief states. (2) Some things may be stored in LTM, but neither as beliefs nor as goals. For example, a sentence may be salted away in LTM because we like the sound of it, or just because it has a sort of staying power in the imagination.[5] This does not mean that we believe the sentence. (3) Some contents stored in LTM are so *weak*—whether through decay, repression, interference, or what have you—that they are no longer retrievable, even with the best of retrieval cues. It is not very plausible to say that these contents are still believed.

Argument (2) is not entirely persuasive. When a sentence is stored, there may always be one or more beliefs associated with it, such as 'I have heard this sentence before', or 'This sentence was uttered on such-and-such an occasion'. However, elements (1) and (3) seem decisive enough. But what do these points establish? Only that *not all* states of LTM are belief states; we may still retain the view that some—presumably many—states of LTM are belief states.

Turn now to the second objection, which claims that not all dispositional beliefs are LTM states. Daniel Dennett, for one, is inclined to say that we have *indefinitely many* beliefs that are not explicitly stored in LTM (or elsewhere). His examples include: "New York is not on the moon, or in Venezuela"; "Salt is not sugar, or green, or oily"; "Tweed coats are not made of salt"; "A grain of salt is smaller than an elephant."[6] These are all propositions a person may never think of, and hence are not stored in LTM. Still, they are things he probably believes.

Personally, I find this claim unconvincing. If a person has never thought whether New York is in Venezuela, then he does not already believe that New York is in Venezuela. If he has never asked himself whether zebras wear codpieces in the wild, then he does not already believe that zebras don't wear codpieces in the wild. He may be disposed to assent to these propositions unhesitatingly, the moment they are queried. But this just shows he has beliefs from which these conclusions would be readily *inferred*. It does not show he already believes each conclusion, prior to the question being raised.

I acknowledge, however, that many philosophers do not share my intuitions. They hold there are non-occurrent beliefs that also are not explicitly represented in LTM.[7] Whether or not they are right is not critical here, however. I can accept the notion of nonexplicitly represented beliefs, as long as we also retain the two categories of explicitly represented beliefs, activated and unactivated beliefs. Since I want to restrict attention to these two categories, I will cheerfully leave the issue of nonexplicitly represented beliefs unresolved.

My main point about the distinction between A-beliefs and U-beliefs concerns *normative* epistemic principles; I will come to this in section 10.2. First let me comment, though, on the *descriptive* importance of this distinction. If the notion of belief is to be even moderately useful for predictive and explanatory purposes, the distinction between A-beliefs and U-beliefs must be observed.

Here is how a failure to observe this distinction can derail a prediction. Suppose Melanie is deciding, one Sunday morning, whether to go to the university library to work. She seldom works there on Sundays, but today she needs to read a certain important article there. Now Melanie knows that the library normally opens at 7:00 A.M. She has also noticed, on many occasions, that the library's Sunday hours are different: it only opens at 1:00 P.M. If she were to recall the latter piece of knowledge, she certainly would not make the trek to the library this morning; it would be a waste of time. Alas, she forgets this piece of information and decides to go there after all. When, upon arrival, she sees the posted hours, she upbraids herself as follows: 'Wasn't that silly of me! I *knew* the library doesn't open on Sundays until 1:00'.

Now suppose we worked with a belief-desire model of human decision that countenanced only one kind each of belief and desire. Within each class the only differences in efficacy would rest on strength. Then such a model would presumably predict that Melanie would decide not to go to the library this morning. After all, her corpus of beliefs and desires include the following:

(B1) The library normally opens at 7:00 A.M.
(B2) Today is Sunday.
(B3) On Sundays the library opens at 1:00 P.M.
(D1) It is most desirable to read a certain article soon, which is only obtainable at the library.
(D2) It is desirable to do a good bit of other work too today.
(D3) It is undesirable to waste time going places that don't allow essential work to be done.

Since Melanie believes today is Sunday, and believes that the library does not open before 1:00 on Sundays, the model should predict that she will decide not to go this morning. This would be a wrong prediction, of course, but one to which such a model seems committed.

Once we draw the distinction between A-beliefs and U-beliefs, and take account of the fact that only A-beliefs are efficacious in decision making, this prediction can be reversed. While the items listed above constitute U-beliefs and U-desires—they are part of Melanie's LTM store—they do not all get activated at the time of decision. At the moment of decision, Melanie fails to retrieve the belief that today is Sunday; or fails to retrieve the belief that the library opens at 1:00 on Sundays. The critical *activated* belief at the time is the belief that the library normally opens at 7:00 A.M. Now if a belief-desire model incorporates the A-belief/U-belief distinction, and if it portrays decisions as governed by A-beliefs only, such a model could correctly predict Melanie's decision to go to the library. Clearly, this would be a better variant of the model.

It is a familiar occurrence that people often do what Melanie does—they fail to *access* part of what they know, and therefore perform silly actions. Failure to distinguish U-beliefs and A-beliefs makes it impossible to account for these occurrences.

Turn now to theoretical inference, where the situation is perfectly analogous. Which inferences a cognizer makes is determined not by his beliefs stored in LTM, but by those that get activated, by his A-beliefs. A person's U-belief corpus is enormous, and only a relatively small portion of it is activated at any one time. Cognizers often fail to make connections between elements in this corpus, even though they are relevant to the theoretical tasks at hand.

For example, at least a decade before Fleming's discovery of penicillin, many microbiologists were aware that molds cause clear spots in bacteria cultures; and they knew such a bare spot indicates no bacterial growth. Yet they did not consider the possibility that molds release an antibacterial agent.[8] They apparently failed to activate these beliefs at a single time, juxtapose them, and then make a natural inference. Similar things occur in everyday life, when a person fails to 'put two and two together' to reach (what seems in hindsight) a natural conclusion. One belief lies dormant while the other is activated, and conversely.

10.2. Memory, Inductive Inference, and Rationality

For predictive and explanatory purposes, the A-belief/U-belief distinction is clearly vital. But what is its significance for normative purposes? Consider the *total evidence principle*, as formulated by Carnap and Hempel, for example.[9] Hempel formulates the requirement as follows: "The credence which it is *rational* to give to a statement at a given time must be determined by the degree of confirmation . . . which the statement possesses on the total evidence *available* at the time."[10] What does it mean for evidence to be 'available'? This might mean that the evidence is out there in the world, waiting to be observed or acquired. But this is not, I think, what Hempel means. A more plausible interpretation is: evidence E is available for person S at time t just in case S *possesses* E at t. What does possession of evidence consist in? Presumably, a person possesses evidence E just in case S *believes* E.

Suppose we ignore the distinction between A-beliefs and U-beliefs. Then belief simpliciter comprehends both species of belief. According to the total evidence principle, then, the rational degree of credence to assign a proposition is a function of its confirmation by *all* evidential beliefs held by the cognizer at the time, including all U-beliefs.

Is this plausible? Reflect first on the case of Melanie, though the issue there is one of rational decision rather than rational credence. Melanie forgets—fails to retrieve—the fact that the library opens at 1:00 on Sundays; and so she makes a fruitless trip. Is this decision irrational? That, I suggest, is a misdiagnosis of the episode. In the example, Melanie calls herself 'silly'. But what, exactly, does this come to, and is it an apt self-criticism? Melanie may surely be charged with thoughtlessness, forgetfulness, or carelessness. But not irrationality. There was nothing at fault in her *reasoning*, at any rate; only a flaw in the information she used to make her decision. An additional item of information should have been—or might have been—included in her active data base. What kind of hitch, then, is responsible for its omission? Surely the omission should not be charged to irrationality. This would confuse two different kinds of breakdown. Once we distinguish A-beliefs and U-beliefs, we can correctly identify the breakdown. Melanie's problem is a failure to *activate* all the LTM-stored facts relevant to her decision. This may be a fault of sorts, but it is not a flaw in reasoning.

Applying this point to credence assignments, consider the penicillin example. Microbiologists prior to Fleming neglected to assign any substantial credence to the hypothesis that molds release an antibacterial agent. This was despite the fact that they knew both *(a)* molds cause bare spots in bacteria cultures, and *(b)* bare spots indicate inhibited bacterial growth. Does this show that they were irrational? Again, this would be a poor diagnosis of the episode. They probably failed to put these facts together because they filed them under different categories in LTM. That molds cause bare spots may have been filed under the category of practical laboratory lore, as information on undesirable contamination; whereas the fact that bare spots indicate inhibited bacterial growth may have been filed under the category of microbiological theory.[11] Their failure to retrieve these facts *jointly* was probably due, therefore, to properties of their memory network; or perhaps to procedures they used—or neglected to use—in searching that network. But it is doubtful that this should be chalked up to a failure of reasoning.

Let us not fuss too much over the words to use in characterizing the breakdown. The more interesting question is why a person fails to retrieve relevant facts from LTM. Of course, this question cannot be separated from the question of why people regularly succeed in retrieving relevant facts. It is only because memory retrieval is normally so powerful and efficient that breakdowns like Melanie's are disappointing. Obviously, the two must be studied together.

To explain what transpires in any particular case, at least three things are relevant: (1) the general properties of LTM, (2) the particular individual's history of encoding units into LTM, and (3) the particular sources of activation (which trigger retrieval processes) present on the occasion in question.

Although there is no unanimity among theorists on the general nature of LTM, there is wide agreement that it is a highly organized body of material. A popular approach depicts LTM as a complex network, containing many, many nodes—each containing some sort of cognitive unit—and a complex array of associative pathways, or links, connecting these nodes. These pathways, or links, are established by environmental stimuli and by the cognizer's own internal processing. The particular history of such stimuli and processing can strengthen or weaken memory traces. In particular, additional presentations of a single environmental stimulus tend to strengthen the trace representing that stimulus. Stronger traces have a higher probability *(ceteris paribus)* of retrieval. Paths, or links, also can have different strengths, which also account for retrieval probability. A recent model along these lines is found in Anderson's *The Architecture of Cognition*. I will follow his version of this kind of theory.

Retrieval takes place by means of a process of spreading activation. When a given cognitive unit is activated, the energy embodied in this activation spreads through the memory network along paths from original source or sources to associated materials. Anderson theorizes that each node has a limited capacity for spreading activation, so as more paths are attached to it, the amount of activation that can be spread down any path is reduced. He also assumes that activation spreads from multiple sources at one time; activation converging on one node from multiple sources will add up.

Let us return to the case of Melanie. Since memory traces can have different strengths, it is plausible that the trace underlying the proposition that the library normally opens at 7:00 is much stronger than the trace underlying the proposition that it opens at 1:00 on Sundays. Melanie often goes early to the library on weekday mornings but seldom goes there on Sundays; nor has she had occasion to rehearse the posted hours, although she has learned them and could reproduce them under some circumstances. It would not be surprising, then, if the latter trace is much weaker than the former. Furthermore, it would not be surprising if the paths between the normal-hours representation and the Sunday-hours representation is not particularly strong. If Melanie has seldom used the library on Sundays, and perhaps never before tried to use it on a Sunday morning, she may have done nothing to strengthen these paths. None of these facts points to any epistemic flaw in Melanie's cognitive conduct.

Is there anything Melanie could—and should—have done at the time of decision to activate the Sunday hours trace? Doubtless, had she directly probed her memory with the question 'When does the library open on Sundays?' this would have activated the answer. But if she was not already taking note of the fact that Sunday is special as far as library hours are concerned, why should she have asked herself that question? In short, although she *could* have done things that would have activated the relevant belief, there is no clear indication that she was epistemically culpable or negligent in this failure. In particular, there is no indication that she was irrational.

Although I have given much attention to this example of behavioral decision, the same points carry over to cases of credal decision. In determining the acceptability of a hypothesis, a cognizer must typically appeal to antecedent beliefs. But these beliefs need to be activated before they can be used in inference.

This point conflicts with the epistemological tenets of certain philosophers, specifically with the view I will call *inferential holism*. Some of Quine's writings hint at such a view, but it is most clearly endorsed by Gilbert Harman:

> We have implicitly supposed that inductive inference is a matter of going from a few premises we already accept to a conclusion one comes to accept . . . But this conception of premises and conclusion in inductive inference is mistaken . . . The suggestion that only a few premises are relevant is wrong, since inductive inference must be assessed with respect to everything one believes . . . Our "premises" are all our antecedent beliefs; our "conclusion" is our total resulting view.[12]

This doctrine of inferential holism, which sees inductive inference as involving *all* our prior beliefs and *all* our resulting beliefs, is psychologically most unrealistic. To be sure, there is a complex state of the cognizer that comprises all his prior beliefs and another complex state that comprises all his beliefs in the next moment of time. It is possible to conceive of inference as a transition from one state to the next. But this departs dramatically from the ordinary conception of inference (as a psychological affair, which is what Harman is discussing). We normally think of inference as a *causal process*, in which the premises are all *causally operative* in producing a new belief (or other doxastic change). Yet it is psychologically impossible for all one's beliefs to be causally operative in any process of inferential transformation. Only activated beliefs are causally operative; and one cannot (simultaneously) activate all of one's beliefs.

Normative principles of inductive inference should not, therefore, require cognizers to utilize all of their belief corpus. Inductive inference should be divided into two parts: *(a)* search of LTM, in the effort to activate, or retrieve, relevant evidence; and *(b)* weighing of the activated evidence. Epistemologists have attended almost exclusively to *(b)*, but *(a)* also needs attention. Specifically, what *cues* are given to memory during the search process, and what is the *duration* of the search process? Normative principles might well be introduced in these areas. Furthermore, there is a third kind of activity, which occurs *prior* to *(a)* and *(b)*, and which heavily influences them. This is *(c)* the *encoding* process, which lays down the pathways through which activation spreads in the memory network.

If a person reflects on an item of information, and tries to connect it to other things he knows, this can establish a richer network of associative connections, which will be operative in subsequent retrieval tasks. In other words, a person can deliberately *integrate* an item of information with either a smaller or wider body of belief. Memory research indicates that deeper integration (sometimes called 'depth of processing') can increase recall of an item. But I am here concerned with the *range* of connected items that can be activated by a given item. The scientist who learns a new fact may either (1) simply file it away, or (2) deliberately trace out its implications (if any) for all sorts of other things he knows. This effortful inquiry will often pay off in later inferences. The pathways established thereby will broaden the range of potentially relevant evidence that can subsequently be activated. By the same token, a scientist who fails to engage in such effortful inquiry will fail to activate relevant evidence on later occasions. This failure may result in negligence because he had *earlier* failed to lay down a sufficiently wide set of memory connections.[13]

I am not prepared to propose specific normative principles in this area. I merely emphasize the *im*plausibility of any principles that ignore the difference between A-beliefs and U-beliefs, or the psychological mechanisms that govern activation.

10.3.   *Elaboration and Reconstruction*

I have been assuming, in the foregoing discussion, that activation of material from LTM is always veridical, that what we retrieve from LTM revives episodes or information that were indeed once encoded there. This assumption is untenable. Memory can certainly yield mistakes. The question is: How pervasive is the unreliability of memory, and what specific mechanisms account for such unreliability?

In speaking of memory unreliability, I am speaking of the production of false A-beliefs, somehow produced through memory mechanisms. It is possible, of course, to acquire false beliefs in the first place, and then retain and retrieve these beliefs accurately. In such cases the falsehoods are not due to memory. I am interested in the ways that error may creep into a doxastic corpus specifically through memory mechanisms.

As elsewhere, though, I am not concerned with just reliability; I am equally concerned with power. Even infallible memory mechanisms would not be very valuable, on the whole, if they generated a mere trickle of recollections. Clearly, powerful memory mechanisms are valuable, even at some sacrifice in reliability. Let us inquire into this mix of traits among human memory mechanisms.

Before proceeding, a word about the term 'power'. In talking of memory power, I am using the term slightly differently than before. At least four different dimensions, or components, seem relevant to the power of a memory system. Although these dimensions are generally relevant to the question-answering sense of 'power'—the ability to retrieve a stored item of information is one way to answer a question—the dimensions are not severally reducible to question-answering power.

Here are the four dimensions of memory power I have in mind: (1) How easy is it to *store* information initially in memory? (According to standard theories, not all information acquired by the mind forms a trace in LTM.) Presumably, the easier material can be stored, the greater the memory's power. (2) How *long* does the memory system retain the information? The longer the storage period, the greater the system's power. (3) How *much* information can be concurrently retained in memory? The greater the quantity, the greater its power. (4) How easy is it to *access* stored materials? More specifically, how many different cues or probes will activate the memory trace? The greater the *access range*, the greater the power. For example, if the only probe that will activate the trace of a given stimulus is a re-presentation of the same stimulus, this is very restricted accessibility (mere 'recognition memory'). It is commonly desirable to activate a trace with other cues or probes, and the more the better.

There are many aspects of human memory mechanisms that bear on reliability and power. One such aspect is 'interference', an oft-cited cause of both inability to recall and errors of recall. But in this section I shall concentrate on two other memory processes that psychologists have investigated: *elaboration* and *reconstruction*.

J. D. Bransford, J. R. Barclay, and J. J. Franks studied the ability of subjects to recognize previously presented sentences, such as *The ants were in the kitchen, The ants ate the sweet jelly, The ants in the kitchen ate the jelly which was on the table,* and *The jelly was sweet.*[14] When subjects were subsequently asked to try to recognize sentences, some of which had been presented and others of which had not, they tended to respond on the basis of how much of the total information a test sentence conveyed. They were more likely to *mis*recognize a nonpresented sentence involving *all* the presented semantic information—for example, *the ants in the kitchen ate the sweet jelly which was on the table*—than a shorter sentence which had in fact been presented. Apparently, subjects encode the sentences in a semantic structure that goes *beyond* the individual sentences actually presented. An interpretation is constructed that elaborates upon the information actually presented.

Another example of this elaborative process occurs in an experiment by R. A. Sulin and D. J. Dooling.[15] One group of subjects read the following passage:

Carol Harris was a problem child from birth. She was wild, stubborn, and violent. By the time Carol turned eight, she was still unmanageable. Her parents were very concerned about her mental health. There was no good institution for her problem in her state. Her parents finally decided to take some action. They hired a private teacher for Carol.

A second group of subjects was given the same passage, except that the name *Helen Keller* was substituted for *Carol Harris.* A week after reading the passage subjects were given a recognition test in which they were presented with a sentence and asked to judge whether it was in the passage. One of the critical sentences was *She was deaf, dumb, and blind.* Only 5 percent of the subjects who read the Carol Harris passage accepted this sentence, but 50 percent of the subjects who read the passage as about Helen Keller thought (mistakenly) they had read this sentence. Apparently, the latter subjects had *elaborated* the story they actually read with facts they previously knew about Helen Keller.

These experiments leave it indeterminate whether construction occurs at the time material is originally encoded into LTM or whether a reconstructive inference occurs at the time of test. Other experiments, however, seem to demonstrate that *both* of these phenomena commonly occur.

An additional experiment on the Carol Harris passage by Dooling and R. E. Christiaansen shows that inferences can be made at the time of test.[16] They had subjects study the passage and told them a week later, just before test, that Carol Harris really was Helen Keller. Subjects still made many errors, accepting such sentences as *She was deaf, dumb, and blind.* These subjects were clearly making an inference at the time of test (or recall).

But elaboration at the time of encoding is also well accepted and documented. T. S. Hyde and J. J. Jenkins had subjects read groups of twenty-four words presented at the rate of 3 seconds per word.[17] One group was asked to check whether each word had an *e* or a *g.* The other group was asked to rate the pleasantness of the words. It is reasonable to assume that the pleasantness rating was a task that required more elaborate processing than the letter verification task. In rating a word for pleasantness, subjects had to think about its meaning, which gave them an opportunity to elaborate on it. For instance, a subject presented with *duck* might think, 'Duck—oh yes, I used to feed the ducks in the park; that was a pleasant time'. Subjects rating for pleasantness showed much higher recall than those with the letter verification task. This was apparently due to elaborative processing.

In the experiments just reviewed elaboration and reconstruction often led to false recall judgments. So elaboration and reconstruction seem to foster *un*reliability. This fact is important not only in abstract, theoretical appraisal of memory mechanisms, but also in practical contexts, where we need to decide whether to trust someone else's memory judgments. Such practical exigencies arise in the courtroom, where decisions appeal in part to the memories of eyewitnesses. The memory mechanisms I have been describing offer opportunities for errors in eyewitness testimony, as Elizabeth Loftus has documented.[18]

One problem in eyewitness testimony is simply the period of retention. R. N. Shepard tested thirty-four clerical workers for recognition of pictures after intervals of two hours, three days, one week, and four months.[19] He found that retention of the picture material dropped from 100 percent correct recognition after two hours to only 57 percent correct after four months. The latter figure essentially represents mere guessing. However, not concerned at the moment with retention intervals, I want to look at the impact of reconstruction and elaboration on recall. Loftus cites relevant work on this topic, including some of her own studies. Specifically, she discusses how *post-event* information—information given after a witnessed event occurred—can distort one's recollection of that event.

An early illustration of this phenomenon was presented by C. Bird.[20] During the course of a routine classroom lecture, the instructor was discussing the results of a series of experiments. A well-meaning but not very thoughtful reporter on the local newspaper printed an account of the lecture riddled with errors. Many students read the newspaper account, and nearly all of these thought it was accurate. The instructor gave an exam at the end of the week and after the usual set of exam questions asked students to indicate whether they had read the press account. Those who had read the article made many more errors on the exam. They remembered the erroneous information from the newspaper, assuming they had learned it from the instructor's original lecture.

In several experiments Loftus and colleagues tested subjects to see whether post-event misinformation would distort their later recollection. In one experiment nearly 200 subjects viewed a series of thirty color slides depicting successive stages in an accident involving a car and a pedestrian.[21] The car was a red Datsun shown traveling along a side street toward an intersection, where there was a stop sign for half of the subjects and a yield sign for the others, and where the accident occurred. Immediately after seeing the slides, the subjects were asked some questions, one of which was critical. For half of the subjects the critical question was, *Did another car pass the red Datsun while it was stopped at the stop sign?* The other half of the subjects were asked the same question with *stop sign* replaced by *yield sign*. For some subjects, the sign mentioned was the one they had actually seen: the question gave them consistent information. For the remaining subjects, the question contained misleading information.

Later a recognition test was administered. Pairs of slides were presented and subjects had to indicate which member of each pair they had seen before. The critical pair was a slide depicting the Datsun stopped at a stop sign and a nearly identical slide depicting it at a yield sign. When the intervening question had contained consistent information, 75 percent of the subjects responded accurately. When the question had contained misleading information, only 41 percent responded accurately. If subjects had been simply guessing, they would have been correct about 50 percent of the time; so the misleading information contained in the question reduced their accuracy below the guessing level.

Apparently, people tend to use post-event information to reconstruct episodes they have observed. Furthermore, they are not always able to disentangle the original sources of their information. So even though they acquire certain information (or misinformation) after the event, they often think it was contained in what they saw.

Is this another piece of evidence for the unreliability of the reconstruction process? Superficially, this is so. But we should proceed cautiously. In Loftus's cases, error is introduced into the subjects' cognitive systems by misleading questions provided by the experimenter. The initial fault, then, does not reside in memory, at least not in the *unreliability* of memory. It is true that the mistakes could be averted if the subjects confidently recalled exactly which sign—a stop sign or a yield sign—they originally saw. If so, they presumably would not be misled by the question, for they would reject what the question presupposes. But failure to recall this accurately is a deficiency in memory power, rather than in memory accuracy. Similarly, any failure to disentangle or isolate the original sources of information could more plausibly be attributed to memory power than to memory accuracy. More precisely, it is a limit on power that, in these special circumstances, is partly responsible for inaccuracy. Still, since the error is introduced by an extramemorial source, it is not clear how badly this reflects on the reconstruction process.

Even if the reconstruction process is deemed inaccurate, and the elaboration process is as well, we should not neglect the fact that the elaboration and reconstruction processes make substantial *positive* contributions toward memory power. Even if these processes have flaws as judged by the reliability standard, they provide substantial trade-offs in power.

One way of explaining this is in terms of the so-called depth of processing principle, developed by F. I. M. Craik and R. L. Lockhart.[22] They and other researchers suggest that more fully elaborated material results in better memory, in my terminology, more powerful memory. Manipulations that increase the 'depth' to which information is processed—roughly, the extent to which the subject processes the material's meaning—result in better memory. The Hyde and Jenkins experiment cited above is one such case. Another demonstration is recounted by S. Bobrow and G. H. Bower.[23] They had subjects try to commit to memory simple subject-verb-object sentences. In condition 1 subjects were provided with sentences written by the experimenters. In condition 2 subjects had to generate a sentence themselves, to connect the subject noun and the object noun. In condition 1 the level of recall was 29 percent; in condition 2, 58 percent. Presumably, in generating their own sentences, subjects had to think more carefully about the meaning of the two nouns and their possible interrelationships. This additional mental effort, or deeper processing, seems to have led to more elaborations concerning the nouns, which apparently produced the dramatic difference in recall level.

To illustrate how elaboration can improve recall, consider this example presented by Anderson.[24] Suppose a subject must commit to memory the following sentence:

1. The doctor hated the lawyer.

A subject presented with this sentence is unlikely to deposit only this structure in LTM. He will probably have other thoughts while studying the sentence, which might also be committed to memory. So, he might store the following propositions in addition:

2. The subject studied this sentence in the psychology laboratory one dreary morning.
3. The lawyer had sued the doctor for malpractice.
4. The malpractice suit was the source of the doctor's hatred.
5. This sentence is unpleasant.

He may have thought of proposition 4 because he had another proposition in memory, namely,

6. Lawyers sue doctors for malpractice.

In storing all the above items in LTM, the subject creates a much more complicated memory structure, which incorporates the elaborations on the original sentence.

How can these elaborations lead to better memory? In two ways. First, they provide additional retrieval routes for recall. Suppose that at the time of test, the subject is given the word *doctor* and asked to retrieve the original sentence. The link from the node representing *doctor* to the target node, representing the sentence *The doctor hated the lawyer,* may be too weak to revive the latter. But because elaborations have led to additional associative links, recall may still be possible. From the prompt *doctor,* the subject might recall the proposition that the lawyer sued the doctor for malpractice. And from here the subject might be able to recall the target node. Thus, an alternative retrieval route may succeed if the more direct one fails.

A second way in which elaboration aids memory is that it can enable someone to infer the target information. For example, the subject who cannot immediately recall the target sentence from the prompt *doctor* might think as follows:

I cannot remember the target sentence but I can remember conjecturing that it was caused by the lawyer suing the doctor for malpractice and I can remember it was a sentence with a negative tone.

From this he might infer that the target sentence was *The doctor hated the lawyer.* L. M. Reder and R. J. Spiro have argued that in real life a great deal of inference is involved in recall.[25] Talk of retrieval or activation may be somewhat misleading, then, if the so-called remembered beliefs are heavily influenced by inferential reconstruction.

In looking for epistemological consequences, we should not rush to the conclusion that elaboration and reconstruction yield unjustified beliefs. Whether the processes would be licensed by a right J-rule system depends on their contribution to such a system's truth ratio. If both elaboration and reconstruction are well constrained by prior information in LTM, if the latter information is true, and if the inferential processes are suitable, the contribution to the rule system's truth ratio may well be acceptable. (Of course, this will also depend on the chosen degree of reliability needed for justifiedness.)

Notice too that there are all sorts of amounts and styles of elaboration and reconstruction that could be discriminated. Some of these amounts and styles would have a more deleterious effect on truth ratios than others. A right J-rule system might license processes incorporating some amounts and styles of elaboration and reconstruction, but not others.

The processes of elaboration and reconstruction exemplify a situation that we have encountered before and will encounter again: a trade-off between reliability and power. It is clear that these processes (can) purchase increases in memory power, though perhaps at some cost in reliability. Our native, uncritical procedures seem content with the purchase price, and nothing in my principles of epistemological appraisal dispute its appropriateness.

Actually, though, it is not clear that there is always a net trade-off, that power and reliability always conflict. Although I often speak of acquiring power at the cost of reliability, power can also *foster* reliability in a J-rule system. At least a case for this suggestion is readily made, in connection with inductive inference. First, the more experiences a person correctly recalls, the larger the number of true beliefs available as premises for inductive inference. Second, the larger the number of true premises employed in inductive inference (that is, the greater the total evidence that gets used), the greater the likelihood of arriving at true conclusions. So there are ways in which recall power can promote the overall reliability of a cognitive system, or the reliability of a set of J-rules. To some degree, then, power supports reliability, and does not conflict with it.

10.4. Belief Perseverance

In this section I examine mechanisms of belief 'perseverance': mechanisms that retain beliefs even after supporting evidence has been totally undermined. Certain psychologists have not only studied perseverance empirically, but evaluated it epistemologically. I explore their empirical findings and raise questions about their epistemic evaluation. On the surface perseverance has little to do with memory. But perseverance may be largely the result of the process of elaboration, discussed in the previous section. Hence, epistemic evaluation of perseverance must go hand in hand with evaluation of elaboration.

Perseverance has been studied mainly by Lee Ross and his colleagues. I draw extensively on the discussion of the phenomenon in his and Richard Nisbett's *Human Inference: Strategies and Shortcomings of Social Judgment*.[26] In an early study by Ross, M. R. Lepper and H. Hubbard subjects were given the task of distinguishing authentic from inauthentic suicide notes.[27] As they worked, they were provided with false feedback after each trial. This feedback indicated that, overall, they had performed at close to an average level, at a level much above average (success condition), or at a level much below average (failure condition). This feedback was simply manipulated by the experimenters, and had nothing to do with a subject's actual performance. Subjects were later thoroughly debriefed concerning the random nature of their feedback. They were told that their feedback had been false, and were shown the experimenter's instruction sheet assigning them to the success, failure, or average performance condition. Subsequent to this debriefing, subjects were asked to fill out a postexperimental questionnaire on which they had to estimate their actual performance at the task, to predict their probable success on related future tasks, and to rate their ability both at the suicide discrimination task and at other related tasks involving social sensitivity.

Nisbett and Ross report that this first experiment revealed a "remarkable degree" of postdebriefing perseverance. Even after debriefing, subjects who had initially been assigned to the success condition continued to rate their performance and abilities far more favorably than did subjects whose initial feedback had indicated average performance, while subjects initially assigned to the failure condition showed the opposite pattern of results.

To replicate this perseverance phenomenon, a second experiment was undertaken, which included both actor subjects and observer subjects (viewing the events from behind a one-way mirror). The observer subjects witnessed the initial (false) feedback presentations to the actors and the later debriefings given by the experimenter. They were later asked to rate the actors' success and ability. Also, two additional experimental conditions were incorporated, yielding three in all. One group of subjects was given no debriefings. A second group of subjects was given outcome debriefings, the same sort of debriefings as in the first experiment. A third group of subjects was given process debriefings, which not only told them about the random assignment and false feedback, but provided an extensive discussion of the perseverance phenomenon, the processes that might contribute to it, and the potential personal relevance and costs of erroneous impression perseverance.

Results from this experiment are shown in Figure 10.1. Among the subjects who were given outcome debriefings, there was still substantial perseverance of the initial impressions for both actors and observers. But much of the initial impression was changed as a result of the debriefings. When subjects were given process debriefings, the initial impressions were eliminated (or overridden) much more completely, except for observer subjects. Ross and colleagues have done similar experiments involving other tasks, and these too show the perseverance effect to some degree or other.[28]

Why does perseverance occur, when it does? And how should the phenomenon be evaluated epistemically? These two questions are intertwined, on my approach to epistemic evaluation, because the evaluation of a belief state is a function of the *processes* that generate it.

Nisbett and Ross consider two kinds of possible explanations of the perseverance phenomenon. The first, emotional commitment to one's beliefs,

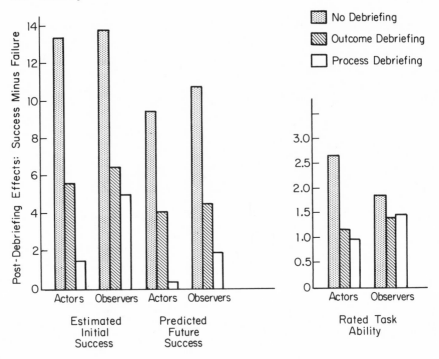

Figure 10.1

they find unsatisfactory, preferring more purely information-processing explanations. The second explanation, which they endorse, is that subjects search for additional information in memory to support the initial (false) feedback, and such information, once found, continues to support the initial impression even after the feedback is discredited.

Another possible explanation not considered by Nisbett and Ross is that the subjects do not fully trust the experimenter's debriefing. Such distrust would be reasonable. After all, the experimenter admits he has lied to them already. Why not entertain the possibility that the debriefing is itself a deception? I will not pursue this suggestion further, however.

Let us return to Nisbett and Ross's explanatory hypothesis, which they amplify as follows. Consider a hypothetical subject Jane, who receives feedback suggesting that she is uncannily successful at the suicide note discrimination task. She has no trouble generating additional 'evidence' that seems consistent with her apparent social sensitivity. Her reasonably good performance in her abnormal psychology course, her ability to make new friends easily, and her increasing sense of confidence and assurance as she progressed in the suicide note task, all might be seen as further evidence of such powers. She can also easily find causal explanations of her performance: her familiarity with the writings of a famous novelist who recently committed suicide, or her part-time job as a paramedical assistant, or her open relationship with her parents all might explain her high level of ability at a task requiring social sensitivity. Once these additional facts or explanations are generated, they are found convincing, and they remain to support her assessment of her ability even after she receives a debriefing from the experimenter.

Although there is no direct support for this account of the perseverance phenomenon, I agree that it is quite plausible. In the remainder of my discussion I will assume that this sort of process underlies the phenomenon. Notice, though, that this process can be redescribed as an instance of *elaboration*. Jane is finding other things in memory with which her apparent good performance on the suicide note task coheres. She is finding a meaning in this good performance by linking it up to other (putative) facts in her life or traits she possesses.

Let us now turn to the normative appropriateness of this sort of process. Nisbett and Ross are highly critical of it, seeing it as an instance of two habits, or propensities, which they deem normatively wrong. First, they see it as an instance of *confirmation bias*. They cite a rich research literature "that shows the operation of a variety of encoding and decoding biases that favor confirmation of prior hypotheses or beliefs over disconfirmation . . . People tend to recognize the *relevance* of confirming cases more readily than that of disconfirming ones, and therefore tend to *search for* such cases in evaluating their hypotheses."[29] They cite experiments by P. C. Wason and P. N. Johnson-Laird, M. Snyder and W. B. Swann, and Snyder and M. Cantor, in support of this claim.[30]

Second, they see the hypothetical process as an instance of searching for *causal explanations*, which are too readily generated and accepted even when the evidence for them is skimpy or nonexistent. Such explanations have a marked effect, they say, even when later undermined. They cite an experiment by L. Ross, M. R. Lepper, F. Strack and J. L. Steinmetz in which subjects were asked to place themselves in the position of a clinical psychologist trying to understand and predict a patient's behavior.[31] Subjects were given an authentic clinical case history, and some were asked to use this case history to explain a critical event in the patient's life, whereas other subjects were not asked to give any such explanation. After the explanation task subjects were informed that the events they had been asked to explain were purely hypothetical, and that there was no available information about the later life of the patient. Then subjects were asked to assess the likelihood of a number of possible events in the patient's later life, including the critical events. The subjects' likelihood estimates revealed a marked effect of the explanation task. Subjects who had explained an event rated it as more probable (even after debriefing) than subjects who had not explained it.

We should not accept Nisbett and Ross's characterizations of people's habits too uncritically. Concerning confirmation bias, for example, they themselves admit that some research indicates that confirming instances are not always more 'available' to a theory holder than disconfirming ones. As R. Hastie and P. A. Kumar noted, surprising or incongruent events may be attended to and stored in memory more often than expected or hypothesis-confirming events.[32] Concerning causal explanation, it is not clear just *how* readily people manufacture causal explanations. That they readily invent causal explanations when given such a task by an experimenter hardly shows that they always invent them spontaneously, even on the slimmest of evidence. Clearly, much empirical work remains to be done on these matters.

Turning to the normative question, suppose that people regularly search for other material in memory that coheres with, or even explains, some newly acquired belief. Is this good or bad? An epistemologist might disagree with Nisbett and Ross's negative assessment on the grounds that search for coherence is a *desirable* epistemic trait, and that the search for possible causal explanations is one piece in such a coherence search. Such searches are a legitimate—perhaps even a required—phase of belief formation. Unless a cognizer checks for coherence, his chances of true belief formation are greatly reduced. (For some further discussion of this point, see Chapter 15.)

Of course, we should distinguish between *attempts* to assess coherence and the specific procedures used for assessing coherence. Perhaps Nisbett and Ross mean to be critical of the specific procedures people use, not their proclivity to investigate the question of coherence. But three responses should be made here. First, since many debriefed subjects *do not* suffer from belief perseverance, as the studies show, these subjects may be using perfectly acceptable procedures (even by Nisbett and Ross's standards). Second, among the subjects who do persist with their initial belief, despite debriefing, their coherence-determining procedures may be all right. Maybe they legitimately found reasons to bolster this belief (even if the belief is false). Third, we should be quite prepared to learn that subjects differ from one another in their coherence-determining procedures; that some of them fail to conform to any right system of J-rules whereas others do so conform. After all, subjects differed in their post-debriefing test responses, so they should not all be lumped together. Nisbett and Ross have a tendency to make blanket statements about human traits, without full allowance for observed variation in subject responses.

However, there is a further point, specially connected to memory, that I have yet to stress. I remarked above that the tendency to look for antecedent beliefs which cohere with a new item of information may be classified as elaboration: the cognizer seeks to connect the new item with other things previously stored in memory. In the previous section we saw that elaboration serves to *strengthen* memory, that is, to improve recall at later junctures. This increase in memory power is surely an epistemically desirable outcome. It should be weighed as one factor in the overall normative assessment of the process in question. If it is significant enough, it may render the process, on balance, normatively acceptable.

There are several complications that need mentioning here. First, I have not offered any principles for overall normative assessment. I have only offered a criterion of justifiedness, and this does not incorporate the element of power. (Arguably it should; but for now let's put that aside.) However, we also saw at the end of section 10.3 that power can positively contribute toward reliability. So elaboration may enhance reliability *via* its enhancement of power, and this could bolster its claim for admissibility by a right system of J-rules. Nisbett and Ross, although they speak frequently of "human judgmental failings" and even "perversity," offer no principles for normative evaluations.[33] Perhaps they would not count power as a relevant factor at all, for normative purposes. And perhaps they would not accept the truth-ratio consequentialism that I have proposed. This just underlines the need for general criteria of epistemic evaluation.

Suppose we focus, though, on my own criterion of justifiedness. It is a very delicate matter to decide just which processes, among those presently at issue, should be approved by a system of J-rules. Since it is always possible that a newly acquired belief is false, how much *should* such beliefs be strengthened in memory? How much should they be combined with other material in memory to generate new beliefs? In the case of Jane, should the subject combine the (apparent) fact that she has performed well on a certain task with other facts in memory to make inferences about her general traits (for example, her social sensitivity)? When focusing on these experimental cases, where it is a datum—to the reader!—that the newly acquired belief is false, it is all too easy to say that the belief should not have been combined with others to generate further inferences. We are inclined to say this because *we* know that the belief is false. But a J-rule system needs to authorize *general* processes. A general process of finding coherent beliefs and making new inferences may have a high truth ratio, as long as the class of input beliefs has a high enough truth ratio. In short, a right J-rule system might well sanction just what many (even most) of the subjects in Ross's experiments do. Many of those subjects arrive at errors; but these errors are only a tiny sample of the set of cases that determine the relevant truth ratio.

I have been discussing the normative status of belief perseverance in terms of the (hypothetical) processes that are actually at work. But perhaps this is the wrong angle. Instead of focusing on what subjects *do* that they shouldn't, perhaps we should focus on what subjects *fail* to do that they should.

At time t_1, Jane forms a belief (based on feedback) about her task performance; call this p. At time t_2, she infers from p (plus other beliefs that p activates) something about her general ability in a certain domain; call this q. At time t_3, she is debriefed: she is told that p is really false, that her performance at the task did not have the property she was led to believe. What should she do now? There is an initial feeling that she should go back and revise both her belief in p and her belief in q. In section 10.5 I will raise queries about what such revision could consist in. The question to be addressed now is: Is Jane obliged to go back in order to revise her belief in p and her belief in q?

When Jane is debriefed, this activates her belief in p, and it is plausible to hold that this belief should be revised. But the debriefing may not activate her belief in q, or her beliefs in any other propositions that are partly traceable to her belief in p. So it may not occur to her to revise any of these other beliefs. Is this a culpable omission? Does her failure to backtrack and recover those other beliefs, and then revise them, render those beliefs unjustified?[34]

Notice that my basic theory of justifiedness does not imply that merely because Jane's belief in q at t_2 is justified, it is also justified at t_3. My framework does not guarantee automatic continuity in justifiedness, even for a belief that remains inert in LTM. Possibly, a right system of J-rules would require a cognizer to backtrack *whenever* new beliefs are acquired, to make selected revisions in antecedently entrenched beliefs. If these old beliefs are retained, contrary to this requirement, they become unjustified.

But would a right rule system really make such a requirement? It should first be stressed that a rule system cannot simply say: 'Revise all U-beliefs that have been undermined by new evidence'. For this injunction does not specify any *basic cognitive processes*, and only such processes are allowed in the rules. What a rule may do is instruct the cognizer to *search* LTM for old beliefs that could be undermined by the new evidence, or perhaps to search LTM for old beliefs that were originally generated by beliefs one has now abandoned. The rule could then say that any beliefs so identified should be abandoned.

A rule formulated in one of these ways would certainly be admissible. But one could conform with such a rule and not succeed in weeding out all (or even many) of the beliefs that are the proper targets of the search. First, even if one searches for old beliefs under the heading 'beliefs that the new evidence undermines', the search might not yield much. Second, if one searches under the heading 'beliefs that originated from beliefs now abandoned', then again the search might yield sparse results. For then one must be guided by *beliefs* about the origins of one's beliefs; yet one might not keep track of the origins very well, or might not activate these beliefs. (Recall my discussion to this effect in section 10.3.) There might be any number of beliefs satisfying this description that one does not identify as such and therefore does not identify as a belief that needs to be abandoned. In short, a person could abide by rules of this sort, fail to abandon some of the indirectly undermined beliefs, yet not be justificationally remiss.

Although not uncongenial, this is a result that may seem counterintuitive until one considers the feasibilities of available cognitive operations. When one considers feasibilities, it is an open question whether a right rule system would *oblige* a cognizer *continually* to search for old beliefs in LTM that might be weeded out in light of new evidence. Since one acquires massive quantities of new evidence (new perceptual beliefs) at every waking moment, conformity to such a requirement would be very costly in cognitive resources; so costly that it could well reduce the overall truth ratio of one's belief corpus. And it would almost certainly put a crimp in other cognitive tasks. Hence, it is a dubious normative precept.[35]

Notice that much more modest belief revision principles are possible than the ones scouted above. A simple rule might say that if one activates an old belief in q, and if one (actively) believes that this belief wholly stems from now abandoned evidence, then one is required to abandon q. But this is a far cry from the general maxim to search LTM *continually* for possibly discredited beliefs. Here is another case, then, in which facts about the structure of memory, and what it takes to activate materials in memory, have direct bearing on normative precepts.

10.5. *Retaining, Forgetting, and Revising*

As emphasized in section 10.3, primary epistemology is interested in memory power as well as reliability. As was indicated there, memory power is a multidimensional affair. It can be measured by ease of storage, by duration of retention, by quantity of retainable information, and by range of accessibility. Without trying to construct a single measure from these dimensions, I wish to inquire further into the determinants of memory power. I have already commented on the impact of elaboration. But there is much research on other influential factors, such as the *context* of encoding and the *spacing* of multiple encodings. As a sample of this work, let us look at the 'spacing effect'.

When facts are studied on multiple occasions, the temporal spacing of these occasions is important, as S. A. Madigan found in an experiment on the free recall of single words.[36] Forty-eight words were presented at the rate of 1.5 seconds per word. Some were presented once and others twice. After study, subjects were asked to recall as many words as they could, and of course they recalled a higher proportion of those studied twice. Of interest here are the data for the twice-presented words. In Figure 10.2 the data for the twice-presented condition are plotted as a function of *lag*, the num-

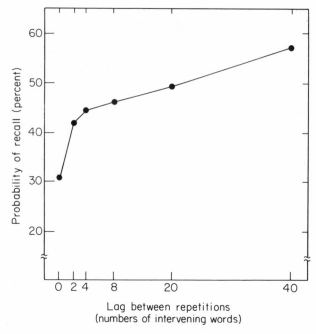

Figure 10.2. Recall probability of twice-presented words.

ber of intervening words between the two presentations. Probability of recall increases systematically with lag. It is a very robust and powerful phenomenon. There is a rapid increase over the initial lag, the benefit increases to lags of forty intervening items, and there is no reason to think this is an upper limit. The improvement of memory with increase in lag between study episodes is known as the *spacing effect*.

In Chapter 1 I distinguished regulative from nonregulative styles of epistemic appraisal, the former designed to guide deliberate conduct and the latter designed to appraise cognitive states and operations from a purely theoretical standpoint. Most of my discussion has been, and will continue to be, confined to the nonregulative style. However, results of cognitive psychology are sometimes usable to devise practical, action-guiding rules. The spacing effect is one such result. One obvious application is that a student who wishes to prepare for an exam during a semester, and who has time to study the material twice, should maximize the lag between the two study periods. Other such pieces of advice can be derived from other experimental results on encoding variability and spacing; but I will not explore these any further.[37]

I wish to turn now to the nature of forgetting. It is natural to suppose that forgetting simply consists in *losing* material from memory. Many memory theorists do indeed postulate that traces in LTM decay, but decay is just a weakening of memory material, not its wholesale disappearance. A popular conjecture among cognitive psychologists is that one never really loses information from LTM; one only loses access to it. Loss of access, it is also conjectured, is primarily due to *interference*. To give these theses some plausibility, let us begin by looking at interference effects.

Interference effects have been extensively studied with paired-associate materials. One group of subjects learns two lists of paired associates, in which the first item of a pair occurs in both lists. For example, the first list might contain *cat-43* and *house-61*, and the second list *cat-82* and *house-37*. The control group studies the same first list; but its second list does not contain the same initial words. In general the first group does not do as well as the control group on retention tests administered after a considerable delay. This is attributed to interference: members of the first group learn interfering associations to the initial items.

It is difficult to test the conjecture that all forgetting is due to interference, not to the total loss of memory traces. W. Penfield's well-known stimulation of the temporal lobes led patients to report memories that they were unable to report in normal recall—such as events from their childhood.[38] But it is hard to know whether these reports uncovered genuine memories. More persuasive evidence comes from experiments by T. O. Nelson, who studied relearning of old items that had been forgotten.[39] His results are consonant with the suggestion that forgotten memories are nevertheless still there, only not easily accessible.

If we suppose that this popular conjecture is correct, then there are implications to be traced for certain epistemic norms philosophers often enunciate. It is common for epistemologists and philosophers of science to say that when an old belief has been undermined by new evidence, it should be abandoned. It is also common to talk about a 'corpus' of belief as if it were a blackboard with a list of sentences written upon it. When new evidence infirms a sentence, it should be stricken or deleted from the corpus; it should be erased from the blackboard. However, a long-standing belief is just a state of LTM. If psychologists are right that there is never any real *loss* of material from LTM, all this talk of abandoning, deleting, striking, or erasing prior beliefs cannot be literally realized.

This idea is explicitly embraced by D. E. Rumelhart, P. Lindsay, and D. A. Norman:

> A basic axiom followed in the development of the system is that, although new information can always be added to the memory, nothing already present can be erased. Excluding physical or physiological damage, we find no evidence whatsoever to support the notion that the material in LTM can ever be deliberately forgotten.[40]

If this is right, what does belief revision, or change in belief, consist in? Surely there is some phenomenon of belief revision, even if it is not literally the erasure or replacement of an old belief. What it is, I suggest, is the 'superimposition' of new content over, or alongside, old. New associative links are established that are intended to be stronger than the old, and to have contrary contents. For example, suppose you believe for a long time (as all the books used to show) that brontosauruses had very small heads. Later evidence is unearthed to show that they did not have such small heads after all. What happens, when you learn this, is that a new associative path is added, leading from the node for brontosaurus to the node for moderate-sized head. Perhaps you also add a note, or correction, to the old small-headedness node, which says: 'No, no, this is wrong'. Later, if asked the size of brontosauruses' heads, you might initially retrieve 'small head'. But then you will retrieve the correction as well and inhibit any such verbal response. When 'moderate-sized head' is also retrieved, that response is made verbally. Still later, after the new material is frequently repeated, for example, the 'small-head' node may not be activated at all; it might be totally interfered with by the 'moderate-sized head' node.

All this conforms with the discussion by Rumelhart, Lindsay, and Norman:

> If material cannot be erased from LTM, then it will contain contradictions and "temporary" structures. The intermediate incorrect steps one follows in solving a complex problem (one that takes a considerable amount of time and thought) will be remembered permanently, along with the final, correct path. The retrieval processes must evolve to deal with these contradictions and irrelevancies.[41]

If the connection between 'brontosaurus' and 'small head' is still there, in LTM, is it a belief? We better not say so, else we will have to ascribe inconsistent *beliefs* to the cognizer, and this is not the sort of situation that invites ascription of inconsistency. But this is not a serious problem. As long as the connection between 'brontosaurus' and 'moderate-sized head' is stronger than the old connection, and as long as the note, or correction, pathway remains strong, only the latter materials deserve to be called beliefs. But don't we need a label for the LTM state that consists in the old, uneradicated connection between 'brontosaurus' and 'small head'? Although there is no good provision for this sort of state in ordinary language, I have frequently stressed the inadequacies of ordinary-language taxonomies of the mental. I will call this sort of state a *credal residue*.

Credal residues are important to acknowledge because, like a phoenix, they can be reborn—as beliefs. Suppose a recently added correction and newly added content become weaker than the old associative pathway. That is, upon first hearing the new evidence, you resolve to make the new content be your *real* opinion, but unfortunately, your memory does not co-operate; it does not retain the new content in sufficient strength. 'Bronto-saurus' cues now activate the old node ('small head') without activating either the correction ('No, no; this is wrong') or the new node ('moderate-sized head'). The new belief is forgotten, and the credal residue resumes its ascendancy. What can we now say about this credal residue? I think the only reasonable thing to say is that it has reacquired its old status as a belief.

What is the justificational status of a credal residue that reemerges as a belief? There is some temptation to call it unjustified. After all, its content has been rejected on a previous occasion, and only the failure to retrieve this rejection allows the content to reemerge in an ascendant form. This answer would make sense if it were possible to expunge beliefs. A theory of justification might say that striking such a belief from one's corpus is mandatory; and if this is not done, then the preserved belief is unwarranted. However, since we have denied the psychological feasibility of belief erasure, it is not clear how we could accommodate the view that the reascendant credal residue is unjustified.

One way of trying to rationalize the label 'unjustified' within our framework is to point out that the target case of belief recreation crucially involves a process of forgetting (forgetting some *other* material). It might be urged that the process of forgetting generally inhibits reliability, and therefore would not be authorized by a right system of J-rules.

How would it be argued that forgetting inhibits, or reduces, reliability? There are really two forms, or manifestations, of forgetting. One manifestation is simply a failure to retrieve a once stored item. This manifestation does not involve the production of a *false* A-belief; rather, it merely involves the *absence* of an A-belief. The second manifestation of forgetting, though, is *erroneous* retrieval. This arises from interference. Suppose a subject has studied a paired-associate list, including the item *cat-43*. Later he studies another list that includes *cat-82*. Learning of the second list interferes with the first. So when he is subsequently asked to recall items on the first list, he erroneously retrieves *cat-82*. This process of interference is responsible for error.

The present case of credal residue is really a form of such interference (only it features 'proactive' inhibition rather than 'retroactive' inhibition). Earlier learning of the connection between 'brontosaurus' and 'small head' interferes with the subsequent learning of the connection between 'bronto-saurus' and 'moderate-sized head', so that the latter is no longer retrieved. When it is recognized that such a process of interference works against reliability, we can see that a rule permitting such a process might be a poor candidate for inclusion in a right system of J-rules. Hence, beliefs formed by such a process would not be justified.

All this is a way of supporting the claim that a reascendant credal residue could be counted as an unjustified belief. But there is a problem with this analysis. Although interference clearly can produce false A-beliefs, it can also work to promote true beliefs. According to my earlier account, the way in which the mind revises its old beliefs is by adding new informational pathways and getting them to dominate the old pathways by means of interference. In many of these cases the beliefs resulting (in part) from interference will be *true*. So it is not evident whether interference generally promotes unreliability, or how seriously it breeds unreliability.

It is thus premature to expect that interference processes generally would be excluded by right J-rule systems. Hence, it is questionable whether my theory implies that reascendant credal residues are always unjustified. I do not think it obvious that this is the intuitively correct judgment anyway. The whole matter needs further reflection and investigation. At this juncture I leave this as one among many problems for future explorations of primary epistemics to pursue.

chapter 11

Constraints on Representation

11.1. Epistemology and Representation Formation

In order to believe something, it must first be present in the mind; some *mental representation* must be constructed that is a candidate for doxastic acceptance or nonacceptance. The question is, How does the mind perform such constructions? Is the construction of representations a random, haphazard affair? Or is it governed by a fixed set of rules and principles? Is there at least some set of *preferred* patterns and styles of constructional activity?

Of all philosophers, Kant laid the greatest emphasis on the mind's constructional activity. Forms of intuition and categories of understanding were viewed as constraining what the mind could represent. Recent trends in cognitive science have been drawing similar conclusions. The sorts of constraints in question are different from the Kantian ones, and the methods of studying them form a sharp contrast. Where Kant used transcendental methods, cognitive science uses theoretico-empirical methods. But there is a striking similarity of perspective. In this chapter I shall discuss certain constraints on representation that seem to emerge from work in cognitive science. Then I shall assess the epistemological ramifications of such constraints.

There are, of course, many domains of cognition and arguably many forms of representation. Representational constraints need not be similar, nor present to the same degree, for different domains or for different forms of representation. Every perceptual system, for example, might have its own peculiar constraints; and constraints on nonperceptual, purely propositional, representations may have little in common with constraints on perceptual representations. There may be specialized constraints on grammatical representations, with no parallel in other domains. All this is open to investigation. But in this chapter I shall propose a number of similarities in representational constraints that appear to cut across several domains.

Suppose it were established that the mind's activity in forming representations is fairly sharply constrained. How might this be evaluated along the dimensions I have sketched? First, there is a danger that such constraints would be distorting. This might reduce reliability. Second, there might be truths that the system is incapable of representing. In Fodor's terminology the system might be "epistemically bounded."[1] This apparently would imply a limitation on the system's power. These, among others, are the sorts of liabilities that representational constraints might engender. But there are also significant assets that constraints might possess. All these will be surveyed after I present some styles of constraints that current research suggests.

11.2. Partitions and Hierarchies

The neorationalist approach to language acquisition, inspired by Noam Chomsky, is undoubtedly the arena of cognitive science that most intensively explores constraints on representation. Chomsky describes the underlying idea as follows:

> It is clear that the language each person acquires is a rich and complex construction hopelessly underdetermined by the fragmentary evidence available . . . This fact can be explained only on the assumption that these individuals employ highly restrictive principles that guide the construction of grammar . . . Powerful constraints must be operative restricting the variety of languages.[2]

Language acquisition , however, is not the main area that I shall explore, for several reasons. First, the literature there is vast and technical, and would take us far afield. Second, precisely because it is so intensively researched, it may be instructive to choose examples from less familiar domains. Third, language acquisition may have very specialized properties, which reduce its usefulness for illustrative purposes. So I shall concentrate my efforts elsewhere. Nonetheless, a few remarks on grammatical representation will be ventured later in the chapter.

Virtually all theories of mental representation assume that the mind somehow decomposes experience into parts, that it somehow partitions or segments the world into convenient units. It is also assumed that the mind engages in 'synthesizing' activities: constructing new units and structures out of antecedently formed units. Kant, of course, laid great emphasis on the mind's synthesizing activity, specifically the mind's propensity to structure experience in terms of material objects. In this section I shall focus on some selected unitizing and constructional operations that cognitive psychologists are investigating. In particular, I shall look at some hypotheses about the ways in which human beings partition objects and events into subunits, hypotheses which (in many cases) attribute a strong preference for groups of representations that admit of *hierarchical* organization.

Let me begin with hierarchical structuring. The literature is replete with descriptions of data structures, or cognitive units, that are organized hierarchically. Units are embedded in higher-level units, which are in turn embedded in yet higher-level units.

Many examples of hierarchically structured representations are linked to natural language.

(1) The phrase structure of sentences is hierarchical. A sentence is the highest level unit, subordinating noun phrases and verb phrases, which in turn subordinate nouns, verbs, and other grammatical units. While these units are categories of word sequences, not of mental units, the universality of these categories in public codes implicates a hierarchical organization of associated mental representations.

(2) Another domain in which hierarchical structuring is widely postulated is semantic memory. The popular semantic memory 'networks' stress a class-inclusion structure in commonsense concepts.[3] Class-inclusion arrays such as <physical object – living thing – animal – mammal – dog – collie> are ubiquitous in natural languages. These taxonomical systems are probably manifestations of deep-seated representational mechanisms of the human cognitive system.[4]

Hierarchicalization is by no means confined to representations associated with natural language. It is found in the representation of all sorts of visual and temporal materials.

(3) In the case of visual cognitive units smaller visual parts are embedded in larger ones.[5]

(4) In the case of temporal strings shorter units are subordinated to longer ones.[6]

Detailed discussion of these domains of representation will follow shortly. Many other domains are also the subjects of postulated hierarchicalization.

(5) In story understanding plots are said to be represented hierarchically, with smaller episodes embedded in larger ones.[7]

(6) The organization of behavior is achieved by hierarchical networks of motives and submotives, plans and subplans.[8]

(7) Problem-solving tasks are structured by means of problems and subproblems.[9]

Turning now to some details, let us begin with visual materials. It is easy to portray visual representation—in both perception and imagery—in terms of multiple layers of embedding. Take the representation of a standing person. The whole is an elongated, ellipse-shaped object, oriented vertically. At a finer level of resolution, the parts of the body are delineated: a head, a torso, two arms, and two legs. Each of these parts has global properties. But each can also be considered a whole with further parts. The head, for example, has eyes, ears, a mouth, and a nose.

An example from A. Stevens and P. Coupe testifies to the storage of imagistic information by hierarchically layered parts.[10] When asked which is farther west, Reno or San Diego, the typical subject mistakenly chooses San Diego. The natural explanation is that San Diego and Reno are encoded as subunits of California and Nevada respectively, and California is pictured as west of Nevada on one's mental map of the continent.

Several of the experimental studies I shall review are not only concerned with hierarchical organization; they also postulate preferences for patterns that accord with Gestalt principles. So before turning to these studies, let me mention and illustrate these well-known Gestalt principles, originally postulated for perception. Some of the principles are illustrated in Figure 11.1. In part A we perceive four pairs of lines rather than eight separate lines. This illustrates the principle of *proximity:* elements close together tend to organize into units. Part B illustrates the same principle. Five columns of dots are seen rather than five rows, because the dots in a column are closer together than the dots in a row. Part C illustrates the principle of *similarity:* objects that look alike tend to be grouped together. In C we tend to see five rows of alternating O's and X's, even though the rows are spaced similar to those in B. Part D illustrates the principle of *good continuation*. We perceive part D as two lines, one from x to y and the other from w to z, although there is no reason why this could not represent another pair of lines, one from x to z and the other from y to w. But the line from x to y displays better continuation than the line from x to z, which has a sharp turn. Part E illustrates the principles of *closure* and *good form*. We see the drawing as one circle occluding another circle, although the occluded object could have many other possible shapes.

It is time to consider some representative studies of hierarchical organization and partition of visual materials. G. H. Bower and A. L. Glass studied subjects' styles of partitioning unfamiliar line drawings.[11] In principle, a given line drawing could be mentally dissected into all kinds of parts. But in fact, they proposed, only certain subpatterns are 'naturally' represented as parts. Bower and Glass predicted that a natural part should serve as a strong retrieval cue for the original, whole pattern; whereas an unnatural fragment, even one of equal size, should lead to poorer recall of the original whole. After their subjects studied a set of original drawings, they were tested for recall on fragments which the experimenters had categorized as 'good', 'mediocre', or 'bad' (misleading). The experimental results were that good cues had about five times more retrieval power than bad cues.

Bower and Glass chose the good, bad, and mediocre fragments by application of Gestalt rules of common direction and minimal angle. As we have seen, the rule of common direction, or good continuation, states that line

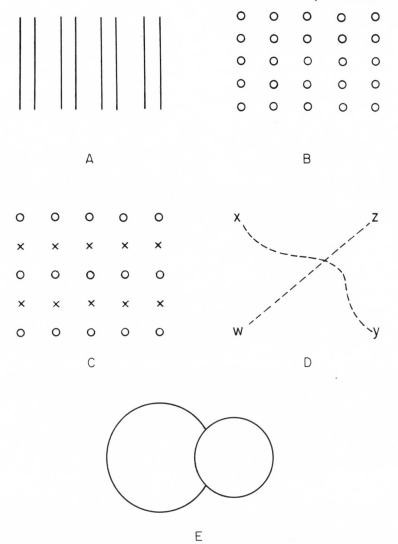

A

B

C

D

E

Figure 11.1

segments continuous in the same direction are combined and encoded as a single structural unit. The rule of minimal angle says that when three or more segments intersect at a point, the two with the minimal angle between them are combined to form a single structural unit. Referring to Figure 11.2 and assuming that part segmentation accords with these rules, the figure in A is parsed into the parts shown in B, and the figure in C is parsed

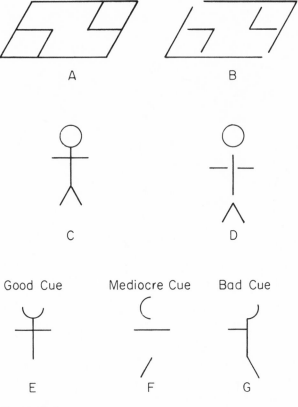

Figure 11.2

into the parts shown in D. Using this theme, Bower and Glass constructed picture fragments of C such as E, F, and G. E should be a good cue, F a mediocre cue, and G a bad cue. Experimental results confirmed this prediction.

A similar set of results was reported by Stephen Palmer.[12] Like Bower and Glass, Palmer suggested that only certain subparts are 'natural', or 'good', decompositions of a larger figure. He devised a measure of goodness based on Gestalt principles of grouping: proximity, closedness, connectedness, continuity, and so forth. Figure 11.3 displays some of the whole figures and respective parts he used, where the parts are rated for degrees of goodness: high (H), medium high (MH), medium (M), medium low (ML), and low (L). Palmer then conducted a series of experiments to see whether observed results conformed with the part ratings his scheme predicted. One experiment asked subjects to divide figures into their natural parts. A second task was to rate goodness of identified parts within figures. A third experiment was a reaction-time experiment. A fourth experiment involved a 'mental synthesis' task, in which subjects were instructed to construct a figure mentally from parts. Palmer found substantial evidence for the kinds of selective organization in perception and imagery that he had postulated.

Although one might suppose these styles of representation are peculiar to vision, quite similar styles are found in the representation of sequences of events. With an eye toward studying hierarchical representation of *serial* patterns, Frank Restle devised a formalism congenial to such representation.[13] Let $E = [1\ 2\ 3\ 4\ 5\ 6]$ be a set of elementary events, where '1', '2', and so on, comprise the alphabet for representing these elementary events. Let X be a sequence of events from this set; for example, $X = <1\ 2>$. A set of operations on this set is then introduced: *repeat* (R) of X, *mirror image* (M) of X, and *transposition +1* (T) of X. Each operation generates a new sequence from a given sequence and then concatenates the old and the new. For example, $R<1\ 2> = <1\ 2\ 1\ 2>$; relative to the alphabet specified above, $M<2\ 3\ 4> = <2\ 3\ 4\ 5\ 4\ 3>$; and $T<2\ 3> = <2\ 3\ 3\ 4>$. In this fashion a lengthy and complex series can be represented economically by multiple embedding. For example, $T<1> = <1\ 2>$; $R<T<1>> = <1\ 2\ 1\ 2>$; $T<R<T<1>>> = <1\ 2\ 1\ 2\ 2\ 3\ 2\ 3>$; and $M<T<R<T<1>>>> = <1\ 2\ 1\ 2\ 2\ 3\ 2\ 3\ 6\ 5\ 6\ 5\ 5\ 4\ 5\ 4>$. Using sequences constructed in this way, Restle and Brown found evidence that subjects mentally encode temporal patterns in accord with a hierarchical structure indicated by the recursive format.[14]

A number of writers have recently proposed that musical cognition reveals hierarchically organized representations. F. Lerdahl and R. Jackendoff, for instance, hold that at least four components of the experienced listener's musical intuitions are hierarchical.[15] 'Grouping structure' expresses a hierarchical segmentation of a piece into motives, phrases, and

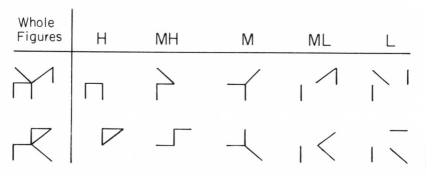

Figure 11.3

Figure 11.4

sections. 'Metrical structure' expresses the intuition that the events of the piece are related to a regular alternation of strong and weak beats at a number of hierarchical levels. And so on.

Diana Deutsch and John Feroe also suggest that people represent pitch sequences in tonal music in abstract form.[16] To illustrate their argument, consider the pitch sequence shown in Figure 11.4. A musically sophisticated performer (or listener) would represent this sequence at two or more levels of description. At the lowest level there is a representation of the entire presented sequence. At the next (higher) level the representation would feature an arpeggio that ascends through the C major triad (C-E-G-C). This more abstract representation registers the fact that the entire sequence can be viewed as the four notes of this triad each preceded by a neighbor embellishment. At this higher level of representation, the embellishments are deleted. The resulting hierarchical structure may be presented in tree form as in Figure 11.5. Drawing on ideas of earlier authors, Deutsch and Feroe propose that tonal music is represented with the help of several different (mental) 'alphabets': major scale alphabets, minor scale alphabets, the chromatic alphabet, and the triad alphabets. Different alphabets can be used at

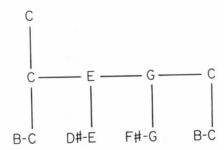

Figure 11.5

different levels of representation of the very same passage. Whereas the first-level representation in the foregoing example occurs in the chromatic alphabet, the second-level representation could use the major triad alphabet. In the major triad alphabet, C-E-G-C is a sequence of *successive* elements. Employment of multiple alphabets facilitates conformity with laws of figural goodness. (Like other authors I have cited, Deutsch and Feroe postulate Gestalt-like laws of goodness.) For example, pitch sequences are more efficiently perceived when their components combine to produce unidirectional pitch changes and changes proximal in pitch. By treating the sample passage in the major triad alphabet, it can be represented as a sequence of successive—proximal—notes.

A major hypothesis of Deutsch and Feroe is that music sequences are stored hierarchically, and that a performer generates a learned composition by accessing it in a top-down fashion. There are close analogies here, which Deutsch and Feroe note, with Chomsky's system of grammar. In music these ideas were anticipated by Heinrich Schenker,[17] who in turn credits C. P. E. Bach's *Essay on the True Art of Playing Keyboard Instruments.*[18]

In addition to these studies of hierarchicalization in specific domains, John Anderson postulates hierarchical organization as a pervasive cognitive phenomenon.[19] Anderson points out that even more complex structures can result when a single element occurs in several different hierarchical structures, thereby joining them to produce a "tangled hierarchy." Furthermore, hierarchies can also contain units of multiple representational types: imaginal, temporal, and propositional. Finally, he postulates, people can retrieve elements from a hierarchical structure either through a top-down process—starting with the top structure and unpacking successively lower layers of elements—or in a bottom-up manner—starting with a bottom node and retrieving higher-level units.

Not all studies of partitioning invoke Gestalt principles or a preference for hierarchicalization, however. Donald Hoffman and colleagues have proposed principles of shape partitioning independent of either Gestalt ideas or hierarchicalization.[20] Hoffman's initial proposal is based on the observation that when two arbitrarily shaped surfaces are made to interpenetrate, they always meet at a contour of concave discontinuity with their tangent planes. A straw in a soft drink, for example, forms a circular concave discontinuity where it meets the surface of the drink. A candle in a birthday cake is another example. Hoffman then proposes, as an initial rule of partitioning: divide a surface into parts along all contours of concave discontinuity with the tangent plane.

This rule does not always define a unique partition. But that fact leads to a prediction: when no unique partition is defined, it should be perceptually ambiguous how the object is partitioned. This prediction is confirmed with reference to the elbow shaped block in Figure 11.6. The only concave dis-

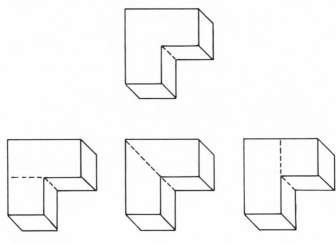

Figure 11.6

continuity is the line in the crook of the elbow. The rule does not define a unique partition of the block. As predicted, there are three plausible ways to cut the block into parts, all relying on the contour defined by the partitioning rule.

The foregoing rule does not help with entirely smooth surfaces. Hoffman therefore develops the following partitioning rule: divide a surface into parts at loci of negative minima of each principal curvature along its associated family of lines of curvature. As applied to the shape in Figure 11.7, this yields the indicated partitioning contours (dashed lines).

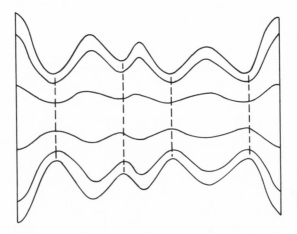

Figure 11.7

Let me close this section with a slightly different topic: not constraints on the representation of parts, but constraints on the representation of *motion*. Shimon Ullman has studied principles that underlie the visual system's interpretation of a sequence of two-dimensional stimuli (for example, dots of light on a movie screen).[21] How does a subject 'see' such a succession of stimuli? One issue is how the subject 'matches' the parts of one frame in a motion picture with parts of a succeeding frame. Which parts of the subsequent frame are viewed as identical to parts of a preceding frame? And does the subject interpret these event sequences as representing a single three-dimensional object in motion or in change? If so, what governs the choice of a three-dimensional interpretation?

Ullman claims that the visual system displays at least three innate preferences: (1) In interpreting which dot elements match in successive arrays, there is a preference for seeing motion to nearest neighbors. (2) In deciding what matching to impute, motion along straight lines is preferred. (Notice that these first two principles echo Gestalt principles of proximity in space and common direction.) (3) Any set of elements undergoing two-dimensional transformation that has a unique interpretation as a rigid body moving in space should be so interpreted. This third principle is a version of the preference for seeing visual arrays as solid 'bodies', a theme that many philosophers have stressed.[22]

Earlier work had shown how humans can retrieve structure from motion. For instance, if a transparent beach ball with tiny light bulbs mounted randomly on its surface is set spinning in a dark room, one immediately perceives the correct spherical layout of the lights. When the spinning stops, so does the perception of the spherical array. How does one see the correct three-dimensional array when infinitely many three-dimensional structures are consistent with the moving two-dimensional retinal projection? Ullman showed mathematically that if the visual system exploits the laws of projection, and 'assumes' that the world contains rigid objects, then in principle a correct interpretation can be obtained. In particular, three views of four noncoplanar light bulbs are enough to solve the problem.

However, in cases of 'biological motion' studied by Gunnar Johansson, one does not have four noncoplanar points.[23] When small light bulbs are attached to the major joints of a walking person, there are at best only pairs of rigidly connected points, such as the ankle and the knee, or the knee and the hip. Nonetheless, the visual system does recognize a walking person from such information. Hoffman and Bruce Flinchbaugh suggested that if the visual system makes a further assumption—the 'planarity' assumption—displays of gait of this sort can be correctly interpreted from three snapshots of just two points.[24] Thus, the visual system appears to have very specific constraints—probably innate computational mechanisms—for constructing shape representations.

11.3. Operations and Analogies

These last examples illustrate specific principles, or operations, that the mind seems to realize in constructing visual representations. But even the earlier examples, identifying preferred partitions, seem to reflect specific operations or transformations for the generation of representations.

The proximity rule might reflect an operation that searches for adjacent elements within a pattern and that constructs partitions which group these elements together. Another preference cited by the Gestalt psychologists, but not previously mentioned here, is the preference for *symmetry*. This preference might reflect an operation that looks for, or tends to generate, inversions or mirror images. I have noted the role of such an operation in musical patterns, but it also seems to underpin aesthetic responses to symmetry in ornamental and even intellectual creations. Again, the preference for hierarchical orderings may reflect such operations as 'abstraction' and 'globalization', or their inverses, 'specification' and 'localization'. All of these operations may function in one or more of the following contexts: *(a)* perception, *(b)* storage and retrieval from memory, and *(c)* imaginative construction of new representational units out of preexisting units.

For my purposes, it is not crucial to fix the representation-forming operations precisely. What interests me here is the hypothesis that there is a determinate and fairly *narrow* set of such operations, roughly of the kind I have culled from the surveyed literature. Indeed, it is equally worth assessing the implications of a weaker hypothesis, namely, that there is a fairly wide set of available operations, or transformations, but also a *preference ordering* among them. On this hypothesis the system's control processes effect a priority ordering among the transformations, so that higher-ranked ones get applied earlier and therefore have a greater frequency of application.

Intimations of a narrow set of operations, at least for certain domains, are contained in the research I have presented. Deutsch and Feroe suggest that a great deal of observed pitch sequences in traditional music can be reconstructed in terms of elementary operations such as sameness in pitch, next in pitch (within a specified scale, or alphabet), predecessor in pitch, transposition of a phrase, inversion (mirroring) of a phrase, and so on. Similarly, of course, Chomsky and other grammarians postulate a fairly narrow set of operations to account for grammatical structures. Chomsky also suggests that analogous representational constraints may underlie art forms.

Certain conditions on the choice and arrangement of linguistic expressions characterize literary genres intelligible to humans, with aesthetic value for humans; others do not . . . In these and many other domains, a certain range of possibilities has been explored to create structures of marvelous intricacy, while others are never considered, or if explored, lead to the production of work that does not conform to normal human capacities.[25]

Citing Marshall Edelson,[26] Chomsky notes that Freud made similar proposals in his work on dreams. In Edelson's interpretation Freud's psychoanalysis was a sort of science of semiology, a dream being created by principles he calls "the dreamwork," which produce the manifest content of dreams from latent dream thoughts. Ultimately, Chomsky proposes a "universal grammar" of scientific theorizing, by which he apparently means a set of hypothesis-constructing operations, which I intend to include in my discussion. Although the literature I have adduced focuses mainly on operations concerning visual or auditory patterns, the class of representation-forming operations I mean to address include operations that take concepts or hypotheses as inputs and generate new hypotheses as outputs.

Notice that my conjecture is independent of the issue of modularity of mind. If the mind is modular, it would be natural to expect that distinct modules have distinct sets of operational, or transformational, repertoires. But a nonmodular theory is also compatible with a highly constrained set of operations. Nothing said here is intended to take sides on the modularity issue.

Distinct repertoires of operations might be associated with distinct representational codes, as opposed to distinct modules. Anderson, who opposes mental modularity, endorses a multiplicity of codes and takes these codes to have different sets of operations.[27] Specifically, he postulates three types of representation: temporal strings, spatial images, and abstract propositions. For temporal strings, he suggests three probable operations: *(a)* combination of objects into linear strings, *(b)* insertion, and *(c)* deletion. For imagery, he mentions synthesis of existing images and rotation. For abstract propositions, he lists insertion of objects into relational slots and filling in of missing slots. He clearly thinks that the representational types, or codes, differ in their transformational repertoire.

The next theme I wish to discuss is *analogy*, which I shall link with the theory of natural operations. Analogy is a large topic, which has burgeoned in recent years. No attempt at comprehensive coverage of the literature is therefore contemplated. Furthermore, I will lump together the notions of analogy, similarity, and metaphor, though these can doubtless be distinguished.

The ubiquity of the similarity construct in psychology has been remarked upon by Amos Tversky: "The concept of similarity is ubiquitous in psychological theory. It underlies the accounts of stimulus and response generalization in learning, it is employed to explain errors in memory and pattern recognition, and it is central to the analysis of connotative meanings."[28] Other cognitive scientists have emphasized the centrality of analogy in (among other areas) the phraseology of everyday language, and the strategies of problem solving.

A recent book by George Lakoff and Mark Johnson traces the pervasiveness of analogy—or metaphor—in ordinary language and thought.[29] A sample metaphorical pattern involves orientational metaphors: expressions rooted in spatial orientations, such as up-down, in-out, front-back, on-off, deep-shallow, and central-peripheral. Innumerable expressions for nonspatial properties and events are built upon these orientational notions. For example, happy is up, sad is down ('I'm feeling up', 'That boosted my spirits', 'My spirits rose', 'You're in high spirits', 'I'm feeling down', 'He's really low these days', 'My spirits sank'); health and life are up, sickness and death are down ('He's at the peak of health', 'He's in top shape', 'He's sinking fast', 'His health is declining'); having control or force is up, being subject to control or force is down ('I have control over her', 'I am on top of the situation', 'He's at the height of his power', 'He is under my control', 'He fell from power', 'He is low man on the totem pole'); good is up, bad is down ('Things are looking up', 'We hit a peak last year, but it's been downhill ever since', 'Things are at an all-time low', 'He does high-quality work'). According to Lakoff and Johnson, a vast expanse of our conceptual territory is rooted in analogical extensions of more primitive conceptual contents. The linguistic patterns, then, may be taken as evidence for the pervasive employment of some sort of analogy-constructing operation in the cognitive system.

The use of analogy in problem solving is also widely remarked upon. G. Polya recommends searching for analogies as a strategy for solving mathematical problems.[30] Analogical test items of the form A:B as C:D are widely used in intelligence testing, since a grasp of these sorts of relationships seems to develop quite early.

Experimental studies of problem solving also reveal a strong influence of similarity judgments in problem-solving strategies. In many problems a person's task is to find a way of getting from one state in a 'problem space' to the goal state. Typically, a long series of states must be traversed. How does the human problem solver choose, in any given state, what state to move to next? Apparently, people are strongly influenced by similarity. They choose to move into new states that are more similar to the goal state than the present state, and more similar to the goal state than are other possible candidates.

Here is an illustration reported by M. E. Atwood and P. G. Polson.[31] Subjects were given the following water jug problem.

> You have three jugs, which we will call A, B, and C. Jug A can hold exactly 8 cups of water, B can hold exactly 5 cups, and C can hold exactly 3 cups. A is filled to capacity with 8 cups of water. B and C are empty. We want you to find a way of dividing the contents of A equally between A and B so that both have 4 cups. You are allowed to pour water from jug to jug.

Atwood and Polson asked which move subjects would prefer, starting from the initial state. Would they prefer to pour from A into C, thereby yielding state 2 (below); or would they prefer to pour from A into B, thereby yielding state 3?

State 2:   A(5)   B(0)   C(3)
State 3:   A(3)   B(5)   C(0)

Twice as many subjects preferred the move to state 3 as preferred the move to state 2. Notice that state 3 is quite similar to the goal, since the goal is to have 4 cups in both A and B, and state 3 has 3 cups in A and 5 cups in B. By contrast, state 2 has no cups of water in B. This illustrates a tendency to move to states that are as similar as possible to the goal state.

Recent work on scientific theory construction, both by cognitive scientists and by historians of science, also explores the role of analogy, or similarity. For example, several authors trace the development of Darwin's theory to his finding an analogy between Malthus's theory of human population growth and the growth of species.[32]

Analogy is often treated as a separate representation-forming device, and we could certainly place it alongside the other operations tentatively listed earlier. In other words, where it is assumed that one representation (be it a concept, a theory, an idea for a problem solution, or what have you) is obtained from another by some sort of operation, one candidate operation might be that of analogy. This might be regarded as a *primitive,* irreducible operation. But I want to advance the proposal that the analogy operation is analyzable in terms of other operations.

One way of trying to flesh out this proposal would be to treat analogical representation formation as a *substitution* operation. Take Bohr's model of the atom, for example. This representation might be derived 'by analogy' from a representation of the solar system. Wherein does the analogical construction consist? The suggestion would be that it consists in substituting *(a)* a nucleus for the sun, *(b)* electrons for the planets, and *(c)* nuclear forces for the gravitational force.

Is this approach plausible? A criterion of adequacy for any such theory would seem to be this: if representation R* is obtained from R 'by analogy', then R* (or, rather, its putative referent) should be judged quite similar, or analogous, to R, at least by the cognizer in question. But not every (mental) substitution yields a representation of a subjectively similar object. If R is a representation of a swan, and R* is obtained by first deleting everything in R except (a representation of) the eyes and then substituting (a representation of) a tiger, the new representation R* is hardly very similar to, or analogous to, the original.

What further constraints can be placed, then, on substitutions to yield a match with intuitive judgments of resemblance or similarity? One possibility is to employ the notion of 'natural parts'. The greater the naturalness of the parts preserved under replacement, the greater the subjective similarity of the resulting representation.

I doubt, however, that judged analogies or similarities can be adequately recovered by the substitution operation, even conjoined with this additional device. Other high-ranking or 'preferred' operations, in addition to substitution, might have to be invoked. For example, assume that reversal, or inversion, relative to some natural axis or alphabet is a high-ranking transformation. Then an object obtained from another object by such a reversal would be judged rather similar to it.

With this in mind, we might try to generalize the approach along the following lines:

> The contents of representations R and R* are similar—receive a high similarity rating—if and only if the content of one is obtainable from the content of the other by application of a *high-ranking* cognitive transformation (or combination of transformations).

Lance Rips points out, in a personal communication, that one source of evidence for this account of similarity is that different transformations yield representations similar to the original one but not themselves similar. For example, the concept 'cold' might be considered similar to 'hot' (from one perspective), via an 'opposites' transformation. Also, 'warm' is similar to 'hot', via a 'next-to' transformation. But 'warm' and 'cold' are not subjectively similar.[33]

Notice the analogy between this idea and one employed by topologists. In topology two figures are said to be topologically equivalent (homeomorphic) just in case one can be obtained from the other by some sort of topological operation.

If this line of analysis proved promising, it might be exploited by turning it on its head. (I owe this suggestion, and the example that follows, to Charles Chastain.) Instead of studying similarity in terms of transformations, one could study transformations in terms of judged similarities. For example, given perceived similarities among faces, one might try to identify high-ranking transformations by seeing which would account for those similarity judgments.

These are some tentative thoughts about analogy. Their relevance stems from my interest in representation-forming operations. If analogy is related to such operations in the manner proposed, we gain new avenues for getting at the repertoire of operations. Furthermore, given the apparent ubiquity of similarity, or analogy, in cognitive phenomena, identification of this repertoire—and the most preferred members of it—is quite important for cognitive science.

11.4. *Epistemic Assets and Liabilities*

It is time to turn to epistemological issues, which will occupy the rest of the chapter. My epistemological reflections will be directed at the sorts of representation-forming operations presented in the preceding sections. To be more specific, I will inquire into the epistemic implications of having a narrowly constrained set of representation-forming operations of these kinds. I start, in this section, with a survey of assorted assets and liabilities that might be associated with such a set. In the next section I will explore the role of such operations in the evaluative dimension of *originality*. Finally, in section 11.6, I will examine the relevance of such operations to epistemic *justification*.

Consider the mind's propensity to segment objects and events into parts, such as spatial and temporal parts, and its possession of a rather narrow set of partitioning preferences. What assets might be associated with such representation-forming properties? Hoffman and Richards discuss a number of such assets.[34]

First, an articulation of an object into parts is useful because one never sees an entire object in one glance. Excepting transparent objects, back sides are never visible. Moreover, even an object's front side is often partially occluded by things interposed between it and the observer. By segmenting an object into parts, and storing associations between the object and its several parts, one can effect a recognition of the object by the visible subset of its parts.

Another virtue of the mind's propensity to decompose an object into a hierarchy of parts concerns the nonrigidity of objects. A hand can assume different postures, for example, a clenched fist, an outstretched hand, or a hand giving a victory sign. How well would the mind manage recognition if it only had a representational device like a template? Not so well. A template of an outstretched hand would correlate poorly with a clenched fist or a hand giving a victory sign. Templates would have to be proliferated to handle the many possible configurations of the hand. This would be unparsimonious and a waste of memory. By comparison, decomposition of objects into parts promotes efficient recognition.

These points pertain to the general strategy of decomposition into a hierarchy of parts. But what about the hypothesized *narrowness* of part preferences? To understand the advantage there, imagine the demands on memory and on the matching process if every time one looked at an object one saw different parts. A face, for example, which at one instant appeared to be composed of eyes, ears, a nose, and a mouth, might later metamorphose into a potpourri of eye-cheek, nose-chin, and mouth-ear parts—a gruesome and unprofitable transmutation. No advantage would accrue for allowing such repartitions. In fact, they would be uniformly deleterious to the task of recognition.[35] Hence, the narrowness of constraints on partitioning also seems to be useful.

In terms of my list of epistemic virtues, the foregoing advantages fall under the heading of aids to power (or perhaps power and reliability). The mechanism of decomposition into a hierarchy of parts helps one answer the question 'What is that?' asked of a perceived, or partially perceived, object. The more such questions can correctly be answered, the greater the power of the cognitive system.

Thus far we have reflected on parts, and hierarchies of parts. But hierarchicalization in general must be considered. Not all hierarchies are part hierarchies. The mind's general affinity for hierarchicalization, however, has advantages in power. Many intellectual tasks benefit from flexibility in the 'grain', or 'level of resolution', of analysis. Which details about an object are relevant and which are irrelevant varies from task to task. If I want to use a computer for word processing, I shall of course be concerned with its microcharacteristics. But if I only want to use it as a paperweight, I can restrict my attention to its global size and weight. The mechanism of hierarchicalization facilitates flexible transitions from level to level; and it creates the potential for the creation of handy superordinate and subordinate groupings *ad libitum*.

Hierarchicalization also contributes to power through its associated mnemonic deployment. This is dramatically illustrated by the case of a Carnegie-Mellon student, reported by K. A. Ericsson, W. G. Chase, and S. Fallon.[36] After training an hour a day for eighteen months, this student increased his memory span for digits to 79. That is, he could memorize and accurately reproduce a random string of 79 digits! According to the authors, there was still a short-term working memory store with a capacity of 4 items, a memory space that had not been affected by practice. The other 75 items were held in a complex hierarchical mnemonic structure of subunits in LTM, each of which held 3 or 4 items. The key unit at the bottom level of the hierarchy was a three- or four-digit string usually associated with the time for running a race. (The subject was a keen runner with a large number of categories of races, from half mile to marathon.) For example, the string '3492' would be stored as '3 minutes 49.2 seconds—nearly a world record for the mile'. The mnemonic system for digits would not generalize to other materials, of course, and his span for consonants remained at 6. Clearly, it was the inventive use of hierarchical organization that made possible his mnemonic feat for digits.

The mnemonic assets of hierarchicalization are also well displayed in the execution of extended courses of action. This concerns the *timeliness* of mental representation. For effective guidance of action, a plan or representation of the action needs to be brought into working memory. But working memory has a severely restricted capacity, so a large, detailed plan would not 'fit'. To execute such a plan, however, a cognizer can partition the plan into subplans. If the relevant subplans are activated at suitable junctures, the entire plan can be executed piece by piece. But this requires that the larger, superordinate plan be suitably linked in memory to appropriate subplans. This is achieved by hierarchical representation of plan and subplans, and the retrieval of microunits from macrounits in accordance with this hierarchical organization.

Musical performance is a vivid case in point. The piece to be performed is represented in LTM at various levels, encompassing different sized segments of the work. As the musician proceeds through the performance, representations appropriate to each passage are accessed. These are detailed enough for guidance of behavior but small enough for accurate retention in working memory. Deutsch and Feroe underline this point as follows:

> Several investigators have shown that for serial recall of a string of items, performance levels are optimal when such a string is grouped by the observer into chunks of three or four items each . . . When segments of tonal music are notated on the present [hierarchical] system, there emerges a very high proportion of chunks of three or four items each . . . As pitch sequences become more elaborate, they are represented as on a larger number of hierarchical levels, but the basic chunk size does not appear to vary with changes in sequence complexity. This chunking feature therefore serves to reduce memory load.[37]

Thus far I have mentioned only virtues of the partitioning and hierarchicalization mechanisms. But one might ask, aren't there any vices? For example, doesn't the presence of *restricted* styles of decomposing wholes into parts reduce power and flexibility? This issue may be discussed in terms of Fodor's notion of "epistemic boundedness": the inability of a cognitive system even to represent—and *a fortiori* its inability to believe—certain truths. If a cognitive system has a fixed set of representation-forming operations, there must be representations it is incapable of generating. This appears to imply a limitation on power.

Actually this is not so, at least on my definition of power. On my definition a system is completely powerful if it can answer (correctly) *every question it can ask*. This does not imply that it can answer every question. In other words, complete power does not entail unboundedness. Therefore, boundedness does not entail the absence of complete power.

Setting this point aside, how serious a defect is the absence of total power? Not much. When talking about finite minds, it is not an alarming defect that omniscience is beyond reach. That's just the nature of the beast. The more important question is: Is it capable of getting true answers to the sorts of questions it actually wants to answer, to the sorts of problems it actually wants to solve? On this point there is no glaring deficiency in the representational operations under discussion.

Notice, in this connection, that the Gestalt principles might be best interpreted as *preferred* operations or default procedures, rather than mandatory operations. Take the wholes and parts that Palmer used in some of his experiments (shown in Figure 11.3). The parts are rated for goodness as either high, medium high, medium, medium low, or low. Subjects gave ratings to the parts that accorded with Palmer's Gestalt-inspired metrics. But subjects can 'see' each of them as a part of the whole, even the lowest ranking parts. It is just harder to see them as parts. So people are not incapable of parsing the whole into the inferior segments; those parsings are just less 'natural' or obvious.

Still, isn't it a vice of the system that it has preferences for certain parsings? Doesn't it inevitably betoken a *distortion* in the system's noetic relation with the world? Doesn't it mean that the mind can't mirror the world, and doesn't this necessarily breed error as well as ignorance?

Representational preferences do preclude mirroring, but mirroring is not required for truth. You do not have to get every truth to get some truths. Partitioning and synthesizing preferences may indeed imply that some 'correct' parts and wholes do not get constructed. But the preferred parts and wholes may be perfectly accurate as far as they go.

Sometimes, however, preferences do produce error, not just partial ignorance. Gestalt preferences induce the visual system to complete, or fill in, the stimuli it encounters, thereby achieving 'good continuation', even when the real figure has discontinuities or gaps. This is indeed distortion. Interpretation of two-dimensional arrays as three-dimensional solid objects can also lead to error—when the real stimuli are only dots of light.

But how serious are these error possibilities? As long as the organism's environment is full of solid objects, which generally do instantiate good continuation, these error prospects will not be systematic. In terms of the *actual environment* of human beings, the preferences seem to be highly reliable. Indeed, the mathematical proofs by Ullman, Hoffman, and their colleagues, mentioned in section 11.2, show that under certain conditions like rigidity and planarity, the hypothesized visual principles are perfectly accurate. (To be more precise, the probability of error has a measure of 0—which does not imply the impossibility of error.)

Even if highly constrained representation-forming devices can lead to error, there may be compensating gains in speed. This is worth illustrating in connection with language learning. In acquiring a first language, the learner may be thought of as generating grammatical hypotheses on the basis of linguistic 'texts' (discourses) to which he or she has been exposed. Language-learning theorists in the Chomskyan tradition conjecture that human dispositions of hypothesis generation—conceptualized as functions from texts to hypothesized grammars—are quite restricted. Such dispositions could not lead to correct identification of all possible languages.[38]

However, although this implies a limit on power, it may be accompanied by gains in speed. A learning function that cannot learn every language may nonetheless be able to learn many languages—including actual natural languages—much more rapidly than more powerful learning functions. Specifically, it may be able to do what the normal child can do: learn a first language in three years. This trade-off between speed and power may well be worthwhile, given our limited lifespan.

Returning now to constraints on partitioning, is there anything useful about the specific partitioning principles human beings seem to manifest (as judged by the evidence in section 11.2)? I have no inkling of the benefits or costs to the organism taken singly, but a definite plus can be assigned to the sharing of a narrow set of principles by species members, no matter what the principles. The plus is associated with *social coordination.* Shared partitions promote successful communication; and successful communication provides enormous epistemic advantages.

The sort of point I have in mind is made, in its essentials, by Quine, who stresses the uniformity of people's innate quality spacings.[39] We might carry this over to a uniformity of innate partitioning principles. If the young child had a very different set of innate quality spacings from its elders, it might associate different mental units with its elders' words than the elders do. This would make it hard to achieve mutuality in sense or reference. Where the parent individuates in terms of rabbits, the child might individuate by rabbit-stages. Or the discrepancy might be even greater. This would certainly make successful intercourse hard to achieve. (I here assume, unlike Quine, that it is determinate which style of mental individuation in fact characterizes a person.) But where innate partitioning principles are shared and relatively small in number, the prospects for successful communication are greatly enhanced. Such communication has immeasurable epistemic benefits: innumerable truths, and truth-acquiring methods, can be learned from others via language. A noncommunicating creature would be at a severe epistemic disadvantage. Thus, the mere sharing of highly constrained partitioning operations—whatever they may be (within limits)—seems to be a great epistemic boon.

11.5. Originality

Although it is scarcely touched by philosophical epistemology, 'originality' is a widespread term of evaluation in intellectual affairs. It is a dimension commonly invoked in the evaluation of both intellectual products—books, articles, ideas, and hypotheses—and intellectual producers. Since the progress of knowledge depends on the production of *new* knowledge, and since this characteristically depends on original ideas (not merely new evidence for old ideas), originality is a proper subject of epistemological study.

Of course, originality is also present in the sphere of the arts, which may not fall under the rubric 'intellectual', and may therefore fall outside epistemology. But that needn't perturb us.

What do we mean when we call an idea 'original'? One broad meaning is that it is an idea nobody else has had before; at any rate, it is an idea that the thinker did not get from anyone else. But there is another, narrower sense of the term. Within the class of ideas that are not *directly* borrowed from others and are not mere duplicates, some strike us as more inventive, clever, surprising, imaginative, or creative than others. These we deem 'original'. Other ideas, which are equally nonduplicates, seem pedestrian, obvious, and trite. The term 'original' is withheld from these. But how do we distinguish the inventive ideas from the pedestrian, the imaginative from the hackneyed?

Apparently we have some tacit *metric* by which we measure originality. Some ideas seem more 'distant' from socially available ideas, harder to think up on one's own. Other ideas, even if they are original in the broad sense, seem easy to think up; they seem 'closer' to what has already been formulated. But what underlies this metric? What makes some ideas seem close to their predecessors, and easier to think up, and others more distant and difficult? The answer is related to human representation-forming operations.

Suppose, as I have suggested, that human beings have a fairly delimited set of representation-forming operations, and a (substantially) fixed ranking of these operations. In addition, assume that in any scientific or cultural milieu the stock of ideas antecedently available to cognizers is essentially the same. Then all new ideas must result from transformations of the same initial stock of ideas. If this is correct, one should expect certain new ideas to occur independently to many workers in a given field. Members of the discipline all have roughly the same stock of initial information and previously tried ideas; and they share a set of problems they wish to solve. So when the highest-ranking—or most 'natural'—operations are applied to their initial stock of ideas, many people will come up with the same (or very similar) new thoughts. But these will be the most *obvious* thoughts, the most straightforward extensions of preexisting ideas.

The sociologist of science Robert Merton has remarked on the prevalence of multiple discoveries in science: the same discovery being made at roughly the same time by several independent researchers.[40] In fact, I would add, the number of historically *significant* multiples surely underestimates the prevalence of the phenomenon. Scientists and scholars are constantly coming up with similar ideas; but many of these do not get published or do not get published by everyone who thinks of them. People's minds run in very much the same channels.

How, then, are truly original ideas created? And why do certain individuals seem particularly adept at such inventiveness? Four possibilities come to mind. (1) Perhaps the ranking of operations is not completely fixed, or universal. Perhaps certain operations, which are unusual or low-ranking for most people, are higher in rank for others. The latter individuals apply these 'unusual' operations more readily, and hence come up with ideas that others find surprising and inventive. (2) Although there may be no interpersonal difference in the ranking of operations, perhaps some individuals try a larger number of operations, turning eventually to unusual operations that most people do not try at all. This could result in ideas that strike others as departures from the commonplace. (3) Perhaps the important difference lies in the combinations, or permutations, of operations that certain people employ. What distinguishes the creative thinker from the humdrum thinker may be the transformational combinations, or permutations, he or she utilizes.

All three of these possibilities are ways in which *control* mechanisms that select representational operations may differ interpersonally. A fourth possibility is that one of our prior assumptions is inaccurate, namely, the assumption that people have the same stock of initial ideas on which to operate. While there is doubtless much overlap in such antecedent resources, there are also differences. Hence, (4) perhaps the distinguishing character of creative people is that they apply the same operations to unusual sets of initial ideas, thereby producing unusual outputs.

Whether this is an exhaustive list of possibilities does not much matter. It is clearly important to the understanding of creativity to determine which of these—or other—possibilities are primarily responsible for differences in creativity. This is a future task for cognitive science, though continuous with work already undertaken on basic representation-forming operations.

But how is this relevant to epistemology? One dimension of epistemological appraisal is the assessment of problem-solving procedures. But problem-solving procedures, as I stressed in Chapter 6, include the formation of representations that are candidate solutions to problems. When problems are difficult and previously unsolved by others, this may mean that unusual solution candidates need to be constructed. Hence, cognitive procedures involved in such construction fall under the scope of epistemology.

11.6. Justification

Originality and creativity are nonstandard topics for traditional epistemology. Other, more traditional, dimensions of appraisal to which the study of representation-forming operations is also germane include justification, which can be illuminated by the psychology of representation formation slightly differently from the reliability considerations already adduced.

It is widely suggested that a person is justified in believing hypothesis p if p would be a good explanation of certain observed phenomena and there is no equally good alternative explanation. But this principle is not quite right. Even if there *is* an alternative explanation, we would not deny that a person's belief in p is justified unless it is reasonable to expect him to think up the alternative explanation. A person is justified in placing credence in a good explanatory hypothesis that occurs to him, as long as any alternative explanation is excessively hard to construct (from his prior belief corpus).

Suppose a child (a ten-year-old, say) has never paid close attention to objects partly immersed in water. Suppose also that he has never heard of laws of optical refraction or other such physical laws. Suppose he now sees an oar half immersed in water and notices that it looks bent. He concludes that it *is* bent. It never occurs to him that there might be a law of physics which implies that a straight object partly immersed in two different media, such as water and air, should look bent. He does not form a representation of any such alternative explanation of the oar's apparent bentness. Is his belief in the oar's being bent justified or unjustified? I think it *is* justified. Given his background information, it would be very difficult to think up any alternative hypothesis to explain the oar's apparent bentness.

Suppose you too see the apparently bent oar, but you are familiar with laws of optical refraction; yet you too conclude that the oar is bent. Then we would say that your belief is unwarranted. You ought to be able to construct the alternative explanation, which should inhibit your belief (at least the 'central-system' belief).

Consider another example. Is Othello justified in believing that Desdemona was unfaithful? Apparently, Othello does not construct any alternative explanation of Iago's insinuations, of Desdemona's loss of her handkerchief, and so on. It does not occur to Othello that Iago might be a villainous fellow, that Iago's being passed over for promotion might make him vindictive and lead him to deceive Othello about Desdemona. Most of Shakespeare's viewers doubtless find in Othello a singular paucity of imagination. It is easy to construct alternative hypotheses to the unfaithfulness hypothesis, but Othello fails to do so. Hence, his belief is unwarranted.

The point I wish to stress in all such cases is that judgments of justifiedness or unjustifiedness depend on the *ease* or *difficulty* of thinking up rival hypotheses. When a scientist's belief in a certain theory is subsequently shown wrong by the invention of a new and vastly more powerful theory, this need not undermine the justifiedness of the earlier belief (that is, the justifiedness of the first theory being believed *at* the earlier time). It depends on how hard it would have been for him to *create* the rival theory then.

The ease or difficulty of creating alternative hypotheses is a function of both one's antecedent conceptual and doxastic corpus, and the naturalness, or likelihood, of a suitable combination of representation-forming operations producing these alternative hypotheses from this corpus. Our intuitive judgments of justifiedness and unjustifiedness, I believe, rest partly on a tacit grasp of the ease or difficulty of constructing relevant rival hypotheses. However, if we want to spell out the basis for these intuitive judgments, we need to identify the repertoire of operations and their standard preference ordering. That would give us a systematic ground for the indicated judgments. But this is a job for cognitive psychology.

How do these comments on justifiedness relate to reliability? The idea is this. A belief-forming process that incorporates consideration of competing explanatory hypotheses is much more reliable than a similar belief-forming process without concern for competing hypotheses. So only the former can be expected to be licensed by suitable rules of justifiedness.

It is not clear, however, that such rules would require a cognizer to construct *all possible* competing hypotheses. At any rate, on the 'resource-relative' conception of justifiedness, a person's belief is justified just in case it is produced by a process that is reasonably reliable relative to the resources of the human cognitive system. Justifiedness is judged by the use of processes that are as reliable as can be expected, given the native endowments of human cognizers. Among the relevant endowments are those for hypothesis construction. Relative to these resources (and some initial corpus of concepts and beliefs), some rival hypotheses are easy to construct and others are difficult. The aforementioned conception of justifiedness is sensitive to this relative ease or difficulty. A detailed identification of the dimensions of ease and difficulty, however, rests with psychology, for only psychology can illuminate the representation-forming repertoire available for these tasks.

chapter 12

Internal Codes

12.1. Sense-Linked and Sense-Neutral Codes

It is natural to think of mental representation as occurring in different internal codes, or code systems, some of which are associated with particular sense modalities such as vision. In addition to visual *perception,* there is visual *recollection* (for example, visually recalling one's lover's face) and visual *imagination* (for instance, picturing a possible move in a chess game). These cognitive events ostensibly share a representational form: they are all, in some sense, 'visual'. Other cognitive events similarly form natural families: a family of *auditory* representations (recalling a passage from Brahms third symphony), a family of *motor* representations (recalling 'by feel' what finger is used to type the letter *f*), and a family of *sense-neutral* representations (recalling the meaning of *untersagen*).

A given code might be employed in at least four different phases of cognition: (1) perception, (2) LTM, (3) recall, or activation, from LTM, and (4) manipulation or transformation, in active memory, of materials generated from LTM. When a code is *sense-linked*—for example, visual—then phases (3) and (4) would ordinarily be called 'imagistic'. One generates from LTM a visual image of one's lover's face, or transforms imagistically a certain chess configuration.

The questions I wish to raise in this chapter are the following. Assuming that there are, indeed, different internal codes or code systems—in particular, sense-linked code systems—what are the epistemic properties of these systems? Suppose that, in addition to some sense-linked code systems, there is a sense-neutral code system (what psychologists often call a 'propositional' code). Then how do epistemically relevant properties of sense-linked systems compare with those of the sense-neutral system? How do they compare on such dimensions as reliability, power, speed, and so on?

Since I include perception as one stage of a given code's employment, the topic of the present chapter in principle includes perception. But I have already touched on perception in Chapter 9. And since no sense-neutral code occurs in perception, there is no basis for *comparing* sense systems with sense-neutral systems at the perceptual stage. I shall therefore concentrate on the three other stages at which different codes might be employed: retaining material in LTM, recalling material from LTM, and constructing new ideas, scenarios, and possibilities in imagination.

The history of epistemology bears witness to the distinction I have sketched between sense-linked and sense-neutral codes or code systems. Often, of course, different terminology was used in describing these code systems. The language of 'faculties', for example, was quite common. In whatever terminology, oppositions were drawn between 'sensibility' and 'understanding', 'intuition' and 'reason', 'percepts' and 'concepts', 'sensation' and 'judgment'. Admittedly, many of these oppositions are primarily concerned with perception, rather than the other cognitive stages I have delineated. Still, it is not too much of a stretch to view these oppositions in the guise I have just been presenting.

The British empiricists and associationists certainly viewed the later stages I have mentioned—retention, recall, and imagination—as closely related to perception. Locke, for example, thought of ideas lodged in memory as the "same" as ones previously perceived:

> This further is to be observed, concerning ideas lodged in the memory, and upon occasion revived by the mind, that they are not only (as the word *revive* imports) none of them new ones, but also that the mind takes notice of them, as of a former impression, and renews its acquaintance with them as with ideas it had known before.[1]

The notion that images are like weak percepts is found in Hume:

> Those perceptions, which enter with most force and violence, we may name *impressions*, and under this name I comprehend all our sensations, passions and emotions, as they make their first appearance in the soul. By *ideas* I mean the faint images of these in thinking and reasoning.[2]

Similarly for James Mill:

> . . . by shutting my eyes see him no longer, I can still think of him. I have still a feeling, the consequence of the sensation, which, though I can distinguish it from the sensation, and treat it as not the sensation, but something different from the sensation, is yet more like the sensation, than anything else can be; so like, that I call it a copy, an image, of the sensation; sometimes, a representation, or trace, of the sensation.[3]

The classical empiricist theory, however, is not a perfect example of the model of mind I favor. The empiricists apparently rejected sense-neutral codes altogether. They viewed *all* thought as derivative from, or decomposable into, sense-produced materials. In contemporary terminology the only internal codes they countenanced were sense-linked codes. If this view were accepted, there could be no epistemic comparison between sense-linked and sense-neutral codes, because there would not *be* any sense-neutral codes.

Although I part company with classical empiricists in their rejection of sense-neutral codes, I agree with them in their acceptance of sense-linked codes. This view, of course, contrasts with that of many philosophers and psychologists of the twentieth century. Many theorists posit only a single, sense-neutral code and reject the presence of multiple codes, especially sense-linked ones. They claim that all cognition takes place in a 'propositional', or 'symbolic', code. If this claim were correct, there would again be no basis for attempting to compare the epistemic properties of different codes, for there would not be different codes.[4]

To get a feel for the dispute between single-coders and multiple-coders, let us briefly survey some of the sample controversies, first among philosophers and then among psychologists. Although the dominant view of twentieth-century philosophy sharply distinguished sense-experience from belief, dissenters began to arise in the last twenty years. D. M. Armstrong and George Pitcher proposed a belief theory of perception, that perceptual experience is the acquisition of beliefs (or dispositions to believe).[5] In a similar vein J. M. Shorter and Daniel Dennett held that imagery is a matter of describing rather than picturing.[6] These philosophers, then, proposed a unification of the sensuous and the cognitive. But unlike the empiricists, who sought unity by reducing the cognitive to the sensory, these philosophers sought unity in the opposite direction: by reducing the sensuous to the cognitive (or propositional).

Parallel developments have occurred in psychology. As we saw in Chapter 9, cognitive psychologists tend to view perceptual and percept-derived events as 'information'-bearing events. In the early 1970s this was made explicit in the theory that all cognitive processing is essentially propositional, a view championed by (among others) John Anderson and Gordon Bower, Herbert Simon, H. H. Clark and W. G. Chase, and M. Minsky and S. Papert.[7] Part of the impetus for the propositional view was the computer analogy. Computer feats impressed theorists with the power of digital coding. It showed what could be done, say, with lists and list processing. Further momentum came from the neurobiological work on feature detectors cited in Chapter 9. This research suggested that even at low levels of processing, the nervous system selects slices of information about environmental objects. The conclusion drawn by the aforementioned group of researchers was that the mind processes information with a *single* code—often called a 'propositional' code. Even perception and imagery could be handled in terms of propositional, or digital, encoding. Alternatively, imagery was dismissed as a mere 'ephiphenomenon'.[8]

Meanwhile, other psychologists were postulating and unearthing evidence for multiple codes. J. S. Bruner, R. O. Oliver and P. M. Greenfield postulated three developmentally linked forms of thought: enactive (or motor), iconic, and symbolic.[9] In their scheme the baby uses only the enactive format; the young child uses imagery as well; but in the adult abstract, symbolic thought predominates. Extremely influential research on imagery was done by Roger Shepard and associates.[10] In famous experiments Shepard and colleagues gave subjects problem-solving tasks involving pairs of perspective line drawings of three-dimensional objects, as in Figure 12.1. Subjects were asked whether the objects in each pair were the same or not, that is, whether they could be made congruent by a physical rotation. For 'same' cases, subjects' reaction times increased according to a remarkably linear function of the angular difference in portrayed orientation. The strong suggestion—confirmed by introspective reports—was that subjects 'image' one of the objects rotating in space, and then imaginatively determine whether the two objects would coincide. This mental rotation seems to involve a kind of mental object—an image—quite different from a set of propositions. And it seems to involve a process—rotation—quite different from one that would be appropriate to propositions.

This sort of research has fueled a lively controversy that continues unabated. Does imagery constitute a distinct form, or code, of mental representation, over and above a generally acknowledged propositional form of representation? Does the mind have a pictorial, or 'analog', way of representing states of affairs, as well as a descriptional, or depictional, mode of representation? The most persistent critic of imagistic representation, Zenon Pylyshyn, has offered theoretical and empirical reasons to question this form of representation, and has (along with many others) produced alternative explanations of experimental findings using a propositional, or digital, model.[11] Stephen Kosslyn and colleagues have generated intriguing new findings on imagery and a set of theoretical replies to Pylyshyn.[12] Thus, the battle lines have been drawn.

Figure 12.1

Since I regard the multiple code theory as extremely natural and attractive, and since I (therefore) wish to explore the epistemological significance of multiple codes, I want to put in some good words for the multiple code hypothesis. In other words, I do not want to merely *assume* its correctness; rather, I want to lend support to it. There are different ways of formulating the central hypothesis, however, and I do not mean to endorse the hypothesis in *all*—or even the most popular—of its renderings. Much of the debate has centered on topics I regard as incidental to epistemological purposes. I shall endorse only a modest variant of the multiple code approach. To explicate this variant, and set it against the backdrop of the recent controversy, is the task of the next section.

12.2. The Imagery Controversy: Some Ambiguities

There are two main ways of stating the nub of the imagery dispute. In one formulation the dispute is whether imagery is (in some sense) 'pictorial' or 'descriptional'. On this formulation proponents of imagery claim that it involves something like picturing, while opponents try to reduce the experience of imagery to propositional or sentencelike representations. Variants of this formulation are *(a)* that imagery involves a spatial, or quasi-spatial, medium of representation; and *(b)* that it constitutes an analog representation of what it depicts. These variants are not obviously equivalent, either to each another or to the original, *pictorial* characterization. There are also difficulties in stating just what an 'analog' mode of representation consists in. Still, despite these ambiguities, this family of formulations contrasts sharply with the second kind of formulation.

In the second main formulation imagists maintain that imagery is essentially like perception. It employs the same code, medium, or system of representation as the corresponding form of perception; at least it shares some of the resources and machinery of the corresponding sense modality. We may call this the *perception-similitude* formulation of the dispute.[13]

The perception-similitude formulation is significantly weaker than the pictorialist formulation. In particular, it does not imply that imagery is either pictorial, spatial, or analog. It just says that imagery is *akin* to perception—leaving it open what perception is like.

Can descriptionalists accept the perception-similitude thesis? Can they accept the claim that imagery shares the same code, medium, or system of representation as its corresponding perceptual faculty? It might seem, at first, that they can. After all, descriptionalists maintain that even perception is descriptional. If imagery is like perception, it too is descriptional. So why need they dispute the perception-similitude thesis?

They *do* need to oppose this thesis if they want to retain their insistence on a single code. According to the perception-similitude thesis, visual imagery shares the code or resources of visual perception. But ordinary 'abstract' (sense-neutral) thinking presumably does not share that code or those resources. Nor do auditory images. Hence, if the perception-similitude thesis is correct, there are *distinct* codes or code-systems. Thus the descriptionalist, to the extent that he wants to cleave to a single code, should not be receptive to the perception-similitude thesis.

For my purposes, I do not care to endorse or defend the pictorial formulation of the imagist position, although this has received the lion's share of attention. It suffices for my purposes to endorse and defend the perception-similitude thesis—or, for that matter, any other thesis that guarantees *multiple, informationally distinct* code systems. However, let us see just what imagists have been claiming. We will find considerable ambiguity in their writings, but no matter. It is open to us to select whichever aspects of their position seem most secure, and most significant from an epistemological point of view.

The most sustained and detailed defender of the imagist position is Stephen Kosslyn. Many of his writings contain phrases and models that strongly insinuate an acceptance of the pictorialist thesis. He has introduced the idea that visual images are like displays on a cathode ray tube (CRT), and he and his colleagues characterize images as "spatial displays" in active memory.[14] In his book *Image and Mind* Kosslyn talks explicitly about images as occurring in an "internal spatial medium,"[15] and he calls his position "quasi-pictorialist."[16]

Yet Kosslyn and colleagues also say that the CRT model is just that—a model—and they do not mean that images are exactly like a display on a CRT. In *Image and Mind* Kosslyn says that picture talk in connection with imagery is just a *metaphor:*

> Images are not physical objects. Unlike a picture, an image cannot be dropped, carried under one's arm, and so on . . . If images pass through intermediate orientations when they seem to "rotate," for example, they do not do so for the same reasons that a rotating physical object passes through intermediate states.[17]

> No researcher in the field would seriously argue that images are pictures; pictures are concrete objects that exist in the world, while images are ethereal entities that occur in the mind.[18]

> What researchers usually mean when they talk of having pictures in one's head is that one has retrieved, or generated from memory, representations *like those that underlie the experience of seeing* . . . Image representations are *like those that underlie the actual experience of seeing something,* but in the case of mental imagery these representations are retrieved or formed from memory, not from immediate sensory stimulation.[19]

Whereas the earlier phrases I quoted strongly suggest the pictorialist thesis, these passages—especially the italicized clauses—support only the perception-similitude thesis. The latter interpretation is bolstered by passages in which Kosslyn indicates what he means by '*quasi*-pictorial':

> We can think of the mind's eye as a processor that interprets quasi-pictorial representations (*that is, those underlying visual perceptual experiences*) in terms of "conceptual" categories.[20]

Unfortunately, it is by no means clear that the perception-similitude interpretation is Kosslyn's final, considered intent. In a very recent paper, "The Medium and the Message in Mental Imagery," he certainly seems to endorse the analog and spatiality themes:

> The distinction between a representation and a medium has proven important in the study of visual mental imagery. Although no serious researcher today maintains that images are actual pictures in the head, some still find it reasonable to posit quasi-pictorial representations that are supported by a medium that *mimics a coordinate space*. On this view, images are not languagelike "symbolic" representations but bear a *nonarbitrary correspondence to the thing represented*. Partly because of the primitive origins of this idea, many people seem wary of it. But the idea that images are a special kind of representation that *depicts* information and occurs *in a spatial medium* is not patently ridiculous, and in fact can be developed in a very coherent way that violates neither philosophical nor empirical considerations.[21]

Ambiguities in the imagists' position are found in Shepard's work as well as Kosslyn's. Shepard's talk of "rotating" mental images suggests a spatial posit. Shepard and Chipman's endorsement of "second-order isomorphism" may also appear to confirm a spatial analog construal of their position. The term 'analog' is explicitly used by Shepard. But more recent passages invite only a perception-similitude interpretation. In a 1978 article Shepard writes:

> Most basically, what I am arguing for here is the notion that the internal process that represents the transformation of an external object, just as much as the internal process that represents the object itself, is in large part the same whether the transformation, or the object, is merely imagined or actually perceived.[22]

Similarly, Shepard and Cooper write:

> The isomorphism that we do claim is a more abstract, "second-order" one . . . namely, that the brain is passing through an ordered series of states that (whatever their neurophysiological nature) *have much in common with the perceptual states* that would occur if the appropriate physical object were presented in successively more rotated orientations in the external world.[23]

Turning now to Pylyshyn, it is clear that his favorite targets in the imagist position are the analog and spatiality themes, or the general idea that there is some nonsymbolic, nonpropositional medium or code. As far as the perception-similitude thesis goes, his stance is more ambiguous. In his most recent statement, "The Imagery Debate: Analog Media versus Tacit Knowledge," Pylyshyn appears to *accept* a large chunk of the perception-similitude view:

> It is my view that there is only one empirical hypothesis responsible for the predictive success of the whole range of imagistic models . . . *When people imagine a scene or an event, what goes on in their minds is in many ways similar to what goes on when they observe the corresponding event actually happening* . . . The claim that imagery is (in some ways) like perception has predictive value because it enables us to predict that, say, it will take longer to mentally scan longer distances, to report the visual characteristics of smaller imagined objects, to rotate images through larger angles, . . . and so on.[24]

However, Pylyshyn indicates that this (the italicized statement) is not *all* that Kosslyn and colleagues maintain. They also claim that imagery involves use of a distinctive form of representation, or a distinctive medium or mechanism. And he is unpersuaded of the alleged characteristics of such a form of representation.

Since even the chief antagonist of the imagist position seems to accept the perception-similitude thesis, perhaps I need not offer an extended defense of it. However, let me cite some of the experimental evidence that supports a close connection between vision and visual imagery, and supports the contention that they both utilize some of the same specialized resources.[25]

First, there is C. W. Perky's old demonstration that people can confuse imaging with perceiving.[26] Then there is recent work by Shepard, R. A. Finke, and others, showing that imagery and perception share much of the same physiological machinery.[27] Yet another impressive experiment is a refinement of the McCollough Effect. In the standard McCollough Effect test subjects first see patterns of black and red vertical stripes, and black and green horizontal stripes, for about 10 minutes. They are then presented with test patterns of black and white horizontal and vertical stripes. Subjects report seeing green on the vertical white stripes and red on the horizontal white stripes. In a variation on the McCollough Effect experiment Finke and J. Schmidt found that similar results can be obtained when subjects merely *imagine* black vertical stripes on the red patch and black horizontal stripes on the green patch![28] Another striking effect of a similar sort is this. It is known that visual acuity for vertical stripes is better than for oblique stripes. If subjects are asked to say when the stripes blur as the experimenter moves them farther away, they report being able to distinguish vertical stripes from farther away than oblique stripes. N. Pennington and Kosslyn found—amazingly—that this effect occurs with *imaginary* stripes as well![29] This is rather dramatic evidence that imagery is subserved by the same code as visual perception.

All this evidence strongly supports the contention that some distinctive code system is shared by visual perception and visual imagery, a code not deployed by nonsensory thought or by perception and imagery in other modalities. Of course, at some deep level, all internal representations, or code systems, have a common basis, namely, electrochemical activity of neurons. But there can be distinct code systems at a higher level, even if there is a common bottom-level realization. (The same piece of computer hardware can run distinct programs and implement many programming languages.) Moreover, for the purposes of (primary) epistemology, it is sufficiently noteworthy that, at *some* level, there are code systems with informationally distinctive properties. That is the idea I shall be elaborating in the rest of the chapter.

The next questions we need to ask are: What are the informationally distinctive properties of sense-linked code systems, and what are the epistemological ramifications of these properties? How does the visual code system, for example, differ from the nonsensory code system? Here the theories developed by Kosslyn and others should prove helpful.

12.3. Code Systems and Cognitive Tasks

Before turning to sensory and nonsensory code systems, let us consider some theoretical aspects of code systems in general. Notice that I use the phrase 'code *system*', not just '*code*'. By 'code system', I mean to designate not simply a symbol system, possessing some formal and semantic properties, but also a set of resources associated with the *employment* of a symbol system, for example, the medium in which it occurs, the operations or processes that can be applied to it, and so on. Examples of such resources will be provided shortly.

It is standardly assumed that a code has both a syntax and a semantics. Although both of these notions become especially problematic when applied to cognitive codes, let us start with some possible semantic differences between different codes. The question is not how codes (cognitive or otherwise) *get* their semantic properties, but what *kinds* of semantic properties they can have. Stephen Palmer proposes three ways in which codes, or representational schemes, can differ semantically.[30]

First, two codes can differ in terms of the *type of information* they can represent, specifically, the sorts of 'dimensions' they can represent. Dimensions might be height, color, distance, pitch, or handedness. One code might be capable of representing a certain group of dimensions while another code can represent only a proper subset of those dimensions or a completely disjoint group of dimensions.

Second, even if two codes are capable of representing the very same set of dimensions, they can differ in terms of *resolution*. In one code, for example, only two possible values of length might be representable: short and long. In another code, the length dimension may be representable in a hundred, or infinitely many, different values.

Third, codes can differ in terms of *uniqueness*. A code might provide order information, making it ordinal. Or it may only offer information about same-different relations, making it merely nominal. Other kinds of uniqueness determinations may be borrowed from measurement theory.

Semantic properties of codes are obviously of epistemic interest, but they are not the only properties important to epistemics. Other important properties connected with codes, however, are really properties of code *systems* rather than codes themselves. For example, how much information and what kinds of information can a code represent at a given time? What are the limits, if any, on the information that can be represented conjointly or concurrently? Constraints of this sort are imposed not by the syntax of the code itself, but by the code's syntax plus the *medium* in which the code is contained. Suppose the medium is restricted to a single page of print. Then although the code is capable, in principle, of representing, say, a million different pieces of information, perhaps only thirty of these are conjointly representable in the medium.

There are other important features of code systems of epistemic interest. For instance, how easily do representations in a specified code get preserved, or retained, and how easily do they get lost? Again, how easily is one representation mistaken for another or confused with it? Answers to these questions might differ from code system to code system.

It should be obvious that the theory of representation must concern itself with code systems and not just codes. This is clearly recognized by cognitive scientists, although the phrase 'code system' is my own. (Others might prefer the term 'computational system', but this has fewer of the right connotations, I believe, for my purposes.) One attempt to develop a theory of code systems is found in Kosslyn. Since he uses it to discuss visual imagery, presentation of that theory should be instructive.[31]

In characterizing a code system, Kosslyn distinguishes two kinds of 'structures'—*data structures* and *media*—and two kinds of 'processes'—*comparisons* and *transformations*. Data structures are the information-bearing representations in any processing system. They can be specified by reference to three properties: their format, content, and organization. The format is determined by *(a)* the nature of the 'marks' used in the representation (such as ink, magnetic fluxes, or sound waves) and *(b)* the way these marks are interpreted. The format specifies whether a representation is composed of primitive elements and relations and, if so, specifies their nature. The content is the information stored in a given data structure. Any given content can be represented using any number of formats. The organization is the way elementary representations can be combined. The format of a representation constrains the possible organizations but does not determine them. For example, propositional representations can be ordered into various kinds of lists and networks.

A medium does not carry information in its own right; rather it is a structure that supports data structures. A page, a television screen, and even the air are media—supporting ink, glowing phosphor, and sound patterns, respectively. Media can be specified by reference to their formatting and accessibility. The formatting places restrictions on what sorts of data structures can be supported by a medium. A short-term store, for example, might have five 'slots' that take 'verbal chunks'—but not visual images. Accessibility characteristics dictate how processes can access data structures within a medium. The slots of a short-term store, for instance, might be accessible only in a given sequence.

Kosslyn indicates that all properties of the media and the data structures are defined in the context of a particular processing system. Even though structures have an independent existence, and their nature imposes constraints on the kinds of processes that can be used, structures attain their functional properties only vis-à-vis the operation of particular processes.

Among the classes of processes, it will be recalled, are comparison and transformation processes. Comparison processes compare two data structures, or parts thereof, and return a match or mismatch decision, or a measure of their degree of similarity (defined over a specific metric). Transformation processes can either alter a given data structure by changing its contents (for instance, by adding or deleting items on a list), by reorganizing the structure, or by leaving the structure intact but using it as an impetus to replace or supplement it with a new data structure.

There are many questions one might ask about this general theory, especially concerning its treatment of interpretation or content. But let us proceed directly to Kosslyn's theory of visual imagery, a particular code system. Images, says Kosslyn, have two major components. The *surface representation* is a quasi-pictorial representation that occurs in a spatial medium: this representation 'depicts' an object or scene and underlies the experience of imagery. The *deep representation* is the information in LTM that is used to generate a surface representation.

The properties of the surface image are in part a consequence of the properties of the medium in which it occurs, which Kosslyn calls the *visual buffer*. The visual buffer functions as if it were a coordinate space. This 'space' is not an actual physical one but a functional space defined by the way processes access the structure. The processes that operate on an image access the medium in such a way that local regions are separated from each other by different numbers of locations. Information is represented by selectively activating local regions of the space. The visual buffer has a limited extent and specific shape, and hence can support only representations depicting a limited visual arc. (This makes sense if this medium is also used in perceptual processing.) The visual buffer has a grain, resulting in a limited resolution. Thus, portions of subjectively smaller images are more diffi-cult to classify. Representations within the visual buffer are transient and begin to decay as soon as they are activated. This property results in the medium's having a capacity defined by the speed with which parts can be generated and the speed with which they fade; if too many parts are imaged, the ones activated initially will no longer be available by the time the later ones have been imaged.

Concerning the format of the data structure, Kosslyn says this. The pri-mary characteristic of representations in this format is that every portion of the representation must correspond to a portion of the object such that the relative interportion distances on the object are preserved by the distances among the corresponding portions of the representation. One implication of this characteristic is that size, shape, orientation, and location information are not independent in this format—in order to depict one, values on the other dimensions must be specified. (When a term like 'distance' is used to refer to surface images, it refers to functional relations among regions in the visual buffer. Increased distance will be represented by increased numbers of locations in the visual buffer.)

Kosslyn postulates two types of representations in LTM that can be used to generate images: literal and propositional representations. Literal infor-mation consists of encodings of how something looked; an image can be generated merely by activating an underlying literal encoding. Proposi-tional information describes an object, scene, or aspect thereof and can also be used to generate a surface image. The literal LTM medium does not function as if it were a coordinate space. Rather, it stores information in nonspatial units analogous to the files stored on a computer. In Kosslyn's computer simulation model files store lists of coordinates specifying where points should be placed in the surface matrix to depict the represented objects.

Turning to the *processes* postulated by the theory, Kosslyn lists four classes of imagery processing: (1) those involved in image *generation;* (2) those involved in image *inspection;* (3) those involved in image *transforma-tion;* and (4) those that determine when imagery will be used spontaneously in retrieving information from LTM. For example, images are often trans-formed incrementally, passing through intermediate points along a trajec-tory as the orientation, size, or location is altered. This is called a *shift* transformation.

This completes my summary of Kosslyn's theory. As indicated in section 12.2, its most controversial ingredient is the spatial medium, or visual buffer. But for my *epistemological* purposes, this element is not of para-mount importance. What is of interest to me are answers to questions like the following: What can the visual code system contribute to cognitive problem solving? What can it do that another (for example, nonsensory) code system cannot do? How reliable is the visual code system; or how reliable are specific operations, or combinations of operations, within this system? Since Kosslyn himself and other participants in the controversy have been so concerned with the *ontological* issues (especially the nature of the medium), there has not been sufficiently systematic treatment of these epistemological issues, though they have not been entirely neglected. I wish to urge a reversal of the emphasis. Let me first survey some of the epistemologically relevant materials provided by writers on imagery, and then identify questions for future research.

There are two kinds of ways in which visually coded materials can help in cognitive tasks. First, there is storage of visual materials in LTM and the retrieval of them (in imagistic form). Second, there is deployment of various operations on representations in the visual buffer. Of course, many cognitive tasks deploy both of these sorts of resources.

Concerning storage and retrieval from LTM, consider the following task described by Kosslyn. Suppose you are asked how many windows there were in the living room of your previous residence. If you are like most subjects, you probably have this information stored only in visual form. You need to generate from LTM an image of your former living room, and then count the number of windows. Few people have a purely propositional memory of the windows in their former living room. Only visually stored information enables them to answer the question. So there is heavy reliance on *LTM's* use of the visual code. But part of the task requires scanning the generated image while one counts the windows. This includes an operation on representations *in the visual buffer.*

Visual materials seem to be well retained in LTM, which accounts for the use of imagery as a mnemonic device. This is most vividly illustrated by the historically popular 'method of loci', the origin and nature of which are related by Kosslyn:

> The Ancient Greek Simonides, the story goes, was performing his role as bard and orator at a banquet when he was called outside to receive a message. At just that time, the ceiling collapsed, mangling all the dinner guests beyond recognition. When asked to recount who the hapless victims were, Simonides discovered that he could mentally picture the table and "walk around it," seeing all those seated with his mind's eye. Simonides reportedly found it quite easy to name all those in attendance by employing this technique, and went on to develop it as a general way of improving one's memory. The product of Simonides' and his methodological descendants' efforts is usually called the "method of loci." The method of loci involves first selecting a series of familiar places, among which one can imagine walking in sequence. Then, when one is trying to memorize a list, one imagines walking from place to place and "leaving" an image of each item in the list at each successive location. When later recalling the list, one then walks by the loci, and "sees" what is present at each one.[32]

Let us turn now to uses of imagery in the visual buffer alone, without (significant) reliance on LTM. In this category are the "mental rotation" tasks explored by Shepard and colleagues. Given the task of deciding whether certain line drawings depict congruent three-dimensional objects (see Figure 12.1), virtually all subjects imagine the rotation of one of the depicted objects, compare the two imagined objects, and then offer an answer. Significantly, subjects' performances on this task are extremely accurate. In Shepard's initial experiments nearly 97 percent of the 12,800 recorded responses of the eight subjects were correct, with error rates for individual subjects ranging from 0.5 percent to 5.7 percent.[33]

Shepard also emphasizes the significant record of image-assisted creativity in the annals of science.[34] The theory of relativity is said to have had its inception when the young Albert Einstein performed his epochal *Gedanken* experiment of imaging himself traveling along with a wave of light at 186,-000 miles per second. James Watson's account of how he and Francis Crick deciphered the double-helical structure of DNA contains still more specific references to mental performances involving imagery, such as his sudden, crucial realization that under an appropriate rotation in space an adenine-thymine pair had the same shape as a guanine-cytosine pair. And the conjoint inventions of the self-starting, reversible induction motor and the polyphase system of electrical distribution burst upon the Hungarian-born inventor Nicola Tesla in imagistic form. Tesla had an almost hallucinatory vision of the rotating magnetic field that would be induced by a circle of electromagnets, each energized by the same alternating current but successively shifted in phase.

These major creative feats are not necessary to establish the significance of image-assisted thinking in science. It is the common practice of average scientists both to draw diagrams and to think in terms of imaged diagrams. Most scientists would be greatly handicapped by any stricture against diagrammatic imagery in their scientific thought processes. Outside science, examples of image-assisted tasks are also plentiful as blackberries. One such example is chess. Chess players typically find it convenient to picture the chessboard configuration that would be generated by a move sequence they are contemplating. This helps them determine favorable or unfavorable prospects of such a sequence.

In all of these cases, it is quite clear that imaging *helps*. It enables one to get information one could not get otherwise, either at all, or with equal facility. Not all uses of imagery, though, are helpful or accurate. A familiar case is the untrustworthiness of imagery as a test of possibility. The fact that one cannot imagine, that is, picture, a chiliagon does not demonstrate the impossibility of a chiliagon.

Other cases of unhelpful, or merely pseudohelpful, imaging are presented by Pylyshyn.[35] Imagine holding in your two hands, and then simultaneously dropping, a large and a small object, or two identically shaped objects of different weights. Which object in your image hits the ground first? Imagine a transparent yellow filter and a transparent blue filter side by side. Now imagine slowly superimposing the two filters. What color do you see in your image through the superimposed filters? Imagine a glass half full of sugar and another nearly full of water. Imagine the sugar being poured into the glass with water in it. Examine your image to see the extent to which the resulting height of water rises (if at all).

As these cases are designed to illustrate, the answers you give from your imaging will only be as good as your knowledge of physical laws. Clearly, what you imagine in these cases will be guided by your beliefs about physical principles: principles of gravity, of color mixture, and of chemical solutions involving sugar and water. Pylyshyn stresses that, in these cases, it is this knowledge—presumably propositional, or 'symbolic' knowledge—that would guide your imagination. Imagery does not *naturally* obey physical laws, just in virtue of its intrinsic medium or mechanism. If you get correct answers to the foregoing questions, it is only because you have (possibly tacit) knowledge of the relevant physical laws. Pylyshyn contends that *all* answers or solutions provided by imagination are of this kind. Imagery can simulate perception because we have had a lot of perceptual encounters with the world, and therefore know how things look when subjected to certain changes or transformations. If this is right, imagery per se contributes little or nothing to our cognitive success. Its apparent contribution is really attributable to tacit, symbolic knowledge.

Pylyshyn uses such considerations to argue against any analog mechanism as a piece of "functional architecture," on the grounds that functional architecture must be *cognitively impenetrable,* that is, nonalterable by propositional content states.[36] The cognitive impenetrability criterion is problematic and cannot be explored here in detail. But it is not clear to me why, even if imagistic operations need to be selected or even guided by propositional beliefs, this would undermine their epistemic significance. There may still be kinds of tasks that cannot be accomplished without imagistic processes, even if these need guidance by propositional knowledge.

However, Pylyshyn's challenge instructively dramatizes the questions: What, precisely, are the contributions that imagery can make to problem solving or question answering? Do these contributions (if any) accrue from intrinsic features of imagery-related mechanisms, as opposed to background knowledge? If so, *which* intrinsic features? What generalizations can be made about the kinds of problems or tasks for which imagery has epistemic utility?

Starting with visual coding of information in LTM, one possibility is that LTM is better with visually coded information than with propositionally coded information. LTM might, for example, be able to hold visually coded information longer; or LTM might be able to preserve it more accurately. In this connection we should note a study by Ralph Haber in which subjects were exposed to 2,560 slides of randomly chosen natural scenes, each slide being exposed for 10 seconds.[37] Recognition performance approached 90 percent one hour after the original exposure. Haber remarks that the results suggest that recognition of pictures is "essentially perfect." Furthermore, work by Mary Potter indicates that 10 seconds of exposure is more than subjects need. Potter reports that subjects' performance in the Haber paradigm asymptotes at an exposure interval of about 2 seconds per slide.[38]

Even if LTM were not better with visually coded material than sense-neutral material, visually coded material could still be an epistemic asset. As long as material happens to have only a visual encoding, utilization of that material can enhance total cognitive performance. (This assumes, at any rate, that retention of such material is sufficiently reliable.) But if recall of visual material is better than that of nonsensory materials, cognizers should prefer visual encoding and actively promote it. The historical success of the method of loci suggests that this may well be true (at least for some individuals), though the matter needs to be addressed in a systematic, experimental fashion.

Results of such a prospective investigation might bear on another sort of epistemological application. Suppose there is a conflict between two of your apparent memories, one of them a propositional recollection and one of them an image. Which ostensible recollection should be given greater credence? This has direct bearing on the selection of a right system of J-rules.

Let us turn next to the deployment of imagery in STM (or the visual buffer). What are the scope and limits of its fruitful uses? Why does it seem to be so useful, say, for the chess player? And how would this extend to other tasks? One possibility is that the *quantity* of information graspable in imagistic form exceeds what can be held in STM in nonimagistic form. Perhaps imagery's way of representing information about size, shape, orientation, and location interdependently gives it special advantages on this score. And this possibility raises new questions: What differences are there in the way visual coding 'chunks' or 'unitizes' information about space? Is this mode of chunking what confers special advantages? How does the rate of fading of imagistic information compare with that of other information in short-term, or active, memory? Is imagistic information easier to retain than other kinds of codes? (Is this what makes people think of imagery as especially vivid?)

Another tempting explanation of imagery's utility is the cognizer's ability to project changes in *certain* parts of a contemplated scene or scenario, and then 'read off' the results of these changes for the system in question. Just how accurate this kind of operation is and what its accuracy depends upon needs to be determined, as does the extent, if any, to which it depends on the sort of tacit knowledge Pylyshyn postulates.

In all of these areas we should bear in mind the three dimensions of epistemic value I have stressed throughout: reliability, power, and speed. In each area we should ask: How reliable is the use of visual coding? How powerful is it? In particular, can it help generate correct answers to questions that could not be generated without its deployment? Finally, how can visual coding increase the speed of problem solving? Similar questions should of course be asked about other sense-linked codes: the acoustic code, the motor code, and the like.

12.4. Mathematics and Sensuous Imagination

Most of the foregoing discussion has focused on the virtues of visual coding. Imagery seems highly useful for many cognitive tasks, even if the basis of this utility needs further investigation. Historically, though, imagery has had a checkered reputation. It has often been viewed with suspicion or downright hostility. I cannot leave the topic of imagery without appraising the merits of this opposition.

One source of concern has centered on mathematics. Perceptual and imagistic thinking was once assigned a pivotal position in mathematics, especially geometry. Kant, for example, viewed geometry as knowable by means of quasi-perceptual apprehension, or intuition. But the last century has largely rejected Kant's philosophy of mathematics, and with it the reliance on intuition, or sensuous imagination. This rejection was hastened by the growth of formal approaches to mathematics, approaches that were partly sparked by discovery of the non-Euclidean geometries. The alternatives to Euclidean geometry persuaded people that the senses and sensory imagination cannot certify controverisal axioms or postulates. Development of formal accounts of proof also persuaded people that knowledge of mathematics rests on systems of language, not perceptual or quasi-perceptual intuitions. The tools of mathematical thought should therefore be confined to logic and abstract reasoning, not imagery or sensuous intuition.

A second source of worry is the apparent seductiveness of sense-linked thinking. People of science may bemoan the fact that the mind is often unmoved by discursive argumentation or statistical facts, but easily swayed by dramatic, sensorily vivid materials, even when the latter are of questionable probity. This danger is scouted by the 'epistemo-psychologists' Richard Nisbett and Lee Ross, who berate our cognitive system's susceptibility to "concrete," "vivid" data and its relative weakness at processing "pallid," or "abstract," materials.[39] This leads them to a pessimistic view of our native cognitive system, at least that portion of the system which responds to vivid, sensory stimuli. This might be taken as a warning, or even a proscription against the use of sense-coded information.

These cautionary statements must be assessed by primary epistemology. Just what is the proper use of sense-linked materials? In this section I explore this question in connection with mathematics, and in section 12.5 I examine the contentions of Nisbett and Ross.

Can sense-linked thinking play any role in the cognition of mathematics? Doubtless there have been sound reasons for challenging the role once assigned to sensuous intuition in mathematics. Such intuition turned out to be deceptive in so many areas of the discipline that claims of 'self-evidentness' allegedly vouchsafed by sensory intuitions are properly greeted with skepticism. Here is an illustration of the point.

It used to be thought that (sensuous) intuition forced us to acknowledge that no curve could fail to have a tangent at *any* of its points. It was believed that a curve must possess an exact slope, or tangent, if not at every point, at least at an overwhelming majority of them. But this is not so. Karl Theodor Weierstrass invented a curve that lacks a precise slope or tangent at any point. Intuition would tell us that there cannot be such a curve. But, as elsewhere, intuition fails us.

Examples of this sort properly fuel doubts about the epistemic role of sensory imagination. These doubts are easily carried too far, however. There are many alternative roles that imagery, or sense-linked thinking, might play in the epistemology of mathematics. These different roles must be considered, lest conclusions be drawn too hastily.

The push toward greater formalization of mathematics in the past century seems to exclude imagistic thinking from the discipline, since formalization is naturally associated with 'abstract' thought or with linguistic forms of representation. Indeed, the general emphasis on proof in mathematics seems to be congenial only to propositional and logical thinking, not sensory imagination or imagistic representation. Let me therefore pause to dispel some confusions on this topic.

In confronting this topic we should not forget the distinction between primary and secondary epistemology. In the context of mathematics secondary epistemology would be concerned with the study of proper *methods* for establishing mathematical truths, including various methods of proof. The secondary epistemology of mathematics would be concerned, for example, with the propriety of nonconstructive versus constructive proof procedures. But this would still leave many questions for primary epistemology about the proper mental *processes* for arriving at, and understanding, proofs.

Setting aside disputes over the status of axioms and controversies over the proper notion of 'proof', let us assume that a proof of a mathematical proposition is a necessary component of anyone's being justified in believing it. Still, such a proof can only be an instrument or method of justification. To be justified in believing the proposition, a person must also employ certain mental processes suitably directed at such a proof. The mere existence of the proof does not suffice for the believer's being justified. He must at least believe that such a proof exists. But mere belief is not enough either. He must believe this justifiably. Such justification might come from someone else's authoritative say-so, in which case the relevant mental processes are those that infer the existence of the proof from this testimony plus other background beliefs. Suppose, however, that his justified belief arises from firsthand study of the proof. Then some mental operations must be employed that make him justified in believing that this is a proof of the proposition in question.

The typical case is one where the cognizer reads the proof, and this obviously involves perception. So perceptual processes are among those typically involved in the acquisition of mathematical knowledge. (This needn't undermine the familiar claim that mathematics is *a priori*, since this notion might be defined in terms of the *possibility* of nonperceptual knowledge.) What other mental processes would typically be involved? Clearly, it is important to remember previous steps of the proof, and to remember the inference rules. These memories might involve visually coded representations of those steps and rules. One would also have to recognize, of each step, that it is indeed an application of relevant rules to previous theorems. This sort of recognition could also involve imagistic representations. In short, a suitable—that is, justification-conferring—set of mental operations might well include imagistic thinking (at least for some people on some occasions). Nothing in the notion of 'following', or 'understanding', a proof excludes imagistic representation from a role in such a process.

It is worth remarking in this connection that visually imaged spatial layouts may be used as analogies for an indefinite assortment of problems, including logical problems. That such imagistic strategies are quite common has been hypothesized by Janellen Huttenlocher, among others.[40] Huttenlocher presented subjects with tasks of the following sort:

Arthur is taller than Bill.
Tom is shorter than Bill.
Is Arthur taller than Tom?

The subjects in Huttenlocher's experiments describe themselves as proceeding as follows.

First, they say, they arrange the two items given them in the first premise. Sometimes Ss [subjects] describe this array as horizontal and sometimes as vertical. For vertical arrays, Ss claim that they start "building" at the top and work towards the bottom. For horizontal arrays they claim to start at the left and work towards the right . . . The goals are to identify the third item and to determine its position with respect to the other two items.[41]

Huttenlocher's hypothesis that subjects solve these sorts of logic problems with spatial imagery is controversial. (It has been challenged, for example, by H. H. Clark.)[42] But it illustrates how mental operations in 'checking' the correctness of a proof might employ spatial imagery, even though the content of the proof has nothing whatever to do with spatial matters.

This discussion shows how imagery could figure in the justification stage of the epistemology of mathematics. But my conception of epistemology comprehends not only the justification stage of inquiry, but all aspects of problem solving (see Chapter 6). On this conception the epistemology of mathematics should include not merely the process of doxastic 'decision'— of deciding which statements of mathematics to believe, or which alleged proofs to accept as proofs—but all facets of the construction of mathematical ideas and 'products'. Primary epistemology, in particular, should study the components that may (properly) go into any of the following cognitive processes or activities: forming or grasping mathematical concepts; inventing mathematical conjectures; and constructing (or trying to construct) proofs of conjectured theorems.

Let us consider how sense-linked processes—or even perception itself— might enter these activities. First of all, a number of proposed accounts of the basic subject matter of mathematics either require or emphasize sense-linked cognition in the formation or grasp of mathematical *concepts*. David Hilbert maintained, for example, that the subject matter of mathematics is *expressions:* either physical marks or imageable marks. He therefore held that the content of mathematics (at least in the simplest cases) is *anschaulich*—a German word that means both visual and intuitive.[43]

Among current writers, several vaguely physicalistic theories of mathematics are propounded, each implying that the grasp of mathematical concepts is, or can be, closely affiliated with perceptual and imagistic representations. This seems to be the view, for example, of Michael Resnik (although details of his view are difficult to pinpoint).[44] Resnik holds that mathematics is about abstract *patterns*. We begin by experiencing physical objects as patterned, an experience that involves visual, auditory, or other sensory modes. Mathematical discourse is constructed by abstracting from concrete patterns. Nonetheless, thinking about abstract entities is frequently accompanied by retention of the visual, auditory, and other sensory images that led to the abstract conceptions.

Philip Kitcher's view has affinities with Resnik's.[45] Kitcher holds that mathematics is about certain activities or operations, such as collecting, segregating, and correlating. Rudimentary arithmetic truths, he says, are true in virtue of "collective" operations, which can be learned by perceptual experience. Thus, the child learns that if one performs the collective operation called "making two," then performs on different objects the collective operation called "making three," then performs the collective operation of combining, the total operation is an operation of "making five." Arithmetic, he says, is about "permanent possibilities of manipulation." Acts of collecting need not, however, be physical. We can collect objects in thought without moving them about. Kitcher goes on to characterize mathematics as some sort of *idealization* of various operations. Still, the general view is congenial to the idea that the content of mathematics is grasped in the first instance by acts of perception and spatial imagination.

Penelope Maddy has also taken a position congenial to this outlook. She holds that certain sets exist in space and time, and that numerical truths about such sets can be acquired by perception.[46]

Turn next to the invention of mathematical conjectures. This too can be assisted by spatial imagination. Even if the true subject matter of mathematics is completely abstract, as platonists contend, or purely formal, as formalists contend, a cognizer may best be able to construct and assess plausible hypotheses about this subject matter by thinking about possible models or instantiations. This may involve spatial imagery. Although geometry and topology may not be about actual physical objects or relations among objects, one of the best ways to think about geometrical and topological hypotheses, and assess their initial plausibility, is by imagining possible models of the conjectures in question. The same point holds for set theory, group theory, and other branches of mathematics.

Even if the proper subject matter of mathematics consists of abstractions from concrete objects and events, it may assist a cognizer in grasping these abstractions—and envisaging new ones—to imagine instances from which the abstractions are derived. There is plenty of anecdotal evidence that learners grasp abstract ideas better if they are given concrete exemplars, such as diagrams and illustrations, of the ideas. Perhaps the mind performs abstractions more easily on sense-derived representations. Take the basic idea of an ordering, for example. We first encounter orderings through spatial and temporal experiences. We see objects lined up in a row; we hear a series of sounds in temporal succession. The general notion of an order, so fundamental to mathematics, is plausibly abstracted from these sensory representations. The process of framing new mathematical conjectures may similarly involve sense-linked representations of various kinds of patterns. Perhaps this is what the famous mathematician G. H. Hardy had in mind by his remark, "A mathematician, like a painter or a poet, is a maker of patterns."[47]

Finally, how might imagistic thinking find its way into attempts to construct proofs of conjectured theorems? In trying to construct a proof it helps to represent the general structure, outline, or contours of the envisaged proof. Many cognizers may find that such a representation consists in an imaged spatial structure. Obviously, this is not a logically necessary component, nor perhaps even a psychologically necessary component, of proof discovery. But anything that contributes to a cognizer's problem-solving power is epistemologically relevant, on my view. And imagery could well be a noteworthy contributor to the power of solving proof-construction problems (such as, 'Is there a proof of T?' or 'What is a proof of T?'). While this point does not affect any of the ontological, or foundational, questions in mathematics, it is certainly germane to the primary epistemology of mathematics.

12.5. *Vividness, Pallidness, and Norms*

Let us now examine Nisbett and Ross's allegations of a "disproportionate" impact of vivid, or sensorily coded, representations. They start by reminding us of the powerful impact of vivid writing, how social movements have been influenced by books like Harriet Beecher Stowe's *Uncle Tom's Cabin* and Upton Sinclair's *The Jungle.* Although there were probably more authoritative, better reasoned, and more factual writings on the same topics that these books addressed, their vivid, concrete, and absorbing writing had more impact. Nisbett and Ross contend that, in general, vivid information exerts a disproportionate impact on belief as compared with pallid and abstract propositions of substantially greater probative and evidential value.[48] People have a tendency to "weight" vivid information more heavily, and this, they imply, is counternormative.

Note that Nisbett and Ross's "vividness" construct cannot be *equated* with sense-linked codes. They themselves analyze vividness into several components, including *(a)* emotional interest, *(b)* concreteness and imagery provokingness, and *(c)* proximity in a sensory, temporal, or spatial way. Only component *(b)* and part of *(c)* are directly germane to the focus of this chapter. Still, the overlap with my present concerns is large, and their discussion raises important questions for primary epistemology.

Nisbett and Ross cite several experimental studies to illustrate the comparative impact of vivid information. The following two studies give the flavor of the point. W. C. Thompson, R. M. Reyes, and G. H. Bower asked subjects to read testimony from a drunk driving trial.[49] The vividness of the testimony was manipulated so that half read pallid prosecution testimony and vivid defense testimony while the other half read vivid prosecution testimony and pallid defense testimony. For example, a pallid version of prosecution evidence stated that the defendant staggered against a table, knocking a bowl to the floor. In the vivid version the action was described as knocking "a bowl of guacamole dip" to the floor and "splattering guacamole all over the white shag carpet." Subjects were then asked to indicate their judgment of the defendant's guilt, both immediately after reading the testimony and the following day. The immediate judgment of guilt did not show any effect of the vividness manipulation, but the delayed judgments did (at least when the defendant was portrayed as having good character). Subjects exposed to vivid prosecution testimony shifted toward guilty verdicts, and subjects exposed to vivid defense testimony shifted toward not-guilty verdicts. (However, delayed judgment did not show any effect of the vividness manipulation for a bad character defendant.)

In an experiment by R. Hamill, T. D. Wilson, and R. E. Nisbett, subjects were given a description of a single welfare case.[50] The description painted a vivid picture of social pathology: an obese and irresponsible woman who had been on welfare for many years, lived with a succession of 'husbands', in a home full of dirty and delapidated plastic furniture, with cockroaches walking about in the daylight, and so on. In a second set of conditions this description was omitted, and subjects were given statistics showing that the median stay on welfare was two years, and that only 10 percent of recipients remained on welfare rolls for four years or longer. The pallid statistical information, however, had no effect on subjects' opinions about welfare recipients; but the vivid description of *one* welfare family prompted subjects to express more unfavorable attitudes toward recipients. So a questionably informative case history had greater effect on inferences than dull statistics.

Anecdotal evidence supporting the vividness-impact hypothesis includes the following two items (originally given by Nisbett, E. Borgida, R. Crandall, and H. Reed.)[51] (1) Mastectomies performed on Mrs. Ford and Mrs. Rockefeller in the fall of 1974 produced a flood of visits to cancer detection clinics, whereas widely disseminated statistics about the lifetime risk for breast cancer had never produced a comparable impact. (2) While all physicians are aware of the statistical evidence linking cigarette smoking to cancer, only physicians who diagnose and treat lung cancer victims are quite unlikely to smoke; and radiologists have the very lowest rate of smoking. So informational vividness seems to influence even sophisticated people who have been exposed to the most probative data.

Why does vividness have this (putatively) large impact? One factor cited by Nisbett and Ross is that vivid information is more likely to be stored and retrieved than pallid information.

> There is good evidence that informational concreteness and imaginability promote recognition and recall. A number of investigators have shown that memory of pictures is astonishingly good and is markedly better than memory of either words or sentences . . . This superiority of picture retention is shown at every retention interval from a few minutes to several months. In addition, Paivio . . . has shown that recognition and recall of concrete words . . . are substantially better than of abstract words . . .
>
> Imagery also enables better retention of arbitrarily yoked concepts. Bower . . . showed that simple paired-associate learning is greatly facilitated when subjects are given instructions to link the stimulus word to the response word using images. For example, if subjects are required to learn the stimulus-response pair "dog-bicycle," their learning is aided greatly by creating an image linking the two terms (for example, a mental picture of a dog riding a bicycle).[52]

Nisbett and Ross cite other possible explanatory factors, beyond good retention. For example, vivid materials may convey more information; or they may recruit connected information by means of memory links; or they may remain longer in (conscious) thought.

Before proceeding to reflect on these possible causes of the impact of sense-linked materials, I should note that many of Nisbett and Ross's conjectures about vividness have been challenged on empirical grounds. Doubts about their empirical support are expressed by Shelley Taylor and Suzanne Thompson in a review of the literature.[53] Eight studies, they report, have directly tested the concreteness hypothesis, manipulating vividness through concrete and colorful language. Seven found no differences in attitudes as a function of the appeal. Four studies employed photographs as manipulations of vividness and found no differences between the picture/no picture conditions. Thirteen studies compared the impact of videotaped information with identical or similar information presented through other media (such as oral or written presentations). Of these, six found no differences in persuasive impact of various media; five found video presentations to be more effective, but only under limited conditions; one found print to have more impact than either television or audio presentations; and one found radio to be a more persuasive medium than television.

Concerning imagery, Taylor and Thompson indicate that actual studies contradict expectations that imageable vivid material will influence judgments more. The one area where the so-called vividness effect *is* supported by empirical studies concerns case histories. Case history information does seem to have a persuasive impact on judgments, when contrasted with base-rate or abstract information. However, the extent to which this finding speaks to the vividness effect is questionable. One possibility, they say, is that subjects are underutilizing base-rate or other statistical information, which they do not understand well, rather than overusing case history information. Perhaps subjects can readily discern the causal relevance of case history information to the judgments they make, but are less able to see the causal relevance when information is presented statistically. However this empirical debate is settled, these last points are extremely important for the *normative* assessment of the use of imaged materials, to which I now proceed.

Nisbett and Ross entitle their chapter on vividness "Assigning Weights to Data: The 'Vividness' Criterion." The implication is that cognizers frequently have both vivid and pallid data equally before their minds, that they understand them equally, but just assign greater weight to the former. However, this is an implausible description even of the cases they describe, and an inaccurate account of even (some of) their own diagnoses. In several of the studies they cite, subjects are given either vivid or pallid information, but not both. Thus, they are not preferring one kind of information over the other. They are just operating separately either with the vivid information or with the pallid. Now it may well be (as Taylor and Thompson suggest) that the subjects tend to underutilize the pallid, statistical information. But this does not show that they are doing anything wrong in deploying their vivid, concrete, sensorily imageable information. Consider the women who, upon learning of the well-publicized mastectomies of Mrs. Ford and Mrs. Rockefeller, visit cancer detection clinics. Surely this is not an obvious cognitive *error* on their part. Maybe their earlier failure to take similar action upon reading statistical data on breast cancer was irrational. So why is positive responsiveness to the case histories of Mrs. Ford and Mrs. Rockefeller counternormative?

Suppose sensorily coded data indeed have more influence over inference and action than nonsensorily coded data. Does this betoken any epistemic flaw in the handling of sensorily coded data? That is not obvious. As Nisbett and Ross themselves emphasize, one factor responsible for this situation is that sensorily coded data are better retained and recalled. But, surely, there is nothing counternormative about accurate and efficient recall of genuinely learned facts! There cannot be any epistemic objection to the memory system for being good at remembering sensorily coded information.

Where, then, can the fault lie? It could lie, as Nisbett and Ross's chapter title intimates, in the handling of the total 'clump' of information available. But how is that faulty? If the pallid statistical information is not well *remembered*, it seems perfectly proper to rely only on the other information, which *is* remembered. The executive portion of the mind, we assume, can only operate on activated materials. It is blameless if it fails to draw conclusions from materials once encountered but no longer available. One could say that there is a flaw in the *memory* system: it ought to recall statistical information better. However, even if we sympathize with this wish, how would it reflect ill on the accurate retention and retrieval of imaged information?

A further point—also suggested by Taylor and Thompson—should be stressed. Perhaps statistical information just is not well *understood*. This could influence either how well it is remembered (that is, poorly), or how much it is used when it is remembered. Recall (from Chapter 10) that strength of retention seems to be influenced by depth of processing. Poorly comprehended material will not be processed deeply, because one does not know what connections to establish between it and previous items in LTM. This possibility would accommodate the fact that, as Taylor and Thompson note, many studies do not show appreciable inferiority of printed material. Perhaps it is only the complexity of statistical materials that make them poorly remembered, not the fact that they are not sensorily coded.

Suppose that statistical information is recalled but poorly understood, and the executive system fails to draw permissible conclusions from it. Is this counternormative? It might be argued, on the one hand, that the system ought to understand statistical data better. Perhaps, but on the other hand, is there anything wrong with the refusal to draw conclusions from information which, as a matter of fact, *is not* well understood? I should think not. To draw conclusions in this situation amounts to random guessing or groping in the dark. That is not likely to promote reliability.

What about the suggestion, then, that the system behaves counternormatively if it fails to understand statistical data? My reaction—to be elaborated upon in later chapters—is that it is unreasonable to require this of the system's basic architecture. Just because some species of information would be cognitively useful, it does not follow that a system is poorly designed if it is not equipped with an innate propensity to grasp that information. (If the information is in principle ungraspable by the system's architecture, that is another matter. This is not in question here.) Granted, statistical information is something it is good for human beings to *learn* to understand and utilize. (This might even be a principle of secondary epistemology.) Failure to understand statistics at the outset, however, is not obviously a flaw in the system's fundamental architecture.

This topic, however, transcends the issue of sense-linked thinking. Is there evidence that something is wrong with our cognitive system's *use* of sensory codes? For example, is its use highly unreliable, or does it contribute to unreliability? As I have emphasized, the recall strength of sensorily coded materials is hardly a defect. The most that Nisbett and Ross are entitled to claim, I think, is that (1) sensory information is likely to concern individual, concrete cases, and (2) the system has a tendency to draw unwarranted conclusions from small samples (for example, isolated case histories). However, there is no necessary connection between sensorily coded information and sample size. Imagery can, in principle, carry information about large numbers of cases. For that matter, it can encode and store information about statistical tendencies: it can help represent and remember diagrams or charts that present statistical patterns. Moreover, if the system does tend to make improper inferences from small samples, that is not a problem with sensory coding per se. It is far from clear, then, that operations governing sensory codes are deficient or defective.

One moral of this discussion—encountered in previous chapters as well—is that a very complex bundle of operations needs to be surveyed and appraised in order to construct even a small piece of a right system of J-rules. It is because of this complexity that I have eschewed any attempt to present and defend any particular J-rule system. The reader may be able to extract from my discussions any number of candidate operations that might (or might not) be permitted by a system of J-rules. A proper appraisal of such a system, though, must weigh the consequences of the system *as a whole.* This contrasts with the (self-confessed) propensity of Nisbett and Ross to underline the dangers and costs of certain cognitive operations (in the present case, deployment of sense-linked materials), not to weigh their overall performance in the context of a complete cognitive system.

chapter 13

Deductive Reasoning

13.1. Logicality, Rationality, and Intelligence

The last two chapters concerned aspects of mental representation. I now return to a more traditional preoccupation of epistemology: the formation of belief (or partial belief) as it occurs in reasoning or inference. This chapter tackles deductive reasoning.

We saw in Chapter 5 that the question of deductive norms is complicated by the fact that people sometimes have false beliefs. Given this fact, it is not a generally correct policy to infer any and every deductive consequence of what you antecedently believe. If you suddenly recognize that some proposition p follows from your prior beliefs, you might reasonably conclude, not that p is worthy of belief, but that some previously believed proposition or propositions should be rejected. In this chapter I want to avoid this kind of complication. Therefore, rather than discuss deductive reasoning in the context of an entire belief corpus, I shall isolate the topic of deduction by focusing on judgments about the deductive validity of arguments. This is convenient for another reason: most of the psychological literature on reasoning focuses on argument validity.

What is the epistemological significance of *psychological* research on deductive reasoning? What can normative epistemology learn from psychology? Doesn't pure logic distinguish good deductive reasoning from bad, that is, valid deductive reasoning from invalid? And isn't this all that epistemology needs?

I made a start on answering these questions in Chapter 5. Even setting aside the problems of whether and when to make deductions from prior beliefs—a question to which pure logic offers no answer—logic alone yields no theory of justified belief. Although logic gives principles for deciding whether an argument is valid or invalid, it gives no principles for deciding whether a person who correctly ascribes validity (or invalidity) to a given argument makes that ascription *justifiably*. The theory presented in Chapter 5 says that whether a cognizer's belief is justified depends on the basic psychological processes he uses to form this belief. The psychology of reasoning is relevant to justifiedness, then, because it inquires into the basic cognitive processes that can occur in reasoning.

The epistemological significance of the psychology of reasoning is also linked to the evaluative dimension of *rationality*. Epistemology is presumably interested in such issues as: (1) Are human beings rational? (2) If they aren't perfectly rational, how rational are they? What are their flaws, or deficiencies, in matters of rationality? (3) How can human rationality be improved, or ameliorated? It is evident that the psychology of reasoning should be relevant to these questions, since whether, or to what degree, humans are rational presumably depends on their (contingent) psychological traits.

There is also another reason why psychology is relevant. The very *standards* for rationality cannot be specified without recourse to psychological facts. Plausible standards of rationality cannot be introduced by reflection on logic alone. They need to appeal to basic psychological capacities of human beings. Let me elaborate this point.

On one popular approach to epistemology the field should proceed by advancing certain ideal models, which encapsulate what a perfect cognizer would be like. It would then evaluate human cognitive performance by reference to such an idealized agent. The strategy of idealization is familiar from science, where ideal models are often introduced. The classical gas laws only hold for 'ideal' gases; the laws of classical economics only govern 'perfect' competition; and models of grammatical competence idealize away defects of performance. These idealization strategies, of course, are directed at explanatory and predictive ends, not evaluative or normative pursuits. But idealization may well serve normative undertakings as well. This strategy was formulated, for example, by Carnap:

> *Rational credence* is to be understood as the credence function of a completely rational person X; this is, of course, not any real person, but an imaginary, idealized person.[1]

How would this approach run for logical, or deductive, rationality? It might seem easy, at first blush, to say how it would run. If one tries to keep the approach plausible, however, it quickly encounters difficulties and ambiguities.

The first possible ideal model is *logical omniscience*. A being is logically omniscient, we might say, if and only if *(a)* it believes of every logical truth that it is a logical truth, and *(b)* it believes nothing to be a logical truth that is not a logical truth. One question about this conception is the scope of the term 'logical'. Does logic include second-order as well as first-order theory? Does it include recursive function theory, proof theory, model theory, and all kinds of deviant and intensional logics? Obviously, many of these branches of logic are indistinguishable from mathematics. But, on this ideal conception of rationality, a cognizer would be irrational—or at least less than completely rational—if he were ignorant of any facts of these disciplines. Yet that seems counterintuitive in the extreme. Why should failure to know (all the truths of) certain, highly specialized branches of mathematics make one *irrational?* Clearly, failure to know all the truths of topology or group theory would not make one irrational, or even less than fully rational. (Lots of these truths, of course, have not yet been discovered by anyone.) Why should failure to know all truths of recursive function theory make one irrational, or even less than fully rational?

Even if the scope of logic is restricted to classical first-order theory, the logical omniscience model seems ill-motivated. Consider a being who does not believe all truths of (first-order) logic simply because he has not had much interest in logic, and therefore has not devoted much attention to determining its set of truths. Such a being might still have ideal logical capacities, even though he is not logically omniscient. Certainly he should not be deemed irrational, or less than completely rational, just because he has not exercised those capacities. A better conception of ideal logicality, then, would be one that specified the sorts of logical tasks that an ideally logical being *could* execute.

However, there are several different kinds of logical tasks that can be specified. So if we seek to define an ideally logical being (ILB) in terms of some set of logic tasks it is capable of performing, we need to choose the tasks in question. To simplify matters, restrict attention to semantic tasks, specifically those concerning implication, or argument validity. Even with this restriction, tasks may be divided into two classes: Wh-tasks and Y/N-tasks. Wh-tasks pose questions of the form: 'What conclusions follow from this set of premises?' Y/N-tasks pose questions of the form: 'Does *this* (specified) conclusion follow from these premises—yes or no?'

Starting with Wh-tasks, two levels of performance suggest themselves as possible candidates for marks of an ILB. (1) An ILB might be defined as one who, for any set of premises, would generate and believe *all and only* the conclusions that follow from that set. (2) More weakly, an ILB might be defined as a being who, for any set of premises, would generate and believe *only* conclusions that follow from that set. In other words, on the first of these conceptions an ILB must have the capacity to provide a complete, or exhaustive, list of correct implications; whereas on the second conception an ILB need only have the capacity to produce a sound list, not necessarily a complete one. The latter would demonstrate total reliability in the production of implications, but not total power. Indeed, the list of correct conclusions could be as short as you please (even null?).

Reference to Y/N-tasks would provide a different characterization of an ILB. An ILB could be defined as a creature who, for any queried argument

<p, q>—where p is the premise set and q the conclusion—would correctly determine whether <p, q> is valid and would believe that answer.

Needless to say, one could select an even stronger conception of an ILB by requiring capacities to perform *all* of these tasks (at the highest level of performance). But let us look at the individual tasks, since some of these alone may be too strong for the purposes at hand.

How adequate are any of these conceptions of an ILB as a model of rationality? The model that requires an ILB to generate and believe all implications of a queried premise set obviously requires belief in infinitely many propositions, since any premise set has infinitely many consequences. On the approach to belief I have advocated, this immediately disbars human beings. But this, like previous proposals, is very counterintuitive. Should mere finitude of belief capacity imply that a being is irrational, or even incompletely rational? To the extent that I have definite intuitions about 'rationality', this requirement seems far too strong.

The second Wh-task model, however, does not have this drawback. It merely requires an ILB to construct (and believe) a sound list of implications, which can be as short as you please. This model, however, might well be regarded as too weak. What if a certain creature could only identify implications of the form (p or r) for any premise p? Is this sufficient for perfect rationality? I think not. This demonstrates only a low level of logical proficiency.

Turn next to the Y/N-task model. This criterion implies that a being is rational only if it can decide the validity or invalidity of any argument in first-order logic—which, of course, includes general quantification theory. But general quantification theory is not decidable, as Alonzo Church proved. There is not (and cannot be) any effective, algorithmic procedure for deciding validity or invalidity. There is a mechanical procedure that will unfailingly show any valid argument valid: if an argument is valid, the routine that shows validity will terminate. If the argument is not valid, though, the routine can go on and on without any decision.

Is it reasonable to characterize rationality in a manner that transcends computational possibility? This is very dubious. If there is no possible procedure that would ensure the execution of a specified set of tasks, how can anyone be called 'irrational' who lacks the capacity to execute those tasks? Such a degree of idealization is surely excessive.

We could lower the requirements still further. We could just require of an ILB determination of *consistency*. Or we could require determination of validity for truth-functional arguments only, where effective decision procedures do exist (for example, using truth tables).

Suppose there exist effective procedures for solving certain kinds of logic problems but a cognizer fails to use any such procedure. Does it follow that he is irrational, or imperfectly rational? Here I wish to inject a new element into the discussion: speed. Suppose that the only effective procedure for solving a certain class of problems would be very slow for a certain subclass of those problems, so that use of the procedure for that class of cases would not yield an answer in the being's lifetime. Is a being who uses a noneffective procedure instead—a procedure not guaranteed to produce a correct answer, but which might produce one in a timely fashion—is such a being irrational? Christopher Cherniak considers a cognizer who wishes to test a system of propositional beliefs (beliefs involving no quantificational structure) for consistency, and his whole belief corpus contains (only) 138 beliefs. The truth table method provides an effective procedure for testing this corpus for consistency. But if each line of the truth table for the conjunction of these statements can be checked in the time a light ray takes to traverse the diameter of a proton—an appropriate cycle time for an ideal computer—a truth-tabular consistency test would still take more time than the estimated twenty billion years from the dawn of the universe to the present![2]

As this example illustrates, the theoretical adequacy of a method is hardly equivalent to practical adequacy or efficiency. Should we say, nonetheless, that creatures who use noneffective procedures when effective procedures exist are imperfectly rational? Again, that seems wrong. Switching to the evaluative term 'intelligent', I feel even greater confidence in saying that fast but noneffective procedures may be more intelligent than effective but laborious procedures. (Notice that 'slow' is one approximate synonym of 'unintelligent'.)

The general topic of speed of computation is currently studied under the title of 'computational complexity'.[3] Complexity theory studies the practical feasibility or unfeasibility of algorithms. An algorithm's feasibility is evaluated in terms of whether its execution time grows as a polynomial function of the size of input instances of the problem. If it does, the algorithm is generally treated as computationally feasible; if it increases faster, usually as an exponential function, the algorithm is regarded as computationally intractable. Such intractability turns out to a large extent to be independent of how the problem is represented and of the computer model involved.

The problem of determining whether a truth-functional argument is valid belongs to a set of problems called 'NP-complete'.[4] While NP-complete problems have not been proven inherently to require exponential time, they are strongly conjectured to do so; and hence are thought to be computationally intractable. So complexity theory suggests that even some comparatively simple reasoning tasks cannot *feasibly* be performed in ways guaranteed to be correct. Thus, it seems implausible to say that human beings are 'irrational' or 'unintelligent' just because they fail to possess, or utilize, algorithms for such tasks.

Reflections on the speed desideratum, and on the sketched results of complexity theory, suggest the difficulty of giving an unambiguous characterization of an ILB. Even if we could agree on some such characterization, though, I question whether it is a sensible requirement for 'perfect rationality', or 'perfect intelligence', that one should be an ILB. The point I now have in mind is one I hinted at earlier. Suppose we could identify a set of optimal logical operations. Does it follow that someone who fails to possess or deploy these operations (in appropriate task situations) is unintelligent (or imperfectly intelligent)? This ignores an alternative, and much more plausible, diagnosis: that he lacks a perfect education or training in logic.

An oft-voiced criticism of IQ tests is that they really test acculturation or acquired knowledge, rather than intelligence. This makes it clear that, intuitively, intelligence consists in a 'raw' ability to learn or perform other cognitive feats. It is to be distinguished from acquired skills and information. If a person lacks optimal logical operations, that need not be ascribed to suboptimal intelligence, any more than a failure to deploy optimal operations for solving topology problems betrays suboptimal intelligence. In both cases we might well say that optimal operations are things to be learned, not things we expect to find in a creature's cognitive architecture.

However, it is certainly plausible to hold that some, at least minimal, logical abilities are required for learning, and for general problem solving. So unless a creature has at least those minimal abilities, as part of its cognitive architecture, it would indeed count as irrational or unintelligent. But it is not obvious that there is some *unique* minimal set of logical abilities that is requisite for learning and problem solving. A number of distinct sets of abilities might each suffice.

There are two ways one might proceed at this point. One might explore the minimal logical abilities necessary for rationality by constructing various sets of such abilities, implementing them on computers, and seeing how well they can learn, solve problems, and so on. This is the route taken by (some) practitioners of artificial intelligence. Another route is to examine the fundamental logical endowments of human beings, on the assumption that human architecture includes only rudimentary logical abilities. These abilities enable people to learn and solve problems, but do not generally confer the highest attainable logical skill without formal *instruction* in logical concepts and techniques. Nonetheless, since these abilities suffice for what we ordinarily call rationality or (moderate) intelligence, we can identify a baseline for these evaluative predicates by exploring the native logical endowments of human beings. And this exploration belongs to the psychology of reasoning.

The distinction I have been drawing between basic logical abilities and acquired logical abilities might be paralleled by a distinction between basic rationality and acquired rationality, or between basic intelligence and acquired intellectual skill. We might then say that it is the job of primary epistemology to identify the components of basic rationality or basic intelligence; whereas the identification of the methods and techniques appropriate to acquired rationality or acquired logical skill would fall to secondary epistemology. Since my goal is to construct a primary epistemology, it is the contours of basic rationality or basic intelligence that will be explored. In this investigation the psychology of reasoning has a natural place.

13.2. Basic Reasoning Abilities

What are people's 'basic', 'natural', or 'intuitive' logical abilities? An optimistic view is that people are *constitutionally* good logicians. People's natural reasoning proclivities are not only 'precursors' of formal logic, but carry people quite far on logical tasks even without formal instruction. No doubt, formal training can augment people's repertoire of deductive strategies (for example, the *reductio ad absurdum* technique); it can show them how to deal with complex problems systematically; and it can increase their speed in solving logic problems. But, according to this optimistic view, native logic abilities are fundamentally quite sound and moderately powerful. Formal training only polishes these abilities, makes them more systematic, and explains underlying theoretical principles.

A pessimistic view, by contrast, would hold that people are constitutionally so illogical that they can only become logical by being completely 're-programmed'. Even more pessimistic, it might be held that we are natively such bad logicians that even formal training cannot eradicate our fundamental logical flaws. I do not know of anyone who holds this last view, but something rather like it has been held about people as intuitive statisticians or probability assessors. Not only do people have a very poor intuitive grasp of statistical principles, it has been held, but even those highly trained in statistics persist in certain blunders (see Chapter 14). A similarly bleak view of human logical endowments is conceivable as well.

It is hard to hold a completely bleak view of human educability in logic. At a minimum, large numbers of people are capable of learning to 'do' logic, in the sense that they can pass formal logic courses, which involves solving many problems and answering many questions correctly. But do they really understand what they are doing? Many a logic instructor feels that a large proportion of students can only do problems mechanically, without true understanding. And if our constitutional logical endowments were so strong, shouldn't formal logic be easy and perspicuous to everyone?

I want to shift the question now from understanding to justification. When people study formal logic, they presumably come to believe in the correctness of the procedures they follow. But are these beliefs justified? According to my theory of justifiedness, justification involves (at least) primary justifiedness, that is, the use of approved *basic* processes. Does our constitutional endowment provide suitable basic processes?

To be more concrete, suppose someone has heard promulgated certain logical principles, and he adopts those principles. Suppose these principles, or 'methods', are formally correct. Then even if he uses those methods to determine the validity of a given argument, his belief in the argument's validity may not be justified. In particular, his belief is not justified unless he has acquired the methods appropriately, for example, by justifiably believing them to be correct (see Chapter 5). But in order for a belief in a method's correctness to be justified, it must have been arrived at (or subsequently reinforced) by an approved set of basic cognitive processes. Justification must ultimately rest on basic processes.

Three possibilities now unfold. First, primary justifiedness vis-à-vis logical principles may arise from the application of some sort of *native* deductive processes. Second, primary justifiedness vis-à-vis logical principles may arise from application of nondeductive processes. Third, people may not be justified vis-à-vis these principles at all. They may lack any permissible set of basic operations to qualify for justification. Let me examine these possibilities briefly.

Here is one way a person might come to believe in the soundness of modus ponens (the first possibility). He first constructs a truth table and notes that whenever two sentences of the forms P and (If P then Q) are both true, then the sentence of the form Q is also true. He then argues as follows: (1) In every possible situation in which both P and (If P then Q) are true, Q is true too. (2) *If,* in every possible situation in which both P and (If P then Q) are both true, Q is true too, *then* the inference schema <P; If P then Q; therefore Q> is sound. Therefore (3), the inference schema <P, If P then Q; therefore Q> is sound. Obviously, this argument is an application of modus ponens. But if this is part of a natural, or basic, inferential routine, it could well be approved by a right system of J-rules. Some might see a danger of circularity here. That seems to be the worry of Lewis Carroll in his famous dialogue "What Achilles Said to the Tortoise."[5] My theory of justifiedness, however, gives no grounds for such a concern.

The second possibility is the conferral of justifiedness by a nondeductive process. For example, someone hears the soundness of modus ponens propounded by a certain authoritative figure, such as the teacher of his logic course. His reliance on this personage might be a specimen of good *inductive* reasoning. Perhaps he has independently verified, on previous occasions, the particular speaker's credibility, or the credibility of any lecturer employed by the school or university he attends. Then his belief in the principle's correctness might be justified.

But what about authorities themselves? How are their beliefs in logical procedures justified? If we do not have native deductive processes to do the job, are there suitable nondeductive processes that do not appeal to the authority of others? In earlier eras epistemologists turned to 'intuitions' about logic to salvage the situation. But nobody has ever made it clear what kind of cognitive process an 'intuition' is. Nor is it clear what would enable intuitions to confer justifiedness. On my theory intuitions would have to be very reliable. But what is the nature of an intuition that might give it reliability? Lacking answers to these questions, appeal to intuitions is not at all appealing.

The third possibility is that there are *no* basic processes by which belief in logical principles can be arrived at justifiably. This possibility, of course, would be savored by the skeptic.

So far I have mainly been conceiving logical endowments as inference rules, procedures, or transformational routines. But there is another general category in which our logical endowments might be described. This is the set of logical *concepts*, or *operators*, that are native parts of our cognitive equipment (assuming that some concepts must be native). Does our native conceptual repertoire feature the concepts of implication and consistency? Does it have the standard repertoire of operators familiar from formal logic: 'not', 'if-then', 'if and only if', 'or', 'there exist some', and the like?

Most of the research on the psychology of reasoning has concentrated on the repertoire of inference procedures. But the category of logical concepts is just as fundamental. It is often suggested, of course, that people are not familiar with the material conditional. But it is also questionable whether they have an antecedent hold on the logician's concept of validity or logical implication. One possible explanation of why logic is difficult (for some students) is that the concepts of logic do not have precise analogues in our native system of thought. Learning logic, on this scenario, is not just a matter of translating new notation into the language of thought. Formal logic benefits people because it introduces a new array of concepts and displays prototypes of argumentation not already contained in thought.

In the section that follows, I shall examine some selected work in the psychology of reasoning that bears on the issues I have just broached, especially the question of justifiedness. Very little of this, however, will deal with native logical concepts, since less research has been done on this notoriously difficult topic.[6] In fact, the entire topic of reasoning is very difficult, and the research I shall sample will not manage to answer (to everyone's satisfaction) all the questions I have raised. Nonetheless, this research gives illuminating hints at the sorts of answers that would be of interest.

13.3. *Mental Logic versus Mental Models*

There are two main competing theories in the current psychology of deductive reasoning: the *mental logic* theory and the *mental models* theory. Roughly, the mental logic theory seeks to explain people's performance on logic tasks by positing mental inference rules that carry out mental derivations. This approach assumes that people possess internal deduction schemata, such as mental analogues of the ones found in Gentzen- or Jaskowski-style natural deduction systems. They might include rules like modus ponens, conjunction introduction, universal instantiation, and so on, that are familiar from introductory texts in predicate logic. Theories of this type have been proposed by P. N. Johnson-Laird, D. N. Osherson, M. D. S. Braine, and Lance Rips.[7] The mental models approach claims that deductive reasoning is a matter not of mental proofs, but of mental models. Roughly, people allegedly construct a kind of inner 'semantics' of an argument's premises, and attempt to manipulate the constructed model or models to assess the argument's validity. The chief proponent of this approach is Johnson-Laird, who has now renounced his own earlier endorsement of the mental logic doctrine.

The best recent development of the mental logic theory is Rips's article "Cognitive Processes in Propositional Reasoning." This will serve as our prototype of this approach. Rips's article outlines a computer model of propositional reasoning, intended to simulate the processes of untrained subjects in deciding the validity of arguments. The model is nicknamed "ANDS," for "A Natural Deduction System." Although it incorporates many of the sorts of rules used in natural deduction systems, it also features routines that control the steps which are taken in trying to construct a proof. Natural deduction inference rules only say what inferences are permitted from what previous steps. They do not instruct, guide, or control a person's application of such rules for the task at hand. But consider the situation of a person who is asked whether a specified conclusion logically follows from a given set of premises, for example, whether the conclusion below follows from the premise:

If there is not both an M and a P on the blackboard, then there is an R.
(Therefore)   If there is no M, then there is an R.

Even if a person in some sense 'possesses' a list of inference rules, these do not say when they should be applied in trying to construct a proof of a conclusion from some premises. Some sort of control system is needed. Such a system will guide the agent in a *goal-directed* manner, toward constructing a proof of the specified conclusion from the specified premise. Nothing in a standard natural-deduction system corresponds to such a goal-directed system. Only such goal-directedness can enable an agent to solve predesignated problems, either in logic or in other areas.

Reasoning in ANDS means constructing a proof in working memory. The two chief components of these proofs—called "trees"—are the *assertion tree* and the *subgoal tree*. An assertion tree encodes a natural-deduction proof (or part of a proof). It records the logical steps leading from the premises to the conclusion of an argument. The subgoal tree may be thought of as the reverse pathway from the conclusion to the premises. Typically, ANDS proves its theorems from "outside in," working alternately backward from the conclusion (in the subgoal tree) and forward from the premises (in the assertion tree). The subgoal tree has no obvious counterpart in formal logic proofs. Subgoals keep the proof procedure aimed in the direction of the argument's conclusion rather than allowing it to produce implications at random from the premises. (This basic idea is due to A. Newell and H. A. Simon.)[8]

ANDS' inference routines control its proof endeavors by placing new assertions and subgoals in memory—these are the actions instigated by the routines. Each routine consists of a set of conditions that must be checked against the memory trees to determine whether the routine applies. If all the conditions are met, then a series of actions are carried out that modify the trees in specific ways. The routines are tested for applicability in a fixed order, and the first routine whose conditions are fulfilled is then carried out.

Here are two examples of ANDS' inference routines, formulated in a condition-action format. (This format resembles the format of production systems, which I will explore in Chapter 17.) Corresponding to ordinary modus ponens, ANDS has two inference routines, R1 and R2:

R1 (modus ponens, backward version)
    Conditions: 1. Current subgoal = q
               2. Assertion tree contains IF p, q
    Actions: 1. Set up subgoal to deduce p
               2. If Subgoal 1 is achieved, add q to assertion tree.

R2 (modus ponens, forward version)
    Conditions: 1. Assertion tree contains proposition x = IF p, q
               2. x has not been used by R1 or R2
               3. Assertion tree contains proposition p
    Actions: 1. Add q to assertion tree.

Forward and backward routines occur in several prior artificial intelligence theorem provers, such as D. Hewitt's PLANNER, and D. V. McDermott and G. J. Sussman's CONNIVER.[9]

Notice that backward rules like R1 are not passive implementations of logical principles; they incorporate heuristics that specify the sorts of proof strategies which are likely to pay off. This illustrates why logic, narrowly considered, does not suffice for intelligence, which embodies the capacity for goal-directed activity. Logic per se does not provide goal-oriented problem-solving strategies even in logic tasks! (Actually, many logic textbooks do include practical suggestions for finding proofs, for example, Quine's techniques of the "fell swoop" and the "full swap" in *Methods of Logic*.[10] But these are not strictly part of a natural deduction system or an axiomatic system.)

To make ANDS more realistic, Rips adds the assumption that his fourteen inference routines are *unavailable* on some proportion of trials (where unavailability may be due to failure to retrieve a rule, to recognize the rule as applicable, or to apply it properly). He assigns a probability to each routine to indicate its (degree of) availability. He then assumes that subjects, asked to judge the validity or invalidity of an argument, will attempt to construct a mental derivation. If they successfully deduce the conclusion, they will judge the argument to be valid. Otherwise, they will either guess at the answer or simply declare the argument invalid. Other factors—such as misperceiving or misunderstanding part of the argument—could keep subjects from finding a correct proof. But Rips assumes, for simplicity, that these sources of error are negligible compared to rule availability.

To make precise predictions of subjects' responses to various arguments, Rips formulates an equation that embodies two main elements: the probability that a subject will construct a proof—and therefore answer 'valid'—and the probability that he won't construct a proof but will *guess* the answer 'valid'. After assigning values to the pertinent parameters—the availability probabilities of each of the rules and the guessing parameter—the model makes specific predictions for particular problems.

In one experiment subjects were given 104 arguments to assess for validity. Among the valid arguments in this experiment, subjects correctly judged them valid on about 51 percent of trials, with scores for individual arguments varying from about 17 to 92 percent. (The arguments clearly spanned a wide range of difficulty for the subjects.) For the invalid arguments, the percentage of (incorrect) 'valid' responses was about 23 percent. These observed percentages came out very close to the percentages predicted by the model for each of the problems. In addition to this sort of test of the model, Rips provides other empirical evidence in the form of *(a)* protocols of a subject while working on a problem, and *(b)* memory for proofs.

Granted that the evidence cited in Rips's article provides substantial support for the theory, there are problems and questions that can be raised. Of substantial interest, at least for my purposes, is the fact that Rips's model posits no fallacious or incorrect inference propensities. All rules embodied in the fourteen routines are sound. (Rips indicates that the routines are not intended to be exhaustive; but he does not suggest that any fallacious routines might be added.) True, the model allows for erroneous judgments; but these can only arise from guesses that are offered when no proof is found. There is plenty of other ostensible evidence, however, of fallacious inference propensities, at least for some people. Furthermore, there are certain kinds of sound inference rules—for example, modus tollens—that seem to be poorly grasped by many subjects. (Interestingly, Rips omits any modus tollens rule from his routines.) One would like to know why modus tollens is not so well grasped by human beings as other inference principles. Are there some deeper-lying facts about mental logic that explain this? If so, they are wholly neglected by the present approach. I will return to this issue in section 13.4.

We come now to the mental models theory. According to this approach, reasoning is not a matter of applying abstract logical rules at all; it is a matter of creating and manipulating internal analogues. The internal analogues 'simulate' what is asserted in the premises and conclusion. By manipulating these simulations, allegedly, one arrives at a judgment of validity or invalidity, or at a conclusion that appears to follow from the specified premises. This approach has something in common with other developments in cognitive science that stress inner representations of concrete instances, or exemplars, such as the prototype theory of concepts.

The best developed version of the mental models approach to reasoning is presented by Philip Johnson-Laird, in *Mental Models*.[11] As he explains it, the models people use to reason "are more likely to resemble a perception or conception of the events (from a God's-eye view) than a string of symbols directly corresponding to the linguistic form of the premises . . . The heart of the process is interpreting premises as mental models that take general knowledge into account, and searching for counterexamples to conclusions by trying to construct alternative models of the premises."[12]

How, in particular, would this be done?[13] Suppose you are given a pair of syllogistic premises and are asked to produce a conclusion that follows from these premises. (This is the standard task that Johnson-Laird has used in his experiments, rather than the task of deciding the validity of a full argument, with conclusion specified.) For example, you may be given the following:

(1)   Some of the artists are not beekeepers.
      All of the clerks are beekeepers.
      _____

      Therefore, ???

According to the theory, the first thing to do is to interpret the individual premises, and you do this by configuring a set of mental exemplars that correspond to particular artists, beekeepers, and clerks. The theory stipulates that the model for the first premise is the one in (2), and the model of the second premise is that of (3).

(2)   artist
      artist
      _____

      (artist) = beekeeper
              beekeeper

(3)   clerk = beekeeper
      clerk = beekeeper
              (beekeeper)
              (beekeeper)

In these diagrams the exemplars are indicated by words, though the words themselves have no significance other than to differentiate exemplars of different types. To indicate identity among the exemplars, you place an equality (or identity) sign between them. So the equal sign between clerks and beekeepers in (3) represents the fact that those clerks also are beekeepers. In (2) the artists above the line are those that are definitely not beekeepers. However, the parenthesized artist below the line symbolizes the possibility that there may be an artist who is a beekeeper. In (3) both of the clerk exemplars are beekeepers and there may or may not be beekeepers who are not clerks.

After you form these representations of the premises, you have to combine them into a unified model of the problem as a whole. One such model might be:

(4)   artist
      artist
      _____

      (artist) = beekeeper = clerk
                 beekeeper = clerk
                 (beekeeper)
                 (beekeeper)

In order to generate a conclusion to the syllogism, you then try to 'read' from this model the relationships that hold between the 'outer' terms: 'artists' and 'clerks'. Two conclusions that suggest themselves on the basis of the unified model is 'Some artists are not clerks' and 'Some clerks are not artists'. However, to be sure that these candidate conclusions really follow, you need to check that there are no alternative models of the premises that make these conclusions false.

Johnson-Laird claims that his theory can successfully predict the difficulty people have in producing correct conclusions.

> The major source of difficulty should be the construction and evaluation of alternative models. This process places an additional load on working memory—the memory system that is used for holding the mental models while they are manipulated. The greater the number of models to be considered, the harder it should be to construct and to evaluate them. Hence, the task should be harder when it is necessary to construct two models, and harder still when it is necessary to construct three models.[14]

These predictions are borne out by experiments that Johnson-Laird did with various colleagues. In one experiment, for example, twenty students at Teachers College, Columbia University were given all sixty-four possible pairs of syllogistic premises. For the premise pairs requiring one model to be constructed to yield the correct conclusion, 92 percent of the correct (valid) conclusions were drawn. Of the premise pairs requiring two models, 46 percent of the correct conclusions were drawn. And of the premise pairs requiring three models, 27 percent of the correct conclusions were drawn.[15]

Johnson-Laird also believes—quite plausibly—that a good theory of reasoning should explain children's ability at reasoning. With this in mind, he did an experiment on syllogistic reasoning involving two groups of intelligent children: one group of nine- to ten-year-olds and another group of eleven- to twelve-year-olds. Unlike most adults, these children could only (in the main) draw valid conclusions that depended on constructing one mental model. The older group responded correctly on 58 percent of the one-model problems—there were eight such problems and a child had to get four of them right to perform reliably better than chance. Not one of the older subjects drew a correct conclusion to the two-model problem or to the six three-model problems. The younger group responded correctly to 41 percent of the one-model problems, three subjects (16 percent) responded correctly to the two-model problem, and not a single subject responded correctly to the three-model problems. This seems to conform to Johnson-Laird's predictions about relative difficulty, and perhaps supports the idea of locating difficulty in memory load (since children may have deficits compared to adults in that respect).

How plausible is the mental models approach? In "Mental Muddles" Rips makes some telling criticisms. The central question is whether mental models can replace mental inference rules. Mental modelers get rid of traditional inference rules, Rips charges, only at the expense of positing some rules of their own. Procedures are necessary to specify how the models should be used to represent the premises, how these premise models should be combined, how one combined model should be transformed into another, and how potential conclusions should be evaluated for consistency with a combined model. The rules that make use of elements in a model have to respect properties that seem like those of logical syntax. The equal sign, for example, has to be interpreted in a way that enforces the idea that the two tokens refer to the same object. So manipulation of mental models is not fundamentally different from manipulation of mental propositions. It seems, then, that the rules that operate on the models must *be* inference rules. If so, the contrast Johnson-Laird sets up between mental logic and mental models collapses.

It might be replied that some of this criticism applies specifically to Johnson-Laird's version of the mental models approach, but may not generalize to all variants of this approach. The underlying theme of the mental models approach is intuitively very attractive, even if Johnson-Laird's particular version seems problematic. Still, the sort of challenge Rips poses would seem to be germane to any specimen of the mental models approach.

Rips also raises some technical problems about Johnson-Laird's models, which cast doubt on his principles for counting the number of models required for a given premise pair. But I will not go into this matter. It should also be noted that Johnson-Laird only applies his leitmotif to *syllogistic* reasoning. It is not clear how it would apply to sentential logic or to predicate logic generally.

13.4. *Justification and Natural Logic*

Given the research of Rips, Johnson-Laird, and many others in the field, what are the grounds for either optimism or pessimism about our native logical endowments? What appears to be the extent of human ability to have *justified* beliefs about logical subject matter, even without formal training in logic? What precisely are the operations that can yield such justifiedness? Even a first pass at these questions will require a critical assessment of the research I have summarized in the previous section, and related work as well.

I will start with Rips's approach and then proceed (more briefly) to Johnson-Laird's. On the surface Rips's model—if it is correct—offers substantial ground for optimism. It depicts the human cognizer as possessing a set of inference routines that all embody *sound* inference rules, such rules as modus ponens, DeMorgan's law, disjunctive syllogism, *and*-elimination, *and*-introduction, *or*-introduction, law of excluded middle, and the like. Though Rips does not suggest that these routines suffice—even in principle—to solve all (propositional) logic problems, the soundness of the rules apparently guarantees perfect reliability. This would be just the sort of characteristic that can confer justifiedness.

But there are several questions and doubts to be raised. First, do the inference routines really guarantee reliability? How can that be so, since the model's predictions came quite close to the subjects' observed performances, and yet these performances involved rather high error rates? How is this possible, and what are the implications for justifiedness?

Second, is a Rips-style model really correct? Do people have only sound inference routines? How is that compatible with other evidence of psychologists (and logic teachers) that untrained subjects are prone to commit various sorts of fallacies and mistakes? What do these fallacies and mistakes imply about the prospects for justifiedness?

Third, Rips's model would be grounds for optimism about our constitutional logical endowments only if the model really depicts people's *native* processes. But it is not clear that it does. (Nor does Rips explicitly claim that it does.)

Concerning the third issue, notice that even if subjects do use the sorts of routines featured in Rips's model, these routines are not obviously 'native' or 'basic'. They could be acquired 'methods' that subjects have evolved or picked up. To be sure, the subjects in Rips's experiments had had no formal training in logic (that is, no logic coursework). Still, the experiments were done on college students (typically at good undergraduate institutions, like the University of Chicago), and any college student has many layers of acculturation imbedded in his or her thinking. Examples of proof procedures would have been encountered in mathematics courses, even in high school geometry courses. And smatterings of logic inevitably appear in many books and lectures outside of so-called logic courses. So while Rips's empirical data—including the protocol data and memory-for-proofs data—may indeed support his model, they leave it entirely open whether the operations in question are *natural* inferences. But only the properties of natural inference concern us here. Although this point is extremely important for our purposes, let us waive it in the remainder of the discussion, turning to the other issues concerning Rips's theory and results.

First, what are we to make of the appreciable number of errors that subjects in Rips's experiment made? How is that compatible with the soundness of the routines he postulates? In the experiment to which I alluded in section 13.3, the subjects correctly judged valid arguments to be valid on only about 51 percent of the trials; so their responses on valid arguments were wrong about 49 percent of the time. On problems involving invalid arguments, their responses were wrong about 23 percent of the time. These are not very high truth ratios, and certainly not perfect ratios.

The main explanation is that soundness of the routines only guarantees that whenever an ostensible proof is constructed (of the conclusion from the premises), the argument is genuinely valid. So whenever a subject judges an argument valid because of a proof he has constructed, the judgment will be correct. But there are also occasions when a subject fails to construct a proof, either because the argument is invalid, and hence there is no proof of the conclusion from the premises, or because his routines have not succeeded in devising a proof despite the argument's validity. With a proof unavailable, however, it seems that the subject must guess at the argument's validity. This is where error possibilities creep in.

An initial point to be made, then, is that subjects performing these sorts of tasks do not always use the same sequences of operations. So we should not assume that the overall performance of the subjects as a group, or even the overall performance of any single subject, represents the truth ratio of a single process (or sequence of operations). Furthermore, it is compatible with the prevalence of erroneous responses that *certain* operation sequences are perfectly reliable; errors that occur may be wholly assignable to *other* operation sequences. In particular, any operation sequence that consists of (*a*) using one of the inference routines in ANDS, (*b*) producing thereby a proof of the target conclusion from the target premises, and (*c*) inferring therefrom a belief in the argument's validity, is a perfectly reliable operation sequence or process. This is just the sort of process that would presumably be licensed by a right J-rule system. By contrast, any operation sequence whose final stage incorporates a mere guess presumably would not be very reliable and would not be licensed by a right J-rule system.

By 'guess', I here mean a process that fixes a *belief.* There is another sense of 'guess' that simply involves the choice of a verbal response, unaccompanied by a genuine belief. Many of the subjects' responses in Rips's experiment may have been guesses in this second sense, because subjects were *forced* to respond either 'valid' or 'invalid'. But since the present discussion focuses on processes that yield justified or unjustified beliefs, I am only concerned with guesses in the sense that triggers beliefs. (Notice that if many of the responses were just guesses in the second sense—mere verbal responses not registering genuine beliefs—then the number of subjects' false beliefs was not as high as the data suggest.)

It might be argued that when a subject tries to construct a proof, fails, and infers that the argument is invalid, this last inference is not a mere guess. It is an *inductive inference*, perhaps of an 'explanatory' variety. It might run: 'I tried a variety of ways of constructing a proof, but none of them worked. The best explanation of this failure is that there is no proof. Therefore, the argument is not valid'. This is indeed one way a subject might reason. It is not obvious, though, whether this would be an approved process of reasoning. What it shows, however, is that even in Rips's model there might be justified beliefs in propositions concerning logical subject matter that are justified by inductive rather than deductive inference processes. Actually, it seems to be a consequence of Rips's model that the only way in which a person can justifiably believe in an argument's *in*validity is by this sort of inductive inference. The ANDS model offers no way of *proving* invalidity.

I can now summarize the implications of Rips's model as follows. If this model is right—and right about our *basic* reasoning processes—there clearly are some operation sequences used to form beliefs in argument validity that would be licensed by a right J-rule system. Specifically, where a person constructs a proof by means of any sequence of (officially designated) routines incorporated in Rips's model, and infers validity of the target argument from this proof, then this belief is presumably justified. But it leaves open the possibility that people have no available operations for judging argument invalidity that would be permitted by a right J-rule system. Or, if there are such operations, they must have a significant inductive component. This last possibility is especially interesting. Could it be that for some judgments of logic, people have to use inductive processes to arrive at justified beliefs? Shades of John Stuart Mill!

We come next to the plausibility of a Rips-style model. How, in particular, does it square with (apparent) evidence of fallacies and mistakes of various kinds? Consider fallacies that are sufficiently prevalent to have received labels, such as 'denying the antecedent' and 'affirming the consequent'.

Some data on this matter are found in a study by Rips himself and a colleague.[16] Subjects were asked to evaluate eight types of "conditional syllogisms," shown in Table 13.1. Subjects were asked to judge whether the conclusion was "always" true, "sometimes" true, or "never" true, given the premises. As the figure shows, subjects could apply modus ponens quite successfully. But there was considerable evidence of tendencies to 'deny the

Table 13.1   Percent of total responses for eight types of conditional arguments.

Argument	Always	Sometimes	Never

1. $P \supset Q$
   P
   $\therefore Q$
	100[a]	0	0

2. $P \supset Q$
   P
   $\therefore \sim Q$
	0	0	100[a]

3. $P \supset Q$
   $\sim P$
   $\therefore Q$
	5	79[a]	16

4. $P \supset Q$
   $\sim P$
   $\therefore \sim Q$
	21	77[a]	2

5. $P \supset Q$
   Q
   $\therefore P$
	23	77[a]	0

6. $P \supset Q$
   Q
   $\therefore \sim P$
	4	82[a]	14

7. $P \supset Q$
   $\sim Q$
   $\therefore P$
	0	23	77[a]

8. $P \supset Q$
   $\sim Q$
   $\therefore \sim P$
	57[a]	39	4

Source: L. J. Rips and S. L. Marcus, "Supposition and the Analysis of Conditional Sentences," in M. A. Just and P. A. Carpenter, eds., *Cognitive Processes in Comprehension* (Hillsdale, N.J.: Erlbaum, 1977).
   a. The correct response.

antecedent' and 'affirm the consequent'. In problem 4, 21 percent mistakenly said that the conclusion would always be true; and in problem 5, 23 percent erroneously said that its conclusion would always be true. These cases invite the query: What processes were those subjects undergoing that led them to their incorrect answers? How are those processes to be explained on Rips's approach? Perhaps answers are to be sought in more 'primitive' operations, which could explain why subjects go wrong in these ways, as well as why they go right in many other cases.

Notice that subjects also had considerable trouble with modus tollens, a rather elementary inference form (from the vantage point of an expert). In problem 8, 39 percent of the subjects failed to see that the conclusion would always be true, given those premises. Of course, failure to possess modus tollens as an inferential rule, or routine, is not a fallacy. However, it again invites the conjecture: perhaps there are more primitive operations that *underlie* the fact that modus ponens, say, is so easily grasped whereas modus tollens is often ignored.

Attempts have been made to explain some of the fallacious propensities in terms of 'misunderstandings' of the conditional. Experiments by J. E. Taplin and H. Staudenmayer suggest that many subjects interpret the conditional as being what logicians would call the 'biconditional'.[17] If so, they would not really be making a fallacious inference. But the failure to apply modus tollens cannot be explained away in this fashion, since it is a legitimate principle even if the conditional is interpreted as a biconditional.

In addition to the fallacies mentioned above, fallacies are frequently made on classical syllogisms. The following invalid syllogisms, for example, are often accepted as valid:

Some A's are B's.
Some B's are C's.
　Therefore, some A's are C's.

No A's are B's.
No B's are C's.
　Therefore, no A's are C's.

To account for this pattern of errors, R. S. Woodworth and S. B. Sells proposed the "atmosphere hypothesis," which stated that the logical terms—'some', 'all', 'no', and 'not'—create an atmosphere that predisposes subjects to accept conclusions with the same terms.[18] For example, subjects are predisposed to accept a positive conclusion to positive premises and a negative conclusion to negative premises. When the premises are mixed, subjects prefer a negative conclusion. Although the atmosphere hypothesis captures some of the trends in the data on syllogistic reasoning, it does not represent the whole story. It certainly raises doubts, though, about the notion that people's inference routines embody only sound inference rules.

Another well-known case of logical errors is found in Wason's "selection

Figure 13.1

task."[19] In the central experiment from this research, four cards were shown to subjects (see Figure 13.1). Subjects were told that a letter appeared on one side of each card and a number on the other. They were asked to consider the following rule, which referred only to these four cards: "If a card has a vowel on one side, then it has an even number on the other side." The task was to decide exactly which cards had to be turned over to determine the correctness or incorrectness of the rule.

Forty-six percent of the subjects elected to turn over the *E* and the *4*, which is a wrong combination of choices. The *E* card does have to be turned over, but the *4* card does not, since neither a vowel nor a consonant on the other side would falsify the rule. Only 4 percent elected to turn over the *E* and the *7*, which is the correct answer. (An odd number behind the *E* or a vowel behind the *7* would falsify the rule.) Another 33 percent of the subjects elected to turn over the *E* only. The remaining 17 percent made other incorrect choices.

There are two main types of error in this task. First, subjects often turn over the *4*, which is not necessary. Second, there is almost total failure to appreciate the necessity of turning over the *7*. Admittedly, not all of these mistakes need be attributed to application of unsound inference routines; they might be attributed to omission of sound routines. But they again cause one to wonder whether all the manipulations subjects are performing can be accounted for by the kind of routine repertoire that Rips postulates.

Let us turn briefly now to Johnson-Laird. It is hard to compare his theory to that of Rips for several reasons. First, it deals primarily with syllogistic reasoning, whereas Rips's model deals with propositional reasoning. Second, the tasks Johnson-Laird gave his subjects were Wh-tasks ('What conclusions follows from these premises?'), not Y/N tasks ('Is this argument valid?'). Third, Johnson-Laird does not really present any *routines* by which subjects are alleged *(a)* to construct 'models', or 'interpretations', of the premises and contemplated conclusion, and *(b)* to check whether they have considered all relevant models. His description of the operation sequences that subjects undergo is therefore quite sketchy.

Given this sketchiness, my treatment of the theory must be a bit speculative. It seems, though, as if nothing corresponding to deduction-framed routines are part of the process envisaged by the theory. In particular, first, nothing of that sort seems to be at work when subjects attempt to construct interpretations of the premises. Second, nothing of that sort seems to be at work when subjects decide whether they have constructed *all* the alternative interpretations that are possible for the premises in question. So far, then, there is nothing corresponding to the soundness of Rips's inference routines to assure high reliability. Of course, processes need not be sound (in the technical sense) in order to be sufficiently reliable for justificational purposes. So we cannot conclude that Johnson-Laird's approach, if correct, would preclude justifiedness. We need to know more details about the processes it postulates.

This much seems clear, however. Johnson-Laird's picture of the processes used in deductive reasoning tasks depicts them as *very similar* to processes used in other kinds of cognitive tasks, such as natural language understanding. In all such tasks there are operations of construction and rearrangement of mental 'tokens', which represent relevant contents of the task. (Of course, the sharing of this feature does not imply that the operations are otherwise exactly alike. But Johnson-Laird's main theme is this similarity.) Thus, on Johnson-Laird's approach, the processes involved in deductive tasks are not at all *sui generis*.

Given the many questions I have raised, no definite conclusions can reasonably be drawn at this point about the justificational potential of the basic processes we use in deductive reasoning tasks. Of course, this inconclusive state of affairs is no cause for embarrassment in cognitive psychology. The questions are, obviously, intrinsically very difficult. What is clear is that primary epistemology needs answers to these questions, and that, at least in principle, they can be answered by cognitive psychology.

13.5. *The Dichotomy in Epistemology versus the Unity of Cognition*

In this section I draw some implications from our discussion for a long-standing dichotomy in the history of epistemology. A sharp demarcation has traditionally been drawn between 'truths of reason' and 'matters of fact'. Allegedly, the epistemologies of these two realms are significantly different. In particular, the epistemology of logic and mathematics is said to differ sharply from the epistemology of 'empirical' subject matters. I want to challenge this sharp dichotomy from the vantage point of this chapter's material. Quine, of course, has famously challenged the same dichotomy,[20] but the grounds of my challenge are quite different from Quine's.

A number of labels are used—and sometimes uncritically assimilated—in addressing this dichotomy. These labels come in pairs: 'a priori' and 'a posteriori'; 'empirical' and 'nonempirical'; 'necessary' and 'contingent'; and 'analytic' and 'synthetic'. Several of these distinctions are not really *epistemological* distinctions. The distinction between the necessary and the contingent is metaphysical; and the distinction between the analytic and the synthetic is semantic. However, for the sake of argument (at least), I shall grant the legitimacy of these distinctions. I will even concede, for the sake of argument, that statements (or facts) of logic differ from 'empirical' statements on these metaphysical or semantic dimensions. But even if it is conceded that truths of logic are necessary or analytic truths, it is an open question what follows from this about the epistemology of logic.

Actually, I do not wish to deny *all* epistemological differences between questions of logic and questions of (what is normally called) 'empirical science'. After all, I too have presupposed some such distinction in claiming that epistemology should invoke the help of empirical sciences. What would be the significance of this claim if there were no contrast between the empirical sciences and other disciplines? It may be, however, that the differences between disciplines are mainly differences in their secondary epistemologies, in the methods appropriate to each. At the level of primary epistemology, they may still have much in common. This weaker thesis is the one I will defend. Even this weaker position, however, parts company with the traditional style of dichotomizing epistemology.

One of the traditional claims is that truths of reason and matters of fact differ on the dimension of *certainty:* unlike matters of fact, truths of reason can allegedly be known with certainty. Quine challenges this principle of differentiation by first equating certainty with immunity from revision and then denying that any statements are so immune. I agree with the certainty challenge, but not because I equate certainty with immunity from revision. (I would also reject the equation of 'analytic statement' with 'statement immune from revision'; but that is another matter.)

As an epistemic (rather than a doxastic) notion, certainty is best understood as the highest possible level of justifiedness or warrant. The theory of justifiedness, as I have formulated it, does not admit *levels,* or *grades,* of justifiedness. But the spirit of the theory lends itself to such an extension. A belief can be regarded as certain if and only if it is caused by perfectly reliable—infallible—cognitive processes (or infallible processes together with infallible methods). Let us ask, then, whether logic belongs in a separate epistemic category because it is knowable with certainty.

The suggestion that truths of logic are so knowable could derive plausibility from the idea that there are *mechanical methods* for determining truths of logic, since mechanical methods are infallible. But, of course, Church's Theorem shows that there are not mechanical methods for determining invalidity in general quantification theory. Moreover, as we have seen (in section 13.1), complexity theory suggests that many other problems in logic are not computationally tractable, that is, are not solvable by mechanical procedures in a human being's lifetime.

Another point is that although mechanical methods may be 'intrinsically' infallible, in the sense that if you use a mechanical procedure or algorithm *correctly* you cannot go wrong, there is still the cognitive task of using it correctly. This involves the use of cognitive processes, and it is unlikely that any of these are infallible. You can misperceive marks and misremember what has occurred in previous steps. You can also mistake a putative algorithm for a genuine one; so your belief that you are proceeding, or have proceeded, algorithmically—by means of a method that yields correct results—is liable to error. According to my theory, the status of certainty is only attainable by the use of infallible cognitive processes (and perhaps, if methods are necessary, infallible methods as well). Yet infallible cognitive processes are no more available for the subject matter of logic than for other subject matters.

This point is not new. Hume wrote: "In all demonstrative sciences the rules are certain and infallible; but when we apply them, our fallible and uncertain faculties are very apt to depart from them, and fall into error."[21] Similarly, Descartes noted the problem of memory in connection with reasoning.[22] But while the point is old, it is nonetheless germane.

Can one distinguish the epistemic status of logic from that of other subject matters by appealing to the *greater* certainty, or reliability, of logic-linked processes—even if they are not perfectly reliable? My discussions in the preceding sections make this very dubious. First, there is the evidence of certain fallacious inference propensities. Second, at least Johnson-Laird's picture of the processes deployed in logic tasks do not make them appear notably reliable. They are not obviously more reliable than, say, perceptual processes.

Let us turn now to the distinction between the *a priori* and the *a posteriori*. This distinction has traditionally been applied to two different kinds of objects: *truths* and (pieces of) *knowledge*. Philosophers sometimes speak of 'a priori truths', and they sometimes speak of things being 'known a priori'. It is generally conceded, though, that knowledge is the primary locus of *a priority*. Truths are dubbed *a priori* only in a derivative sense: when it is possible to *know* them *a priori*.

The standard explication of *a priori* knowledge is knowledge that does not involve, or depend upon, perception, or 'experience'. However, other baggage is often added to the term 'a priori'. In particular, it is often taken to entail certainty. If so, we have already had grounds for denying that logical truths are (generally) knowable *a priori*. But let us unload this excess baggage (certainty) and focus on the alleged irrelevance of perception to logic.

Here is an argument for disputing the general knowability of logic without perception. Note first that in actual practice logicians learn new logical truths by reading the proofs others have constructed, and constructing their own proofs with pencil and paper. These activities involve perception. The *a priorist* would contend, however, that perceptual reliance on inscriptions is in principle dispensable. One could, in principle, frame all the relevant representations in the mind. But is this true? Do human cognitive capacities enable one to construct, or follow, a complex proof in the mind with sufficient reliability to qualify for knowledge? That is doubtful. It is universally acknowledged that short-term, or working, memory is limited in capacity. When this capacity is exceeded, error rates increase sharply. It seems likely, therefore, that many phases (even single steps) of a truly complex proof will involve more material than can reliably be maintained in working memory. Therefore, a logical truth whose proof involves that degree of complexity can only be known with the help of external inscriptions, hence, only with the help of perception.[23]

Would it be too hasty to conclude that truths of logic are not generally knowable *a priori*? Could one distinguish the realms of the *a priori* and *a posteriori* by saying that propositions known *a posteriori* are, or can be, known by perceiving the known facts themselves, not just inscriptions related to them? And could one say that, by contrast, *a priori* knowledge only utilizes perception as an 'aid'—that there is no perception of the target truths themselves?[24] This obviously will not work. Some facts known *a posteriori*—for example, facts involving electrons and nomological facts generally—cannot themselves be perceived. So this approach would not draw the line where it is intended to be drawn.

Could one say that truths of reason are *sui generis* inasmuch as they *could* be known by beings (such as God) without any perceptual faculties at all? This criterion also would not draw the demarcation properly. Perhaps God could know contingent facts without perception—by some sort of nonsensuous intuition or clairvoyance.

The prospect of distinguishing the two realms in terms of perceptual knowability seems dim. There is no need to deny, though, that *simple* logical truths may be humanly knowable without any perception, and this trait may indeed contrast with contingent truths about external matters. Even granting this point, though, can it sustain the *a priorist's* hope? No. The traditional hope of the *a priorist* is to draw an epistemological dichotomy between the *entire* realm of logic and mathematics, on the one hand, and the realm of contingent fact, on the other. This hope cannot be sustained by the nonperceptual knowability of a small subset of logical truths.

Notice also that perception is only one of many cognitive faculties. Even if it is granted that the epistemology of logic does not encourage the *same* role for perception as does the epistemology of contingent matters, there is extensive sharing of other cognitive operations (or types of operations.) This sharing raises the question, Why harp so persistently on differences concerning the role of perception while downplaying the shared utilization of other faculties?

It is important in this connection to bear in mind the central place of problem solving, or question answering, in my account of epistemology. The epistemology of any 'realm' X is a matter not just of how one is *justified* in believing propositions concerning X, but of how one *finds* answers—and proofs of answers—to questions concerning X. In the realm of logic, for example, it is not just a matter of how one can be justified in believing that something is a proof of a specified conclusion from specified premises; it is also a matter of how one goes about searching for such a proof (without knowing beforehand whether there is one). Similarly, the epistemology of logic consists not just of what it takes to know that a specified conclusion follows from specified premises, but also of how one goes about *constructing* propositions that answer the question, Which conclusions follow from those premises?

Let us examine features that the epistemology of logic shares with the epistemology of 'empirical' subject matters. Although I have stressed the proof aspects of Rips's theory, which may be distinctive of logical or mathematical subject matter, even Rips's model has significant features that would be shared by processes used on empirical topics. Recall first the goal-directed routines and the control system that specifies an order in which routines are to be tested for applicability. Many of the posited routines, especially the 'backward' routines, are heuristics that constitute strategies likely to pay off. Precisely analogous heuristics can be expected for empirical domains as well. Of course, these would not be proof-construction heuristics; but they would be heuristics for finding evidence that bears on the question at hand.

The very existence of counterpart heuristics in different domains strongly suggests the possibility that the specific heuristics Rips postulates are not native. They may be acquired in the way other domain-specific heuristics are acquired. This topic of the acquisition of heuristics (or 'condition-action' pairs) will be treated in Chapter 17, where I will discuss 'production systems' generally and the acquisition of new productions in particular. It is reasonable to expect that while the details of heuristics differ from domain to domain, the underlying process of heuristic acquisition (and heuristic retention) is the same across domains. If this is correct, then both the psychology of logic and the psychology of empirical subject matters have roots in the same (second-order) processes of heuristic learning.

Let us look next at the role of memory in logic problem solving. Recall that Rips assumes that the postulated routines are not always *available* and do not have equal availability probabilities. Unavailability of a routine may be due to several sources, he says. For example, one may simply fail to retrieve it from memory. Or one may fail to recognize its applicability. These same sorts of cognitive obstacles doubtless crop up in empirical domains as well. A cognizer is always facing the problem of trying to retrieve (from

LTM) the most relevant heuristics, rules of thumb, or procedures. Presumably, the factors that facilitate or inhibit retrieval in the logic domain are the same as those in the other domains. For instance, if one has recently used a given heuristic to solve an *analogous* problem, one may be more likely to retrieve that heuristic in the present task. This role of analogy will operate in all domains of inquiry, logic included.

Finally, let us turn to the task of constructing possible answers to logic questions. This is a nontrivial task when the question is, What conclusion (or conclusions) follows from these premises? In Johnson-Laird's experiments he found that one major factor affecting syllogistic inference (previously unmentioned here) is the figure of the premises. This "figural effect" is a bias towards certain forms of conclusion. In particular, people are much more prone to infer an A-C conclusion from A-B and B-C premises, or to infer a C-A conclusion from B-A and C-B premises, than to draw inferences in other figures.[25] Johnson-Laird conjectures that this is due to basic processes of working memory, that working memory operates on a "first in, first out" basis. It is easier, for example, to recall a list of digits in the order in which they were presented—the first digit recalled first, the second digit recalled second, and so on—than in the opposite order. If this is right, then hypothesis formation in logic is a special case of much more general cognitive operations.

We saw in section 13.4 that the main theme of Johnson-Laird's theory—construction and manipulation of models—posits processes that are used for all sorts of cognitive tasks. If correct, this would certainly confirm the point being stressed in this section. Needless to say, the entire topic deserves fuller treatment. The exact extent of *shared* cognitive operations in logic tasks and in empirical tasks requires more experimental and theoretical spadework. I have illustrated the idea, however, that the cognitive ingredients of problem solving, at a deep level of analysis, are fundamentally similar across different domains. Hence, the classical attempt to dichotomize epistemology is fundamentally misguided, another example of the potential impact of psychological work on epistemological theory.

chapter 14

Probability Judgments

14.1. *What Can Psychologists Tell Us?*

In the last decade or so, psychological research on probability judgments has led to the claim that procedures commonly used in arriving at these judgments are counternormative. Several writers formulate the matter by suggesting that people's intuitive processes of probability judgment are 'irrational'. This chapter addresses the findings of this research and their evaluative implications.

The most important and influential research in this area has been done by Amos Tversky and Daniel Kahneman, who are themselves rather cautious in phrasing their conclusions. However, their language has intimations of counternormativeness. They speak of the "biases" of certain cognitive processes, of cognitive "illusions," of large and systematic "errors," and of "violations" of rules or laws (of statistics or probability theory) that they ostensibly regard as normatively correct.[1] Kahneman and Tversky also say that "for anyone who would wish to view man as a reasonable intuitive statistician, [their] results are discouraging."[2] Expositors of this and related research, such as Richard Nisbett and Lee Ross, make similar or stronger claims. They write of human failure to employ normatively correct inferential strategies;[3] of "departures from normative standards of inference";[4] and of "profound systematic, and fundamental errors in judgments and inferences."[5] Nisbett and E. Borgida write of "bleak implications for human rationality."[6] P. Slovic, B. Fischoff, and S. Lichtenstein assert that "people systematically violate principles of rational decision-making when judging probabilities, making predictions, or otherwise attempting to cope with probabilistic tasks."[7] Furthermore, in commentaries on L. Jonathan Cohen's paper "Can Human Irrationality Be Experimentally Demonstrated?"[8] none of these researchers dispute Cohen's assertion that they view their research results as signs of human irrationality. Apparently, that interpretation is close to the mark.

What can psychologists do, or tell us, that concerns rationality or other dimensions of intellectual appraisal? I have pursued this question, of course, through much of this book. At this point it may be helpful to approach it from a slightly different angle, more directly dovetailing with the work of people like Tversky and Kahneman.

First of all, the psychologist can arrange experiments in which subjects answer certain questions, and he can report these responses. Second, the psychologist can often say what proportion of these responses are true or false; and presumably he can say whether the responses are consistent or coherent. It is not obvious that this second sort of issue is *always* within the psychologist's sphere of competence. In perceptual experiments the psychologist tells us the true properties of the presented stimuli; he is presumed to be authoritative (enough) on that matter. In other kinds of experimental tasks, though, the truth or falsity of the subjects' responses may be more controversial. For example, whether specific probability judgments are true or false is entangled in controversial issues about the interpretation of probability sentences. So what a psychologist might say on this score could be disputed by others.

Third, the psychologist can offer hypotheses about the cognitive processes that underlie the observed responses. That is, he can theorize about the procedures, mechanisms, strategies, or heuristics that must be leading the subjects to respond as they do. Of course, any proffered explanatory hypothesis is open to empirical dispute. How well does it explain the evidence? What competing model might explain the evidence as well, or better?

Fourth, there is the question of the normative status of the subjects' responses; or the normative status of their using certain procedures, and failing to use others, in arriving at their responses. This question, it seems to me, falls outside the domain of psychology, narrowly construed. It is not the job of empirical science to make normative judgments (whether ethical, aesthetic, or epistemological). When it comes to epistemic normative judgments, this is the task of epistemology.

However, if certain epistemic rules or principles are agreed upon, then the psychologist may be in a position to tell us whether or not human beings conform with these rules or violate them, and with what frequency or in what circumstances. But if there is any dispute about which normative principles are correct, this dispute goes outside the realm of psychology per se.

Of course, I have been contending that principles of primary epistemology are partly determined by psychological facts. So on my view the psychologist can help epistemology ascertain correct normative principles. And the very sorts of experiments in question may help do this. But this flows from the criteria of rightness (at least J-rule rightness) that I have defended, and the defense of such criteria falls outside psychology altogether.

In the present context, then, there are three points I wish to stress about the psychologist's role. First, it is certainly possible that the psychologist might tell us things about human cognitive performances which imply (together with correct normative principles) that people's beliefs or probability estimates are frequently, even characteristically, unjustified, irrational, or otherwise counternormative. (Here I disagree sharply with Cohen.) But second, the psychologist is not necessarily authoritative on what the correct normative principles are. So if he makes any claims about such principles, those are open to dispute. Third, since I have argued that epistemic rules, or norms, should specify acceptable (and unacceptable) cognitive processes, the psychologist can help arrive at such rules by trying to uncover what sorts of cognitive processes are available to the human organism.

14.2. *Empirical Findings*

Turning now to specific empirical findings and tendered explanatory hypotheses in the area of probability judgments, it seems there are two main classes of results and explanations. First, people persistently show ignorance of facts of probability theory, or neglect these facts in the course of various cognitive tasks, even when they are highly relevant. It is not just untrained subjects who do this; so do people with considerable formal training in probability and statistics. Second, it is hypothesized that people use a different set of intuitive strategies, or heuristics, to make probability judgments, rather than the probability calculus. The one most commonly alleged is the 'representativeness' heuristic. Let us examine these results in detail.

Concerning ignorance or misconceptions of probability and statistics, Tversky and Kahneman cite the following phenomena.[9] (1) People are often insensitive to prior probabilities. When asked to estimate the probability that Steve is a librarian rather than a farmer, they tend to rely on the similarity of Steve's personality profile to the stereotypes of farmers and librarians, while ignoring 'base-rate' information, that is, information about the number of farmers and librarians in the population. (2) People tend to be insensitive to sample size. They do not realize that a smaller sample is more likely to stray farther from a population statistic than a larger sample. (3) People seem to expect that events generated by a random process will represent that randomness. For example, people regard the sequence of coin tosses H-T-H-T-T-H to be more likely than the sequence H-H-H-T-T-T and more likely than H-H-H-H-T-H, even though all three are equiprobable. (4) People are insensitive to the phenomenon of regression toward the mean, despite its ubiquity. Suppose, for example, that a large group of children have been examined on two equivalent versions of an aptitude test. If one selects ten children from among those who did best on one of the two versions, he will usually find their performance on the second version to be somewhat disappointing. Conversely, if one selects ten children from among those who did worst on one version, they will be found, on the average, to do somewhat better on the other version. But people do not expect such regression in many contexts where it is bound to occur; and when they recognize regression, they often invent spurious causal explanations for it, claim Kahneman and Tversky.

In "Extensional versus Intuitive Reasoning" Tversky and Kahneman study people's insensitivity to a basic law of probability theory: the conjunction rule. This rule states that a conjunctive event A and B can never be more probable than either of its conjuncts. This is because the set of possibilities associated with the conjunction must always be included within the set of possibilities associated with each conjunct. The probability that it will be windy and rainy tomorrow cannot be greater than the probability that it will be windy, nor greater than the probability that it will be rainy. However, people's intuitive judgments of probability often violate the conjunction rule. They frequently make groups of probability estimates in which the probability of a conjunction is rated higher than the probability of one of its conjuncts.

Here is a partial description of a typical experiment in which violations of the conjunction rule were commonly found. Subjects were given a personality sketch of a fictitious individual, Linda, followed by a set of possible occupations and avocations she might pursue.

> Linda is thirty-one years old, single, outspoken, and very bright. She majored in philosophy. As a student, she was deeply concerned with issues of discrimination and social justice, and also participated in antinuclear demonstrations.
>
>> Linda is a teacher in elementary school.
>> Linda works in a bookstore and takes Yoga classes.
>> Linda is active in the feminist movement.
>> Linda is a psychiatric social worker.
>> Linda is a member of the League of Women Voters.
>> Linda is a bank teller.
>> Linda is an insurance salesperson.
>> Linda is a bank teller and is active in the feminist movement.

Asked to rank the probabilities of Linda's current activities, including being a bank teller (T), being active in the feminist movement (F), and their conjunction (T and F), the great majority of subjects ranked the conjunction T and F as more probable than T, one of its conjuncts.

Tversky and Kahneman did three types of experimental tests of the conjunction rule: indirect tests, direct-subtle tests, and direct-transparent tests. In the indirect tests one group of subjects evaluated the probability of the conjunction and another group evaluated the probability of its constituents. No subject compared a conjunction to its constituents. In the direct-subtle tests subjects did make this comparison, but the inclusion relation between the events was not emphasized. In the direct-transparent tests the format highlighted the relation between the conjunction and its constituents. In all three kinds of tests, even the transparent tests, violation of the conjunction rule was very high. Using the Linda description with undergraduates at the University of British Columbia, 85 percent of respondents in a transparent test indicated that T and F was more probable than T.

To probe the depth of this phenomenon, Tversky and Kahneman asked subjects to indicate which of the following two arguments they found more convincing (hoping they would recognize the validity of the conjunction rule when it was expressly formulated):

Argument 1.   Linda is more likely to be a bank teller than she is to be a feminist bank teller, because every feminist bank teller is a bank teller, but some women bank tellers are not feminists, and Linda could be one of them.

Argument 2.   Linda is more likely to be a feminist bank teller than she is likely to be a bank teller, because she resembles an active feminist more than she resembles a bank teller.

The majority of subjects (65 percent) chose the resemblance argument, (2), over the extensional argument, (1).

Modest success in loosening the grip of the conjunction fallacy was achieved by asking subjects to choose whether to bet on T or on T and F. The subjects were given Linda's description with the following instruction:

If you could win ten dollars by betting on an event, which of the following would you choose to bet on? (Check one.)

'Only' 56 percent of the responses in this task violated the conjunction rule.

Many of the respondents in the foregoing studies were statistically naive. Does statistical education eradicate the fallacy? The answer is not entirely clear. In one study indirect and direct-subtle tests were given not only to naive respondents, but to informed and sophisticated respondents, the informed group being first-year graduate students or professional students who had had one or more courses in statistics, and the sophisticated group being doctoral students in the decision science program at Stanford University, who had taken advanced courses in probability, statistics, and decision theory. The sophisticated and informed groups did not perform (much) better than the naive group. Eighty-nine percent of the naive subjects, 90 percent of the informed subjects, and 85 percent of the sophisticated subjects violated the conjunction rule.

In another study, however, statistical education did seem to have an appreciable effect. Sixty-four graduate students of social sciences at the University of California, Berkeley and at Stanford University, all with credit for several statistics courses, were given a transparent version of the Linda problem. For the first time in this series of studies, less than half of the respondents committed the fallacy—'only' 36 percent. But even this seems fairly high, given the subjects' statistical sophistication.

The hypothesis proposed by Tversky and Kahneman to explain the findings I have summarized is the 'representativeness' heuristic. Both in the studies where subjects were insensitive to prior probabilities (base rates) and in the conjunction fallacy studies, subjects' probability estimates were apparently guided by the degree to which the person in question was representative of, or similar to, the classes defined by the queried events or outcomes. For example, the description of Linda presumably made her representative of an active feminist and unrepresentative of a bank teller. Presumably, she was also more representative of a feminist bank teller than a bank teller. Indeed, in many experiments on the conjunction fallacy, subjects were explicitly asked to rank various outcomes both for representativeness and for probability. The correlation between the mean ranks of probability and representativeness were typically extremely high, often greater than .95. Tversky and Kahneman also propose the representativeness heuristic as an explanation of misconceptions of chance. People's (mis)estimates of coin toss likelihoods, they suggest, is due to their expectation that coin toss sequences will be representative of the random generating process.

What, exactly, is 'representativeness'? It turns out to be a rather multifaceted relation. In "Judgments of and by Representativeness" Tversky and Kahneman discuss this relation in some detail.[10] They say that representativeness is a relation between a process or model M and some instance or event X, associated with that model. The model in question could be of a person, a fair coin, or the world economy, and the respective outcomes might be a comment, a sequence of heads and tails, or the present price of gold. Normally, the sample or act is said to be representative of the population or person. But these roles can be reversed, and we can say that the occupation of librarian is representative of a person.

They then distinguish four types of cases in which representativeness can be invoked: (1) M is a class and X is a value of a variable defined in this class. For example, the mean income of college professors might be representative of that class. (2) M is a class and X is an instance of that class. In this case, John Updike might be regarded as a representative American writer. (3) M is a class and X is a subset of M. The set of psychology students might be more representative of the entire student body than the set of astronomy students. (4) M is a (causal) system and X is a (possible) consequence. For example, M can be the U.S. economy and X the rate of inflation, or M can be a person and X an act performed by M (such as divorce, suicide, professional choice).

In early work Tversky and Kahneman suggested that people rely exclusively on the similarity of a sample to its population parameters to make probability judgments. Now they make a more moderate hypothesis: predictions and probability judgments are "highly sensitive" to representativeness, though not completely dominated by it. The magnitude of the appeal to representativeness depends on the nature of the problem, the characteristics of the design, the sophistication of the respondents, and the presence of suggestive clues or other demand characteristics.[11]

Given the multifacetedness of the representativeness relation, and the multiple determinants of whether, or to what degree, people rely on it, it is not clear that any very specific hypothesis concerning the reliance on representativeness is currently proposed. Rather, it is a more general suggestion that people 'often' rely on representativeness, or something of this sort. But however frequently this reliance is made, there is the suggestion that any appeal to representativeness in making probability judgments is counternormative. There is also the claim that failure to employ correct probabilistic and statistical rules is counternormative. This normative claim is what I address next.

14.3. Probability and Rationality

Since the evaluative term 'rational' has been introduced in this context, let me start with that term. Many theorists view the 'violation' of probabilistic or statistical rules as a specimen of irrationality. They think of the probability calculus, along with logic, as a constituent of rationality. Cognitive activity that violates the probability calculus—probabilistic 'incoherence'—is deemed irrational. Violation of the conjunction rule would be a salient case in point.

Tversky and Kahneman, it should be noted, avoid such an outright claim. In their conjunction fallacy paper, at any rate, they offer a descriptive definition of 'fallacy' and eschew its use as an evaluative epithet. They define a judgment as a 'fallacy' when "most of the people who make it are disposed, after suitable explanation, to accept the following propositions: *(a)* They made a nontrivial error, which they would probably have repeated in similar problems, *(b)* the error was conceptual, not merely verbal or technical, and *(c)* they *should* have known the correct answer or a procedure to find it."[12] However, even Tversky and Kahneman make evaluative judgments in other passages and writings; and other theorists are certainly less circumspect or continent.

Now no one should dispute the notion that probability theory and statistics can be extremely valuable intellectual tools and methods. Certainly I do not wish to dispute this. But their connection with 'rationality' is a less straightforward matter. In discussing this issue I will concentrate on probability theory, where there is a clear-cut and well-accepted mathematical theory. Statistics, by contrast, is a large set of diverse methods and techniques, the foundations of which are extremely controversial and problematic. Of course, the *application* of probability theory to issues in (normative) epistemology is also very controversial. But at least the mathematical theory is compact and manageable.

In this section there are two main groups of questions I shall raise. (1) Is probabilistic coherence an epistemic desideratum? Is incoherence a defect? If so, why? How serious a defect is it? And (2) assuming that probabilistic incoherence is a defect, is it a defect in *rationality?* In the next section I will talk about justifiedness, though not exclusively in connection with coherence and incoherence.

Before turning to these questions, we need to distinguish different ways of interpreting probability judgments. Two main approaches will concern us here: *objective* and *subjective* approaches. According to the objective approach, a probability is some sort of objective property of things, for example, the chance that a certain type of event will occur. Theorists have sought to explicate the notion of chance in various ways, especially in terms of long-run relative frequencies, or propensities. I will not explore these attempts in detail, nor the difficulties they encounter. But on the objectivist approach, when a person says, for example, that the probability of rain tomorrow is .75, he makes a statement about the objective chance of rain tomorrow. Assuming the person is sincere, he expresses a belief (an ungraded belief) in the proposition that the chance of rain tomorrow is .75. The proposition that he believes is a proposition about chances, and such a proposition presumably has a truth-value (at least according to the objectivist). Hence, the person's belief in the probabilistic proposition is either true or false (and more or less accurate).

According to the subjectivist approach, a probability is just a state of mind: a degree to which a person believes something, or the firmness of his conviction. Thus, when a speaker says that the probability of rain tomorrow is .75, he does not make a statement about the objective chance of rain. The probability qualifier is not construed as appearing *within* the proposition he believes. Rather, it characterizes the *strength* of the belief. What he believes—the content of his belief—is that it will rain tomorrow; the probability qualifier just registers the firmness, or confidence, with which he believes it.

It is also possible to combine these two approaches. A person might have subjective probabilities in objective probability propositions. That is, he might have degrees of confidence in propositions about objective chances. (This is one possible application of the notion of 'probabilities of probabilities'.)

In addition to the objective and subjective interpretations, there are the *logical* and *epistemic* interpretations of probability. The logical interpretation refers to degrees of inductive support, or confirmation, between pairs of propositions. In other words, it applies to arguments construed as sequences of premises and conclusions. The existence of such degrees of inductive support is problematic. But, in any case, inductive support does not figure prominently in the topic that presently concerns us. Thus, I will give the notion of logical probability no further attention.

There are various ways of defining the notion of epistemic probability. In the context of my theory an epistemic probability is best understood as a probability that it is rational, or justified, for a cognizer to assign, given his evidential situation. The concept of epistemic probability thereby invokes some evaluative epistemic notion—either rationality or justifiedness—that distinguishes it from the other probability notions considered thus far. However, such an evaluation must apply either to beliefs in objective probability propositions or to subjective probability states. In a sense, then, no new kind of probability is introduced by the phrase 'epistemic probability'. It is just an evaluation of one of the two kinds of probability-related doxastic states already presented: either a belief in a proposition about chance or a subjective probability state.[13] Although we are certainly interested in the evaluative appraisal of such doxastic states, in so being we are not really invoking a further species of probability. So I will dispense with the phrase 'epistemic probability'.

We now have the relevant possible interpretations of probability judgments. Before turning to the normative status of probabilistic incoherence, though, it is instructive to address the normative status of *logical inconsistency*, that is, the normative status of having a set of (ungraded) beliefs in inconsistent propositions.

Is logical consistency an epistemic desideratum? Is inconsistency a defect? If so, why? One oft-cited reason is that a person who believes inconsistent propositions would be entitled to infer any proposition whatever, since anything follows from a contradiction. But it has not so far been established that a right system of J-rules (or rationality rules) would entitle a person to draw any or every logical consequence of what he antecedently believes, even if he appreciates that it is a consequence. Hence, there need be no cause for alarm on this score.

A second possible reason for regarding inconsistency as a defect is that anyone who believes inconsistent propositions thereby believes at least one falsehood. So, on any verific consequentialist approach to epistemic value, there is at least some *bad-making* feature of being inconsistent. (Note that verific consequentialism might also be needed to make full sense of the first objection to inconsistency. What is so bad, we may ask, about inferring any proposition whatever from your antecedent corpus of beliefs? Presumably, it is bad because addition of randomly chosen propositions to one's belief corpus is likely to yield lots of false beliefs, which is bad according to verific consequentialism.)

But how bad is it, after all, to believe *one* falsehood? Not very, it would seem. So inconsistency cannot thus far be convicted of being a serious epistemic defect. Of course, while inconsistency only *guarantees* one falsehood, having an inconsistent set of beliefs will frequently involve much more than one falsehood. If you have arrived at your inconsistent conclusions by inference, not only will (at least) one of those conclusions be false, but so, probably, will some of the premises that led to the conclusion or conclusions. (If the inference was deductive, then at least one of those premises *must* be false.) In this way inconsistency will tend to carry with it some larger quantity of falsehoods, although it cannot be said, in general, how many. Thus, inconsistency should not be dismissed lightly, though it is hard to say, on verific grounds, just how nasty an infection it is.

Notice that consistency is not necessarily markedly superior to inconsistency in terms of false-belief avoidance. This can be put as follows. Consistency is, of course, a necessary condition for *total* avoidance of false belief. But it is only a necessary condition, not a sufficient one. Having a consistent set of beliefs does not guarantee total avoidance of false belief. In fact, it does not guarantee avoidance of false belief at all. A set of consistent beliefs can all be false.

These points have consequences for what one can and cannot expect to achieve if one discovers that one's belief corpus is inconsistent and tries to revise the corpus to rid it of this property. In general, it is not clear which of an inconsistent set of beliefs should be abandoned. In eliminating some of these beliefs, then, you cannot be assured you will eliminate false ones. Removal of inconsistency eliminates the guarantee of errors, but it does not guarantee the elimination of errors.

It is not so obvious, then, that elimination of inconsistency should be a cardinal epistemic precept. Even if you discover an inconsistency, it may be all right to keep these beliefs 'on hold', especially if you have no inkling at the moment which of the beliefs are least defensible. Why not retain them all, at least for the nonce, until a good reassessment of their relative merits can be made? Maintenance of an inconsistent set of beliefs need not be irrational, even when you are aware of the inconsistency. Many would argue that you should at least reduce your degrees of *confidence* in the inconsistent propositions, and perhaps this is right. But for the present we are dealing with the binary, or ungraded, category of belief.

It is even clearer that inconsistency of beliefs need not be irrational when this results from failure to notice the inconsistency. Failure to discover inconsistency is not always a mark of irrationality. Axiomatizations of logical theory by Frege and by Quine were both inconsistent in ways that did not reveal themselves immediately to many who used each axiomatization extensively. Were all the people who failed to notice these inconsistencies irrational? That seems like a misplaced epithet. Or consider mathematicians who believed, before Russell's paradox, in the axiom of comprehension of set theory, that for every formulable condition, there is a set whose members are just the things fulfilling that condition. Russell's paradox showed that this axiom implies contradictions; but were those who believed in the axiom prior to Russell's discovery of the paradox irrational? Surely not. Inconsistencies are often extremely difficult to detect; and failure to detect them need not betoken irrationality.

An example from another domain may help solidify this point. The artist M. C. Escher is famous for drawings that appear, on initial perusal, to depict a consistent scene. But close inspection gradually reveals that there is no possible coherent interpretation. Is a viewer who fails (even for some time) to recognize the scene's incoherence irrational? I think not. Doubtless, such a viewer fails to notice something of importance, but this hardly warrants the charge of irrationality.

None of these comments is intended to deny that a right set of epistemic rules—either at the primary or the secondary level—might require attempts to discover and remove inconsistencies in some contexts, perhaps many contexts. Shaping your belief corpus with an eye toward consistency is doubtless an effective way of increasing reliability. If one's perceptual beliefs are usually true, then forming further beliefs consistent with these is presumably a helpful way of working toward new beliefs with a high truth ratio. My point has only been to put the seriousness of inconsistency into a better, more measured, perspective.

Bearing these points about inconsistency in mind, let us turn now to questions about probabilistic incoherence. Here we must deal separately with objectivist and subjectivist interpretations of probability judgments. On an objectivist interpretation probabilistic incoherence is just a special case of inconsistency. Suppose you judge that the probability of its being rainy tomorrow is .60, and that the probability of its being rainy and windy tomorrow is .75. On the objectivist interpretation this means that you believe both Q, 'The chance of its being rainy tomorrow is .60', and Q*, 'The chance of its being rainy and windy tomorrow is .75.' Since *chances* obey the probability calculus (all objectivists assume this much), these propositions are inconsistent; they cannot both be true. (At least they are mathematically if not logically inconsistent.) So probabilistic incoherence in this case is just inconsistency. As we have seen, however, inconsistency is not necessarily the most flagrant or serious epistemic defect. It is not clearly epistemically objectionable in every case. Similarly cautious normative conclusions should be made for probabilistic incoherence.

When we move to the subjectivist interpretation of probability judgments, the matter is somewhat different. Probabilistic incoherence is no longer a case of believing logically inconsistent (or mathematically inconsistent) propositions. In the foregoing example the subjectivist would not interpret you as believing propositions Q and Q*. Rather, he would interpret you as having degrees of confidence in a different pair of propositions, namely, .60-confidence in 'It will be rainy tomorrow' and .75-confidence in 'It will be rainy and windy tomorrow'. *These* propositions are not inconsistent (either logically or mathematically).

On the subjectivist approach, then, it cannot be said that incoherence is a defect *because* it guarantees at least one false belief. Why, then, is it a defect? The most popular argument for the defectiveness of (subjective) probabilistic incoherence is the Dutch Book argument. On the standard approach a person's degrees of belief generate quotients at which the cognizer is prepared to make corresponding bets. A Dutch Book is a set of betting odds that guarantee a net loss no matter which propositions turn out to be true. The Dutch Book argument says that it is bad to have incoherent degrees of belief because if you do, it is possible for an opponent to make a Dutch Book against you.

But this argument has many weaknesses, as has been noted in the literature. One is not always in a betting situation. And what is wrong with maintaining incoherent subjective probabilities if there is no opportunity or occasion for anyone to make a set of bets with you? Furthermore, even if the context is ripe for betting, maybe it is sensible to leave yourself open to a Dutch Book if it would be very uneconomical in terms of your time and effort to guarantee against one. Besides, even if an opponent could make a Dutch Book, there is no guarantee he would. He might not be clever enough to do this; and there are many situations in which it would be silly of him to bet Dutch Book style to ensure a small gain.[14]

Finally, we can separate degrees of belief from betting odds. It might be defensible to have incoherent degrees of belief if one were careful not to engage in sets of bets that would necessarily yield a net loss. This would be analogous to retaining a set of inconsistent beliefs but carefully avoiding any temptation to infer random conclusions simply because contradictions entail anything. Of course, standard *dispositional* theories of degrees of belief would disallow (on conceptual grounds) the separation of belief degrees and betting propensities. But such dispositional theories are highly questionable, as I will argue in Chapter 15.

Wherever the foregoing arguments ultimately lead, let us suppose that it is a defect to make incoherent probability judgments, either on the objectivist or the subjectivist interpretation. Still, would such a defect be a mark of *irrationality?* I am inclined to answer, no. Consider the following: probability theory is a branch of mathematics, like other branches of mathematics. Failure to have learned or mastered other branches of mathematics is not normally taken as a shortcoming in rationality. Nor is the failure to recognize every concrete application of such branches. By parity of treatment, it would be wrong to view every deficiency in grasping or applying probability theory as a specimen of irrationality.

Until the time of Cantor, there was a general misunderstanding of the concept of infinity. People offered many arguments on the subject that with the hindsight of our improved grasp of the infinity concept, would be viewed as fallacious. But it would be misleading to say that these misunderstandings betrayed irrationality. People just do not come naturally to the properties of the infinite; and until intellectual giants clarified this concept, there were many confusions. The same could be said of the concept of probability. The modern concept of probability did not begin to be clarified until the seventeenth century, and a full axiomatization of probability theory was not achieved until the twentieth century. So it is hardly surprising if the naive, untrained person should find it difficult to arrive at an adequate conception of probability, or chance phenomena, all by himself. Similarly, consider the fact that many different sorts of geometries are self-consistent. This fact is not likely to be noticed by the uninitiate. Yet that is hardly ground for calling people (even partly) 'irrational'.

What about people who have proper training in probability and statistics? One of the interesting findings of Tversky and Kahneman is that even such people frequently violate probabilistic rules. However, the evidence here is not without ambiguities. As we saw in the previous section, the results of one study showed well-trained ('sophisticated') subjects performing about as badly as untrained ('naive') subjects. But in another experiment, trained subjects did quite a bit better. Only a third (36 percent) of the Berkeley and Stanford graduate students who had had several advanced statistics courses committed the conjunction fallacy when the test was 'transparent'. Moreover, as we will see in the next section, even naive subjects do better when they are given problems that call attention to the class inclusion structure of the problem.

Even 36 percent may seem like a high proportion for people with extensive formal education of the relevant kind. But it is not a trivial matter to recognize all the facts or principles you have learned that might be relevant to a given cognitive task. Recall the examples in Chapter 10 concerning the Sunday library hours and the relation between mold and bacteria. In hindsight it may be easy to say that Melanie and the microbiologists should have pulled certain facts from LTM and applied them to the case at hand. But this is only easy with hindsight, when we already start with the target facts or principles clearly in mind. In the context of problem solving the accessing of relevant, previously learned principles is not a trivial matter. Furthermore, as argued in Chapter 10, failure to access relevant facts is not plausibly construed as a defect in rationality, even if it is some sort of cognitive defect.

If *these* are not instances of irrationality, what on my view would count as specimens of irrationality? As I have stressed earlier, I have no positive account of (ir)rationality to offer. However, I am inclined to hold two things: *(a)* irrationality is a defect in basic *processes,* not simply a failure to have learned or fully mastered intellectual tools; and *(b)* not every defect in basic processes is a defect in rationality. In particular, the defect must have something to do with basic 'reasoning' processes, not just memory retrieval processes, for example.

Notice that I am not arguing that people *are* natively rational in matters of probability. I am only saying that the matter cannot now be settled, because we do not presently have an acceptable account of rationality and irrationality, especially native rationality and irrationality. Pending a satisfactory account, we are not in a position to conclude from Tversky and Kahneman's evidence that people are irrational. Notice in particular that people are capable of learning probability theory and of applying it correctly in many applications. The fact that they are misled or confused in a special class of applications does not obviously make them irrational. Naturally, it would help our theoretical plight if I had an account of rationality to offer. Unfortunately, I find this a rather misty notion. Although I find many popular requirements for rationality unacceptable, I have no good substitutes to offer in their place.

I have been focusing on rationality because that is the term of appraisal most widely used by other writers on this topic. This is an appropriate juncture, however, to switch to another term of appraisal, 'justifiedness', for which I *have* offered a positive account. The question is, how do people's beliefs or credences about probability fare on the justifiedness dimension?

14.4. Probability and Justifiedness

In considering justifiedness, we must bear in mind the two distinct components of justifiedness posited by my theory: *primary* justifiedness and *secondary* justifiedness. As far as secondary justifiedness (S-justifiedness) goes, it is certainly possible that respondents who fail to use proper probabilistic methods when they are applicable should have their resulting beliefs denied the status 'S-justified'. If so, these beliefs will not be fully justified, since full justifiedness requires S-justification. However, I have not offered a firm account of S-justifiedness. There is an unresolved question of whether someone *unexposed,* or not amply exposed, to proper methods, should have his beliefs denied the status of S-justified. So there is some question of whether to fault naive subjects who fail to employ proper probabilistic considerations. But the beliefs of amply trained respondents who fail to apply proper methods certainly seem to merit the charge of secondary unjustifiedness.

Of course, there are no grounds for concluding that people's probabilistic beliefs are never fully justified. Although the research I have surveyed focuses on probabilistic errors, it has not been shown that people never apply probabilistic methods properly. Tversky and Kahneman themselves admit that the problem tasks in their studies were deliberately constructed to elicit conjunction errors, and they do not provide an unbiased estimate of the prevalence of these errors.[15]

Under what conditions do people succeed in grasping and applying probabilistic methods, and under what conditions do they fail? The root difficulty in understanding and applying probabilistic ideas seems to be that people do not naturally think of probabilities in terms of *classes* of possibilities, and therefore do not think in terms of class inclusion, even when it is relevant. As Tversky and Kahneman express it, people do not generally represent probabilities "extensionally." This suggestion is supported by several studies, including some reported by Tversky and Kahneman themselves, who gave the following health survey problem to statistically naive students at the University of British Columbia.

> A health survey was conducted in a sample of adult males in British Columbia, of all ages and occupations. Please give your best estimate of the following values:
>> What percentage of the men surveyed have had one or more heart attacks?
>> What percentage of the men surveyed both are over the age of fifty-five and have had one or more heart attacks?

This problem produced substantial conjunction errors: 65 percent of the respondents assigned a higher estimate to the second question than to the first. However, a subtly different version of the health survey problem given to naive subjects produced very different results. This version read:

> A health survey was conducted in a sample of 100 adult males in British Columbia, of all ages and occupations. Please give your best estimate of the following values:
>> How many of the 100 participants have had one or more heart attacks?
>> How many of the 100 participants both are over the age of fifty-five and have had one or more heart attacks?

In this version only 25 percent of the subjects violated the conjunction rule. Furthermore, this portion was reduced to a record 11 percent when subjects first estimated the number of participants over fifty-five years of age prior to estimating the conjunctive category. Evidently, an explicit reference to the number of individual cases encourages subjects to set up a representation of the problem so that class inclusion is readily perceived and appreciated.

Other writers have explored the question of when subjects use reasonably accurate statistical heuristics. R. E. Nisbett, D. H. Krantz, C. Jepson, and Z. Kunda indicate that reasonably good statistical heuristics are used when *(a)* the sample space and the sampling process are clear, and *(b)* the role of chance in producing events is clear.[16] Similarly, although subjects are often oblivious to statistical factors like base rates, Fischhoff, Slovic, and Lichtenstein showed that subjects become sensitive to base rates when they encounter successive problems that vary in this critical variable.[17]

As far as secondary justifiedness goes, people are evidently *capable* of using correct probabilistic methods. They often do not use them, even when they have been trained; but sometimes they do. Hence no universally bleak conclusion about secondary justifiedness of probabilistic judgments is warranted. Thus far, there are no grounds for the eager skeptic to rejoice.

But how does this conclusion affect *primary* justifiedness? How adequate are the basic processes that get deployed in connection with probability tasks? Are they so poor as to be excluded by all right J-rule systems? Or are some of them sanctionable by a right J-rule system? Much of the work in this field has centered on the representativeness heuristic, which bears the brunt of the attack on native processes in probability judgment. Recall from section 14.2, however, that Tversky and Kahneman no longer claim that people rely exclusively on representativeness in making probability judgments. They now say that predictions and probability judgments are "highly sensitive" to representativeness, not completely dominated by it. There must, then, be *other* processes that get deployed in such tasks.

In "Extensional versus Intuitive Reasoning" Tversky and Kahneman speak of people using a "holistic, singular and intuitive" manner of evaluating probabilities.[18] This phrase, though, does not identify any specific cognitive process. In another article they explain their use of 'intuitive' as follows. A judgment is called 'intuitive' if it is reached "by an informal and unstructured mode of reasoning, without the use of analytic methods or deliberate calculation."[19] But this is a largely negative characterization, which still does not identify the specific processes at work. There is no assurance, moreover, that only one such process is used. Maybe a number of processes can be used, some more reliable than others. In particular, some reliable processes may be employed by sophisticated cognizers when they correctly identify problems as susceptible to probabilistic methods and then apply those methods appropriately.

But what about the representativeness heuristic? Doesn't the evidence suggest that it is frequently used? And doesn't this seem to be a basic process that would be barred from any right J-rule system? First, a point of terminology. The term 'heuristic' connotes a deliberately chosen shortcut procedure. In the present case the process is not deliberately chosen and is not seen as a shortcut. So I will speak instead of a representativeness 'routine'—an R-routine.

I do not wish to deny that use of the R-routine leads to errors in the class of cases to which Tversky and Kahneman draw our attention. Specifically, when subjects rank the probability of a conjunction as higher than the probability of a conjunct, this is clearly an error. (At least it is an error if this ranking expresses a belief in a comparative objective probability statement, and if each event has a genuine objective probability.) However, it does not follow from this that the R-routine is not admissible in a right J-rule system. Perhaps the R-routine is *generally* quite reliable, though it breeds errors in this subclass of cases. A case can be made for just this thesis by contemplating the possibility that the R-routine is a facet of the general use of matching operations, or similarity assessments, in cognition.

Matching operations may well be a fundamental part of cognitive processing; and matching of an object X to a model M seems to be the core of the R-routine, as Tversky and Kahneman view it. Another way of putting this idea is in terms of similarity assessments. The use of similarity is a ubiquitous facet of human cognition (as noted in Chapter 11), and is particularly stressed in recent work on *concepts* and *categorization*. Let us explore this latter research, as a prelude to the discussion of the R-routine in probability judgments.

Cognitive psychologists investigate the psychological representations and processes that underlie the use and comprehension of (natural-language) words, especially common nouns for ordinary objects like 'bird' or 'chair'. A popular theory is that people mentally represent the properties in question by means of 'prototypes', and that they decide how an object should be categorized by assessing the similarity of the object to the category's prototype.

The chief rationale for this theory is the ubiquity of 'typicality' effects. For example, subjects find it natural to rate the subsets or members of a category with respect to how typical each is of the category. Such ratings were first reported by L. J. Rips, E. J. Shoben, and E. E. Smith and by E. Rosch.[20] Rosch had subjects rate the typicality of members of a category on a 1-to-7 scale, where 1 meant very typical and 7 very atypical. Subjects were extremely consistent. In the bird category 'robin' got an average rating of 1.1, and 'chicken' 3.8; 'football' was rated a very typical sport (1.2) but weightlifting was not (4.7); 'carrot' was rated a very typical vegetable (1.1), and 'parsley' a less typical one (3.8). Other typicality effects include these: *(a)* categorization is faster with more typical test items; *(b)* typical members of a concept are the first ones learned by children; and *(c)* typical members of a concept are likely to be named first when subjects are asked to produce all members of a category.

Typicality effects are to be expected if subjects represent a category in terms of a prototype, and if categorization proceeds by judging similarity to prototype. There are also several variants of the prototype theory that would all invoke similarity assessments, or matching processes, in categorization.[21]

What is important for my purposes is that judgments of similarity, or feature matching, are fundamental ingredients of the categorization process. If this general idea is correct, the use of representativeness is an extremely pervasive facet of human cognition. Whenever objects or events are categorized as belonging (or not belonging) to this or that concept, representativeness is employed. Furthermore, as long as cognizers apply this routine to perceptually detected features of the object, as long as the cognizer's prototype of the category corresponds closely enough to the prototypes used by other members of the linguistic community, and as long as the routine of matching to prototype is executed properly, virtually all the categorization judgments made in this manner will be *true!* Objects judged to be members of the concept Y will really be members of Y—that is, will really qualify under the lexical label, as it is used by the linguistic community. In short, this use of the R-routine will be *highly reliable.*

If the R-routine is so reliable for this large class of cases, the *general* routine might be endorsed by a right system of J-rules, despite the fact that the routine generates errors in some of its applications. For purposes of comparison, consider the case of perceptual processes that sometimes breed illusion. (Tversky and Kahneman themselves draw the analogy between judgmental illusions and perceptual illusions.) Presumably, the processes responsible for well-known illusions like the moon illusion or the Ames-room illusion are generally reliable processes. As such, they would presumably be sanctioned by a right J-rule system, despite the fact that they undoubtedly breed false judgments in the designated contexts. Thus, even in the illusion cases, a cognizer's belief is justified, though it is of course false. Similarly, if the R-routine is simply part of a generally reliable judgmental process, the beliefs it generates on probabilistic subject matter might still be justified, even if they are false.

Actually, this needs to be qualified. The most we could conclude is that these beliefs have primary justifiedness. They could still be denied the status of secondary justifiedness, because of failure to deploy learned probabilistic methods. The same point would hold for the perceptual cases. If an adult believes that the moon hovering over the horizon is genuinely bigger this evening than at other times, we would not accord this belief the status 'justified'. We would surely hold that the report of his visual system (his 'visual belief') should be overridden by his central system, by appealing to facts or methods he has learned from past experience. Similarly, even if the R-routine is permitted by a right system of J-rules (at the primary level), someone who has studied probability theory might be held accountable for failure to employ correct probabilistic methods to revise his initial, intuitive judgment.

There is another, more important, reason why the foregoing analysis might not suffice for justifiedness. We have been supposing that there is a *single* process that employs matching, or the R-routine; but this is dubious. Arguably, there are significant distinctions between the process used in categorization and the process used in the probability judgment cases. Although both employ a common component of similarity assessment, or matching, there are points of difference.

First, in the categorization cases, all (or most) critical features of the target object are known to the cognizer. If you see a robin flitting about, you can detect most of the features critical to its being or not being a bird. But when a subject seeks to judge whether Linda is (probably) a bank teller, or a feminist and a bank teller, he lacks information about critical features of Linda. He does not know whether Linda is employed, whether she is employed in a bank, and so on. So the relationship between the known features of the object (the features given by the personality sketch) and the target properties (feminist, bank teller, feminist and bank teller) is quite different. In categorization cases the cognizer tries to decide whether exemplification of the known features *qualifies* the individual for the target property. In the probability judgment cases it is assumed that the known features do not qualify the individual for the target property. The only question is whether they make it *likely* that this property is instantiated. And if the two uses of the R-routine are different, we really have two different processes before us. Clearly, one might be permitted by a right J-rule system while the other one isn't permitted.

We cannot conclude, then, that the use of representativeness in probabilistic tasks does yield justified beliefs. Nevertheless, that possibility is not definitively precluded. Grounds for deep pessimism are therefore premature. Moreover, since representativeness has not been shown to be the *sole* process available in confronting probability questions, the prospects for justified beliefs in this domain are brightened still more. Undoubtedly there are signs of trouble. But the gloomy diagnosis of a (local) skeptic is not yet vindicated, at least as far as justifiedness is concerned.

chapter 15

Acceptance and Uncertainty

15.1. Acceptance and Subjective Probabilities

What kinds of doxastic categories are appropriate for the human mind, and hence for human epistemology? This is a question that cannot be answered *a priori;* nor should it be answered by uncritical acceptance of the categories of ordinary language. It should be answered only with the help of cognitive science. Thus, as I suggested at the beginning of Part II (in Section 9.1), epistemology needs contributions from cognitive science to select its descriptive apparatus for doxastic states. This chapter begins by exploring this topic.

Like many works in epistemology, this work has regularly deployed a binary notion of belief. A person either believes a proposition, or he doesn't. Another label for binary belief is *acceptance.* Other epistemologists, however, think of belief, or credence, as a graded, or quantitative, notion. This is commonly expressed in the language 'subjective probabilities', and 'personal probabilities'. On this view there are varying degrees of confidence one can have in a proposition, widely represented as points on the interval from 0 to 1.

The question I now wish to ask is: Are *both* of these credal-state notions—binary belief and graded belief—psychologically legitimate? If not, we need to know which one is legitimate; or if so, we need to know what their connection is. In particular, are they two entirely different psychological categories (or continua)? Or do they somehow fit with one another into a single psychological category?

From an introspective standpoint I find the notion of acceptance, or unqualified belief, quite plausible. There seem to be many propositions I just *believe,* without any (salient) doubt or reservation. This would include propositions about my present address, about the university at which I am employed, and about the names of the Democratic and Republican candidates for President in the 1984 election.

At the same time, there are many cases in which we are inclined to believe a proposition, but feel some hesitancy. The evidence points toward its truth, but is not conclusive; or there is contrary as well as supporting evidence. In such cases we have tangibly qualified beliefs, prompting such verbalizations as '*I think* it is going to rain, but I'm not sure', or 'It will *probably* rain, but it might not'. Such cases seem to force the admission of graded beliefs.

Many writers admit both subjective probabilities and acceptance.[1] Although the psychological status of these states is all too often ignored, they seem to be viewed as entirely distinct psychological categories. But this perspective is unsatisfying. The two kinds of states—binary belief and graded belief—seem too intimately tied with one another for this view to be plausible.

How, then, do we accommodate both sorts of states within an adequate psychology? What would be an integrated psychological account of both acceptance and subjective probabilities? A first attempt might be to identify acceptance with a subjective probability of 1. In other words, belief is identified with *maximal conviction*.

There are at least three difficulties with this. First, many propositions a person can plausibly be described as 'believing' are not accepted with maximal conviction. I would describe myself as believing—without qualification—that Ronald Reagan was the Republican candidate for President in 1984 and Walter Mondale the Democratic candidate. But I would not say that there is nothing of which I am *more* confident. Second, it is standard theoretical practice to reserve the probability 1 for propositions that are true in all possible cases, that is, for tautologies or necessary truths. (I here set aside infinite domains, where this principle does not hold.) But it then seems pathological for people to assign 1 to contingent propositions, which are not true in all possible cases. Yet people obviously *do* accept contingent propositions. So the proposed account of acceptance automatically imputes to people a pathological practice. Third, according to standard approaches, it is impossible (at least by use of Bayes's theorem) to revise a probability assignment of 1 conditional on the receipt of new evidence. It would appear, then, that the acceptance of, or belief in, a proposition would be unrevisable. Yet people clearly do revise their beliefs.[2]

A second approach is to choose some threshold less than 1, for example, .95, and say that any degree of credence at or above this threshold is an (unqualified) belief or acceptance. One problem with this is that the choice of a threshold seems entirely arbitrary and artificial, whereas belief seems to a psychologically natural and well-defined state, not carved out artificially from a continuous range of credal intensities. Furthermore, this construal would unfairly ascribe inconsistent beliefs to people. This point is made by Gilbert Harman, in an adaptation of the well-known lottery problem.[3] Consider a 100-ticket lottery, and suppose that a man has a subjective probability of .99, with respect to each ticket, that the ticket will lose. On the present proposal this would be interpreted as *acceptance* of the proposition that the ticket will lose, for each such proposition. Yet he also accepts the proposition that some ticket will win, so the current proposal forces us to ascribe to him inconsistent acceptances. That seems unfair. Nothing in the initial description of him warrants the conclusion that he has inconsistent beliefs.

Thus far I have worried about finding mutually comfortable niches for both subjective probabilities and acceptance. But now I want to turn to problems for the subjective probability interpretation of credal uncertainty. In other words, granted that there is some psychological reality to the notion of tentative, hesitant, or incomplete conviction, is this correctly or best described in terms of the probability calculus? I wish to question this descriptive assumption, generally associated with (subjective) Bayesianism.

One problem is the empirical evidence *against* the notion that people conform their beliefs to the probability calculus. One piece of evidence, intensively discussed in Chapter 14, concerns the principle of probability theory that the probability of a conjunction cannot exceed that of any of its conjuncts, a rule people readily violate. Similarly, according to standard models, the probability of any tautology, or necessary truth, is 1; and the probability of a contradiction, or impossible proposition, is 0. But people are not always maximally confident in every tautology or maximally confident in rejecting every contradiction. When they do not recognize a tautology or a contradiction, they may have quite different degrees of confidence in them.

Next, consider whether it is plausible that humans should have a psychological mechanism that fixes credal states in accord with the probability calculus. Remember, I am here regarding subjective probability as a *descriptive* theory, one that is intended to hold for all human beings, whatever their age or educational background. Subjective credences must therefore be fixed by native mechanisms. Are there any native mechanisms that would make credal states behave like probabilities? To assume there are is to assume there are native mechanisms for making arithmetic calculations of the kind needed for determining probabilistic relations. But native mechanisms do not seem adequate for even the simplest arithmetic. Most arithmetic needs to be culturally acquired by explicit instruction; it is not programmed into the organism. Admittedly, there might be mechanisms that simulate arithmetic computation at a preconscious level, just as visual mechanisms apparently simulate mathematical operations in determining distance or in computing the trajectory of an object flying toward you. But there is no clear evidence of credence-fixing mechanisms that simulate the probability calculus in this way.

Many theorists of subjective probability might reply that the subjective probability model is descriptively tenable as long as there is a procedure for ascribing such states to the organism on the basis of overt choice behavior, including expressed preferences or indifferences vis-à-vis gambles. A number of such procedures, of course, are proposed in the literature.[4] This literature includes a number of 'representation theorems', which prove that if certain preference axioms are satisfied, then there exists a set of subjective probabilities that can be imputed to a decision maker. To be more precise, if these axioms are satisfied, there exists a subjective probability function P and a desirability function D such that, when 'subjective expected utility' (SEU) is calculated in terms of them, an item X will be preferred to an item Y if and only if SEU (X) > SEU (Y).

There are several problems with this approach. First, the mere fact that subjective probabilities *can* be imputed to a cognizer does not establish any psychological reality to those imputed states. Lots of different models of internal states and processes could be consistent with choice behavior. Just because a given assignment of desirability and subjective probability is possible does not show that there is any genuine psychological reality to this assignment. The epicycles of Ptolemaic astronomers kept their theory consistent with observed planetary trajectories, but that did not establish the astronomical reality of those postulations.

Second, in the present case, there are empirical doubts about some of the preference axioms presupposed by the representation theorems. For example, Tversky found systematic and predictable intransitivies of preference,[5] and K. R. MacCrimmon reported violations of most of Leonard Savage's postulates.[6] Moreover, many of the popular approaches to subjective probability assignments presuppose that choice is determined by SEU; but this presupposition is empirically quite doubtful. For example, in one of Tversky and Kahneman's experiments subjects were asked to choose between gambles A and B (Choice I), and then between C and D (Choice II).

Choice I A = $1,000 with probability .5, or $0 with probability .5
   B = $400 with probability 1

Choice II C = $1,000 with probability .1, or $0 with probability .9
   D = $400 with probability .2, or $0 with probability .8

Nearly all subjects chose B over A, and C over D, and analogous results were obtained using different payoffs and probabilities. These results present grave difficulties for the assumption that choice follows SEU.[7] To the extent that subjective probability assignments are predicated on standard decision theory, there are serious grounds for doubts about their empirical worth.

There is a method for determining subjective probabilities that does not explicitly presuppose SEU: the Dutch Book method. This determines a subjective probability by taking the highest odds one is willing to offer for a bet on p—let's say a to b. Then the degree of belief in p is fixed as a/a + b.

For example, if one would bet on p at maximum odds of 3 to 1, then the assigned degree of belief in p is .75. What justifies this method? The assumption is that if degrees of belief are fixed this way, and bets made accordingly, then no Dutch Book can be made against one.

This justification, however, is very weak. At most it shows that *rational* degrees of belief would reflect maximum betting odds. But we are interested in actual degrees of belief, which may not be rational. A person may be willing to bet at unrealistically high odds because he likes risky situations, or unwilling to bet at odds as high as his true confidence level because he dislikes betting. So his real degree of belief may not coincide with his maximum betting odds.

Finally, note that the different proposed methods for 'operationalizing' subjective probability are not equivalent. They would not yield the same assignments in the same cases.[8] Which of these nonequivalent operationalizations of subjective probabilities should be chosen? Clearly they cannot all correctly limn the structure of inner mental reality. Once this is recognized, however, one is forced to wonder whether *any* of them do.

In conclusion, there are numerous reasons for doubting that subjective uncertainty can be correctly captured by applications of the probability notion. There is, of course, a widespread view to the contrary. But perhaps this merely arises from the allure of a precise mathematical tool—the probability calculus—which dangles the prospects of a tidy and elegant theory. This makes it extremely tempting to try to devise a workable application. But there are scant grounds for thinking that any such theory does capture psychological reality.

Let me emphasize that what I am challenging here is the use of probabilities as an account of *credal uncertainty*. I am not challenging the idea that probabilistic concepts can occur in the propositional contents of people's credal states. There may well be legitimate notions of objective probability, or chance, as indicated in Chapter 14. People may learn these notions and incorporate them into various propositions, some of which become the objects of belief. A person might accept the propositional content 'It probably won't rain today', or 'It's more likely to rain today than to snow'. I have no objection against such 'propositionalized' treatments of uncertainty. But the aim of subjective Bayesianism, of course, is to replace objective probabilities with probabilities construed as psychological states. This is the theoretical orientation I mean to challenge.

15.2. Winner-Take-All Networks

In the spirit of psychological realism, what might be a better way to model uncertainty, and how could we achieve an *integrated* model of acceptance as well as uncertainty? Recent work in the 'new connectionist' literature suggests a promising avenue.

New connectionism is an approach to cognition with two main emphases. First, it assumes that enough is known about brain structure to offer a serious constraint on hypotheses about cognition. It is a necessary exercise for anyone proposing a cognitive theory to provide at least an argument to show that the brain could work in the way the theory requires.[9] Second, new connectionism assumes that an important array of neural processes are parallel as opposed to sequential; this parallel processing involves the use of massive numbers of neural units and connections.

One critical argument for this approach appeals to basic properties of neurons and considerations of computational speed. The basic computation speed of neurons is a few milliseconds, yet they must account for complex cognitive behaviors carried out in a few hundred milliseconds. So entire complex behaviors are carried out in less than a hundred time steps. However, current artificial intelligence and simulation programs, which are largely sequential, require millions of time steps. Hence, these sequential models seem inadequate.[10]

Let us examine one way of developing connectionism, the one formulated by Jerome Feldman and Dana Ballard and by Lokendra Shastri and Feldman.[11] Their approach includes a particular kind of neural network—the 'winner-take-all' network—which provides, I shall argue, a fruitful way of conceptualizing acceptance and uncertainty. In this section, then, I first sketch the general connectionist framework of Feldman and colleagues. Next I present the winner-take-all (WTA) idea. Third, I suggest how WTA networks may provide a good model for acceptance and uncertainty. In the following section I shall raise some normative questions about WTA networks as belief-fixing mechanisms.

Feldman and colleagues develop a standard model of an information processing "unit," based on the current understanding of neurons. A unit may be used to model anything from a single neuron (or neuron part) to a major subsystem of neurons. The exact realization of a unit is left intentionally vague. Attention is focused on the computational properties of units and networks of units.

Units communicate with the rest of a network by transmitting a simple value. A unit transmits the same value to all units to which it is connected. The output value is closely related to the unit's *potential,* and is best described as a level of activation, such as firing frequency. A unit's potential reflects the amount of activation the unit has been receiving from other units. For concreteness, think of a unit as a single neuron, having multiple dendrites, or dendritic sites, each of which receives inputs from other neurons. This is illustrated in Figure 15.1.

All inputs are weighed and combined in a manner specified by *site functions* and a *potential function,* in order to update a unit's potential. The computational behavior of units can be described in terms of these main variables:

p = a continuous value called *potential*
v = an *output* value (approximately 10 discrete values)
i = a vector of *inputs* i_1, i_2, ..., i_n

Two functions define the values of potential and output at time t + 1 based on the values at time t:

$$p_{t+1} \longleftarrow P(i_t, p_t, q_t)$$
$$v_{t+1} \longleftarrow V(i_t, p_t, q_t)$$

The arrow notation is borrowed from the assignment statement of programming languages. The value at time t + 1, to the left of the arrow, is determined by the values of the variables at time t, represented by the expression to the right of the arrow. Time is broken into discrete intervals. The variable q ranges over a small set of states that a unit can be in; for purposes of this exposition, though, these states can be ignored. Also, while the output function relates the output v to several variables, the authors frequently treat it as just the rounded value of p, the potential. I shall follow that practice here.

A unit does not treat all inputs uniformly. Units receive inputs via connections, or links, and each incoming link has an associated weight. A unit weighs each input using the weight on the appropriate link. A weight may have a negative value, which corresponds to an *inhibitory* link. This is important, since inhibition is a basic neural mechanism, and many of the constructions that interest us are networks featuring mutual inhibition (or lateral inhibition), a phenomenon widely found in nature.

As indicated earlier, each unit may have more than one input site, and incoming links are connected to specific sites. Each site has an associated site function. These functions carry out local computations based on the input values at the site, and it is the result of this computation that is processed by the functions P and V.

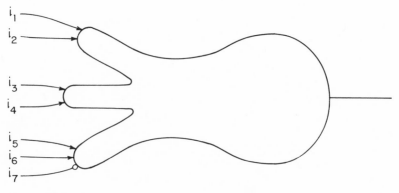

Figure 15.1

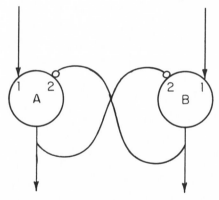

A₁ receives an input of 6 units, then 2 per time step

B₁ receives an input of 5 units, then 2 per time step

t	P(A)	P(B)
1	6	5
2	5.5	4
3	5.5	3.5
4	6	3
5	6.5	2
6	7.5	1
7	9.5	0
8	Sat	0

Figure 15.2

To illustrate these ideas, let a unit be a neuron with dendrites that receive inputs. Each dendrite can be thought of as an alternative enabling condition: if it receives enough inputs, it activates the neuron. The firing frequency of the neuron might be the maximum of the firing rate at any one of its dendritic sites. The formula for this unit's potential could be written as follows:

$$p_{t+1} \longleftarrow p_t + \text{Max} \ (i_1 + i_2; \ i_3 + i_4; \ i_5 + i_6 - i_7)$$

This is shown in Figure 15.1. The minus sign associated with i_7 indicates that it is an inhibitory input.

Drawing on these ideas, I will illustrate a configuration of symmetric units that mutually inhibit one another. First, consider Figure 15.2, containing two units, A and B, each with two input sites. Suppose the initial input to site A_1 is 6, after which that site receives 2 inputs per time step. Suppose B_1 receives an initial input of 5, and then 2 inputs per time step.

Notice that each unit transmits an inhibitory input to its mate, at site 2. Suppose further that the weights at the sites are as follows. The weight at site 1 is 1, and the weight at site 2 is −.5. Then at each time step, each unit changes its potential by adding the external input value and subtracting half the output value of its mate. So we have the equation:

$$p_{t+1} = p_t + i_1 - (.5)i_2.$$

Finally, assume that the output variable v takes the discrete values: 0, . . ., 9; and that v is always the rounded value of the potential p.

The result, as indicated in the table in Figure 15.2, is that the potential and output of unit B are gradually reduced to 0, while unit A gradually in-

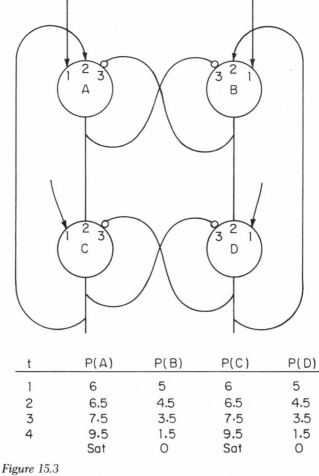

t	P(A)	P(B)	P(C)	P(D)
1	6	5	6	5
2	6.5	4.5	6.5	4.5
3	7.5	3.5	7.5	3.5
4	9.5	1.5	9.5	1.5
	Sat	0	Sat	0

Figure 15.3

creases its potential and output to a saturation point. There the system stabilizes.

Another symmetric configuration involves *coalitions* of units, shown in Figure 15.3. The idea here is that units A and C form a coalition with mutually reinforcing connections. This coalition competes with another coalition comprised of B and D. Competition between the coalitions is determined by their mutual inhibition. As in the previous example, such mutual inhibition results in convergence toward a stable state, but here the convergence is faster: convergence occurs in only four time steps. This system is described by the following equations and specifications:

$w_1 = 1$, $w_2 = .5$, $w_3 = -.5$
$v = \text{round}(p)$
$p_{t+1} = p_t + i_1 + .5(i_2 - i_3)$
A, C start at 6; B, D start at 5
A, B, C, D have no external input for $t > 1$

Competing coalitions of units is a central organizing principle behind many of Feldman and colleagues' models and is critical to our topic. To illustrate this principle psychologically, consider two visual interpretations of the Necker cube, shown in Figure 15.4. At each level of visual processing, there are mutually contradictory units representing alternative possibilities. The dashed lines denote the boundaries of coalitions that embody the alternative interpretations: one interpretation depicts the A-D-H-E face as closer to the viewer, the other depicts the B-C-G-F face as closer. In the Necker cube example, though, there may be no convergence on a stable value. Instead, there can be the familiar phenomenon of figure *reversal*, with the two interpretations oscillating in relative strength.

Of special interest to me are the WTA networks. These exhibit the properties of convergence and stable states illustrated in Figures 15.2 and 15.3. The basic idea motivating WTA networks, as Feldman and Ballard explain it, is that cognitive systems make *decisions*. This includes behavioral decisions, such as turning left or right and fight-or-flight decisions; but it also includes cognitive decisions, such as the interpretation of ambiguous words or images. I am interested in WTA networks because I view them as promising models of acceptance, or (binary) belief.

The critical property of a WTA network is that only the unit with the highest potential (among a set of contenders) will have output above zero after some settling time. An example of a WTA network is one that operates in one time step for a set of contenders each of which can read the potential of all the others. Each unit in the network computes its new potential according to the rule:

$p \longleftarrow$ If $p > \max(i_j)$, then p; otherwise 0.

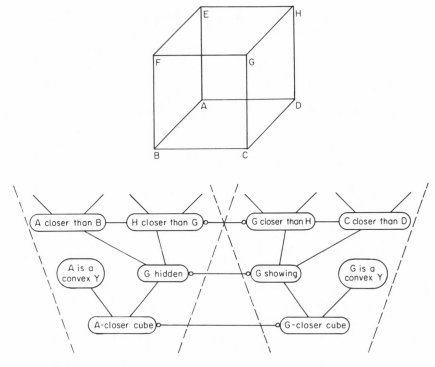

Figure 15.4

In other words, each unit sets itself to zero if it knows of a higher input.[12] This general idea is illustrated in Figure 15.5. The inhibitory connections guarantee that each unit stops if it 'sees' a higher value. This is fast and simple, though probably not terribly realistic. However, there are other ways in which a WTA network might be realized.

The basic idea of acceptance, as I view it, is that a proposition is accepted only when all rivals, or contraries, are rejected. This is well captured by the idea that all rival hypotheses, or interpretations, have their activity levels reduced to zero. This does not necessarily mean that these competing hypotheses cannot later be reactivated. But acceptance marks the emergence of a *decisive* winner, not a hypothesis that merely has *more* strength than its competitors. At the same time, belief must also be a reasonably stable, or settled, state. If one's attitude is continually fluctuating, one does not yet have a belief. Roughly this account of belief was endorsed by C. S. Peirce, who viewed belief as a "calm" and "satisfactory" state, in the nature of a "habit."[13]

This account of acceptance carries with it a plausible account of its com-

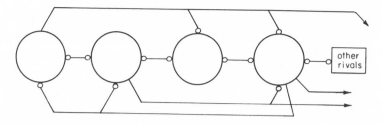

Winner-Take-All
Each unit stops if it sees a higher value

Figure 15.5

plement: *uncertainty*. Uncertainty is to be viewed as a condition of continuing competition among rival alternatives, whose relative attractiveness—here interpreted in terms of activity level—is still in flux. It is an unstable state, which has not yet converged on any one contender. This depiction of uncertainty is phenomenologically appealing. Uncertainty is irresolution or indecision: a condition in which competing ideas battle one another, without one clearly besting the others.

Apart from introspective appeal, this approach has the virtue of unifying the treatment of cognition and *choice* (or volition). The phenomenon of uncertainty is as central to the volitional domain as it is to the doxastic. The difference, of course, is that volition, or choice, is directed at behavioral alternatives, competing plans of action, rather than at hypotheses or propositions. But here too, I propose, uncertainty consists in the absence of a clear-cut winner. There is continued oscillation among the set of contenders; or at least multiple contenders are kept 'on hold', while deliberation continues. As long as such rivalry persists, there is the feeling of hesitancy, of tentativeness, of 'not having made up one's mind'. Felt uncertainty is the sense of continuing competition among contenders, whereas acceptance is the victory of one contender over all others. This parallel treatment of volitional and doxastic decision fits well with the plausible conjecture that the same types of computing mechanisms subserve decision making in both domains.

Perhaps the clearest cases of cognitive acceptance occur in perception. Perceptual systems normally deliver just one interpretation to consciousness, having somehow eliminated all competitors, even when some of these are quite viable. In the famous Ames room there are two seemingly viable interpretations of the visual input, but the visual system decisively selects just one, which portrays the room as normal and the two individuals in it as dramatically different in size. As it happens, this interpretation is false.

What interests me here, though, is simply the making of a decisive, categorical choice. Ambiguous figures like the Necker cube, which induce interpretive reversals, are comparatively rare.

I believe that the nonperceptual systems also tend to favor categorical doxastic choice. Although doxastic uncertainty or indecision is more common here than in the perceptual domain, there is a built-in preference for finding 'winners'. Thus, contrary to what the standard subjective probability model suggests, acceptance is a natural, highly prevalent doxastic state, not a radical or pathological state, as judged by the normal operating characteristics of the system. This idea was anticipated by Peirce, who viewed uncertainty, or "doubt," as an "irritation" of which the system seeks to rid itself by replacing it with belief.

Several other features of the neuropsychological models proposed by Feldman and colleagues suggest properties of doxastic activity different from those implied by typical subjective probability approaches. First, although their models do have a place for degrees of confidence—represented by the magnitude of a unit's output value (for example, its firing frequency)—there is no assumption that the degrees of confidence among a set of contenders must *add up* to a fixed value. This contrasts with the probability model, in which the sum of all mutually exclusive possibilities must be 1.[14]

Second, mutual-inhibition models of the sort I have canvassed tend to depress the level of activity of (most) units, which results in rapidly changing levels of confidence (at least until some stable point is reached). I think this accounts for the familiar fact that people find it quite difficult to specify precise degrees of confidence on the basis of introspection, or even to make comparative assessments of confidence. Typically, the activity level associated with competing alternatives changes too quickly. This contrasts with subjective probability approaches, which usually assume definite degrees of confidence.

At this point, an objection arises. Surely people *are* capable of making precise probability estimates, at least if pressed; and they often settle on precise odds in placing bets. How are these activities compatible with my theory? The crucial point here is that judgments of probability need not always, or even typically, be expressions of subjective confidence. They may be assessments of objective chance (as indicated at the end of section 15.1). In making probability estimates of tomorrow's weather, or a patient's prospects for recovery, or the outcome of a horse race, people assess objective chances, for which known (or believed) *frequencies* provide relevant clues. Where probability estimates are anchored to frequencies, rather than to introspected credal intensities, definite numerical values are more easily formulated.

The proposed account of uncertainty focuses on events accessible to consciousness, or on events occurring in active memory. But what about the phenomenon of uncertainty in LTM? Does this too consist in nonconverging, often fluctuating, levels of activation among competing hypotheses? The proper treatment of uncertainty for LTM may be quite different—a possibility that current models of subjective probability ignore entirely. Indeed, I suspect that there is not any corresponding phenomenon of uncertainty in LTM at all. Everything in LTM may be in a 'settled' state, without ongoing competition. (It is noteworthy, in this regard, that theories of LTM do not feature a strength variable marking belief intensity. Variables representing 'strength' are commonly found, but these mark something like associative strength between nodes in a network, which concerns the probability of one node activating another. In other words, the strength variable concerns likelihood of retrieval, not firmness of conviction.)

I do not mean to deny the presence in LTM of something functionally similar to degrees of uncertainty. But what is there, I conjecture, is information stored (without reservation!) that is related to manifestations of uncertainty. First, people may store information about previous entertainings of competing hypotheses or past weighings of various strands of evidence. When the question is raised anew, they retrieve these contents and recycle the old thoughts, giving rise to renewed uncertainty. All this is compatible with memories being stored as states of binary belief, not as degrees of confidence. Second, people may store information about previous *objective probability* estimates. When such beliefs about previous estimates are retrieved, they tend to reassign those estimates, unless new information is encountered.

The first of these proposals may provide a simple explanation of the observed tendency of beliefs to become more confident over time (when no new evidence is acquired). A person may *forget* some of the considerations once raised in favor of a weak hypothesis, which fared relatively poorly in previous competitions. Indeed, one may fail altogether to retrieve a weak contender, since it will probably have received less attention in previous deliberations. When competition is renewed, it is easier for the formerly ascendant hypothesis to win once again, even more quickly and decisively, since there is less material in mind to compete with it.

I have here sketched a model of acceptance and uncertainty that I regard as psychologically plausible. Its account of credal uncertainty is better, I think, than that of standard subjective probability models. Its neat accommodation of acceptance, which seems to be a psychologically robust phenomenon, also gives it superiority over those models. Finally, it fits within a general framework that can make claims for neural realism.

As I have stressed, this theory of credal uncertainty does not account for all phenomena commonly treated under this rubric. In particular, it gives no systematic treatment of 'propositionalized' uncertainty, that is, doxastic attitudes whose propositional content involves notions of objective chance or likelihood. However, for purposes of primary epistemology, a theory of credal uncertainty is central; and that is what my (admittedly rough) model aims to capture.[15]

15.3. Epistemic Evaluation of WTA Networks

The model I have sketched of acceptance and uncertainty is a purely descriptive model, underwriting the appropriateness of the doxastic category of acceptance. It is now time, however, to turn to evaluative issues. Granted that human cognition produces categorical (as opposed to graded) beliefs, how satisfactory are the native mechanisms of belief formation? Proceeding on the assumption that human cognition widely employs WTA processes, how good, epistemically, are these processes? Most important, can they yield *justified* beliefs?

To answer this question, of course, we need an assessment of the truth ratio that WTA processes would tend to generate. We cannot make such an assessment, however, without more information. First, we need an exact specification of the WTA process or processes. Does even the slightest difference in strength between two rival units reduce the weaker rival to zero? That is what the model sketched in section 15.2 provides. But alternatives to that model are readily available. There might be some constant d, such that a given unit's strength is reduced to zero only when the strength of a rival unit exceeds it by at least d. If d is fairly large, it is hard for a unit to become a winner. This property might serve to forestall rash beliefs, thereby increasing the truth ratio. Hence, the existence and the exact value of such a d-parameter would be critical determinants of the truth ratio of any WTA network.

Second, we need more information about rivalry, or competition. Consider a lottery example. Suppose there is a 1,000-ticket lottery and S considers the proposition, 'Ticket no. 1 will lose'. Which propositions are its 'rivals'? (For convenience I speak of propositions, rather than the units that represent the propositions, as rivals.) If a proposition's rivals are only its *contraries*, presumably this proposition is much stronger than any of its rivals. The chief rival is, 'Ticket no. 1 will win'. This presumably has much less support than 'Ticket no. 1 will lose', so the latter will be accepted. However, suppose the rivals of a proposition p include any proposition q that is negatively relevant to it, meaning any proposition q such that the probability of p given q is smaller than the prior probability of p.[16] Then 'Ticket no. 2 will lose', 'Ticket no. 3 will lose', and so on, are all rivals of 'Ticket no. 1 will lose'. Since all these rivals are tied in strength, no rival will be reduced to zero, and none will be *accepted*.

Many epistemologists would be cheered by this last prospect, since they deem it inappropriate to accept the hypothesis 'Ticket no. 1 will lose'. Whether or not this is so, the point is that we cannot determine whether a WTA mechanism *would* have this result unless we are given more information about how rivalry, or competition, is established. How does the mind-brain decide which propositions to treat as rivals or competitors, that is, which ones get represented by mutually inhibiting computing units?

A third question to raise about a WTA process is how it performs when information is very sparse. Although the only evidence on a given issue may favor a given hypothesis, this evidential support may nonetheless be (intuitively) weak. Does the supported hypothesis still get accepted, because all rivals have zero strength? Such a mechanism would not be conducive to a high truth ratio.[17]

Fourth, even were these issues resolved, the truth ratio of a WTA process alone cannot be assessed. One critical complementary process, or set of processes, is the process or processes by which initial strengths are assigned to units. If these processes assign strengths to units in a manner highly sensitive to truth, the WTA process might be justificationally viable. But if no such truth-sensitive complementary processes are available, it would not be viable.

This shows that one cannot assess a WTA process for truth ratio all by itself. But that should come as no surprise. Remember that, within my theory of justifiedness, single rules authorizing single processes are not assumed to have a determinate truth ratio. I speak only of the truth ratio of an entire rule-system, authorizing an entire set of cognitive processes. The important question to ask, then, is whether a WTA process can be complemented by other processes that are *jointly* sanctionable by a right rule system, in virtue of a high enough truth ratio. Thus far, nothing obviously precludes WTA processes from being licensed by a right J-rule system.

There are other materials in the connectionist approach that bear on this issue and that are worth examining. In particular, there is the idea of *mutually reinforcing coalitions* (recall the illustrations in Figures 15.3 and 15.4). I suggest that this idea may correspond to the epistemologist's conception of coherence. It may provide support for the notion that coherence-deploying mechanisms are part of our basic cognitive equipment. These coherence-deploying mechanisms may also serve to promote a high truth ratio.

By 'coherence' I here mean some sort of *positive* relationship—not merely logical compatibility—the details of which would have to be worked out elsewhere. In outline, it might come to something like this. Some combinations of events or states of affairs are conceptualized as a unity because they instantiate previously encountered patterns. For example, they match familiar schemas, frames, scripts, or scenarios. To the extent that a hypothetical event or state can be fitted into such a unity with other hypothetical events or states, these form a set of mutually reinforcing possibilities: a *coalition*. Furthermore, the larger and more detailed such a coalition, the greater the amount of reinforcement each hypothesis (unit) receives from the remaining members. Thus, a comprehensive and detailed scientific theory would have a high degree of coherence. Of course, no member of a coalition can raise the strength of others unless it gets some strength from outside the coalition; presumably, the external sources of excitation are ultimately traceable to perception. Thus, perception as well as coherence will serve as a major determinant of strength.

How can coherence, or coalition formation, serve as a guide or indicator of truth? First, since a necessary condition of a hypothesis' being true is its compatibility with other truths, the absence of coherence may be a good sign of falsity. 'Isolated' hypotheses cannot benefit from reinforcement by other coalition members, so they are ultimately rejected. Furthermore, if coalitions are formed under some previously established patterns—schemas, frames, scripts, scenarios, and so on—instances of which have been frequently encountered in the past, there is evidence that this pattern has a non-negligible prior probability of occurrence. Thus, a coalition will represent not merely an abstract conjoint possibility, but also an instance of a type with a non-negligible chance of recurrence. So, on the present conceptualization, coalitions register 'induction' from past observation—in the form of inductively based schemas, scripts, and so on—as well as the other ingredients previously cited.[18]

Although membership in a strong coalition is a useful test of truth, it obviously is not a sufficient indicator of truth. Suppose a rival hypothesis also belongs to a strong coalition. That ought to raise doubts about the truth of the target hypothesis. Allowing groups of coalitions to compete may thus be a useful device for selecting *true* hypotheses as winners.

Until now I have directed all attention to a single dimension of epistemic appraisal, justifiedness, and its associated standard, reliability. But what of the other standards of appraisal that interest us: speed and power? Any facet of a WTA mechanism that *delays* acceptance obviously works against speed. For example, the larger the d-parameter, the more it takes for the mechanism to reject rivals. On average, it will take longer for the mechanism to select a winner. Similarly, the more the cognitive system seeks and creates competing coalitions, which might give an initially favored hypothesis a run for its money, the slower the system will be in selecting a winner. Of course, both of these traits would enhance reliability; but there would be a loss in speed.

It seems likely that the human system has a speed-sensitive design, not just a reliability-sensitive design. In language understanding, for example, the hearer processes sentences very rapidly, normally selecting a unique grammatical parsing and a unique semantic interpretation for each sentence, even where there are (in principle) several alternative parsings and readings. (Of course, if there is a special language module, this fact may not speak to doxastic decisions in other domains. But it is certainly suggestive of a design that is oriented toward speed considerations.)

The core of a WTA device may also be seen as sensitive to considerations of power. The fundamental impact of a WTA device is to remove clutter from active memory. As long as rivals are competing with a given hypothesis, active memory will be cluttered with items requiring processing resources. This makes it more difficult to move on to other questions that could be answered. Selection of a winner settles an issue and allows the mind to proceed more quickly to the rest of its agenda, enabling it (in principle) to solve a larger number of problems.

What I have said thus far shows that a WTA mechanism is cogenial to the desiderata of speed and power, but not incompatible with achieving high reliability. Other epistemologists, however, have not viewed the idea of 'acceptance' so favorably. Here is a kind of objection they might raise against acceptance, against a process that selects one hypothesis as a winner while reducing the strengths of rival hypotheses to zero.

As background, notice that many theorists are attracted by what may be called a *pragmatic* criterion of evaluation (recall section 5.4). An example of a pragmatic criterion is one that evaluates cognitive processes by their impact on desire satisfaction. Decision theory stresses that a cognizer's subjective probabilities are among the factors that determine the choice of behavior. And behavior, of course, may be more or less successful in obtaining outcomes the agent desires. Now it may be suggested that an optimal cognitive system is one that so selects behavior as to optimize (the agent's) desire satisfaction, or payoffs. Is a WTA mechanism optimal according to this standard?

One problematic feature of a WTA mechanism leaps out in this context. It is in the nature of a WTA mechanism to reduce the strength of all but one of a set of competitors to zero. Doesn't this entail a loss of critical information, and won't this produce nonpragmatic, or nonprudential, choices? Consider an example. You are driving on a two-lane road, and there is little traffic in the opposite direction. You are now caught on a hill behind a slow truck, and you are pressed for time. Should you try passing the truck, even though you cannot see over the hill? The sparsity of traffic traveling the opposite way suggests that the hypothesis 'A car is coming over the hill', is much weaker in strength than its rival, 'No car is coming over the hill'. It appears, then, that a WTA mechanism would reject the former hypothesis and accept the latter. Once these doxastic decisions are plugged into your behavioral decision matrix, it looks like a decision to pass the truck will be made. Yet this seems likely to be a nonpragmatic, or nonprudential, choice. In particular, if the objective probability that a car is coming is, say, .15, and if you act this way repeatedly in similar situations, the long-run performance of these mental mechanisms will probably lead to a very bad pay-off. This kind of case can obviously be generalized. It then begins to look as if the WTA process of acceptance has very bad properties, at least as judged by a pragmatic standard.

There are at least two ways of countering this objection, granting (for argument's sake) the appropriateness of a pragmatic standard. First, an acceptance process does not necessarily *preclude* retention of probabilistic information. As stressed in section 15.2, information about chances may be accepted and therefore preserved for decision-making purposes. In the driving example you could accept the proposition 'The chance that a car is coming in the opposite lane is .15'. The prevalance of WTA processes, then, does not entail the suppression of all probabilistic information. Admittedly, such preservation of information about chances involves belief contents that invoke an *objective* probability notion, which is philosophically controversial. But if sense cannot be made of objective probabilities, it is not clear that the prudential criticism can be properly motivated in the first place. Certainly the form of criticism advanced above relies on objective probabilities.

Second, there is a possible mechanism, a complementary mechanism, that would avert the apparent shortcoming of an acceptance process. Suppose there is an allied cognitive mechanism that is sensitive to possible pay-offs with *extreme values:* very rewarding or very threatening outcomes. This mechanism increases the activation level of any contemplated hypothesis h that is believed to make some extreme payoff likely. That is, h's activation level is increased if the cognizer believes that some extreme payoff would be likely if h were true. Such heightened activation would tend to prevent h from being rejected, would keep it 'in contention', and hence not ignored during behavioral choice. In the foregoing example the threat of a fatal accident heightens the activation level associated with 'A car is coming'. This keeps it from being rejected, and keeps its negation from being accepted. Thus, the choice of the 'don't pass' option is promoted. (I do not offer any specific model of how a choice would then be made. But such models could readily be constructed.)

I suspect that human beings *do* have some such mechanism. Indeed, it may be just the mechanism that accounts for wishful thinking and fearful thinking. The present analysis shows how such a mechanism can have prudential merit—even if it has attendant liabilities for reliability. If a cognizer *believes* hypotheses largely because they would, if true, fulfill his fondest dreams or deepest fears, these beliefs are unlikely to have a high truth ratio. But if such hypotheses are kept from being rejected and therefore ignored, because of their potentially extreme consequences, one's behavioral decisions may be prudentially more effective. Thus, an acceptance mechanism with built-in sensitivity to extreme values may facilitate prudentially effective choices, at any rate, choices that avoid disasters and capitalize on major opportunities.

The familiar Bayesian approach divides human decision making into two entirely separate processes: (1) processes of *doxastic* choice, and (2) processes of *behavioral* choice. The outputs of (1) are subjective probabilities. These serve, along with utilities, as inputs to (2). The utilities, or preferences, however, only play a role in (2), not in (1). According to Bayesianism, desires, aversions, fears, and so on, do not affect the selection of subjective probabilities, or any other doxastic choices.

I am painting a rather different picture. I am suggesting that actual psychological mechanisms are not segregated in the foregoing fashion. Utilities can affect doxastic decisions. Of course, this is only intended as a descriptive theory, not as a normative theory. In particular, I agree that whenever fears or desires infect doxastic choice, this is likely to reduce reliability. However, it may be good from the standpoint of *pragmatic effectiveness*. Nature appears to have a different way of getting people to make pragmatic behavioral decisions, even at the attendant cost of worsening their doxastic decisions.[19]

Suppose it were conceded, however, that an acceptance mechanism is inferior, on the whole, to a subjective probability mechanism. Still, human beings may well be stuck with an acceptance mechanism. Why, then, expend theoretical energy exploring the properties of mechanisms it might be nice to have if we do not in fact have them? Why spend time bemoaning the actual machinery of our minds if there is nothing we can do about it? Why not seek the best procedures that are realistically available to human cognition? This is what the 'resource-relative' stance sketched in Chapter 5 would advocate. There, of course, I was concerned exclusively with justifiedness, whereas epistemology in general should also be prepared to deal with other evaluative dimensions, including ones that impinge on behavioral choice. In any event, if acceptance mechanisms, or WTA mechanisms, are basic, inherent features of our cognitive architecture, epistemology should be concerned with how best to utilize these mechanisms. It should not expend too much energy over subjective probability models that, though arguably 'ideal', are not realizable by human beings.

chapter 16

Belief Updating

16.1. Psychological Realism

How do human beings respond to new evidence that bears on previous beliefs they hold? How do they revise, or update, their beliefs? Are these processes of belief updating at all satisfactory from a normative point of view? I touched on belief revision—or, rather, the lack of revision—in Chapter 10, in discussing Ross's work on belief perseverance. But that work did not purport to provide a general model of belief updating. In this chapter I present a general model of updating and examine its normative implications.

The most popular model of updating is Bayesian conditionalization.[1] Its popularity is primarily in its normative or prescriptive quality, but it also has appeal as a descriptive model, perhaps because of the dearth of systematic alternatives. However, conditionalization as a descriptive model of updating seems to presuppose that human beings are natively equipped for performing highly sophisticated probabilistic calculations, or for simulating such calculations. My discussions in Chapters 14 and 15 raise serious doubts about this. I therefore want to examine a recent and more plausible model of belief updating, one proposed by Hillel Einhorn and Robin Hogarth.[2] This has the advantage of much greater psychological realism. It can be taken seriously as a description of *basic* psychological processes people use to change their degrees of belief in response to new evidence.

The Einhorn-Hogarth model assumes degrees of belief that can be scaled on the unit interval, something like subjective probabilities. I raised objections to subjective probabilities in Chapter 15. However, in the present chapter I shall waive these objections and go along with the acceptance of such states, in order to present and weigh the implications of the Einhorn-Hogarth model. Although that model presupposes (something like) subjective probabilities, it does not assume manipulation of such probabilities in accordance with Bayes's Theorem or other laws of the probability calculus. So it has at least greater realism than standard models, in my view.

It should be emphasized that the nonrealization of conditionalization at the level of *processes* is compatible with the use of conditionalization—or other uses of the probability calculus—at the level of *methods*. If someone learns Bayes's Theorem and a rule (such as the Jeffrey rule) of conditionalization, and if that person has, say, (ungraded) beliefs in objective probabilities, he can certainly apply his acquired rule to arrive at new objective probability estimates. I am not disputing a psychological capacity to learn and apply probabilistic rules in this fashion. But here, as elsewhere in the book, I am concerned in the first instance with native processes; and it is doubtful that our native processes involve anything like Bayesian conditionalization.

16.2. The Anchoring-and-Adjustment Model

Einhorn and Hogarth propose that people revise their beliefs by a process of adjustment from an anchor. One's current attitude toward a given hypothesis provides an anchor, from which adjustments are made upon receipt of new information. Once the adjustment is accomplished, the new attitude becomes the anchor for any subsequent information. The crucial idea in their model is that adjustments work by means of a "contrast," or "surprise," effect. The stronger one's antecedent belief in h, the greater the downward adjustment if new negative evidence is received. To borrow a boxing metaphor, the bigger one's initial confidence, the more it will fall. Analogously, the weaker one's antecedent belief in h, the greater the upward adjustment if new positive evidence is received. This contrast assumption leads to some interesting predictions, borne out by experimental data.

To explain the Einhorn-Hogarth model in more detail, I will start with their model for adjustments upon receipt of negative evidence. This is what they call their "discounting" model. Let

S_0 = the initial strength of belief in some hypothesis $(0 \leq S_0 \leq 1)$;

$s(a_k)$ = the strength of the kth piece of negative evidence, a_k $(0 \leq s(a_k) \leq 1)$;

S_k = the strength of belief in the hypothesis after k pieces of negative evidence $(0 \leq S_k \leq 1)$.

It is assumed that people have some way of assessing whether new evidence is positive or negative and quantifying the strength of that evidence (assigning some degree of confirmatory or disconfirmatory import to the evidence). Einhorn and Hogarth make no specific suggestions about this process, and I too shall simply take it as a given.

To illustrate the process, consider the effect of the first piece of negative evidence, a_1, on one's position. Assuming that

w_0 = an adjustment weight associated with the initial strength of belief,

the resulting strength of belief, S_1, after the first piece of negative evidence is given by

$$S_1 = S_0 - w_0\, s(a_1). \tag{1}$$

The adjustment weight reflects the importance given to negative evidence in the discounting process. But the adjustment weight is a function of the anchor at the given time. (Note that the anchor and adjustment weight have the same temporal subscript.) The rationale for this is explained as follows. Imagine that your initial confidence is weak and a strong piece of negative evidence is revealed. Since your confidence is already low, the new information cannot reduce S_0 very much (in absolute terms). But if your initial confidence in the hypothesis is very high, the reduction of strength by the *same* piece of evidence would be larger. This is the basis of the contrast, or surprise, component of the model.

Reconsider equation (1) and ask what happens when a second piece of negative evidence is received. The new position is given by

$$\begin{aligned} S_2 &= S_1 - w_1\, s(a_2) & \text{(2a)} \\ &= S_0 - w_0\, s(a_1) - w_1\, s(a_2). & \text{(2b)} \end{aligned}$$

Equation (2a) can be generalized as follows:

$$S_k = S_{k-1} - w_{k-1}\, s(a_k). \tag{3}$$

Now consider the functional relation between the strength of the anchor and the adjustment weight (the "adjustment weight function"). It is assumed that bigger anchors have larger adjustment weights. This implies that the adjustment weight function is a monotonically increasing function of the size of the anchor. To illustrate this, Einhorn and Hogarth posit a simple form often found in psychophysical judgments, that is,

$$w_{k-1} = (S_{k-1})^{\alpha} \qquad (\alpha \geqslant 0). \tag{4}$$

In this equation α is a parameter that reflects one's attitude toward disconfirming evidence. Its value may vary across individuals. To appreciate the role of α, consider Figure 16.1. Note that the adjustment weight is monotonically increasing with the size of the anchor *regardless* of the value of α. When a hypothesis is believed to degree 0, it cannot be adjusted below 0. When the anchor is 1, the adjustment weight is 1; so a 'certain' belief is adjusted solely by the strength of negative evidence. When $\alpha > 1$, the adjustment weight is less than the anchor. (Since the degree of belief is typically less than 1, an exponent larger than 1 makes the adjustment weight smaller than does an exponent smaller than 1.) As α increases beyond 1, and the adjustment weight therefore gets smaller, negative evidence receives corre-

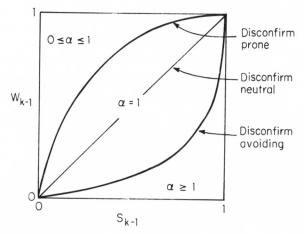

Figure 16.1

spondingly less weight in the discounting process. People with an α greater than 1 are labeled as "disconfirmation avoiding," since they give relatively less weight to negative evidence. When $0 \le \alpha < 1$, adjustment weights are large and initial positions are strongly discounted by negative information. People with such attitudes are "disconfirmation prone." When $\alpha = 1$, a "disconfirmation neutral" attitude is assumed.

The full discount model is now obtained by substituting (4) into (3) to obtain:

$$S_k = S_{k-1} - (S_{k-1})^\alpha \, s(a_k). \tag{5}$$

The discount model implies that the strength of a belief after the kth piece of negative evidence is a function of three factors: (1) the size of the anchor, S_{k-1}; (2) the strength of negative evidence, $s(a_k)$; and (3) an adjustment weight, which is a function of the anchor and one's attitude toward disconfirming evidence (α).

A model for adjustments in response to new *positive* evidence is exactly parallel to the discounting model. Einhorn and Hogarth call it the "accretion" model. The form of the model is given by

$$S_k = S_{k-1} - r_{k-1} \, s(b_k), \tag{6}$$

where

r_{k-1} = the adjustment weight for positive evidence

and

$s(b_k)$ = the strength of the kth piece of positive evidence, b_k $\quad (0 \le s(b_k) \le 1)$.

Equation (6) follows the same general form as the discount model except that the final position results from an anchoring and upward adjustment process. The basic assumption in the accretion model is that weak beliefs are increased more by positive evidence than are strong beliefs. The same positive evidence 'helps' a weaker position more than a stronger one. As in the discounting model, Einhorn and Hogarth posit a simple form to capture the monotonically decreasing relation between r_{k-1} and s_{k-1}. In particular, they propose the following relation:

$$r_{k-1} = (1 - s_{k-1})^\beta \qquad (\beta \geqslant 0). \tag{7}$$

The adjustment weight function is shown in Figure 16.2. The parameter β is interpreted as reflecting one's "attitude toward confirming evidence." When $\beta > 1$, confirming evidence is given a relatively small weight. In fact, as β increases, the weight for confirming evidence approaches 0. When $0 \leqslant \beta < 1$, confirming evidence is given a large weight, reflecting a "confirmation prone" attitude. When $\beta = 1$, the attitude is labeled as "confirmation neutral." Obviously, the role of β in the accretion model is directly analogous to the role of α in the discount model. The full accretion model is obtained by substituting (7) into (6):

$$S_k = S_{k-1} + (1 - S_{k-1})^\beta \, s(b_k). \tag{8}$$

To develop an updating model for both positive and negative evidence, Einhorn and Hogarth simply combine the discount model for negative evidence and the accretion model for positive evidence. The resulting *mixed evidence* model uses whichever adjustment process is appropriate for the

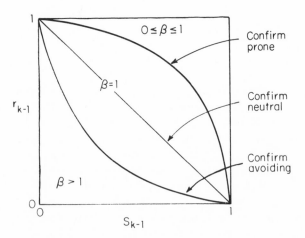

Figure 16.2

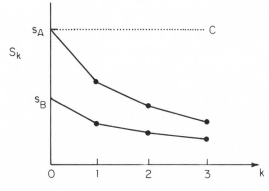

Figure 16.3

evidence at hand. When the evidence is negative, the discount model is used; when the evidence is positive, the accretion model is used.

Let us now consider some implications of the model for the kinematics of belief. First, consider the convergence of beliefs when two people have different initial positions but receive the same evidence. Start with the receipt of negative evidence. This can be illustrated by Figure 16.3. When $k = 0$, the initial positions for persons A and B are shown as S_A and S_B, respectively. If A and B have the same attitude toward disconfirming evidence, note what happens after receipt of the first piece of negative evidence. Since person A has a higher initial position, the decrease in his or her belief is greater than that for person B. This is because bigger anchors have larger adjustment weights. Indeed, the slopes of the lines connecting S_k over k (for the same strength of evidence) will decrease at a faster rate for A than for B. This means that at each successive adjustment, the difference in final positions gets smaller and will eventually converge.

Although convergence of beliefs occurs when persons have different starting points and the same attitude toward disconfirming evidence, divergence can occur when the α's are not equal. Consider person C, whose initial position is the same as A's but whose α is very high. Since C gives little weight to negative evidence, Figure 16.3 shows his or her beliefs to be unchanged (or very slightly changed) over the k pieces. This leads to divergence of beliefs between A and C given the same evidence. However, as k increases, the two positions will converge toward zero unless C gives zero weight to negative evidence. Analogous points about convergence and nonconvergence hold for the receipt of positive evidence under the accretion model.

Moving to the consequences of mixed evidence, a major implication of the contrast approach is *strong recency effects* in belief change. To see why, consider the strength of belief after receiving one piece each of positive and negative information. Consider the difference between the belief strength after receiving them in the positive-negative order, $S(+,-)$, as compared with the strength after receiving them in the negative-positive order, $S(-,+)$. Figure 16.4 shows the effects of these two orders at different starting levels, S_{01} and S_{02}. When the initial belief is at S_{01}, the two orders are shown in the top half of the figure. Compare the effects of the $(+,-)$ and the $(-,+)$ orders. Note that the slope of the line connecting $S_{k=0}$ and $S_{k=1}$ in the $(-,+)$ order is less steep than when negative evidence occurs in the $(+,-)$ order. The reason is that the same negative evidence has a larger discounting weight after the positive evidence because of the contrast effect. Similarly, the slope of $S_{k=1}$ to $S_{k=2}$ in the $(-,+)$ order is steeper than the slope for positive evidence from the initial position. These differences in slopes lead to crossing lines that resemble fish tails. The fish-tail pattern implies recency effects since the final position after the $(+,-)$ order is lower than for the $(-,+)$ order. The prediction of recency effects does not depend on one's initial position, as illustrated in the lower half of the figure.

Another implication of the model concerns the relative effect of presenting multiple pieces of evidence simultaneously instead of sequentially. Simultaneous presentation of two or more pieces of negative evidence, for example, results in greater discounting than presentation of these same pieces one after another. Thus, the contrast or surprise effect is 'diluted' by sequential processing.

Experiments done by Einhorn and Hogarth, and by J. D. Shanteau, support these *order-effect* implications. In two of Einhorn and Hogarth's own experiments, subjects were given four scenarios, each scenario consisting of an initial description (the "stem") and four additional pieces of information

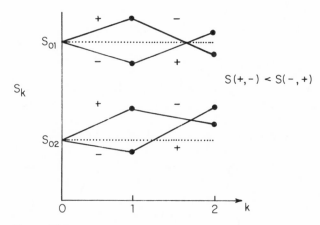

Figure 16.4

presented in separate paragraphs. The scenarios concerned a defective stereo speaker thought to have a bad connection, a baseball player whose hitting had dramatically improved after a new coaching program, and so on. In each case the stem provided information concerning a target causal hypothesis, for example, whether the coaching had caused the player's hitting improvement. At the end of the stem, subjects were asked to rate the likelihood of the suspected factor being the cause of the outcome, on a rating scale from 0 to 100. After responding to this question, subjects were presented with four pieces of additional information regarding the causal hypothesis. These consisted of two pieces of positive information and two pieces of negative information. The new information was presented in either a positive-negative order $(+,+,-,-)$ or a negative-positive order $(-,-,+,+)$. After this new information was presented, subjects were again asked to rate the likelihood that X caused Y.

The order in which information was presented had a large recency effect, as the theory predicts. The mean change in belief is .155 for the positive-negative order, while the mean change in belief for the negative-positive order is .057. This was replicated in a slightly different design, where the mean change for $(+,+,-,-)$ was .184 while the change for $(-,-,+,+)$ was .088.

Einhorn and Hogarth also reanalyze data from an experiment by Shanteau.[3] Shanteau's tasks involved probabilistic inference and probabilistic estimation on the basis of information drawn from urns containing proportions of colored beads. These tasks tested both the recency effect hypothesis and the dilution effect hypothesis (that sequential processing of the different components of a body of evidence will have a smaller effect on beliefs than simultaneous presentation of that same evidence). The data from Shanteau's experiment bear out both of these hypotheses, as illustrated in Figures 16.5 and 16.6. Figure 16.5 shows the prevalance of fish tails, indicating recency effects throughout these data. Figure 16.6 shows that simultaneous presentation leads to more extreme responses for *both* positive and negative evidence.

Among the large set of order-effect data obtained by numerous researchers, there are data indicating primacy as well as recency effects. In order to account for primacy effects, Einhorn and Hogarth add another element to their model: *attention*. To understand this element, imagine reading a long and complex book. At the outset, attention is high, fatigue is low, and information is scrutinized carefully. As one continues, however, attention may begin to wane and information that occurs later in the book receives less careful consideration. Such a process, in which attention decreases with serial position, means that evidence occurring early has more influence than the same evidence would if it occurred late. The primacy effect—the greater impact of early information—may therefore be explained by "attention decrement." This idea has been developed in detail

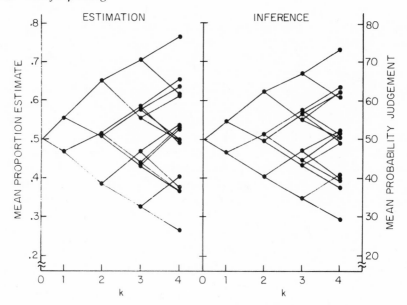

Figure 16.5

by N. H. Anderson.[4] Einhorn and Hogarth proceed to incorporate the attention-decrement factor into their theory.

I will not pursue the details of this theoretical refinement. Suffice it to say that attention decrement works in the opposite direction from the contrast or surprise factor in that the latter leads to recency effects, whereas attention decrement leads to primacy effects. The net effect of these opposing

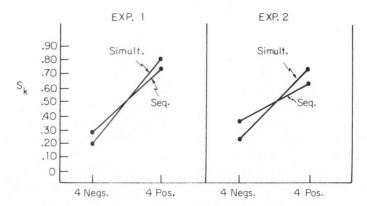

Figure 16.6

forces can result in primacy, recency, or neither, depending on the exact values of the relevant parameters.

16.3. *Justification and Calibrational Convergence*

Let us now inquire into the normative status of the anchoring-and-adjustment process that Einhorn and Hogarth postulate. Can such a process, if it indeed exists as a basic psychological process, confer justification? Would it be permitted by a right system of J-rules?

A complaint might immediately be lodged against the anchoring-and-adjustment (A-and-A) process: it produces *order effects*. Surely, the objection would run, the order in which evidence is presented should make no difference to the resulting doxastic states. 'No order effects' ought to be a formal, *a priori* principle of adequacy for any belief-updating process. But the A-and-A process clearly violates this principle. It can yield either recency or primacy effects, and it can produce the dilution effect, in which sequential presentation of multiple pieces of evidence has less impact on belief change than simultaneous presentation. Given these 'biases', the A-and-A process should be ruled out immediately as justificationally unacceptable.

This objection would be right if a *formalist* principle like 'no order effects' were appropriate. But I am very dubious about the validity of such a principle. Various formal principles of rationality have been proposed in the philosophical and social scientific literature, principles for the rationality of belief and the rationality of choice. But I am unpersuaded of their (unconditional) correctness. Two such formal principles encountered in earlier chapters were noninconsistency and probabilistic coherence. In both cases I gave reasons for rejecting these principles as (categorical) principles of rationality or of justification. Another example of a formal principle, in the theory of rational choice, is the requirement of transitivity of preference. It too has been called into question, at least in social choice theory.[5]

Clearly, the general approach to justifiedness I favor, verific consequentialism, does not necessarily imply such 'formalist' principles. Principles requiring noninconsistency or probabilistic incoherence do not function as high-level, categorical principles in my theory. At most they would have to be derived (as lemmas) from the more fundamental, verific consequentialist, family of criteria. However, such derivations, as we saw in previous chapters, are very much in doubt. Similarly, I am dubious about the derivability of the no-order-effects principle. It is not obvious how it would follow from the verific consequentialist criterion I have defended, in particular, from the good-calibration variant that applies to degrees of belief. Nor does it follow from a new variant of this approach that I shall introduce shortly. It remains to be asked whether the A-and-A process, in particular, is compatible with these calibrationist criteria of justifiedness. This is the topic to which we should now turn.

Before addressing this question, I should mention parenthetically that order effects associated with the contrast or surprise process can be mitigated by the attention-decrement process. This is an intriguing observation made by Einhorn and Hogarth. As noted at the end of section 16.2, the contrast or surprise factor and the attention-decrement factor are forces working in opposite directions, the former toward recency effects and the latter toward primacy effects. If the bias from the contrast or surprise process were exactly offset by the bias from attention decrement, the net effect might be zero. Perhaps, then, the contrast or surprise process does not necessarily breed (net) recency effects. However, it would be remarkable if the two sorts of biases *exactly* offset one another.

Let us now ignore the no-order-effects principle and ask how the contrast or surprise process, or more generally, the entire set of A-and-A processes, would fare under the good-calibration criterion. Recall that good calibration was defined for a system of J-rules. Whether such a system is well calibrated is a function of the partial beliefs, or subjective probabilities, that would be produced if cognizers used processes that conform with that system. Consider the set of partial beliefs that would be so produced, and partition them into separate classes for each degree of belief D (or classes spanning small ranges of degrees of belief). The system is well calibrated just in case the proportion of truths within each class is approximately the same as the degree of belief of that class. For example, given the class of subjective probabilities equaling .60 that would be produced in a realization of the rule system, approximately 60 percent of the propositions assigned this subjective probability must be true.

The main point to be made here is that there isn't any reason why an A-and-A process described by Einhorn and Hogarth could not perform adequately, as judged by the good-calibration criterion. Hence, there isn't any reason why it could not be approved by a right J-rule system. Note in particular that the good-calibration criterion only requires that for each strength of belief D, the truth ratio of beliefs of strength D that would result from an approved set of processes should be *approximately* D. I see no reason why an A-and-A process of belief revision could not satisfy this requirement, especially if the margin of approximation is fairly loose.

Of course, the generic A-and-A process is not solely responsible for achieving proximity to good calibration. This depends on at least two other factors. First, it depends on the processes for assessing evidence: processes for deciding (a) whether a given piece of evidence bears positively or negatively on the target hypothesis, and (b) how *weighty* a piece of evidence it is. Einhorn and Hogarth's model presupposes such decisions but is silent about their details. Obviously they are critical in determining the calibrational adequacy of belief updating procedures. Second, calibrational adequacy also depends on the values of α and β, parameters of the adjustment weight functions. I will focus on this second factor.

Recall that different values of α and β represent different attitudes toward disconfirmation and confirmation respectively. Extreme values of α and β represent either extreme proneness toward disconfirmation or confirmation, or extreme avoidance of disconfirmation or confirmation. Any of these extreme values might militate against good calibration.

Reflecting on this point, the general A-and-A model should be construed, for our purposes, as picking out not a single process, but rather a family of belief-updating processes. Members of the family will differ in terms of differences in attitudes toward confirmation and disconfirmation. It is unlikely that all members of this family would perform well as judged by the good-calibration criterion. But some members of this family might perform adequately. Thus, *some* A-and-A processes, or contrast or surprise processes, could be justificationally admissible according to verific consequentialism. People who use *these* A-and-A processes can have justified (partial) beliefs. But partial beliefs updated by extreme confirmation proneness, or by extreme disconfirmation avoidance, will not be justified.

Some comments on Bayesian conditionalization might be apt at this juncture. There is nothing in my account which suggests that Bayesian conditionalization would not also be a justificationally acceptable process. If Bayesian conditionalization were a basic psychological process of belief updating, it could be sanctioned by a right J-rule system. (Recall that my metatheory allows multiple right J-rule systems.) Of course, the mere use of Bayesian conditionalization would not by itself ensure good calibration. Highly inaccurate conditional probabilities could lead to poor calibration, despite conformity with conditionalization rules. But conditionalization per se might be justificationally admissible; that is, combined with *suitable* processes of forming conditional subjective probabilities, it might produce good calibration.

As I have said, however, there is good reason to believe that Bayesian conditionalization is not a native psychological process. And as I have stressed, it is unlikely that human beings have the native capacity to make probabilistic calculations of the sort conditionalization requires. Furthermore, it is very doubtful that conditionalization rules would be generally applicable. Conditionalization requires that a cognizer have a *prior* assessment of the conditional probability of the target hypothesis on the evidence in question. But use of conditionalization then requires that a cognizer have a conditional probability assignment for *any* piece of evidence he might receive in the future, which is certainly unrealistic. Nobody can anticipate all possible evidence that might be encountered.

Returning now to A-and-A processes, advocates of the no-order-effects principle might interject the following point. Granted that some members of the A-and-A family might fit into a well-calibrated rule system, couldn't a belief-updating procedure that did not feature the contrast or surprise mechanism help form an even *better* calibrated system? In other words, wouldn't a process with no order effects be even a better component of a coordinated set of processes, according to calibration consequentialism?

This may be true (though it would have to be established). Even so, two replies are in order. First, although an abstractly possible process of this sort might be better, human beings may possess no such process—not, at any rate, as part of their native cognitive equipment. Second, the criterion of rightness for J-rule systems is not *comparative*. Even if one rule system were better calibrated than another, it would not follow that the less well-calibrated one is not right. According to my criterion, a J-rule system is right if it is sufficiently well calibrated. It cannot be demoted from this status by finding a better calibrated system (especially one that licenses processes that are just abstractly possible). True enough, one might try to refine my approach so as to admit 'degrees' of rightness or degrees of justifiedness. Then superior calibrational properties might be used to rank alternative sets of processes. But even this would not mean declaring order-effect processes wholly nonjustificational.

I have said that *some* members of the A-and-A family might be justificationally admissible according to calibration consequentialism. But further reflection makes this somewhat doubtful. Indeed, no belief updating process might be admissible by this criterion. This suggests that a revised criterion of J-rule rightness might be in order.

The difficulty is created by the fact that a person might encounter only one or two pieces of evidence, perhaps 'small' pieces of evidence, that bear on hypothesis h. One's subjective probability vis-à-vis h will therefore be based on very slender grounds. Now consider a large class of such cases. Even if cognizers respond to such evidence with one of the better members of the A-and-A family of processes (that is, one with moderate α and β parameters), is it really likely that the resulting truth ratio of their beliefs will be well calibrated? That is doubtful. Just one or two applications of even a good belief-updating process may not lead in the direction of truth, especially if the evidence is quite weak. This raises doubts about whether any A-and-A process would qualify for justificational approval under calibration consequentialism. Moreover, this is a potential problem for any belief-updating process! It is not peculiar to the family of A-and-A processes. Yet it seems unreasonable to preclude all such processes. If repeated use of a process would lead to good calibration, or would gradually *converge* on good calibration, that ought to suffice to vindicate the process. The process ought not be (justificationally) prohibited just because one or two applications of it would not yield good calibration.

One possible way to meet this difficulty is to point out that a string of uses of a given A-and-A process might be viewed as a single process. N applications of the A-and-A process is a large conjunctive process, and where N is large enough, such a process might make a suitable contribution to good calibration. However, it is not clear that this would work for any fixed N. Since pieces of evidence can vary widely in relevance, there may be no fixed number of applications that will do the job.

An alternative solution is to introduce a different variant of the calibration approach: *calibrational convergence.* A set of process rules will be called calibrationally convergent if and only if the more frequently they are applied, the closer the resulting truth ratio of beliefs to perfect calibration. (A more precise definition could be given using the mathematical notion of a limit.) We might then propose that a system of J-rules is right if it is calibrationally convergent. This requirement is obviously weaker than our original calibration criterion and might be more attractive for that reason.

A possible refinement of this approach would introduce speed of convergence as a justificationally pertinent factor. If two sets of rules are both calibrationally convergent but the use of one would converge faster than the other, the former might plausibly be deemed epistemologically preferable. Although my metatheoretical structure does not explicitly accommodate degrees of justification or comparative justifiedness, such notions are intuitively quite plausible. We might say that (partial) beliefs formed in accordance with the former set of rules are more justified than beliefs formed in accordance with the latter. For example, beliefs that result from updatings by an A-and-A process with optimal values of α and β may be called *more* justified than beliefs that have been updated by an A-and-A process with suboptimal α and β values. But even the latter may be justified to some degree.

I shall not try to develop this theme in detail. However, let me comment on its kinship with sundry other approaches in the philosophy of science and the theory of epistemic norms. Many philosophers of science have suggested that even if good scientific method need not bring us to the truth, its repeated use should at least bring us closer to the truth. C. S. Peirce is famous for this suggestion, although he went on—very implausibly—to *define* truth as the (set of) opinion(s) toward which inquiry leads. My idea of calibrational convergence as a test for justifiedness is a cousin of this suggestion. Another close relative of my proposal is Hans Reichenbach's "pragmatic" justification of induction.[6] Reichenbach appealed to the possibility of an inductive method converging toward a true value, or producing gradually better approximations through repeated use.

Karl Popper's theory of "corroboration" is another case in point. A theory is better corroborated the more often it survives attempts to falsify it. To be sure, Popper stresses that degree of corroboration is a function not just of the number of corroborating instances, but also of their severity.[7]

Still, the core idea of making an epistemic judgment rest on *successive* applications of a method is present here too.

The diachronic approach to epistemic evaluation has also been popularized by Imre Lakatos. He proposed that we appraise scientific research programmes by their historical progressiveness.[8] On Larry Laudan's permutation of this idea a research tradition may be evaluated by the "general progress," or the "rate of progress," of a research tradition in solving problems over time.[9]

I do not wish to endorse any of these specific proposals in the philosophy of science literature. I merely call attention to the fact that the kernel of my idea—judging a method by its *repeated* use—has enjoyed significant popularity among philosophers.

An emphasis on diachronic properties of a process or method is also urged by Robin Hogarth.[10] Hogarth argues that the biases of judgmental processes revealed in "discrete," isolated incidents may be outweighed by the merits of those processes when they are used "continuously" (repeatedly) over time, with feedback.

Although I shall not develop the calibrational convergence approach in further detail, I regard it as significant for two reasons. First, it brings into prominence an important way of evaluating judgmental processes and methods, namely, evaluating their success over time, through repeated application. Second, it shows the versatility of the general reliabilist and calibrationist approach to epistemic norms. If the criterion of rightness proposed in Chapter 5 does not strike one as fully correct, the verific approach still allows for variations in many directions. Calibrational convergence is one such promising direction.

chapter 17

Production Systems and Second-Order Processes

17.1. *Anderson's Production System Theory*

In this chapter I focus on a general framework for describing cognition: the *production system* framework. I choose this framework for two reasons. First, it provides a very general approach to cognition, and it is worth asking how our standards of evaluation can be applied to such a general approach. Second, it is especially useful in discussing a topic introduced in Part I but heretofore neglected in Part II, namely, second-order processes. We saw in Part I that both knowledge and justifiedness depend on how belief-forming processes, or methods, are learned or acquired. But thus far I have said very little about processes governing such learning or acquisition. The production system framework provides an excellent sample treatment of such second-order processes, as I will show in section 17.3.

The basic claim of the production system framework is that human cognition may be conceptualized in terms of a set of condition-action pairs, called 'productions'. A *condition* specifies some data patterns, and if elements matching these patterns are in working memory, then the production can apply. The *action* component of a production specifies what to do in that state. The standard action is to add new data elements to working memory. A typical production rule, stated informally, might be:

> IF person 1 is the father of person 2
>   and person 2 is the father of person 3
> THEN person 1 is the grandfather of person 3.

This production would apply if 'Fred is the father of Bill' and 'Bill is the father of Tom' were active in working memory. The system would make the inference to 'Fred is the grandfather of Tom' and deposit this fact in working memory. This may be understood as *forming a belief*.

Production systems can be traced back to the proposals of E. L. Post,[1] but modern production systems began with A. Newell's work in the early sixties, formulated later in Newell and H. A. Simon's *Human Problem Solving*.[2]

From the start, production systems have had an ambiguous status, being in part programming languages for computer science and in part psychological theories. I am interested in them, of course, in the latter guise. I shall concentrate on perhaps the best developed psychological theory within the production system tradition: that of John Anderson in *The Architecture of Cognition.*[3] Anderson started his work in this mode in an earlier book, *Language, Memory, and Thought,* where he called his system "ACT."[4] The more recent version, which I shall examine, is called "ACT°."

To illustrate the idea of a production system, Anderson provides a hypothetical set of productions, usable for doing addition. Let's see how such a set of productions might be deployed to solve the following addition problem:

```
 614
 438
+683
????
```

Here is the hypothetical set of productions.

P1   IF the goal is to do an addition problem
     THEN the subgoal is to iterate through the columns of
               the problem.

P2   IF the goal is to iterate through the columns of an addition
               problem
          and the rightmost column has not been processed
     THEN the subgoal is to iterate through the rows of that
               right-most column
          and set the running total to 0.

P3   IF the goal is to iterate through the columns of an
               addition problem
          and a column has just been processed
          and another column is to the left of this column
     THEN the subgoal is to iterate through the rows of
               this column to the left
          and set the running total to the carry.

P4   IF the goal is to iterate through the columns of an addition
               problem
          and the last column has been processed
          and there is a carry
     THEN write out the carry
          and POP the goal.

P5   IF the goal is to iterate through the columns of an addition
               problem

and the last column has been processed and there is no carry

THEN POP the goal.

P6 IF the goal is to iterate through the rows of a column
and the top row has not been processed

THEN the subgoal is to add the digit of the top row to the running total.

P7 IF the goal is to iterate through the rows of a column
and a row has just been processed
and another row is below it

THEN the subgoal is to add the digit of the lower row to the running total.

P8 IF the goal is to iterate through the rows of a column
and the last row has been processed
and the running total is a digit

THEN write the digit
and delete the carry
and mark the column as processed
and POP the goal.

P9 IF the goal is to iterate through the rows of a column
and the last row has been processed
and the running total is of the form 'string digit'

THEN write the digit
and set carry to the string
and mark the column as processed
and POP the goal.

P10 IF the goal is to add a digit to another digit
and a sum is the sum of the two digits

THEN the result is the sum
and mark the digit as processed
and POP the goal.

P11 IF the goal is to add a digit to a number
and the number is of the form 'string digit'
and a sum is the sum of the two digits
and the sum is less than 10

THEN the result is 'string sum'
and mark the digit as processed
and POP the goal.

P12 IF the goal is to add a digit to a number
and the number is of the form 'string digit'
and a sum is the sum of the two digits

and the sum is of the form '1 digit'
and another number sum° is the sum of 1 plus string
THEN the result is 'sum° digit°'
and mark the digit as processed
and POP the goal.

The conditions of these productions are given by the IF parts and their actions by the THEN parts. Figure 17.1 illustrates the flow of control among the productions in that set. Application of this set of productions is controlled by the setting of goals. Figure 17.1 basically shows which productions respond to which goals and which productions set which goals. Applied to the addition problem mentioned above, application of the production system would run as follows. Production P1, the first to apply, sets a subgoal to iterate through the columns. Production P2 then changes the subgoal to add the digits of the rightmost column and sets the running total

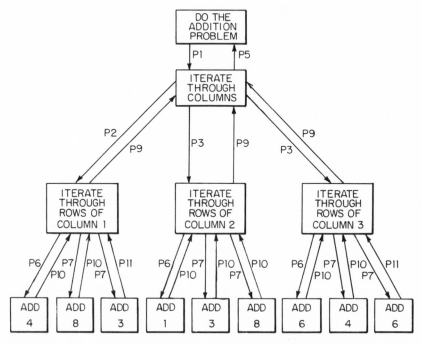

Figure 17.1. A representation of the flow of control among the various goals. The boxes correspond to goal states and the arrows to productions that can change these states. The goal at the origin of the arrow corresponds to the goal that elicits the production, and the goal at the terminus of the arrow corresponds to the goal that is set after the application of the production. Control starts with the top goal.

to 0. Then production P6 sets the new subgoal to add the top digit of the row (4) to the running total. In terms of Figure 17.1 this sequence of three productions has moved the system down from the top goal of doing the problem to the bottom goal of performing a basic addition operation. The system has four goals stacked, with attention focused on the bottom goal.

At this point production P10 applies, which calculates 4 as the new value of the running total. In doing this it retrieves from the addition table (in LTM) the fact that $4 + 0 = 4$. Production P10 also pops the goal of adding the digit to the running total. 'Popping' a goal means shifting attention from the current goal to the one above it in the hierarchy. In this situation attention will return to iterating through the rows of the column. Then P7 applies, which sets the new subgoal of adding 8 to the running total. P10 applies again to change the running total to 12, then P7 applies to create the subgoal of adding 3 to the running total, then P11 calculates the new running total as 15. At this point the system is back to the goal of iterating through the rows and has processed the bottom row of the column. Then production P9 applies, which writes out the 5 in 15, sets the carry to the 1, and pops back to the goal of iterating through the columns. At this point the production system has processed one column of the problem. This should suffice to illustrate the application of these productions.

In Anderson's ACT* theory three memories are postulated: working memory, declarative memory, and production memory. Working memory contains the information that the system can currently access, consisting of information retrieved from long-term declarative memory as well as temporary structures deposited by encoding processes and the actions of productions. Working memory is declarative knowledge, permanent or temporary, that is in an active state. Declarative memory contains declarative knowledge that may not be in an active state. Production memory contains the set of productions, or procedures, available to the system. In a mature human cognizer, Anderson puts the number of productions somewhere between the tens of thousands and the tens of millions.

The interactions between these memories is illustrated in Figure 17.2. Most of the processes depicted here involve working memory. *Encoding* processes deposit information about the outside world into working memory; *performance* processes convert commands in working memory into behavior. The *storage* process can create permanent records in declarative memory of the contents of working memory and can increase the strength of existing records in declarative memory. The *retrieval* process retrieves information from declarative memory. In the *match* process data in working memory are put into correspondence with the conditions of productions. The *execution* process deposits the actions of matched productions into working memory. The whole process of production matching followed by execution is referred to as *production application*. Note that the arrow

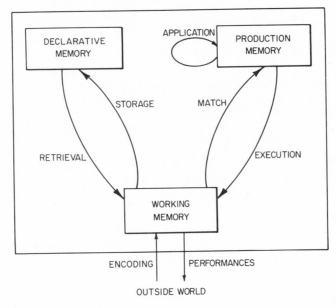

Figure 17.2

marked 'application' cycles back into the production memory box, reflecting the fact that new productions are learned from studying the history of application of existing productions. This involves the idea of *procedural learning*, which I shall explore in sections 17.3 and 17.4.

I will not summarize all the basic principles of ACT*, but let me mention a few salient ones. Since all activities of productions require activation—only activated data can be matched with production conditions—an important question concerns the *sources* of activation. What Anderson calls "source nodes" are the "springs" from which activation flows throughout the system. Nodes can become source nodes in several ways. First, they can be created by the perception of objects in the environment. Second, elements deposited in working memory by a production's action become transient source nodes. These are "internal" sources. They stay active for a brief period of time and then cease to be sources. A special goal element, however, permits one internal source that is not so transient, and this enables the system to maintain focus on a current goal.

A critical issue concerning the flow of cognitive activity is the selection of productions that get matched. Given what has been said thus far, it would seem possible for incompatible productions to match data in working memory, and for all to get applied. But this is assumed to be psychologically unrealistic. Rival productions are not allowed to apply simultaneously. What, then, are the principles for conflict resolution, for choosing the production that does get applied? ACT* involves several such principles.

First, ACT* allows the conditions of a production to be applied when its condition is matched only partially, not fully. However, a full match is preferred to a partial match, and among partial matches, more complete matches are preferred to less complete matches.

Any number of phenomena, Anderson says, point to the fact that productions can be evoked by partial matches. Faces change but still can be recognized. We can recognize partial lexical patterns, as in Figure 17.3, and this seems best explained by the concept of partial matching. Many errors described by Donald Norman[5] also can be explained by partial matching. For instance, there is the case of a person who threw a dirty shirt by mistake into the toilet rather than into the hamper. Apparently a 'hamper-matching' pattern partially matched the toilet.

A second principle for production selection concerns the relative strength of rival productions. Stronger productions are preferred to weaker productions. The determinants of production strength will be examined in section 17.3.

A third principle for production selection is the specificity principle. It states that when two productions match the same data, preference is given to the production with the more specific condition. Condition A is more specific than condition B if A matches in a proper subset of the situations where condition B would match. This principle handles cases of exceptions to rules, as in productions P1 and P2 below.

P1   IF the goal is to generate the plural of a noun
        THEN say the noun *s*.

P2   IF the goal is to generate the plural of *man*
        THEN say *men*.

Production P1 gives the general rule for pluralizing a noun, while P2 gives the exception for *man*. The specificity principle enables the exception to take precedence over the general rule. There are two ways in which one production can be more specific than another. One possibility is that the more specific one contains additional clauses in its condition. The second is that the production contains additional tests about a data structure, as in the foregoing example.

A fourth principle concerning production selection involves goal dominance. Many productions contain in their conditions tests for the current

RONALD REAGAN

Figure 17.3

goal. There can be only one current goal active in the system at a time. Productions that refer to the current goal take precedence over productions that might otherwise apply. A goal-directed production that matches the current goal applies more rapidly and reliably, but if it does not match the current goal, it will not apply no matter how well the rest of its condition matches. If a number of goal-directed productions match the current goal, the principles of degree of match, strength, and specificity select the one that will apply.

These are some of the main features of ACT°. More of its features will be presented in section 17.3. Let me now turn (briefly) to some evaluative reflections on the features of ACT° introduced thus far.

17.2. Production Architecture: Reliability, Speed, and Power

Are productions belief-forming processes? It might seem as if they are. Application of a production often involves the insertion of new data structures into working memory. Such an insertion seems to be the formation of a belief (at least in many cases). So a production—or the *application* of a production—seems to be a belief-forming process. Since primary epistemology is concerned with the reliability of belief-forming processes, it apparently should be concerned with the reliability of individual productions or groups of productions.

However, a moment's reflection should indicate that productions are not (in general) belief-forming 'processes' in my special use of this term. They are not, in particular, *basic* cognitive processes. In general, individual productions are learned, highly task-specific procedures. They are not part of the fixed, native architecture of the cognitive system. This is sufficient grounds for their not being basic processes. They are (in general) what I have called 'methods' rather than processes. (There are possible exceptions. Some productions may be original, innate features of the system. *These* could count as basic processes. But since ACT° has nothing to say about such productions, I will ignore them in my discussion.)

The reliability of methods may be relevant to the *secondary* justifiedness of beliefs formed by those methods. But method reliability is not relevant to the *primary* justifiedness of these beliefs (see section 5.3). In this work, at least in Part 2, my concern with justifiedness is restricted to primary justifiedness. Hence, since productions are methods rather than processes, we need not be concerned with the reliability properties of productions.

Are there any features of a production system architecture, then, which *do* interest primary epistemology? Yes, two kinds of features. First, a production system architecture includes basic processes for *using* productions already in the system's repertoire. Second, a production system architecture has processes for *adding* productions to the repertoire and selectively increasing or decreasing the *strengths* of productions (strengths that in turn affect when the productions are applied). Clearly, all of these processes are of interest to primary epistemology. In this section I shall reflect on (some of) the processes in ACT* for using productions.

Processes for using methods are included under the category of 'first-order' processes. Processes for acquiring new methods, and for deleting or modifying them in various ways, would fall under the category of 'second-order' processes (see sections 5.3 and 5.7). Thus far I have only presented first-order processes of ACT*. So in this section my evaluative comments on production *use* are confined to such first-order processes. An exposition of ACT*'s second-order processes will be given in the next section; an evaluation of them will appear in section 17.4.

Let us turn now to the reliability of the processes for using a repertoire of productions. This includes the processes for selecting which productions to apply on given occasions as well as the process of application itself. Of course, the reliability of selection and application processes cannot be completely isolated from the reliability of the productions on which they operate. In the interest of simplicity, though, let us assume that all productions in a person's repertoire are perfectly reliable. How, then, would selection and application processes affect reliability?

One important point to note here is the partial matching feature of ACT*. Even if all the productions are perfectly reliable, error can creep in through partial matching. A new belief can be formed in working memory by application of a production that does not really fulfill a preexisting condition. This amounts roughly to taking a sound inference procedure and misapplying it.

A partial matching process will typically reduce overall reliability. Does this mean that any cognitive architecture that realizes ACT* has a feature that precludes its approval by a right J-rule system? Not necessarily. This will depend on two factors: the degree of reliability required for justifiedness, and the degree of match that constitutes the minimal threshold for production application. In section 17.1 I stressed the comparative principle for production selection: *ceteris paribus*, productions with a higher degree of match are preferred to productions with a lower degree of match. But ACT* also includes a cutoff feature: below a certain level of match, a production will not be selected at all. Obviously, this cutoff level is important for reliability.

However, even if the cutoff level of a given architecture allows too much error, as judged by a rightness criterion with a fixed truth-ratio requirement, this does not mean that *no* belief formed under this architecture is justified. When productions are selected in virtue of a sufficiently high degree of match—high enough to satisfy the specific rightness criterion—then beliefs so formed may be justified. In *those* cases the minimal cutoff point is not the causally operative degree of match. (Recall my discussion of this sort of case in Chapter 3.)

Although partial matching is a potential liability from the standpoint of reliability, it is probably an asset from the standpoints of speed and power. Apropos of speed, the cognizer does not have to search or wait for all features of a pattern to match before applying a production. He can recognize stimuli when they have been only partly observed. This is presumably a significant timesaver. (ACT°'s pattern matcher responds faster to more complete matches, *when* more complete matches are available. But this does not conflict with the point I am making.)

Apropos of power, the principle of partial matching allows the cognizer to deal successfully with the commonly found stimuli that only partly match stored conditions, whether through occlusion, change, deformation, or the like. Examples of occlusion were mentioned in Chapter 11. Examples of change and deformation include two that were mentioned in the previous section: a face that has changed since previous encounters, and deformed lexical patterns such as the one in Figure 17.3. Without partial matching, the cognizer could not correctly answer the questions, 'Who is that?' or 'What does that say?' questions he wants to answer in these examples. Thus, partial matching can enhance power.

Another feature of ACT° architecture that is highly congenial to question-answering power is *goal-directed* processing. Complicated questions require complicated operations to obtain (correct) answers. Frequently, many different facts have to be retrieved (or obtained), and complex algorithms or heuristics need to be applied. All of this takes time and mental organization. The mind needs to stick to the problem at hand and keep from getting distracted. It also needs to perform operations in an appropriate sequence and to keep track of significant relationships. The goal-directed structure of the ACT° architecture facilitates satisfaction of these requisites. The goal structure solves the focus-of-attention problem by allowing the *current* goal to be a prime *source* of activation. And the provision for hierarchical goals facilitates the necessary seriality in the control of cognition.

In the arithmetic example given in section 17.1 we saw how cognition may be controlled by hierarchically ordered goals. This explains how the organism can engage in *planning,* a topic that has engrossed many cognitive scientists. Like the dominant view of planning in cognitive science,[6] this depicts the top-down aspect of planning: the process starts with high-level goals and refines them stepwise into achievable actions. But Anderson remarks that his ACT° system can also accommodate bottom-up, data-driven phenomena.

Data-drivenness is accommodated by the fact that perception can serve as a source node, that is, a source of activation which can redirect attention. Furthermore, ACT° is designed to reflect the fact that even planning can involve bottom-up components. This has been stressed by B. Hayes-Roth and F. Hayes-Roth in their conception of *opportunistic planning.*[7] In studying how subjects plan a series of errands around town, these researchers found evidence of the subjects' proceeding unsystematically and multi-directionally in their planning space, seeking to develop the most promising aspects of their plan as the occasion permits. Subjects thereby mix low-level and high-level decision making, instead of proceeding in a strictly hierarchical fashion. Anderson tries to capture such possibilities in ACT*. If the resulting procedures are indeed psychologically correct, it is an open question how they affect the general power of the ACT* architecture. Clearly, however, the goal-linked properties of this architecture are importantly connected to the epistemically significant dimension of question-answering, or problem-solving, power.

17.3. Procedural Learning

As I remarked earlier, what concerns primary epistemology is not only processes that use productions but also those that govern production acquisition and adjustment of production strength. In this section I give an exposition of the processes governing acquisition and strength adjustment. Anderson discusses them under the heading *procedural learning.* In my framework they fall into the category of second-order processes, because they control the acquisition and modification of methods.

Notice that the label 'second-order' is apt to cause confusion. One might suppose that second-order processes are only relevant to secondary epistemology. But this is incorrect. Since a second-order process is a kind of basic process, its status is exclusively of interest to primary epistemology—including the question of primary justifiedness. It is essential to keep the contrasts between *(a)* first-order and second-order processes and *(b)* primary and secondary epistemology (or justifiedness) sharply distinct. Secondary epistemology, including the theory of secondary justifiedness, is concerned with properties of methods, not with properties of second-order processes.

Let us now turn to the mechanisms of procedural learning built into ACT*. Anderson first draws a sharp distinction between two kinds of 'knowledge': *declarative* knowledge and *procedural* knowledge. This dichotomy is reflected in two of the memories depicted in Figure 17.2—declarative memory and production memory—which store the two kinds of knowledge. The content of procedural knowledge is productions: knowledge about how to do things. The phrase 'how to do things' first brings to mind motor skills, because these are the most concrete examples of procedural knowledge. But motor skills like riding a bike or typing are not the prime focus of the ACT* theory, although they are included within procedural knowledge. In Anderson's theory the focus is on cognitive skills such as decision making, mathematical problem solving, and language generation. This focus also suits my main concerns.

In addition to the declarative-procedural dichotomy, Anderson draws a clear distinction between the nature of fact-acquiring processes and production-acquiring processes. It is not possible, he says, simply to add a production in the way that one simply encodes a fact or cognitive unit. Procedural learning occurs only in executing a skill; one learns by doing. This is one reason why procedural learning is much more gradual than declarative learning.

Notice that a skill can be embodied in two ways—either declaratively or procedurally. For example, a declarative encoding of a recipe can be used to guide cooking behavior with the help of a general recipe-following set of productions. In this case the declarative information expressed by the recipe is used as a set of instructions. When, in this fashion, existing productions use declarative knowledge to guide behavior, there is an "interpretive" embodiment of a skill. Once this knowledge has been applied interpretively a number of times, a set of new productions can be "compiled" that apply the knowledge directly. At this stage, there arises a "procedural" embodiment of the skill.

One might wonder why new productions are compiled at all, if skills can be embodied interpretively. Anderson replies that interpretive application of declarative knowledge has serious costs in time and working-memory space. The process is slow because interpretation requires retrieving declarative information from LTM and because an interpreter's individual production steps are small in order to achieve generality. The interpretive productions also require that the declarative information be represented in working memory, and this can place a heavy burden on working-memory capacity (which is much more restricted than declarative LTM or production memory). Subjects' errors and slowness on various tasks can be attributed to working-memory errors. Students keep repeating the same information over and over again as they lose critical intermediate results and have to recompute them. Building up new, task-specific productions greatly increases efficiency in terms of both time and working-memory demands.

Anderson divides the process of creating new productions into two subprocesses: *composition* and *proceduralization*. Composition takes a sequence of productions and collapses them into a single production that has the effect of the sequence. This speeds up the skill considerably by creating new operators that embody the sequences of steps used in a particular problem domain. Proceduralization builds versions of the productions that no longer require the domain-specific declarative information to be retrieved into working memory. Rather, the essential products of these retrieval operations are built into the new productions themselves.

One example Anderson gives concerns dialing a telephone number.[8] At first, a person might use the following two productions to begin dialing a telephone number. (In what follows, the abbreviation 'LV' stands for 'local variable'.)

P1 IF the goal is to dial LVtelephone-number
     and LVdigit1 is the first digit of LVtelephone-number
  THEN dial LVdigit1.

P2 IF the goal is to dial LVtelephone-number
     and LVdigit1 has just been dialed
     and LVdigit2 is after LVdigit1 in LVtelephone-number
  THEN dial LVdigit2.

The process of composition, operating on these two productions, could create a "macroproduction":

P1&P2 IF the goal is to dial LVtelephone-number
     and LVdigit1 is the first digit of LVtelephone-number
     and LVdigit2 is after LVdigit1
  THEN dial LVdigit1 and then LVdigit2.

A composed production like P1&P2 still requires that the information (in this case, the phone number) be retrieved from declarative memory, held in working memory, and matched to the second and third clauses in P1&P2. Proceduralization eliminates clauses (in the condition of a production) that require information to be retrieved from declarative memory and held in working memory. In P1&P2 the second and third condition clauses would be eliminated. The local variables that would have been bound in matching these clauses are replaced by the values they are bound to in the special case. For example, if this and related productions are repeatedly applied in dialing Mary's telephone number, which is 432-2815, procedularization would eventually build a macroproduction that dials the full number:

P° IF the goal is to dial Mary's number
  THEN dial 4-3-2-2-8-1-5.

In using this production, one no longer has to retrieve Mary's number from declarative memory, match it to the conditions of a production, and thereby use up working memory space with it. The number is part of the production itself. This knowledge-specific procedure makes it easier for the system to simultaneously perform a second concurrent task that does make working-memory demands.

There are two other processes of building new productions that Anderson discusses, although he considers them under the heading "tuning" (thereby grouping them, somewhat oddly, with the processes that affect production strength). These processes are *generalization* and *discrimination*. Generalization is a process in which production rules become broader in their range of applicability, and discrimination is one in which the rules becomes narrower. Strictly, this means that *new* productions, either broader or narrower, are constructed.

Generalization may be illustrated by an example from the game of bridge. While bridge players often learn rules of play from expert instruction, the following example assumes that the person has compiled some special-case production rules from experience. Two such rules might be:

P1   IF I am playing no trump
           and my dummy has a long suit
      THEN try to establish that suit
           and then run that suit.

P2   IF I am playing spades
           and my dummy has a long suit
      THEN try to establish that suit
           and then run that suit.

ACT° will create a generalization of these productions:

P3   IF my dummy has a long suit
      THEN try to establish that suit
           and then run that suit.

It is certainly useful to generalize overly specific procedures. But it is even more necessary to restrict the range of overly general procedures. The discrimination process tries to restrict the range of application of a production—actually, construct a new production—to just the appropriate circumstances. This requires that the cognizer have examples of (ostensibly) correct and incorrect applications of the production. The discrimination process remembers and compares the values of the variables in the correct and incorrect applications. It chooses a variable for discrimination among those that have different values in the two applications. Having selected a variable, it looks for some attribute that the variable has in only one of the situations. A test is added to the condition of the production for the presence of this attribute.[9]

The feature selected for discrimination is determined by comparing the variable bindings in the successful and unsuccessful production applications. A variable is selected on which the applications differ, and features are selected to restrict the bindings. Anderson says that the probability of choosing the right feature to discriminate upon depends on the similarity of the successful and unsuccessful situations. The more similar they are, the fewer the distracting possibilities, and the easier it is to identify the critical feature. This is the idea of near misses, discussed for example by P. H. Winston.[10]

A prerequisite for discrimination is that the system have feedback indicating that a particular production has misapplied. In principle, Anderson says, a production application could be characterized as being in one of three states—known to be incorrect, known to be correct, or correctness unknown. However, the mechanisms implemented in ACT° do not distinguish between the second and third states. If a production applies and there is no feedback about its success, it is treated as if it is a successful application.

There are two basic ways in which ACT° can determine that a production application is in error. One is through external feedback, and the other is through internal computation. In the external feedback situation the learner may be directly told that his behavior is in error or he may infer this by comparing his behavior to an external referent (such as a model or a textbook answer). In the internal computation case the learner must ascertain that an output of the production contradicts prior or subsequently formed beliefs, or that a goal has failed. In either case the feedback is only indirectly about the production. It is directly about the action of the production that entered into working memory.

It should be emphasized that whenever new productions are created, whether by generalization, discrimination, or composition, they do not replace previous productions. They just coexist with the latter, which are never replaced. However, although productions are never deleted, even when they are seen to be incorrect, they can remain or become very weak. Comparatively weak productions may seldom or never get applied (since they lose out to stronger rivals). Thus, even though incorrect productions remain in the repertoire, their existence need not be deleterious.

This brings us to the question of how productions gain or lose strength. Anderson offers an algebra for strength determination. When first created, a production has a strength of 1. Each time it applies, its strength increases by 1. However, when a production applies and receives negative feedback, its strength is reduced by 25 percent. Because a multiplicative adjustment usually produces a greater change in strength than an additive adjustment, this 'punishment' has much more impact than a reinforcement. Anderson adds that although his exact strengthening and weakening values are somewhat arbitrary, the general relationships are important.

Anderson has several further principles that affect strengths of productions, and I will not mention them all. One additional principle, though, should be explained. The ACT theory posits a power-law decay principle for the strength of units in declarative memory, and a similar power-law decay principle is included for production strength. Thus, productions lose strength over time through disuse.

17.4. Epistemic Assessment of Second-Order Processes

It is time for an epistemic evaluation of ACT°'s processes of production acquisition and tuning. First of all, let us recall from Chapter 5 the proposals for evaluating second-order processes. Focusing on primary justifiedness, I argued that the theory of primary justifiedness depends crucially on two kinds of criteria of rightness: a criterion of rightness for first-order processes and a criterion of rightness for second-order process. Although I gave scant attention to the rightness of second-order processes, this was discussed in section 5.7, where I suggested that a rightness criterion for second-order processes might naturally invoke some notion of second-order reliability, or metareliability.

Backing up a bit, we may characterize a second-order process as a process that controls the acquisition of new methods, or otherwise governs the repertoire of methods available for use in the cognitive system. Next, a second-order process may be called 'metareliable' in case, roughly, the methods it tends to acquire and preserve have sufficiently good reliability properties; or if it tends to *improve* the reliability properties of the method repertoire over time.

In section 5.7 two kinds of proposals were made. The first proposal was that a second-order process is metareliable if and only if the proportion of reliable methods it tends to acquire is sufficiently high. In other words, the ratio of reliable methods to all methods it would acquire meets or exceeds some specified threshold. For example, if the threshold is set at .80, then a second-order process is deemed metareliable if and only if 80 percent of the methods it would acquire are reliable. (This presupposes a threshold for fixing a categorical, binary concept of reliability.)

A second kind of proposal concerning metareliability focused on diachronic improvements in method repertoire. This proposal presupposed that second-order processes effect modifications, replacements, and deletions of methods. One conception, then, would consider a second-order process metareliable in case its operation *always* yields improvements in reliability. Modifications of methods must always increase their reliability; replacements must always substitute more reliable for less reliable methods; and simple deletions must delete only (comparatively) unreliable methods.

A weaker and more plausible variant would not require *all* modifications, replacements, and deletions to effect improvements in reliability. It may be deemed sufficient that a high enough proportion of them should yield increases in reliability.

To obtain a unified criterion of evaluation, one would have to decide how to balance, or integrate, appraisals of method acquisition and appraisals of method refinement (including modification, replacement, and deletion). It is not obvious how this should be done. At first blush, method acquisition seems quite important. If a second-order process permits many unreliable processes to be created, that seems to be a critical defect. But further reflection raises doubts on this score. If unreliable methods are promptly modified, replaced, or simply deleted, perhaps it is not so bad that unreliable methods are easily created.

The matter is further complicated by the possibility—introduced here by Anderson's production system theory—that methods can vary in *strength*. If methods vary in strength, as productions allegedly do, it may be harmless for unreliable methods to remain in a system's repertoire, as long as *(a)* they are very weak, and *(b)* weak methods do not get applied when they conflict with stronger rivals. The strength variable was not contemplated when my proposals in Chapter 5 were advanced. Once introduced, it complicates the conception of metareliability still further.

The last complication is, of course, directly relevant to the learning and tuning processes within ACT*. ACT* has no process for *deleting* productions. This might look like a serious flaw. But the tuning processes of ACT* do yield adjustments in strength. In particular, they (ostensibly) favor strength reductions for unreliable productions. Since strength reduction lowers the frequency or probability of production application, perhaps these learning and tuning processes are not so inadequate from the standpoint of metareliability (or justifiedness).

I am not prepared to propose any unified criterion of J-rightness for second-order processes. But as my several proposals indicate, I assume that a rightness criterion for second-order processes will involve some sort of metareliability standard. Although I am not advancing any single rightness criterion for second-order processes, we can still examine the learning and tuning processes of ACT*, with an eye to their metareliability, as measured by any of the standards we have canvassed. Before proceeding to this examination, though, two comments are in order.

First, we should not assume that second-order processes can be evaluated in isolation. Like their first-order brethren, second-order processes are interdependent. The effects of any given process partly depend on complementary processes that are at work. So these processes should be evaluated collectively: the proper unit of evaluation is really a system, or set, of second-order processes. Nonetheless, we can inspect second-order processes individually to see what contribution they might make to a larger system of second-order processes.

Second, our interest should not be restricted to meta*reliability*. It should encompass meta*power* and meta*speed* as well. Justifiedness mainly concerns reliability. But justifiedness is not the only notion of epistemic importance. Intelligence, as embodied in power and speed, is also important. Hence, the capacity of learning and tuning processes to generate and strengthen faster and more powerful methods is an epistemically positive feature.

With these points in mind, let us now examine the several learning and tuning processes incorporated in ACT*. First, consider the building of new productions by composition and compilation. If this has the psychological properties claimed by Anderson, then it enhances at least the speed and power of cognitive skills. Speed is increased because the relevant information for solving the problem no longer needs to be retrieved from declarative memory nor entered into working memory. Power is increased because fewer demands are made on working-memory space. This allows that space to be used for other, concurrent cognitive tasks, thereby increasing overall power.

The impact on reliability is somewhat mixed, although in the long run it appears to be positive. Anderson notes that the transition phase from declarative to procedural embodiment of a skill often breeds the most errors. But these are eventually corrected. Moreover, he emphasizes that heavy use of working-memory space produces errors, so the bypassing of working memory effected by proceduralization should increase reliability.

The fact that new productions can only be compiled when their components have already been applied successfully is another feature of the ACT° processes conducive to metareliability. It means that merely arbitrary productions will not be constructed. Nor will they be constructed just from verbal instructions, which might possibly be misunderstood or mistaken.

I turn now to the production-building processes of generalization and discrimination. Both of these processes can sometimes produce incorrect, meaning unreliable, productions. Overgeneralization is a well documented phenomenon in the language acquisition literature. It occurs with both syntactic rules and natural-language concepts. Discrimination can also fail by introducing inappropriate restrictive conditions, as discussed in section 17.3.

Strength-adjustment processes are ones by which such errors can be mitigated. If overgeneralizations or misdiscriminations are detected, that is, if negative feedback follows their application, then they are reduced in strength by 25 percent. Also, in many such cases, new productions are introduced to handle (more correctly, it is hoped) the same tasks. With these rival productions in place, the old mistaken productions tend to lose out and not get applied. Such disuse leads to gradual decay.

Is it clear, though, that strength-adjustment processes can adequately compensate for the errors of production-creation processes? This depends partly on just how meta-*un*reliable the production-creation processes are, and partly on the effectiveness of feedback processes.

With these questions in mind, consider the process of discrimination. According to Anderson's description, the discrimination algorithm randomly chooses a variable for discrimination from among those that have different values in successful and unsuccessful applications. It then looks for some attribute that the variable has in only one of the situations, a successful situation, and adds this condition to the production. But it appears that correct identification of such an attribute is largely a chance affair. True, a discriminated production yields the same belief ('action') as the original production in the restricted situation; so the discrimination process does not impose an unreliable production over a reliable one. But it is problematic whether improvements will be secured very often.

The matter of feedback is also delicate. Feedback itself is not infallible. Indeed, what Anderson calls "internal" feedback is especially susceptible to error. So it cannot be assumed that productions whose applications yield positive, or non-negative, feedback are *ipso facto* reliable.

Thus, we cannot in general certify that because a production has survived the operation of strength-adjustment processes and still remains fairly strong, it is therefore reliable. However, there may be a greater likelihood that strong productions are more reliable than weak ones. A production can only have attained substantial strength by being applied repeatedly without incurring (much) negative feedback. High strength indicates that a production has weathered the test of repeated applications and come through more or less unscathed. A history of 'failure to fail', of trials without detected error, may be a good indicator of genuine reliability. (The idea here is analogous to Karl Popper's account of corroboration. On Popper's account a theory is corroborated to the extent that it survives tests without falsification.)

This also suggests another idea similar to one mentioned in section 16.3. Setting aside the rightness criterion for second-order processes, what sort of J-rules should be contemplated for second-order processes? What I wish to stress is that a J-rule can permit certain *sequences* of processes but not other sequences. For example, in connection with ACT*, a J-rule system is not forced to choose between sanctioning *single* applications of the strengthening process and refusing to sanction the strengthening process at all. It could decide to license a sequence of, say, twenty strengthenings of a given production, but not license shorter sequences of strengthenings.

Suppose it does this. Then if a belief is formed by application of some production P, and P is applied as a result of having a certain strength T, and its strength T resulted from (at least) twenty applications on P of the strengthening operation, then the belief would qualify for justifiedness as far as second-order processes are concerned. By contrast, if the belief is formed by application of P*, and P*'s strength only resulted from, say, seven strengthenings, then the belief would not qualify for justifiedness.

Whatever the ultimate upshot of such deliberations, we have here a clear example of how the learning and tuning processes of ACT* could be evaluated from the standpoint of primary epistemology or primary epistemics. I have not, of course, presented a final formulation of a rightness criterion for second-order processes. This leaves my treatment extremely tentative. Nonetheless, it should be evident how such a criterion could be applied. I should also stress, once again, that perhaps neither ACT* nor any other production system framework provides a descriptively correct cognitive psychology. And if it does not, then the evaluation of ACT* is not a serious epistemological goal. Still, ACT* provides a *very instructive example* of how the enterprise of primary epistemics should be conducted, especially with respect to second-order processes.

Conclusion: Primary Epistemics and Cognitive Science

I HAVE NOW completed the task of Part II: to provide some detailed specimens of primary epistemology or primary *epistemics*. Needless to say, these chapters do not purport to be a final embodiment of primary epistemics. They are, as billed in section 9.1, only first steps in the subject. The enterprise should of course continue with new developments in a number of directions.

It is a bit misleading to call the present chapters 'first' steps in primary epistemics. As indicated in the Introduction, there are earlier conceptions and traditions with which primary epistemics has close affiliations, including the psychologistic epistemologies of the seventeenth through the nineteenth centuries and W. V. Quine's conception of "naturalistic epistemology." However, only the accomplishments and prospects of contemporary cognitive science make feasible a serious execution of primary epistemics. Although the general conception of primary epistemics could have been advanced in previous centuries (and was indeed adumbrated by Locke and Hume), comparable opportunities for scientifically grounded analysis of mental operations were not then available.

What further developments should be expected in primary epistemics? First and most obvious, developments are to be expected in substantive cognitive science—changes in theoretical posture as well as refinements in empirical detail. The 1980s are witnessing new approaches to memory, and these can be expected to burgeon. Linkages to neural constructs are bound to be strengthened. Whether such a schema as the production system framework continues to be fruitful only time will tell. Whether the mind is importantly modular is equally a matter for future cognitive science to determine. New developments in cognitive theory mean changes in the posited repertoire of fundamental operations, or changes in the precise properties of these operations. Such changes could require significant revisions in empirical material of the kind discussed in Part II.

Second, new developments should be encouraged in primary epistemics even with a completely *static* cognitive science. After all, epistemics undertakes to draw evaluative conclusions about cognitive processes. Even if cognitive theory is held fixed, considerable work must be done in assessing the reliability, power, and speed of the components of the cognitive repertoire. There is the task of determining what right J-rule systems, if any, can be devised for this repertoire. Can some (or all) of the processes belonging to this repertoire be deployed in a way that satisfies a specified truth ratio criterion? Are there more than one set of processes that can do this? If so, what are they? Even holding a posited cognitive repertoire constant, answers to these questions are not so easy to give; and revisions in putative answers are naturally to be expected.

Third, developments are needed in the formulation of evaluative criteria. My own proposals, which have been deliberately flexible, would profit from some tightening. As an example, let me review my treatment of justifiedness. I began in Chapter 5 by proposing a family of alternative rightness criteria for *belief*-forming processes. My calibrational approach to *degrees of credence*, in Chapter 5, was also rather exploratory. Further proposals for a calibrational approach to degree of credence were advanced in Chapter 16, but these too were quite tentative. Finally, Chapter 17 surveyed alternative criteria for second-order processes—all involving metareliability—but none was definitely endorsed. The criteria for J-rule rightness, then, clearly warrant further attention.

Looking beyond criteria of justifiedness, more detailed standards of evaluation may be proposed for other dimensions of evaluation, such as intelligence or rationality. I have made a few suggestions on these matters, but more remains to be done. Again, while I have expressed doubts about a *unified* criterion of epistemic appraisal, perhaps other theorists could invent and defend such a measure, integrating such standards as reliability, power, and speed. This would certainly be within the spirit of the general enterprise.

Proposals for revising criteria of evaluation can come from different sources. One is general reflection on the ordinary use of the relevant evaluative terms. Another might be progress in empirical psychology, which highlights factors that could be missed in purely abstract reflection. An example was given in Chapter 17, in the discussion of rightness criteria for second-order processes. We had earlier supposed that rightness criteria would concern only the acquisition and retention of methods. But consideration of ACT* drew our attention to the strength variable. It became plausible to suppose that a satisfactory J-rule criterion for second-order processes might invoke some factor like strength, or probability of employment.

Another avenue of development lies in possible *applications* of primary epistemics. I have presented the evaluative enterprise as a 'theoretical' rather than a 'regulative' one. But there are some prospects for deliberate control of cognitive operations, should this prove advisable. Habits in deployment of the cognitive repertoire may be amenable to inculcation and training. There may be techniques for promoting the use of certain sequences or patterns of operations over others. If primary epistemics distinguishes superior from inferior processes, it is natural to try to promote the better over the worse. A challenge is then extended to educational theory to devise techniques for achieving this end.

There is, then, a substantial agenda for the future of primary epistemics, and for offshoots from it. Exciting prospects lie ahead for a collaboration between philosophy and a variety of cognitive disciplines.

In recent years philosophers have laid the groundwork for a working relationship between cognitive science and the philosophy of mind. The argument here is that cognitive science is equally important (though in different ways) to epistemology. However, my conception of epistemology is even broader than this. At the *social* level it would intersect with yet other disciplines outside of philosophy proper. A full argument for this thesis, however, must await a future volume.

Notes

Illustration Credits

Author Index

Subject Index

Notes

Introduction

1. Ludwig Wittgenstein, *Philosophical Investigations*, trans. G. E. M. Anscombe (New York: Macmillan, 1953), para. 309.

2. W. V. Quine, "Epistemology Naturalized," in *Ontological Relativity and Other Essays* (New York: Columbia University Press, 1969), p. 82.

3. Donald Campbell, "Evolutionary Epistemology," in Paul Schilpp, ed., *The Philosophy of Karl Popper*, vol. 1 (La Salle, Ill.: Open Court, 1974), p. 413.

4. Two other recent works that treat epistemology in some sort of psychologistic vein are Gilbert Harman's *Thought* (Princeton: Princeton University Press, 1973) and Fred Dretske's *Knowledge and the Flow of Information* (Cambridge, Mass.: MIT Press, 1981). But the approaches of these authors are quite different from mine. For example, instead of drawing on psychology to reach epistemological conclusions, Harman's main strategy is to use epistemological judgments to reach psychological conclusions. Specifically, he seeks to decide what inferences people make by seeing what inferences must be postulated to account for our judgments of whether or not they 'know' (see *Thought*, pp. 20–23.) This seems to me to get the relation between psychology and epistemology backward. Dretske refines a popular term of cognitive theory—'information'—and puts it to epistemological use. But his theory assigns no systematic role to empirical psychology; nor does he conceive of epistemology as an evaluative discipline.

5. Although it is not clear that Quine intends to neglect the evaluative dimension, his actual characterizations of naturalistic epistemology do not expressly introduce this dimension. See, for example, "The Nature of Natural Knowledge," in Samuel Guttenplan, ed., *Mind and Language* (Oxford: Clarendon Press, 1975).

6. Otto Neurath, "Protokollsätze," *Erkenntnis*, 3 (1932):206.

7. Francis Bacon, *Novum Organum* (1620), bk. 1, sect. 2.

8. John Locke, *An Essay concerning Human Understanding* (1690), introduction, sect. 4.

9. David Hume, *A Treatise of Human Nature* (1739), introduction.

10. On Carnap's sharp separation, see *The Logical Syntax of Language*, trans. Amethe Smeaton (London: Routledge and Kegan Paul, 1937), sect. 72, esp. pp. 278–279. Reichenbach's distinction appears in *Experience and Prediction* (Chicago: University of Chicago Press, 1938), pp. 6–8.

11. Quine, "Epistemology Naturalized," p. 83.

12. Thomas Kuhn, *The Structure of Scientific Revolutions*, (Chicago: University of Chicago Press, 1962).

13. *Philosophical Investigations*, for example, para. 486.

14. Richard Rorty, *Philosophy and the Mirror of Nature* (Princeton: Princeton University Press, 1979), pp. 170, 174.

1. The Elements of Epistemology

1. Richard Rorty, *Philosophy and the Mirror of Nature* (Princeton: Princeton University Press, 1979), p. 308.

2. See especially Karl Popper, *The Logic of Scientific Discovery* (London: Hutchinson, 1959) and *Conjectures and Refutations* (New York: Harper & Row, 1963).

3. See my "What Is Justified Belief?" in George Pappas, ed., *Justification and Knowledge* (Dordrecht: D. Reidel, 1979); reprinted in Hilary Kornblith, ed., *Naturalizing Epistemology* (Cambridge, Mass.: MIT Press, 1985).

4. I draw here on a distinction made by Holly Smith, in her article "Making Moral Decisions," forthcoming in *Nous*. Smith talks of two roles, or functions, that a principle, especially a moral principle, might have: a "theoretical" role and a "first-person practical" role.

5. One example is Descartes, in his *Rules for the Direction of the Mind*. In an earlier work I considered a conception of justification that was linked to action-guiding principles—what I there called 'doxastic decision principles'. (See "The Internalist Conception of Justification," in Peter French, Theodore Uehling, Jr., and Howard Wettstein, eds., *Midwest Studies in Philosophy*, vol. 5, *Studies in Epistemology*, Minneapolis: University of Minnesota Press, 1980.) In this book, however, my account of justification does not invoke such decision principles.

6. Notice that appraisal, or assignment of normative status, needn't involve a judgment of praiseworthiness or blameworthiness. Thus, one might judge a certain belief to be justified without implying that the cognizer merits praise for it; and one might judge a belief to be unjustified without implying blame or condemnation. Praise and blame are in order where *voluntary* performances have been executed. But many cognitive processes culminating in belief are not voluntary.

2. Skepticism

1. A classification of types of skepticism is given by George Pappas in "Some Forms of Epistemological Scepticism," in George Pappas and Marshall Swain, eds., *Essays on Knowledge and Justification* (Ithaca: Cornell University Press, 1978). For a historical overview of skepticism, see Richard Popkin, "Skepticism," in Paul Edwards, ed., *The Encyclopedia of Philosophy*, vol. 7 (New York: Macmillan, 1967). A critical survey of skeptical arguments is given by Nicholas Rescher in *Scepticism* (Totowa, N.J.: Rowman and Littlefield, 1980).

2. Sextus Empiricus, *Outlines of Pyrrhonism*, trans. R. G. Bury (London: Heinemann, 1933).

3. See Peter Klein, *Certainty: A Refutation of Scepticism* (Minneapolis: University of Minnesota Press, 1981).

4. See Popkin, "Skepticism," p. 454.

5. Immanuel Kant, *Critique of Pure Reason*, 2nd ed. (1787).

6. Perhaps Plato's own worry about change, however, was a little different.

7. David Hume, *Enquiry into the Human Understanding* (1748).

8. Bertrand Russell, *The Analysis of Mind* (New York: Macmillan, 1921).

9. *Outlines of Pyrrhonism*, vol. 1, pp. 163–164.

10. Perhaps Nelson Goodman's new riddle of induction can be viewed as a skeptical argument in this general category. Cf. *Fact, Fiction, and Forecast*, 2nd ed. (Indianapolis: Bobbs-Merrill, 1965). For every inductive conclusion, there are alternative conclusions with seemingly parallel support. Of course, Goodman presents his riddle not so much as a problem about justification, but rather as a problem of how to describe our inductive practice. But it still can be viewed as a skeptical puzzle. As such, it would not quite fit into the 'alternative *explanation*' category I expound in the text, but neither does it fit so naturally into the possibility-of-error category.

11. George Berkeley, *A Treatise concerning the Principles of Human Knowledge* (1710) and *Three Dialogues between Hylas and Philonous* (1713).

12. John Stuart Mill, *An Examination of Sir William Hamilton's Philosophy* (1865).

13. See Hilary Putnam, *Meaning and the Moral Sciences* (London: Routledge and Kegan Paul, 1978) and *Reason, Truth and History* (Cambridge: Cambridge University Press, 1981).

14. I first developed a causal approach in "A Causal Theory of Knowing," *The Journal of Philosophy*, 64 (1967):355–372; reprinted in George Pappas and Marshall Swain, eds., *Essays on Knowledge and Justification* (Ithaca: Cornell University Press, 1978). Some problems facing this particular theory are discussed in other selections reprinted in the same collection. There will be more on the causal approach in Chapter 3.

15. See Gilbert Harman, *Thought* (Princeton: Princeton University Press, 1973).

16. Sydney Shoemaker, *Self-Knowledge and Self-Identity* (Ithaca: Cornell University Press, 1963).

17. Barry Stroud, "Transcendental Arguments," *The Journal of Philosophy*, 65 (1968):241–256.

18. The most famous sources for these attacks are W. V. Quine, "Two Dogmas of Empiricism," in *From a Logical Point of View* (Cambridge, Mass.: Harvard University Press, 1953) and *Word and Object* (Cambridge, Mass.: Technology Press of MIT, 1960).

19. There is also psychological evidence challenging the notion that word meanings are mentally represented as necessary and sufficient conditions. For a review of this evidence, see Edward Smith and Douglas Medin, *Categories and Concepts* (Cambridge, Mass.: Harvard University Press, 1981).

20. I do not deny that *some* skeptical arguments might challenge the rationality or justifiedness of even partial beliefs. But the more familiar lines of argument are directed at knowledge, certainty, or 'acceptance'.

21. It should also be noted that certain questions about knowledge and justification can be studied with little or no concern for skepticism. For example, how should knowledge be analyzed in a way that meets the Gettier problems? This question about knowledge has little connection to skeptical concerns. Similarly, there is the question: what is the *structure* of epistemic justification? Is it foundationalist or coherentist? This problem can also be investigated with little concern for skepticism. It may be assumed that we *do* have justified beliefs in some fashion or other; it just remains to be shown how that justification arises. I have not stressed these points because they will not be *central* to the continuing discussion.

3. Knowledge

1. Some people object to using 'cause' in the analysis of knowledge because that notion is itself philosophically problematic. But we can make progress in understanding one concept by using others, even if the latter also invite analysis. In particular, it is useful to analyze epistemological notions in terms of nonepistemological ones, as in the present case. One comment on my view of causation is in order. I do not presume that causation implies determinism. Hence, while knowledge cannot be attained if beliefs are wholly uncaused, knowledge is possible in a nondeterministic universe.

2. D. M. Armstrong, *Belief, Truth and Knowledge* (Cambridge: Cambridge University Press, 1973). Also see Marshall Swain, *Reasons and Knowledge* (Ithaca: Cornell University Press, 1981).

3. I will not reproduce all the details of Armstrong's account, which gets rather intricate. (See *Belief, Truth and Knowledge*, pp. 192ff.) But I do not believe that any of his qualifications ultimately save his approach.

4. Armstrong gives a somewhat similar case, attributed to Ken Waller. (Cf. *Belief, Truth and Knowledge*, pp. 178–179.) But my case is a bit different, and is not (I believe) open to the same rejoinder as he gives to Waller's. For more on the reliable-indicator versus reliable-process approach—applied, however, to the theory of *justification*—see Frederick Schmitt, "Justification as Reliable Indication or Reliable Process," *Philosophical Studies*, 40 (1981):409–417.

5. Frank Ramsey, *The Foundations of Mathematics and Other Logical Essays* (London: Routledge and Kegan Paul, 1931).

6. These terms are borrowed from Colin McGinn, "The Concept of Knowledge," in Peter French, Theodore Uehling, Jr., and Howard Wettstein, eds., *Midwest Studies in Philosophy*, vol. 9, *Causation and Causal Theories* (Minneapolis: University of Minnesota Press, 1984). In earlier drafts of this chapter I used the phrases 'generic' and 'situation-specific' reliability. But I prefer the 'global' and 'local' terminology.

7. Robert Nozick, *Philosophical Explanations* (Cambridge, Mass.: Harvard University Press, 1981), chap. 3.

8. Fred Dretske, "Conclusive Reasons," *The Australasian Journal of Philosophy*, 49 (1971):1–22. Also see his *Knowledge and the Flow of Information* (Cambridge, Mass.: MIT Press, 1981). It is not clear that Dretske's theory should be viewed as a specimen of the reliable-*process* approach since it places little importance on the causal production of belief.

9. Actually, the core of the thermometer example is taken from Dretske's own paper "Conclusive Reasons." Nonetheless, it is easily turned against his account.

10. Alvin Goldman, "Discrimination and Perceptual Knowledge," *The Journal of Philosophy*, 73 (1976):771–791.

11. Edmund Gettier, "Is Justified True Belief Knowledge?" *Analysis*, 23 (1963):121–123, showed that even when a true belief is justified, it may not qualify as knowledge. In particular, his examples were ones in which a true belief in p is justifiably inferred from a false but justified belief in q. Later writers presented other sorts of examples in which justified true beliefs fail to be items of knowledge. A review of this literature, and attempted solutions to the analysis of knowledge, is found in Robert Shope, *The Analysis of Knowing* (Princeton: Princeton University Press, 1983).

12. Brian Skyrms, "The Explication of 'X knows that p'," *The Journal of Philosophy*, 64 (1967):373–389.

13. An account of knowledge along these lines was formulated in an unpublished paper of mine, "Inferential Knowledge," first presented at Princeton University in 1974.

14. See Alvin Goldman, "Innate Knowledge," in Stephen Stich, ed., *Innate Ideas* (Berkeley: University of California Press, 1975) and "What Is Justified Belief?" in George Pappas, ed., *Justification and Knowledge* (Dordrecht: D. Reidel, 1979).

15. McGinn, "The Concept of Knowledge," p. 536.

16. Ibid., pp. 536–538.

17. McGinn does offer general methodological reasons why a counterfactual condition is not appropriate. These are interesting but not conclusive, and I will not enter into a discussion of them here.

18. See McGinn, "The Concept of Knowledge," pp. 533–535.

19. If one adopts a fine-grained theory of individuating process tokens, more than one token will cause the belief. But on any theory many *types* will be involved, which is the source of the problem.

20. This point was first made by Frederick Schmitt in comments on Richard Feldman's "Reliability and Justification," a paper presented at the 1983 Western Division meeting of the American Philosophical Association.

21. Especially Feldman, in "Reliability and Justification," and also John Pollock, in "Reliability and Justified Belief," *Canadian Journal of Philosophy*, 14 (1984):103–114.

22. However, since these algorithms are eventually called 'methods' rather than 'processes', it is a bit odd to call an acquisition process a *second-order* process. Since nothing hinges on this terminological point, though, I will let the terminology stand.

23. If Humperdink applies this algorithm repeatedly and finds by independent criteria that it yields correct answers, and if this sustains or supports his continued use of the algorithm, then his possession and deployment of the algorithm is overdetermined. Moreover, one of the determining processes is a good one. In this case, by contrast with the case in the text, Humperdink's application of the algorithm can yield knowledge. In the text I assume that the *sole* cause of his algorithm deployment is his blind faith in Fraud.

24. For more on the psychology of procedure acquisition, see Chapter 17.

25. Further discussions of this topic appear in section 5.7 and Chapter 17.

26. Cf. Gettier, "Is Justified True Belief Knowledge?"

27. Keith Lehrer and Thomas Paxson, Jr., "Knowledge: Undefeated Justified True Belief," *The Journal of Philosophy*, 66 (1969):225–237.

28. Fred Dretske, "Epistemic Operators," *The Journal of Philosophy*, 67 (1970):1007–1023, and Nozick, *Philosophical Explanations*, pp. 204–211, 227–229.

29. "The Concept of Knowledge," pp. 542ff.

30. See William Alston, "Level-Confusions in Epistemology," in Peter French, Theodore Uehling, Jr., and Howard Wettstein, eds., *Midwest Studies in Philosophy*, vol. 5, *Studies in Epistemology* (Minneapolis: University of Minnesota Press, 1980).

31. W. V. Quine, "The Nature of Natural Knowledge," in Samuel Guttenplan, ed., *Mind and Language* (Oxford: Oxford University Press, 1975), p. 68.

4. Justification: A Rule Framework

1. I was reminded of this practical context for justification judgments by I. T. Oakley's paper "Should Epistemology Be Naturalized?" presented at the University of Arizona in 1985. The practice of making "head-world" inferences of the indicated sort is stressed in Stephen Schiffer, "Truth and the Theory of Content," in H. Parret and J. Bouverese, eds., *Meaning and Understanding* (Berlin: Walter de Gruyter, 1981) and Hartry Field, "Mental Representation," *Erkenntnis*, 13 (1978):9–61, though without attention to the relevance of justifiedness in such inferences.

2. I do not mean to beg the question of a possible connection between rightness and general acceptance. If there is such a connection, though, it would have to be established.

3. My full theory really requires J-rule systems that include obligations as well as permissions (see section 5.6). But I shall concentrate on permissions.

4. Conditions for justified belief, or knowledge, proposed by some writers would violate this constraint. See, for example, Wilfrid Sellars, "Empiricism and the Philosophy of Mind," in *Science, Perception, and Reality* (London: Routledge and Kegan Paul, 1963), esp. p. 168, and Laurence BonJour, "Can Empirical Knowledge Have a Foundation?" *American Philosophical Quarterly*, 15 (1978):1–15. Ernest Sosa properly diagnoses such violations in "The Raft and the Pyramid," in Peter French, Theodore Uehling, Jr., and Howard Wettstein, eds., *Midwest Studies in Philosophy*, vol. 5, *Studies in Epistemology* (Minneapolis: University of Minnesota Press, 1980), sect. 8.

5. On the idea of level-confusions, see William Alston, "Level-Confusions in Epistemology," in Peter French, Theodore Uehling, Jr., and Howard Wettstein, eds., *Midwest Studies in Philosophy*, vol. 5, *Studies in Epistemology*.

6. John Rawls, *A Theory of Justice* (Cambridge, Mass.: Harvard University Press, 1971).

7. John Austin, *The Province of Jurisprudence Determined* (1832).

8. H. L. A. Hart, *The Concept of Law* (Oxford: Oxford University Press, 1961).

9. On this point, see Jules Coleman, "Negative and Positive Positivism," *The Journal of Legal Studies*, 11 (1982):139–164.

10. Ludwig Wittgenstein, *Philosophical Investigations*, trans. G. E. M. Anscombe (New York: Macmillan, 1953).

11. Thomas Kuhn, "Second Thoughts on Paradigms," in *The Essential Tension* (Chicago: University of Chicago Press, 1977).

12. Richard Rorty, *Philosophy and the Mirror of Nature* (Princeton: Princeton University Press, 1979).

13. Nelson Goodman, *Fact, Fiction, and Forecast*, 2nd ed. (Indianapolis: Bobbs-Merrill, 1965), and Rawls, *A Theory of Justice*, pp. 20–21, 46–51.

14. However, to the extent that a criterion is tested by the intuitive acceptability of the criterion's consequences, psychology might be indirectly relevant in the assessment of *certain* candidate criteria.

15. Rudolf Carnap made the most systematic attempt to develop an inductive logic, in *Logical Foundations of Probability*, 2nd ed. (Chicago: University of Chicago Press, 1962). But few theorists now regard that sort of approach as very promising.

16. Cf. John Pollock, "Epistemology and Probability," *Synthese*, 55 (1983):231–252.

17. I know of nobody who formulates precisely this idea. But it has thematic affinities with Descartes's project and with the working practice of some inductive logicians, such as Carnap in *Logical Foundations of Probability* and "The Aim of Inductive Logic," in Ernest Nagel, Patrick Suppes, and Alfred Tarski, eds., *Logic, Methodology and Philosophy of Science*, vol. 1 (Stanford: Stanford University Press, 1962).

18. 'Absolutism' can also designate the view that moral rules are *exceptionless*. This sense of the term does not interest me here.

19. A recent collection of papers on this topic is Martin Hollis and Steven Lukes, eds., *Rationality and Relativism* (Cambridge, Mass.: MIT Press, 1982).

20. Stephen Stich and Richard Nisbett, "Justification and the Psychology of Human Reasoning," *Philosophy of Science*, 47 (1980):188–202.

21. Explicit formulation of such rules, or principles, is found in Roderick Chisholm, *Theory of Knowledge*, 1st and 2nd eds. (Englewood Cliffs, N.J.: Prentice-Hall, 1966, 1977).

22. Even radical methodological gulfs, such as those separating theologically and scientifically oriented thinkers, may best be construed in objectivist, truth-linked terms. For example, the religious thinker supposes that certain texts or alleged revelations are the best guides to truth on certain topics, whereas the scientific theorist holds that scientific methodology is verifically optimal on all subjects.

23. Critical discussions of moral relativism and subjectivism may be found in the following: G. E. Moore, *Ethics* (London: Oxford University Press, 1912); Philippa Foot, "Moral Relativism," The Lindley Lecture, University of Kansas (1978); Phillip Montague, "Are There Objective and Absolute Moral Standards?"

in Joel Feinberg, ed., *Reason and Responsibility*, 5th ed. (Belmont, Calif.: Wadsworth, 1981); and Walter Stace, "Ethical Relativism," in ibid.

For an incisive critique of epistemological cultural relativism, see Hilary Putnam's discussion of Rorty's brand of relativism, in "Why Reason Can't Be Naturalized," in *Realism and Reason* (Cambridge: Cambridge University Press, 1983).

24. See John Pollock, "A Plethora of Epistemological Theories," in George Pappas, ed., *Justification and Knowledge* (Dordrecht: D. Reidel, 1979).

25. Admittedly, I disclaim any general association between judgments of justifiedness and praise or blame (see Chapter 1, note 6). But we needn't exclude praise and blame entirely. At any rate, casting the issue in these terms is a useful *device* for crystallizing intuitions about the kind of case cited.

26. *Philosophy and the Mirror of Nature*, p. 170.

27. The distinction between *primary* and *secondary* justification will be expounded in section 5.3.

28. See Gilbert Harman, *Thought* (Princeton: Princeton University Press, 1973), pp. 27–29.

29. The only exceptions are some proposals on 'secondary' justifiedness.

30. A good exposition of the essentials of foundationalism (plus one kind of variant on the main theory) can be found in William Alston, "Two Types of Foundationalism," *The Journal of Philosophy*, 73 (1976):165–185.

31. See Roderick Firth, "Coherence, Certainty, and Epistemic Priority," *The Journal of Philosophy*, 61 (1964):545–557, and Mark Pastin, "Modest Foundationalism and Self-Warrant," *American Philosophical Quarterly*, monogr. ser. no. 4 (1975):141–149.

32. Keith Lehrer, *Knowledge* (Oxford: Oxford University Press, 1974), pp. 78–79.

33. *Philosophy and the Mirror of Nature*, for example, pp. 163, 211–212.

34. This possibility has not been raised in the literature, to my knowledge.

35. I will examine some empirical evidence on this score in section 9.4.

5. Justification and Reliability

1. Belief retention over time is not automatically permitted. As new beliefs arise, they may incriminate old ones, whose continuation is no longer appropriate.

2. A system is right only if all the permissions it delivers, using any of its rules or combinations thereof, are acceptable (though the permitted beliefs needn't all be true). If a given member of system R delivers unacceptable permissions, perhaps in combination with other members of R, then R is not right. Hence, if a given rule is not capable of delivering only acceptable permissions when combined with *any* other set of rules, then it does not belong to any right system.

3. Gilbert Harman, *Thought* (Princeton: Princeton University Press, 1973), p. 157.

4. It is a delicate question just what 'abandonment' of belief consists in, psychologically speaking. I shall broach this question in Chapter 10. Meanwhile, I treat it as if it were unproblematic.

5. Proponents of relevance logic would deny that the argument from an in-

consistent set of premises to a random conclusion is valid. They would propose a revision in the standard treatment of validity. (Cf. Alan Anderson and Nuel Belnap, Jr., *Entailment*, vol. 1, Princeton: Princeton University Press, 1975.) But no such revision is needed to save the intuition that a person is not justified in *inferring*—forming a belief in—a random conclusion from inconsistent premises. All that's needed is the recognition that facts of validity have no straightforward implications for belief-forming license.

6. Strictly, the nonjustifiedness of Claude's belief in y only shows that there is no right system containing the target rule plus the rules that licensed Claude's belief in x. Does it show that there is no right system *at all* to which this rule belongs? Well, no constraints were placed on the system that licensed his belief in x. Any arbitrary system could have been supposed. Hence, there is *no* system to which the target rule might belong which would be right. The entire argument, of course, rests on the presumed correctness of the framework principle, (P1°) or (P3°); but these seem quite unobjectionable.

7. There are nice metaphysical questions about the nature of processes. I am not sure that calling processes 'causal chains' captures exactly what needs to be said about processes. But since I lack satisfactory answers to the relevant questions, I will proceed without any further, detailed account of processes.

8. See Christopher Cherniak, "Feasible Inferences," *Philosophy of Science*, 48 (1981):248–268.

9. The point I have highlighted in this section has not gone wholly unnoticed. For example, Carl Hempel writes: "Formal logic tells us that if a given set of statements is true then such and such other statements are true as well; but it does not tell us what statements to believe or to act on. Indeed, the notion of accepting certain statements, like the notion of total evidence, is pragmatic in character and cannot be defined in terms of the concepts of formal deductive or inductive logic" ("Inductive Inconsistencies," in *Aspects of Scientific Explanation*, New York: Free Press, 1965, p. 66). Still, the significance of the point has not been widely appreciated. Nor has the relevance of psychological processes been generally acknowledged.

10. Rudolf Carnap, *Logical Foundations of Probability*, 2nd ed. (Chicago: University of Chicago Press, 1962).

11. I have misgivings about characterizing basic processes as *unacquired* processes. What about processes acquired through maturation, or the triggering of innate propensities? Couldn't these still be considered *basic* processes? Perhaps so. What I mainly mean to exclude from the class of processes are the acquired skills, strategies, heuristics, and algorithms—especially task-specific ones—that are encoded either as explicitly accepted instructions or as automatic procedures (see Chapter 17). These are what I think of as 'methods'. A fully satisfactory formulation of the process/method distinction, however, has eluded me. I shall rely throughout on an informal grasp of this distinction.

12. See Daniel Kahneman, Paul Slovic, and Amos Tversky, eds., *Judgment under Uncertainty: Heuristics and Biases* (Cambridge: Cambridge University Press, 1982), and Richard Nisbett and Lee Ross, *Human Inference: Strategies and Shortcomings of Social Judgment* (Englewood Cliffs, N.J.: Prentice-Hall, 1980). This material will be explored in Part II, especially Chapter 14.

13. On this point see Roderick Firth, "Epistemic Merit, Intrinsic and Instrumental," in *Proceedings and Addresses of the American Philosophical Association*, 55 (1981):5–23.

14. Keith Lehrer's coherence theory of justification, in *Knowledge* (Oxford: Oxford University Press, 1974), seems to be a specimen of weak coherentism. With one qualification, to be explained below, Lehrer's theory says that a belief is justified if the proposition believed is viewed by the cognizer as having a better chance of truth than its competitors (see p. 212). But when a person believes any proposition, he views it as having a better chance at truth than its competitors (at least the competitors he thinks of). So even an idle dreamer's beliefs will satisfy this condition. Lehrer's theory does contain the qualification that the belief should be viewed from the cognizer's 'corrected' doxastic system, which is obtained by deleting beliefs the cognizer would not retain as a "veracious inquirer," that is, as an "impartial and disinterested truth-seeker." But suppose a fantasizer honestly believes—again, through fantasy—that fantasizing is the optimal method for getting the truth. Then he is genuinely seeking truth (impartially and disinterestedly); so his actual belief system is not subject to any correction. But then the "veracious-inquirer" condition does no real work, and we are left with the counterintuitive result obtained earlier.

Perhaps Lehrer would say that what counts as veracious belief formation must not be judged by the inquirer's own lights, but by the facts of the matter. In that case dreaming and fantasizing would not be methods of a veracious inquirer, and this man's doxastic system would require drastic correction. But if this is the proper interpretation of the view, it comes out more as closet reliabilism than as subjective coherentism. Reference to the 'corrected doxastic system' really masks a thoroughly reliabilist viewpoint.

Lehrer no longer subscribes to the view expressed in *Knowledge*. His more recent position comes somewhat closer to reliabilism. This position is formulated in "A Self Profile," in Radu Bogdan, ed., *Keith Lehrer* (Dordrecht: D. Reidel, 1979), pp. 84–85. There he characterizes 'complete' justification as the conjunction of 'personal justification'—his old notion—plus 'verific justification'. Roughly, a belief in p is 'verifically' justified just in case it coheres with the cognizer's *true* beliefs. But this notion of verific justification—and hence the notion of complete justification—is excessively strong. A belief inferred from false premises is in danger of being unjustified solely because the premises are false. But, surely, the mere falsity of previous beliefs should not endanger justifiedness. If believing those premises was justified, and if the inferences were appropriate, then the resulting beliefs should also be justified. Falsity of the premises endangers knowledge, but not justifiedness. Hence, this strategy for introducing truth into the justification picture does not work.

15. See Richard Jeffrey, *The Logic of Decision*, 2nd ed. (Chicago: University of Chicago Press, 1983), chap. 11.

16. Lewis's term for this stronger notion of coherence is "congruence"; see *An Analysis of Knowledge and Valuation* (La Salle, Ill.: Open Court, 1946), p. 338. Chisholm's term for the same concept is "concurrence"; cf. *Theory of Knowledge*, 1st ed. (Englewood Cliffs, N.J.: Prentice-Hall, 1966), chap. 3; 2nd ed. (Englewood Cliffs, N.J.: Prentice-Hall, 1977), chap. 4.

17. John Pollock also speaks of negative and positive coherence, in "A Plethora of Epistemological Theories," in George Pappas, ed., *Justification and Knowledge* (Dordrecht: D. Reidel, 1979). But his terminology marks a somewhat different distinction.

18. See Carl Hempel, "Deductive-Nomological vs. Statistical Explanation," in Herbert Feigl and Grover Maxwell, eds., *Minnesota Studies in the Philosophy of Science*, vol. 3 (Minneapolis: University of Minnesota Press, 1962); Jaakko Hintikka and J. Pietarinen, "Semantic Information and Inductive Logic," in Jaakko Hintikka and Patrick Suppes, eds., *Aspects of Inductive Logic* (Amsterdam: North-Holland, 1966); Isaac Levi, *Gambling with Truth* (New York: Knopf, 1967); Risto Hilpinen, *Rules of Acceptance and Inductive Logic* (Amsterdam: North-Holland, 1968); and Lehrer, *Knowledge*.

19. See Levi, *Gambling with Truth*, chap. 4.

20. My framework principle, (P3°), employs a categorical notion of justification, so I cannot easily incorporate this point into the current formulation of the theory. But this feature could probably be revised to accommodate degrees of justifiedness.

21. Apart from accounting for intuitions in all these cases, the truth ratio, or reliabilist, theory of justifiedness holds out the prospect of coping satisfactorily with the Humean riddle of induction. Although it does not fit naturally at this juncture, let me sketch an approach to this problem, predicated on the correctness of the reliabilist theory.

I propose to divide the traditional problem of induction into two problems. The first is: Can we have justified beliefs based on inductive inference? The second is the problem of *second-order* justifiedness: Can we have a justified belief that we can have justified beliefs based on inductive inference? I think it quite possible that Hume himself, and many followers of Hume, confused the first problem with the second. At least they have held that a positive answer to the first depends upon a positive answer to the second. I disagree with this contention. Nonetheless, the second problem is significant; and there is no reason why one could not take the conjunction of these problems as *the* problem of induction.

If the reliability theory is correct, the first problem is not terribly serious. At least it is 'logically' possible to have justified beliefs based on inductive inference, whether or not it is humanly possible. Suppose we have a (basic) inductive process with a sufficiently high truth ratio, at least a process whose output beliefs would be true often enough if its input beliefs were true. Then this process could be permitted by a right system of J-rules. Hence, beliefs generated by this process could be justified, as long as the input beliefs to the process were justified. A critical point here is that our framework principle imposes no iterative requirement. A person's belief is justified if it *is* permitted by a right rule system (I ignore the no-undermining clause for simplicity); the person does not also have to be justified in believing that the belief is so permitted.

This takes care of the first problem of induction. But what about the second? If we stick to the framework principle, there is no reason why a belief in the justification-conferring power of induction could not be justified as a result of the self-same inductive process! If the indicated inductive process *is* permitted by a right rule system, then one might apply that same permitted process to beliefs in the process's past successes, and draw the conclusion that the process is successful (reliable) *in general*. From this one could permissibly infer that the process is permitted by right rules.

Of course, this inductive justification of induction is staunchly resisted by defenders of Hume. The familiar charge is one of circularity. But how would this charge be formulated in terms of my general theory? It would have to be couched as a further restriction on justifiedness, to be incorporated into a new framework principle. It might run: 'No belief about the permissibility of a process is justified if the belief results from that selfsame process'. But does this restriction have any plausibility? Surely not. It seems quite arbitrary. Would one say that a person could not be justified in believing in the validity of modus ponens if he used modus ponens to arrive at this belief? (Here I waive the point that modus ponens isn't really a *process*.) Acceptance of this stricture leads to the dilemma posed by Lewis Carroll, in "What the Tortoise Said to Achilles," in *Mind*, vol. 4 (1895), pp. 278–280. But there is no good reason to accept it. If a process deserves to be permitted, then its permission should extend to all subject matter, including its own performance and its own permissibility.

Another attempt to address the problem of induction in a reliabilist vein is made by James Van Cleve, in "Reliability, Justification, and Induction," in Peter French, Theodore Uehling, Jr., and Howard Wettstein, eds., *Midwest Studies in Philosophy*, vol. 9, *Causation and Causal Theories* (Minneapolis: University of Minnesota Press, 1984). Van Cleve has an instructive discussion of circularity. He says that an argument is *viciously* circular only if it is *epistemically* circular. He then distinguishes *premise* circularity and *rule* circularity, as possible sources of epistemic circularity. He indicates that the critical argument in the case of induction does not suffer from premise circularity, and that rule circularity is not really a source of epistemic circularity. I will not rehearse these arguments but commend them to the interested reader.

22. This phrase is used by Hilary Kornblith, in "Justified Belief and Epistemically Responsible Action," *The Philosophical Review*, 92 (1983):33–48. However, Kornblith uses it to express a different theory than the one intended in the text. Kornblith's own theory is that a belief is justified just in case it is guided by a *desire* to believe the truth. Such a theory is extremely weak, though. If a cognizer is sufficiently benighted, such a desire may lead to very weird processes or 'evidence-collecting' activities. It is questionable whether beliefs formed from such processes or activities are justified. Furthermore, the theory may also be too strong. Perceptual beliefs may presumably be justified; yet such beliefs are not controlled or guided by a *desire* to believe the truth.

Let me return to the theory intended in the text: a truth-ratio maximization theory, relativized to human cognitive endowments. There are various possible refinements of this approach. Suppose, for example, that the best human perceptual processes can secure a truth ratio of .99, but the best human inductive processes can only secure a truth ratio of .65. The simple maximizing criterion might then disallow rule systems that sanction inductive processes, on the ground that inductive processes would reduce the truth ratio below an otherwise attainable maximum. This is (arguably) counterintuitive. However, the simple maximizing criterion might be replaced by a more sophisticated criterion, which maximizes *within a category*. For example, a criterion could license the best perceptual belief-forming processes, the best inductive belief-forming processes, the best memorial belief-forming processes, and so on. This approach would encounter some difficulties—how, exactly, should the categories be selected?—but it is still attractive.

23. As formulated, (ARI) has a problem. It presupposes that each J-rule system has a unique truth ratio. This is plausible if we consider only *actual* instantiations of the permitted processes (by all cognizers, past, present, and future), assuming these are finite. But presumably a truth ratio should be fixed by possible as well as actual instantiations. For one thing, we want to allow a system to have a nonzero truth-ratio *propensity* even though its authorized processes are never actually instantiated. However, this makes the assumption of a unique truth ratio extremely doubtful. There are *many* possible ways of instantiating a permitted set of processes. Because of the permissive nature of the rules, one pattern of instantiation might use a given subset of permitted processes (for example, inductive processes) very often, while another pattern of instantiation might use this subset sparingly. Let us call any pattern of permitted instantiations of a given system a *compliance profile* of that system. The problem is that it is most unlikely that all compliance profiles of a system have the same truth ratio. But if a rule system's truth ratio is not *invariant* under diverse compliance profiles, the system does not have a unique truth ratio.

One way to handle this problem is to require, for rightness, that *all possible* compliance profiles of the target system meet the threshold truth ratio. (An exception could be made for the 'null' profile, which does not use any of the permitted processes. This is a compliance profile in the sense that it does not *violate* the rule system. But the truth ratio of this profile is 0.) This is a very stringent requirement. A milder way of handling the problem is to require only that the *median* truth ratio of all the compliance profiles meet the threshold. But this seems too weak. The worst truth ratio might be too low.

A third solution is to adopt the previous condition as necessary, but add a further requirement that the amplitude of departures from the median value must not be too great. To borrow a term from Brian Skyrms, the rule system should be quite *resilient*. (Cf. *Causal Necessity*, New Haven: Yale University Press, 1980, p. 11. However, Skyrms's notion of resiliency is defined for probabilities.) Obviously, many other measures of these sorts could be proposed, so the problem appears soluble. But I will not try to pick a particular solution; I will simply assume that (ARI) can be reformulated with a satisfactory solution.

Notice that similar problems would arise for resource-relative criteria, such as a maximizing criterion. In fact, here the problems would be trickier because one would have to compare various systems, each with multiple compliance profiles. One possible solution is a 'maximax' solution: the system with the highest maximum compliance profile is best. Another possible solution is a 'maximin' condition: the system with the highest minimum compliance profile is best. Again, I will not try to pick any particular solution from these candidates.

24. I assume that a system's truth ratio is relatively invariant across different normal worlds.

25. Saul Kripke, *Naming and Necessity* (Cambridge, Mass.: Harvard University Press, 1980), and Hilary Putnam, "The Meaning of 'Meaning'," in *Mind, Language and Reality* (Cambridge: Cambridge University Press, 1975).

26. Peter Unger, *Philosophical Relativity* (Minneapolis: University of Minnesota Press, 1984), pp. 84ff. Unger does not endorse normal-world chauvinism. His own positive theory is quite different and ultimately supports a relativistic approach to conceptual analysis. I am not embracing this aspect of his discussion.

27. Hilary Putnam, "It Ain't Necessarily So," in *Mathematics, Matter and Method* (Cambridge: Cambridge University Press, 1975).

28. Hilary Putnam, "Why Reason Can't Be Naturalized," in *Realism and Reason* (Cambridge: Cambridge University Press, 1983).

29. Laurence BonJour, "Externalist Theories of Empirical Knowledge," in Peter French, Theodore Uehling, Jr., and Howard Wettstein, eds., *Midwest Studies in Philosophy*, vol. 5, *Studies in Epistemology* (Minneapolis: University of Minnesota Press, 1980).

30. See, for example, my "What Is Justified Belief?" in George Pappas, ed., *Justification and Knowledge* (Dordrecht: D. Reidel, 1979). Actually, BonJour focuses his criticism on Armstrong's version of reliabilism, in *Belief, Truth and Knowledge* (Cambridge: Cambridge University Press, 1973), although Armstrong does not advance a theory of *justification*.

31. See Keith Lehrer and Stewart Cohen, "Justification, Truth, and Coherence," *Synthese*, 55 (1983):191–207; John Pollock, "Reliability and Justified Belief," *Canadian Journal of Philosophy*, 14 (1984):103–114; Stewart Cohen, "Justification and Truth," *Philosophical Studies*, 46 (1984):279–295.

32. At times I have been tempted to handle demon-world cases by saying that beliefs in that world are not 'really' justified; they are merely 'apparently' justified (see section 4.3). If this response were intuitively plausible, reliabilism could dispense with the normal-worlds theory. However, while some people find this solution intuitively appealing, many do not.

33. Sarah Lichtenstein, Baruch Fischhoff, and Lawrence Phillips, "Calibration of Probabilities: The State of the Art to 1980," in Daniel Kahneman, Paul Slovic, and Amos Tversky, eds., *Judgment under Uncertainty: Heuristics and Biases* (Cambridge: Cambridge University Press, 1982), p. 307.

34. The main problem is whether good calibration is *sufficient* for justifiedness. The following example illustrates the problem. Suppose a weather forecaster predicts a 20 percent chance of rain every day, despite the fact that meteorological indicators differ from day to day. If the long-run proportion of rainy days in the area is 20 percent, this forecaster's predictions are well calibrated, by definition. But it is questionable whether these predictions are justified, or otherwise normatively sound.

One possible way of strengthening the calibration requirement is suggested by Morris DeGroot and Stephen Fienberg, in "Assessing Probability Assessors," in S. Gupta and J. Berger, eds., *Statistical Decision Theory and Related Topics, III*, vol. 1 (New York: Academic Press, 1982). Following DeGroot and Fienberg, let m denote the relative frequency of days on which it rains, and let v(x) be the probability that a forecaster's prediction on a randomly chosen day will be x (or the proportion of days on which his prediction is x). We can now characterize the previous weather forecaster as having the following probability function:

$$v(m) = 1,$$
$$v(x) = 0 \quad \text{for } x \neq m.$$

In other words, where the relative frequency of rain is .20, the probability of this forecaster making a 20 percent chance of rain prediction on a given day is 1. This man is a *least refined*, though well-calibrated, forecaster. Contrast him with another well-calibrated forecaster, characterized by the following probability function:

$$v(1) = m,$$
$$v(0) = 1-m,$$
$$v(x) = 0 \quad \text{for } x \neq 0, 1.$$

The only probabilities of rain that this forecaster ever specifies are 0 and 1, and since he is well calibrated, his predictions are always correct. This man is referred to as a *most-refined* forecaster. (In meteorology, the first forecaster is said to exhibit zero sharpness and the second is said to exhibit perfect sharpness.)

Now it clearly seems too strong to require, for justificational rightness, that a rule system yield *maximal refinement* as well as good calibration. But some threshold of refinement might be set, as a further condition for rightness beyond good calibration. This seems feasible since DeGroot and Fienberg develop a condition for determining whether one well-calibrated forecaster is more refined than another.

For another attempt to use calibration to explicate epistemic standards, see Bas van Fraassen, "Calibration: A Frequency Justification for Personal Probability," in R. Cohen and L. Laudan, eds., *Physics, Philosophy and Psychoanalysis* (Dordrecht: D. Reidel, 1983).

35. Hilary Putnam, "Why Reason Can't Be Naturalized," in *Realism and Reason* (Cambridge: Cambridge University Press, 1983), p. 231.

36. Roderick Firth, "Epistemic Merit, Intrinsic and Instrumental," p. 19.

37. Ibid., p. 17.

6. Problem Solving, Power, and Speed

1. My emphasis on relief from ignorance bears some similarity to Isaac Levi's emphasis on relief from "agnosticism" (see his *Gambling with Truth*, New York: Knopf, 1967). But the latter denotes relief from the absence of belief (or from the weakness of belief) while the former denotes relief from the absence of true belief.

2. Larry Laudan, *Progress and Its Problems* (Berkeley: University of California Press, 1977).

3. John Dewey, *Logic: The Theory of Inquiry* (New York: Henry Holt, 1938).

4. Karl Popper, *Objective Knowledge* (Oxford: Oxford University Press, 1972); Thomas Kuhn, *The Structure of Scientific Revolutions* (Chicago: University of Chicago Press, 1962); Imre Lakatos, "Falsification and the Methodology of Scientific Research Programmes," in Imre Lakatos and Alan Musgrave, eds., *Criticism and the Growth of Knowledge* (Cambridge: Cambridge University Press, 1970); and Laudan, *Progress and Its Problems*.

5. Jaakko Hintikka, "On the Logic of the Interrogative Model of Scientific Inquiry," *Synthese*, 47 (1981):69–83.

6. Sylvain Bromberger, "Why-Questions," in Robert Colodny, ed., *Mind and Cosmos* (Pittsburgh: University of Pittsburgh Press, 1966); and Bas van Fraassen, *The Scientific Image* (Oxford: Oxford University Press, 1980).

7. "Why-Questions," pp. 90–91.

8. Nuel Belnap, Jr., and Thomas Steel, Jr., *The Logic of Questions and Answers* (New Haven: Yale University Press, 1976).

9. For further treatment of the semantics of questions and answers, see Jaakko Hintikka, "The Semantics of Questions and the Questions of Semantics," *Acta Philosophical Fennica*, 28 (1976), issue 4.

10. Discussions of problem solving in artificial intelligence portray it as getting to an end state from some initial state. For surveys of this topic, see Patrick Winston, *Artificial Intelligence* (Reading, Mass.: Addison-Wesley, 1977); Nils Nilsson, *Principles of Artificial Intelligence* (Palo Alto, Calif.: Tioga, 1980); and Elaine Rich, *Artificial Intelligence* (New York: McGraw-Hill, 1983).

11. See Belnap and Steel, *The Logic of Questions and Answers*, pp. 5, 109–121.

12. *Progress and Its Problems*, p. 24.

13. Cf. Lakatos, "Falsification and the Methodology of Scientific Research Programmes"; Laudan, *Progress and Its Problems;* and Thomas Nickles, "Scientific Discovery and the Future of Philosophy of Science," in Thomas Nickles, ed., *Scientific Discovery, Logic, and Rationality* (Dordrecht: D. Reidel, 1980).

14. Actually, pursuit may not be wholly different from the components mentioned above. A decision to pursue a specific research program is arguably predicated on the cognizer's judgment of which program is most promising (in my interpretation, most likely to lead to truth), which is a species of doxastic decision. Having selected a research program, the scientist usually needs to generate new hypotheses under the aegis of that program and then devise tests of these hypotheses. So pursuit can itself be broken down into subcomponents, perhaps of the same variety as previously mentioned.

15. Paraphrased from Michael Posner, *Cognition: An Introduction* (Glenview, Ill.: Scott, Foresman, 1973), pp. 150–151.

16. Alternative modes of framing outcomes also have significant ramifications for choice behavior, as shown in Amos Tversky and Daniel Kahneman, "The Framing of Decisions and the Psychology of Choice," *Science*, 211 (1981):453–458, and Daniel Kahneman and Amos Tversky, "Choices, Values, and Frames," *American Psychologist*, 39 (1984):341–350. However, representations for behavioral choice do not concern me here.

17. G. Polya, *How to Solve It*, 2nd ed. (Princeton: Princeton University Press, 1971), pp. 10, 209.

18. *Cognition*, pp. 151–152. The example is drawn from C. N. Cofer, "The Role of Language in Human Problem Solving," paper presented at a conference on human problem solving, New York University, 1954.

19. Cf. A. de Groot, *Thought and Choice in Chess* (The Hague: Mouton, 1965), and William Chase and Herbert Simon, "The Mind's Eye in Chess," in William Chase, ed., *Visual Information Processing* (New York: Academic Press, 1973).

20. Walter Kintsch and T. A. van Dijk, "Toward a Model of Text Comprehension and Production," *Psychological Review*, 85 (1978):363–394.

21. Mary Gick and Keith Holyoak, "Analogical Problem Solving," *Cognitive Psychology*, 12 (1980):306–355.

22. For reviews of artificial intelligence approaches to strategies, see the works cited in note 10.

23. The relevance of real-time constraints is discussed further in Chapter 13.

24. Actually, this is open to challenge. On some conceptions justificational status depends on how well one collects evidence. See Hilary Kornblith, "Justified Belief and Epistemically Responsible Action," *Philosophical Review*, 92 (1983):33–48. It may also depend on how well one generates alternative hypotheses. I explore this suggestion in Chapter 11.

7. Truth and Realism

1. Putnam's principal writings in this area are: *Meaning and the Moral Sciences* (London: Routledge and Kegan Paul, 1978); *Reason, Truth and History* (Cambridge: Cambridge University Press, 1981); and several papers in *Realism and Reason* (Cambridge: Cambridge University Press, 1983). Dummett's major works in this area are: several papers in *Truth and Other Enigmas* (Cambridge, Mass.: Harvard University Press, 1978); "What Is a Theory of Meaning? (II)," in Gareth Evans and John McDowell, eds., *Truth and Meaning* (Oxford: Oxford University Press, 1976); *Elements of Intuitionism* (New York: Oxford University Press, 1977); and "Realism," *Synthese*, 52 (1982):55–112.

2. Dummett, "Realism," p. 55.

3. Ibid., p. 55 and elsewhere.

4. Dummett comments on the case of empty singular terms, but says this *is* a kind of antirealism, the contrasting opposite of which is a realism of a Meinongian kind. I find this implausible.

5. See Hilary Putnam, "On Truth," in Leigh Cauman et al., *How Many Questions?* (Indianapolis: Hackett, 1983). Also cf. Scott Soames, "What Is a Theory of Truth?" *The Journal of Philosophy*, 81 (1984):411–429.

6. *Reason, Truth and History*, chap. 3.

7. "Realism and Reason," in *Meaning and the Moral Sciences*.

8. *Meaning and the Moral Sciences*, p. 125.

9. See Dummett, "Realism," p. 69.

10. C. S. Peirce, "How to Make Our Ideas Clear," in Justus Buchler, ed., *Philosophical Writings of Peirce* (New York: Dover, 1955), p. 38. Note that this is, strictly, a doxastic definition, not an epistemic one. It only invokes agreement in opinion, whether or not this is justified or rational.

11. *Reason, Truth and History*, p. 55.

12. *Meaning and the Moral Sciences*, p. 125.

13. Brian Loar, "Truth Beyond All Verification," in Barry Taylor, ed., *Essays on Michael Dummett* (The Hague: Martinus Nijhoff, forthcoming).

14. See William Wimsatt, "Robustness, Reliability and Multiple-Determination in Science," in M. Brewer and B. Collins, eds., *Knowing and Validating in the Social Sciences* (San Francisco: Jossey-Bass, 1981). Among several works by Campbell, he cites D. T. Campbell and D. Fiske, "Convergent and Discriminant Validation by the Multi-Trait Multi-Method Matrix," *Psychological Bulletin*, 56 (1959):81–105, and T. D. Cook and D. T. Campbell, *Quasi-Experimentation* (Chicago: Rand-McNally, 1979). The relevant works by R. Levins are "The Strategy of Model Building in Population Biology," *American Scientist*, 54 (1966):421–431, and *Evolution in Changing Environments* (Princeton: Princeton University Press, 1968).

15. See especially "What is a Theory of Meaning? (II)," p. 116.

16. Some critical discussions of Dummett's proposals include Loar, "Truth Beyond All Verification"; Colin McGinn, "Realist Semantics and Content-Ascription," *Synthese*, 52 (1982):113–134; Michael Devitt, "Dummett's Anti-Realism," *The Journal of Philosophy*, 80 (1983):73–99; and Gregory Currie and Peter Eggenberger, "Knowledge and Meaning," *Nous*, 17 (1983):267–279.

17. Ludwig Wittgenstein, *Tractatus Logico-Philosophicus*, trans. C. K. Ogden and F. P. Ramsey (London: Routledge and Kegan Paul, 1922).

18. *Reason, Truth and History*, pp. 52–53. Note, however, that in earlier work Putnam had endorsed the notion of kinds being *in the world*. See "On Properties," in Nicholas Rescher et al., eds., *Essays in Honor of Carl G. Hempel* (Dordrecht: D. Reidel, 1970).

19. Nelson Goodman, *Ways of Worldmaking* (Indianapolis: Hackett, 1978).

20. Ibid., p. 138.

21. Cf. Hilary Putnam, "Reflections on Goodman's *Ways of Worldmaking*," *The Journal of Philosophy*, 76 (1979):611.

22. See Putnam, "Realism and Reason," pp. 123–126, in *Meaning and the Moral Sciences*, and *Reason, Truth and History*, chap. 2.

23. Alvin Plantinga, "How To Be an Anti-Realist," in *Proceedings and Addresses of the American Philosophical Association*, 56 (1982):47–70.

24. A similar characterization of scientific realism, minus the third thesis, is given by Bas van Fraassen, in *The Scientific Image* (Oxford: Oxford University Press, 1980): "Science aims to give us, in its theories, a literally true story of what the world is like; and acceptance of a scientific theory involves the belief that it is true" (p. 8).

25. More generally, Michael Dummett has observed that various kinds of reductionisms can be compatible with realisms about those domains (see "Realism," p. 75).

26. Cf. Putnam, Lecture II, in *Meaning and the Moral Sciences*, where he draws on unpublished work by Boyd; Richard Boyd, "Scientific Realism and Naturalistic Epistemology," in P. D. Asquith and R. N. Giere, eds., *PSA 1980*, vol. 2 (East Lansing, Mich.: Philosophy of Science Association, 1981): and W. H. Newton-Smith, *The Rationality of Science* (London: Routledge and Kegan Paul, 1981).

27. Larry Laudan raises doubts about the historical record in "A Confutation of Convergent Realism," *Philosophy of Science*, 48 (1981):19–49.

28. *Meaning and the Moral Sciences*, pp. 24–25, 37.

29. Parenthetically, we should be reminded that past applications of a method do not exhaust the class of applications relevant to reliability. These would include present and future cases as well as counterfactual cases. But there is no reason to suppose that historical uses of scientific methods would be unrepresentative of long-run truth properties, as long as the very same methods are in question.

30. This point has a connection with what has been called "verisimilitude," or "truth-likeness." However, I do not mean to commit myself to any particular definition of verisimilitude, or to the prospects for a workable definition along the lines initiated by Popper. This is a very complicated issue. For some proposed definitions and critiques of verisimilitude, see Karl Popper, *Objective Knowledge*

(Oxford: Oxford University Press, 1972); Ilkka Niiniluoto, "Truthlikeness in First-Order Languages," in Jaakko Hintikka et al., eds., *Essays on Mathematical and Philosophical Logic* (Dordrecht: D. Reidel, 1979), and "Scientific Progress," *Synthese*, 45 (1980):427–462; W. H. Newton-Smith, *The Rationality of Science;* Pavel Tichy, "On Popper's Definition of Verisimilitude," *British Journal for the Philosophy of Science*, 25 (1974):155–160, and "Verisimilitude Revisited," *Synthese*, 38 (1978):175–196; and Laudan, "A Confutation of Convergent Realism."

8. The Problem of Content

1. See W. V. Quine, *The Roots of Reference* (La Salle, Ill.: Open Court, 1973), p. 35.

2. In "Mental Representation," in Ned Block, ed., *Readings in Philosophy of Psychology*, vol. 2 (Cambridge, Mass.: Harvard University Press, 1981), Hartry Field takes the belief relation to be a composite of two other relations: a relation between a person and an internal sentence, and a relation between the sentence and a proposition. For a recent defense of the view that takes propositions to be the only objects of belief, see Robert Stalnaker, *Inquiry* (Cambridge, Mass.: MIT Press, 1984).

3. Hilary Putnam, "Computational Psychology and Interpretation Theory," in *Realism and Reason* (Cambridge: Cambridge University Press, 1983).

4. Paul Churchland, "Eliminative Materialism and the Propositional Attitudes," *The Journal of Philosophy*, 78 (1981):67–90. Also see Patricia Smith Churchland, "A Perspective on Mind-Brain Research," *The Journal of Philosophy*, 77 (1980):185–207.

5. Imre Lakatos, "Falsification and the Methodology of Scientific Research Programmes," in Imre Lakatos and Alan Musgrave, eds., *Criticism and the Growth of Knowledge* (Cambridge: Cambridge University Press, 1970).

6. Cf. Ned Block and Jerry Fodor, "What Psychological States Are Not," in Ned Block, ed., *Readings in Philosophy of Psychology*, vol. 1 (Cambridge, Mass.: Harvard University Press, 1980); Ned Block, "Troubles with Functionalism," in ibid.; Joseph Owens, "Functionalism and Propositional Attitudes," *Nous*, 17 (1983):529–549; Stephen Stich, *From Folk Psychology to Cognitive Science: The Case Against Belief* (Cambridge, Mass.: MIT Press, 1983); and Stephen Schiffer, *Remnants of Meaning*, in preparation.

7. See Ernest Nagel, *The Structure of Science* (New York: Harcourt, Brace & World, 1961), chap. 11.

8. Kenneth Schaffner, "Approaches to Reduction," *Philosophy of Science*, 34 (1967):137–147.

9. See David Hull, *Philosophy of Biological Science* (Englewood Cliffs, N.J.: Prentice-Hall, 1974), chap. 1. Hull himself, though, is cautious about any such derivability.

10. Jerry Fodor, "Special Sciences, or The Disunity of Science as a Working Hypothesis," in Block, ed., *Readings in Philosophy of Psychology*, vol. 1.

11. Stich, *From Folk Psychology to Cognitive Science*, pp. 135–136.

12. Daniel Dennett, *Content and Consciousness* (New York: Humanities Press, 1969), p. 183.

13. See *Inquiry*, pp. 62–67.

14. Saul Kripke, "A Puzzle about Belief," in Avishai Margalit, ed., *Meaning and Use* (Dordrecht: D. Reidel, 1979).

15. For further discussion of this point, see Brian Loar, "*De Dicto* Ascription and the Content of Names in Thought," forthcoming, and Ruth Barcan Marcus, "Rationality and Believing the Impossible," *The Journal of Philosophy*, 80 (1983):321–338.

16. Tyler Burge, "Individualism and the Mental," in Peter French, Theodore Uehling, Jr., and Howard Wettstein, eds., *Midwest Studies in Philosophy*, vol. 4, *Studies in Metaphysics* (Minneapolis: University of Minnesota Press, 1979).

17. Terence Horgan and James Woodward, "Folk Psychology Is Here to Stay," *The Philosophical Review*, 94 (1985):197–226.

18. *From Folk Psychology to Cognitive Science*, p. 231.

19. I obviously have not exhausted all challenges to content. Two salient examples are W. V. Quine's indeterminacy of translation argument, in *Word and Object* (Cambridge, Mass: MIT Press, 1960), chap. 2, and Saul Kripke's problems about meaning or intending, in *Wittgenstein on Rules and Private Language* (Cambridge, Mass.: Harvard University Press, 1982). These arguments would require extensive examination, which cannot be undertaken here. Among the many discussions of Quine's indeterminacy thesis, a recent one I find congenial is Peter Unger's, in *Philosophical Relativity* (Minneapolis: University of Minnesota Press, 1984), pp. 15–20. This draws partly on Hilary Putnam's paper "The Refutation of Conventionalism," in *Mind, Language and Reality* (Cambridge: Cambridge University Press, 1975).

20. See Hilary Putnam, "The Meaning of 'Meaning'," in *Mind, Language and Reality*.

21. See Jerry Fodor, "Methodological Solipsism Considered as a Research Strategy in Cognitive Psychology," in *Representations* (Cambridge, Mass.: MIT Press, 1981).

22. Ibid., p. 227.

23. Ibid., p. 231.

24. "Propositional Attitudes," in *Representations*, p. 183.

25. *Representations*, p. 30.

26. This interpretation was suggested to me by Robert Harnish.

27. *From Folk Psychology to Cognitive Science*, chap. 8.

28. Cf. Tyler Burge, "Individualism and Psychology," presented at the 1984 Sloan Conference at the Massachusetts Institute of Technology.

29. This is suggested by Hartry Field, in "Thought Without Content," presented at the 1984 Sloan Conference at the Massachusetts Institute of Technology.

30. See Zenon Pylyshyn, *Computation and Cognition* (Cambridge, Mass.: MIT Press, 1984).

31. Robert Cummins, *The Nature of Psychological Explanation* (Cambridge, Mass.: MIT Press, 1983).

32. *Word and Object*, p. 59.

33. Donald Davidson, "Psychology as Philosophy," in *Essays on Actions and Events* (Oxford: Oxford University Press, 1980), p. 237.

34. Ibid., p. 237.

35. Donald Davidson, "On the Very Idea of a Conceptual Scheme," in *Inquiries into Truth and Interpretation* (Oxford: Oxford University Press, 1984), p. 197.

36. Ibid., p. 196.

37. "Thought and Talk," in *Inquiries*, pp. 168–169.

38. Daniel Dennett, "Three Kinds of Intentional Psychology," in R. Healey, ed., *Reduction, Time and Reality* (Cambridge: Cambridge University Press, 1981).

39. Stephen Schiffer, "Truth and the Theory of Content," in H. Parret and J. Bouverese, eds., *Meaning and Understanding* (Berlin: Walter de Gruyter, 1981); Field, "Mental Representation," sect. 5; Brian Loar, *Mind and Meaning* (Cambridge: Cambridge University Press, 1981), chap. 8; Fred Dretske, *Knowledge and the Flow of Information* (Cambridge, Mass.: MIT Press, 1981); and Jerry Fodor, "Psychosemantics, or: Where Do Truth Conditions Come From?" forthcoming. At least one of these writers—Schiffer—no longer subscribes to his earlier position.

40. Christopher Cherniak, "Minimal Rationality," *Mind*, 90 (1981):161–183.

41. This and other criticisms of charity principles are presented by Paul Thagard and Richard Nisbett, in "Rationality and Charity," *Philosophy of Science*, 50 (1983):250–267.

42. For other arguments to this effect, see Colin McGinn, "Charity, Interpretation, and Belief," *The Journal of Philosophy*, 74 (1977):521–535.

9. Perception

1. Irvin Rock, *The Logic of Perception* (Cambridge, Mass.: MIT Press, 1983); see chap. 1, especially pp. 17–19. David Marr is even better known for positing multiple perceptual stages and outputs (see his *Vision*, San Francisco: W. H. Freeman, 1982). But Marr's perceptual stages do not exemplify the kind of distinction I wish to emphasize here.

2. For example, see Marr, *Vision*, pp. 339–343.

3. D. H. Hubel and T. N. Weisel, "Receptive Fields, Binocular Interaction, and Functional Architecture in the Cat's Visual Cortex," *Journal of Physiology*, 166 (1962):106–154; J. Y. Lettvin, H. R. Maturana, W. S. McCulloch, and W. H. Pitts, "What the Frog's Eye Tells the Frog's Brain," *Proceedings of the IRE*, 47 (1959):1940–51.

4. G. C. Kinney, M. Marsetta, and D. J. Showman, *Studies in Display Symbol Legibility*, pt. 21, "The Legibility of Alphanumeric Symbols for Digitalized Television" (Bedford, Mass.: Mitre Corp., 1966), no. ESD-TR-66-117.

5. My discussion here and below draws on John R. Anderson, *Cognitive Psychology and Its Implications* (San Francisco: W. H. Freeman, 1980).

6. R. M. Warren, "Perceptual Restorations of Missing Speech Sounds," *Science*, 167 (1970):392–393.

7. G. A. Miller and S. Isard, "Some Perceptual Consequences of Linguistic Rules," *Journal of Verbal Learning and Verbal Behavior*, 2 (1963):217–228.

8. Jerry Fodor, *The Modularity of Mind* (Cambridge, Mass.: MIT Press, 1983).

9. Ibid., p. 69; emphases are mine.

10. Zenon Pylyshyn, *Computation and Cognition* (Cambridge, Mass.: MIT Press, 1984).

11. See Rock, *The Logic of Perception*, pp. 12–13.

12. Rock also clearly acknowledges this (see Ibid., chap. 11).

13. Thomas Kuhn, *The Structure of Scientific Revolutions* (Chicago: University of Chicago Press, 1962). Other well-known proponents of the theory-ladenness of perception include N. R. Hanson, *Patterns of Discovery* (Cambridge: Cambridge University Press, 1958), and Nelson Goodman, *Ways of Worldmaking* (Indianapolis: Hackett, 1978).

14. This point is elaborated in Jerry Fodor, "Observation Reconsidered," *Philosophy of Science*, 51 (1984):23–43, an article I encountered after completing the bulk of this chapter.

15. G. Reicher, "Perceptual Recognition as a Function of Meaningfulness of Stimulus Material," *Journal of Experimental Psychology*, 81 (1969):275–280.

16. D. D. Wheeler, "Processes in Word Recognition," *Cognitive Psychology*, 1 (1970):59–85.

17. E. Tulving, G. Mandler, and R. Baumal, "Interaction of Two Sources of Information in Tachistoscopic Word Recognition," *Canadian Journal of Psychology*, 18 (1964):62–71.

18. *The Logic of Perception*, chap. 2.

19. See especially J. J. Gibson, *The Perception of the Visual World* (Boston: Houghton Mifflin, 1950) and *The Senses Considered as Perceptual Systems* (Boston: Houghton Mifflin, 1966).

20. It does not matter to my present considerations whether the hypothesized top-down processing is *intramodular* or *extramodular.* Fodor has argued that studies of context effects in speech perception—studies of Cloze values—are compatible with his view that speech perception has access only to information *within* a language perception module. What is being accessed, according to Fodor, is only information about lexical items, something *internal* to the language recognition module (see *Modularity of Mind*, pp. 77–80). This issue is not critical for my present purposes, however. What concerns me here is the implications of top-down processing for speed and reliability, whether the top-down processing is intramodular or not.

21. *Modularity of Mind*, p. 70.

22. *The Logic of Perception*, p. 2.

23. The first two of these assumptions are built into John Anderson's model in *The Architecture of Cognition* (Cambridge, Mass.: Harvard University Press, 1983). He expresses them in the terminology of "productions" and production "application." I bypass the productions formulation here; but I will return to production systems, and to the theme of partial matching, in Chapter 17.

24. A good presentation of F-ism along these lines is found in William Alston, "Two Types of Foundationalism," *The Journal of Philosophy*, 73 (1976):165–185. Also see Ernest Sosa, "The Raft and the Pyramid: Coherence versus Foundations in the Theory of Knowledge," in Peter French, Theodore Uehling, Jr., and Howard Wettstein, eds., *Midwest Studies in Philosophy*, vol. 5, *Studies in Epistemology* (Minneapolis: University of Minnesota Press, 1980).

25. On this topic see Roderick Firth, "Coherence, Certainty, and Epistemic Priority," *The Journal of Philosophy*, 61 (1964):545–557, and Mark Pastin, "Modest Foundationalism and Self-Warrant," in George Pappas and Marshall Swain, eds., *Essays on Knowledge and Justification* (Ithaca, N.Y.: Cornell University Press, 1979).

26. See John Pollock, "A Plethora of Epistemological Theories," in George Pappas, ed., *Justification and Knowledge* (Dordrecht: D. Reidel, 1979).

27. Cf. Roderick Chisholm's notion of "concurrence," in *Theory of Knowledge*, 2nd ed. (Englewood Cliffs, N.J.: Prentice-Hall, 1977), p. 83. I referred to other versions of positive coherence in Chapter 5.

28. See Pollock, "A Plethora of Epistemological Theories," p. 102.

29. Since there can be multiple right J-rule systems, on my theory, one right system might be F-ist and another right system might be C-ist. This suggests the commonly ignored possibility that *both* F-ism and C-ism might be right. But it is also possible that F-ism could be viewed as the doctrine that *all* right J-rule systems have a certain F-ist property; and C-ism could say that all right J-rule systems have a certain C-ist property. On this approach the possibility of multiple right systems would not provide for the cotenability of F-ism and C-ism.

30. See Fodor, *Modularity of Mind*, p. 107.

10. Memory

1. For example, see my *A Theory of Human Action* (Englewood Cliffs, N.J.: Prentice-Hall, 1970; Princeton: Princeton University Press, 1976), chap. 4.

2. See Robert Crowder, "The Demise of Short-Term Memory," *Acta Psychologica*, 50 (1982):291–323.

3. John Anderson, *The Architecture of Cognition* (Cambridge, Mass.: Harvard University Press, 1983), chaps. 1, 3.

4. I argued for this sort of distinction in an earlier paper, "Epistemology and the Psychology of Belief," *The Monist*, 61 (1978):525–535.

5. See Daniel Dennett, "Brain Writing and Mind Reading," in *Brainstorms* (Montgomery, Vt.: Bradford Books, 1978).

6. Ibid., p. 45.

7. For example, see Robert Cummins, "Inexplicit Representations," forthcoming in Myles Brand and Robert Harnish, eds., *The Representation of Knowledge and Belief* (Tucson: University of Arizona Press).

8. This case is borrowed from Christopher Cherniak, "Rationality and the Structure of Human Memory," *Synthese*, 57 (1983):163–186.

9. Rudolf Carnap, *Logical Foundations of Probability*, 2nd ed. (Chicago: University of Chicago Press, 1962), and Carl Hempel, "Inductive Inconsistencies," in *Aspects of Scientific Explanation* (New York: Free Press, 1965).

10. "Inductive Inconsistencies," p. 64; my emphases.

11. Cf. Cherniak, "Rationality and the Structure of Human Memory," pp. 164–165.

12. Gilbert Harman, *Thought* (Princeton: Princeton University Press, 1973), pp. 158–159.

13. The complexity of the time course of culpability is discussed by Holly

Smith in "Culpable Ignorance," *The Philosophical Review*, 92 (1983):543–571. It is clear that normative judgments in the epistemic sphere should be sensitive to such complexities of time.

14.   J. D. Bransford, J. R. Barclay, and J. J. Franks, "Sentence Memory: A Constructive versus Interpretive Approach," *Cognitive Psychology*, 3 (1972):193–209.

15.   R. A. Sulin and D. J. Dooling, "Intrusion of a Thematic Idea in Retention of Prose," *Journal of Experimental Psychology*, 103 (1974):255–262.

16.   D. J. Dooling and R. E. Christiaansen, "Episodic and Semantic Aspects of Memory for Prose," *Journal of Experimental Psychology: Human Learning and Memory*, 3 (1977):428–436.

17.   T. S. Hyde and J. J. Jenkins, "Recall for Words as a Function of Semantic, Graphic, and Syntactic Orienting Tasks," *Journal of Verbal Learning and Verbal Behavior*, 12 (1973):471–480.

18.   Elizabeth Loftus, *Eyewitness Testimony* (Cambridge, Mass.: Harvard University Press, 1979).

19.   R. N. Shepard, "Recognition Memory for Words, Sentences and Pictures," *Journal of Verbal Learning and Verbal Behavior*, 6 (1967):156–163.

20.   C. Bird, "The Influence of the Press upon the Accuracy of Report," *Journal of Abnormal and Social Psychology*, 22 (1927):123–129.

21.   E. F. Loftus, D. G. Miller, and H. J. Burns, "Semantic Integration of Verbal Information into a Visual Memory," *Journal of Experimental Psychology: Human Learning and Memory*, 4 (1978):19–31.

22.   F. I. M. Craik and R. S. Lockhart, "Levels of Processing: A Framework for Memory Research," *Journal of Verbal Learning and Verbal Behavior*, 11 (1972):671–684.

23.   S. Bobrow and G. H. Bower, "Comprehension and Recall of Sentences," *Journal of Experimental Psychology*, 80 (1969):455–461.

24.   John Anderson, *Cognitive Psychology and Its Implications* (San Francisco: W. H. Freeman, 1980), pp. 193–194.

25.   L. M. Reder, "The Role of Elaborations in Memory for Prose," *Cognitive Psychology*, 11 (1979):221–234, and R. J. Spiro, "Constructing a Theory of Reconstructive Memory: The State of the Schema Approach," in R. C. Anderson, R. J. Spiro, and W. E. Montague, eds., *Schooling and the Acquisition of Knowledge* (Hillsdale, N.J.: Erlbaum, 1977).

26.   Richard Nisbett and Lee Ross, *Human Inference: Strategies and Shortcomings of Social Judgment* (Englewood Cliffs, N.J.: Prentice-Hall, 1980).

27.   L. Ross, M. R. Lepper, and M. Hubbard, "Perseverance in Self Perception and Social Perception: Biased Attributional Processes in the Debriefing Paradigm," *Journal of Personality and Social Psychology*, 32 (1975):880–892. This and other articles by Ross and colleagues are summarized by Nisbett and Ross, in *Human Inference*, pp. 176ff.

28.   However, Nisbett and Ross sometimes overstate the results of these experiments. For example, they write: "The evidence suggests that [Francis] Bacon was correct in his assertion that 'the human understanding when it has once adopted an opinion draws all things to support and agree with it' . . . Conflicting evidence is treated as if it were supportive of beliefs, impressions formed on the basis of early evidence survive exposure to inconsistent evidence presented later,

and beliefs survive the total discrediting of their evidence base" (p. 179). This summary statement does not do justice to the facts of the experiment I have just reviewed. After all, most of the initial impressions in this experiment were successfully eliminated by process debriefings, and some of the effects of the initial impressions were eliminated by outcome debriefings. Admittedly, there are many other studies in their chapter on which Nisbett and Ross's summary statement draws. But, all in all, the evidence they marshal does not support the very strong statement quoted from Bacon. And their next sentence suggests that conflicting evidence is *always* treated as if it were supportive of beliefs, that beliefs *always* survive the discrediting of their evidence, and so on; whereas, in fact, these things only *sometimes* happen.

29. Ibid., p. 181.

30. P. C. Wason and P. N. Johnson-Laird, *Psychology of Reasoning: Structure and Content* (London: Batsford, 1965); M. Snyder and W. B. Swann, "Behavioral Confirmation in Social Interaction: From Social Perception to Social Reality," *Journal of Experimental Social Psychology*, 14 (1978):148–162; and Snyder and N. Cantor, "Testing Theories about Other People: Remembering All the History that Fits," unpublished manuscript, University of Minnesota, 1979.

31. L. Ross, M. R. Lepper, F. Strack, and J. L. Steinmetz, "Social Explanation and Social Expectation: The Effects of Real and Hypothetical Explanations upon Subjective Likelihood," *Journal of Personality and Social Psychology*, 35 (1977):817–829.

32. R. Hastie and P. A. Kumar, "Person Memory: Personality Traits as Organizing Principles in Memory for Behavior," *Journal of Personality and Social Psychology*, 37 (1979):25–38.

33. *Human Inference*, p. 167.

34. The literature on artificial intelligence contains a good bit of discussion of belief revision and dependency-directed backtracking. See Jon Doyle, "A Model for Deliberation, Action, and Introspection," (Cambridge, Mass.: MIT Artificial Intelligence Laboratory, 1980), no. TR-581; Doyle, "A Truth Maintenance System," *Artificial Intelligence*, 12 (1979):231–272; and R. M. Stallman and G. J. Sussman, "Forward Reasoning and Dependency-Directed Backtracking in a System for Computer-Aided Circuit Analysis," *Artificial Intelligence*, 9 (1977):135–196. I cannot pursue this technical literature in detail. But the complications involved in a system of backtracking show that it may be excessive to require ubiquitous backtracking. At a minimum this may prove excessive from a resource-relative perspective.

35. Similar ideas are expressed by Gilbert Harman, in "Positive versus Negative Undermining in Belief Revision," *Nous*, 18 (1984):39–49. My own thoughts on this were arrived at independently.

36. S. A. Madigan, "Intraserial Repetition and Coding Processes in Free Recall," *Journal of Verbal Learning and Verbal Behavior*, 8 (1969):828–835.

37. See Anderson, *Cognitive Psychology and Its Implications*, chap. 7.

38. W. Penfield, "The Interpretive Cortex," *Science*, 129 (1959):1719–25.

39. T. O. Nelson, "Savings and Forgetting from Long-Term Memory," *Journal of Verbal Learning and Verbal Behavior*, 10 (1971):568–576.

40. D. E. Rumelhart, P. Lindsay, and D. A. Norman, "A Process Model for

Long-Term Memory," in E. Tulving and W. Donaldson, eds., *Organization of Memory* (New York: Academic Press, 1972), pp. 231–232.

41. Ibid., p. 232.

11. Constraints on Representation

1. Jerry Fodor, *Modularity of Mind* (Cambridge, Mass.: MIT Press, 1983), p. 120.

2. Noam Chomsky, *Reflections on Language* (New York: Pantheon, 1975), pp. 10–11.

3. Cf. A. M. Collins and M. R. Quillian, "Retrieval Time from Semantic Memory," *Journal of Verbal Learning and Verbal Behavior*, 8 (1969):240–247, and A. M. Collins and E. F. Loftus, "A Spreading-Activation Theory of Semantic Processing," *Psychological Review*, 82 (1975):407–428.

4. For studies of the formal properties of natural-language taxonomies, see Fred Sommers, "The Ordinary Language Tree," *Mind*, 68 (1959):160–185 and "Types and Ontology," *Philosophical Review*, 72 (1963):327–363. See also Frank Keil, *Semantic and Conceptual Development* (Cambridge, Mass.: Harvard University Press, 1979).

5. D. Navon, "Forest before Trees: The Precedence of Global Features in Visual Perception," *Cognitive Psychology*, 9 (1977):353–383; and P. H. Winston, "Learning Structural Descriptions from Examples," in P. H. Winston, ed., *The Psychology of Computer Vision* (New York: McGraw-Hill, 1975).

6. R. A. Bjork, "All-or-None Subprocesses in the Learning of Complex Sequences," *Journal of Mathematical Psychology*, 5 (1968):182–195; H. A. Simon and K. Kotovsky, "Human Acquisition of Concepts for Sequential Patterns," *Psychological Review*, 70 (1963):534–546; and J. G. Greeno and H. A. Simon, "Processes for Sequence Production," *Psychological Review*, 81 (1974):187–196.

7. W. A. Kintsch and T. A. van Dijk, "Toward a Model of Text Comprehension," *Psychological Review*, 85 (1978):363–394.

8. G. A. Miller, E. H. Galanter, and K. H. Pribram, *Plans and the Structure of Behavior* (New York: Holt, Rinehart and Winston, 1960); Alvin Goldman, *A Theory of Human Action* (Englewood Cliffs, N.J.: Prentice-Hall, 1970; Princeton: Princeton University Press, 1976).

9. G. W. Ernst and A. Newell, *GPS: A Case Study in Generality and Problem Solving* (New York: Academic Press, 1969); A. Newell and H. A. Simon, *Human Problem Solving* (Englewood Cliffs, N.J.: Prentice-Hall, 1972); H. A. Simon, "Complexity and the Representation of Patterned Sequences of Symbols," *Psychological Review*, 79 (1975):369–382.

10. A. Stevens and P. Coupe, "Distortions in Judged Spatial Relations," *Cognitive Psychology*, 10 (1978):422–437.

11. G. H. Bower and A. L. Glass, "Structural Units and the Redintegrative Power of Picture Fragments," *Journal of Experimental Psychology: Human Learning and Memory*, 2 (1976):456–466.

12. Stephen Palmer, "Hierarchical Structure in Perceptual Representation," *Cognitive Psychology*, 9 (1977):441–474.

13. Frank Restle, "Theory of Serial Pattern Learning: Structural Trees," *Psychological Review*, 77 (1970):481–495.

14. F. Restle and E. Brown, "Organization of Serial Pattern Learning," in G. Bower, ed., *The Psychology of Learning and Motivation: Advances in Research and Theory,* vol. 4 (New York: Academic Press, 1970).

15. F. Lerdahl and R. Jackendoff, *A Generative Theory of Music* (Cambridge, Mass.: MIT Press, 1983). Work on this theme has also been done by Carol Krumhansl and colleagues. See C. L. Krumhansl and E. J. Kessler, "Tracing the Dynamic Changes in Perceived Tonal Organization in a Spatial Representation of Musical Keys," *Psychological Review,* 89 (1982):334–368, and Krumhansl and R. N. Shepard, "Quantification of the Hierarchy of Tonal Functions within a Diatonic Context," *Journal of Experimental Psychology: Human Perception and Performance,* 5 (1979):579–594.

16. Diana Deutsch and John Feroe, "The Internal Representation of Pitch Sequences in Tonal Music," *Psychological Review,* 88 (1981):503–522.

17. Heinrich Schenker, *Free Composition,* ed. and trans. Ernst Oster (New York: Longman, 1979).

18. C. P. E. Bach, *Essay on the True Art of Playing Keyboard Instruments,* ed. and trans. W. J. Mitchell (New York: Norton, 1949).

19. John Anderson, *The Architecture of Cognition* (Cambridge, Mass.: Harvard University Press, 1983).

20. See Donald Hoffman, "The Interpretation of Visual Illusions," *Scientific American,* 249 (1983):154–162, and Hoffman and W. A. Richards, "Parts of Recognition," *Cognition,* 18 (1984):65–96.

21. Shimon Ullman, *The Interpretation of Visual Motion* (Cambridge, Mass.: MIT Press, 1979).

22. Ibid., chap. 4.

23. See Gunnar Johansson, "Visual Motion Perception," *Scientific American,* 232 (1975):76–88.

24. Reported in Hoffman, "The Interpretation of Visual Illusions," p. 157.

25. Noam Chomsky, *Rules and Representations* (New York: Columbia University Press, 1980), p. 252.

26. Marshall Edelson, "Language and Dreams: *The Interpretation of Dreams* Revisited," *Psychoanalytic Study of the Child,* 27 (1972):203–282.

27. *The Architecture of Cognition,* chap. 2.

28. Amos Tversky, "Features of Similarity," *Psychological Review,* 84 (1977):327–352.

29. George Lakoff and Mark Johnson, *Metaphors We Live By* (Chicago: University of Chicago Press, 1980).

30. G. Polya, *How to Solve It* (Princeton: Princeton University Press, 1957).

31. M. E. Atwood and P. G. Polson, "A Process Model for Water Jug Problems," *Cognitive Psychology,* 8 (1976):191–216.

32. For other attempts to study the role of analogy in theory construction, see D. Gentner, "The Structure of Analogical Models in Science" (Cambridge, Mass.: Bolt, Beranek and Newman, 1980), report no. 4451; L. Darden, "Artificial Intelligence and Philosophy of Science: Reasoning by Analogy in Theory Construction," in Peter Asquith and Thomas Nickles, eds., *PSA 1982,* vol. 2 (East Lansing, Mich.: Philosophy of Science Association, 1983); and Mary Hesse, *Models and Analogies in Science* (Notre Dame, Ind.: University of Notre Dame Press, 1966).

33. Something like this may be behind the evidence about similarity presented

in A. Tversky and I. Gati, "Similarity, Separability, and the Triangle Inequality," *Psychological Review*, 89 (1982):123–154.

34. "Parts of Recognition," p. 67.

35. Here too I have drawn from "Parts of Recognition," pp. 75–76.

36. K. A. Ericsson, W. G. Chase, and S. Fallon, "Acquisition of a Memory Skill," *Science*, 208 (1980):1181–82.

37. "The Internal Representation of Pitch Sequences in Tonal Music," pp. 518–519.

38. Cf. D. N. Osherson, M. Stob, and S. Weinstein, "Learning Theory and Natural Languages," *Cognition*, 17 (1984):1–28; E. M. Gold, "Language Identification in the Limit," *Information and Control*, 10 (1967):447–474; K. Wexler and P. Culicover, *Formal Principles of Language Acquisition* (Cambridge, Mass.: MIT Press, 1980); R. J. Matthews, "The Plausibility of Rationalism," *The Journal of Philosophy*, 81 (1984):492–515.

39. W. V. Quine, "Natural Kinds," in *Ontological Relativity and Other Essays* (New York: Columbia University Press, 1969), and *The Roots of Reference* (La Salle, Ill.: Open Court, 1973), p. 23.

40. See Robert Merton, "Singletons and Multiples in Science," in *The Sociology of Science* (Chicago: University of Chicago Press, 1973).

12. Internal Codes

1. John Locke, *An Essay concerning Human Understanding* (1690), bk. 2, chap. 10, sect. 7.

2. David Hume, *A Treatise of Human Nature* (1739), bk. 1, pt. 1, sect. 1.

3. James Mill, *Analysis of the Phenomena of the Human Mind* (1829) p. 52.

4. Talk of a 'propositional code' implies that the mind has a form of representation that *uses* propositions. It suggests that propositions or propositionlike entities are vehicles of thought. This is quite different from the (milder) view that *what* is represented in thought are propositions. This latter view is silent about *how* the mind represents. It can be construed as merely holding that propositions are an appropriate extrinsic index of thought, not that propositions are mental instruments. (Cf. Robert Stalnaker, *Inquiry*, Cambridge, Mass.: MIT Press, 1984, chap. 1.)

Unfortunately, it is far from clear just what vehicles, instruments, or data structures are being postulated by a theorist who talks of a propositional code. Must the vehicles be like sentences? In what respects like sentences? Despite this lack of clarity, I shall continue to employ the terminology of propositional codes with regularity. It must be insisted, however, that the charge sometimes leveled against image theorists, that they are insufficiently explicit about the nature of the code they postulate, can also be turned against (some) proposition theorists. They too are insufficiently specific about the kind of representational vehicles to which they are committed.

5. D. M. Armstrong, *Perception and the Physical World* (London: Routledge and Kegan Paul, 1961), and George Pitcher, *A Theory of Perception* (Princeton: Princeton University Press, 1971).

6. J. M. Shorter, "Imagination," *Mind*, 61 (1952):528–542, and Daniel Dennett, *Content and Consciousness* (New York: Humanities Press, 1969). Similar

views on imagery may be associated with Wittgenstein's *Philosophical Investigations* (New York: Macmillan, 1953).

7. John Anderson and Gordon Bower, *Human Associative Memory* (New York: V. H. Winston, 1973); Herbert Simon, "What is Visual Imagery? An Information Processing Interpretation," in L. W. Gregg, ed., *Cognition in Learning and Memory* (New York: Wiley, 1972); H. H. Clark and W. G. Chase, "On the Process of Comparing Sentences against Pictures," *Cognitive Psychology*, 3 (1972):472–517; and M. Minsky and S. Papert, "Artificial Intelligence Progress Report" (Cambridge, Mass.: MIT Artificial Intelligence Laboratory) memo no. 252.

8. See Zenon Pylyshyn, "What the Mind's Eye Tells the Mind's Brain: A Critique of Mental Imagery," *Psychological Bulletin*, 80 (1973):1–24.

9. J. S. Bruner, R. O. Oliver, and P. M. Greenfield, *Studies in Cognitive Growth* (New York: Wiley, 1966).

10. R. N. Shepard and S. Chipman, "Second Order Isomorphisms of Internal Representations: Shapes of States," *Cognitive Psychology*, 1 (1970):1–17; Shepard and J. Metzler, "Mental Rotation of Three-Dimensional Objects," *Science*, 171 (1971):701–703; Shepard and C. Feng, "A Chronometric Study of Mental Paper Folding," *Cognitive Psychology*, 3 (1972):228–243; Shepard, "Form, Formation, and Transformation of Internal Representations," in R. L. Solso, ed., *Information Processing and Cognition: The Loyola Symposium* (Hillsdale, N.J.: Erlbaum, 1975).

11. "What the Mind's Eye Tells the Mind's Brain"; see also Zenon Pylyshyn, "Imagery and Artificial Intelligence," in C. W. Savage, ed., *Perception and Cognition: Issues in the Foundations of Psychology* (Minneapolis: University of Minnesota Press, 1978); "The Rate of 'Mental Rotation' of Images: A Test of a Holistic Analogue Hypothesis," *Memory and Cognition*, 7 (1979):19–28; "The Imagery Debate: Analogue Media versus Tacit Knowledge," *Psychological Review*, 88 (1981):16–45; *Computation and Cognition* (Cambridge, Mass.: MIT Press, 1984), chaps. 7–8.

12. Stephen Kosslyn, "Scanning Visual Images: Some Structural Implications," *Perception and Psychophysics*, 14 (1973):90–94; "Information Representation in Visual Images," *Cognitive Psychology*, 7 (1975):341–370; "Measuring the Visual Angle of the Mind's Eye," *Cognitive Psychology*, 10 (1978):356–389; *Image and Mind* (Cambridge, Mass.: Harvard University Press, 1981); Kosslyn and J. R. Pomerantz, "Imagery, Propositions, and the Form of Internal Representations," *Cognitive Psychology*, 9 (1977):52–76; Kosslyn, S. Pinker, G. E. Smith, and S. P. Shwartz, "On the Demystification of Mental Imagery," *Behavioral and Brain Sciences*, 2 (1979):535–581; reprinted in Ned Block, ed., *Imagery* (Cambridge, Mass.: MIT Press, 1981).

13. Both the pictorialist formulation and the perception-similitude formulation are presented by Ned Block, in his introduction to Block, ed., *Imagery*; also see his "Mental Pictures and Cognitive Science," *Philosophical Review*, 92 (1983):499–541.

14. See Kosslyn, Pinker, Smith, and Shwartz, "On the Demystification of Mental Imagery," in Block, ed., *Imagery*, p. 132.

15. *Image and Mind*, p. 33.

16. Ibid., pp. 30, 31.

17. Ibid., p. 13.

18. Ibid., p. 18.

19. Ibid., p. 18; my emphasis.

20. Ibid.; my emphasis.

21. Stephen Kosslyn, "The Medium and the Message in Mental Imagery," in Block, ed., *Imagery*, p. 207; my emphases.

22. R. N. Shepard, "The Mental Image," *American Psychologist*, 33 (1978):135.

23. R. N. Shepard and Lynn Cooper, *Mental Images and Their Transformations* (Cambridge, Mass.: MIT Press, 1982), p. 14; emphasis added.

24. Zenon Pylyshyn, "The Imagery Debate: Analog Media versus Tacit Knowledge," in Block, ed., *Imagery*, pp. 199–201.

25. Much of this evidence is culled from Block's introduction to Block, ed., *Imagery*.

26. C. W. Perky, "An Experimental Study of Imagination," *American Journal of Psychology*, 21 (1910):422–452. Also see S. J. Segal and V. Fusella, "Influence of Imaged Pictures and Sounds on Detection of Visual and Auditory Signals," *Journal of Experimental Psychology*, 83 (1970):458–464.

27. For summaries, see Shepard, "The Mental Image," and R. A. Finke, "Levels of Equivalence in Imagery and Perception," *Psychological Review*, 87 (1980):113–139.

28. R. A. Finke and M. J. Schmidt, "Orientation-Specific Color Aftereffects following Imagination," *Journal of Experimental Psychology: Human Perception and Performance*, 3 (1977):599–606.

29. N. Pennington and S. M. Kosslyn, "Measuring the Acuity of the Mind's Eye," (in preparation); reported by Block in his introduction to Block, ed., *Imagery*.

30. Stephen Palmer, "Fundamental Aspects of Cognitive Representation," in E. Rosch and B. Lloyd, eds., *Cognition and Categorization* (Hillsdale, N.J.: Erlbaum, 1978).

31. I paraphrase my presentation from Kosslyn, "The Medium and the Message in Mental Imagery."

32. *Image and Mind*, p. 277. (The original source misspells 'Simonides'; I have corrected it here.) Kosslyn credits A. Paivio, *Imagery and Verbal Processes* (New York: Holt, Rinehart and Winston, 1971).

33. Shepard and Cooper, *Mental Tasks and Their Transformations*, p. 36.

34. See Shepard and Cooper's introduction to *Mental Images and Their Transformations*, pp. 6–7. For further treatment of this theme, see Judith Wechsler, ed., *On Aesthetics in Science* (Cambridge, Mass.: MIT Press, 1978).

35. See "The Imagery Debate: Analog Media versus Tacit Knowledge," and *Computation and Cognition*.

36. Cf. *Computation and Cognition*, chap. 5.

37. Ralph Haber, "How We Remember What We See," in Richard Atkinson, ed., *Contemporary Psychology: Readings from Scientific American* (San Francisco: W. H. Freeman, 1971).

38. Personal communication from Mary Potter to Jerry Fodor, reported in Fodor, *Modularity of Mind* (Cambridge, Mass.: MIT Press, 1983), pp. 62–63.

39. Richard Nisbett and Lee Ross, *Human Inference: Strategies and Shortcomings of Social Judgment* (Englewood Cliffs, N.J.: Prentice-Hall, 1980), chap. 3.

40. See Janellen Huttenlocher, "Constructing Spatial Images: A Strategy in Reasoning," in P. N. Johnson-Laird and P. C. Wason, eds., *Thinking* (Cambridge: Cambridge University Press, 1977).

41. Ibid., pp. 89–90.

42. H. H. Clark, "Linguistic Processes in Deductive Reasoning," in Johnson-Laird and Wason, eds., *Thinking*.

43. David Hilbert, "On the Infinite," in Paul Benacerraf and Hilary Putnam, eds., *Philosophy of Mathematics* (Englewood Cliffs, N.J.: Prentice-Hall, 1964).

44. Michael Resnik, "Mathematics as a Science of Patterns: Epistemology," *Nous*, 16 (1982):95–105. A similar view appears to have been maintained by the Bourbaki mathematicians.

45. See Philip Kitcher, *The Nature of Mathematical Knowledge* (New York: Oxford University Press, 1984), chap. 6.

46. Penelope Maddy, "Perception and Mathematical Intuition," *The Philosophical Review*, 89 (1980):163–196.

47. G. H. Hardy, *A Mathematician's Apology* (Cambridge: Cambridge University Press, 1941), p. 24.

48. *Human Inference*, pp. 44–45.

49. W. C. Thompson, R. M. Reyes, and G. H. Bower, "Delayed Effects of Availability on Judgment," unpublished manuscript, Stanford University, reported in Nisbett and Ross, *Human Inference*, p. 52.

50. R. Hamill, T. D. Wilson, and R. E. Nisbett, "Ignoring Sample Bias: Inferences about Collectivities from Atypical Cases," unpublished manuscript, University of Michigan, reported in Nisbett and Ross, *Human Inference*, p. 57.

51. R. E. Nisbett, E. Borgida, R. Crandall, and H. Reed, "Popular Induction: Information is Not Always Informative," in J. S. Carroll and J. W. Payne, eds., *Cognition and Social Behavior* (Hillsdale, N.J.: Erlbaum, 1976).

52. *Human Inference*, pp. 51–52.

53. Shelley Taylor and Suzanne Thompson, "Stalking the Elusive 'Vividness' Effect," *Psychological Review*, 89 (1982):155–181.

13. Deductive Reasoning

1. Rudolf Carnap, "The Aim of Inductive Logic," in E. Nagel, P. Suppes, and A. Tarski, eds., *Logic, Methodology and Philosophy of Science* (Stanford: Stanford University Press, 1962), p. 307.

2. Christopher Cherniak, "Computational Complexity and the Universal Acceptance of Logic," *The Journal of Philosophy*, 81 (1984):739–758.

3. I draw here on Cherniak's article, "Computational Complexity and the Universal Acceptance of Logic." Among other papers on this topic that he cites are two easily accessible articles: H. Lewis and C. Papadimitriou, "The Efficiency of Algorithms," *Scientific American*, 238 (1978):96–109, and L. Stockmeyer and A. Chandra, "Intrinsically Difficult Problems," *Scientific American*, 240 (1979):140–159.

4. For an explanation of the notion of an NP-complete problem, see Cher-

niak, "Computational Complexity and the Universal Acceptance of Logic," p. 744.

5. Lewis Carroll, "What Achilles Said to the Tortoise," *Mind*, 4 (1895):278–280.

6. For some treatments of this topic, however, see H. H. Clark, "Semantics and Comprehension," in T. A. Sebeok, ed., *Current Trends in Linguistics*, vol. 12 (The Hague: Mouton, 1974), on the topic of negation; P. N. Johnson-Laird and J. Tagart, "How Implication Is Understood," *American Journal of Psychology*, 2 (1969):367–373, on the topic of conditionals; and S. Fillenbaum, "Mind Your *p*'s and *q*'s: The Role of Content and Context in Some Uses of AND, OR, and IF," in Gordon Bower, ed., *The Psychology of Learning and Motivation*, vol. 11 (New York: Academic Press, 1977).

7. P. N. Johnson-Laird, "Models of Deduction," in R. J. Falmagne, ed., *Reasoning: Representation and Process in Children and Adults* (Hillsdale, N.J.: Erlbaum, 1975); D. N. Osherson, "Logic and Models of Logical Thinking," in ibid.; M. D. S. Braine, "On the Relation between the Natural Logic of Reasoning and Standard Logic," *Psychological Review*, 85 (1978):1–21; and L. Rips, "Cognitive Processes in Reasoning," *Psychological Review*, 90 (1983):38–71.

8. A. Newell and H. A. Simon, *Human Problem Solving* (Englewood Cliffs, N.J.: Prentice-Hall, 1972).

9. D. Hewitt, "Description and Theoretical Analysis (Using Schemata) of PLANNER" (Cambridge, Mass.: MIT Artificial Intelligence Laboratory, 1972), no. AI-TR-258; D. V. McDermott and G. J. Sussman, "The CONNIVER Reference Manual" (Cambridge, Mass.: MIT Artificial Intelligence Laboratory), memo no. 259.

10. W. V. Quine, *Methods of Logic* (New York: Holt, Rinehart and Winston, 1950, 1959).

11. Philip Johnson-Laird, *Mental Models* (Cambridge, Mass.: Harvard University Press, 1983).

12. Ibid., pp. 53–54.

13. Here my exposition of Johnson-Laird partly follows Lance Rips's "Mental Muddles," in Myles Brand and Robert Harnish, eds., *The Representation of Knowledge and Belief* (forthcoming).

14. *Mental Models*, p. 104.

15. Ibid.; also reported in P. N. Johnson-Laird and M. J. Steedman, "The Psychology of Syllogisms," *Cognitive Psychology*, 10 (1978):64–99.

16. L. J. Rips and S. L. Marcus, "Supposition and the Analysis of Conditional Sentences," in M. A. Just and P. A. Carpenter, eds., *Cognitive Processes in Comprehension* (Hillsdale, N.J.: Erlbaum, 1977).

17. J. E. Taplin and H. Staudenmayer, "Interpretation of Abstract Conditional Sentences in Deductive Reasoning," *Journal of Verbal Learning and Verbal Behavior*, 12 (1973):530–542.

18. R. S. Woodworth and S. B. Sells, "An Atmosphere Effect in Formal Syllogistic Reasoning," *Journal of Experimental Psychology*, 18 (1935):451–460.

19. See P. C. Wason and P. N. Johnson-Laird, *Psychology of Reasoning: Structure and Content* (London: Batsford, 1965; Cambridge, Mass.: Harvard University Press, 1972), chaps. 13 and 14.

20. The *opus classicus* here is W. V. Quine, "Two Dogmas of Empiricism," in *From a Logical Point of View* (Cambridge, Mass.: Harvard University Press, 1953).

21. David Hume, *A Treatise of Human Nature* (1739), bk. 1, pt. 4, sect. 1.

22. Cf. René Descartes, *Regulae*, especially rules 7 and 11.

23. On similar issues, see Philip Kitcher, *The Nature of Mathematical Knowledge* (New York: Oxford University Press, 1984), chap. 2.

24. This possibility was raised by Holly Smith.

25. See *Mental Models*, p. 109.

14. Probability Judgments

1. These quotations are taken from Amos Tversky and Daniel Kahneman, "Extensional versus Intuitive Reasoning: The Conjunction Fallacy in Probability Judgment," *Psychological Review*, 90 (1983):293–315.

2. Daniel Kahneman and Amos Tversky, "Subjective Probability: A Judgment of Representativeness," in D. Kahneman, P. Slovic, and A. Tversky, eds., *Judgment under Uncertainty: Heuristics and Biases* (Cambridge: Cambridge University Press, 1982), p. 46. Several other papers by Tversky and Kahneman, also reprinted as chapters of this volume, strike similar themes, including "Judgment under Uncertainty: Heuristics and Biases," "Belief in the Law of Small Numbers," and "On the Psychology of Prediction".

3. Richard Nisbett and Lee Ross, *Human Inference: Strategies and Shortcomings of Social Judgment* (Englewood Cliffs, N.J.: Prentice-Hall, 1980), p. 3.

4. Ibid., p. 6.

5. Ibid.

6. R. E. Nisbett and E. Borgida, "Attribution and the Psychology of Prediction," *Journal of Personality and Social Psychology*, 32 (1975):935.

7. P. Slovic, B. Fischhoff, and S. Lichtenstein, "Cognitive Processes and Societal Risk Taking," in J. S. Carroll and J. W. Payne, eds., *Cognition and Social Behavior* (Hillsdale, N.J.: Erlbaum, 1976), p. 169.

8. L. Jonathan Cohen, "Can Human Irrationality Be Experimentally Demonstrated?" *The Behavioral and Brain Sciences*, 4 (1981):317–331. Commentaries on this paper, including ones by Fischhoff, Kahneman, Nisbett, and Tversky, appear in the same journal issue, pp. 331–359.

9. These are summarized in "Judgment under Uncertainty: Heuristics and Biases," and in the other articles cited in note 2, which are reprinted in Kahneman, Slovic, and Tversky, eds., *Judgment under Uncertainty*.

10. Amos Tversky and Daniel Kahneman, "Judgments of and by Representativeness," in Kahneman, Slovic, and Tversky, eds., *Judgment under Uncertainty*.

11. Ibid., pp. 88–89.

12. "Extensional versus Intuitive Reasoning," p. 304.

13. However, the phrase might be applied to states that a cognizer could be in, not just to states he is in. That is, the phrase may refer to a state it *would* be rational, or justified, for him to be in, even if he is not actually in it.

14. A survey of these issues is found in Ellery Eells, *Rational Decision and Causality* (Cambridge: Cambridge University Press, 1982).

15. "Extensional versus Intuitive Reasoning," p. 311.

16. R. E. Nisbett, D. H. Krantz, C. Jepson, and Z. Kunda, "The Use of Statistical Heuristics in Everyday Inductive Reasoning," *Psychological Review*, 90 (1983):339–363.

17. B. Fischhoff, P. Slovic, and S. Lichtenstein, "Subjective Sensitivity Analysis," *Organizational Behavior and Human Performance*, 23 (1979):339–359.

18. See p. 310.

19. Daniel Kahneman and Amos Tversky, "On the Study of Statistical Intuitions," in Kahneman, Slovic, and Tversky, eds., *Judgment under Uncertainty*, p. 494.

20. L. J. Rips, E. J. Shoben, and E. E. Smith, "Semantic Distance and the Verification of Semantic Relations," *Journal of Verbal Learning and Verbal Behavior*, 12 (1973):1–20; and E. Rosch, "On the Internal Structure of Perceptual and Semantic Categories," in T. E. Moore, ed., *Cognitive Development and the Acquisition of Language* (New York: Academic Press, 1973).

21. See Edward Smith and Douglas Medin, *Concepts and Categories* (Cambridge, Mass.: Harvard University Press, 1981).

15. Acceptance and Uncertainty

1. Varying terminologies make it unclear to whom, exactly, this position can be attributed. But it seems to be attributable at least to Isaac Levi, *Gambling with Truth* (New York: Knopf, 1967), and to Keith Lehrer, *Knowledge* (Oxford: Oxford University Press, 1974).

2. In *The Enterprise of Knowledge* (Cambridge, Mass.: MIT Press, 1980), Isaac Levi proposes a theory intended to rationalize the revision of subjective probabilities equal to 1. For criticisms of this theory, however, see reviews of the book by Patrick Maher, *Philosophy of Science*, 51 (1984):690–692, and by Mark Kaplan, *The Philosophical Review*, 92 (1983):310–316.

3. Gilbert Harman, *Thought* (Princeton: Princeton University Press, 1973), p. 118; also Mark Kaplan, "A Bayesian Theory of Rational Acceptance," *The Journal of Philosophy*, 78 (1981):305–330.

4. For a survey, see Ellery Eells, *Rational Decision and Causality* (Cambridge: Cambridge University Press, 1982), chaps. 1, 2.

5. Amos Tversky, "Intransitivity of Preferences," *Psychological Review*, 76 (1969):31–48.

6. K. R. MacCrimmon, "Descriptive and Normative Implications of the Decision-Theory Postulates," in K. Borch and J. Mossin, eds., *Risk and Uncertainty* (New York: St. Martin's, 1968).

7. Cf. Amos Tversky, "A Critique of Expected Utility Theory," *Erkenntnis*, 9 (1975):163–173, and Daniel Kahneman and Amos Tversky, "Prospect Theory: An Analysis of Decision under Risk," *Econometrica*, 47 (1979):263–291.

8. I owe this point to John Pollock.

9. See David Rumelhart and Donald Norman's introduction to Geoffrey Hinton and James Anderson, eds., *Parallel Models of Associative Memory* (Hillsdale, N.J.: Erlbaum, 1981).

10. See J. A. Feldman and D. H. Ballard, "Connectionist Models and Their Properties," *Cognitive Science*, 6 (1982):206.

11. Ibid., and Lokendra Shastri and J. A. Feldman, "Semantic Networks and

Neural Nets" (Rochester: University of Rochester, Computer Science Department, 1984), technical report no. 131. Also see Feldman, "A Connectionist Model of Visual Memory," in Hinton and Anderson, eds., *Parallel Models of Associative Memory.*

12. Actually the *formula* seems to imply that a unit sets itself to zero if it knows of a higher *or equal* input. But I assume that Feldman and Ballard mean just a higher input, which is what they say (p. 228).

13. See C. S. Peirce, "The Fixation of Belief" and "How To Make Our Ideas Clear," in Justus Buchler, ed., *The Philosophical Writings of Peirce* (New York: Dover, 1955).

14. There is a nonstandard model of probability, proposed by A. P. Dempster and G. A. Shafer, in which this requirement is relaxed. See Dempster, "A Generalization of Bayesian Inference," *Journal of the Royal Statistical Society,* ser. B, 30 (1968):205–247, and Shafer, *A Mathematical Theory of Evidence* (Princeton: Princeton University Press, 1976). However, I focus on the standard model.

15. Notice that a theory of propositional uncertainty could include not only propositional contents with explicit probability values, but also modal propositions like 'It *might* rain today'.

16. Cf. Lehrer, *Knowledge,* chap. 8.

17. The problem of little or no information is mentioned in Shastri and Feldman, "Semantic Networks and Neural Nets," pp. 26–28.

18. Use of scenarios in bolstering the strength of hypotheses has been criticized by Tversky and Kahneman, on the grounds that they can lead to conjunction errors. See their article "Extensional versus Intuitive Reasoning," *Psychological Review,* 90 (1983):293–315. For example, groups of subjects (in 1982) estimated the probability of "a massive flood somewhere in North America in 1983, in which more than 1,000 people drown" and the probability of "an earthquake in California sometime in 1983, causing a flood in which more than 1,000 people drown." The estimates of the conjunction—earthquake and flood—were significantly higher than estimates of the flood. Presumably, a reminder that a devastating flood could be caused by an earthquake made the conjunction—a 'coherent' sequence—seem more probable. Similarly, Tversky and Kahneman note, a plausible story of how a victim might have been killed by someone other than the defendant may convince a jury of the existence of reasonable doubt. An attorney can fill in guesses regarding unknown facts, such as motive or mode of operation, thereby strengthening a case through improving its coherence, and a political analyst can improve scenarios by adding plausible causes and representative consequences. All such uses of coherence-promoting scenarios are regarded by Tversky and Kahneman with suspicion.

These examples may illustrate how *certain* uses of coherence can lead cognizers astray. But they hardly foreclose the prospect that some versions of the coherence processes in question could help a set of processes achieve a reasonably high truth ratio, high enough to qualify for admission into a right system of J-rules. Indeed, it is not even clear that these examples are (all) misuses of coherence. Maybe subjects' estimates of the chances of flood alone were not very accurate. Being reminded that a flood can be caused by an earthquake could improve the accuracy of one's estimate of flood chances—and of earthquake-plus-flood chances.

19. Speaking of 'nature's way', it is worth noting the existence of WTA mecha-

nisms elsewhere in nature. Consider, for example, the WTA mechanisms of *mating* found in certain species. Elk and bighorn sheep have battles among their males to determine dominance within the herd. The females of the herd all mate exclusively with the single victorious male. This mechanism has some obvious genetic advantages. It allows the genes of only the strongest or most battleworthy male to be transmitted to subsequent generations. It also has some apparent disadvantages: it does not make use of the entire gene pool of the male population. The viability of such species, however, suggests that this is a tenable mating mechanism. Analogous advantages of WTA mechanisms in cognition may also be identified.

16. Belief Updating

1. One variant of conditionalization is that presented by Richard Jeffrey in *The Logic of Decision*, 2nd ed. (Chicago: University of Chicago Press, 1983), chap. 11.

2. Hillel Einhorn and Robin Hogarth, "A Contrast Model for Updating Beliefs," University of Chicago, Center for Decision Research (1984). I am grateful to Professors Einhorn and Hogarth for allowing me to present material from this unpublished paper.

3. J. D. Shanteau, "An Additive Model for Sequential Decision Making," *Journal of Experimental Psychology*, 85 (1970):181–191.

4. N. H. Anderson, *Foundations of Information Integration Theory* (New York: Academic Press, 1981).

5. For example, see Amartya Sen, *Collective Choice and Social Welfare* (San Francisco: Holden-Day, 1970), chap. 10, and C. Plott, "Axiomatic Social Choice Theory: An Overview and Interpretation," *American Journal of Political Science*, 20 (1976):511–596.

6. Hans Reichenbach, *Theory of Probability* (Berkeley: University of California Press, 1949), pp. 470–482.

7. See Karl Popper, *The Logic of Scientific Discovery* (London: Hutchinson, 1959), p. 267.

8. Imre Lakatos, "Falsification and the Methodology of Scientific Research Programmes," in Imre Lakatos and Alan Musgrave, eds., *Criticism and the Growth of Knowledge* (Cambridge: Cambridge University Press, 1970).

9. Larry Laudan, *Progress and Its Problems* (Berkeley: University of California Press, 1977), pp. 196ff.

10. Robin Hogarth, "Beyond Discrete Biases: Functional and Dysfunctional Aspects of Judgmental Heuristics," *Psychological Bulletin*, 90 (1981):197–217.

17. Production Systems and Second-Order Processes

1. E. L. Post, "Formal Reductions of the General Combinatorial Decision Problem," *American Journal of Mathematics*, 65 (1943):197–268.

2. A. Newell and H. A. Simon, *Human Problem Solving* (Englewood Cliffs, N.J.: Prentice-Hall, 1972); also see Newell, "Production Systems: Models of Control Structures," in W. G. Chase, ed., *Visual Information Processing* (New York: Academic Press, 1973).

3. John Anderson, *The Architecture of Cognition* (Cambridge, Mass.: Harvard University Press, 1983).

4. John Anderson, *Language, Memory, and Thought* (Hillsdale, N.J.: Erlbaum, 1976).

5. Donald Norman, "Categorization of Action Slips," *Psychological Review,* 88 (1981):1–15.

6. See G. A. Miller, E. Galanter, and K. H. Pribram, *Plans and the Structure of Behavior* (New York: Holt, Rinehart and Winston, 1960), and Newell and Simon, *Human Problem Solving.*

7. B. Hayes-Roth and F. Hayes-Roth, "A Cognitive Model of Planning," *Cognitive Science,* 3 (1979):275–310.

8. The following two productions and macroproduction are quoted from *Architecture of Cognition,* pp. 235–236.

9. Anderson also discusses what he calls "action discrimination," as opposed to "condition discrimination," but I will ignore that.

10. Cf. P. H. Winston, "Learning Structural Descriptions from Examples" (Cambridge, Mass.: MIT Artificial Intelligence Laboratory, 1970), no. AI-TR-231, and "Learning to Identify Toy Block Structures," in R. L. Solso, ed., *Contemporary Issues in Cognitive Psychology: The Loyola Symposium* (Washington, D.C.: Winston, 1973).

Illustration Credits

Figure 9.1: redrawn from O. G. Selfridge, "Pattern Recognition and Modern Computers," in *Proceedings of the Western Joint Computer Conference* (New York: Institute of Electrical and Electronics Engineers, 1955), p. 92. Copyright © by the American Federation of Information Processing Societies.

Figure 9.2: redrawn from Irvin Rock, *The Logic of Perception* (Cambridge, Mass.: MIT Press, 1983), p. 309.

Figure 9.3: redrawn from Stephen Palmer, "Symmetry, Transformation, and the Structure of Perceptual Systems," in J. Beck, ed., *Organization and Representation in Perception* (Hillsdale, N.J.: Erlbaum, 1982), p. 122.

Figure 10.1: redrawn from L. Ross, M. Lepper, and M. Hubbard, "Perseverance in Self Perception and Social Perception: Biased Attributional Processes in the Debriefing Paradigm," *Journal of Personality and Social Psychology*, 32 (1975):887. Copyright © 1975 by the American Psychological Association. Adapted by permission of the publisher and author.

Figure 10.2: redrawn from Stephen Madigan, "Intraserial Repetition and Coding Processes in Free Recall," *Journal of Verbal Learning and Verbal Behavior*, 8 (1969):829.

Figure 11.1: redrawn from John Anderson, *Cognitive Psychology and Its Implications* (San Francisco: W. H. Freeman, copyright © 1980), p. 53.

Figure 11.2: redrawn from G. H. Bower and A. L. Glass, "Structural Units and the Redintegrative Power of Picture Fragments," *Journal of Experimental Psychology: Human Learning and Memory*, 2 (1976):459, 460. Copyright © 1976 by the American Psychological Association. Adapted by permission of the publisher and author.

Figure 11.3: redrawn from Stephen Palmer, "Hierarchical Structure in Perceptual Representation," *Cognitive Psychology*, 9 (1977):452.

Figures 11.4 and 11.5: redrawn from Diana Deutsch and John Feroe, "The Internal Representation of Pitch Sequences in Tonal Music," *Psychological Review*, 88 (1981):504, 505. Copyright © 1981 by the American Psychological Association. Adapted by permission of the publisher and author.

Figures 11.6 and 11.7: redrawn from Donald Hoffman, "The Interpretation of Visual Motion," *Scientific American*, 249 (1983):157, 159. Copyright © 1983 by Scientific American, Inc. All rights reserved.

Figure 12.1: redrawn from Roger Shepard and Lynn Cooper, *Mental Images and Their Transformations* (Cambridge, Mass.: MIT Press, 1982), p. 21.

Figure 13.1: redrawn from P. C. Wason and P. N. Johnson-Laird, *Psychology of Reasoning: Structure and Content* (Cambridge, Mass.: Harvard University Press, 1972), p. 173.

Figures 15.1–15.5: redrawn from J. A. Feldman and D. H. Ballard, "Connectionist Models and Their Properties," *Cognitive Science*, 6 (1982):213, 219, 221, 229.

Figures 16.1–16.6: redrawn from Hillel Einhorn and Robin Hogarth's unpublished paper "A Contrast Model for Updating Beliefs," with the authors' permission.

Figures 17.1–17.3: redrawn from John Anderson, *The Architecture of Cognition* (Cambridge, Mass.: Harvard University Press, 1983), pp. 10, 19, 132.

Author Index

Subject Index